Windows® Server® 2008 Active Directory® Resource Kit

Stan Reimer, Conan Kezema, Mike Mulcare, and Byron Wright
with the Microsoft Active Directory Team

PUBLISHED BY
Microsoft Press
A Division of Microsoft Corporation
One Microsoft Way
Redmond, Washington 98052-6399

Library of Congress Control Number: 2008920569

Printed and bound in the United States of America.

1 2 3 4 5 6 7 8 9   QWT   3 2 1 0 9 8

Distributed in Canada by H.B. Fenn and Company Ltd.

A CIP catalogue record for this book is available from the British Library.

Microsoft Press books are available through booksellers and distributors worldwide. For further information about international editions, contact your local Microsoft Corporation office or contact Microsoft Press International directly at fax (425) 936-7329. Visit our Web site at www.microsoft.com/mspress. Send comments to rkinput@microsoft.com.

Acquisitions Editor: Martin DelRe
Developmental Editor: Karen Szall
Project Editor: Maureen Zimmerman
Editorial Production: Custom Editorial Productions, Inc.
Technical Reviewer: Bob Dean, Technical Review services provided by Content Master, a member of
ˉM Group, Ltd.
ˉ: Tom Draper Design

ˉt No. X14-15141
No. X14-14924

To the three wonderful women in my life—Rhonda, Angela, and Amanda.
Your love and encouragement keep me going.

— *Stan Reimer*

I dedicate this book to the love of my life, Rhonda, and our precious sons,
Brennan and Liam. Thank you for your continuous support and for
being the reason that I do what I do. I also dedicate this book
to the rest of my family, who are still trying to figure out
what I actually do for a living.

— *Conan Kezema*

To my family—Nancy, James, Sean, and Patrick. Thanks
always for your encouragement and support.

— *Mike Mulcare*

Tracey, Samantha, and Michelle, you are the reason I keep
it going. Darrin, thanks for holding down the fort.

— *Byron Wright*

Contents at a Glance

Contents at a Glance

Table of Contents

What do you think of this book? We want to hear from you!

Microsoft is interested in hearing your feedback so we can continually improve our books and learning resources for you. To participate in a brief online survey, please visit:

www.microsoft.com/learning/booksurvey/

Part II **Designing and Implementing Windows Server 2008 Active Directory**

5 **Designing the Active Directory Domain Services Structure** **143**

What do you think of this book? We want to hear from you!

Microsoft is interested in hearing your feedback so we can continually improve our books and learning resources for you. To participate in a brief online survey, please visit:

www.microsoft.com/learning/booksurvey/

Acknowledgments

by Stan Reimer (for the team):

First of all, I want thank my coauthors for their hard work on this book. When I was first asked to lead this writing project, I looked around for the right people to work with me on this book and I couldn't have picked a better team.

Secondly, I want to thank the folks at Microsoft Press. This team includes Martin DelRe, the program manager, who kept poking us until we agreed to do this project, Karen Szall, the content development manager, and Maureen Zimmerman, the content project manager. I am sure that the problems we had keeping to the schedule on this book caused a few headaches for this group, but they were amazingly supportive and encouraging all the way through. Maureen had an amazing knack for reminding us when materials were due without making it feel like nagging.

Thanks to Bob Dean, the technical reviewer, for his valuable comments. Production for this book was professionally handled by Custom Editorial Productions Inc., with Linda Allen as the project manager, Cecilia Munzenmaier as the copy editor, and many others who toiled away in the background. As writers, we get to have all of the fun at the beginning of the process; these folks are still working on this long after we are done.

A Resource Kit doesn't come together without a lot of interaction with the product groups at Microsoft, as well as other technical experts, such as Directory Services MVPs. All of the chapters in this book have been reviewed by these experts and many of these experts contributed to the Direct from the Source, Direct from the Field, or How It Works sidebars that you will enjoy reading in this book. These reviewers and contributors include:

James McColl, Mike Stephens, Moon Majumdar, Judith Herman, Mark Gray, Linda Moore, Greg Robb, Barry Hartman, Christiane Soumahoro, Gautam Anand, Michael Hunter, Alain Lissoir, Yong Liang, David Hastie, Teoman Smith, Brian Lich, Matthew Rimer, David Fisher, Bob Drake, Rob Greene, Andrej Budja, Rob Lane, Gregoire Guetat, Donovan Follette, Pavan Kompelli, Sanjeev Balarajan, Fatih Colgar, Brian Desmond, Jose Luis Auricchio, Darol Timberlake, Peter Li, Elbio Abib, Ashish Sharma, Nick Pierson, Lu Zhao, and Antonio Calomeni.

by Conan Kezema:

Special thanks to my fellow coauthors for their hard work on this book. I would also like to thank Stan for the many opportunities he has provided over the years; he is a great friend and mentor.

Introduction

Welcome to the *Windows Server 2008 Active Directory Resource Kit*, your complete source for the information you need to design and implement Active Directory in Windows Server 2008.

The *Windows Server 2008 Active Directory Resource Kit* is a comprehensive technical resource for planning, deploying, maintaining, and troubleshooting an Active Directory infrastructure in Windows Server 2008. While the target audience for this Resource Kit is experienced IT professionals who work in medium-sized and large-sized organizations, anyone who wants to learn how to implement and manage Active Directory in Windows Server 2008 will find this Resource Kit invaluable.

One of the new features in Windows Server 2008 Active Directory is that the term *Active Directory* now covers a lot more territory than it did in previous iterations of this directory service. What was previously called Active Directory in Windows 2000 and Windows Server 2003 is now called Active Directory Domain Services (AD DS), and several more directory service components have been included under the Active Directory umbrella. These include Active Directory Lightweight Directory Services (AD LDS), Active Directory Certificate Services (AD CS), Active Directory Rights Management Services (AD RMS), and Active Directory Federation Services (AD FS).

Within this Resource Kit you'll find in-depth technical information on how Active Directory works in Windows Server 2008. In addition, you will find detailed task-based guidance for implementing and maintaining the Active Directory infrastructure. You'll also find numerous sidebars—contributed by members of the Active Directory product team, other directory experts at Microsoft, and directory services MVPs—that provide deep insight into how Active Directory works, best practices for designing and implementing Active Directory, and invaluable troubleshooting tips. Finally, the companion CD includes deployment tools, templates, and many sample scripts that you can use and customize to help you automate various aspects of managing Active Directory in enterprise environments.

Overview of Book

This book is divided into the following five parts with the following chapters:

Part I – Windows Server 2008 Active Directory Overview

- **Chapter 1 – "What's New in Active Directory for Windows Server 2008"**   This chapter provides an overview of the new features that are available in Windows Server 2008. If you know Windows Server 2003 Active Directory, this is a good place for you to get a quick overview of some of the new material that will be covered in this book.

- **Chapter 2 – "Active Directory Domain Services Components"**   This chapter provides an overview of Active Directory Domain Services—if you are somewhat new to Active Directory, this is a great chapter to get you started on the terms and concepts that make up AD DS.

- **Chapter 3 – "Active Directory Domain Services and Domain Name System"**   One of the most critical components that you need in order to make AD DS work efficiently is a properly implemented DNS infrastructure. This chapter provides information on how to do this.

- **Chapter 4 – "Active Directory Domain Services Replication"**   In order to work with AD DS, you will need to understand replication. This chapter provides all of the details of how AD DS replication works and how to configure it.

Part II – Designing and Implementing Windows Server 2008 Active Directory

- **Chapter 5 – "Designing the Active Directory Domain Services Structure"**   Before deploying AD DS, you need to create a design that meets your organization's requirements. This chapter provides the in-depth information that you will need to do that planning.

- **Chapter 6 – "Installing Active Directory Domain Services"**   Installing AD DS on a Windows Server 2008 computer is pretty easy, but there several variations on how to perform the installation. This chapter describes all of the options and the reasons for choosing each one.

- **Chapter 7 – "Migrating to Active Directory Domain Services"**   Many organizations are already running a previous version of Active Directory. This chapter provides the details on how to deploy Windows Server 2008 domain controllers in this environment, and how to migrate the Active Directory environment to Windows Server 2008.

Part III – Administering Windows Server 2008 Active Directory

- **Chapter 8 – "Active Directory Domain Services Security"**   AD DS provides the core network authentication and authorization services in many organizations. This chapter describes how AD DS security works and the steps you can take to secure your AD DS environment.

- **Chapter 9 – "Delegating the Administration of Active Directory Domain Services"**   One of the options in implementing AD DS is that you can delegate many administrative tasks to other administrators without granting them domain level permissions. This chapter describes how AD DS permissions work and how to delegate them.

- **Chapter 10 – "Managing Active Directory Objects"**   Most of your time as an AD DS administrator will be spent managing AD DS objects like users, groups and organizational units. This chapter deals with how to manage these objects individually, but also provides details on how to manage large numbers of these objects by using scripts.

■ **Chapter 11 – "Introduction to Group Policy"**   A central component in a Windows Server 2008 network management system is Group Policy. With Group Policy, you can manage many desktop settings as well as configure security. This chapter begins by explaining what Group Policy objects are and shows how to apply and filter Group Policy objects.

■ **Chapter 12 – "Using Group Policy to Manage User Desktops"**   One of the important tasks you can perform with Group Policy is configuring user desktops. In Windows Server 2008 and Windows Vista, there are several thousand Group Policy settings available. This chapter describes not only how to apply the policies, but also which policies are most important to apply.

■ **Chapter 13 – "Using Group Policy to Manage Security"**   Another important task that you can perform with Group Policy is applying security settings. This includes settings that will be applied to all users and computers in the domain as well as settings that can be applied to individual computers or users. This chapter provides the details on how to configure security by using Group Policy.

Part IV – Maintaining Windows Server 2008 Active Directory

■ **Chapter 14 – "Monitoring and Maintaining Active Directory"**   This chapter prepares you to maintain your Active Directory infrastructure after you deploy it. This chapter covers how to monitor your AD DS environment, and how to maintain the AD DS domain controllers.

■ **Chapter 15 – "Active Directory Disaster Recovery"**   Because of the central role that AD DS has in many corporations, it is critical that you know how to prepare for and recover from disasters within your AD DS environment. This chapter details how you can do this.

Part V – Identity and Access Management with Active Directory

■ **Chapter 16 – "Active Directory Lightweight Directory Services"**   AD LDS is one of the new server roles that is included under the Active Directory umbrella in Windows Server 2008. AD LDS is designed to be an application directory—this chapter describes how you can deploy and manage your AD LDS environment.

■ **Chapter 17 – "Active Directory Certificate Services"**   AD CS can be used to provide the public key infrastructure that provides digital certificates that are so critical for many network security implementations. This chapter describes how to plan and implement AD CS.

■ **Chapter 18 – "Active Directory Rights Management Services"**   AD RMS provides the tools to apply persistent usage policies to information that stays with the information even as it is moved around or outside the organization. This chapter details how to implement AD RMS.

■ **Chapter 19 – "Active Directory Federation Services"**   AD FS provides a means to enable users to access multiple Web-based applications in their organization or in other organizations while only authenticating once. This chapter describes the AD FS deployment scenarios and how to implement them.

Document Conventions

The following conventions are used in this book to highlight special features and usage:

Reader Aids

The following reader aids are used throughout this book to point out useful details:

Reader Aid	Meaning
Note	Underscores the importance of a specific concept or highlights a special case that might not apply to every situation
Important	Calls attention to essential information that should not be disregarded
Caution	Warns you that failure to take or avoid a specified action can cause serious problems for users, systems, data integrity, and so on
On the CD	Calls attention to a related script, tool, template, or job aid on the companion CD that helps you perform a task described in the text
More Info	Points out Web sites or other related material that you can access to get more details about a topic described in the text
Security Alert	Emphasizes information or tasks that are essential for maintaining a secure environment or identifies events that indicate a potential security incident

Sidebars

The following sidebars are used throughout this book to provide added insight, tips, and advice concerning Windows Server 2008 Active Directory:

Sidebar	Meaning
Direct from the Source	Contributed by experts at Microsoft to provide "from-the-source" insight into how Active Directory in Windows Server 2008 works, best practices for planning and implementing the Active Directory server roles, and troubleshooting tips
Direct from the Field	Contributed by directory service MVPs to provide real-world insight into best practices for planning and implementing the Active Directory server roles and troubleshooting tips
How It Works	Provides unique glimpses of Windows Server 2008 Active Directory features and how they work

Command-Line Examples

The following style conventions are used in documenting command-line examples throughout this book:

Style	Meaning
Bold font	Used to indicate user input (characters that you type exactly as shown)
Italic font	Used to indicate variables for which you need to supply a specific value (for example, *filename* can refer to any valid file name)
`Monospace font`	Used for code samples and command-line output
%SystemRoot%	Used for environment variables

Companion CD

The companion CD is a valuable addition to this book. Many of the tools and resources mentioned in the chapters are on the CD itself; you can access other tools and resources via links from the CD.

For documentation of the contents and structure of the companion CD, see the Readme.txt file on the CD.

Management Scripts

A set of scripts to manage Active Directory is included on the CD. Among them are scripts to get information about Active Directory objects and scripts to create or modify these objects. These scripts all require Windows PowerShell. The following scripts are included on the CD:

- **AddUserToGroup.ps1**   Adds a user account to a group in the same OU

- **CreateAndEnableUserFromCSV.ps1**   Creates an enabled user account by reading a .csv file

- **CreateGroup.ps1**   Creates a group in Active Directory in the OU and domain specified

- **CreateObjectInAD.ps1**   Creates an object in Active Directory

- **CreateOU.ps1**   Creates an organizational unit in Active Directory

- **CreateUser.ps1**   Creates a user account in Active Directory

- **EnableDisableUserSetPassword.ps1**   Enables or disables a user account and sets the password

- **GetDomainPwdSettings.ps1**   Obtains the password policy settings for a domain

- **GetModifiedDateFromAD.ps1**   Lists the last modified date of a specific user onto a local or remote domain

- **ListUserLastLogon.ps1**   Lists the last logon date of a specific user onto a local or remote domain

- **LocateDisabledUsers.ps1**   Locates disabled user accounts in a local or remote domain

- **LocateLockedOutUsers.ps1**   Locates locked out user accounts a local or remote domain

- **LocateOldComputersNotLogon.ps1**   Locates computer accounts in a local or remote domain that have not logged on for a specified number of days

- **LocateOldUsersNotLogOn.ps1**   Scans a local or remote domain for user accounts that have not logged onto the domain for an extended period of time that is specified in days

- **ModifyUser.ps1**   Modifies user attributes in Active Directory

- **QueryAD.ps1**   Queries Active Directory for objects such as users, groups, computers, and so on

- **UnlockLockedOutUsers.ps1**   Unlocks user accounts that are locked out

In addition to these scripts, many of the chapters contain references to additional scripts that perform the management tasks included in that chapter.

Full documentation of the contents and structure of the companion CD can be found in the Readme.txt file on the CD.

Using the Scripts

The companion CD includes scripts that are written in VBScript (with a .vbs file extension) and Windows PowerShell (with a .ps1 file extension).

The VBScript scripts on the companion CD are identified with the .vbs extension. To use those scripts, double-click them or execute them directly from a command prompt.

The Windows PowerShell scripts require that you have Windows PowerShell installed and that you have configured Windows PowerShell to run unsigned scripts. You can run the Windows PowerShell scripts on Windows XP SP2, Windows Server 2003 SP1, Windows Vista, or Windows Server 2008. In order for the scripts to work, all computers must be members of a Windows Server 2008 domain.

 Note   For information about the system requirements for running the scripts on the CD, see the System Requirements page at the end of the book.

Find Additional Content Online

As new or updated material becomes available that complements your book, it will be posted online on the Microsoft Press Online Windows Server and Client Web site. Based on the final build of Windows Server 2008, the type of material you might find includes updates to book content, articles, links to companion content, errata, sample chapters, and more. This Web site will be available soon at *http://www.microsoft.com/learning/books/online/serverclient*, and will be updated periodically.

Digital Content for Digital Book Readers: If you bought a digital-only edition of this book, you can enjoy select content from the print edition's companion CD.
Visit http://go.microsoft.com/fwlink/?LinkId=109208 to get your downloadable content. This content is always up-to-date and available to all readers.

Resource Kit Support Policy

Every effort has been made to ensure the accuracy of this book and the companion CD content. Microsoft Press provides corrections to this book through the Web at the following location:

http://www.microsoft.com/learning/support/search.asp.

If you have comments, questions, or ideas regarding the book or companion CD content, or if you have questions that are not answered by querying the Knowledge Base, please send them to Microsoft Press by using either of the following methods:

E-mail:

rkinput@microsoft.com

Postal Mail:

Microsoft Press

Attn: Windows Server 2008 Active Directory Resource Kit

One Microsoft Way

Redmond, WA 98052-6399

Please note that product support is not offered through the preceding mail addresses. For product support information, please visit the Microsoft Product Support Web site at the following address:

http://support.microsoft.com

Part I
Windows Server 2008 Active Directory Overview

Chapter 1

What's New in Active Directory for Windows Server 2008

What's New in Active Directory Domain Services

Although much of what you will need to know in order to manage an Active Directory domain remains the same from previous versions of the directory service implementation, such as Windows 2000 and Windows Server 2003, several new and compelling features will offer the administrator greater control and security over the domain environment. This chapter will review six enhancements to the Active Directory Domain Service (AD DS), as well as four new roles that Active Directory can and will play in your enterprise.

Read-Only Domain Controllers (RODC)

One of the new features in Windows Server 2008 is the option to deploy a read-only domain controller (RODC). This new type of domain controller, as its name implies, hosts read-only partitions of the Active Directory database.

An RODC makes it possible for organizations to easily deploy a domain controller in scenarios where physical security cannot be guaranteed, such as branch office locations, or in scenarios where local storage of all domain passwords is considered a primary threat, such as in an application-facing role, or when used in conjunction with the Windows 2008 Server Core installation option.

Organizations that can guarantee the physical security of a branch domain controller might also deploy an RODC because of its reduced management requirements that are provided by such features as Administrator Role Separation.

Because RODC administration can be delegated to a domain user or security group, an RODC is well suited for a site that should not have a user who is a member of the Domain Admins group. RODCs have the following characteristics.

Read-Only AD DS Database

Except for account passwords, an RODC holds most of the Active Directory objects and attributes that a writable domain controller holds. However, changes cannot be made to the database that is stored on the RODC. Changes must be made on a writable domain controller and then replicated back to the RODC.

Local applications that request Read access to the directory can obtain access. Lightweight Directory Application Protocol (LDAP) applications that request Write access receive an LDAP referral response. This response directs them to a writable domain controller, normally in a hub site.

RODC Filtered Attribute Set

Only some attributes are replicated to the RODC. You can dynamically configure a set of attributes, called the RODC filtered attribute set, so that its attributes are not replicated to an RODC. Attributes that are defined in the RODC filtered attribute set are not allowed to replicate to any RODCs in the forest.

A malicious user who compromises an RODC can attempt to configure it in such a way that it tries to replicate attributes that are defined in the RODC filtered attribute set. If the RODC tries to replicate those attributes from a domain controller that is running Windows Server 2008, the replication request is denied. Therefore, as a security precaution, you should ensure that forest functional level is Windows Server 2008 if you plan to configure the RODC filtered attribute set. When the forest functional level is Windows Server 2008, an RODC that is compromised cannot be exploited in this manner because domain controllers that are running Windows Server 2003 are not allowed in the forest.

Unidirectional Replication

Because no changes are written directly to the RODC, no changes originate at the RODC. Accordingly, writable domain controllers that are replication partners do not have to pull changes from the RODC. This means that any changes or corruption that a malicious user might make at branch locations cannot replicate from the RODC to the rest of the forest. This also reduces the workload of bridgehead servers in the hub and the effort required to monitor replication.

RODC unidirectional replication applies to both AD DS and Distributed File System (DFS) Replication. The RODC performs normal inbound replication for AD DS and DFS Replication changes.

Credential Caching

Credential caching is the storage of user or computer credentials, including the user password expressed as a number of hashed values. By default, an RODC does not store user or computer credentials. The exceptions are the computer account of the RODC and a special (and unique) krbtgt account that each RODC has.

You can configure credential caching on the RODC by modifying the Password Replication Policy for the specific domain controller. For example, if you want the RODC to cache the credentials for all users in the branch office who routinely log on in the office location, you can add all user accounts for users in the branch office to the Password Replication Policy. In this way, users will be able to log on to the domain controller even if the wide area network (WAN) connection to a writable domain controller is unavailable. Likewise, you can add all of the branch office computer accounts, so that these accounts can authenticate to the RODC even when the WAN link is down. In both of the previous scenarios, the WAN connection to a writable domain controller must be available during the first logon for the credentials to be cached to the RODC.

Administrator Role Separation

You can delegate local administrative permissions for an RODC to any domain user without granting that user any user rights for the domain or other domain controllers. This permits a local branch user to log on to an RODC and perform maintenance work on the server, such as upgrading a driver. However, the branch user cannot log on to any other domain controller or perform any other administrative task in the domain. In this way, the ability to effectively manage the RODC in a branch office can be delegated to a branch user without compromising the security of the rest of the domain.

Read-Only DNS

You can install the DNS Server service on an RODC. An RODC is able to replicate all application directory partitions that DNS uses, including ForestDNSZones and DomainDNSZones. If the DNS server is installed on an RODC, clients can query it for name resolution as they query any other DNS server.

However, the DNS server on an RODC does not support client updates directly. Consequently, the RODC does not register name server (NS) resource records for any Active Directory–integrated zone that it hosts. When a client attempts to update its DNS records against an RODC, the server returns a referral. The client can then attempt the update against the DNS server that is provided in the referral. In the background, the DNS server on the RODC attempts to replicate the updated record from the DNS server that made the update. This replication request is only for a single object (the DNS record). The entire list of changed zone or domain data does not get replicated during this special replicate-single-object request. To enhance security, the branch office RODC needs to register its DC records (as time server, ldap host, kdc host, etc.) with a Windows Server 2008 DC. If the RODC then gets compromised, it will not be able to change DNS records and impersonate another DC, or to advertise itself to clients outside its own site.

Active Directory Domain Services Auditing

To better manage AD DS for an organization, it is valuable to not only know what objects have been modified, but to know both their current and previous values. In previous versions of AD DS, there was a single audit policy: Audit directory service access. Windows Server 2008 has additional subcategories of directory service auditing. This feature offers greater logging information on success and failure events within the AD DS. In Windows Server 2008, the Audit directory service access policy is now divided into four subcategories:

- Directory Service Access
- Directory Service Changes
- Directory Service Replication
- Detailed Directory Service Replication

In Windows Server 2008, this global audit policy is enabled by default. The subcategory Directory Service Changes, also enabled by default, is set to log success events only. You can control what operations to audit by modifying the system access control list (SACL) on the appropriate directory service objects. For auditing directory service changes, the following capabilities are now available:

- When a successful modify operation is performed on an attribute of an object, AD DS logs the previous and current values of the attribute. If the attribute has more than one value, only the values that change as a result of the modify operation are logged.

- If a new object is created, values of the attributes that are populated at the time of creation are logged. If attributes are added during the create operation, those new attribute values are logged.

- If an object is moved within a domain, the previous and new location (in the form of the distinguished name) is logged. When an object is moved to a different domain, a create event is generated on the domain controller in the target domain.

- If an object is undeleted, the location to which the object is moved is logged. In addition, if attributes are added, modified, or deleted during an undelete operation, the values of those attributes are also logged.

Note   Although the global audit policy: Audit directory service access is enabled using the Group Policy Management console, there is no GUI available in Windows Server 2008 to view or set AD DS audit policy subcategories. To view or set audit policy subcategories, use the command-line tool Auditpol.exe. For more information on using Auditpol.exe to enable individual subcategories, see Chapter 8, "Active Directory Domain Services Security," as well as the "Windows Server 2008 Auditing AD DS Changes Step-by-Step Guide" at *http://technet2.microsoft.com/windowsserver2008/en/library/a9c25483-89e2-4202-881c-ea8e02b4b2a51033.mspx?mfr=true.*

Fine-Grained Password Policies

In Windows Server 2000 and Windows Server 2003, both password policy and account lockout settings for all users in the domain are controlled by the Default Domain Policy. To create a separate password policy or account lockout setting for specific users in the domain once required either the creation of additional domains or the creation of password filters. In Windows Server 2008 AD DS, *fine-grained password policies* are now available to specify multiple password policies within a single domain. This enables members of the Domain Admins group to create separate password policy and account lockout settings for different types of users in the domain. For example, a domain admin can create a stricter password policy for a power users group, who have more privileged access, and then a less-strict password policy for average users.

Fine-grained password policies in Windows Server 2008 can be applied either to user objects or to global security groups. You cannot apply fine-grained password policy directly to an Organizational Unit (OU). To create a different password policy for members of the OU, apply the password policy to a global security group that is logically mapped to the OU (a *shadow group*). If you move a user from one OU to another, you must update the membership of the shadow group if you want the user to be controlled by the password policy of the new OU (or to no longer be affected by the policy of the old OU).

Storing Fine-Grained Password Policies

Two new object classes are created in the AD DS schema to store fine-grained password policies: Password Settings Container (PSC) and Password Settings. Password Settings objects (PSOs) are stored in the PSC. The PSC is created by default in the System container in the domain—and it cannot be moved, renamed, or deleted. A PSO has attributes for all the settings that can be defined in the Default Domain Policy (except Kerberos settings). These settings include attributes for the following password settings:

- Enforce password history
- Maximum password age
- Minimum password age
- Minimum password length
- Passwords must meet complexity requirements
- Store passwords using reversible encryption

These settings also include attributes for the following account lockout settings:

- Account lockout duration
- Account lockout threshold
- Reset account lockout after

In addition, a PSO has the following two new attributes:

- **PSO link**   This is a multivalued attribute that is linked to users and/or group objects.

- **Precedence**   This is an integer value that is used to resolve conflicts if multiple PSOs are applied to a user or group object.

> **Note**   When adding a domain controller running Windows Server 2008 to an existing Active Directory domain, be sure to run Adprep to extend the Active Directory schema to include the two new object classes that fine-grained password policy requires. The Adprep command-line tool will prepare the schema for the changes required to support AD DS in Windows Server 2008. For more information on using Adprep, see Chapter 6, "Installing Active Directory Domain Services," as well as the "Step-by-Step Guide for Fine-Grained Password and Account Lockout Policy Configuration" at *http://technet2.microsoft.com/windowsserver2008/en/library/2199dcf7-68fd-4315-87cc-ade35f8978ea1033.mspx*.

Resultant Set of Policy for Fine-Grained Password Policy

Fine-grained password policy settings can be applied both to the user objects and global security groups. Resultant Set of Policy (RSOP) can only be calculated for the user object. If multiple PSOs are linked to a user or group, the resultant PSO that is applied is determined as follows:

1. A PSO that is linked directly to the user object is the resultant PSO. If more than one PSO is linked directly to the user object, a warning message is logged in the event log and the PSO with the lowest precedence value is the resultant PSO.

2. If no PSO is linked to the user object, the global security group memberships of the user and all PSOs that are applicable to the user based on those global group memberships are compared. The PSO with the lowest precedence value is the resultant PSO. (If there are multiple lowest precedence values, then the PSO GUID would be used for defining the order in which they are applied.)

3. If no PSO is obtained from conditions (1) and (2), the Default Domain Policy is applied.

There are three settings applied directly to the user object that will always override the settings that are applied through the fine-grained password policy. You can set these bits in the *userAccountControl* attribute of the user object:

- Reversible password encryption required

- Password not required

- Password does not expire

These bits override the settings in the resultant PSO that is applied to the user object (just as these bits override the settings in the Default Domain Policy in Windows 2000 and Windows Server 2003).

Restartable Active Directory Domain Services

Restartable AD DS in Windows Server 2008 enables the administrator to perform functions that are performed offline without having to restart the domain controller. In previous versions of Windows Server, offline functions, such as offline defragmentation of the database, required a restart of the domain controller in Directory Services Restore mode. In Windows Server 2008, you can stop the AD DS and perform the necessary updates, while other services running on the server (such as Dynamic Host Configuration Protocol [DHCP]) remain unaffected and available to satisfy user requests even while the AD DS is stopped. Keep in mind that dependent services such as DNS and KDC will not function without AD DS; dependent services will be stopped when the AD DS is stopped.

The three possible states for a domain controller running Windows Server 2008 are as follows:

- **AD DS Started**   In this state, AD DS is started. For clients and other services running on the server, a Windows Server 2008 domain controller running in this state is the same as a domain controller running Windows 2000 Server or Windows Server 2003.

- **AD DS Stopped**   In this state, AD DS is stopped. Although this mode is unique, the server has some characteristics of both a domain controller in Directory Services Restore Mode and a domain-joined member server.

- **Directory Services Restore Mode**   This mode is unchanged from Windows Server 2003.

You can easily start and stop the AD DS using the Services component of the Computer Management MMC snap-in or otherwise stop the service the same way as any other service that is running locally on the server.

Database Mounting Tool

The database mounting tool (Dsamain.exe) enables you to view snapshots and backups of AD DS data to determine which backup or snapshot contains the appropriate data to be restored. Previously, in earlier versions of AD DS running on the Windows 2003 or Windows Server 2003 operating system, administrators would have to restore multiple backup sets to determine which set contained the data necessary to restore. This process required a restart of the domain controller in Directory Services Restore Mode and did not provide a means to compare data stored in backups taken at different points in time. Although the database mounting tool cannot be used to restore the data to the AD DS, it can be used to simplify the process of identifying modified information and selecting the backup to be restored without incurring service downtime.

You will use the database mounting tool to expose the snapshot volume (created using Ntdsutil or the Volume Shadow Copy Service) as an AD.dit file. You can then use an LDAP tool, such as LDP.exe (which is included with Windows Server 2008), to browse the snapshot just as you would any live domain controller.

User Interface Improvements

Windows Server 2008 introduces several improvements to the AD DS interface. The Active Directory Domain Services Installation Wizard now includes advanced options to better support the installation of RODCs. The AD DS installation process has been streamlined and simplified. In addition, the management tools (MMC Active Directory Sites and Services snap-in) provide controls for new features in AD DS, such as Password Replication Policy for RODCs.

Improvements in the AD DS Installation Wizard

Although you can use the new Add Roles Wizard to configure the server for the AD DS role and to install the necessary files to start the AD DS installation, you will still need to run AD DS Installation Wizard by using the Dcpromo.exe command. New in Windows Server 2008 on the AD DS Installation Wizard Welcome page is the option to run the wizard in Advanced mode, instead of having to use the /adv switch when entering the Dcpromo.exe command from the Run command or command line.

The additional installation options in advanced mode include the following:

- Creating a new domain tree
- Using backup media from an existing domain controller in the same domain to reduce network traffic that is associated with initial replication
- Selecting the source domain controller for the installation, which enables you to control which domain controller is used to initially replicate domain data to the new domain controller
- Defining the Password Replication Policy for an RODC

The new Active Directory Domain Services Installation Wizard also includes the following improvements:

- By default, the wizard now uses the credentials of the user who is currently logged on. You are prompted for additional credentials if they are needed.
- When you create an additional domain controller in a child domain, the wizard now detects whether the infrastructure master role is hosted on a global catalog server in that domain, and it prompts you to transfer the infrastructure master role to the domain controller that you are creating if it will not be a global catalog server. This helps prevent misplacement of the infrastructure master role.
- On the Summary page of the wizard, you can export the settings that you have selected to a corresponding answer file that you can use for subsequent operations (installations or uninstallations). This method is less error-prone than manually creating an unattended installation file.

- You now can omit your administrator password from the answer file. Instead, type **password=*** in the answer file to ensure that the user is prompted for account credentials.

- You can prepopulate the wizard by specifying some parameters on the command line, reducing the amount of user interaction that is required with the wizard. Command-line parameters are also required when installing AD DS in Windows Server 2008 Server Core.

- You now can force the demotion of a domain controller that is started in Directory Services Restore Mode.

Improvements to the AD DS Management Tools

There have been several improvements to the Active Directory Sites and Services snap-in to simplify managing the AD DS. First, a new Password Replication Policy tab has been added to the domain controller Properties sheet that can be used to see what passwords have been sent to an RODC and which passwords are currently stored on the RODC. This tab will also indicate which accounts have authenticated on the RODC to determine whether or not to allow password replication. In addition, a Find command has been added to the toolbar and to the Action menu of the snap-in. This will enable administrators to determine what site a domain controller is located in to better troubleshoot replication problems.

A number of tools, including Ldp, Repadmin, and Nltest, that were part of the support tools or were otherwise available in the Windows Server 2003 Resource Kit are now included in the standard installation of Windows Server 2008 and are available by installing the DC roles. These same tools can be used to manage both AD DS and AD LDS (formerly Active Directory Application Mode [ADAM]). There is an option to only install these tools during installation.

Additional Active Directory Service Roles

In addition to AD DS, you can deploy a computer running the Windows Server 2008 operating system in four additional Active Directory Service roles. The four additional AD Service roles are as follows:

- Active Directory Certificate Services Role (AD CS)
- Active Directory Federation Services Role (AD FS)
- Active Directory Lightweight Services Role (AD LS)
- Active Directory Rights Management Services Role (AD RMS)

This section will briefly describe the functionality that is available by configuring the server with these AD Service roles. In later chapters you will learn the design implications of installing multiple service roles on a single computer running the Windows Server 2008 operating system, as well as the detailed functionality of each service role.

To deploy these service roles on a computer running the Windows Server 2008 operating system, you will use the Server Manager console. Several of these service roles require that the server first be configured as a domain controller while others require that it be installed into an existing Active Directory forest.

Active Directory Certificate Services Role

The AD CS role is used to create, distribute, and manage public key certificates to secure network resources. Public key certificates can be issued to users, devices or computers, and services, and AD CS functions to bind the identity of the person, device, or service to a corresponding private key that is unique to that object.

There are several enhancements in AD CS in Windows Server 2008 in the management and revocation of certificates in scalable environments:

- **Cryptography Next Generation (CNG)**   CNG provides a set of APIs that are used to perform basic cryptographic operations, such as creating hashes and encrypting and decrypting data. It is also used to create, store, and retrieve cryptographic keys.

- **Web enrollment**   Web enrollment allows users to connect to a CA by means of a Web browser in order to request certificates, retrieve Certificate Revocation Lists (CRLs), and perform smart card certificate enrollment.

- **Online Responder service**   The Online Responder service enables clients to check the revocation status of a digital certificate by using the Online Certificate Status Protocol (OCSP) rather than Certificate Revocation Lists (CRLs). When a client requests a certificate revocation status from the Online Responder service, the server evaluates the status of the certificate and sends back a signed response containing just the requested certificate status information. Alternatively, when a CRL is used, the entire list of revoked certificates is downloaded to the client.

- **Network Device Enrollment Service (NDES)**   NDES allows routers, switches, and other network devices that do not have network accounts to obtain certificates.

- **Enterprise PKI (PKIView)**   PKIView is an MMC snap-in available in AD CS for Windows Server 2008 used to monitor and troubleshoot the health of all certification authorities (CAs) in a public key infrastructure (PKI). The PKIView snap-in provides a graphical indication of the health and status of all CAs in the environment.

- **Restricted enrollment agent**   The restricted enrollment agent is a new functionality in Windows Server 2008 that limits the permissions that users designated as "enrollment agents" have for enrolling smart card certificates on behalf of other users. This feature is only available in Windows Server 2008 Enterprise.

■ **Certificate-related Group Policy settings**   There are new certificate-related Group Policy settings in AD CS that can be administered using the Group Policy Management console (GPMC). This GP setting can be used to:

   ❑   Deploy intermediate certification authority (CA) certificates to client computers.

   ❑   Prevent users from installing applications that have been signed with an unapproved publisher certificate.

   ❑   Configure network timeouts for large CRLs, as well as extend CRL expiration times.

When you deploy a CA in AD CS, you can deploy an Enterprise CA or a stand-alone CA. An Enterprise CA is tightly integrated with AD DS, which enables you to automate many of the tasks for certificate enrollment and renewal. If you deploy an Enterprise CA, you must deploy it on a Windows Server 2008 computer that is a member of an AD DS domain.

The AD CS components can be deployed on a single server or distributed across multiple servers. In a small enterprise, you may deploy all the roles except the Online Responder service on a single computer and dedicate one computer as an Online Responder. In large enterprises with complex digital certificate requirements, you may deploy several CAs, including subordinate CAs, and Online Responders on separate computers. The number of servers that you deploy in your environment will depend on a number of variables, including the volume of certificate requests, the number and location of CAs, and the applications that require certificates in the environment. These applications include Secure/Multipurpose Internet Mail Extensions (S/MIME), secure wireless networks, virtual private network (VPN), Internet Protocol security (IPsec), Encrypting File System (EFS), smart card logon, Secure Socket Layer/Transport Layer Security (SSL/TLS), and digital signatures.

To increase flexibility in supporting the PKI of the organization, single or multiple Online Responders may be deployed. Multiple Online Responders can be deployed to support one or more CAs, and a single Online Responder can support multiple CAs. For greater fault-tolerance and to support remote certificate revocation requests (branch-office scenarios), Online Responders can be deployed as an array. One member of the array must be designated as the array controller. Although each Online Responder in an array can be configured and managed independently, in case of conflicts, the configuration information for the array controller will override configuration options set on other array members.

Active Directory Federation Services Role

Active Directory Federation Services (AD FS) is a server role in the Windows Server 2008 operating system that is used to extend AD DS's account authentication functionality beyond the boundary of an AD FS forest and across multiple platforms, including both Windows and non-Windows environments. AD FS is well suited for Internet-facing applications or any environment where a single user account will need to access resources on different networks.

In these scenarios, users may be prompted for credentials whenever they try to access an application that is using a different authentication source (for example, in another organization or in a different forest, such as a perimeter network forest in the same organization).

When you implement AD FS, you can implement a federated trust between two different organizations or between two different forests. This federated trust enables users to use the security credentials from their own forest when accessing an application in an environment outside their forest. The federated trust is configured between resource organizations (organizations that own and manage resources and applications that are accessible from either the Internet or other third-party networks) and the account organizations (organizations that own and manage the user accounts that will then be granted access to the resources in the Resource Organizations). In this scenario, AD FS offers a single sign-on (SSO) access to resources in the resource organization to users who have been authenticated in the account organization. SSO enables users to log on to the local network and receive a security token that will provide them with access to resources on different networks that have been configured to trust those accounts. Even within a single organization with separate networks and security boundaries, users will appreciate the convenience of having an SSO for accessing all appropriate network resources. AD FS is suitable both within large organizations with separate resource and account organizations and outside the firewall: AD FS is Internet-scalable to support access requests from users accessing resources using a Web browser.

There are several different components that comprise AD FS in Windows Server 2008:

- **Federation Service**   The Federation Service comprises one or more federation servers that share a common trust policy. You use federation servers to route authentication requests from user accounts in other organizations or from clients that may be located anywhere on the Internet.

- **Federation Service Proxy**   The Federation Service Proxy is a proxy to the Federation Service in the perimeter network (also known as a demilitarized zone and screened subnet). The Federation Service Proxy uses WS-Federation Passive Requestor Profile (WS-F PRP) protocols to collect user credential information from browser clients, and it sends the user credential information to the Federation Service on their behalf.

- **Claims-aware agent**   You use the claims-aware agent on a Web server that hosts a claims-aware application to allow the querying of AD FS security token claims. A claims-aware application is a Microsoft ASP.NET application that uses claims that are present in an AD FS security token to make authorization decisions and personalize applications.

- **Windows token-based agent**   You use the Windows token-based agent on a Web server that hosts a Windows NT token-based application to support conversion from an AD FS security token to an impersonation-level, Windows NT access token. A Windows NT token-based application is an application that uses Windows-based authorization mechanisms.

One of the several improvements in AD FS in Windows Server 2008 is the installation process. Unlike AD FS in Windows Server 2003 R2, in which you needed to use Add Or Remove Programs to install AD FS, in Windows Server 2008, AD FS is installed like the other server roles—by using Server Manager. AD FS requires a directory service and can use either AD DS or Active Directory Lightweight Directory Services (AD LDS) as the directory. Additional improvements in the Windows Server 2008 release of AD FS are the tight integration between AD FS and Office SharePoint Server 2007 for membership and role providers, and AD RMS for sharing rights-protected content with trusted external partners.

Once you have installed AD FS, you will manage the service using the Microsoft Management Console (MMC). To manage both the Federation Service and Federation Service Proxy role services, use the Active Directory Federation Services snap-in.

Active Directory Lightweight Directory Services Role

The Active Directory Lightweight Directory Services (AD LDS), formerly known as Active Directory Application Mode (ADAM), is a Lightweight Directory Access Protocol (LDAP) directory service that can replace AD DS functionality in some scenarios, or be deployed together with AD DS. AD LDS is specifically used to provide directory services for deploying directory-enabled applications, without the dependencies of AD DS. Using AD LDS, you can deploy a lightweight directory service without domains or forests (as those are AD DS requirements), and you can support separate schemas for each instance of AD LDS you deploy. AD DS is limited to a single schema across the entire forest.

There are several scenarios in which you may want to deploy AD LDS:

- **Providing an enterprise directory store**   AD LDS is used to store application-specific data, which is only relevant to the enterprise application. This information can be stored on the same server as the application, or it can be replicated to multiple AD LDS servers across the enterprise. AD LDS can store just the configuration data for the enterprise application, whereas AD DS can be used to store the security principal data—which will reduce the amount of application-specific user-account databases across the network.

- **Providing an extranet authentication store**   AD LDS is a good candidate for this authentication store because it can store user account data that are not Windows security principals but that can be authenticated with LDAP simple binds. Web clients can access portal-based applications using a simple LDAP directory services.

- **Providing a configuration store for distributed applications**   In this scenario, an AD LDS instance that serves as the application's configuration store is bundled with a distributed application. This way, application designers do not have to be concerned about the availability of a directory service before the installation of the application. Instead, they can include AD LDS as a part of their application's installation process to ensure that the application has access to a directory service immediately upon installation. The application then configures and manages AD LDS entirely on its own or partially, depending on the application's exposure to the AD LDS management, and it uses AD LDS to address its various data requirements.

> **Note**   The Edge Transport Server role in Exchange Server 2007 is one example of an application that uses AD LDS. When you install this server role, AD LDS is automatically installed and configured to support the server role.

■ **Migrating legacy directory-enabled applications**   You can deploy AD LDS to serve and provide support for the legacy applications that rely on X.500-style naming, while you can use AD DS in the enterprise to provide a shared security infrastructure. You can use a metadirectory or configure synchronization between AD LDS and AD DS to automatically synchronize the data in AD DS and AD LDS for a seamless migration experience.

After you add the AD LDS server role to your server using Server Manager, you will create AD LDS instances and application partitions by using the Active Directory Lightweight Directory Services Setup Wizard. You can install several instances of AD LDS on a single server, with each instance using a different schema. Within each instance, you can configure multiple application partitions. After creating the instances and partitions, you can manage them using any LDAP management tools, such as the ADSI Edit MMC snap-in or LDP.exe.

Active Directory Rights Management Services Role

The Active Directory Rights Management Services Role (AD RMS) is used to augment an organization's existing security solution by providing an object-based persistent usage policy. AD RMS extends that security solution to include persistent usage policies that can protect sensitive corporate data, such as word-processing documents, customer data, e-mail messages, and financial data. The security restrictions for a specific file follow the document wherever it is moved and are not assigned to the container in which the document is stored (unlike ACLs).

Using AD RMS, network users can restrict the ability to copy, print, or forward sensitive data. This enables you to send confidential e-mail messages, so that the recipient can open and read the message but will not be able to cut, copy, or forward the message to other recipients, including any attachments included with the message. Confidential corporate communications remain confidential by restricting e-mail recipients from forwarding rights-protected communications. AD RMS also disables the ability to copy permissions-restricted data and then paste it into a nonrestricted e-mail message or document.

There are several enhancements to AD RMS in Windows Server 2008 over Windows Rights Management Services (RMS) that will improve administration of the service and will extend its functionality outside of the organization. The new features are:

■ **Improved installation and administration experience**   AD RMS is included with Windows Server 2008 and is installed as a server role. The earlier versions of RMS were provided as a separate installation available from the Microsoft Download Center. Additionally, AD RMS administration is now done through an MMC snap-in console, which is much easier to use than the Web interface used in the previous version of RMS. Additionally, with the inclusion of AD RMS administration roles, the AD RMS console displays only the parts of the console that the user can access. For example, a user who is using the AD RMS Template Administrators administration role is restricted to tasks that are specific to AD RMS templates. All other administrative tasks are not available in the AD RMS console.

- **Self-enrollment of the AD RMS cluster**   AD RMS cluster can be enrolled without having to connect to the Microsoft Enrollment Service. Through the use of a server self-enrollment certificate, the enrollment process is done entirely on the local computer. This new feature eliminates the operational dependency on the enrollment service and also allows AD RMS to operate in a network that is entirely isolated from the Internet.

- **Integration with AD FS**   AD RMS and AD FS have been integrated such that enterprises are able to leverage existing federated relationships to collaborate with external partners. In earlier versions of RMS, the options for external collaboration of rights-protected content were limited to Windows Live ID (formerly Microsoft Passport). Integrating AD FS with AD RMS provides the ability to establish federated identities between organizations and share rights-protected content, without requiring a deployment of AD RMS in both places.

- **New AD RMS administrative roles**   The ability to delegate AD RMS tasks to different administrators is needed in any enterprise environment and is included with this version of AD RMS. Three administrative roles have been created: AD RMS Enterprise Administrators, AD RMS Template Administrators, and AD RMS Auditors. The new AD RMS administrative roles give you the opportunity to delegate AD RMS tasks without giving full administrative control over the entire AD RMS cluster.

The AD RMS-enabled client must have an AD RMS-enabled browser or application, such as Microsoft Word, Outlook, or PowerPoint in Microsoft Office 2007. In order to create rights-protected content, Microsoft Office 2007 Enterprise, Professional Plus, or Ultimate is required. Windows Vista includes the AD RMS client by default, but other client operating systems must have the RMS client installed. The RMS client with Service Pack 2 (SP2) can be downloaded from the Microsoft Download Center and works on versions of the client operating system earlier than Windows Vista and Windows Server 2008. For additional security, AD RMS can be integrated with other technologies such as smart cards.

> **Note**   Recipients of rights-protected messages who are not running an e-mail application that supports messages with restricted permission, such as Microsoft Office 2003 or Microsoft Office 2007, can view these messages by downloading the Rights Management Add-on for Internet Explorer from the Microsoft Download Center at *http://www.microsoft.com/down-loads/details.aspx?FamilyId=B48F920B-5AF0-46B4-994F-2F62582CC86F&displaylang=en*. This download is required for recipients using Web mail applications, for example.

AD RMS is installed on a computer running the Windows Server 2008 operating system. When the AD RMS server role is installed, the required services are installed. Internet Information Services (IIS) is a required service. AD RMS also requires a database, such as Microsoft SQL

Server, which can be run either on the same server as AD RMS or on a remote server located within the same AD DS forest. In addition, AD RMS and AD FS have been integrated to allow enterprises to leverage existing federated relationships to collaborate and secure information with external partners.

Summary

This chapter introduced the new features of AD DS, as well as the server roles that are available in Windows Server 2008. Understanding these new features and server roles will equip directory services administrators with the information necessary to evaluate the migration to Windows Server 2008 and Active Directory and to plan for the new functionality that Windows Server 2008 will provide in their organization.

Chapter 2

Active Directory Domain Services Components

As an Active Directory Domain Services (AD DS) administrator, you will spend much of your time configuring user and group accounts that are located in organizational units or container objects, which are located in a domain. When you configure these objects, you are actually making changes to a database file that is stored on the domain controller hard drive. In most circumstances, you will not directly interact with the physical AD DS database; rather you will use the AD DS management tools to modify the logical objects stored in the database.

Microsoft Windows Server 2008 AD DS includes both a physical component and a logical organization of objects in the directory. In terms of its physical structure, AD DS consists of a single database file on the hard disk of each of the domain controllers that host the service. The logical structure of AD DS consists of the containers that are used to store the directory service objects (such as directory partitions, domains, and forests) in the enterprise. In this chapter, you will learn about the physical components that make up the AD DS. Then, you will look at the logical structure of an AD DS implementation. A solid understanding of the physical structure of the directory service is important, but your understanding of the logical structure is vital to successful implementation and management of your directory service infrastructure. It is this logical structure of the directory service that you will interact with on a daily basis.

AD DS Physical Structure

AD DS data is stored primarily as a single database file. The database file is stored on domain controllers, which provide access to the database for administrators and provide directory service functionality such as authentication and authorization for other users and computers. When implementing AD DS, you can add as many domain controllers as are needed to support the directory services needs of the organization.

All domain controllers in a domain provide essentially the same services. However, there are five specific roles that can be located on only one domain controller at a time. These roles are known as *flexible single-master operation roles*. AD DS also enables unique domain controller roles for global catalog servers and read-only domain controllers. In this section you will look at both the AD DS data store and the domain controllers that host it.

The Directory Data Store

All the data in the AD DS database is stored in a file named Ntds.dit and the transaction logs on the domain controller. These data files are stored by default in the %SystemRoot%\NTDS folder on the domain controller. These files store all the directory information for the domain, as well as information that is shared by all domain controllers in a given organization. Global catalog servers also store the global catalog data in the same files.

> **Note**   Although you will rarely directly interact with the AD DS data files, you do need to understand how AD DS manages the database, and you may need to work with the files during disaster recovery. You will learn more about how to maintain and recover the AD DS database in Chapter 14, "Monitoring and Maintaining Active Directory," and Chapter 15, "Active Directory Disaster Recovery."

The AD DS data store is implemented on every domain controller in the forest. The AD DS data store consists of several components that are shown in Figure 2-1.

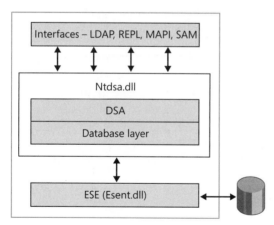

Figure 2-1   The AD DS data store includes several components.

Table 2-1 provides a description of the data store components.

Table 2-1   Data Store Components

Component	Description
Interfaces	Client computers, administrators, and other domain controllers cannot communicate directly with the database. The data store supports the following interfaces for directory clients and other directory servers to communicate with the data store: ■ **Lightweight Directory Access Protocol (LDAP)** LDAP v3 is the most common interface used by directory clients to locate information in the directory store. LDAP v3 is backward compatible with LDAP v2. Clients can use port 389 (the standard LDAP port), port 636 (LDAP secured by SSL), port 3268 (for global catalog lookups), and port 3269 (Global catalog LDAP secured by SSL) to access the LDAP interface. Clients can also use UDP Port 389 for both LDAP and Netlogon (this interface is used to locate domain controllers). ■ **Replication (REPL) and domain controller management interface** The REPL management interface is used by AD DS management tools and during replication between domain controllers. This interface provides functionality for finding data about domain controllers, converting the names of network objects between different formats, and manipulating service principal names (SPNs) and DSAs. This interface is accessible through Remote Procedure Calls (RPCs) and through SMTP (only for SMTP based replication). ■ **Messaging API (MAPI)** MAPI is used by messaging clients such as Outlook to access the Microsoft Exchange Server data stored in the data store. Exchange Server 2000 and later use the AD DS data store to store all recipient information, and the MAPI interface enables messaging clients to access the Global Address List (GAL). MAPI uses RPC communication. ■ **Security Accounts Manager (SAM)** SAM is a proprietary interface for connecting to the DSA on behalf of clients that use Windows NT 4.0 or earlier. These clients use Windows NT 4.0 networking APIs to connect to the DSA through SAM. SAM communication also uses RPC communication.
Directory Service Agent (DSA) (Ntdsa.dll)	The DSA (which runs as Ntdsai.dll on each domain controller) provides the data store access interfaces. In addition, the DSA enforces directory semantics, maintains the schema, guarantees object identity, and enforces data types on attributes. When clients or other domain controllers need to access the directory store, they used one of the supported interfaces to connect (bind) to the DSA and then search for, read, and write to AD DS objects and their attributes.

Table 2-1   Data Store Components *(continued)*

Component	Description
Database layer	The database layer resides in Ntdsai.dll and provides an internal interface between the DSA and the directory database. The DSA cannot directly connect to the database; applications go through the database layer. The database layer also provides an object view of the directory database, making the data accessible to the DSA as a set of hierarchical containers.
	The database layer is also responsible for the creation, retrieval, and deletion of individual records (objects), attributes within records, and values within attributes.
ESE (Esent.dll)	The Extensible Storage Engine (ESE) is a Windows component that is used by AD DS, as well as by several other Windows components, as an interface to the database. The ESE is responsible for indexing the data in the database file and for transferring the data in and out of the database. It also maintains the rows and columns that comprise the database. Its purpose is to enable applications to store and retrieve data. The ESE also implements the transactional process for committing changes to the database.
Database files	The data store stores directory information in a single database file. In addition, the data store also uses transaction log files, to which it temporarily writes uncommitted changes, as well as committed transactions prior to committing them to the database.

Note   A second copy of the Ntds.dit file is located on every domain controller in the %SystemRoot%\System32 folder structure. This version of the file is the distribution copy (default copy) of the directory database and is only used to install AD DS. This file is copied to the server when Microsoft Windows Server 2008 is installed so that the server can be promoted to a domain controller without having to access the installation media. When the Active Directory Domain Services Installation Wizard (Dcpromo.exe) is run, the Ntds.dit file is copied from the System32 folder to the NTDS folder. The copy stored in the NTDS folder then becomes the live copy of the directory data store. If this is not the first domain controller in the domain, this file will be updated from other domain controllers in the domain through the replication process.

Domain Controllers

By definition, any computer running Windows Server 2008 that maintains a copy of the AD DS database is a domain controller. Domain controllers provide authentication services for the domain as well as directory lookup services. With several exceptions, which are detailed later in this chapter, all domain controllers are created equal. Using the multimaster replication process described in Chapter 4, "Active Directory Domain Services Replication," every domain controller in the domain maintains an up-to-date copy of the domain database and is capable of making changes to the database.

In addition to the domain controllers that host AD DS, there are several special-purpose domain controllers that AD DS requires to perform certain functions. These are the global catalog servers and the operations masters. In addition, Windows Server 2008 supports read-only domain controllers (RODCs).

Global Catalog Servers

The global catalog is a partial, read-only replica of all other domain directory partitions in the forest. The additional domain directory partitions are partial because only a limited set of attributes is included for each object. By including only the attributes that are most used for searching, every object in every domain in the forest can be represented in the database of a single global catalog server. The global catalog provides the ability to efficiently locate objects from any domain even if the forest contains multiple domains and domain trees. Searches that use the global catalog are faster because they do not involve referrals to different domain controllers.

The global catalog is stored on domain controllers that have been designated as global catalog servers and is distributed through multimaster replication.

Whether or not an attribute is replicated to the global catalog is determined by the schema. The attributes that are included to the global catalog are identified in the schema as the partial attribute set (PAS). The PAS is identified by the *isMemberOfPartialAttributeSet* attribute: if this attribute is set to *true*, then the attribute will be included in the global catalog.

Administrators can add attributes to the global catalog by using the Active Directory Schema snap-in. You may choose to add an attribute to the global catalog if you anticipate that users will need to search for objects across multiple domains by using a specific attribute. For example, the *Department* attribute is not added to the global catalog by default. If you want users to be able to search for users by department in multiple domains, then you should consider adding the attribute to the global catalog.

To add an attribute to the global catalog, access the attribute properties in Active Directory Schema and select the Replicate This Attribute To The Global Catalog option. This will set the value of the *isMemberOfPartialAttributeSet* parameter on the attribute to *true*. Figure 2-2 shows the interface used to configure an attribute as a member of the PAS.

Caution Use caution when adding attributes to the global catalog. When you add an attribute to the global catalog, the global catalog must be recalculated in all domains in the forest and the updated information must be replicated to all global catalog servers. This is particularly important if your environment contains Windows 2000 domain controllers. When a new attribute is added to or removed from the global catalog on a Windows 2000 domain controller, the domain controller will rebuild and re-replicate the *entire* global catalog. Windows Server 2003 and later domain controllers only replicate the delta (that is, the attribute that was added to or removed from the PAS). In a large organization with multiple domains, this may require significant processor and network utilization. In most cases, you will make changes to the PAS only if it is required by a specific application. For example, installing Exchange 2000 Server, or later versions of Exchange Server, will add many new attributes to the global catalog.

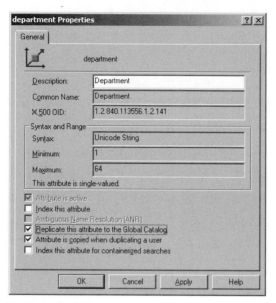

Figure 2-2   You can add the *Department* attribute to the global catalog by using the Active Directory Schema MMC.

The first domain controller installed in the forest is automatically configured as a global catalog server. Additional domain controllers can be designated as global catalog servers during the installation of AD DS or by selecting the Global Catalog Server option in the Active Directory Sites and Services administrative tool.

> **Note**   In most cases, you should configure a global catalog server in each office location that is configured as an AD DS site. This will optimize the logon process for users in that office. Chapter 5, "Designing the Active Directory Domain Services Structure," provides guidance on the number of global catalog servers you will need to deploy and where to locate them.

Global catalog servers are important for several reasons. One reason is that they are used for making AD DS searches more efficient. Without a global catalog, search requests received by a domain controller for an object in a different domain would result in that domain controller referring the query to a domain controller in the object domain. This search would be possible only if the search query included the domain where the object is located. Because the global catalog contains a complete list of every object in the forest, the global catalog server can respond to any query using an attribute that has been replicated to the global catalog without needing to refer to another domain controller.

> **Note**   Global catalog queries are identical to any other LDAP query against a Windows Server 2008 domain controller. The only difference is that the global catalog query uses TCP port 3268 rather than TCP port 389, which is the standard LDAP port. If a domain controller that is also a global catalog server receives a query on port 389, it will not search the global catalog for objects in other domains.

Global catalog servers are also used when processing user logons. Every time a user logs on to a domain, a global catalog server is contacted. This is because nonglobal catalog domain controllers do not contain any information about universal group membership. Universal groups can contain user and group accounts from any domain in a particular forest. Since universal group membership is forest-wide, group membership can only be resolved by a domain controller that has forest-wide directory information—the global catalog. In order for an accurate security token to be generated for the user seeking authentication, the global catalog must be contacted to determine the user's universal group membership.

Note   Windows Server 2008 supports a feature known as *universal group membership caching* that makes it possible to log on to a Windows Server 2008 network without contacting a global catalog. Universal group membership can be cached on nonglobal catalog domain controllers after a user has logged on to that domain controller. After this information is obtained from a global catalog, it is cached on the domain controller for the site indefinitely and is periodically updated (by default every 8 hours). Enabling this feature results in faster logon times for users in remote sites, as the authenticating domain controllers do not have to access a global catalog. Chapter 5 goes into more detail on planning and configuring universal group membership caching.

Global catalog servers are also required to process user logons when users use a User Principal Name (UPN) to log on. UPNs enable users to log on to computers in any domain in a forest by using a consistent user name. The UPN format is *username@domainname*, but the domain name does not need to be the domain that contains the user account. In order to identify the user's domain, the UPN must be resolved in the global catalog.

Read-Only Domain Controllers

Read-only domain controllers (RODC) are another special type of domain controller available in Windows Server 2008 AD DS. RODCs host read-only versions of the AD DS database and provide all of the authentication and authorization services provided by other domain controllers.

RODCs are primarily designed to be deployed in branch offices scenarios where the physical security of the domain controller cannot be ensured, or in scenarios where the local storage of domain passwords is considered a security risk. RODCs can also contain read-only versions of the AD DS integrated DNS zones and can be configured as global catalog servers.

Note   For additional security, consider deploying RODCs on Windows Server 2008 Server Core installation option. This installation option does not provide any graphical administration tools. In addition, as RODCs may be deployed in sites that are not considered secure, you should not deploy any regular domain controllers in these sites.

Credential Caching on RODCs

One of the configuration options available on an RODC is credential caching. Credential caching refers to the storage of the password that is associated with security principals. All writable domain controllers have access to all security principal credentials. To provide additional security for an RODC, you can restrict which credentials are cached on an RODC.

By default, no credentials other than the RODC computer account and a special krbtgt account are stored on the RODC. This means that the RODC must have an available connection to a writable domain controller whenever a user or computer authenticates to the RODC. When the RODC receives the authentication request, it forwards the request to a writable domain controller.

You can modify the default credential caching configuration by configuring the Password Replication Policy for RODC. For example, you might consider configuring the Password Replication Policy so that the credentials for all user, computer, and service accounts in the branch office are cached on the RODC. When you modify the Password Replication Policy, passwords will be cached on the RODC after the next successful logon of a security principal identified in the policy. After an account is successfully authenticated, the RODC attempts to contact a writable domain controller at the hub site and requests a copy of the appropriate credentials. The writable domain controller recognizes that the request is coming from an RODC and consults the Password Replication Policy in effect for that RODC. If the Password Replication Policy allows it, the writable domain controller replicates the credentials to the RODC, and the RODC caches them. After the credentials are cached on the RODC, the RODC can directly service that user's logon requests until the credentials change or until the Password Replication Policy changes.

By limiting credential caching on the RODC, you can limit the potential exposure of credentials if the RODC is stolen. Typically, only a small subset of domain users has credentials cached on any given RODC. Therefore, in the event that the RODC is stolen, only those credentials that are cached can potentially be abused. In that case, you can use Active Directory Users and Computers to easily identify which credentials are cached on the server, and reset the passwords for all of those accounts.

To support the RODC Password Replication Policy, Windows Server 2008 AD DS includes new attributes that are assigned to an RODC. These attributes include the following:

- *msDS-Reveal-OnDemandGroup*   This attribute identifies a group whose members are permitted to have their credentials cached on the RODC.

- *msDS-NeverRevealGroup*   This attribute identifies a group for which the credentials for all group members are blocked from being cached on the RODC. By default, this attribute contains all administrator accounts. This attribute does not impact the ability of these security principals to authenticate using the RODC.

- *msDS-RevealedList*   This attribute is a list of security principals for which the RODC has cached credentials.

■ *msDS-AuthenticatedToAccountList* This attribute contains a list of security principals in the local domain that have authenticated to the RODC. You can determine which computers and users are using the RODC for logon by accessing the RODC properties in Active Directory Users and Computers. This enables you to refine the Password Replication Policy for the RODC.

Delegating Administrative Permissions on RODC

Another feature available with RODCs is Administrator Role Separation, which enables you to configure a delegated local administrator for the RODC without granting any domain level permissions. The delegated administrator can log on to an RODC to perform maintenance work on the server such as upgrading a driver. However, the delegated administrator would not be able to log on to any other domain controller or perform any other administrative task in the domain. Consider delegating administrative permissions on the RODC if the domain controller is located in a branch office that does not have any domain administrators on site.

Security Alert RODC delegated local administrators have direct access to the Active Directory Domain Services database files, and as such, they could potentially crack all information stored in the RODC, including cached credentials. Delegated local administrators should still be highly trusted individuals.

Note You can add the delegated local administrator to the RODC when you run the Active Directory Domain Services Installation Wizard. When you delegate local administrator permissions, the user account is not added to any extra security group. Instead, the user or group name is kept in an attribute on the RODC computer object in AD DS, which is used when that user tries to log on to the RODC. Note that the delegated local administrator credentials are not cached by default on the RODC. This means that the delegated local administrator will not be able to log on to the RODC if a writable domain controller is not available. Consider modifying this setting if local administration is required in the RODC when a WAN link fails. To add local administrators to the RODC administrative groups after AD DS is configured, use the Dsmgmt.exe command-line tool. For complete details, see Chapter 6, "Installing Active Directory Domain Services."

RODC Limitations

Some domain controller options that are available for writable domain controllers are not available on an RODC. An RODC cannot be configured as:

■ **An operations master role holder** Operations master role holders must be able to write information to the AD DS database. For example, the schema master must be able to write definitions for new object classes and attributes. The relative ID (RID) master must be able to write the values of RID pools that are allocated to other domain controllers. Because of the read-only nature of the AD DS database on an RODC, it cannot act as an operations master role holder.

■ **A bridgehead server**   Bridgehead servers are servers that are designated to replicate changes from and to other sites. Because RODCs can only receive changes through replication and cannot send replication updates, they cannot act as a bridgehead server for a site. If you deploy an RODC in a site with other domain controllers in the same domain or forest, one of the other domain controllers will be configured as the bridgehead server for the site.

On the Disc   You can use the ListDomainControllers.ps1 Windows PowerShell script on the CD to list all of the domain controllers in your domain and global catalog servers in your forest. If you are running Windows PowerShell on a Windows Server 2008 computer, you must configure the PowerShell script execution policy to allow unsigned certificates by running the Set-ExecutionPolicy RemoteSigned command. Also, you need to provide the full path when running a Windows PowerShell script.

For examples of Visual Basic Scripting Edition (VBScript) scripts that you can use to obtain AD DS information, see the Script Center Script Repository Web site at *http://www.microsoft.com/technet/scriptcenter/scripts/default.mspx?mfr=true*.

Operations Masters

AD DS is designed as a multimaster replication system. This requires that all domain controllers other than RODCs have Write permissions for the directory database. This system works well for most directory operations, but for certain directory operations a single authoritative server is required. The domain controllers that perform specific roles are known as operations masters, and each has a flexible single-master operations (FSMO, pronounced *fizz-mo*) role. The domain controllers that hold operations master roles are designated to perform specific tasks to ensure consistency and to eliminate the potential for conflicting entries in the AD DS database. The five operations master roles in AD DS are as follows:

■ Schema master

■ Domain naming master

■ RID master

■ PDC emulator

■ Infrastructure master

The first two roles, schema master and domain naming master, are per-forest roles. This means that there is only one schema master and only one domain naming master for every forest. The other three roles are per-domain roles; there is one of these operations master roles for each domain in the forest. When you install AD DS and create the first domain controller in the forest, it will possess all five of these roles. Similarly, as you add domains to the forest, the first domain controller in each new domain will also acquire the per-domain operations master roles. As you add domain controllers to a domain, you can transfer these roles to other domain controllers.

Schema Master

The schema master is the only domain controller that has Write permissions to the directory schema. To make any change to the schema, the administrator (who must be a member of the Schema Admins security group) must be connected to the schema master. If a modification to the schema is attempted on a domain controller other than the schema master, it will fail. After a change has been made, schema updates are replicated to all other domain controllers in the forest.

The schema master is identified by the value of the *fSMORoleOwner* attribute on the root object of the schema partition. By default, the first domain controller installed in a forest assumes the schema master role. This role can be transferred at any time using the Active Directory Schema snap-in or by using the Ntdsutil command-line utility.

Domain Naming Master

The domain naming master is the domain controller that manages the addition and removal of all directory partitions in the forest hierarchy. The domain controller that has the domain naming master role must be available when you:

- **Add or remove domains**   When you create or remove a child domain or new domain tree, the installation wizard contacts the domain naming master and requests the addition or deletion. The domain naming master is responsible for ensuring that domain names are unique. If the domain naming master is unavailable, you cannot add domains or remove them from the forest.

- **Add or remove application directory partitions**   Application directory partitions are special partitions that can be created on domain controllers running Windows Server 2003 or Windows Server 2008 to provide storage for dynamic application data. If the domain controller hosting the domain naming operations master role is not available, you cannot add or remove application directory partitions from the forest.

- **Add or remove cross-reference objects**   When a new forest is created, the schema, configuration, and domain directory partitions are created on the first domain controller in the forest. A cross-reference object is created for each directory partition in the Partitions container in the configuration directory partition (*CN=partitions,CN=configuration, DC=forestRootDomain*). As new domains or application directory partitions are created, an associated cross-reference object is also created in the Partitions container. If the domain naming master is unavailable, you cannot add or remove cross-reference objects.

- **Validate domain rename instructions**   When you use the domain rename tool, Rendom.exe, to rename an AD DS domain, the tool must be able to access the domain naming operations master. When you run the tool, the XML-encoded script containing the domain rename instructions is written to the *msDS-UpdateScript* attribute on the Partitions container object (*CN=partitions,CN=configuration,DC=ForestRootDomain*) in the configuration directory partition. In addition, the new DNS name of each domain being renamed is also written by Rendom.exe to the *msDS-DnsRootAlias* attribute on the cross-reference object (class *crossRef*) corresponding to that domain. Both of these objects are stored in the Partitions container, and the container can only be updated on the domain controller holding the domain naming operations master role for the forest.

The domain naming master is identified by the value of the *fSMORoleOwner* attribute on the Partitions container object. By default, the first domain controller installed in a forest assumes the domain naming master role. This role can be transferred at any time using the Active Directory Domains and Trusts snap-in or by using the Ntdsutil command-line utility.

RID Master

The RID master is a per-domain operations master role. It is used to manage the RID pool to create new security principals throughout the domain, such as users, groups, and computers. Each security principal is issued a unique security identifier (SID) that includes a domain identifier, which is the same for all SIDs in the domain, and a relative identifier (RID), which is unique for each security principal. Because security principals can be created on any domain controller with a writable copy of the directory, the RID master is used to ensure that two domain controllers do not issue the same RID. The RID master issues a block of relative identifiers (RIDs), called the RID pool, to every domain controller in the domain. When the number of available RIDs in the RID pool on any domain controller begins to run low (below about 100), a request is made for another block of RIDs from the RID master. When this happens, the RID master issues a pool of about another 500 RIDs to the domain controller.

If the RID master is unavailable for a period of time, the process of creating new accounts on specific domain controllers may be interrupted. The mechanism for requesting a new block of RIDs is designed so that this should not happen, because the request is made before all of the available RIDs in the RID pool are exhausted. However, if the RID master is offline and the requesting domain controller depletes the remainder of its RIDs, account creation will fail. To re-enable account creation, either the RID master role holder must be brought back online, or the role must be transferred to another domain controller in the domain.

The RID master is identified by the value of the *fSMORoleOwner* attribute on the object in the domain partition whose class is *rIDManager*. By default, the first domain controller installed in a new domain assumes the RID master role. This role can be transferred at any time using the Active Directory Users and Computer snap-in or by using the Ntdsutil command-line utility.

PDC Emulator

The PDC emulator role operates as a primary domain controller (PDC) for pre-Windows 2000 operating systems. Windows NT member servers and client computers must be able to communicate with a PDC to process password changes. In addition to providing services for older clients, the PDC emulator also plays an important role in replicating passwords.

> **Note**   In Windows 2000 and Windows 2003 Active Directory, one of the important roles for the PDC Emulator is to act as the PDC for down-level (Microsoft Windows NT 3.51 or Windows NT 4.0) backup domain controllers (BDCs). Because Windows Server 2008 does not support coexistence with pre-Windows 2000 domain controllers, this functionality is no longer relevant.

Even if no Windows NT member servers or client computers exist in the domain, the PDC emulator has a role in maintaining password updates. All password changes made on other domain controllers in the domain are sent to the PDC emulator using urgent replication. If a user authentication fails on a domain controller other than the PDC emulator, authentication is retried on the PDC emulator. If the PDC emulator has accepted a recent password change for the account, authentication will succeed. When a user successfully authenticates on a domain controller where the previous attempt failed, the domain controller notifies PDC emulator of the successful authentication. This resets the lockout counter at the PDC emulator in case another client attempts to validate the same account by using a different domain controller.

The PDC emulator is identified by the value of the *fSMORoleOwner* attribute on the root object of the domain partition. By default, the first domain controller installed in a new domain assumes the PDC emulator role. This role can be transferred at any time using the Active Directory Users and Computers snap-in or by using the Ntdsutil command-line utility.

Infrastructure Master

The infrastructure master is responsible for updating the cross-domain group-to-user references. This operations master role ensures that changes made to object names (changes to the common name attribute, *cn*) are reflected in the group membership information for groups located on a different domain. The infrastructure master maintains an up-to-date list of these references, and it then replicates this information to all other domain controllers in the domain. If the infrastructure master is unavailable, the cross-domain group-to-user references will be out of date.

The infrastructure master is identified by the value of the *fSMORoleOwner* attribute on the Infrastructure container in the domain partition (*CN=Infrastructure, DC=domain*). By default, the first domain controller installed in a new domain assumes the infrastructure master role. This role can be transferred at any time using the Active Directory Users And Computers snap-in or by using the Ntdsutil command-line utility.

> **On the Disc**   To display which domain controllers in your forest and domain hold the FSMO roles, run the ListFSMOs.ps1 Windows PowerShell script on the CD.

Transferring Operations Master Roles

Operations master roles can be moved between domain controllers either to better optimize domain controller performance or to substitute a domain controller if a role holder has become unavailable. The process for doing this will depend on the role being transferred. Table 2-2 lists the tools that are used to transfer the five operations master roles.

Table 2-2   Tools for Managing the Operation Master Roles

Operations Master Role	Administration Tool
Schema master	Active Directory Schema
Domain naming master	Active Directory Domains And Trusts
RID master, PDC emulator, and infrastructure master	Active Directory Users And Computers

To transfer an operations master role, there must be connectivity to both the current and proposed role holder domain controllers. In the event of server failure, the current role holder may not be available to complete a role transfer. In this case, the role can be seized. Seizing operations master roles is not a preferred option and should be done only if absolutely necessary. You should only seize an operations master role if it is indicated that the domain controller hosting this role will be unavailable for an extended period. More information on seizing operations master roles is provided in Chapter 15.

> **Note**   The operation master roles can be moved to any other domain controller in the domain. The only restriction on operation master placement is that the infrastructure master role should not be installed on a domain controller that is also a global catalog server if the forest contains multiple domains, unless every domain controller in the domain is also a global catalog server. By default, the first domain controller in a forest is both a global catalog server and holds the infrastructure master role. When you install the second domain controller in the domain and that domain controller is not a global catalog server, the Active Directory Domain Services Installation Wizard prompts you to move the infrastructure master to the new domain controller during the AD DS installation.

The Schema

The schema defines every class and attribute that can be stored in AD DS. Every object in AD DS is an instance of a class. Examples of classes are "user" or "group." Before an object can be created in AD DS, its class must first be defined in the schema. The schema also enforces a number of rules regarding the creation of objects in the database.

There is one schema per forest. However, a copy of the schema is replicated to every domain controller in the forest. This way, every domain controller has quick access to any class or attribute definition that it might need, and every domain controller uses the same definition when it creates a given object. The data store relies on the schema to provide class and attribute definitions, and the data store uses those definitions to enforce data integrity. The result is that all objects are created uniformly, and it does not matter which domain controller creates or modifies an object because all domain controllers use the same schema definitions.

Schema Components

The schema is made up of *classSchema* objects and *attributeSchema* objects. The *classSchema* objects are definitions that are stored in the schema and are used to define classes. Classes define groups of attributes that have something in common. An example of a class is the *User* class. The *User* class includes a variety of attributes, including the user's logon name, first name, last name, and password. Any time a new user account is created, the directory uses the *User* class to define how the object will be configured. Settings determined by the *User* class include attributes the object can and must have and which classes can be its superior in the AD DS hierarchy. Every user object that is created uses those attributes.

The schema also defines the attributes that can be stored for each class. Attributes are defined globally in AD DS as *attributeSchema* objects, and each class can use multiple globally defined attributes. For example, a user account object has a number of attributes that are used to store various pieces of data that are related to a user account, such as a logon name attribute and a password attribute. Each of these attributes is defined by attribute objects that also have their own definition that specifies information such as the type of data that they store and the minimum and maximum length or value. The directory service uses *attributeSchema* objects to define the type of the data stored in attributes for each object of a given class and to enforce the constraints defined in the *attributeSchema* (for example, string length range).

The *classSchema* object specifies the attributes that are associated with the object. The specification includes all of the attributes that can be associated with the object, which can be broken into four categories:

- *mustContain* attributes, which include mandatory attributes that must be present on any object that is an instance of this class

- *mayContain* attributes, which include optional attributes that may be found on an object that is an instance of this class

- *systemmayContain* attributes, which are optional attributes configured during object creation, and which cannot be modified after the object has been created

- *systemmustContain* attributes, which are mandatory attributes configured during object creation, and which cannot be modified after the object has been created

Additionally, the *classSchema* object specifies hierarchy rules that determine the possible parents in the directory tree of an object that is an instance of the class. For example, as shown in Figure 2-3, a computer object can only be created in the *container, domainDNS*, or *organizationUnit* objects.

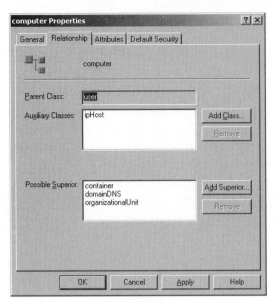

Figure 2-3   The schema defines where objects can be created in AD DS.

Finally, the type of data that can be stored in AD DS for each attribute is defined in the schema as the attribute's *syntax*. The *User* class contains an attribute titled *displayName*, and the syntax for this attribute is defined as a string value that accepts any alphanumeric character. The value for each attribute included with an instance of a class must meet the syntax requirements for that attribute.

The AD DS schema supports inheritance of classes. All schema objects are organized hierarchically. Because of this hierarchical structure, any class is able to inherit all of the characteristics of its parent class. For example, as shown in Figure 2-3, the *Computer* class is actually a subclass of the *User* class. As such, the *Computer* class inherits all of the attributes associated with the *User* class. The *Computer* class is then associated with the attributes specific to the *User* class. Using the Active Directory Schema snap-in, you can see the organization of class inheritance and the hierarchy of the object classes. This system of inheritance makes it much easier for administrators to create new object classes, because they do not have to define every attribute that is associated with a new class. The new object simply inherits all the attribute associations of a suitable parent class.

Modifying the Schema

The AD DS schema contains the most commonly used classes and attributes to support an enterprise directory services implementation. In order to support applications that need to store information in AD DS, the schema was designed to be extensible. In other words, it can be modified, or *extended*, to include new class and attribute objects that an organization might need.

The schema is most often extended to meet the needs of an Active Directory–enabled application. A good example of this is Microsoft Exchange Server 2007, which makes more than a thousand modifications to the schema to enable AD DS to support Exchange Server.

> **Note**   Before you can install Exchange 2000, Exchange 2003, or Exchange 2007, you must modify the schema. The Exchange installation files include several LDIF files that, when imported, make the required schema changes. If you are deploying a different application that requires you to modify the schema, you should only modify the schema using LDIF files that have been thoroughly tested. This will help prevent you from making mistakes in modifying the schema.

How It Works: Indexing for Optimized Searches

The directory data store can be indexed to improve the efficiency of searches. Indexing is specified as part of the schema definition of an attribute (such as *Description* or *given-Name*). When an attribute is indexed, all occurrences of that attribute will be included in the index. Some attributes are indexed by default, and the administrator can configure additional attributes to be indexed. Multiple types of indexing are available, depending on how the attribute will be used in searches:

- **Basic indexing**   The value(s) of the attribute is indexed so that queries requesting objects with a specific value for that attribute will run quickly.

- **Containerized indexes**   Similar to basic indexing, but also indexes the objects by container. This enables a query to quickly evaluate all the child objects in a container to determine if any match the requested attribute value.

- **Tuple indexes**   Used on string attributes so that substring searches specifying that attribute will run quickly. For example, applying a tuple index to the *Description* attribute would allow queries such as "return all objects whose *Description* attribute contains the string 'Fabrikam' anywhere in it" to execute efficiently. Maintaining tuple indexes can consume a large amount of resources, so they should be enabled sparingly.

- **Subtree indexes**   Enables a special type of Active Directory search, known as virtual list view, to execute quickly. These are similar to containerized indexes but include not only the immediate children of the container but also all the grand-children, great-grandchildren, and so on. Like tuple indexes, subtree indexes can be expensive to maintain.

Administrators can enable indexing on attributes that aren't indexed by default, based on the needs of their organization. Basic and containerized indexes can be enabled using the Active Directory Schema snap-in. However, tuple and subtree indexes require you to manually set the value of the *searchFlags* attribute on the *attributeSchema* objects defining the attributes you want to index.

> Tuple indexing and how to enable it are discussed in more detail at *http://msdn2.microsoft.com/en-us/library/ms676931.aspx*. The *searchFlags* attribute, including the values to set for tuple and subtree indexes, is discussed at *http://msdn2.microsoft.com/en-us/library/ms679765.aspx*.
>
> *Matthew Rimer*
>
> *Senior SDE, US-Directory and Service Business*

Apart from using Active Directory-enabled applications, administrators can extend the schema using a variety of other methods. The schema can be extended in a batch mode using command-line administrative tools, including the LDAP Data Interchange Format Directory Exchange (LDIFDE) tool and the Comma Separated Value Directory Exchange (CSVDE) tool. The schema can also be extended programmatically, using Active Directory Service Interfaces (ADSI) and Microsoft Visual Basic scripts.

Finally, the schema can be modified from the Windows Server 2008 user interface (UI) using the Active Directory Schema snap-in. For example, an organization may need to keep records of employee start dates. It could maintain the employee start date as an attribute of the user object in AD DS. By default, AD DS does not include this attribute. To have this attribute available when each new user object is to be created, the attribute would first be defined in the schema.

To use the Active Directory Schema snap-in, you must first register the snap-in by executing the Regsvr32 Schmmgmt.dll command from the command line and then add the Active Directory Schema snap-in to an MMC. You must be a member of the Schema Admins global group to modify the schema using this interface.

> **Caution**   Although you can deactivate changes that you make to the schema, you can never remove new classes or attributes that you create in the schema. You should make changes to the schema only after careful planning and thorough testing in a test forest. Ensure that your schema changes are compatible with current and future applications that require schema changes.

Creating a New Attribute

To use the Active Directory Schema snap-in to add a new attribute to the schema and associate it with the *User* class object, perform the following steps:

1. Open the Active Directory Schema snap-in.

2. Select the Attributes folder in the tree pane.

3. From the Action menu, click Create Attribute.

4. At the Schema Object Creation warning dialog box, click Continue.

5. In the Create New Attribute dialog box, supply information for the Identification section:

    ❑ Common Name

    ❑ LDAP Display Name

    ❑ Unique X500 Object ID

    ❑ Description

6. In the Syntax and Range section, supply information for:

    ❑ Syntax

    ❑ Minimum

    ❑ Maximum

    ❑ Select whether or not the new attribute is a Multi-Valued attribute.

> **Note**   Further information about the content of each field is available by selecting the field's text box and then pressing the F1 function key.

Figure 2-4 shows how to create a new attribute using the Active Directory Schema snap-in.

7. After creating the new attribute, you must associate the attribute with the class object. To do this, select the Classes folder in the tree pane.

8. Locate the class object to which you want to add the attribute, right-click the object, and click Properties.

9. On the Attributes tab, click Add, and add the new attribute that you created.

> **Note**   Adding a new attribute to the schema does not mean that the attribute will automatically be accessible from any of the administrative tools. The administrative tools like Active Directory Users And Computers only show some of the attributes for each class and do not show any attributes you add. If you want the new attribute to appear in an administrative tool, you must either modify the existing tool or create your own. For information on how to modify and create administrative tools, see "Extending the User Interface for Directory Objects" at *http://msdn2.microsoft.com/en-us/library/ms676902.aspx*. ADSIEdit will display new attributes because the list of available attributes on an object is dynamically loaded from the schema.

Figure 2-4   Creating the *EmployeeStartDate* attribute in AD DS.

Direct from the Source: Implementing Schema Updates

After creating new attributes, you should not take for granted that the new attributes will be immediately available in the schema. Schema attributes and classes internally dictate the structure of the database. The creation of new classes or attributes has a much bigger performance impact on the domain controller compared to other regular operations. Given the importance of schema for the system, the whole schema content is always cached in memory. When the schema is updated, the cached copy of the schema must be updated before the new attributes or classes are available. By default, AD DS waits for five minutes after the last change is made to the schema before updating the cache.

The main schema extensions scenario is when new directory enabled software is installed (for example, when installing Exchange Server or when you run Adprep to update a Windows 2000 or 2003 forest to prepare for Windows Server 2008). In these scenarios, multiple changes are made to the schema in sequence in a short period of time. In many cases, the changes to the schema have dependencies—for example, one schema change may create a new attribute, and other change will assign the new attribute to a class.

When creating the LDIF files to update the schema, it is recommended that the schema extension developer include a signal to AD DS to refresh the schema cache before using references to just created attributes or classes. This can be done by setting the *rootDSE* attribute *schemaUpdateNow* to *1*. Most of the sch*.ldf files that are used by Adprep do this. For example, the sch43.ldif file updates the schema cache after new attribute creation and before they are referenced by new classes. To update the schema cache, the file contains the following lines:

```
DN:
changetype: modify
add: schemaUpdateNow
schemaUpdateNow: 1
-
```

Elbio Abib, SDE II

X.500 Object IDs

The *X.500 OID* namespace is a hierarchical naming structure that identifies a unique number for each *classSchema* and *attributeSchema* in a directory service. Using the X.500 Object Identifier (OID), every object in every directory services structure can be uniquely identified. The *X.500 OID* namespace definition includes directories other than AD DS, but AD DS is an X.500-based directory service.

This namespace can be represented either in dotted notation (numeric) or in string notation. For example, the organization object class (with an LDAP display name of *organization*) is identified by the X.500 OID 2.5.6.4. The numeric representation of this object class uniquely identifies this object within the X.500 hierarchy.

To view the X.500 OID, you can use either the Active Directory Schema snap-in or the ADSI Edit snap-in. To view the X.500 OID for the *Organization classSchema* object, use ADSI Edit to open the schema container and scroll down to the distinguished name of the *classSchema*: *CN=Organization*.

One of the concerns about modifying the schema is the possibility that two applications will make incompatible modifications to the schema by both attempting to add a class or attribute object with the same name or OID. The goals of the OID are to be able to uniquely identify any object or attribute in AD DS and to ensure that no other schema object uses the same OID.

To accomplish this identification, organizations planning to create new OIDs should register with the International Standards Organization (ISO), the American National Standards Institute (ANSI), or with Microsoft. When you register, the standards organization or Microsoft assigns you part of the OID space, which you can then extend to suit your needs. For example, your company may be granted a number such as 1.2.840.*xxxx*. This number is arranged hierarchically and can be broken down as follows:

1–ISO

2–ANSI

840–United States

xxxx–A unique number identifying your company

After you have been granted the number, you can manage your own part of the hierarchy. For example, if you create a new attribute called *Employee Start Date*, you could assign it a number such as 1.2.840.*xxxx*.12.

AD DS conforms to the OID standards. For example, the OID for a contact in AD DS is 1.2.840.113556.1.5.15. The first three parts of the number have been assigned to ISO, ANSI, and the United States, respectively. ANSI then assigned 113556 to Microsoft, who assigned 1 to Active Directory, 5 to Active Directory classes, and 15 to the *Contact* class.

Important   You must ensure that any changes you make to the schema have a unique OID to ensure that your changes will not be incompatible with future changes. One way to ensure uniqueness is to obtain a unique identifier for your company. Another attribute that must be unique when you make a schema change is the *LdapDisplayName* attribute. Before making a schema change, ensure you understand all of the rules for making these changes.

Deactivating Schema Objects

Although extending the schema is a straightforward operation, careful planning should be done before implementing such changes. After the schema has been extended, or an existing class or attribute has been modified, these changes are not reversible. Objects in the schema cannot be deleted. If you do make an error when extending the schema, you may choose to disable (deactivate) the object. In Windows Server 2008, schema objects that are deactivated can be used again if necessary, and new schema objects can be created with the same LDAP display name or OID as a deactivated object.

There are several points to keep in mind regarding deactivating schema class and attribute objects. First, you cannot deactivate *Category 1*, or *base schema*, objects. Second, you cannot deactivate an attribute that is a member of a class that is not also deactivated. This restriction prevents errors in creating new instances of the nondeactivated class if the deactivated attribute is a required attribute.

Note   If your forest is set at the Windows Server 2003 functional level, you can create a new object that uses the same identification attribute values (that is, *attributeID, governsID, lDAPDisplayName, mAPIID,* or *schemaIDGUID*) as a defunct schema object, as long as the new object's distinguished name is unique. This makes it possible to deactivate a schema object and then create an entirely new schema object as if the old object were actually deleted.

To deactivate either a class or an attribute object, set the Boolean value of the *isDefunct* attribute of the schema object to *true*. This can be accomplished by using a tool such as ADSI Edit. Figure 2-5 illustrates how to deactivate the *EmployeeStartDate* attribute created in the example given earlier. You can also deactivate an AD DS attribute by clearing the Attribute Is Active check box when viewing the attribute properties in the Active Directory Schema snap-in.

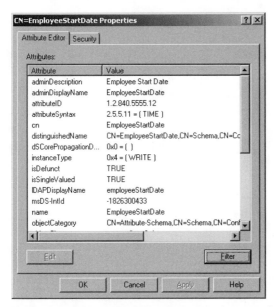

Figure 2-5   Using ADSIEdit.msc to deactivate a schema attribute.

After a schema object has been deactivated, it is treated in all respects as if it does not exist. The error messages that are returned if an attempt is made to create a new instance of a defunct class or attribute are the same as when there is no existing class or attribute in the schema. Additionally, the only modification that can be made to a deactivated schema object is to reactivate it. To reactivate the defunct schema object, simply set the *isDefunct* attribute to *false* or enable the Attribute Is Active check box. After a defunct schema object has been reactivated, it can be used again to create new instances of the class or attribute. There are no adverse effects of this deactivation/reactivation process.

AD DS Logical Structure

After you install AD DS in your network environment and begin to implement the appropriate AD DS design for your business purposes, you will be working with the logical structure of AD DS. The logical structure displays the configuration of domains, organization units, and other AD DS objects in a way that is independent of the AD DS physical components, such as the domain controllers or the AD DS data store located on each domain controller. The AD DS logical structure includes the following components:

- Partitions
- Domains
- Domain trees
- Forests
- Sites
- Organizational units

This section provides an introduction to these components. It will also discuss the concept of trusts, which are used to enable access to resources for security principals that are stored in different domains. In Chapter 5, you will learn how and why these structural components are used to achieve specific business goals (such as secured access to resources) and optimize network performance.

AD DS Partitions

As described earlier, the AD DS database is stored in one database file on the hard disk of each domain controller. The information stored in the directory database is divided into multiple logical partitions, with each partition storing different types of information. AD DS partitions are also called *naming contexts* (NCs). AD DS partitions are visible through use of a tool such as Ldp.exe or ADSI Edit, as shown in Figure 2-6.

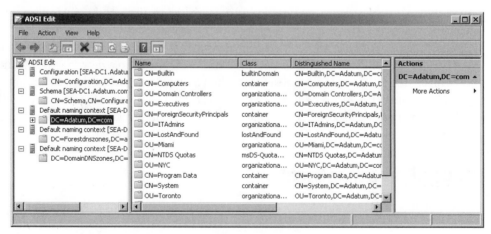

Figure 2-6   AD DS partitions that are visible using ADSIEdit.msc.

AD DS and LDAP

Lightweight Directory Access Protocol (LDAP) is both an access protocol and an object identification model in Windows Server 2008 AD DS. As an object identification model, LDAP uses a hierarchical format to identify each object in AD DS. This hierarchical format starts at the directory partition level and includes each logical component in the hierarchy to uniquely identify each object. This is known as a distinguished name. For example, a user account can be identified by using the following LDAP distinguished name:

CN=Yvonne McKay,OU=Marketing,OU=Miami, DC=ADatum,DC=com

Each part of the LDAP name is identified by the object type. These parts are known as relative distinguished names (RDN), and the object type is known as the RDN attribute. For example, *cn* refers to common name, *ou* refers to organizational unit, and *dc* refers to domain component. Using this naming convention, you can specifically reference and access objects within an LDAP-compliant directory service such as AD DS. The LDAP protocol and directory model (but not the naming syntax) are defined by RFC 2251 "Lightweight Directory Access Protocol (v3)," which is available at *http://www.ietf.org/rfc/rfc2251.txt*.

LDAP is also an access protocol and application programming interface (API) for accessing information in AD DS. As an API, LDAP is implemented in Windows Server 2008 AD DS in the Wldap32.dll. Within an application or script, you can access any object in AD DS by using the LDAP path. For example, to refer to a specific OU within a Windows PowerShell script, you would use the following syntax:

```
$objADSI = [ADSI]"LDAP://OU=Marketing,OU=Miami,DC=ADatum,DC=com"
```

To administer AD DS using LDAP, you can use an LDAP-compliant administration tool, such as Ldp.exe, which is installed with Windows Server 2008. Using Ldp.exe, you can bind, or connect, to AD DS by its Transmission Control Protocol (TCP) port number and display the LDAP display name of each attribute, class, and object. To connect to AD DS using Ldp.exe and display the attributes of a user object, connect to the AD DS domain controller using TCP port 389, expand the container or organizational unit, and then double-click the distinguished name of the user.

Domain Directory Partition

The domain directory partition contains all of the domain information, including information about users, groups, computers, and contacts. Essentially, anything that can be viewed through the Active Directory Users and Computers administrative tool is stored in the domain directory partition.

The domain directory partition is automatically replicated to all domain controllers in the domain. The partition contains the information that each domain controller needs to authenticate users.

Configuration Directory Partition

The configuration directory partition contains the information about the configuration of the entire forest. For example, all of the information about sites, site links, and replication connections are stored in the configuration directory partition. Other applications may also store information in the configuration partition. For example, Exchange Server 2007 stores all of its configuration information in the AD DS configuration directory partition rather than in its own directory service.

Because the configuration directory partition contains information about the entire forest, it is replicated throughout the entire forest. Each domain controller contains a writable copy of the configuration directory partition, and changes to this directory partition can be made on any domain controller in the organization. This means that the configuration information is then replicated to all the other domain controllers. When the replication is fully synchronized, every domain controller in the forest will have the same configuration information.

Schema Directory Partition

The schema directory partition contains the schema for the entire forest. As described earlier in this chapter, the schema is a set of rules detailing what types of objects can be created in AD DS as well as rules about each type of object.

The schema directory partition is replicated to all domain controllers in the entire forest. However, only one domain controller, the schema master, has a writable copy of the schema directory partition. All changes to the schema must be made on the schema master; the changes are then replicated to all other domain controllers.

Global Catalog Partition

The global catalog partition is not a partition in the same sense as the other partitions. The global catalog partition is stored in the database like the other partitions, but administrators cannot enter information directly into this partition. The global catalog is a read-only partition on all global catalog servers, and it is built from the contents of the domain databases. Each attribute in the schema has a Boolean value named *isMemberOfPartialAttributeSet*. If this value is set to *true*, the attribute is replicated to the global catalog.

Application Directory Partitions

The last type of partition in Windows Server 2008 AD DS is the application directory partition, or Non-Domain Naming Context (NDNC). Application directory partitions are used to store application-specific information. The advantage of using application directory partitions rather than one of the other AD DS partitions is that the replication scope for the application directory partitions can be controlled. If the partition is being used to store directory information, the information might be fairly dynamic. By defining which domain controllers will host a replica of the application directory partition, you can limit the amount of replication traffic that is created on the network. The domain controllers that receive a replica of the application directory partition can be in any domain or site in the forest.

Application directory partitions can store any type of AD DS object except security principals. Also, because application directory partitions are created to control where the data is replicated, none of the objects in the application directory partition can be replicated to the global catalog partition.

By default, no application directory partitions are created in AD DS. However, if you choose to install DNS on the first domain controller in the forest when you install AD DS, two application directory partitions named ForestDnsZones and DomainDnsZones are created for the Domain Name System (DNS) server service. In addition to creating application directory partitions for DNS, you can also create these partitions for other applications.

More Info   For more information on these DNS application directory partitions, see Chapter 3, "Active Directory Domain Services and Domain Name System."

The naming scheme for application directory partitions is identical to other AD DS directory partitions. For example, the LDAP name for the configuration directory partition in the ADatum.com forest is *CN=Configuration,DC=ADatum,DC=com*. If you create an application directory partition called AppPartition1 in the ADatum.com domain, its DNS name is *DC=AppPartition1,DC=ADatum,DC=com*. Application directory partitions are quite flexible in regard to where you can create the partition, or more accurately, what the naming context for the partition will be. For example, you can create an additional application directory partition under the AppPartition1 partition resulting in a partition with a name of *DC=AppPartition2, DC=AppPartition1,DC=ADatum,dc=com*. You can even create an application directory partition with a DNS name that is not contiguous with any domain in the forest. You can create an application directory partition in the ADatum.com domain that has a DNS name of *DC=AppPartition*. In effect, this creates a new tree in the forest.

Note   Choosing the DNS name for the application namespace does not affect the functionality of the application directory partition in any way. The only difference will be in the configuration of the LDAP client that is accessing the partition. Application directory partitions are designed for LDAP access, so the client must be configured to search the right namespace on the server.

One of the complicating factors when creating an application directory partition is maintaining permissions to the objects in the partition. With the default partitions in AD DS, the permissions are automatically assigned. When an object is created in the domain directory partition, the Domain Admins group is automatically assigned full permissions to the object. When an object is created in the configuration directory partition or schema directory partition, user and group accounts from the forest root domain are assigned permissions. Because an application directory partition can be replicated to any combination of domains in the forest, this default way of assigning permissions does not apply. Although it is easy to assign a group like Domain Admins full control of the objects in the partition, what is not clear is which domain is the default domain. To deal with this issue, application directory partitions are always created with a security descriptor reference domain. This domain becomes the default domain that is used to assign permissions to objects in the application directory partition. If an application directory partition is created under a domain directory partition, the parent domain is used as the security descriptor reference domain, in effect creating an inheritance of permissions. If the application directory partition creates a new tree in the forest, the forest root domain is used as the reference domain.

> **Note**   Normally, the application directory partitions will be created by the installation of an application that requires the use of an application directory partition. Also, the application installation procedure should allow for the creation of additional replicas on other domain controllers. Although you can create application directory partitions using Ntdsutil, you would normally not expect to do this in a production environment. The procedures for managing application directory partitions are described in the Windows Server 2008 Help And Support Center. For detailed information on application directory partitions, including how to access them programmatically, see "Application Directory Partitions" at *http://msdn2.microsoft.com/en-us/library/ms675020.aspx*.

Domains

The domain is the most basic building block in the AD DS model. When you install AD DS on your first computer running Windows Server 2008, you create a domain. A domain serves as an administrative boundary, and it also defines the boundary of certain security policies. The domain structure should be based on the administrative requirements of an organization, such as the delegation of administrative authority, and operational requirements, such as the need to control replication. For example, all members of the Domain Admins in a domain have full administrative access to all objects in that domain, but do not by default have administrative access to objects in other domains.

Within AD DS, domains define the following:

- **Replication boundaries**   Domain boundaries are replication boundaries for the domain directory partition and for the domain information stored in the Sysvol folder on all domain controllers. Whereas other directory partitions like schema, configuration, and the GC are replicated throughout the forest, the domain directory partition is replicated only within one domain. By partitioning data in a very large organization into multiple domains in the same forest, you can manage replication traffic between domain controllers. Information that is stored in the domain partition is replicated to all other domain controllers in the domain, but is not replicated to domain controllers in other domains.

■ **Security policy boundaries**   Some security policies can only be set at a domain level. These policies, such as password policies, account lockout policies, and Kerberos ticket policies, apply to all domain accounts.

> **Note**   In Windows Server 2008, you can define fine-grained password policies that override the default domain account policies for specific users. However, you cannot apply fine-grained password policies to container objects, only to individual user accounts or security groups.

■ **Resource access boundaries**   Domain boundaries are also boundaries for authentication and authorization services. A domain provides authentication services for all of its accounts in order to facilitate logons and single sign-on access control to shared resources within the boundaries of the domain. By default, users in one domain cannot access resources in another domain unless they are explicitly given the appropriate permissions.

■ **Trust boundaries**   A domain is the smallest container within AD DS that can be used in a trust relationship. Trusts are used to enable the authentication and authorization services so that users in one domain can access resources in another domain. Within a forest, trust relationships are automatically created between the forest root domain and any tree root domains on the one hand, and all child domains that are subordinate to the forest root domain on the other.

> **Security Alert**   Domain boundaries are not security boundaries—the actions taken by an administrator in one domain can impact all other domains in the forest. To create a security boundary, you must create separate forests. For more information, see Chapter 5.

AD DS domains within a forest are hierarchically organized. The first domain in the enterprise is known as the *forest root domain,* and it is the starting point for an AD DS namespace. For example, the first domain in the A. Datum organization is ADatum.com. This first domain can either be a *dedicated* or a *nondedicated* root domain. A dedicated root, also known as an *empty root,* is one that is used as an empty placeholder to start AD DS. The only accounts that are contained in the dedicated root domain are the default domain user and group accounts, such as the Administrator account and the Domain Admins global group. A nondedicated root domain is one in which actual user and group accounts are created. The reasons for selecting either a dedicated or nondedicated forest root are discussed in Chapter 5.

All other domains in the forest exist either as *peers* to the root domain or as *child* domains. *Child domains* share the same AD DS namespace as the parent domain (the root domain). For example, if the first domain in the A. Datum organization is named ADatum.com, a child domain in this structure might be named NA.ADatum.com. The NA.ADatum.com domain would be created to manage all of the security principals for the North American locations of the A. Datum organization. If the organization is sufficiently large or complex, additional child domains, such as Sales.NA.ADatum.com, might be required. Figure 2-7 illustrates the parent-child domain hierarchy for the ADatum organization.

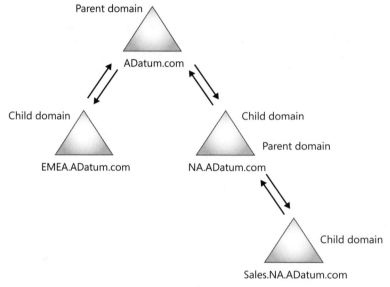

Figure 2-7   Parent-child domain model for A. Datum Corporation.

When domains are installed in parent-child configuration, the resulting model is called a *domain tree*. A domain tree is one or more domains that share a contiguous namespace. In the ADatum.com forest, NA.Adatum.com shares the Adatum.com namespace with the forest root domain.

You can also implement additional domain trees in the same forest. When you create a new domain tree, you are adding domains to the forest that do not share the same contiguous namespace. For example, A. Datum may have a subsidiary named Trey Research that requires a separate domain. You can add the TreyResearch.com domain to the ADatum.com forest and create a new domain tree. In this scenario, the TreyResearch.com domain is a domain tree root domain.

If further domains are required to satisfy the Trey Research business unit, they can be created as children of the TreyResearch domain tree. See Figure 2-8 for an illustration of the ADatum organization with multiple domain trees.

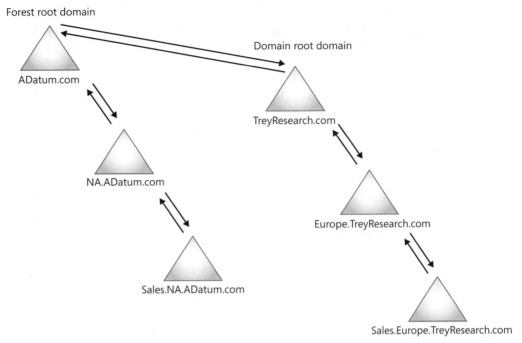

Figure 2-8   A. Datum Corporation with multiple domain trees.

Regardless of whether a single namespace (one domain tree) or multiple namespaces (multiple domain trees) are used, additional domains in the same forest function in exactly the same way. All the domains are still part of the same forest, and all domains share a transitive trust with all other domains in the forest. The creation of additional domain trees is purely an organizational and naming decision, not one that affects functionality. Using multiple trees rather than child domains does have an impact on the DNS configuration (as discussed in Chapter 3).

Locating Objects in Other Domains

Because the information in each domain partition is replicated only to other domain controllers in the same domain, domain controllers must have some means to locate objects in other domains. For example, when a user in one domain tries to access a shared folder in another domain in the forest, the domain controller in the user domain must be able to determine that the other domain exists and must be able to locate the domain controllers in the domain. AD DS uses cross-references to enable every domain controller to be aware not only of its domain, but of all other domains and directory partitions in the forest.

Cross-references are stored as directory objects of the class *crossRef* that identify the existence and location of all directory partitions. In addition, these objects contain information that AD DS uses to construct the directory tree hierarchy. The *crossRef* class includes the following attributes:

- *nCName* The distinguished name of the directory partition that the *crossRef* object references. (The prefix *nC* stands for naming context, which is a synonym for directory partition.) The combination of all *nCName* properties in the forest defines the entire directory tree, including the subordinate and superior relationships between partitions.

- *dNSRoot* The DNS name of the domain where servers that store the particular directory partition can be reached.

For every directory partition in a forest, there is an internal cross-reference object stored in the Partitions container (*CN=Partitions,CN=Configuration,DC=ForestRootDomain*). Because cross-reference objects are located in the Configuration container, they are replicated to every domain controller in the forest, and thus every domain controller has information about the name of every partition in the forest. By using the cross-reference objects, any domain controller can generate referrals to any other domain in the forest.

Forests

A forest is the highest level of the AD DS logical structure hierarchy. An AD DS forest represents a single self-contained directory. The forest is the replication and security boundary for the enterprise. All domains and domain trees exist within an AD DS forest.

An AD DS forest can be defined by what is shared by all domain controllers in the forest. The shared components include the following:

- **A common schema** All domain controllers in the forest will have the same schema. The schema is stored in the schema directory partition in AD DS and is replicated to all domain controllers in the forest. The only way to deploy two different schemas in your organization is to deploy two separate forests.

- **A common configuration directory partition** All domain controllers in the forest have the same configuration container. The configuration partition contains information about the topology of the forest as well as other forest, domain, and domain controller settings. This configuration data includes a list of all domains, trees, and forests and the locations of the domain controllers and global catalogs. The configuration directory partition is also used extensively by Active Directory–enabled applications like Exchange Server.

- **A common global catalog** The global catalog contains information about all of the objects in the entire forest. This makes searching for any object in the forest efficient and enables users to log on in any domain in the forest using their UPN.

■ **A common set of forest-wide operation masters and administrators**   The domain naming master and the schema master are configured at the forest level. Each forest has only one schema master and one domain naming master. In addition, two security groups with unique permissions are created in the root domain for the forest. The Schema Admins group is the only group that has the right to modify the schema, and the Enterprise Admins group is the only group that has the right to perform forest-level actions such as adding or removing domains from the forest. The Enterprise Admins group is also automatically added to each local Administrators group on the domain controllers in every domain in the forest.

■ **A shared trust configuration**   All the domains in the forest are automatically configured to trust all the other domains in the forest.

Figure 2-9 shows the A. Datum forest.

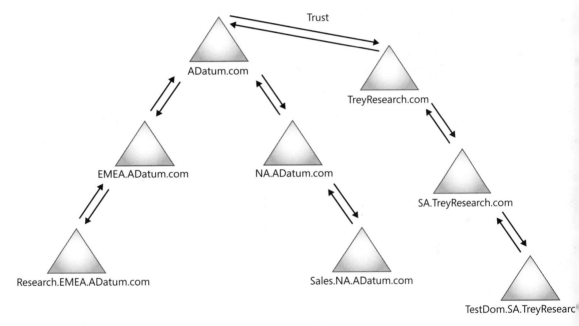

A. Datum Forest

Figure 2-9   A forest can contain multiple domains and trees.

On the Disc   To display information on your AD DS forest and the domains within that forest, run the ListADDSDomains.ps1 Windows PowerShell script on the CD.

Trusts

If no trusts are configured, the domain is the boundary of resource access in an organization. With sufficient permissions, any security principal (for example, a user or group account) can access any shared resource in the same domain. In order for security principals to access shared resources that exist outside of their domain, AD DS trust relationships are utilized. A *trust* is an authentication connection between two domains by which security principals can be authorized to access resources on the other domain.

When a trust is configured between domains, the authentication mechanism for each domain trusts the authentication mechanism for all other trusted domains. If a user or application is authenticated by one domain, its authentication is accepted by all other domains that trust the authenticating domain. Users in a trusted domain have access to resources in the trusting domain, subject to the access controls that are applied in the trusting domain.

> **Note**   Trusts are automatically configured between all domains in a forest. The trusts cannot be removed.

There are several types of trust relationships, including the following:

- Transitive two-way trusts
- Shortcut trusts
- Forest trusts
- External trusts
- Realm trusts

Transitive Two-Way Trusts

All domains in a forest maintain transitive, two-way trust relationships with every other domain in that forest. In the example provided earlier, when the NA.ADatum.com domain is created as a child domain of the root domain ADatum.com, an automatic two-way trust is created between the NA.ADatum.com and the ADatum.com domains. Through this trust, any user in the NA.ADatum.com domain can access any resource in the ADatum.com domain to which permission has been granted. Likewise, if any security principals exist in the ADatum.com domain, they can be given access to resources in the NA.ADatum.com domain.

Within a forest, the trusts are set up as either parent-child trusts or as tree root trusts. An example of a parent-child trust is the trust between the NA.ADatum.com domain and the ADatum.com domain. A *tree root trust* is the trust between two trees in the forest, for example, between ADatum.com and TreyResearch.com.

However, all of the trusts between domains in a forest are also *transitive*. The transitive nature of the trust means that all the domains in the forest trust each other. If the ADatum.com domain trusts the NA.ADatum.com domain, and the EMEA.ADatum.com domain trusts the ADatum.com domain, then transitivity means that the EMEA.ADatum.com domain also trusts the NA.ADatum.com domain. Therefore, users in the NA.ADatum.com domain can access resources in the EMEA.ADatum.com domain and vice versa. The transitive trusts also apply to the tree root trusts. The NA.ADatum.com domain trusts the ADatum.com domain, and the ADatum.com domain trusts the TreyResearch.com domain. Therefore, the NA.ADatum.com domain and the TreyResearch.com domain also share a transitive-trust relationship.

Shortcut Trusts

In addition to the automatic, two-way transitive trusts that are created when a new child domain is created, shortcut trusts can be created between domains in the forest. Shortcut trusts are used to optimize performance when accessing resources between domains that are connected through transitive trusts. A shortcut trust is desirable when there is frequent resource access between domains that are remotely connected through the domain tree or forest. For example, the trusts at A. Datum could be configured as illustrated as Figure 2-10.

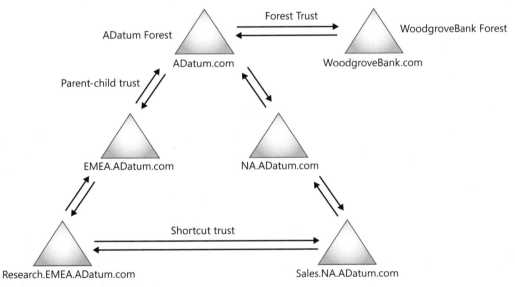

Figure 2-10   Trusts in the ADatum forest.

If a security group in the Research.EMEA.ADatum.com domain has a frequent need to access a shared resource in the Sales.NA.ADatum.com domain, and with only transitive trusts established between the domains, users in the Research.EMEA.ADatum.com domain must be referred to a domain controller in every domain in the tree between them and the domain that contains the resource. This is not efficient if the need is frequent. A shortcut trust is a direct trust that will efficiently enable users in the Sales.EMEA.ADatum.com domain to be referred to a domain controller in the Research.NA.ADatum.com domain—without traversing the entire directory tree to get there. Figure 2-10 illustrates this shortcut trust. Shortcut trusts can be configured as one-way or two-way trusts. Shortcut trusts are not transitive.

Forest Trusts

A *forest trust* is a two-way transitive trust between two separate forests. With a forest trust, security principals in one forest can be given access to resources in any domain in a completely different forest. Also, users can log on to any domain in either forest using the same UPN. Figure 2-10 illustrates a forest trust between the ADatum.com forest and the WoodgroveBank.com forest.

> **Note** In order to configure a forest trust, both forests must be at the Windows Server 2003 forest functional level or higher.

Forest trusts can be very useful in a Windows Server 2008 environment. If an organization requires more than one forest for political or technical reasons, the use of a forest trust means that it is easy to assign access to resources across all the domains, regardless of which forest the user or resource is in. If two companies that have deployed Windows Server 2008 forests merge, the two forests can be logically joined by using the trust.

Although forest trusts do provide some excellent functionality, they are also subject to some limitations:

- Forest trusts are not transitive to other forests. For example, if ADatum.com has a forest trust with WoodgroveBank.com, and WoodgroveBank.com has a forest trust with Fabrikam.com, ADatum.com does not automatically have a forest trust with Fabrikam.com.

- Forest trusts only make authentication possible between forests; they do not provide any other functionality. For example, each forest will still have a unique global catalog, schema, and configuration directory partition. No information is replicated between the two forests—the forest trust just makes it possible to assign access to resources between forests.

- In some cases, you may not want to have all the domains in one forest trust all the domains in another forest. If this is the case, you can set up one-way, nontransitive external trusts between individual domains in two separate forests. As an alternative, you can also configure selective authentication on the forest trust, which means that you must explicitly enable users from a trusted domain to access resources on a server in the trusting domain.

> **More Info** For more information on planning forest trusts, see Chapter 5.

External Trusts

An external trust is a trust relationship that can be created between AD DS domains that are in different forests or between an AD DS domain and a Windows NT 4.0 or earlier domain.

External trusts can be used to provide access to resources in a domain outside of the forest that is not already joined by a forest trust or to create a direct trust between two domains that are joined by a forest trust. An external trust is different from a forest trust in that the external trust is configured between any two domains in either forest, not just between the forest root domains. In addition, external trusts have the following characteristics:

- External trusts are not transitive. Only two domains participate in the trust relationship.

- You must configure both sides of the trust relationship. If you want to configure a two-way trust, you must configure a trust for each direction.

- External trusts enforce SID filtering by default in Windows Server 2008. SID filtering is used to verify that incoming authentication requests made from security principals in the trusted domain contain only SIDs of security principals in the trusted domain. SID filtering ensures that administrators in the trusted domain cannot use the *SIDHistory* attribute to gain unauthorized access to resources in the trusting domain.

Realm Trusts

The last type of trust is a *realm trust*. A realm trust is configured between a Windows Server 2008 domain or forest and a non-Windows implementation of a Kerberos v5 realm. Kerberos security is based on an open standard, and there are several other implementations of Kerberos-based network security systems available. Realm trusts can be created between any Kerberos realms that support the Kerberos v5 standard. Realm trusts can be either one-way or two-way, and they can also be configured to be transitive or nontransitive.

Sites

All of the AD DS logical components discussed so far are almost completely independent of the physical infrastructure for your network. For example, when you design the domain structure for a corporation, where the users are located is not the most important question you need to ask. All the users in a domain may be located in a single office building, or they may be located in offices around the world. This independence of the logical components from the network infrastructure comes about largely as a result of the use of sites in AD DS.

Sites provide the connection between the logical AD DS components and the physical network infrastructure. A *site* is defined as an area of the network where all domain controllers are connected by a fast and reliable network connection. In most cases, a site contains one or more Internet Protocol (IP) subnets on a local area network (LAN) or very high-speed wide area network (WAN) and connected to the rest of the network with slower WAN connections.

 On the Disc   To display information on the sites AD DS forest, run the ListADDSSites.ps1 Windows PowerShell script on the CD.

The primary reason for creating sites is to be able to manage any network traffic that must use slow network connections. Sites are used to control network traffic within the Windows Server 2008 network in three different ways:

- **Replication**   One of the most important ways that sites are used to optimize network traffic is in the management of replication traffic between domain controllers. For example, within a site, any change made to the directory will be replicated within a few minutes. The replication schedule between sites can be managed so that the replication traffic will occur less frequently or during nonworking hours. By default, replication traffic between sites is compressed to conserve bandwidth, while replication traffic within a site is not compressed. (Chapter 4 goes into much more detail on the differences between intersite and intrasite replication.)

- **Authentication**   When a user logs on to a Windows Server 2008 domain from a Windows 2000, Windows XP Professional, or Windows Vista client, the client computer will always try to connect a domain controller in the same site as the client. As discussed in Chapter 3, every domain controller registers site-specific service locator (SRV) records—when the client computer tries to locate a domain controller, it will always query the DNS servers for these site records. This means that the client logon traffic will remain within the site.

- **Site-aware network services**   The third way that sites can preserve network bandwidth is by limiting client connections to site-aware applications and services on the site. For example, by using Distributed File System (DFS), you can create multiple replicas of a folder in different sites on the network. Because DFS is designed to be aware of the site configuration, client computers always try to access a DFS replica in their own site before crossing a WAN link to access the information in another site. As well, Exchange Server 2007 uses the AD DS site configuration to define the message routing topology within the organization. Messages sent between Exchange Servers in the same site will always be sent directly from the source Exchange Server to the destination Exchange Server, even if a message needs to be sent to several servers in the same site. Only single copies of messages are sent between Exchange Servers in different sites, even if the messages are intended for users on several different Exchange Servers in the destination site.

Every computer on a Windows Server 2008 network will be assigned to a site. When AD DS is installed in a Windows Server 2008 environment, a default site called Default-First-Site-Name is created, and all computers in the forest will be assigned to that site unless additional sites are created. When additional sites are created, the sites are linked to IP subnets. When a server running Windows Server 2008 is promoted to become a domain controller, the domain controller is automatically assigned to a site that corresponds to the computer's IP address. If needed, domain controllers can also be moved between sites using the Active Directory Sites and Services administrative tool.

Client computers determine their sites the first time they start up and log on to the domain. Because the client computer does not know which site it belongs to, it will connect to any domain controller in the domain. As part of this initial logon process, the domain controller will inform the client which site it belongs to, and the client will cache that information for the next logon.

> **Note** If a domain controller or a client computer has an IP address that is not linked to a specific site, that computer will be placed in the Default-First-Site-Name site. Every computer that is part of a Windows Server 2008 domain must belong to a site.

As mentioned earlier in this chapter, there is no direct connection between sites and the other logical concepts in AD DS. One site can contain more than one domain, and one domain can cross multiple sites. For example, as shown in Figure 2-11, the Seattle site contains both the ADatum.com domain and the NA.ADatum.com domain. The TreyResearch.com domain is spread across multiple sites.

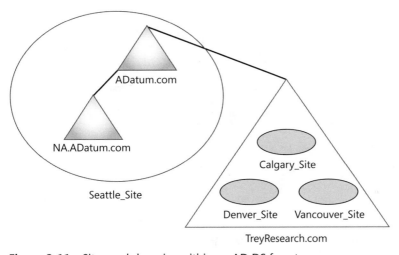

Figure 2-11   Sites and domains within an AD DS forest.

> **Note** Sites are discussed in more detail in several other chapters in this book. Chapter 3 details the role of DNS and sites for client logons. Chapter 4 addresses the role of sites in replication and how to create and configure sites. Chapter 5 goes into detail on designing an optimal site configuration for an AD DS forest.

Organizational Units

By implementing multiple domains in a forest, either in a single tree or in multiple trees, Windows Server 2008 AD DS can scale to provide directory services for almost any size network. Many of the components of AD DS, such as the global catalog and automatic transitive trusts, are designed to make the use and management of this enterprise directory efficient regardless of how big the directory gets.

Organizational units (OUs), however, are designed to make AD DS easier to administer at a smaller scale. OUs are used to make the management of single domains more efficient. A domain might contain tens of thousands of objects (or even millions). Managing this many objects without some means of organizing the objects into logical groupings is very difficult. OUs are used to create a hierarchical structure within a domain. Figure 2-12 shows an example of what the OU structure might look like at A. Datum.

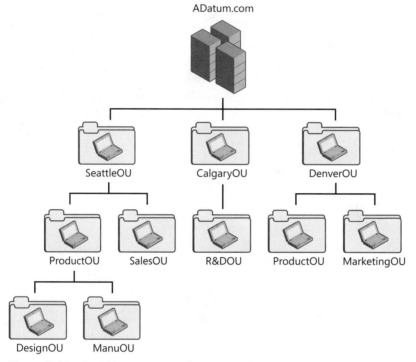

Figure 2-12 An OU structure can have many layers.

OUs are container objects that can contain several types of directory service objects, including the following:

- Computers
- Contacts
- Groups
- inetOrgPerson
- Printers
- Users
- Shared folders
- Organizational units

OUs are used to group objects together for administrative purposes. There are two ways that OUs can be used as administrative units: to delegate administrative rights and to manage a group of objects as a single unit.

Using OUs to Delegate Administrative Rights

OUs can be used to delegate administrative rights. For example, a user can be given the rights to perform administrative tasks for a specific OU. These rights could be high-level rights, in which the user has full control of the OU and all objects in the OU, or the rights can be very limited and specific (such as only being able to reset passwords for users in that OU). The user that has been given administrative rights to an OU does not by default have any administrative rights outside the OU.

The OU structure is very flexible in assigning rights (also called permissions in many Windows dialog boxes and Properties sheets) to objects inside the OU. The OU itself has an access control list (ACL) where you can assign rights for that OU. Each object in an OU and, in fact, each attribute for each object, also has an ACL. This means that you can have extremely precise control of the administrative rights anyone can have in the OU. For example, you can give a Help Desk group the right to change passwords for users in an OU but not to change any other properties for the user accounts. Or you can give the Human Resources department the right to modify any personal information on all user accounts in all OUs but not give them any other rights to any other attributes on the user accounts, or any rights to any other objects. You can also grant rights to individual objects within the OU if there are some objects that you want to have different rights than the other objects in the OU.

Using OUs to Administer Groups of Objects

Another reason for using OUs is to group objects together so that the objects can all be administered the same way. For example, if you want to administer all of the workstations in a department the same way (such as limiting which users have the right to log on to the workstations), you can group all the workstations into an OU and configure the Logon Locally permission at the OU level. This permission is applied to all workstations in that OU. If a collection of users needs the same standard desktop configuration and the same set of applications, the users can be put into an OU and Group Policy can then be used to configure the desktop and to manage the installation of applications.

In many cases, objects in an OU will be managed through Group Policy. Group Policy can be used to lock down user desktops, to give them a standardized desktop, to provide logon and logoff scripts, and to provide folder redirection. Table 2-3 provides a brief list of the types of settings available in Group Policy.

Table 2-3   Group Policy Setting Types

Setting Types	Explanation
Administrative templates	Used to manage registry-based parameters for configuring application settings and user desktop settings, including access to the operating system components, access to control panel, and configuration of offline files.
Security	Used to manage the local computer, domain, and network security settings, including controlling user access to the network, configuring account policies, and controlling user rights.
Software installation	Used to centralize the management of software installations and maintenance.
Scripts	Used to specify scripts that can be run when a computer starts or shuts down, or when a user logs on or off.
Folder redirection	Used to store certain user profile folders on a network server. These folders, such as the My Documents folder, appear to be stored locally but are actually stored on a server where they can be accessed from any computer on the network.
Preferences	Used to manage options related to Windows settings or Control Panel settings, including drive mappings, environment variables, network shares, local users and groups, services, devices, and many more.

Group Policy objects will be most commonly assigned at the OU level. This eases the task of administering the users in the OU because you can assign one Group Policy object—for example, an administrative template policy—to the OU, which is then enforced on all the users or computers in the OU.

> **Note**   OUs are not security principals. This means that you cannot use an OU to assign permissions to a resource and then have all of the users in the OU automatically inherit those permissions. OUs are used for administrative purposes. To grant access to resources, use security groups.

Summary

This chapter introduced the basic physical and logical components of AD DS in Windows Server 2008. Although having an understanding of the physical components is important (especially when dealing with database management, domain controller placement, and schema management), most of the work you will do in AD DS will be with the logical components. Most of the rest of this book deals with the logical structure of AD DS.

Additional Resources

- Chapter 5, "Designing the Active Directory Domain Services Structure," goes into detail about designing the AD DS logical and physical configuration.

- The Domain and Forest Trusts Technical Reference at *http://technet2.microsoft.com/ windowsserver/en/library/92b3b6cb-9eb3-4dd7-b5f6-3fa9be8080821033.mspx?mfr=true* provides details on trusts in an Active Directory. This resource refers to Windows Server 2003, but the way trusts are implemented has not changed significantly in Windows Server 2008.

- The Script Repository: Active Directory Web site located at *http://www.microsoft.com/ technet/scriptcenter/scripts/default.mspx?mfr=true* has several scripts that can be used to enumerate and modify the AD DS objects.

Related Tools

Windows Server 2008 provides several tools that can be used when managing the AD DS logical and physical components. Table 2-4 lists some of these tools and their uses.

Table 2-4   AD DS Management Tools

Tool Name	Description and Uses
Active Directory Users and Computers	Use to configure AD DS domains including configuring and managing OUs and all other domain objects.
Active Directory Domains and Trusts	Use to configure AD DS trusts.
Active Directory Sites and Services	Use to configure sites and replication.
Ntdsutil.exe or Dsbutil.exe	Use to manage the AD DS data store files and to transfer FSMO roles between domain controllers.
ADSI Edit	Use to view and modify the contents of AD DS partitions.

Resources on the CD

- ListDomainControllers.ps1 is a Windows PowerShell script that lists all of the domain controllers in your domain and global catalog servers in your forest.

- ListFSMOs.ps1 is a Windows PowerShell script that lists all of the operations master servers in your forest and domain.

- ListADDSDomains.ps1 is a Windows PowerShell script that lists information about all of the domains in your forest.

- ListADDSSites.ps1 is a Windows PowerShell script that lists information about all of the sites in your forest.

Related Help Topics

- "Managing Trusts" in Active Directory Domains and Trusts help.
- "Managing Forest Trusts" in Active Directory Domains and Trusts help.
- "Understanding Domains" in Active Directory Users and Computers help.

Chapter 3

Active Directory Domain Services and Domain Name System

Microsoft Windows Server 2008 Active Directory Domain Services (AD DS) requires Domain Name System (DNS) to locate resources on a network. Without a reliable DNS infrastructure, AD DS replication between domain controllers on your network will fail, your Microsoft Windows XP and Windows Vista clients will not be able to log on to the network, and servers running Microsoft Exchange Server 2007 will not be able to send e-mail. Essentially, if your DNS implementation is not stable and available, your Windows Server 2008 network will fail. This means you must have a thorough knowledge of DNS concepts and the Windows Server 2008 implementation of DNS if you are going to manage a Windows Server 2008 AD DS environment.

AD DS is tightly integrated with DNS in several ways. First of all, all Microsoft Windows 2000 or later computers use DNS to locate domain controllers in an AD DS environment. This includes client computers that are trying to log on to the network, domain controllers trying to connect to replication partners, or Exchange Servers looking up e-mail recipient information in AD DS. Only after the DNS lookup fails will these computers attempt to use NetBIOS name resolution by using Windows Internet Name Service (WINS), broadcasts, or LMHosts files. Secondly, you can store DNS zone data in the AD DS data store, which provides enhanced functionality and security. In addition, AD DS domain names are DNS names. If your AD DS forest includes several domains in a hierarchical (parent-child) configuration, or in a peer (multiple domain trees) configuration, your DNS implementation should correspond to the AD DS domain implementation.

> **Important**   Because DNS is essential for AD DS, you must become familiar with DNS
> concepts and know how DNS is implemented. If you are not familiar with DNS, you should
> consult some of the excellent resources available on the Microsoft Web site, such as the DNS
> Technical Reference located at *http://technet2.microsoft.com/WindowsServer/en/Library/*
> *6e45e81e-fb44-4a20-a752-ebe740e2acc61033.mspx.*

Integration of DNS and AD DS

AD DS cannot function without a reliable DNS configuration. DNS is critically important in
AD DS because DNS provides the information that computers on the network need to locate
the AD DS domain controllers. This section takes a detailed look at the information that is
stored in DNS and the process that a client computer uses to locate the domain controllers.

> **On the Disc**   Because of the dependency AD DS has on DNS, you should ensure that you
> have current documentation for all DNS zones managed by your company. You can use
> the DNSConfig.xlsx spreadsheet on the CD to document your DNS zone and DNS server
> configurations.

Service Location (SRV) Resource Records

To facilitate the location of domain controllers, AD DS uses service location or SRV resource
records. An SRV record, which is described in RFC 2782, "A DNS RR for Specifying the
Location of Services (DNS SRV)" at *http://www.ietf.org/rfc/rfc2782.txt,* is used to identify
computers that provide services located on a Transmission Control Protocol/Internet Protocol
(TCP/IP) network. In Windows Server 2008, all domain controllers register SRV records in
DNS that identify the computers as providing AD DS related services.

> **Note**   All networks require some means to locate computers that provide domain services. In
> Windows NT, domain logon was based on NetBIOS names. Every domain controller registered
> the NetBIOS name *Domainname* with a *<1C>* as the sixteenth character in the name on the
> network and in Windows Internet Name Service (WINS). When a client tried to log on to
> the network, the client would try to locate the servers that had the domain controller name
> registered. If the client could not locate one of these servers, the logon would fail. In Windows
> 2000 or later, the SRV records are used to locate domain controllers. Without the SRV records,
> these clients will also not be able to log on to the Windows Server 2008 domain. Windows
> Server 2008 domain controllers still register the domain NetBIOS name on the network and in
> WINS if a WINS server is configured.

Every SRV record uses a standard format, as explained in Table 3-1 and as shown in the following example of one of the records used by AD DS:

```
_ldap._tcp.Adatum.com. 600 IN SRV 0 100 389 SEA-DC1.Adatum.com
```

Table 3-1 The SRV Record Components

Component	Example	Explanation
Service	_ldap	The service that this record identifies. This service identifies this server as a server that will respond to LDAP requests.
Protocol	_tcp	The protocol used for this service. It can be either TCP or user datagram protocol (UDP).
Name	ADatum.com	The domain name that this record refers to.
TTL	600	The default Time to Live for this record (in seconds).
Class	IN	The standard DNS Internet class.
Resource Record	SRV	Identifies the record as an SRV record.
Priority	0	Identifies the priority of this record for the client. If multiple SRV records exist for the same service, the clients will try to connect first to the server with the lowest priority value.
Weight	100	A load-balancing mechanism. If multiple SRV records exist for the same service and the priority is identical for all the records, clients will choose the records with the higher weights more often.
Port	389	The port used by this service.
Target	SEA-DC1.ADatum.com	The host that provides the service identified by this record.

Figure 3-1 shows this record in the DNS management console.

Essentially, the information in this record states that if a client is looking for a Lightweight Directory Access Protocol (LDAP) server in the ADatum.com domain, the client should connect to SEA-DC1.ADatum.com.

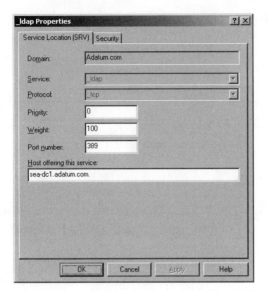

Figure 3-1   Example of an SRV record.

SRV Records Registered by AD DS Domain Controllers

The domain controllers in a Windows Server 2008 domain register many SRV records in DNS. The following list includes all of the records registered by the first server in a forest:

```
Adatum.com. 600 IN A 10.10.10.10
Adatum.com. 600 IN AAAA 2001:4898:28:4:343e:eb57:e7d1:a87c
_ldap._tcp.Adatum.com. 600 IN SRV 0 100 389 SEA-DC1.Adatum.com.
_ldap._tcp.Default-First-Site-Name._sites.Adatum.com. 600 IN SRV 0 100 389
     SEA-DC1.Adatum.com.
_ldap._tcp.pdc._msdcs.Adatum.com. 600 IN SRV 0 100 389 SEA-DC1.Adatum.com.
_ldap._tcp.gc._msdcs.Adatum.com. 600 IN SRV 0 100 3268 SEA-DC1.Adatum.com.
_ldap._tcp.Default-First-Site-Name._sites.gc._msdcs.Adatum.com. 600 IN SRV 0
     100 3268 SEA-DC1.Adatum.com.
_ldap._tcp.64c228cd-5f07-4606-b843-d4fd114264b7.domains._msdcs.Adatum.com.
     600 IN SRV 0 100 389 SEA-DC1.Adatum.com.
gc._msdcs.Adatum.com. 600 IN A 10.10.10.10
     175170ad-0263-439f-bb4c-89eacc410ab1._msdcs.Adatum.com. 600 IN CNAME
     SEA-DC1.Adatum.com.
gc._msdcs.Adatum.com. 600 IN AAAA 2001:4898:28:4:343e:eb57:e7d1:a87c
_kerberos._tcp.dc._msdcs.Adatum.com. 600 IN SRV 0 100 88 SEA-DC1.Adatum.com.
_kerberos._tcp.Default-First-Site-Name._sites.dc._msdcs.Adatum.com. 600 IN
     SRV 0 100 88 SEA-DC1.Adatum.com.
_ldap._tcp.dc._msdcs.Adatum.com. 600 IN SRV 0 100 389 SEA-DC1.Adatum.com.
_ldap._tcp.Default-First-Site-Name._sites.dc._msdcs.Adatum.com. 600 IN SRV 0
     100 389 SEA-DC1.Adatum.com.
_kerberos._tcp.Adatum.com. 600 IN SRV 0 100 88 SEA-DC1.Adatum.com.
_kerberos._tcp.Default-First-Site-Name._sites.Adatum.com. 600 IN SRV 0 100 88
     SEA-DC1.Adatum.com.
_gc._tcp.Adatum.com. 600 IN SRV 0 100 3268 SEA-DC1.Adatum.com.
_gc._tcp.Default-First-Site-Name._sites.Adatum.com. 600 IN SRV 0 100 3268
     SEA-DC1.Adatum.com.
```

```
_kerberos._udp.Adatum.com. 600 IN SRV 0 100 88 SEA-DC1.Adatum.com.
_kpasswd._tcp.Adatum.com. 600 IN SRV 0 100 464 SEA-DC1.Adatum.com.
_kpasswd._udp.Adatum.com. 600 IN SRV 0 100 464 SEA-DC1.Adatum.com.
DomainDnsZones.Adatum.com. 600 IN A 10.10.10.10
DomainDnsZones.Adatum.com. 600 IN AAAA 2001:4898:28:4:343e:eb57:e7d1:a87c
_ldap._tcp.DomainDnsZones.Adatum.com. 600 IN SRV 0 100 389 SEA-DC1.Adatum.com.
_ldap._tcp.Default-First-Site-Name._sites.DomainDnsZones.Adatum.com. 600 IN
     SRV 0 100 389 SEA-DC1.Adatum.com.
ForestDnsZones.Adatum.com. 600 IN A 10.10.10.10
ForestDnsZones.Adatum.com. 600 IN AAAA 2001:4898:28:4:343e:eb57:e7d1:a87c
_ldap._tcp.ForestDnsZones.Adatum.com. 600 IN SRV 0 100 389 SEA-DC1.Adatum.com.
_ldap._tcp.Default-First-Site-Name._sites.ForestDnsZones.Adatum.com. 600 IN
     SRV 0 100 389 SEA-DC1.Adatum.com.
```

> **Note**   When one of the Windows Server 2008 servers is promoted to a domain controller, all of these records are written to a file called Netlogon.dns, which is located in the %systemroot%\system32\config folder. If you do not want to enable dynamic updates on the DNS servers, you can import these records into the DNS zone.

The first part of the SRV record identifies the service that the SRV record points to. The possible services are:

- **_ldap**   AD DS is an LDAP-compliant directory service, with the domain controllers operating as LDAP servers. The _ldap SRV records identify the available LDAP servers on the network. These servers could be Windows Server 2008 domain controllers, previous versions of Windows domain controllers, or other LDAP servers.

- **_kerberos**   The primary authentication protocol for all Windows 2000 and later clients and servers. The _kerberos SRV records identify all the Key Distribution Centers (KDCs) on the network. These could be Windows Server 2008 domain controllers, previous versions of Windows domain controllers, or other KDC servers.

- **_kpasswd**   The _kpasswd SRV record identifies the Kerberos password-change servers on the network (again either Windows Server 2008 domain controllers, previous versions of Windows domain controllers, or other Kerberos password-change servers).

- **_gc**   The _gc SRV record is specific to the global catalog function in AD DS. Only Windows Server 2008 or previous versions of Windows domain controllers that are configured as global catalog servers register this record.

Many of the SRV records also contain a site identifier in addition to the components listed in Table 3-1. One of the reasons for implementing sites is to ensure that the network clients will always try to log on to a domain controller that resides in the same site as the client. The site records are essential for the computers to locate domain controllers in the same site as the client. The process that a client uses to locate the site information is discussed in the next section.

Another essential component of the SRV records is the _msdcs value that appears in many of the records. Some of the services provided by the SRV records are non–Microsoft specific. For example, there could be non-Microsoft implementations of LDAP or Kerberos servers on the network. These servers could also register an SRV record with the DNS server. Windows Server 2008 domain controllers register the generic records (for example, _ldap._tcp.ADatum.com), but the domain controllers also register records containing the _msdcs reference. These records refer only to Microsoft-specific roles, that is, to Windows 2000 and later domain controllers. The records identify the primary function of each server as *gc* (global catalog), *dc* (domain controller), or *pdc* (primary domain controller emulator).

> **Note**   You may notice that the resource records with an _msdcs value appear in a different zone than the other resource records in the DNS management console. The zone name is called _msdcs.*domainname* rather than just *domainname*. If you install DNS on a domain controller when you run the Active Directory Domain Services Installation Wizard on the first domain controller in a domain, the DNS zones are stored in application partitions in the AD DS data store. The _msdcs zone information is stored in an application partition that is replicated throughout the AD DS forest, whereas the domain zone is stored in an application partition that is replicated to all AD DS domain controllers that are also DNS servers. For more detail, see the next two sections in this chapter.

Another record that is registered contains the domain's globally unique identifier (GUID). This record enables a client to locate a domain controller in a domain on the basis of its GUID. The domain GUID record is used to locate domain controllers in the event of a domain rename.

Windows Server 2008 domain controllers also register the following DNS host (A/AAAA) records for the use of LDAP clients that do not support DNS SRV records:

- **DNSDomainname 600 IN A *IPv4Address***   Enables a non–SRV-aware client to locate any domain controller in the domain by looking up an A record. A name in this form is returned to the LDAP client through an LDAP referral. These host records are registered for the AD DS domain name, as well as the ForestDNSZones and Domain DNSZones domain names.

- **DNSDomainname 600 IN AAAA *IPv6Address***   Enables a non–SRV-aware client to locate any domain controller in the domain by looking up an AAAA record. Domain controllers configured with IPv6 enabled do not register the link-local IPv6 address but will register statically configured IPv6 addresses. These host records are registered for the AD DS domain name, as well as the ForestDNSZones and Domain DNSZones domain names.

- **gc._msdcs.DnsForestName**   Enables a non–SRV-aware client to locate any global catalog server in the forest by looking up an A record. A name in this form is returned to the LDAP client through an LDAP referral.

How It Works: SRV Records and RODCs

For security reasons, read-only domain controllers (RODC) and read-only global catalog servers (ROGC) are not enabled by default to register their own DNS records. Instead, the RODC or ROGC sends a DNS update request to a writable Windows Server 2008 domain controller, which validates and then registers the records on behalf of the RODC or ROGC.

In addition, RODCs only register the site-specific LDAP and Kerberos and CName records in DNS. By default, only users in the same site as the RODC site users should be able to discover and use them. This can be achieved by registering *only* site-specific records. ROGCs also register the site-specific GC records. Because RODCs cannot be used to change passwords, the servers do not register Kpasswd records.

Ashish Sharma

SDE II, US-Directory and Service Business

DNS Locator Service

The domain controllers running Windows Server 2008 register some or all of the records described earlier in DNS. These records then play an essential role when a client like Windows 2000 or later tries to log on to the domain. The following steps describe the process that these clients use to log on to the domain:

1. When the user logs on, the client computer sends a remote procedure call (RPC) to the local Net Logon service, initiating a logon session. As part of the RPC, the client sends information such as the computer name, domain name, and site name to the Net Logon service.

2. The Net Logon service uses the domain locator service to call the DsGetDcName() API, passing one of the flag parameter values listed in Table 3-2.

Table 3-2   A Subset of the DsGetDcName Flag Parameter Values

DsGetDcName Flag Values	DNS Record Requested
DS_PDC_REQUIRED	_ldap._tcp.pdc._msdcs.*domainname*
DS_GC_SERVER_REQUIRED	_ldap._tcp.sitename._sites.gc._msdcs.*forestrootdomain-name*
DS_KDC_REQUIRED	_kdc._tcp.sitename._sites.dc._msdcs.*domainname*
DS_ONLY_LDAP_NEEDED	_ldap._tcp.*sitename*._sites._msdcs.*domainname*

> **Note**   In almost all cases, the *DsGetDcName* function also includes the *sitename* parameter. For all of the requests except the DS_PDC_REQUIRED request, the client always makes an initial request using the site parameter. If the DNS server does not respond to the request, the client will send the same request without the site parameter. For example, if the DS_KDC_REQUIRED request is not fulfilled, the client will send a request for the _kdc._tcp.dc._msdcs.*forestrootdomain* record. This can happen when the client site is not configured or not available.
>
> Windows Server 2008 introduces a new flag called DS_TRY_NEXTCLOSEST_SITE. When this flag is set, the client will try to locate a domain controller in the same site as the client. If that fails, the client will use the AD DS site link configuration to locate a domain controller in the next closest site.
>
> Windows Server 2008 introduces another new flag that can be used by the *DSGetDCName* function. This flag, DS_IP_VERSION_AGONISTIC, is used by the client to specify that they want either an IPv4 or IPv6 address. If this flag is not set, the locator will return an IPv4 address.
>
> The client may also pass the *DomainGUID* parameter rather than the domain name to DsGetDcName(). In this case, the client is requesting the _ldap._tcp.*domain-GUID*.domains._msdcs.*forestname* record. This will only happen when a domain has been renamed.

3. The DNS server returns the requested list of servers. The client then sorts the list based on priority. The list of the same priority servers are randomized based on weight. The client then processes the servers list in order. It gets the addresses of each server and sends an LDAP query using UDP port 389 to each of the addresses in the order they were returned. After each packet is sent, the client waits for a response, and if no response is received, it sends a packet to the next domain controller. The client continues this process until it receives a valid response that specifies the requested services (e.g., time service, writable DC) or has tried all of the domain controllers.

4. When a domain controller responds to the client, the client checks the response to make sure that it contains the requested information. If it does, the client begins the logon process with the domain controller.

5. The client caches the domain controller information so that the next time it needs to access AD DS, it does not have to go through the discovery process again.

Direct from the Source: How a Client Determines Availability of a Domain Controller

When a client tries to locate a domain controller after it has received the IP address from DNS, it varies the time it waits for a response based on the number of domain controllers it has already pinged. For the first five domain controllers, it waits for 0.4 seconds, and for next five domain controllers, it waits for 0.2 seconds. After 10 domain controllers have been pinged, the client uses a 0.1 second wait for the remaining requests.

The algorithm is designed to reduce network traffic if possible and also to ensure that the client receives a response in a reasonable time if all the queries fail. The logic is that if the domain controllers are slow because of a high load, the first 10 domain controllers should be able to respond with the longer wait time before the client increases the frequency of requests, which results in increased network traffic.

Ashish Sharma

SDE II, US-Directory and Service Business

How the Client Determines Which Site It Belongs To

Having site-specific records is important in order for AD DS to operate efficiently, because a lot of client network traffic can be limited to a particular site. For example, the client logon process always tries to connect to a domain controller in the client site before connecting to any other sites. So how does the client know which site it belongs to?

The site information for the forest is stored in the configuration directory partition in AD DS, and this information is replicated to all domain controllers in the forest. Included with the configuration information is a list of IP subnets that are associated with a particular site. When the client logs on to AD DS for the first time, the first domain controller to respond compares the client's IP address with the site IP addresses. Part of the domain controller's response to the client is the site information, which the client then caches. Any future logon attempts will include the client site information.

If the client is moved between sites (for example, a portable computer may be connected to a network in a different city), the client still sends the site information as part of the logon. The DNS server will respond with the record of a domain controller that is in the requested site. However, if the domain controller determines that the client is not in the original site based on the client's new IP address, it will send the new site information to the client. The client then caches this information and tries to locate a domain controller in the correct site.

If the client is not in any site that is defined in AD DS, it cannot make site-specific requests for domain controllers.

Direct from the Source: IPv6 Addressing and Site Determination

Windows Server 2008 provides full support for IPv6. This means that the domain controller can use any of the client's IP addresses when determining the client's site. These addresses include the IPv4 address, the global IPv6 address, and the link-local IPv6 address.

> When the domain controller gets a client's IP address, it tries to find the corresponding site in the configuration. By default, the domain controller will use only one of the IP addresses even if both IPv4 and IPv6 addresses are used. Prior to Windows Server 2008, if the provided IP address did not map to a site, the domain controller would return no site mapping to the client. In Windows Server 2008, the domain controller will use both the client's IPv4 and global IPv6 address, and it returns the corresponding site for those addresses if mapped.
>
> This has implications for AD DS site configuration. In previous versions of AD DS, you only had to assign the correct IPv4 subnets to a site. In Windows Server 2008, you should configure both the IPv4 and global IPv6 subnet addresses to a particular site.
>
> *Ashish Sharma*
>
> *SDE II, US-Directory and Service Business*

After a client computer authenticates, it will cache the domain controller information for a default of 15 minutes. If the client computer authenticated when no domain controller was available in its site, it will have authenticated with a domain controller in a different site. This means that the client computer will use the domain controller in a different site for all AD DS lookups for those 15 minutes. To modify this default value, create a REG_DWORD entry named CloseSiteTimeout in the *HKLM\SYSTEM\CurrentControlSet\Services\Netlogon\Parameters* key. You can configure a value of 1 minute to 49.7 days for this entry. Use caution when changing the value of this entry. If the value is too high, then the client may use a domain controller in a different site for a long period of time. If the value is too low, then repeated attempts to find a domain controller can create excessive network traffic.

Automatic Site Coverage

You can create sites in AD DS without installing a domain controller in the site. Or you may create a site that contains domain controllers for one domain, but client computers from a different domain in the forest may need to log on in the site. This means that client computers in the site will need to authenticate to a domain controller in a different site. To ensure that these clients will still choose the best available domain controller, AD DS is designed so that the domain controllers will automatically calculate which domain controllers will register the SRV records for sites that do not have domain controllers. This feature is called automatic site coverage.

Note   Automatic site coverage is a dynamic process. If a domain controller in a particular site is unavailable, other domain controllers will automatically configure the site coverage records for the site.

The domain controllers use the sites and site link information to determine which domain controller will provide coverage for a site with no domain controllers. All domain controllers are aware of all sites, site links, and domain controllers, because this information is stored in the Configuration partition in AD DS. All domain controllers first build a list of target sites, that is, sites that do not have any domain controllers in the local domain controller's domain. The domain controllers then build a list of potential sites that could provide automatic site coverage. This list includes all sites that have domain controllers in the specific domain.

By default, the domain controllers in the site with the lowest cost site links to the target site will provide site coverage. If more than one site is linked with the lowest cost site links, the site with the largest number of domain controllers will provide site coverage. If two or more sites still qualify, the site that is first alphabetically is selected. The domain controllers in the selected site then register the site-specific SRV records for the domain controllers for this domain in the target site.

> **Note**   When you deploy an RODC in a separate site, Windows Server 2003 domain controllers will provide automatic site coverage for the site. This is because Windows Server 2003 domain controllers do not include RODCs in their automatic site calculations. See Chapter 5, "Designing the Active Directory Domain Services Structure," for details on how you can address this issue.

Managing DNS Registration by Using Group Policy

You can manage how AD DS domain controllers register SRV records in DNS by using group policies. To apply these settings to all domain controllers, you can modify the Default Domain Controllers Policy. If you want to apply different policies to domain controllers, you will need to create a new group policy object and then use a filter to apply the group policy to only specified domain controllers. The following table lists the settings that are available. These settings are available in the DC Locator DNS Records folder under Administrative Templates\System\Net Logon.

Group Policy Setting	Description
Domain Controller Address Type Returned	Determines whether the DC Locater returns just IPv4 addresses or IPv4 and IPv6 addresses. By default, both types of addresses are returned, but if this setting is disabled, only IPv4 addresses will be returned.
Dynamic Registration of the DC Locator DNS Records	Determines if Dynamic Registration of the DNS resource records is enabled. These DNS records are dynamically registered by the Net Logon service.
DC Locator DNS records not registered by the DCs	Determines which DNS records are not registered by the Netlogon service. You can restrict domain controllers from registering specific types of records.
Refresh Interval of the DC Locator DNS Records	Specifies the Refresh Interval of the DNS resource records for domain controllers to which this setting is applied.

Group Policy Setting	Description
Weight Set in the DC Locator DNS SRV Records	Specifies the Weight field in the SRV resource records registered by the domain controllers to which this setting is applied.
Priority Set in the DC Locator DNS SRV Records	Specifies the Priority field in the SRV resource records registered by domain controllers to which this setting is applied.
TTL Set in the DC Locator DNS SRV Records	Specifies the value for the Time-To-Live (TTL) field in Net Logon registered SRV resource records.
Automated Site Coverage by the DC Locator DNS SRV Records	Determines whether domain controllers dynamically register DC Locator site-specific SRV records for the closest sites where no domain controller for the same domain exists (or no global catalog for the same forest exists).
Sites Covered by the DC Locator DNS SRV Records	Specifies the sites for which the domain controllers register the site-specific SRV records if no domain controller for the domain is available in the site.
Sites Covered by the GC Locator DNS SRV Records	Specifies the sites for which the global catalog servers should register if no global catalog server for the forest is available in the site.
Sites Covered by the Application Directory Partition Locator DNS SRV Records	Specifies the sites for which the domain controllers hosting the application directory partition should register the site-specific SRV records.
Location of the DCs hosting a domain with a single label DNS name	Specifies if the computers to which this setting is applied attempt DNS name resolution of single-label domain names.
Force Rediscovery Interval	Specifies a time limit when clients will be forced to rediscover domain controllers. Useful when the domain controller configuration changes frequently on a network. By default, clients are forced to rediscover domain controllers every 12 hours.
Ignore incoming mailslot messages used for domain controller location based on NetBIOS domain names	Determines if the domain controller will respond to mailslot responses for more information about the domain controller. Mailslot requests are only used by Window NT or older clients that use NetBIOS names to locate and log on to domain controllers.
Try Next Closest Site	Determines if client computers will automatically try the closest site if a domain controller is not available. By default, clients will request a domain controller in the closest site by using the DC Locater call DS_TRY_NEXTCLOSEST_SITE.

AD DS Integrated Zones

In addition to using DNS to locate domain controllers, Windows Server 2008 can also be integrated with DNS by storing the DNS zone information in the AD DS data store.

Benefits of Using AD DS Integrated Zones

AD DS integrated zones provide a number of advantages:

- **The zone transfer process is replaced by AD DS replication.**   Because the zone information is stored in AD DS, the data is replicated through the normal AD DS replication process. This means that the replication occurs at a per-attribute level so that only the changes to the zone information are replicated. Between sites, the replication traffic can also be highly compressed, saving additional bandwidth. Using an AD DS integrated zone also enables the use of application partitions that can be used to fine-tune the replication of DNS information. In addition, when new domain controllers are added to the domain, the DNS information is automatically replicated to the new domain controller without any further configuration.

- **Integrated zones enable a multimaster DNS server configuration.**   Without AD DS, DNS can support only one primary name server for each DNS zone. That means that all changes to the zone information must be made on the primary name server and then transferred to the secondary name servers. With AD DS integrated zones, each DNS server has a writable copy of the domain information, so that changes to the zone information can be made anywhere in the organization. The information is then replicated to all other DNS servers.

- **Integrated zones enable secure updates.**   If a zone is configured as an AD DS integrated zone, you can configure the zone to use secure updates only. This gives you more control over which users and computers can update the resource records in AD DS.

- **Integrated zones provide additional security.**   Because the DNS zone data is stored in AD DS, you can use access control lists (ACLs) to secure the dnsZone object container in the directory. This feature provides granulated access to either the zone or a specified resource record in the zone.

In some cases, organizations are hesitant to use AD DS integrated zones because DNS must be installed on a Windows Server 2008 domain controller. This can create an additional load on that domain controller. Another issue is that if all client computers in an organization are configured to register their host records in DNS, the AD DS database may contain hundreds of thousands of additional records.

> **Note**   You can combine AD DS integrated zones with secondary zones. For example, you might have three domain controllers in a central location with several remote offices where you do not have a domain controller. If you want to install a DNS server into a remote office, you can install the DNS server role on a member server running Windows Server 2008 and then configure a secondary zone on the DNS server. The secondary server will then accept zone transfers from the AD DS integrated zone.

Default Application Partitions for DNS

When you install DNS while you are promoting the first server in the forest to be a domain controller, two new application directory partitions are created in AD DS. These partitions are the DomainDnsZones partition and the ForestDnsZones partition. DNS zone information is then stored in these directory partitions, rather than in a text file on the DNS server hard disk.

Each of these partitions contains different information and has a different replication configuration. The DomainDNSZones partition contains all of the domain controller records that are important for locating domain controller services within the domain. All of the resource records described previously, except the resource records that include the _msdcs_ value, are stored in the DomainDnsZones partition. The DomainDnsZones partition is replicated to all DNS servers running on domain controllers in a domain.

The ForestDnsZones partition is replicated to all DNS servers running on domain controllers in the forest. The ForestDnsZones partition contains the information that is required for domain controllers and clients to locate domain controller services in other domains in the forest. For example, the ForestDnsZones partition includes a domains subzone that lists all of the domain GUIDs and lists the domain controllers for each of the domains. The ForestDns-Zones partition lists all of the domain controllers by GUID in the entire forest and lists all of the global catalog servers in the forest. The _msdcs subzone is stored in the ForestDnsZones partition.

Note   The DNS application directory partitions are created only if you choose to install DNS when you promote the first domain controller in the domain or forest. If you want to take advantage of DNS application directory partitions after you have already upgraded the domain controller, you must manually create the partition before you can use them. To create the partitions, you can use the DNS Manager or the DNSCmd command-line tool. If you are using the DNS administrative tool, right-click on the DNS server name and select Create Default Application Directory Partitions. If you are using DNSCmd, open a command line and type **dnscmd DNSservername /CreateBuiltinDirectoryPartitions /forest**. This will create the ForestDnsZones partition. To create the DomainDnsZones partition, use **"/domain"** as the last parameter in the command, instead of **"/forest"**. You can create the DomainDNSZones partition for all domains in the forest by running the command with the _/Alldomains_ parameter. Because this command modifies the configuration directory partition in AD DS, you must be logged in as a member of the Enterprise Admins group.

The DNS application partitions can be viewed through the DNS Manager and through tools such as DNSCmd, ADSIEdit.msc, or Ldp.exe. In the DNS Manager (shown in Figure 3-2), the ForestDnsZones partition information is listed in the _msdcs.forestname_ delegated zone. The DomainDnsZones partition is listed in the DomainDnsZone subzone within the _domain-name_ zone. In ADSIEdit.msc, the application partitions can be viewed by connecting to the dc=domaindnszones,dc=_domainname_ partition or the dc=forestdnszones,dc=_forestname_ partition (shown in Figure 3-3).

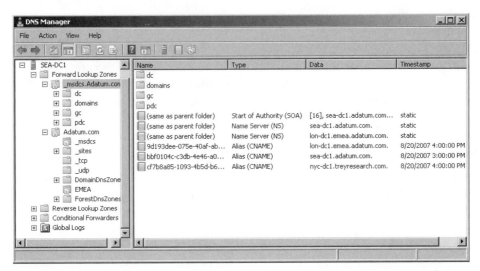

Figure 3-2   The DNS application directory partitions in DNS management console.

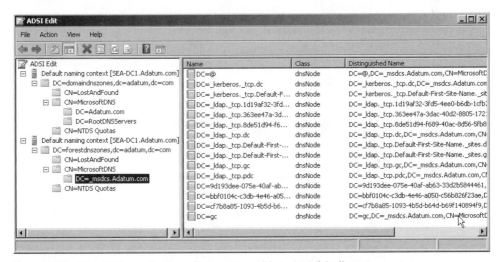

Figure 3-3   The DNS application directory partitions in Adsiedit.msc.

On the Disc   You can use the ListAppPartitions.ps1 Windows PowerShell script on the CD to list the application partitions deployed in your forest and to display which domain controllers have a replica of the partitions. If you are running Windows PowerShell on a Windows Server 2008 computer, you must configure the PowerShell script execution policy to allow unsigned scripts by running the Set-ExecutionPolicy RemoteSigned command. Also, you need to provide the full path when running a Windows PowerShell script.

Managing AD DS Integrated Zones

When you implement AD DS integrated zones, you may need to perform additional DNS management tasks that are not required when using standard DNS zones. These tasks include configuring the AD DS application directory partitions that will contain the DNS zone information, managing and securing dynamic DNS, and configuring record aging and record scavenging.

Configuring DNS Application Partitions

By default, when you install DNS while configuring the first domain controller in a domain, the DNS zone information is stored in the DomainDnsZones and the ForestDnsZones application partitions. However, you can modify the application partition that is used for these zones, or you can store DNS zone information in AD DS when you create new zones on the domain controller. You are given a choice about where to store the DNS information when you create a new zone (see Figure 3-4) or through the Zone Properties sheet in the DNS administrative tool. You are given the following four choices of where to store the DNS information:

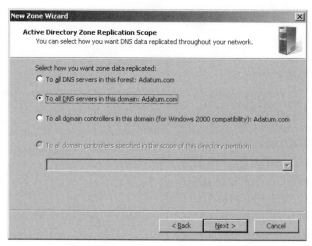

Figure 3-4   Configuring the replication scope for DNS zones.

- **To All DNS Servers In This Forest:** *forestname*   The information is stored in the ForestDnsZones partition, where it is replicated to all DNS servers running on domain controllers in the forest. Use this zone only if users in multiple domains in the forest will need to access this zone information.

- **To All DNS Servers In This Domain:** *domainname*   The information is stored in the DomainDnsZones partition, where it is replicated to all the DNS servers running on domain controllers in the domain. Use this zone if only users in a specific domain require access to the zone information, or if you will be using delegation or forwarding to enable other DNS servers to locate this zone information.

- **To All Domain Controllers In This Domain (for Windows 2000 compatibility):** *domain-name*   The information is stored in the domain directory partition, where it is replicated to all domain controllers in the domain. The difference between this option and the option to store the information in the DomainDnsZones partition is that, in this case, all domain controllers will receive the information while the DomainDnsZones partition is only replicated to domain controllers that are also DNS servers. Because Windows 2000 Server Active Directory does not support application directory partitions, you must use this option if you want to use AD DS integrated zones with Windows Server 2000 domain controllers.

- **To All Domain Controllers Specified In The Scope Of This Directory Partition**   This option is only available if you create an additional application directory partition with its own replication configuration. The DNS information will be replicated to all domain controllers that have a replica of this partition.

Normally, you should not change the default configuration for the AD DS integrated zones. If you have multiple domain controllers in a domain but only some of them are DNS servers, using the DomainDnsZones partition reduces the amount of replication because domain controllers that are not DNS servers do not receive a copy of the zone. The ForestDnsZones partition is replicated throughout the forest, so the DNS information needed to locate all the domain controllers in the forest is replicated to all DNS servers in the forest.

Managing Dynamic DNS

In the past, one difficult aspect of working with DNS was that all the zone information had to be manually entered into the DNS server. However, as described in RFC 2136, DNS servers can now be configured to accept automatic updates to the resource records in the zones. This option is called dynamic DNS (DDNS).

Windows Server 2008 DNS servers support dynamic DNS. By default, all Windows 2000 and later clients, as well as Windows 2000 Server and later computers, automatically update their resource records in DNS. In addition, Windows Server 2008 DNS servers will also accept dynamic record registration from Dynamic Host Configuration Protocol (DHCP) servers. The Windows Server 2008 DHCP server can be configured to automatically update the DNS records for any of its clients, including Microsoft Windows 95, Microsoft Windows 98, Microsoft Windows Me, or Microsoft Windows NT clients.

One of the concerns with dynamic DNS is security. Without some control over who can update the DNS resource records, anyone with access to your network can potentially create a resource record in your DNS zone and then use the record to redirect network traffic. To deal with this, Windows Server 2008 DNS provides for *secure updates*. Secure updates are only available in AD DS integrated zones. With secure updates, you can control who has the right to register and update the DNS records. By default, the members of the Authenticated Users group have the right to update their records in DNS. This means that computers that are members in the domain have the right to update their own DNS records. However, you can change this by modifying the access control list (ACL) for the DNS zone.

> **More Info**   For more information on configuring dynamic DNS, see the DNS Technical
> Reference.

Aging and Scavenging

One of the issues with using AD DS integrated zones and dynamic updates in large enterprise environments is that if you allow all client computers to update their resource records in DNS, you could potentially have thousands of records in DNS which will increase the size of the AD DS database file. If client computers are shut down while still connected to the network, the client computers will release their resource records in AD DS. However, if clients are improperly disconnected from the network, its host (A) RR might not be deleted. To clean up these resource records in AD DS zones, you may choose to configure aging and scavenging.

With dynamic DNS, each resource record added to DNS is given a time stamp based on the current date and time that is set at the server computer. Resource records that have been manually added to DNS are configured with a time-stamp value of zero to indicate that the records should not be deleted by the aging and scavenging process.

By default, aging and scavenging are not enabled for Windows Server 2008 DNS servers and zones. After you enable aging and scavenging, the DNS server will monitor the time for all records since the record was last updated. When the time elapsed for the record refresh exceeds the configured age limit, the record is scavenged from DNS.

Background Zone Loading

As mentioned earlier, one of the potential issues with using AD DS integrated zones and enabling dynamic DNS is that you can have thousands of client computers that register their host records in DNS. When the AD DS domain controller starts or the DNS service is restarted, it must read the DNS zone information from the AD DS data store. In very large organizations, loading the AD DS data store when restarting the DNS server can take an hour or more. The result is that the DNS server is effectively unavailable to service client requests for the entire time that it takes to load AD DS-based zones.

Windows Server 2008 provides a new feature called background zone loading to address this scenario. With the feature, a DNS server can begin responding to DNS client requests while continuing to load zone data from AD DS in the background. When the DNS server starts, it:

- Enumerates all zones to be loaded.
- Loads root hints from files or the AD DS data store.
- Loads all standard DNS zones that are stored in text files rather than in AD DS.

- Begins responding to DNS queries and remote procedure calls (RPCs). If the server receives a query for a zone that is not yet loaded, the DNS server reads the node's data from AD DS and responds to the client query.

- Spawns one or more threads to load the zones that are stored in AD DS.

DNS and Read-Only Domain Controllers

As mentioned earlier, Windows Server 2008 provides read-only domain controllers (RODC). To support RODCs, Windows Server 2008 also supports a new type of DNS zone, the primary read-only zone. When you configure an RODC as a DNS server, it replicates from a writable domain controller a full read-only copy of all of the application directory partitions that DNS uses, including the domain partition, ForestDNSZones, and DomainDNSZones. This ensures that the DNS server running on the RODC has a read-only copy of any DNS zones stored in those directory partitions.

The RODC DNS server responds to client queries just like any other DNS server. However, because the AD DS integrated DNS zones on the RODC are read-only, no changes can be made to the zones on the RODC. The administrator of an RODC can view the contents of a primary read-only zone; however, the administrator cannot make changes to the local copy of the zone. Changes can only be made on a domain controller with a writable AD DS copy. When client computers try to register their host record with the DNS server using dynamic DNS, the client computer is redirected to a DNS server with a writable copy of the DNS zone.

> **Note**   Just like other domain controllers, RODCs can be configured as DNS servers or not. If you do configure an RODC as a DNS server, it will only support primary read-only zones if you use AD DS integrated zones. You can configure the RODC as a DNS server with standard primary or secondary zones. If you implement a primary standard zone on the RODC, it will not be read-only.

Integrating DNS Namespaces and AD DS Domains

All AD DS domain names must be DNS names, and DNS is required for AD DS to function correctly. In a single domain environment, the integration of the DNS namespace and the AD DS name is very simple—you just need to have a DNS server that is authoritative for the DNS zone that is equivalent to the AD DS domain name. However, in an organization with multiple domains, and possibly multiple domain trees in the forest, integrating the DNS namespaces with the AD DS domain names can be more complicated.

> **Important**   Ensuring that the DNS namespace is correctly integrated with the AD DS designs is just as important as ensuring that all of the domain controller SRV records are registered in DNS. In order for domain controllers in different domains in the forest to replicate with each other, they must be able to locate each other in DNS.

> **Note**   This chapter describes the options for integrating DNS namespaces with AD DS domain names in a single forest. Chapter 5 goes into more detail on the design issues related to integrating the AD DS forest into DNS namespaces outside of AD DS.

DNS Delegation

DNS uses a hierarchical namespace and distributed database model. This enables DNS clients to resolve any name in the DNS namespace without requiring that one DNS server host all of the DNS zones in the namespace. For example, if a client connects to a DNS server that is authoritative for the .com top-level domain and requests a server in the ADatum.com domain, the authoritative .com server must have some way of determining which name servers are authoritative for the ADatum.com domain. This is made possible by the use of *delegation records*.

A delegation record is a pointer to a subdomain that identifies the name servers for the subdomain. For example, as shown in Figure 3-5, DNS1.ADatum.com is an authoritative name server for the ADatum.com domain. DNS2 and DNS3 are authoritative name servers for the NA.ADatum.com domain. DNS1 is considered authoritative for the NA.ADatum.com.com domain but does not have all of the resource records for the child domain. However, DNS1 uses a delegation record pointing to DNS2 and DNS3 as the name servers for the child domain. When a client connects to DNS1 requesting information about NA.ADatum.com.com, the server will refer the client to the name servers for the child domain.

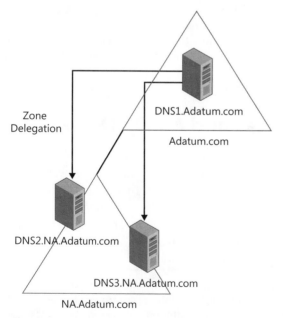

Figure 3-5   Delegated zones link higher level domains with subdomains.

Note   When you install the first domain controller in a domain and configure it as a DNS server, the installation wizard automatically attempts to create a delegation record in the parent DNS zone. For example, if you created a new AD DS domain named Corp.ADatum.com, the Active Directory Domain Services Installation Wizard would attempt to connect to a name server that is authoritative for the ADatum.com domain and then attempt to create a delegation record for the Corp.ADatum.com domain. If the DNS server is not available, or if the account used to run the installation wizard does not have permission to create the delegation record, you will receive the warning shown in Figure 3-6. You can continue the installation and manually configure the delegation record if required.

Figure 3-6   Warning message that creating a delegation record has failed.

Security Alert   If the parent domain for your domain name is an Internet-based DNS server (for example, if when you create the ADatum.com domain, the parent domain is the .com domain hosted on Internet DNS servers), you should not configure a delegation record pointing to your internal DNS servers. The internal DNS zones for your AD DS should never be exposed to the Internet.

Forwarders and Root Hints

The second method for connecting the different layers of the DNS hierarchy together is by using forwarders and root hints. In most cases, forwarders and root hints are used by those DNS servers lower in the DNS namespace to locate information from DNS servers higher up in the hierarchy. Both forwarders and root hints are used by the DNS server to locate information that is not in its zone files. For example, a DNS server may be authoritative for only the ADatum.com domain. When this DNS server receives a query from a client requesting a name resolution in the TreyResearch.com domain, the ADatum.com DNS server must have some way of locating this information.

Forwarders

One way to configure this is to use *forwarders*. A forwarder is simply another DNS server that a particular DNS server uses when it cannot resolve a query. For example, the authoritative name server for ADatum.com might receive a recursive query for the TreyResearch.com domain. If the ADatum DNS server has been configured with a forwarder, it will send a recursive query to the forwarder requesting this information. Forwarders are often used on an organization's internal network. An organization may have several DNS servers with the primary task of internal name resolution. However, users inside the organization are also likely to need to resolve Internet IP addresses. One way to enable this is to configure all the internal DNS servers to try to resolve the Internet addresses. A more common configuration has all the internal DNS servers configured with a forwarder pointing to one DNS server that is responsible for Internet name resolution. This latter configuration is shown in Figure 3-7. All the internal DNS servers forward any query for a nonauthoritative zone to one DNS server, which then tries to resolve the Internet addresses. If a DNS server is configured with more than one forwarder, that DNS server will try all of the forwarders, in order, before trying any other way of resolving the IP addresses.

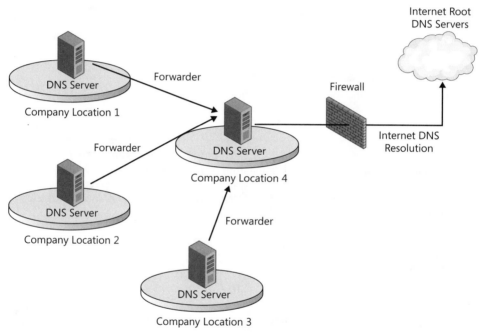

Figure 3-7   Using forwarders for Internet name resolution.

Conditional Forwarding

Windows Server 2008 DNS servers support conditional forward to make the forwarding process more efficient. One of the issues with standard forwarders is that the forwarding process cannot make any distinctions based on domain names. When a client resolver makes a request that the server cannot answer from its cache or zone files, the server sends a recursive query to the list of configured forwarders without being able to choose different forwarders based on the requested domain name.

Conditional forwarding provides exactly this functionality: the DNS server can now forward domain requests to different DNS servers based on domain names. This means that when one of the DNS servers needs to resolve a name in a zone for which it is not authoritative, it can use just the forwarder that is configured for that zone. For example, when a client in the ADatum.com domain needs to locate a resource in the TreyResearch.com domain, it queries the DNS server in the ADatum.com domain. (See Figure 3-8.) The DNS server checks its zone files to determine if it is authoritative for the domain and then checks its cache. If it cannot resolve the name from these sources, it will check the forwarder list. If one of the forwarders is specific for the TreyResearch.com domain, the ADatum.com DNS server will send the recursive query only to that DNS server. If the client computer requests a name resolution for a domain name that does not have a conditional forwarder, the DNS server will use the standard forwarder and then try locating the zone through root hints.

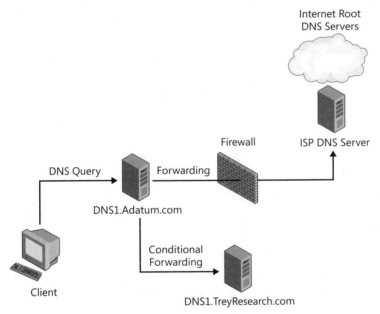

Figure 3-8   Configuring conditional forwarders.

The DNS server will always try to match the most qualified domain name when using conditional forwarding. For example, if you have a conditional forwarder configured for TreyResearch.com and for Europe.TreyResearch.com, and a client makes a request for a server such as Web1.Europe.TreyResearch.com, the DNS server will forward the request to the DNS server for Europe.TreyResearch.com.

Note   Windows Server 2003 also supports the use of conditional forwarders. One of the new features in Windows Server 2008 is the option to store the conditional forwarders in an AD DS integrated zone (See Figure 3-9.) This means that you can simplify the configuration of name resolution within a forest by making the conditional forwarders available to all DNS servers in the domain or in the forest.

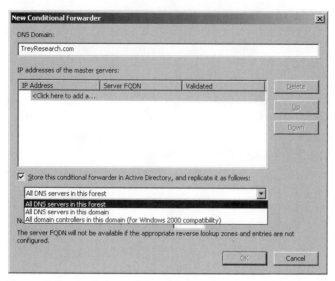

Figure 3-9   Storing conditional forwarders in the AD DS partition.

Root Hints

The second method available to a DNS server for resolving queries for zones for which it is not authoritative is the use of *root hints*. When you install a Windows Server 2008 DNS server that has access to the Internet, the server is automatically configured with a standard list of root servers. These servers are the servers that are authoritative for the root of the Internet namespace. If a DNS server receives a query for a DNS zone for which it is not authoritative, the server will send an iterative query to one of the root servers, initiating a series of iterative queries until the name is resolved or until the server has confirmed that the name cannot be resolved.

> **Note**   The root servers that are automatically configured on the DNS server are copied from the Cache.dns file that is included with the DNS server setup files.

You can add additional DNS servers to the root hint list, including the DNS servers on your internal network.

Stub Zones

Stub zones are another option available in Windows Server 2008 that can be used to simplify the configuration of name resolution across multiple namespaces. A stub zone is similar to a secondary zone. When you set up a stub zone, you must specify the IP address of a primary name server for the zone. The server holding the stub zone then requests a zone transfer from the primary name server. What is different, however, is that the stub zone contains only the

SOA records, the NS records, and the host (A) records for the name servers for the domain, rather than all of the records in the zone.

This enhances name resolution across namespaces without secondary name servers having to be used. When a DNS server is configured with a stub zone, it is not authoritative for the domain. It is just much more efficient at locating the authoritative name server for the specified zone. With stub zones, the DNS server can locate the authoritative name servers for a zone without having to contact the root hint servers.

Another useful function for stub zones is to maintain the name server list for delegated zones. When you set up a delegated subdomain, you must enter the IP address of all the name servers in the delegated domain. If that list of name servers changes—for example, if one of the name servers is removed from the network—you must manually update the delegation record. You can use a stub zone to automate the process of keeping the name server list updated. To configure this in the ADatum.com domain, you would configure a stub zone for the NAmerica. ADatum.com domain on the DNS servers in the ADatum.com domain. You would also configure a delegation record in the ADatum.com zone pointing to the stub zone. As name server records are modified in the child domain, they will be updated automatically in the stub zone. When the ADatum.com DNS servers use the delegation record, they will be referred to the stub zone, so they will always have access to the updated name server information.

How DNS Namespaces and AD DS Domains Are Integrated

With all of the options available for integrating the levels in the DNS namespace, how does Windows Server 2008 do this in an AD DS forest? By default, Windows Server 2008 uses delegation and forwarding to integrate multiple domains and domain trees in the forest with the DNS namespaces.

For example, consider an organization that includes multiple domains and domain trees in a single forest (see Figure 3-10 for an illustration of the forest plan).

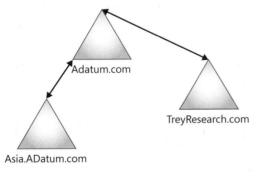

Figure 3-10   A multiple-tree AD DS forest design.

If you install DNS on the domain controllers in each domain and configure the DNS servers to be authoritative for the domain, Windows Server 2008 uses delegation and forwarding to integrate the child domain DNS zone with the parent domain DNS zone. In this example, the Active Directory Domain Services Installation Wizard will create a delegation record on the ADatum.com DNS server pointing to the DNS server in Asia.ADatum.com. The DNS server in Asia.ADatum.com is automatically configured to use the ADatum.com domain as a forwarder. This means that all names can be resolved between these two domains.

The DNS configuration for the new tree in the forest (TreyResearch.com) is a bit more complicated. By default, the DNS server in the TreyResearch.com domain is configured to use the DNS server in the ADatum.com domain as a forwarder. This means that the domain controllers and clients in the TreyResearch.com domain can resolve names in the ADatum.com domain.

However, by default, DNS servers in the ADatum.com cannot resolve names in the TreyResearch.com domain. The easiest way to configure name resolution between the forest root domain and the domain tree root domain is to configure conditional forwarding on the parent root DNS servers. In this case, you can configure the ADatum.com DNS servers with a conditional forwarder for the TreyResearch.com domain. Figure 3-11 shows the resulting DNS integration.

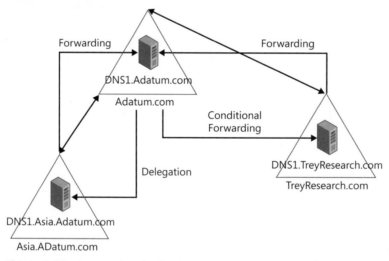

Figure 3-11   Integrating the DNS namespace in an AD DS forest.

Troubleshooting DNS and AD DS Integration

Because of the tight integration between DNS and AD DS, you will often troubleshoot AD DS issues by first ensuring that DNS is functioning correctly. If DNS is not functional or is incorrectly configured, AD DS will appear unavailable to clients and domain controllers.

In order to troubleshoot the DNS/AD DS integration, you need to have a clear understanding of the DNS and AD DS deployment in your environment. This should include the DNS server configuration, the DNS zone configuration (including a listing of the zones that are stored in AD DS application directory partitions), and the zone delegation and forwarding configuration.

Troubleshooting DNS

In most cases, the first steps in troubleshooting the integration of DNS and AD DS will be just general DNS troubleshooting steps. These steps include:

1. Identify the problem. Often the initial problem presented by a user may not be the actual problem. For example, the user may indicate that they cannot access the Internet, but the actual problem may be that the user cannot access a particular Web site, or it may be that the client computer has been disconnected from the network.

2. Determine the scope of the problem. Is only one client computer or only one domain controller experiencing the problem? Or is it all users in a particular office? If only one computer is experiencing the problem, you can focus your troubleshooting on that one computer. If multiple client computers or servers are experiencing the problem, attempt to identify the common element for all computers that are experiencing the problem. Are all the affected computers in the same office, or on the same network segment, or configured to use a particular DNS server?

3. Verify the TCP/IP settings on the client computer or domain controller to ensure that the DNS client is configured to use the correct DNS server. The quickest way to verify the settings is to use the Ipconfig /all command.

4. Verify that the DNS server has the correct information in its zone files. From any computer, you can use the Nslookup.exe utility to determine if a particular record exists in the DNS zone. For details on how to use the Nslookup command, see the "Using NSlookup.exe" Knowledge Base article at *http://support.microsoft.com/kb/200525*.

5. Verify that the DNS suffixes are configured correctly. DNS suffixes are used in two ways in Windows Server 2008 DNS. First of all, DNS suffixes are used when clients try to resolve host names without specifying the fully qualified domain name. When the client computer tries to resolve this name, it will append all of the DNS suffixes configured on the client computer in an attempt to resolve the host name. If the correct DNS suffix is not configured on the computer, the name resolution will fail.

    DNS suffixes are also used by dynamic DNS. By default, the client computer will try to register its host record in the zone identified by the primary DNS suffix that is the DNS name for the computer's domain. You can specify additional DNS suffixes and configure the computer to register its DNS settings in each of the zones identified by the DNS suffix.

6. Verify that the DHCP Client service is enabled and set to start automatically. The DHCP client service is required for dynamic updates to function, even if the computer is configured with static IP addresses and is not using a DHCP server.

7. Use Network Monitor to capture the network traffic between the DNS client and DNS server. If DNS name resolution or dynamic name registration fails, capture the network traffic created by the DNS request on both the client computer and the DNS server. The network capture may indicate a configuration problem (for example, the DNS client is trying to connect to the wrong DNS server) or may indicate a network problem (for example, the client computer is sending the DNS query to the correct server, but the query is being blocked by a firewall or other network setting).

8. Enable the Debug Logging option. You can collect detailed information on the Windows Server 2008 DNS server by enabling debug logging on the server. To enable debug logging, access the DNS server properties in the DNS console and select the check box for Log packets for debugging. The dialog box is shown in Figure 3-12.

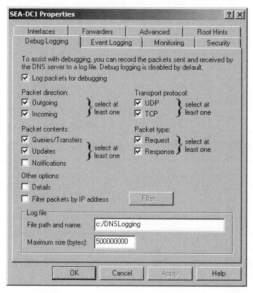

Figure 3-12   Enabling debug logging on a DNS server.

You may want to limit the traffic the logging captures. Filtering packets by IP address can be especially helpful if you want to limit the logging to traffic between the server and a specific DNS server.

9. If dynamic updates are failing, verify that the DNS zone is configured to allow dynamic updates. If the zone is configured to allow only secure updates and the updates are failing, change the zone configuration to allow nonsecure updates to determine whether the problem is with secure updates or with both secure and nonsecure updates. If neither update is working, verify the client TCP/IP configuration and verify the DNS server availability on the network. If only secure updates are failing, then follow these steps:

   a. Verify that hosts are domain members. Dynamic updates are based on Kerberos authentication, which requires that all client computers be domain members.

b. Verify that there is no problem with the machine account of the host trying the update. If the problem is occurring on just one host, remove the host from the domain and rejoin the domain.

c. Verify that a record does not already exist with the same name. By default, records created by one host cannot be modified or removed by a different host. If there is an existing record with the same name, delete the existing record and have the host try to register again.

Troubleshooting SRV Record Registration

In addition to the general DNS troubleshooting steps, you may also need to troubleshoot domain controller registration of the SRV records required to locate the domain controller on the network. If a domain controller is not registering the SRV records in DNS, begin by verifying the TCP/IP settings and DNS zone settings as described above. Also determine if the domain controller is able to successfully register its host and PTR records. If the host and PTR records are registering correctly and only the SRV records are affected, follow these steps:

1. Verify that the domain controller is trying to register the correct records. To do this, stop the Netlogon service on the domain controller and then delete the Netlogon.dnb and the Netlogon.dns files located in the %systemroot%\System32\Config folder. Then start the Netlogon service. Verify that the Netlogon.dns file contains the correct SRV records and verify that these records have been updated in DNS.

2. If the records did not update correctly, examine the System event log for errors. In particular, look for events with event IDs of 5774, 5775, and 5781. Each of these event IDs indicates a problem with the SRV record registration.

> **More Info**   For more information, see Knowledge Base article 259277, "Troubleshooting Netlogon Event 5774, 5775, and 5781," located at *http://support.microsoft.com/kb/259277*.

A common cause for these errors is that a domain controller references itself as a primary DNS server in its TCP/IP properties. When the domain controller starts in this configuration, the Netlogon service may start before the DNS service starts. Because the Netlogon service must register records in DNS and the DNS service is not yet available, errors may occur. In this situation, you can safely ignore the errors because the Netlogon service will again try to register the records in approximately five minutes, at which time it will be successful. The easiest way to avoid this issue is to configure domain controllers to use another DNS server to register the SRV records.

Summary

DNS is an essential network service for Windows Server 2008 networks. Without a stable DNS infrastructure, almost all logon and resource location efforts will fail. As a network administrator for a Windows Server 2008 network, you must become a DNS expert. This chapter discussed specifically the integration of DNS with AD DS.

Best Practices

■ DNS is the foundation for AD DS and other AD DS integrated applications such as Microsoft Exchange Server. When users report issues with these services, a good first step in troubleshooting the issues is to verify that DNS is working correctly.

■ You do not have to use AD DS integrated zones in DNS to support an AD DS deployment. However, because of the tight integration between AD DS and DNS, we recommend that you use AD DS integrated zones for the AD DS deployment, even if you are using other DNS servers for other name resolution services.

■ If you are deploying multiple domains in your organization's forest, and especially if you are deploying multiple domain trees, ensure that all domain controllers in all domains can resolve the DNS names for all other domain controllers in the forest. As a best practice, use zone delegations and conditional forwarding to tie the various DNS namespaces together.

Additional Resources

These resources contain additional information related to this topic:

Related Information

■ Chapter 4, "Active Directory Domain Services Replication," the next chapter in this book, provides details about how AD DS replication works—when you implement AD DS integrated zones, the DNS information is replicated between domain controllers using the same AD DS replication process as any other AD DS information.

■ Chapter 5, "Designing the Active Directory Domain Services Structure," goes into detail on designing the DNS deployment.

■ The DNS Technical Reference located at *http://technet2.microsoft.com/WindowsServer/ en/Library/6e45e81e-fb44-4a20-a752-ebe740e2acc61033.mspx* provides detailed information about DNS as a network service. Use this resource to supplement the AD DS integration content in this chapter.

■ The "What's New in DNS in Windows Server 2008" Web page located at *http://technet2.microsoft.com/windowsserver2008/en/library/0b0bf633-5732-4b39-80 d3-a2a4330acb141033.mspx?mfr=true* provides details on the new features in Windows Server 2008 DNS.

- RFC 2782: "A DNS RR for Specifying the Location of Services (DNS SRV)"
- RFC 2136: "Dynamic Updates in the Domain Name System (DNS UPDATE)"

Related Tools

Windows Server 2008 provides several tools that can be used when managing DNS and troubleshooting DNS issues. Table 3-3 lists some of these tools and when you would use each of the tools.

Table 3-3 DNS Tools

Tool name	Description and Use
Ipconfig.exe	This tool runs on all Windows server and client operating systems.
	Ipconfig displays all current TCP/IP network configuration values and refreshes Dynamic Host Configuration Protocol (DHCP) and DNS settings.
	Use IPconfig to ensure that the client TCP/IP settings are configured correctly. Use this tool when a specific client is not able to resolve DNS names or if the client is unable to register its resource record in DNS.
DNS Console	This tool is installed when the DNS server role is installed.
	The DNS console is used to administer the DNS server role. It can be used to modify all aspects of the DNS Server service, including creating and deleting zones and resource records and forcing replication events between DNS server physical memory and DNS databases. The DNS console can also be used to enable debug logging and test name resolution on a network.
Dnscmd.exe	This tool is installed when the DNS server role is installed.
	Dnscmd is a command-line tool that can be used to view and modify the properties of DNS servers, zones, and resource records. Dnscmd can also be useful for developing scripts for configuring a DNS server.
Dnslint.exe	This tool is a free download from Microsoft. (See *http://support.microsoft.com/ kb/321045* for the download location.)
	This tool can be used to help diagnose common DNS name resolution issues. It can be targeted to look for specific DNS record sets and ensure that they are consistent across multiple DNS servers. It can also be used to verify that DNS records used specifically for AD DS replication are correct.
Network Monitor	Microsoft Network Monitor 3.1 is available as a download from the Microsoft Download Center (see *http://www.microsoft.com/downloads/details.aspx? familyid=18b1d59d-f4d8-4213-8d17-2f6dde7d7aac&displaylang=en*).
	Network Monitor captures data about the packets on a network and logs them for subsequent analysis. The monitored data can be filtered many different ways including protocol, ports, physical addresses, and logical addresses. Network Monitor can be useful in many situations because it displays the actual network packets sent during DNS lookups or DNS zone transfers.

Table 3-3   DNS Tools *(continued)*

Tool name	Description and Use
Nslookup.exe	This tool is included in all Microsoft Windows server and client operating systems.
	Nslookup is used to query DNS servers and to obtain detailed responses. The information obtained using Nslookup can be used to diagnose and solve name resolution problems, verify that resource records are added or updated correctly in a zone, and debug other server-related problems.
Nltest.exe	This tool is included in all Microsoft Windows server and client operating systems.
	This tool can be used to get a list of all domain controllers and query the status of trusts between domain controllers.

Resources on the CD

- ListAppPartitions.ps1 is a Windows PowerShell script that lists all of the application directory partitions in your forest.

- DNSConfig.xlsx is a Microsoft Office Excel spreadsheet that can be used to document the DNS zone and DNS server configuration in your organization.

Related Help Topics

- "Create the Default DNS Application Directory Partitions," in DNS management console help.

- "Understanding Aging and Scavenging," in DNS management console help.

- "Understanding Dynamic Update," in DNS management console help.

- "Troubleshooting DNS," in DNS management console help.

Chapter 4

Active Directory Domain Services Replication

In almost all cases, when you deploy an Active Directory Domain Services (AD DS) domain in Microsoft Windows Server 2008, you should deploy more than one domain controller. Deploying multiple domain controllers in each domain is the easiest and most effective way to provide high availability for the domain controller services. These domain controllers might all be located in one data center at the company head office where they are connected by very fast network connections. Or they might be spread across many locations around the world, with a variety of wide area network (WAN) connections linking the company locations.

Regardless of how many domain controllers a company has or where those domain controllers are located, they must replicate information with each other. If they cannot replicate the information, the directories on the domain controllers will become inconsistent. For example, if a user is created on one domain controller, and that information is not replicated to all the other domain controllers, the user will only be able to authenticate to the domain controller where the account was created.

This chapter describes the process of replication in AD DS. The focus of this chapter is on how replication works; that is, on how the replication topology is created and how domain controllers replicate with each other. By default, when you install AD DS domain controllers, they automatically begin replicating with each other. This default replication topology may not be the most efficient for your organization, so this chapter describes ways that you can modify the replication configuration to meet your company requirements. In addition, this chapter provides guidance on how to troubleshoot AD DS replication.

AD DS Replication Model

As described in Chapter 2, "Active Directory Domain Services Components," AD DS is made up of multiple logical partitions. Replication between the domain controllers with replicas of each partition is handled in exactly the same way for all partitions. When an attribute is changed in the configuration directory partition, it is replicated using the same model and processes as when an attribute is changed in any other partition. The only thing that changes is the list of domain controllers that will receive a copy of the replicated change. Also, replication between domain controllers in the same site is handled differently than it is between domain controllers in different sites, but the essential model does not change. This section describes the replication model used by AD DS.

AD DS uses a multimaster replication model. That means that changes to the AD DS data store can be made on any domain controller except specifically configured read-only domain controllers (RODC). That is, every domain controller except the RODCs has a writable copy of the directory, and there is no single domain controller where all changes have to be made. After a change has been made, it is replicated to all the other domain controllers. This multimaster replication model addresses many important reliability and scalability issues. Because all of the domain controllers provide the same services, no domain controller represents a single point of failure.

> **Note**   As discussed in Chapter 2, AD DS has specific operations master roles that can be held by only one domain controller. These roles represent a single point of failure, but the roles can also be easily moved or seized to another domain controller.

The replication model used by AD DS can be described as being loosely consistent, but with convergence. The replication is *loosely consistent* because not all domain controllers with a replica of a partition will always have identical information. For example, if a new user is created on one of the domain controllers, the other domain controllers will not receive that information until the next replication cycle. The replication always moves towards *convergence*, however. If the system is maintained in a steady state, with no new changes made to the directory for a period of time, all domain controllers will reach a state of convergence where they all have identical information.

The replication model also uses a *store-and-forward* replication process. This means that a domain controller can receive a change to the directory and then forward the change to other domain controllers. This is advantageous when multiple domain controllers in a number of company locations are separated by slow WAN links. A change to the directory can be replicated from one domain controller in one site to a single domain controller in another site. The domain controller that receives the update can then forward the changes to other domain controllers in the second site.

AD DS also uses a *state-based* replication model. This means that each domain controller tracks the state of replication updates. As a domain controller receives new updates (either from changes being made on the domain controller or through replicated changes from another domain controller), the domain controller applies the updates to its replica of the AD DS data store. When another domain controller attempts to replicate information that a domain controller already has, the receiving domain controller can determine by the state of its data store that it does not need to get the duplicate information. The current state of the data store includes metadata that is used to resolve conflicts and to avoid sending the full replica on each replication cycle.

Replication Process

Features such as multimaster replication and store-and-forward replication mean that a domain controller could receive AD DS updates from multiple domain controllers and that AD DS replication traffic could take more than one path between domain controllers. For example, if a change is made to AD DS on DC1, the change could be replicated directly to DC2 and DC3. Because of the store-and-forward replication model, DC2, after receiving the update from DC1, may try to replicate the same change to DC3. AD DS replication is designed to ensure that the replication process is efficient while still providing redundancy.

Update Types

Two types of changes can be made to the AD DS information on a particular domain controller. The first type of update is an *originating update*. An originating update is performed when an object is added, modified, or deleted on a domain controller. The second type of update is a *replicated update*. A replicated update is performed when a change made on another domain controller is replicated to the local domain controller. By definition, there can be only one originating update performed for any particular change, and this occurs on the domain controller where the change is made. This originating update is then replicated to all the domain controllers that have a replica of the affected AD DS partition.

Originating updates occur in AD DS under any of the following circumstances:

- **A new object is added to AD DS**   Adding a new object to AD DS creates an object with a unique *objectGUID* attribute. As well, all values assigned to attributes that are configured for the object are assigned a version number of *1*.

- **An existing object is deleted from AD DS**   When an object is deleted from AD DS, it is marked as deleted, but not immediately removed from the AD DS data store. Only after the tombstone expires on the object is the object actually deleted. For more details, see the section "Replicating Object Deletions" later in this chapter.

- **The attributes for an existing object are modified**   This modification can include adding a new value to an attribute, deleting a value for an attribute, or modifying an existing value. When you change an object, the modify request compares the new value for each attribute with the existing value. If the value for an attribute has not changed, the attribute is not updated. If the value has changed, the attribute is updated and the version number for each updated attribute is incremented by one.

- **An object in AD DS is moved to a new parent container**   If the parent container is renamed, each object in the container is also moved to the renamed container. When an object is moved to another container in AD DS, the only attribute that changes for the object is the *name* attribute, which is changed to reflect the new location in the LDAP hierarchy.

All originating updates to AD DS are *atomic operations*, which means that when an update is committed to AD DS, either the entire transaction is committed and the change is made to the data store, or no part of the update will be committed. For more information on the process of committing changes to the AD DS data store, see Chapter 14, "Monitoring and Maintaining Active Directory."

The Replication Process in Windows Server 2008

Windows Server 2003 introduced several important changes to the replication process that are also available in Windows Server 2008. One change is the linked value replication. In Windows 2000, the smallest unit of replication is an attribute. This means that in some cases, changing one value in a multivalued attribute can create a significant amount of replication traffic. The most common example of this is what happens with *universal group membership*. Because the entire membership list for the universal group is one attribute, adding a single user to the universal group results in significant replication, especially when the group already has several thousand members. In Windows Server 2003 Active Directory and Windows Server 2008 AD DS, multivalued attributes like *group membership* can be updated by replicating only the change to the attribute by using linked value replication.

AD DS uses linked attributes to enable linked value replication. Linked attributes always include a forward link and backward link to create a link between two AD DS objects. The forward link is the linked attribute on the source object (for example, the *member* attribute on the group object), whereas the backward link is the linked attribute on the target object (for example, the *memberOf* attribute on the user object). A backward link value includes the distinguished names of all the objects that have the object's distinguished name set in their corresponding forward link.

The relationships between linked attributes are stored in a separate table in the directory database as link pairs. The matching pair of *Link IDs* ties the attributes together. For example, the *member* attribute has a *link ID* of 2 and the *memberOf* attribute has a *link ID* of 3. Because the *member* and the *memberOf* attributes are linked in the database and indexed for searching, the directory can be examined for all records in which the link pair is *member/memberOf* and the *memberOf* attribute identifies the group.

Another important change in Windows Server 2003 Active Directory is the support for groups of more than 5,000 members. In Windows 2000, groups cannot contain more than 5,000 members because of the attribute-level updates and replication. The practical limit for committing a change to the directory database in one transaction is 5,000. This also defines the maximum number of updates that can be replicated in one update during replication. As a result, the maximum group size in Windows 2000 is 5,000 members. In Windows Server 2008 AD DS, support for modifications of only one value on a multivalued linked attribute removes these restrictions.

Replicating Changes

After an originating update has been committed to AD DS, the change must be replicated to other domain controllers that host a replica of that partition. Within a site, the domain controller where the originating update occurred waits 15 seconds before replicating the changes to its direct replication partners. The 15-second wait occurs so that if multiple updates are committed to the database, they can all be replicated at the same time. This increases the efficiency of the replication. Between sites, the originating update will be replicated to replication partners based on the schedule configured on the site link.

When replicating changes to the directory information, the domain controllers require a mechanism for managing the flow of replication. To optimize AD DS replication, only those changes that need to be replicated between two domain controllers should be sent. To accomplish this, the domain controllers should be able to determine which, if any, changes have not yet been replicated, and then replicate only those changes that are required. AD DS uses a combination of update sequence numbers (USNs), high-watermark values, up-to-dateness vectors, and change stamps to manage directory replication.

Update Sequence Numbers

When an object is updated in the database, an *update sequence number (USN)* is assigned to the update. The USN is specific to the domain controller where the update occurred. For example, if a telephone number update for one user was assigned *USN 5555*, the next change to the domain controller, regardless of which object was modified, would be *USN 5556*. One USN is assigned for each committed change. If multiple attributes are changed with one update (for example, a user's address, telephone number, and office location are all modified at once), only one USN is assigned during the update.

There are three ways that the USN is used when an update is committed. First, the local USN value is stored with the attribute that was updated. The local USN value identifies the USN of the changed attribute. The second way the USN is used is for the object's *uSNChanged* attribute. This attribute is stored with each object and identifies the highest USN for any attribute for the object. For example, suppose a user's telephone number was changed and the USN applied to that change was 5556. Both the local USN and the *uSNChanged* attribute will be set to 5556. If the next update applied to the directory on that server were an address change for the same user, the local USN on the address attribute and the *uSNChanged* attribute for the user object would both be changed to 5557. However, the local USN for the telephone number attribute would remain at 5556, because that was the USN for the last update that changed that particular attribute.

The local USN and the *uSNChanged* attribute are applied for both originating and replicated updates. The last way the USN is used is as the *originating USN* for the attribute. This value is set only for originating updates and is replicated to all other domain controllers as part of the attribute replication. When the telephone number for a user is changed on a server, the USN for the change is assigned to the originating USN value. When the modified telephone number is replicated to another domain controller, the originating USN is sent along with the update, and this value is not modified on the destination domain controller. The local USN and the *uSNChanged* attribute will be modified on the destination domain controller (and will be specific to that domain controller), but the originating USN is not changed until the attribute itself is updated again. The originating USN is used for propagation dampening, which is described later in this chapter.

Viewing USN Information

The USNs for any object can be viewed through different administrative tools included with Windows Server 2008. The easiest way to view the current and original USN values for an object is to use the Active Directory Users And Computers administrative tool. To view this information, turn on Advanced Features under the View menu and then access the Object tab in the object's Properties sheet. Remember that the USN number is domain controller-specific, so that if you view the USN for an object on two different domain controllers, the USN will be different.

One way to view the local USN, originating domain controller, originating USN, and time stamp for any attribute is by using the Repadmin command-line tool. Type **repadmin /showobjmeta** *domaincontrollername objectdistinguishedname* at a command prompt. Figure 4-1 shows the partial output from this command.

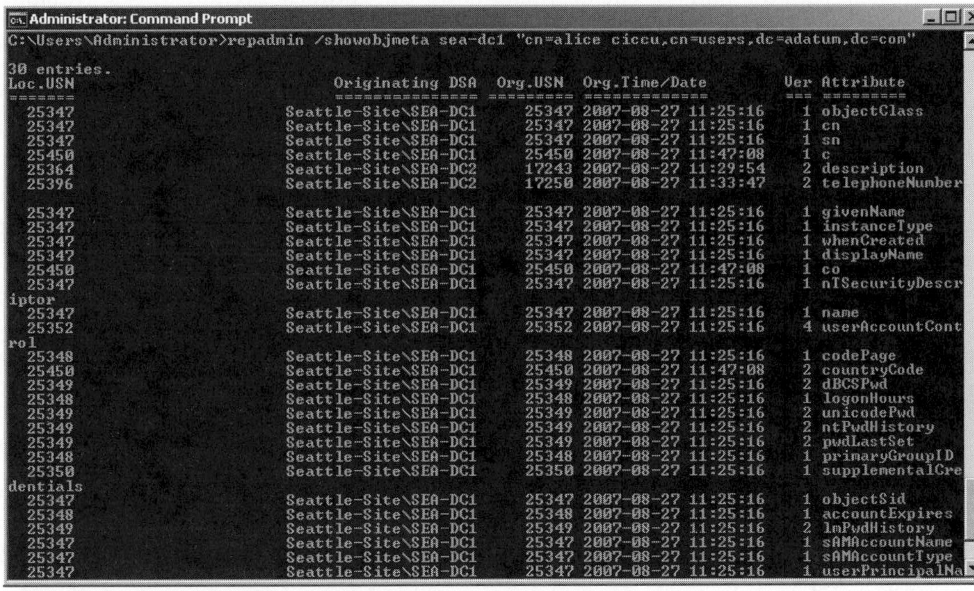

Figure 4-1 Viewing replication metadata using *Repadmin*.

In this output, you can see that the user was created on SEA-DC1, but then the *description* and *telephoneNumber* attributes were modified on SEA-DC2. The originating USNs for all of the attributes except these two are from SEA-DC1, but the originating USNs for the *description* and *telephoneNumber* attributes are from SEA-DC2. However, the local USN numbers are all from SEA-DC1, which is the domain controller where this information was captured. As well, the version number for these two attributes is 2, indicating that the attribute has been modified from the original version.

You can also access the same replication information through the Ldp tool. To do this, connect and bind to a domain controller using Ldp, locate the object, and then right-click the object, select Advanced, and then select Replication Metadata. The replication metadata is the same information as is shown in the Repadmin tool, except that the originating DSA information is shown using the domain controller globally unique identifier (GUID) rather than the display name.

High-Watermark Values

The high-watermark values are used to manage what information is replicated between domain controllers. Each domain controller maintains its own set of high-watermark values for each of its direct replication partners. The high-watermark is just the latest *uSNChanged* value that the domain controller has received from a specific replication partner. When a domain controller sends an update to a replication partner, the *uSNChanged* value is sent along with the update. The destination domain controller retains this *uSNChanged* as the high-watermark value for the replication partner.

The high-watermark values are used during the process of replication. When one domain controller requests updates from another domain controller, the destination domain controller sends its high-watermark value for use by the source domain controller. In effect, the high-watermark is telling the source domain controller which updates the destination domain controller has already received. The source domain controller uses the destination domain controller's high-watermark to filter all of the potential directory updates and sends only the changes with a higher *uSNChanged* value.

> **Note**   A separate high-watermark value is maintained for each directory partition on the domain controller and for each direct replication partner.

Up-to-Dateness Vectors and Propagation Dampening

The up-to-dateness vectors are also used to control what information is replicated between domain controllers. The up-to-dateness vectors are used to keep track of all of the originating updates that a domain controller has received from any domain controller. For example, suppose the telephone number for a user is changed on DC1 and the attribute is given the originating USN of 5556. When this attribute is replicated to DC2, the originating USN is replicated with the updated attribute. Also, the server GUID for DC1 is replicated with the attribute. When DC2 receives this update, it will modify its up-to-dateness vector to show that the latest originating update it received from DC1 is now 5556.

When a destination domain controller requests updates from a source domain controller, it includes its up-to-dateness vectors with the request. The source domain controller then uses this information to filter the list of all possible updates it could send to the destination domain controller. This option is important when there are more than two domain controllers for a directory partition. For example, if DC3 is added to the scenario described in the preceding paragraph, the telephone number change made on DC1 will be replicated to both DC2 and DC3. Now both DC3 and DC2 will have the updated telephone number, and they will modify their up-to-dateness vector to show that the latest update both of them received from DC1 had an originating USN of 5556. About 15 seconds after receiving this update, DC2 will notify DC3 that it has updated information. When DC3 requests the directory updates from DC2, it will include its up-to-dateness vector with the request. In this case, DC2 determines that DC3's up-to-dateness vector for DC1 already has the most recent originating USN. If this telephone number update were the only change made to the directory during this time period, no information would be replicated between the DC2 and the DC3 domain controllers.

This process of limiting the updates sent during replication by using the up-to-dateness vector is called *propagation dampening*. This is an important feature because AD DS is designed to create redundant replication connections between domain controllers. One of the problems with creating the redundant links is that the same updates might be sent to a domain controller from multiple replication partners. This could create a significant amount of unnecessary replication traffic, as well as potentially leading to a situation where the same update is sent repeatedly to all domain controllers (resulting in a replication loop). Propagation dampening using the up-to-dateness vector eliminates this possibility.

The high-watermark and up-to-dateness vector are used together to limit replication traffic. The high-watermark identifies the latest change that a domain controller received from another specific domain controller, so the source domain controller does not need to resend changes. The up-to-dateness vector identifies the most recent changes that have been received from all other domain controllers that contain a replica of the partition, so that the source domain controller does not have to send any directory updates that the destination domain controller has received from another replication partner.

Change Stamps and Conflict Resolution

The last property that is used to manage the replication between domain controllers is a *change stamp*. Whenever an attribute is updated, this modification is marked with the change stamp. The change stamp is then sent with the update when it is replicated to other domain controllers. The change stamp is used to determine which change will be accepted in the case of a replication conflict. The change stamp consists of three components:

- **Version number**   This is used to track the number of changes that have been made to an attribute on an object. When an object is created, the version number on all attributes is set to *0* if the attribute is left blank. When a blank attribute is assigned a value, the version number is incremented to *1*. Whenever the attribute is updated, the version number increments by one each time.

- **Last write time**   This is used to track when the last write occurred to the attribute. The time value is recorded on the server where the attribute is updated and is replicated with the object to other domain controllers.

- **Originating server**   This is the GUID for the server where the last originating update to the attribute was applied.

These three components form the change stamp for every modification to an attribute. When the attribute is replicated to another domain controller, this change stamp information is replicated with the attribute. If an attribute is changed on one domain controller and the same attribute is changed on another domain controller before the update is replicated to the second domain controller, this change stamp is used to determine which attribute is accepted as the final change. If a conflict arises, the decision as to which is the final change is made in the following order:

1. **Version number**   The change with the highest version number is always accepted. This means that if the change on one domain controller is version 3, and the change on the other domain controller is version 4, the version 4 change will always be accepted.

2. **Last write time**   The next value used to determine which value is accepted is the last write time. If the version numbers are identical, the change with the most recent time stamp will be accepted.

3. **Server GUID**   If the version numbers are identical and the time stamps are identical, the server database GUID is used to determine which change is accepted. The change coming from the server with the higher GUID will be accepted. These GUIDs are assigned when the domain controllers are added to the domain and the assignment of the GUID is arbitrary.

The AD DS replication process is able to resolve conflicts that are created when the same attribute on an object is modified on two domain controllers at the same time. However, there are at least two other types of conflicts that can arise:

■ Adding an object or modifying an object on one domain controller at the same time that the container object for the object is deleted on another domain controller: Take an example in which on one domain controller a new user is added to the Accounting organizational unit (OU). At the same time, on another domain controller, another administrator deletes the Accounting OU. In this case, the container will be deleted on all domain controllers through replication, and the object that was added to the deleted container will be moved to the LostAndFound container in AD DS.

■ Adding objects with the same relative distinguished name into the same container: An example of this conflict is when an administrator on one domain controller creates a user object with a relative distinguished name of *Bill* in the Accounting OU, and at the same time, on another domain controller, a user with the same relative distinguished name is moved into the same OU or created in the same OU. In this case, the conflict resolution model will use the GUID assigned to the directory updated to determine which object is kept and which object is renamed. The object with the higher GUID is retained, and the object with the lower GUID is renamed to Bill*CNF:*userGUID*, where the number sign (*) is a reserved character. If the second user object is required, it can be renamed.

Replicating Object Deletions

The replication of object deletions is handled differently in AD DS than other directory updates. When an object like a user account is deleted, the object is not immediately deleted. Rather, a tombstone object is created. The *tombstone object* is the original object where the *isDeleted* attribute has been set to *true*, and most of the other attributes for the object are removed from it. Only a few attributes that are required to identify the object, such as the GUID, SID, SIDHistory, and distinguished name, are retained. Deleted objects are stored in the Deleted Objects hidden container. Every directory partition has a Deleted Objects container.

Note   To view the Deleted Objects container in a directory partition, use a tool like Ldp. After connecting and binding to the directory partition, access the Controls option on the Options menu. In the Controls dialog box, add the Return Deleted Objects control. After adding the control, you will be able to view the CN=Deleted Items container when you view the directory tree.

This tombstone is then replicated to other domain controllers in the domain. As each domain controller receives the update, the modifications that were made on the originating domain controller are applied to each domain controller. The tombstone objects remain in the domain database for a specified period of time, called the *tombstone lifetime*. At the end of the tombstone lifetime, set to 180 days by default, each domain controller removes the tombstone from its copy of the database. This process of removing the tombstones from the database is called *garbage collection*. By default, the garbage collection interval for the forest is set at every 12 hours. This means that every 12 hours, the garbage collection process runs and deletes any tombstones that have passed the tombstone lifetime value.

Note   The default tombstone lifetime in versions of Active Directory before Windows Server 2008 has varied. In Windows 2000 and Windows 2003 Active Directory, the tombstone lifetime was 60 days. In Windows 2003 SP1, this value was increased to 180 days, but it was changed back to 60 days in Windows Server 2003 R2. If you upgrade an existing domain with a 60-day tombstone to Windows Server 2008, the 60-day tombstone lifetime is retained. The tombstone lifetime and the garbage collection interval can be modified using ADSI Edit or Ldp.exe. These properties are configured on the CN=Directory Service,CN=Windows NT,CN=Services,CN= Configuration, DC=*ForestRootDomain* object. The *garbageCollPeriod* and the *tombstone-Lifetime* attributes define these settings. In most cases, these values do not need to be modified.

Linked attributes can result in special cases when deleting objects. When an object is deleted, the following changes are made to the linked attributes:

- All of the forward links on the deleted object are removed. For example, if a group object is deleted, all of the member links on the group object are removed. This means that the group is removed from the *memberOf* back-link attribute on each user that was a member of the group.

- All the back-links on the deleted object are removed. For example, if a user is deleted, the user's distinguished name value is removed from the member attributes of each group object that is named in the *memberOf* attribute of the deleted user.

After the linked attribute has been modified on one domain controller, the updates are replicated to other domain controllers just like any other updates.

Important   Because of how linked attributes are deleted, you have to treat the authoritative restore of these objects differently than if you are restoring objects without linked attributes. For details, see Chapter 15, "Active Directory Disaster Recovery."

Replicating the SYSVOL Directory

Changes to the AD DS data store are made using the process described previously. However, the System Volume (SYSVOL) folder on each domain controller also contains information that is critical to the correct functioning of AD DS. The SYSVOL shared folder contains the following files and folders that must be available and synchronized between domain controllers in a domain:

- **Group Policy settings**   SYSVOL contains a folder with the name of the domain that the domain controller is a member of. In the domain folder is a folder called Policies that contains Group Policy templates and scripts for Windows 2000 or later clients.

- **The NETLOGON shared folder**   This includes system policies (Config.pol or Ntconfig.pol files) and user-based logon and logoff scripts for pre-Windows 2000 network clients, such as clients running Windows 98 or Windows NT 4.0. The NETLOGON shared folder is the Scripts folder in the domain folder.

The contents of SYSVOL folder are replicated to every domain controller in a domain. If the domain is at Windows Server 2003 or lower functional level, the File Replication Service (FRS) is responsible for replicating the contents of the SYSVOL folder between domain controllers. When you upgrade the domain functional level to Windows Server 2008, Distributed File System Replication (DFSR) is used to replicate the contents of the SYSVOL folder. In both cases, the connection object topology and schedule that the Knowledge Consistency Checker (KCC) creates for Active Directory replication is used to manage replication between domain controllers.

> **Note**   Distributed File System (DFS) Replication is a state-based, multimaster replication engine introduced in Windows Server 2003 R2 that supports replication scheduling and bandwidth throttling. DFS Replication uses a new compression algorithm that is known as Remote Differential Compression (RDC). Using RDC, DFS Replication replicates only the differences (or changes) between the two servers, resulting in lower bandwidth use during replication. For more information on DFSR, see the article "Overview of the Distributed File System Solution in Microsoft Windows Server 2003 R2" at *http://technet2.microsoft.com/windowsserver/en/ library/d3afe6ee-3083-4950-a093-8ab748651b761033.mspx?mfr=true.*

Intrasite and Intersite Replication

The description of how AD DS replication works applies to both intrasite and intersite replication. In both cases, the domain controllers use the same processes to optimize the replication process. However, one of the main reasons to create additional sites in AD DS is to manage replication traffic. Because all of the domain controllers within a site are assumed to be connected with fast network connections, replication between these domain controllers is optimized for maximum speed and reduced latency. However, if the replication traffic has to cross a slow network link, conserving network bandwidth is a much more significant issue. Creating multiple sites allows for this conservation of network bandwidth by enabling features such as data compression and scheduled AD DS replication.

Intrasite Replication

The primary goal for replication within a site is to reduce replication latency, that is, to make sure that all domain controllers in a site are updated as quickly as possible. To accomplish this goal, intrasite replication traffic has the following characteristics:

- The replication process is initiated by a notification from the sending domain controller. When a change is made to the database, the sending computer notifies a destination domain controller that changes are available. The changes are then pulled from the sending domain controller by the destination domain controller using a remote procedure call (RPC) connection. After this replication is complete, the domain controller notifies another destination domain controller, which then pulls the changes. This process continues until all the replication partners have been updated.

- Replication occurs almost immediately after a change has been made to the AD DS information. By default, a domain controller will wait for 15 seconds after a change has been made and then begin replicating the changes to other domain controllers in the same site. The domain controller will complete replication with one partner, wait 3 seconds, and then initiate replication with another partner. The reason the domain controller waits 15 seconds after a change is to increase the efficiency of the replication in case additional changes are made to the partition information.

- The replication traffic is not compressed. Because all the computers within a site are connected with fast network connections, the data is sent without compression. Compressing the replication data adds an additional load on the domain controller server. Uncompressed replication traffic preserves server performance at the expense of network utilization.

- Replication traffic is sent to multiple replication partners during each replication cycle. Whenever a change is made to the directory, the domain controller will replicate the information to all direct replication partners, which might be all or some of the other domain controllers in the site.

Modifying Intrasite Replication

In most cases, you will not need to modify how replication works within a site. However, there are some settings that you can modify in specific situations. These settings include:

- **Wait time** If your AD DS forest is running in Windows Server 2003 or Windows Server 2008 functional level, you can modify the time that the domain controller will wait before notifying the first replication partner and before notifying subsequent replication partners. To do this, open the Configuration partition in ADSIEdit and browse to the CN=Partitions,CN=Configuration,DC=*forestname* folder. In the folder, right-click the partition where you want to modify the replication settings. The value for the delay in notifying the first replication partner is stored in the *msDS-Replication-Notify-First-DSA-Delay* attribute. The default value is not displayed but is set at *15 seconds*. The value for subsequent notification delay is stored in the *msDS-Replication-Notify-Subsequent-DSA-Delay* attribute. The default value is *3 seconds*. If your organization contains Windows 2000 Server domain controllers, you must modify the registry on the Windows 2000 Server domain controllers to modify the default settings of *300 seconds* to notify the first replication partner and *30 seconds* for subsequent notifications. You can also use "repadmin *computername* /notifyopt *namingcontext* /first:*timeinseconds* /subs: *timeinseconds*" to set the replication wait times. To reset the wait times to the default values, use the same command with no values assigned to the time settings.

- **Strict replication consistency**   Strict replication consistency determines how outdated objects are replicated from reconnected domain controllers that have not replicated in longer than a tombstone lifetime. For example, if a domain controller that is offline while an object is deleted remains offline for the entire tombstone period, the tombstone is never replicated to the server. When the server is reconnected to the network, it will try to replicate the object to other domain controllers. If the destination domain controller has strict replication consistency enabled, it will not accept the inbound replication of an outdated object. By default, Windows Server 2008 enforces strict replication consistency. You can modify this by setting the value of the HKEY_LOCAL_MACHINE\SYSTEM\CurrentControlSet\ Services\NTDS\Parameters\Strict Replication Consistency key to *0*.

- **Amount of data that is replicated in each replication packet**   By default, the number of objects Windows Server 2008 domain controllers will replicate in a single packet is 1/1,000,000th the size of RAM, with a minimum of 100 objects and a maximum of 1,000 objects. The maximum size of objects that will be replicated is 1/100th the size of RAM, with a minimum of 1 megabyte (MB) and a maximum of 10 MB. You can modify these settings by creating the Replicator intrasite packet size (objects) and Replicator intrasite packet size (bytes) values in the HKEY_LOCAL_MACHINE\System\CurrentControlSet\Services\NTDS\ Parameters path.

Caution   Before making any changes to the default settings for intrasite replication, make sure that you test the changes thoroughly. In most cases, these settings do not need to be modified.

Intersite Replication

The primary goal of replication between sites is to reduce the amount of bandwidth used for replication traffic. This means that intersite replication traffic has the following characteristics:

- Replication is initiated according to a schedule rather than when changes are made. To manage replication between sites, you must configure a site link connecting the two sites. One of the configuration options on the site link is a schedule for when replication will occur. Another is the replication interval setting for how often replication will occur during the scheduled time. If the bandwidth between company locations is limited, the replication can be scheduled to happen during nonworking hours.

■ Replication traffic is compressed down to about 40 percent of the noncompressed size when replication traffic is more than 32 KB in size. To save bandwidth on the network connection, the bridgehead servers in each site compress the traffic at the expense of additional CPU usage.

■ Notifications are not used to alert a domain controller in another site that changes to the directory are available. Instead, the schedule determines when to replicate.

> **Note**   You can disable compression for intersite replication and enable notifications. For more details, see the section titled "Configuring Intersite Replication" later in this chapter.

■ Intersite replication connections can use either an Internet Protocol (IP) or a Simple Mail Transfer Protocol (SMTP) transport. SMTP can be used as a transport protocol only for the configuration, schema, and application directory partitions, not for the domain partition. The connection protocol you use is determined by the available bandwidth and the reliability of the network that connects company locations.

■ Replication traffic is sent through bridgehead servers rather than to multiple replication partners. When changes are made to the directory in one site, the changes are replicated to a single bridgehead server (per directory partition) in that site, and the changes are then replicated to a bridgehead server in the other site. The changes are replicated from the bridgehead server in the second site to all the domain controllers in that site.

■ You can easily modify the flow of replication between sites. Almost every component of intersite replication can be changed.

> **Important**   One of the key elements in designing AD DS is site design. Site design includes planning the number and location of sites plus the configuration of intersite connections to optimize the use of network bandwidth while minimizing the replication latency. Configuration options for the intersite connections are discussed later in this chapter, and site design issues are discussed in Chapter 5, "Designing the Active Directory Domain Services Structure."

Replication Latency

Because of the way replication works in Windows Server 2008 AD DS, it can take some time for a change made on one domain controller to be replicated to all the other domain controllers in an organization. This time lag is called the *replication latency*. In most cases, the replication latency is easy to calculate, especially within a site. As mentioned earlier, any change made to the data store on one domain controller will be replicated to that domain controller's replication partners in about 15 seconds. The destination domain controller will hold that change for 15 seconds and then pass it on to its replication partners. So the replication latency within a site is about 15 seconds times the number of hops the change has to take before reaching all domain controllers. As explained in the next section, the replication topology within a site never requires more than three hops, so the maximum replication latency within a site will usually be less than one minute.

Determining the replication latency between sites is more difficult. First of all, you must calculate the replication latency within the source site. This replication latency is the amount of time it takes for a change made on a domain controller in the site to be replicated to the source site's bridgehead server. After the information arrives at the originating site's bridgehead server, the site link schedule and replication interval determine the amount of time it takes for the information to get to the destination site. The default configuration for site links is to replicate every three hours. If this configuration is not changed, a maximum of three hours will be added to the replication latency. When the information arrives at the bridgehead server in the destination site, the intrasite replication latency for the destination site must be added. In some cases, this replication latency might be unacceptable. To minimize this, you can shorten the replication interval to a minimum of 15 minutes for intersite replication.

Managing replication latency is a matter of balancing the need for a short latency period and bandwidth limitations. If you want the shortest possible latency period, you should put all the domain controllers in the same site, and the replication latency will be about one minute for all domain controllers. However, if your company locations are separated by WAN connections with limited bandwidth, you will require multiple sites so that you can manage network utilization for AD DS replication, but replication latency will be higher.

Urgent Replication

In some cases, the replication latency described in the previous section is too long. In particular, this is the case when a security-related attribute has been modified in the directory. For these situations, AD DS uses *urgent replication,* in which a domain controller forwards the changes immediately to its replication partners. Any domain controller receiving an urgent update will also immediately forward the change. In this way, all domain controllers in the site are updated within seconds. The following types of changes trigger an urgent replication:

- Modifying the account lockout policy for the domain
- Modifying the domain password policies
- Moving the relative identifier (RID) master to a new domain controller
- Changing a Local Security Authority (LSA) secret, such as when the domain controller machine password is modified
- Locking out a user account when a user attempts to log on too many times using an incorrect password

By default, urgent updates apply only to intrasite replication and not to intersite replication. This default handling of urgent updates can be modified by enabling notification for replication between sites.

User password changes are not replicated using the same urgent replication model. Instead, when a user changes his or her password on a domain controller, the password change is immediately replicated directly to the PDC emulator for the domain. This replication crosses site boundaries and does not make use of the bridgehead servers in each site. Instead, the domain controller where the change was made uses an RPC connection to the PDC emulator to update the password. The PDC emulator then updates all the other domain controllers through the normal process of replication. If the user tries to log on to a domain controller that has not yet received the new password, the domain controller will check with the PDC emulator to see if there are any updated password changes for the user before denying the logon.

Replication Topology Generation

One of the keys to understanding AD DS replication is understanding how the replication topology is created. By default, the process of creating the replication topology is handled automatically by AD DS. Although the replication topology can be manually configured, in most cases the default configuration by the system is the best option.

In order for the replication topology to be successfully created, the following components must be in place:

- **Routable IP infrastructure**   In order to configure intersite replication, you need to configure AD DS sites and map the sites to IP subnet address ranges. Domain controllers and client computers use this IP subnet to site mapping when locating domain controllers.

- **DNS**   AD DS replication topology requires DNS in order for domain controllers locate replication partners. DNS also stores SRV resource records that provide site affinity information to clients searching for domain controllers.

- **Netlogon service**   Netlogon is required for DNS registrations. As well, the Netlogon service must be running for AD DS to function.

- **Remote Procedure Call (RPC) connectivity**   AD DS domain controllers must be able to connect to other domain controllers in the same domain by using RPCs. RPCs must be used between domain controllers in the same site and in different sites if the domain controllers are in the same domain. SMTP is an alternative protocol that can be used by domain controllers in different domains and sites.

- **Intersite Messaging**   Intersite Messaging is required for SMTP intersite replication and for site coverage calculations. If the forest functional level is Windows 2000, Intersite Messaging is also required for intersite topology generation.

Knowledge Consistency Checker

Knowledge Consistency Checker (KCC) is the process that runs on every domain controller to create the replication topology within a site and between sites. As soon as a domain controller is added to an AD DS forest, KCC begins creating a replication topology that is both efficient and fault tolerant. As additional domain controllers are added to a site or as additional sites are added, KCC uses the information about servers, sites, site links, and schedules to create the optimal replication topology.

The KCC runs on each domain controller. It uses the forest information stored in the configuration directory partition on each domain controller to create a replication topology. Because all domain controllers use the same configuration information and the same algorithm for creating the topology, the topology is created without direct communication between KCC components on different domain controllers. The KCC communicates with other KCCs only to make an RPC request for replication error information.

KCC also dynamically deals with changes or failures within the replication topology. If one of the domain controllers is offline for a period of time, KCC revises the replication topology to work around the unavailable domain controller. By default, KCC on every domain controller recalculates the replication topology every 15 minutes. You can force KCC to recalculate the replication topology at any time through the Active Directory Sites And Services administrative tool by locating the server where you want to check the replication topology, right-clicking the NTDS Settings container in the server container, selecting All Tasks, and then selecting Check Replication Topology. You can also force the domain controller to recalculate the replication topology by using the Repadmin /kcc *domaincontrollername* command.

Connection Objects

When KCC creates the replication topology, it creates a series of connection objects that are stored in the configuration directory partition of AD DS. The connection objects are direct logical connections between domain controllers that are used to replicate directory information. KCC tries to create a replication topology that is both efficient and fault-tolerant. KCC builds as many connection objects as are required to achieve these goals.

Connection objects are always created as one-way pull connections between two domain controllers. This is because the normal process of replication is always a pull operation where the destination domain controller requests the information from a sending domain controller. In most cases, KCC will build two one-way connections between domain controllers so that information can be replicated either way.

In most cases, the connection objects automatically created by KCC are optimized and you do not need to make any changes. However, in some cases you might want to modify the connection objects. For example, you may need to modify the connection object to aid in troubleshooting AD DS replication.

You can modify the default connection objects in two ways: by modifying some settings on connection objects created by KCC and by adding new connection objects.

Modifying a Connection Object Created by KCC

You can modify the schedule and the source domain controller for a connection object within a site, and you can also modify the transport protocol for connection objects between sites. The connection interface is shown in Figure 4-2. By default, domain controllers within a site will check all their replication partners for missed updates every 15 minutes. You can change that schedule to never check or to check every hour or every half hour. When you modify the connection object, it is renamed from <*automatically generated*> to the object's globally unique identifier (GUID). You can rename the object after modifying it.

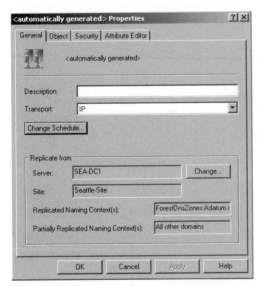

Figure 4-2   Modifying an existing connection object.

Creating a New Connection Object

You can also create an entirely new connection object to force a particular replication topology. When you create a connection object, you are given a choice of which domain controller to pull changes from. You can also modify any of the other settings on the connection agreement.

KCC will not delete or modify any connections that have been manually modified or created. However, KCC will use the manual connection objects as it would use any other connection, and KCC might reconfigure the connection objects in the site to compensate for the manually created connections.

Intrasite Replication Topology

Within a single site, KCC will create a replication topology that includes redundant links. The primary goal for designing AD DS replication is availability and fault tolerance. The unavailability of a single domain controller should not cause AD DS replication to fail. The disadvantage of using redundant links is that a domain controller might receive the same update several times, because each domain controller will have multiple replication partners. As described earlier, AD DS replication uses propagation dampening to avoid multiple updates of the same information.

As domain controllers with replicas of particular AD DS partitions are added to the organization, KCC automatically begins creating the replication topology. This topology forms a replication ring. Figure 4-3 shows an example of a simple network structure with three domain controllers in the same domain and in a single site.

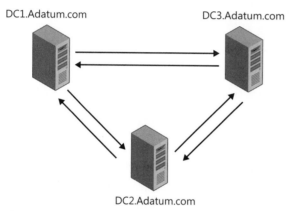

Figure 4-3   A simple replication ring.

As shown in Figure 4-3, KCC creates a replication ring in which every domain controller is configured with two incoming replication connections. If one of the connections is not available, updates can still arrive on the other connection. Also, each domain controller is configured as the source domain controller for two other domain controllers. This creates a redundant ring for each domain controller. As the number of domain controllers with a replica of a particular partition increases, a second principle for creating connections becomes important. KCC will always create a replication topology in which each domain controller in a site is no more than three replication hops away from any other domain controller. As the number of domain controllers with the same directory partition in a site increases beyond seven, extra connection objects are created to decrease the potential number of hops to three or fewer. For example, the site shown in Figure 4-4 has nine domain controllers. It would have a replication topology that would include at least one additional connection.

Replication rings are based on directory partitions. This means that KCC calculates a replication ring for each directory partition. For example, an organization might have multiple domains in a single site and an application directory partition that is replicated to several domain controllers in the site. The configuration could be set up as shown in Figure 4-5.

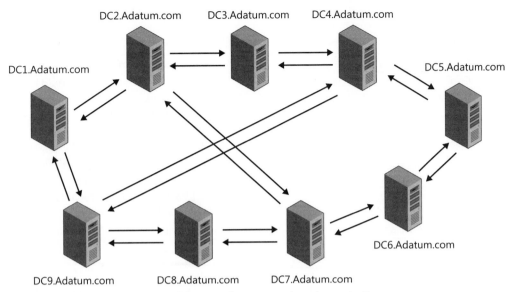

Figure 4-4   A replication ring with more than seven domain controllers.

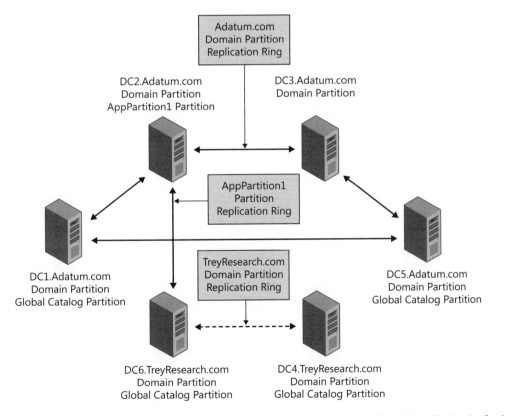

Note: All domain controllers also host a replica of the Configuration and Schema Partitions. The replication ring for the Configuration and Schema Partitions would include all the domain controllers.

Figure 4-5   Replication rings created for each directory partition.

In the scenario illustrated in Figure 4-5, the replication rings shown in Table 4-1 would be created.

Table 4-1   Replication Rings in a Complex Site

Directory Partition	Replication Partners
Configuration directory partition, schema directory partition	All the domain controllers would be included in the replication ring for both the configuration directory partition and the schema directory partition.
ADatum.com domain directory partition	DC1.ADatum.com, DC2.ADatum.com, DC3.ADatum.com, DC5.ADatum.com
TreyResearch.com domain directory partition	DC4.TreyResearch.com, DC6.TreyResearch.com
Global catalog partition	DC1.ADatum.com, DC4.ADatum.com, DC4.TreyResearch.com
AppPartition1 application directory partition	DC2.ADatum.com, DC6.TreyResearch.com

Note   The Domain Name System (DNS) application directory partitions (ForestDnsZones and DomainDnsZones) are also included in the replication topology. To keep the Figure 4-5 scenario from getting too complicated, these partitions are not included in that figure nor in the associated table. As discussed in Chapter 3, "Active Directory Domain Services and Domain Name System," these partitions are treated exactly like other domain directory partitions. Also, the global catalog replication topology is not shown in Figure 4-5. The process of creating a global catalog replication ring is slightly different than for other partitions and will be described in the next section.

The replication connections and replication status can be viewed by using the Repadmin command-line tool with the */showrepl* parameter. Figure 4-6 shows the partial output when running this command on a domain controller in a forest with multiple domains and sites.

The replication ring is a logical concept; the actual replication topology as implemented with the connection objects does not duplicate the replication rings exactly. Although a separate replication ring is created for each directory partition, KCC will not create additional connection objects for each replication ring. Instead, KCC reuses connection objects to use as few connection objects as possible while still creating a replication topology that provides redundancy for each partition. For example, in the scenario illustrated in Figure 4-5, DC2.ADatum.com has a connection object with DC6.TreyResearch.com. This single connection object could be used to replicate the schema partition, the configuration partition, and the AppPartition1 partition, as well as the DNS application directory partitions. You can see which directory partitions are replicated by each connection object by viewing the connection object in Active Directory Sites And Services and Repadmin. As shown in Figure 4-6, you can view the Replicated Naming Context(s) setting on each connection object. You can also use the Repadmin /showconn *servername* to show the partitions that are being replicated by each connection object. Partial output of this command is shown in Figure 4-7. In this figure, you can see that the connection object with SEA-DC2.ADatum.com is being used to replicate the DomainDnsZones, ForestDnsZones, ADatum.com, Configuration, and Schema partitions.

Figure 4-6   Using *Repadmin* to view the replication connections.

Figure 4-7   A single connection object used to replicate multiple directory partitions.

Global Catalog Replication

The global catalog is a different partition than the other partitions in that it is built from all the domain databases in the entire forest. The global catalog itself is read-only on all domain controllers, which means that the information in the global catalog cannot be directly modified by the administrator. The global catalog is just a list of all the attributes that are moved into the global catalog because their *isMemberOfPartialAttributeSet* attribute is set to *true*.

The fact that the global catalog is created from the domain databases also affects the replication ring for the global catalog. Each global catalog server must get the global catalog information from the domain controllers in all domains. For a simple example, see Figure 4-8, which shows a company with two domains and one domain controller in each domain in the same site. Only the DC1.ADatum.com domain is configured as a global catalog server. The global catalog server is also the only domain controller for the ADatum.com domain, so it will extract the global catalog information for ADatum.com from its own domain database. The domain controller in the TreyResearch.com domain has the only copy of that domain directory partition, so DC1.ADatum.com collects the global catalog information for the TreyResearch.com domain from DC2.TreyResearch.com. To extract the information from the TreyResearch.com domain, a connection object is created from DC2.TreyResearch.com to DC1.ADatum.com. This connection is then used to replicate the global catalog information to DC1.ADatum.com.

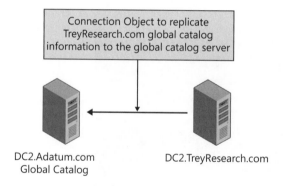

DC2.Adatum.com
Global Catalog

DC2.TreyResearch.com

Figure 4-8   An example of simple global catalog replication.

Figure 4-9 shows a more complicated example of how the global catalog is created and replicated. In this scenario, a connection object is configured from a domain controller in every domain to each global catalog server. For example, DC1.ADatum.com will have an inbound connection object from DC2.ADatum.com, DC4.TreyResearch.com, and DC6.Contoso.com. This connection object is used to build the global catalog on DC1.ADatum.com. Each of the other global catalog servers will have a similar set of connection objects created. Also, a separate replication ring is created for the global catalog partition with all of the global catalog servers.

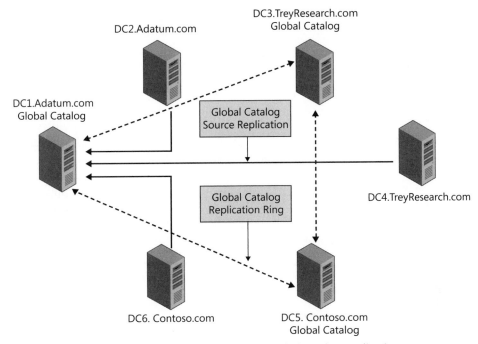

Figure 4-9   An example of a more complicated global catalog replication.

Intersite Replication Topology

When additional sites are added to a forest, the replication topology becomes increasingly complex. In a multisite scenario, a replication topology must be created for each site, and a replication topology must be created for replication between sites. To deal with this complexity, the process for creating connection objects changes for the intrasite replication. Within a site, KCC on each domain controller is responsible for creating the connection objects that it needs to ensure that it has the required replication redundancy for all of its partitions; it then replicates the information about the connection objects to the other domain controllers. Also, the domain controller receives information about the connection objects that have been created by other domain controllers. The next time KCC runs, connection objects might be added, modified, or deleted based on the information the domain controller has received about other connection objects in the site. Eventually, KCCs on all the domain controllers in a site determine the optimal replication configuration.

A similar approach is used when determining the replication topology between sites, except that one domain controller in each site is responsible for developing the intersite topology. KCC on one domain controller in the site is designated as the Inter-Site Topology Generator (ISTG) for the site. There is only one ISTG per site regardless of how many domains or other directory partitions there are in the site. ISTG is responsible for calculating the ideal replication topology for the entire site. This process consists of the following two actions:

- Identifying the bridgehead servers for each directory partition that is present in the site. Replication between sites is always sent from a bridgehead server in one site to a bridgehead server in another site. This means that information is replicated only once across the network connection between the sites.

- Creating the connection objects between the bridgehead servers to ensure that the information is replicated between the sites. Because the replication is configured between bridgehead servers, there are no redundant connection objects configured as there are within a site. However, the ISTG will create connection objects with bridgehead servers in multiple sites if the site links are configured to enable the connections.

When a new site is added to the forest, ISTG in each site determines which directory partitions are present in the new site. ISTG then calculates the new connection objects that will be needed to replicate the required information from the new site. Also, ISTG designates one domain controller to be the bridgehead server for each directory partition. ISTG creates the required connection agreement in its directory, and this information is replicated to the bridgehead server. The bridgehead server then creates a replication connection with the bridgehead server in the remote site, and replication begins.

To see how the replication topology is created between sites, see Figure 4-10. In this example, the forest contains two sites and two domains with domain controllers for each domain in each site. There is also at least one global catalog server in each site. This means that each site contains a directory partition for each of the domains and a global catalog partition, as well as the schema directory partition and the configuration directory partition. Two bridgehead servers would be designated in each site, because each of these partitions must be replicated between the sites. One of the bridgehead servers in each site will be a domain controller in the Adatum.com domain. Another bridgehead server in each site must be a domain controller in the TreyResearch.com domain. In the Figure 4-10 example, DC1.ADatum.com and DC6.Trey-Research.com are also global catalog servers. This means that they will become bridgehead servers to replicate global catalog information between sites. Because the schema directory partition and the configuration directory partition are shared by all domain controllers, one of the existing connection objects can be used to replicate these partitions.

 Note   This discussion of the replication topology is based on the default behavior for AD DS domain controllers. Administrators can modify the default behavior, especially for replication between sites. These modifications and the effect of these changes are discussed later in this chapter.

RODCs and the Replication Topology

RODCs also participate in normal AD DS replication, and connection objects must be created between RODCs and other domain controllers. However, because RODCs have read-only copies of the AD DS database, the KCC will only create single one-way connection objects from a domain controller with a writable copy of the database to the RODC. The RODC can only pull changes from other domain controllers; it can never be configured as a replication source for any connection object.

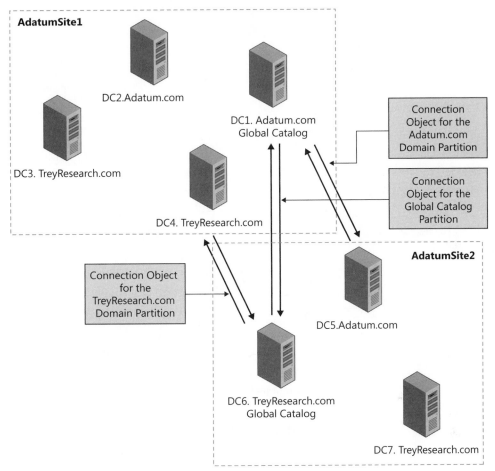

Figure 4-10   Intersite connection objects.

RODC replication is also limited by which domain controllers can be direct replication partners. RODCs can replicate all AD DS partitions except the domain partition from Windows Server 2003 domain controllers. RODCs can also replicate all partitions from another Windows Sever 2008 domain controller, but they must replicate the domain partition from a domain controller running Windows Server 2008. This means that each RODC must have a connection object with a Windows Server 2008 domain controller with a writable copy of the database for the RODC's domain. This also means that when you upgrade a domain from Windows Server 2003, the first Windows Server 2008 domain controller cannot be an RODC.

If the RODC is deployed in a separate site, the Windows Server 2008 should be placed in the nearest site in the topology. Figure 4-11 provides an example of a possible RODC deployment and the connection objects that would be configured.

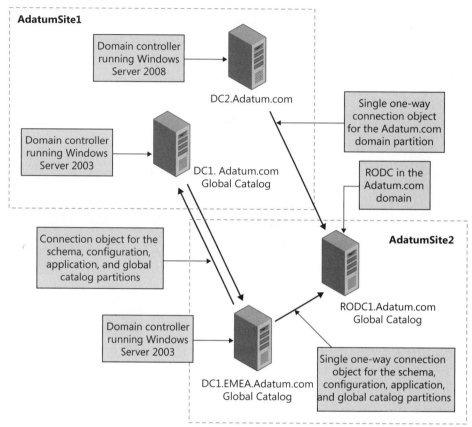

Figure 4-11 Replication connection objects with RODCs.

Configuring Intersite Replication

The most important reason for creating multiple sites in AD DS is to control replication traffic between company locations, especially between locations that are separated by slow WAN connections. As described in Chapter 2, an AD DS site is a network location in which all the domain controllers are connected to each other with fast and reliable network connections. One of the tasks of setting up an AD DS network is determining where to draw the site boundaries and then connecting the sites together.

> **Note** Defining clear criteria for when to create an additional site is difficult because of the large numbers of variables that have to be included in this decision. Chapter 5 goes into detail about when you should consider creating additional sites. That chapter also covers many of the other design issues that you must consider when designing the site topology.

Creating Additional Sites

When AD DS is installed, a single site called the Default-First-Site-Name (the site can be renamed) is created. Because sites are usually based on the company location, you can rename this site to more accurately reflect the location where the domain controllers in the site are located. If additional sites are not created, all subsequent domain controllers will be added to this site as they are installed. However, if your company has multiple locations with limited bandwidth between the locations, you will almost certainly want to create additional sites.

Additional sites are created using the Active Directory Sites And Services administrative tool (see Figure 4-12). To create a new site, right-click the Sites container and then click New Site.

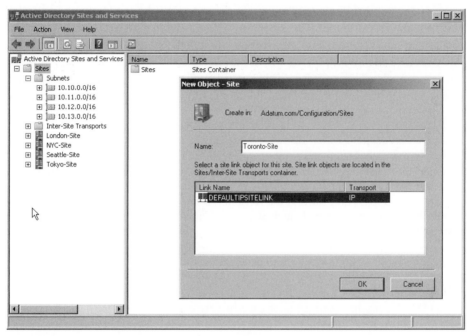

Figure 4-12   Creating a new site in Active Directory Sites And Services.

When you create a new site, you must link the site with an existing site link. This ensures that the site will automatically be included in the replication topology. From the Link Name list, choose which site link will be used to connect this site to other sites.

Each site is associated with one or more IP subnets in AD DS. By default, no subnets are created in AD DS, so you will normally begin by creating all of the subnets associated with the Default-First-Site-Name site. As you create additional sites, also create additional subnets in the Subnets container in Active Directory Sites And Services and associate the subnets with the new site.

On the Disc   As you modify the site configuration, ensure that you document all of the changes you make. You can use the ADDSSites.xlsx job aid on the CD as a template for documenting the site configuration. You can use the ListADDSSites.ps1 Windows PowerShell script on the CD to display information about all of the sites in your forest. Remember that you need to provide the full path when running a Windows PowerShell script, and you may need to modify the PowerShell script execution policy before you can run a script.

For examples of Visual Basic Scripting Edition (VBScript) scripts that you can use to obtain site information, see the Script Center Script Repository Web site at *http://www.microsoft.com/technet/scriptcenter/scripts/default.mspx?mfr=true*.

To move an existing domain controller into the site, right-click the domain controller object in its current Servers container and select Move. You are then given a choice about which site you want to move the domain controller into. If you install a new domain controller and you have more than one site in your forest, you are given a choice about which site to install the new domain controller. The default selection in the Active Directory Domain Services Installation Wizard is to locate the domain controller in the site where the IP subnet matches the domain controller's IP address.

Important   When you move a domain controller to a new site, ensure that you modify the domain controller IP configuration to reflect the new site location. You will also need to refresh the host record in DNS by using the *IPConfig /refreshDNS* command and update the SRV records by stopping and starting the Netlogon service. Verify that you can ping all domain controllers in the domain by fully qualified domain name after completing the domain controller move.

Site Links

The AD DS objects that connect sites together are called *site links*. When AD DS is installed, a single site link—called DEFAULTIPSITELINK—is created. If you do not create any additional site links before you create additional sites, each site is included in this default site link. If all of the WAN connections between your company locations are equal in terms of bandwidth and cost, you can just accept this default configuration. If all the sites are connected by one site link, the replication traffic between all sites will have exactly the same properties. If you make a change on this site link, the replication configuration for all sites will be modified.

On the Disc   As part of documenting your site configuration, ensure that you also document the site link configuration. You can use the ADDSSites.xlsx job aid on the CD. The ListADDSSites.ps1 script on the CD lists the site links associated with each site.

However, in many cases, you might not want to have the replication between all sites configured the same way. For example, if your company locations are linked by different network connections, you may want to replicate AD DS information across network connections with limited available bandwidth less frequently than you do across network connections with more available bandwidth. If you want to be able to configure different replication settings between sites, you must create additional site links and assign the appropriate sites to the site links.

> **Note**   Creating a site link does not replace the work of ISTG; all it does is make it possible for ISTG to do its work. After a site link is in place, ISTG will use the site link to create the required connection objects to replicate all the AD DS partitions between each site.

The following are the configuration options on all site links. Figure 4-13 shows the interface for configuring site links:

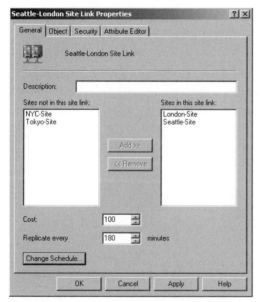

Figure 4-13   Configuring site links.

- **Cost**   The cost for a site link is an administrator-assigned value that defines the relative cost of the site link. The cost will usually reflect the speed of the network connection and the expenses associated with using the connection. This cost is important if there are redundant site links in the organization, that is, if there is more than one path for replication to travel from one site to another. In all cases, the lowest-cost route will be chosen as the replication path.

> **Important**   Creating redundant site links between sites and configuring costs on the site links is only useful if you have multiple WAN connections between the sites. If you only have one network connection between company locations, adding site links provides no benefit.

■ **Replication schedule**   The replication schedule defines what times during the day the site link is available for replication. The default replication schedule allows for replication to occur 24 hours a day. However, if the available bandwidth to a site is very limited, you might want to have replication occur only during nonworking hours.

■ **Replication interval**   The replication interval defines the intervals at which the bridgehead servers check with the bridgehead servers in the other sites to see if there are any directory updates. By default, the replication interval for site links is set at *180 minutes*. The replication interval is only applied during the replication schedule. If the replication schedule is configured to allow replication from 22:00 to 05:00, by default, the bridgehead servers will check for updates every three hours during that time.

■ **Replication transports**   The site link can use either RPC over IP or SMTP as the replication transport. See "Replication Transport Protocols" later in this chapter for more details.

These options provide significant flexibility for configuring replication between sites. However, there are also some mistakes to avoid. To understand how these options work together, consider a company network like that shown in Figure 4-14.

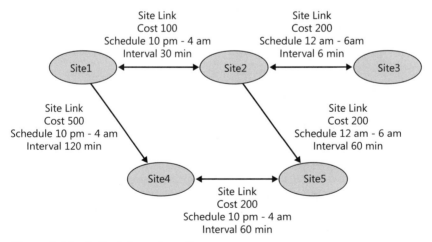

Figure 4-14   A site link configuration.

In Windows Server 2008 AD DS, all site links are considered transitive by default. This means that connection objects can be created between domain controllers that are not in adjacent sites. For example, in Figure 4-14, Site1 has a site link to Site2 and to Site4, and Site2 has a site link to Site3 and Site5. Because of the transitive nature of the site links, this means that domain controllers in Site1 can also replicate directly with domain controllers in Site3 and Site5.

The site link costs define the path that replication traffic will take through the network. When KCC is creating the routing topology, it uses the accumulated costs for all site links to calculate the optimal routing. In the example shown in Figure 4-14, there are two possible routes between Site1 and Site5: the first route is through Site2; the second route is through Site4. The cost to route through Site2 is 300 (100 + 200), and the cost through Site4 is 700 (500 + 200). This means that all replication traffic will be replicated through Site2 unless the connection is not available.

When replication traffic crosses multiple site links, the site link schedules and replication intervals for each site link combine to determine the effective replication window and interval. For example, effective replication will occur between Site1 and Site3 only during the hours of 00:00 to 4:00 (the overlapping time in the schedules), and the effective replication will happen every 60 minutes (the replication interval for the Site2–Site3 site link).

> **Note**   If the schedules for site links do not overlap, it is still possible for replication to occur between multiple sites. For example, if the Site1–Site2 site link is available from 02:00 to 06:00, and the Site2–Site3 site link is available from 22:00 to 01:00, changes to the directory will still flow from Site1 to Site3. The changes will be sent from Site1 to Site2, and then from Site2 to Site3. However, the replication latency would be almost a day in this case, because changes replicated to Site2 at 02:00 would not be replicated to Site3 until 22:00.

Additional Site Link Configuration Options

In addition to the site link configuration options available in Active Directory Sites And Services, you can also configure other site link settings by using ADSIEdit, or by modifying the registry on the domain controllers. For example, you configure the following settings:

- **Turn off compression for intersite replication**   By default, all replication traffic between sites is compressed. However, compressing the traffic places an extra load on the domain controller's processor. If you have sufficient bandwidth between the AD DS sites, you can disable the compression in Windows Server 2008 AD DS.

- **Enable notification for intersite replication**   By default, replication between sites is based on the schedule and replication frequency configured on the site link. You have the option to enable notification for intersite replication. If notification is enabled, the bridgehead server in a site where a change has occurred notifies the bridgehead server in the destination site, and the changes are pulled across the site link. This can greatly reduce replication latency between sites, but will also increase the network traffic between sites.

> To turn off compression or to turn on notification for intersite replication, you must use a tool such as ADSI Edit to modify the Options attribute on either the site link object or the connection object. To turn off compression, set the value of the Options attribute to 4; to turn on notification, set the value to 1.
>
> ■ **Modify the amount of data that is replicated**   You can modify the amount of data that is replicated in each replication packet. By default, the number of objects Windows Server 2008 domain controllers will replicate in a single packet is 1/1,000,000th the size of RAM, with a minimum of 100 objects and a maximum of 1,000 objects. The maximum size of objects that will be replicated is 1/100th the size of RAM, with a minimum of 1 megabyte (MB) and a maximum of 10 MB. You can modify these settings by creating the Replicator inter site packet size (objects) and Replicator inter site packet size (bytes) values in the HKEY_LOCAL _MACHINE\System\CurrentControlSet\Services\NTDS\Parameters path.

Site Link Bridges

In some cases, you might want to turn off the transitive nature of site links by turning off site link bridging and manually configuring site link bridges. When you configure site link bridges, you define which site links should be seen as transitive and which site links should not. Turning off the transitive nature of site links can be useful when you do not have a fully routed network, that is, if all segments of the network are not available at all times (for example, if you have a dial-up or scheduled-demand dial connection to one network location). Site link bridges can also be used to configure replication in situations where a company has several sites connected to a fast backbone with several smaller sites connecting to each larger center using slow network connections. In such cases, site link bridges can be used to manage the flow of replication traffic more efficiently.

> **More Info**   Chapter 5 provides details about when and how to use site link bridges.

When you create a site link bridge, you must define which site links are part of the bridge. Any site links you add to the site link bridge are considered transitive with each other, but site links that are not included in the site link bridge are not transitive. In the example used earlier, a site link bridge could be created for the site links connecting Site1, Site2, Site4, and Site5. All of these site links would then be considered transitive, which means that a bridgehead server in Site1 could replicate directly with a bridgehead server in Site5. However, because the site link from Site2 to Site3 is not included in the site link bridge, it is not transitive. That means that all replication traffic from Site3 would flow to Site2, and from there it would flow to the other sites.

To turn off the transitive site links, expand the Inter-Site Transport container in Active Directory Sites And Services, right-click IP, click Properties, and then clear the Bridge All Site Links option on the General tab of the IP Properties sheet.

> **Caution**   The site link bridging setting affects all site links using the transport protocol where you disable site link bridging. This means that all site link bridging is disabled, and you will now have to configure site link bridges for all site links if you want transitive site connections.

Replication Transport Protocols

Windows Server 2008 AD DS can use one of three different transport protocols for replication:

- **RPC over IP within a site**   All replication connections within a site must use an RPC-over-IP connection. This connection is synchronous, which means that the domain controller can replicate with only one replication partner at any one time. The RPC connection uses dynamic port mapping. The first RPC connection is made on the RPC endpoint mapper port (TCP port 135). This connection is used to determine which port the destination domain controller is using for replication.

> **Note**   If you are replicating the directory information through a firewall or are using routers with port filtering enabled, you can specify the port number that the domain controllers will use for replication. To do this, create the following registry key as a DWORD value and specify any valid port number: HKEY_LOCAL_MACHINE\SYSTEM\ CurrentControlSet\Services\NTDS \Parameters\TCP/IP Port.

- **RPC over IP between sites**   Replication connections between sites can also use RPC over IP. This RPC connection is the same as the intrasite connection with one important exception: by default, all traffic sent between sites is compressed.

> **Note**   When you look at the two types of RPC-over-IP connections in the Active Directory Sites And Services administrative tool, you will notice that they are identified differently in the interface. The RPC over IP within a site is called *RPC*, and the RPC over IP between sites is called *IP*.

- **SMTP between sites**   Replication connections between sites can also use SMTP to replicate information between sites. SMTP can be a good choice as a replication protocol if the WAN links between company locations have very high latency. SMTP uses an asynchronous connection, which means that the domain controller can replicate with multiple servers at the same time.

Configuring SMTP Replication

Configuring SMTP replication is significantly more complicated than configuring RPC over IP replication between sites. With RPC-over-IP replication, domain controllers use built-in components and Kerberos authentication to automatically configure and secure replication.

To configure SMTP replication, complete the following steps:

1. Install the SMTP Server feature on the bridgehead servers in both sites. When you install the SMTP Server feature, required components from the Web Server (IIS) server role are also installed.

2. Install Active Directory Certificate Services and configure the Certification Authority (CA) as an Enterprise CA. The CA will be used to issue certificates to the domain controllers that will be used to sign and encrypt the SMTP messages that are exchanged between domain controllers. When you install an Enterprise CA, it automatically issues domain controller certificates to domain controllers in the same domain as the Enterprise CA. These domain controllers can use the certificates to secure SMTP data. For domain controllers in other domains in the forest, you must manually request a Domain Controller certificate or a Directory Email Replication certificate.

> **Note** You can also purchase certificates from public CAs to be used for SMTP replication.

3. Configure SMTP site links with a cost that is less than any RPC over IP site link connecting between the two sites. The two sites must not have any domain controllers in the same domain.

4. Ensure that SMTP e-mail can be sent between the domain controllers. If the domain controllers can communicate directly by using port 25, no further configuration is required. However, in some cases, the domain controllers may need to forward the SMTP messages to a SMTP bridgehead server rather than directly to the destination bridgehead server.

Configuring Bridgehead Servers

As mentioned earlier, replication between sites is accomplished through bridgehead servers. By default, ISTG automatically identifies the bridgehead server as it calculates the intersite replication topology. To view which domain controllers are operating as bridgehead servers, you can use the *Repadmin /bridgeheads* command. The command output lists all of the current bridgehead servers in each site, including the directory partitions each bridgehead server is responsible for. The command output also displays whether or not the last replication with each bridgehead server was successful.

If you run the *Repadmin /bridgeheads /v* command, the command output displays the last attempted replication for each directory partition on the bridgehead server, as well as the last successful replication time. Figure 4-15 shows the partial output from this command.

In some cases, you might want to control which domain controllers are going to operate as bridgehead servers. Bridgehead server may require additional server resources if there are many changes to the directory information, replication is set to occur frequently, and the organization has hundreds of sites. To configure which servers will be the bridgehead servers, access the computer objects in the Active Directory Sites And Services administrative tool, right-click the server name, and then select Properties. (Figure 4-16 shows the interface.) You are given the option of configuring the server as a preferred bridgehead server for either IP or SMTP transports.

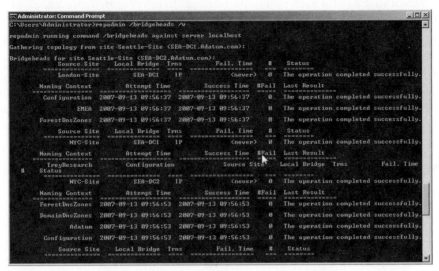

Figure 4-15   Viewing bridgehead server status using *Repadmin*.

> **On the Disc**   If you configure a bridgehead server and then forget that you configured it, you may spend a lot of time troubleshooting AD DS replication if the bridgehead server fails. Ensure that you document preferred bridgehead servers for both types of replication transports in the ADDSSites.xlsx job aid on the CD.

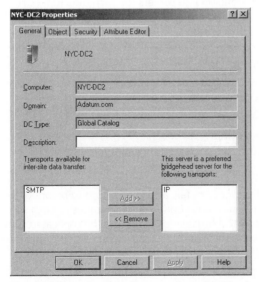

Figure 4-16   Configuring a preferred bridgehead server.

The advantage of configuring preferred bridgehead servers is that you can ensure that the domain controllers you choose will be selected as the bridgehead servers. If you want complete control over which servers are used as bridgehead servers, you must configure a preferred bridgehead server for each partition that needs to be replicated into a site. For example, if a site contains replicas of the ADatum.com domain directory partition, the TreyResearch.com domain directory partition, the global catalog partition, and an application directory partition, you will need to configure at least one domain controller with a replica of each of these partitions. If you do not configure bridgehead servers for all of the partitions, you will get a warning message like the one shown in Figure 4-17, and ISTG will log an event in the event log and then choose a preferred bridgehead server for the partition. You can also configure multiple preferred bridgehead servers. If you do, ISTG will choose one of the identified servers as the bridgehead server.

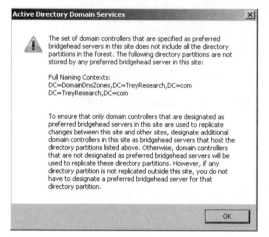

Figure 4-17   Warning message to configure bridgehead servers for each directory partition.

You should configure this option with caution. Configuring preferred bridgehead servers limits the ability of ISTG to choose the bridgehead server—it will always select a server that is configured as a preferred bridgehead server. If this server fails and no other servers have been designated as bridgehead servers for that directory partition, ISTG will not select another bridgehead server and replication will cease until the server is again available or until you have reconfigured the preferred bridgehead server options. If the preferred bridgehead server does fail, you can either remove the server as a preferred bridgehead server and allow ISTG to identify a bridgehead server or choose another preferred bridgehead server.

Caution   If the preferred bridgehead server does fail, and you choose to reconfigure the preferred bridgehead server, you need to make any configuration changes in both sites. Because the bridgehead servers are not available, no information will be replicated between the sites until the configuration changes are made in both sites. To make changes in a remote site, connect to a domain controller in the site in Active Directory Sites And Services.

Troubleshooting Replication

If AD DS replication fails, domain controllers will not be updated with changes made on other domain controllers. This may lead to inconsistent experiences for users and administrators, depending on which domain controller they are connecting to. If password or configuration changes for users are not replicated, users may not be able to log on to the network. If group policy settings or the SYSVOL directory are not replicated, users may experience different group policy settings. Because of the importance of AD DS replication, you should be prepared to troubleshoot AD DS replication issues.

Process for Troubleshooting AD DS Replication Failures

The first step in troubleshooting AD DS replication failures is to identify the reason for the failure. In many cases, it can be difficult to immediately identify why AD DS replication fails, so often troubleshooting is a matter of eliminating possible reasons for failure. As general guidance, complete the following steps:

1. Verify network connectivity. As is the case with most troubleshooting scenarios, start by verifying that the domain controllers can communicate with each other on the network. The network connection might be unavailable or network settings may not be configured properly.

2. Verify name resolution. One of the most common causes for replication errors is that DNS name resolution is failing. If you receive error messages indicating that the RPC server is not available or "Target account name is incorrect" errors, verify that the domain controllers can resolve the target server's FQDN.

3. Test for authentication and authorization errors. If you are receiving access denied errors during replication, then there is a problem with authentication or authorization. To identify the cause of the security error, run the *dcdiag /test:CheckSecurityError / s:DomainControllerName* command, where *DomainControllerName* is the name of the domain controller that you want to test. To test the connection between two domain controllers for replication security errors, run the *dcdiag /test:CheckSecurityError /Repl-Source:SourceDomainControllerName* command. This command tests the connection between the domain controller on which you run the command and the source domain controller (identified by *SourceDomainControllerName*). The output from these commands identifies the security issues between the domain controllers. Fix the issues and then rerun the command to verify that you have addressed the issue.

4. Check the Event Viewer on the affected domain controllers. When replication fails, events describing the nature of the failure are written to the Event Viewer.

5. Check for domain controller performance issues. If a domain controller does not have enough server resources, replication may fail, or the replication queues may back up. For example, if the domain controller runs out of hard disk space on the drive where the AD DS data store is located, the domain controller will not accept replication changes.

In some cases, the domain controller performance may be the cause of delayed replication. To address domain controller performance issues, consider the following:

   a. Move applications or services to another server. If the domain controller is performing multiple roles or running other applications, consider moving the roles or applications to another server on the network.

   b. Distribute AD DS and DNS roles across multiple servers. AD DS integrated DNS zones provide benefits, but running both AD DS services and DNS services on a single computer can cause performance issues. By distributing the load of these services, you may be able to minimize the server performance impact.

   c. Deploy domain controllers with 64-bit hardware. Computers with 64-bit hardware provide significant performance gains over domain controllers with 32-bit hardware.

6. Review and modify the replication topology. In large organizations with thousands of sites, calculating the replication topology can consume the processor resources on the domain controller performing the Inter-Site Topology Generator role. Consider decreasing the number of sites in the organization or configuring dedicated bridgehead servers. Also verify that the AD DS site link configuration corresponds with the actual WAN link configuration in your network. AD DS replication should use the WAN connections with maximum available bandwidth whenever possible.

More Info   Two excellent resources for troubleshooting specific AD DS replication errors are the Troubleshooting Active Directory Replication Problems Web page (*http://technet2 .microsoft.com/windowsserver/en/library/4f504103-1a16-41e1-853a-c68b77bf3f7e1033 .mspx?mfr=true*) and the How to Troubleshoot Intra-Site Replication Failures Web page (*http://support.microsoft.com/kb/249256*).

Tools for Troubleshooting AD DS Replication

Windows Server 2008 provides several tools for troubleshooting AD DS replication. All of these tools are installed on Windows Server 2008 when the server is configured as a domain controller.

Active Directory Sites And Services

In addition to using Active Directory Sites And Services to configure sites and replication, you can also use it perform some basic troubleshooting tasks. These tasks include:

■ **Forcing the KCC to recalculate the replication topology**   To do this, expand the domain controller object in the AD DS site servers container, right-click NTDS Settings, point to All Tasks, and click Check Replication Topology. This forces the KCC to run immediately rather than waiting for the next scheduled update.

- **Forcing a domain controller to pull replication changes**   Locate the domain controller to which you want to pull changes in the site servers container. In the NTDS Settings container under the domain controller, right-click the connection object with the domain controller from which you want to pull changes and then click Replicate Now. If both domain controllers are in the same site, you will get an error message or get a message the replication was successful. If the domain controllers are in different sites, you will get a message telling you that the domain controller will attempt immediate replication. Check the Event Viewer for replication errors.

- **Forcing the replication of the configuration partition from or to a domain controller**   When you right-click the NTDS object under a domain controller other than the domain controller that is the current focus for Active Directory Sites And Services, you can choose to Replicate configuration from the selected DC or Replicate configuration to the selected DC. One of the benefits of using these commands is that the configuration information will be replicated even if no connection object exists between the domain controllers. This option is useful when a replication partner was removed from the domain while a domain controller was offline and the domain controller cannot locate other domain controllers to create new connection objects.

Repadmin

The most useful tool for monitoring and troubleshooting replication is Repadmin. You can use the Repadmin.exe command-line tool to view the replication topology from the perspective of each domain controller. You can also use Repadmin.exe to manually create the replication topology, force replication events between domain controllers, and view the replication metadata and up-to-date state of vectors.

To run the Repadmin command-line tool, use the following syntax:

```
repadmin command arguments [/u:[domain\]user /pw:{password|*}]
```

You need to provide the user account information only if the current logged-on user is not a member of the Domain Admins group.

The following examples use some of the available command arguments for the Repadmin command-line tool:

- To export the replication information on a domain controller to a .csv file, use this syntax:

  ```
  Repadmin /showrepl DC1.Adatum.com /csv>filename.csv
  ```

  This command is useful because you can open the .csv file by using an application like Microsoft Office Excel and search the file.

- To display the replication partners of the domain controller named DC1, use this syntax:

  ```
  repadmin /showreps DC1.Adatum.com
  ```

- To display the highest USN on the domain controller named DC2, use this syntax:

  ```
  repadmin /showvector dc=Adatum,dc=com DC2.Adatum.com
  ```

- To display the connection objects for the domain controller named DC1, use this syntax:

  ```
  repadmin /showconn DC1.Adatum.com
  ```

- To initiate a replication event between two replication partners, use this syntax:

  ```
  repadmin /replicate DC2.Adatum.com DC1.Adatum.com dc=Adatum,dc=com
  ```

- To initiate a replication event for a specified directory partition with all of its replication partners, use this syntax:

  ```
  repadmin /syncall DC1.Adatum.com dc= Adatum,dc=com
  ```

  Running this command will result in the domain controller requesting updates for all directory partitions from all direct replication partners. If you want to force the domain controller to initiate replication of local changes, add the */p* parameter at the end of the command.

Dcdiag

The Dcdiag.exe tool performs a number of tests that check domain controllers for issues that might affect replication. These tests include connectivity, replication, topology integrity, and intersite health tests.

To run the Dcdiag command-line tool, use the following syntax:

```
dcdiag command arguments [/v /f:LogFile /ferr:ErrLog ]
```

In the command, the optional switch */v* directs the command to produce detailed output, */f* directs the output to the log file, and */ferr* redirects fatal error output to a separate log file. To run all of the dcdiag tests on a local computer and display the results in the command prompt window, just type **DCdiag** and press Enter. To check a remote domain controller, run DCDiag /s:*Servername*, where *Servername* is the remote domain controller name.

Following are a few of the tests that can be run using DCDiag:

- **Connectivity**   Tests whether domain controllers are DNS registered, can be pinged, and have LDAP/RPC connectivity.

- **Replications**   Checks for timely replication and any replication errors between domain controllers.

- **NetLogons**   Checks that the appropriate logon privileges exist to allow replication to proceed.

- **Intersite**   Checks for failures that would prevent or temporarily hold up intersite replication and tries to predict how long it will take before the KCC is able to recover. Results of this test are often not valid, especially in atypical site or KCC configurations or at the Windows Server 2008 forest functional level.

- **FSMOCheck**   Checks that the domain controller can contact a KDC, a Time Server, a Preferred Time Server, a PDC, and a global catalog server. This test does not test any of the servers for operations master roles.

- **Services**   Checks if the appropriate domain controller services are running.

- **Kccevent**   Checks that the Knowledge Consistency Checker is completing without errors.

- **Topology**   Checks that the KCC has generated a fully connected topology for all domain controllers.

> **Note**   For detailed information on how to use the Repadmin and DCDiag command-line tools, type the command name followed by **/?**.

Additional Tools

Two standard server administrative tools are also useful for monitoring and troubleshooting replication. The first tool is the Event Viewer. One of the event logs added to all domain controllers is a Directory Service event log. Most of the directory replication-related events are logged in this event log, and this should be one of the first places you look when replication fails.

The Reliability and Performance Monitor tool is useful for monitoring the amount of replication activity happening on the server. When a server is promoted to be a domain controller, the *DirectoryServices* performance object and several file replication performance objects are added to the list of performance counters. These performance counters can be used to monitor the level of replication traffic as well as a wide variety of other AD DS–related activities.

Summary

One of the key aspects to managing Windows Server 2008 AD DS is understanding how replication works. A stable replication environment is crucial in maintaining an up-to-date copy of all directory information on all the domain controllers in the forest, which is essential to ensure consistent user logon and directory search performance. By understanding how replication works within a site and between sites, you can also design and implement the optimal replication configuration.

Best Practices

- Replication within a single site happens automatically and quickly and rarely fails. If all of your company's domain controllers are connected by fast network connections, you should implement a single site.

■ On the other hand, if your company has multiple locations where you install domain controllers, creating additional sites is the easiest and best way to manage AD DS–related traffic across WAN links with limited available bandwidth. Not only do multiple sites limit replication traffic, but they also keep client authentication traffic local.

■ Develop a regular practice of monitoring AD DS replication. Consider using a tool such as the Active Directory Management Pack with System Center Operations Manager to monitor replication on all domain controllers in your site. If you do not have a tool like this, regularly monitor the Directory Service event log and either the DFS Replication event log (if your AD DS forest is at the Windows Server 2008 functional level) or the File Replication Service event log.

■ In most organizations, the most important cause of AD DS replication errors is DNS lookup errors. By integrating DNS with AD DS and taking advantage of the DNS directory partitions, you can minimize the chances of DNS errors.

Additional Resources

These resources contain additional information related to this topic:

Related Information

■ Chapter 14, "Monitoring and Maintaining Active Directory," provides details on using monitoring tools such as Event Viewer and Reliability and Performance Monitor to monitor AD DS domain controllers, including monitoring replication.

■ Chapter 5, "Designing the Active Directory Domain Services Structure," goes into detail on designing the AD DS site configuration.

■ "Troubleshooting Active Directory Replication Problems" is located at *http:// technet2.microsoft.com/windowsserver/en/library/4f504103-1a16-41e1-853a-c68b77bf3f7e1033.mspx?mfr=true*. This Web site provides detailed steps for troubleshooting Active Directory replication issues and links to Knowledge Base articles that address specific Event IDs.

■ The "How to Troubleshoot Intra-Site Replication Failures" Knowledge Base article at *http://support.microsoft.com/kb/249256* provides details on how to troubleshoot intrasite replication errors. This KB article, as well as many of the other KB articles listed next, refers to Windows Server 2003. Many of the steps in troubleshooting AD DS replication have not changed in Windows Server 2008.

■ The "Active Directory Replication Troubleshooter" located at *http://blogs.technet.com/ rbeard47/pages/active-directory-replication-troubleshooter.aspx* provides a detailed step-by-step process for troubleshooting Active Directory replication.

- "Fixing Replication DNS Lookup Problems (Event IDs 1925, 2087, 2088)" at *http://technet2.microsoft.com/windowsserver/en/library/43e6f617-fb49-4bb4-8561-53310219f9971033.mspx?mfr=true* provides detailed information on how to troubleshoot replication errors related to DNS.

- "How to Troubleshoot RPC Endpoint Mapper Errors" (*http://support.microsoft.com/kb/839880*) provides detailed information on how to troubleshoot replication errors related to RPC connectivity.

- "Service Overview and Network Port Requirements for the Windows Server System" (*http://support.microsoft.com/kb/832017*) describes the ports required by most Windows Server services, including AD DS replication. This information is very useful when configuring firewalls between domain controllers.

- "Replication Not Working Properly Between Domain Controllers After Deleting One from Sites and Services" (*http://support.microsoft.com/kb/262561*) describes how to use the Repadmin tool to create manual connection objects to domain controllers that have been removed from Active Directory Sites And Services.

- "Active Directory Replication Technologies" at *http://technet2.microsoft.com/windowsserver/en/library/53998db6-a972-495e-a4e7-e3ca3f60b5841033.mspx* provides detailed information on how AD DS replication works.

- The Script Repository: Active Directory Web site, located at *http://www.microsoft.com/technet/scriptcenter/scripts/ad/default.mspx,* has several scripts that can be used to enumerate and modify the AD DS site and site link configuration.

Related Tools

Windows Server 2008 provides several tools that can be used when managing and trouble-shooting replication. Table 4-2 lists some of these tools and explains when you would use each of the tools.

Table 4-2   AD DS Replication Tools

Tool Name	Description and Use
Dnslint.exe	This tool is a free download from Microsoft. (See *http://support.microsoft.com/kb/321045* for the download location.) This tool can be used to help diagnose common DNS name resolution issues and to verify that DNS records used specifically for AD DS replication are correct.
Nslookup.exe	This tool is included in all Microsoft Windows server and client operating systems. Nslookup is used to query DNS servers and to obtain detailed responses. The information obtained using Nslookup can be used to diagnose and solve name resolution problems, verify that resource records are added or updated correctly in a zone, and debug other server-related problems.
Active Directory Sites And Services	This tool can be used to configure sites and replication and to perform some basic AD DS replication troubleshooting tasks.

Table 4-2   **AD DS Replication Tools** *(continued)*

Tool Name	Description and Use
Repadmin.exe	Use this command-line tool to view the replication topology from the perspective of each domain controller. You can also use Repadmin.exe to manually create the replication topology, force replication events between domain controllers, and view the replication metadata and up-to-date state of vectors.
DCDiag.exe	Use this tool to perform tests that check domain controllers for issues that might affect replication.

Resources on the CD

- ADDSSite.xlsx is a spreadsheet template for documenting AD DS site information.

- ListADDSSites.ps1 is a simple Windows PowerShell script for listing information about all of the sites in your forest.

Related Help Topics

- "Checklist: Configure an Additional Site" in Active Directory Sites And Services help.

- "Checklist: Configure the Intersite Replication Schedule" in Active Directory Sites And Services help.

- "Troubleshooting Active Directory Domain Services Replication" in Active Directory Sites And Services help.

Part II
Designing and Implementing Windows Server 2008 Active Directory

Chapter 5

Designing the Active Directory Domain Services Structure

In many organizations, the Active Directory Domain Services (AD DS) infrastructure may be the single most important component in the IT environment. In these organizations, AD DS provides central authentication and authorization services that enable single sign-on access to many other network services in the organization. This means that it is critical that the AD DS infrastructure be designed so that it addresses as many of the organization's requirements as possible.

This chapter provides an overview of the planning process that you must go through before you deploy Windows Server 2008 AD DS. For the most part, this chapter assumes that you are working with a large corporation with multiple business units and locations. If you are working with a smaller company, many of the concepts discussed here will still apply.

This chapter then looks at the biggest question first: How many forests do you need in your network? From there the chapter moves on to discuss splitting the forests into domains and planning for the domain namespace. Once your domains are in place, you also need to create an organizational unit (OU) structure for each domain. As a parallel activity to creating the AD DS logical structure, you also need to design the physical AD DS components, so this chapter also addresses how to design sites and domain controller placements.

> **Note**   Designing a Windows Server 2008 AD DS infrastructure is not significantly different from designing an Active Directory infrastructure in Microsoft Windows 2000 or Windows Server 2003. Windows Server 2008 AD DS includes several important new features that will affect AD DS design, but many of the core concepts of AD DS have not changed, and many of the design decisions have not changed. If you already have Active Directory deployed, you can use this chapter to review your current design in preparation for upgrading to Windows Server 2008 AD DS.

Defining Directory Service Requirements

Before you can begin designing your organization's directory service, you must first understand why your organization plans to deploy the directory service and the state of the current directory service. Very few organizations deploy a new technology just because it is the latest and greatest option. Before investing in a new technology, managers need to see a clear business benefit. That means that you must understand and be able to clearly explain to business decision makers how a new technology such as Windows Server 2008 AD DS will address existing and new business requirements.

Figure 5-1 shows a checklist of the types of requirements that you need to collect when starting your AD DS design.

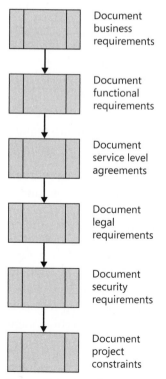

Figure 5-1   Use the AD DS design requirements checklist to determine the information that you need to collect.

> ## Business Involvement in AD DS Design
>
> When you design AD DS for a corporation, it is important to get the company's management involved in the design process. The business users are the primary consumers for the services provided by the Information Technology (IT) infrastructure, so it is essential that your design meet their requirements and have the support of their management.
>
> The amount of involvement in the design process that business units require varies greatly among companies. In almost every organization, however, the involvement includes at least an approval of the high-level goals of the design project. These goals might revolve around issues such as accessibility of information, security, ease of management, and usability. Business managers are also usually involved in high-level and highly visible decisions that cannot easily be changed after deployment. These decisions include how many forests and domains are needed in the network and the number of domain namespaces to be deployed.

Defining Business and Technical Requirements

Organizations invest in technology to solve business problems or to provide new business opportunities. Business requirements typically dictate the reasons a new technology is being implemented within the organization. Technical requirements frequently define how the new technology will be designed and deployed to address the business requirements.

Business Requirements

Business requirements can take many different forms. For example, an organization may need to:

- **Become more efficient**   Most businesses are very competitive and strive to be more efficient than their competitors. When evaluating new technologies, these organizations typically will invest in the technology if it will improve efficiency.

- **Meet an external requirement**   Forces outside an organization, such as the government or business partners, may impose requirements. For example, government regulations may require that organizations ensure the privacy of all user and customer information.

- **Avoid disruptions to business processes**   A current technology may meet most business requirements. However, if it is unreliable, an organization may invest in a new technology that provides the requisite reliability and availability.

- **Explore new business areas or solutions**   Organizations sometimes use technologies to pursue new business opportunities. For example, deploying Web-based tools for selling products and services has significantly increased the business potential for many organizations.

A technology deployment is more likely to address an organization's needs if business requirements are defined clearly and concisely at the project's inception. Additionally, it is easier to measure a project's success if the project team is knowledgeable about the business problems that the project must solve.

Functional Requirements

Functional requirements define a system's expected behavior. Functional requirements are derived from business requirements. Business requirements define the problem to address, while functional requirements define how the proposed technology should solve that problem.

For example, an organization may define a business requirement that all users in all offices must always be able to gain access to shared resources such as an e-mail system or business applications during regular business requirements. The resulting functional requirement may specify the server locations and configurations required to address the business requirement.

Functional requirements are used to create the *functional specification*, which describes the proposed solution in exacting detail and forms the basis for project plans and schedules. The functional specification is important because it:

- **Establishes an agreement between the deployment team and the technology consumer or customer**   This enables the team to determine the correct solution to meet the customer's expectations.

- **Provides in-depth project details to help the team determine if it is building the solution correctly**   This, in turn, makes the solution easier to validate and verify.

- **Enables the team to estimate budgets and schedules**   The quantity of resources and their respective skill sets are difficult to determine without the specific detail that a functional specification provides.

 Note   In addition to functional requirements, every design has nonfunctional requirements. Nonfunctional specifications do not define what the system does but rather how the system will perform and/or the quality of service it will provide. Common nonfunctional requirements include system availability, maintainability, performance, reliability, and scalability.

Service Level Agreements

Service level agreements (SLAs) are understandings between an organization and the group managing the information system infrastructure that define expected performance levels. It is important to define an SLA because it documents the service expectations and requirements that an organization expects the IT department to deliver. SLAs may define several categories of expected performance, including:

- **Availability**   For example, an SLA may require that all users can logon on to the network and access critical applications 99.99 percent of the time during business hours and 99.9 percent of the time during nonbusiness hours.

- **Performance**   For example, an SLA may specify that all users should be able to logon to AD DS within 15 seconds of entering their credentials.

- **Recovery**   For example, an SLA may stipulate that in the event of a single server failure, the services provided by the server will be restored to at least 75% of normal capacity within 4 hours of server failure.

> **Note**   The SLAs that organizations use can vary from informal to very structured. Informal SLAs often are not documented, but rather are general expectations for system performance that are well known. For example, an organization may have an internal, unwritten policy that certain servers should not be restarted during business hours except in cases of emergencies. Formal SLAs typically are documented extensively and detail expectations determined from negotiations between service providers and business customers. These SLAs may define exact expectations for each system component in the system and may include penalties if expectations are not met. Often, the most formal SLAs are negotiated between business customers and outsourced IT providers.

SLAs have a significant impact on a project's scope and budget, so it is important to define them at the project's inception. Business requirements plus functional and nonfunctional requirements typically form the basis for initial SLA negotiations. In most cases, the project team and business sponsors negotiate the final SLA details. Initial requirements may set very high expectations. However, meeting those high expectations can be expensive. For example, if an SLA requires that all users in all offices be able to logon on to AD DS at all times, you may need to deploy fully redundant systems or WAN connections throughout the organization. The cost of this is likely would be prohibitive. Thus, the organization may negotiate a more acceptable performance level at a more reasonable cost.

Legal Requirements

Information systems make it very easy to collect, store, and transmit information. Many countries have imposed compliance requirements that mandate how organizations ensure data confidentiality. Examples of legislation restricting how organizations manage information include:

- United States:
    - Sarbanes-Oxley Act of 2002 (SOX)
    - Gramm-Leach-Bliley Act (Financial Modernization Act)
    - Health Insurance Portability and Accountability Act of 1996 (HIPAA)
    - Uniting and Strengthening America by Providing Appropriate Tools Required to Intercept and Obstruct Terrorism Act of 2001 (USA Patriot Act)
- Canada: The Personal Information Protection and Electronic Documents Act
- Australia: Federal Privacy Act

- Europe: European Union Data Protection Directive (EUDPD)

- Japan: Japan's Personal Information Protection Act

When designing the AD DS infrastructure, you need to consider these legal requirements. In some cases, you will be able to design technical solutions to address the requirements. For example, if all customer information must be kept confidential from all but certain specified users, you may choose to store customer information in a separate Active Directory Domain Services (AD DS) forest or deploy an Active Directory Lightweight Directory Services (AD LDS) instance with strict restrictions on who can access the data. To prevent users from sending confidential data outside the organization, you may implement an Active Directory Rights Management Services (AD RMS) solution.

Technical solutions can rarely address all of the legal requirements. For example, if you use AD RMS to protect confidential data, a user can still use a digital camera to take pictures of the confidential data and send the data outside the organization. Users with access to confidential customer information can still share that information with unauthorized users. To address these issues, organizations must complement the technical solutions with corporate policy-based solutions that clearly specify acceptable actions and consequences for not following acceptable actions.

Security Requirements

All IT deployments will also have security requirements. These requirements become especially important when deploying AD DS because AD DS is likely to be used to secure access to most data, services, and applications on the network.

To identify security requirements, ask the following questions:

- What are the organization's security risks? There are many possible answers to this question, including:

  - Mobile users who travel extensively and must connect to the internal network to gain access to e-mail, applications, or data.

  - Users outside the organization who may require access to Web sites located in a perimeter network and be able to authenticate using their internal AD DS user accounts.

  - Offices that are not physically secure, where malicious users might be able to gain access to the network. Other offices may not have a secure location for storing domain controllers or other servers.

  - A database with confidential customer information that must be accessible to Web applications running in the perimeter network.

- How are the security requirements currently addressed? Almost all organizations have addressed at least some security requirements. For example, virtually all organizations have implemented antivirus solutions and firewalls to protect the internal network from Internet-based attacks.

■ What gaps exist between security requirements and current solutions? These gaps will vary between different organizations. For example, some organizations have deployed applications that require users to authenticate using credentials that are not secure when transmitted on the network. To simplify the user experience in these situations, some organizations will assign the same user name and password for the application as is used to log on to AD DS. This means that if the credentials used to authenticate to the application are compromised, the AD DS credentials are also compromised.

■ What general security requirements or guidelines must the project follow? Most organizations have general security requirements that apply to all projects. These requirements could include:

❑ All servers must be located in a secure server room which can be accessed by only authorized users.

❑ All authentication traffic must be secured while transmitted on the network.

❑ All users who access the internal network through a virtual private network (VPN) must use two-factor authentication.

Security requirements can sometimes conflict with business requirements. For example, a business requirement may state that all users in a particular department must be able to access the internal network through a VPN. The security requirement may state that all VPN users must provide two-factor authentication. If not all users in the department have mobile computers that support two-factor authentication, then there is a conflict between the business requirement and the security requirement.

Security requirements often place restrictions on what a project can accomplish. A technical solution may meet or exceed business requirements, but if the person who is responsible for defining security requirements does not consider it secure, it may need to be revised or the business requirement may need to be removed. In many organizations, some security requirements are not negotiable, while other security requirements may be modified to accommodate a critical business requirement.

Project Constraints

Project constraints define the project's parameters by setting limits on what can be done. For example, if the project has a fixed budget, planners may have to use the equipment they can afford rather than the equipment they consider ideal for the job.

There are three general categories of project constraints:

■ **Resource constraints** A project's budget is a common resource constraint. If the proposed budget cannot meet the projected personnel costs, equipment costs, and software costs, the project cannot continue or may need to be modified to address the restraints. Additionally, a project may have other resource constraints:

❏ The appropriate personnel may not be available or their training may not be sufficient to complete the project.

❏ Computer resources or equipment may not be accessible.

■ **Schedule constraints** A project schedule also may restrict what the project can accomplish. For example, many organizations do not allow changes to the IT environment during specific times, such as during the end of the corporate fiscal year or peak business cycles. If a project is due for completion during one of these periods, the project scope may require modification. Additionally, a project may be constrained by the schedule of other projects.

■ **Feature constraints** Feature constraints can impact a project's start or scope. For example, if an organization is evaluating a new product based on a particular feature and that feature is not available or does not meet the company requirements, the organization may choose to cancel the project. If a particular feature is critical, the project scope may be modified to include the feature.

The project team and business sponsors often negotiate project constraints, as well as business requirements and SLAs. The budget may seem like a firm constraint, but if increasing the budget results in meeting an important business requirement or SLA level, the budget may be adjusted to include the requirement.

Documenting the Current Environment

Once you have gathered the directory service requirements, the next step is to analyze the current network and directory environment. Analyzing the current environment helps determine what needs to change when deploying the new infrastructure. This information provides a starting point for determining the appropriate design and implementation plan for the Windows Server 2008 deployment.

Figure 5-2 shows a checklist of the types of information that you need to collect when starting your AD DS design.

> **Important** As you collect information about the current network infrastructure or any other component in the current environment, you should also ensure that you collect information about any planned changes to the environment. For example, if the WAN links are going to be upgraded before AD DS will be deployed, include this information in your documentation. These changes may interfere with the AD DS deployment because of project dependencies or may result in changes to your design.

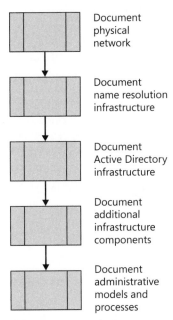

Figure 5-2   AD DS design current environment checklist.

Documenting the Physical Network Infrastructure

When documenting the physical network infrastructure, include the following components:

- **The number, geographic locations, and link speed of all sites where network services exist**   It is important to identify all locations that make up the network infrastructure, such as buildings, campuses, and branch offices. You also must determine the connection types and network speed for each location. It is also important to consider the physical security of the various locations. For branch offices in particular, it is common to have decreased physical security, and this will affect the design choices you have to make.

- **A routing topology map that illustrates the physical sites and the Internet Protocol (IP) subnets in use at those sites**   This map is useful in planning or integrating with the AD DS site design.

- **Bandwidth, latency, and current usage**   Bandwidth is the transmission speed over a network connection in kilobits per second (Kpbs). Latency refers to the time it takes, in milliseconds, to transfer data between two points. Both of these factors combine to determine how much data that can be transmitted in a set time period over the network. This information, as well as the current applications using the network and the number of users at various locations and their use patterns, can be used to create a design for your AD DS implementation that provides a satisfactory user experience.

- **Firewall configuration requirements**   If your organization has deployed firewalls between company locations, document the firewall locations and the firewall rules. Incorrectly configured firewalls can disrupt DNS name resolution, AD DS replication, and authentication.

■ **Nontechnical constraints**   These include geographical, political, or cost-related restrictions resulting from a change or upgrade of network links between sites.

On the Disc   You can use the CurrentNetworkEnviroment.xlsx file on the CD to document the current networking environment. Several tabs in the slide refer to associated network diagrams. One of the best tools for creating network diagrams is Microsoft Office Visio. Four Visio templates that can be used for diagramming LAN and WAN configurations are included on the CD. You can download additional Visio templates from *http://office.microsoft.com/en-us/templates/default.aspx*. A sample WAN diagram (WANDiagram_Sample.vsd) is also included on the CD.

Documenting the Name Resolution Infrastructure

AD DS requires a DNS (Domain Name System) infrastructure so that domain controllers can locate each other and so that client computers can locate domain controllers. When documenting the DNS infrastructure, include the following:

■ What type of DNS software is currently in use? Is it able to handle service (SRV) resource records?

■ Who maintains and administers the organization's internal and external DNS servers and zone information? What are the IP addresses of all DNS servers?

■ Who assigns DNS names and domains within the organization? Is there a centralized authority for DNS namespace planning and control?

■ Where are internal DNS servers located on the network? What zones are stored on each DNS server?

■ How is DNS name resolution across multiple namespaces configured? How are root hints, forwarders, conditional forwarders, stub zones, and delegations used to facilitate name resolution?

■ Are the DNS zones AD DS-integrated?

On the Disc   Refer to the DNS Zone Configuration and the DNS Server Configuration tabs in the CurrentNetworkEnvironment job aid located on the CD to document the current name DNS infrastructure.

Documenting the Active Directory Infrastructure

Most organizations that deploy AD DS will already be running some version of Active Directory. Before starting your AD DS design, ensure that you understand the current environment. When documenting the current Active Directory deployment, include the following:

■ Active Directory forest and domain topology

❑ Does your organization consist of a single forest or multiple forests? If the organization has deployed multiple forests, you may want to explore options for consolidating the forests.

❑   How many domains are implemented in each forest?

❑   What is the purpose of each domain? In order to determine if you can consolidate domains, you need to understand why each domain was created.

❑   If the organization has deployed multiple forests, what rationale does the organization have for maintaining multiple forests? If the rationale for choosing multiple domains is still valid, you will probably have to retain multiple forests. If not, you will be able to explore the option of consolidating forests.

■   Active Directory trust configuration

❑   What trusts are configured in addition to the default trusts configured within an AD DS forest? As you document the trusts, determine the rationale for each trust. Is the rationale still valid?

❑   What trust relationships exist with external domains? Determine whether these trusts are still required or if additional trusts are required.

■   What are the domain and forest functional levels? As you raise the domain and forest functional levels, you gain new features in Active Directory. If the domain and forest functional levels are not at the highest level supported by the operating systems on the domain controllers, why has the functional level not been raised?

■   Active Directory site configuration: Document the current Active Directory site topology, including:

❑   Number of configured sites

❑   Subnet configurations and their site association

❑   IP site links and their member sites

❑   IP site link costs and replication schedules

■   Domain controller and global catalog server configuration: As you analyze each Active Directory site, document the configuration and location of each domain controller and global catalog server. As part of the domain controller documentation, identify which domain controllers are hosting the forest and domain operation master roles.

■   FSMO role holders: AD DS has a number of operation master roles and it is very important to understand which domain controllers in the domain or forest holds them.

■   Time service configuration: Time synchronization is critical in an AD DS environment, so you should review how time service is configured in your forest.

■   Organizational unit (OU) configuration: As you analyze the domain, document the current OU structure. For each OU, document the location in the domain hierarchy, the purpose for each OU, and the delegated permissions and linked Group Policy objects (GPOs).

■   Group Policy configuration: Many organizations use Active Directory Group Policy to provide centralized management and security of users, groups and computers, and other directory objects. Document the GPOs, the purpose for each GPO, the inheritance and filtering settings for each GPO, and the GPO settings.

■ Active Directory groups: Document the group configuration, including the group scope and type, the group owners and membership list, and how the group is used. This is particularly important for all groups with administrative permissions.

On the Disc   You can use the CurrentDirectoryEnviroment.xlsx file on the CD to document the current Active Directory environment.

Current Active Directory Configuration and AD DS Design

An important requirement in AD DS design is balancing the optimal design for a network in which it is currently deployed. As you prepare your AD DS design, consider the current Active Directory design and the implications of migrating from that infrastructure to a different design in AD DS. The current domain structure might not be ideal. However, just upgrading the current domains is significantly easier (and less costly) than creating the ideal AD DS structure and then migrating all of the domain objects to the new domains. This means that you might be forced to work with a less-than-ideal AD DS structure because you are required to upgrade the current domains. Of course, you might also find that the current structure is so far from the ideal structure that it is worth the extra work and cost of restructuring all the domains. Probably the most common scenario will be one where the current structure is almost acceptable, but you would like to make some changes. In this scenario, you might upgrade one or more domains and then merge other domains into the upgraded domains.

As you prepare your AD DS design, consider creating an ideal AD DS design and then create another design based on the optimal upgrade scenario for the current environment. Chances are good that your final design will fall somewhere between the ideal and the optimal designs.

This interaction between an ideal design and what is realistically possible illustrates another important aspect of AD DS design: it is almost always an iterative process. You might start out with one design in mind, and as you gather additional information, you will likely need to modify that design. As you start testing the implementation or migration scenarios, you might again modify your AD DS design.

It is important, however, that some parts of your design be finalized before you begin deployment. Design decisions such as the number of forests and domains as well as the domain namespace design are difficult to change after deployment has started. Other issues, such as final OU design and site design, are fairly easily changed after deployment.

Documenting Additional Infrastructure Components

In addition to the network infrastructure and directory components, you may need to collect information on additional infrastructure components, such as:

■ **Exchange Server implementation**   If your organization has deployed Exchange Server, you will need to document the Exchange Server infrastructure. Exchange Servers and messaging clients have a strong dependency on AD DS that will affect the number and placement of domain controllers and global catalog servers. In addition, if your organization has deployed or is planning on deploying Exchange Server 2007, you will need to consider Exchange message routing when designing the site configuration. For more details on how Exchange Server may influence your AD DS design, see the sidebar, "Exchange Server 2007 and Site Design," later in this chapter.

- **Directory enabled applications** In addition to Exchange Server, document all other directory-enabled applications deployed in the organization. In your documentation, describe whether the application is currently using Active Directory or another directory service, whether the application requires AD DS schema changes, and where the application is deployed.

- **Backup and disaster recovery infrastructure** In most cases, the AD DS domain controllers will need to integrate with the current backup and disaster recovery infrastructure. Collect information on the backup and disaster recovery technology as well as on backup schedules and processes.

- **Additional applications** Create an inventory of the products used in your environment, including antivirus solutions, storage management software, and system management and monitoring tools.

Documenting Administrative Models and Processes

Your organization's administrative structure and processes have great influence on the IT infrastructure design. This is particularly true with an AD DS design because of the flexibility that AD DS provides for delegating administrative tasks. When documenting the administrative model, include the following:

- **Current organizational administrative model** In some organizations, IT management may be centralized, while in other organizations, the responsibilities may be delegated to regional areas or individual business units. The most common approach is a combination of the two, in which some IT functions are centralized, such as network provisioning and security, while other functions, such as user account or desktop computer management, are delegated to geographic or business subdivisions.

- **User account administrative model** In a centralized environment, a single group of administrators may perform these tasks for all users throughout the organization. In a decentralized environment, this responsibility may lie with the departmental team or with some other team, such as the human resources or corporate security departments.

- **Business unit structure** It is not necessary to explore exhaustively the interrelationships between an organization's business units or divisions. However, it is useful to examine some aspects of these relationships. For example:

  ❑ Do separate business units or divisions require security boundaries between them? If so, a multiple-forest design may be required.

❑ What are the requirements for communication between different business units? For example, is a unified directory or address list necessary for the entire organization?

❑ How is cross-unit communication controlled? In other words, which group is responsible for locating and resolving authentication, network, or protocol problems that hinder communication between users and resources in different units?

■ **Troubleshooting processes**   Most large organizations have a well-defined troubleshooting process that may include multiple levels of support. The information about the current troubleshooting processes is useful when you create the deployment plan and also helps to ensure that the appropriate administrators receive the necessary training for troubleshooting the AD DS deployment.

■ **Change control process**   The change control process varies greatly between organizations. Some organizations have not implemented a formal change control process, while others implement strict change requests, approval, and notification processes. Key questions to ask regarding change control processes include:

❑ How does the organization implement IT changes? You need to identify specific processes that take place when changes are implemented.

❑ How are IT infrastructure changes approved? Before changes are made, specific approval may be required by IT managers, enterprise administrators, or security personnel. You need to document who the decision makers are and how they affect the change-approval process.

❑ How are change notifications handled? Before the change takes place, all affected users must be notified of the change and any impact it may cause. It is important to document all current change-notification processes and the requirements specifying when change notifications are required.

❑ What are the emergency escalation notification processes? If issues arise during implementation of the approved change, you will need to know who to contact to provide troubleshooting and recovery procedures.

❑ What are the time frames for making changes that may impact availability? Many organizations limit when critical network services can be changed or taken offline.

❑ What are the risk management processes related to change management? A complete change control process includes a risk analysis and processes for mitigating risks.

Designing the Forest Structure

After collecting the business and technical requirements and documenting the current environment, you are ready to start designing the AD DS infrastructure. Probably the most important decision you need to make early in the design process is how many forests you will create. Deploying a single AD DS forest makes it easy to share and access information within the company. It also makes it easy to centrally manage the entire directory infrastructure.

However, using a single forest for a large corporation also requires a significant degree of cooperation and interdependence between possibly diverse and disconnected business units. Ultimately, the number of forests you deploy depends on what is more important in your company: sharing information with ease across all the domains in the forest or being able to maintain fully isolated control of a part of the directory structure.

Figure 5-3 shows the process for creating a forest design.

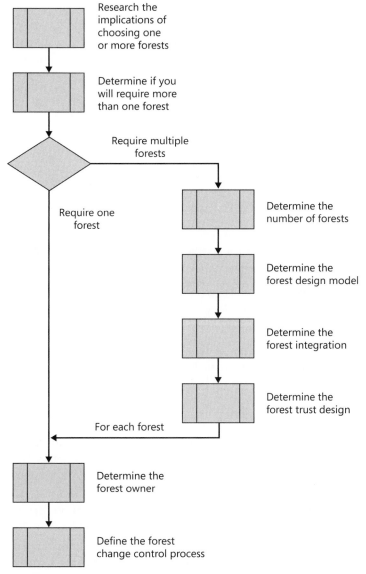

Figure 5-3 Creating a forest design.

Forests and AD DS Design

An AD DS forest is designed to be a self-contained unit. Inside the forest, it is easy to share information and collaborate with other users in the same unit. However, because the forest is a self-contained unit, the actions of one person can potentially impact everyone else in the forest. As you design the highest level of the AD DS infrastructure, you must decide whether you need to deploy one forest or multiple forests. Each forest is an integrated unit because it has the following characteristics:

- **Global catalog**   The forest can have many global catalog servers but has only one global catalog. The global catalog makes it easy to locate objects in any domain in the forest and to log on to any domain in the forest, regardless of which domain hosts your user account.

- **Configuration directory partition**   All domain controllers share the same configuration directory partition. This configuration information is used to optimize replication of information throughout the forest, to store application information for directory-enabled applications, and to share information through application directory partitions.

- **Trusts**   All of the domains in the forest are connected by two-way transitive trusts. There is no option to change this.

> **Note**   One of the best illustrations of the way a single forest is used to make collaboration easier is seen in how Microsoft Exchange 2000 Server and later versions use forests. The forest boundary is also the boundary for the Exchange Server organization. Exchange Server stores most of its configuration information in the configuration directory partition, making it easy to manage message routing throughout a large organization. The global address list (GAL) is made up of all the e-mail recipients in the global catalog. Having a single Exchange Server organization is highly desirable for most companies. Within one organization, calendar information, public folders, and recipient information is accessible to everyone, and many types of collaborations are enabled by default. As soon as you deploy multiple organizations (and multiple forests), these benefits are much more difficult to implement.

Although AD DS makes the sharing of information easier, it also enforces a number of restrictions that require the different business units in a company to cooperate in several different ways. These restrictions include:

- **One schema**   All the domains in the forest share a single schema. Although this sounds simple enough, this might be the most important reason for a corporation to deploy multiple forests. If one business unit decides to deploy an application that modifies the schema, all business units are affected. This can become overwhelming if 20 business units decide that they want to deploy applications that modify the schema. Every schema modification must be tested to ensure that it does not conflict with other schema changes.

■ **Change control policies**   Because changes made to the forest can affect every domain and because most significant changes should only be performed in a centralized manner, a well-defined change control policy must be in place.

■ **Centralized administration**   Choosing to deploy a single forest means that some components of network administration must be centralized. For example, the only group with the right to change the schema is the Schema Admins group. The only group with the right to add and remove domains from the forest is the Enterprise Admins group. Both of these groups exist in the forest root domain and the actions of these administrators will impact the entire forest. The Enterprise Admins group is automatically added to the domain local Administrators group on every domain controller in the forest. For some companies, this type of centralized administration is not acceptable.

■ **Trusted administrators**   Deploying a single forest requires a degree of trust from all administrators in all domains. Any administrator with the rights to administer a domain controller can make changes that will affect the entire forest. This means that all domain administrators must be highly trusted. You can reduce the risk of administrators making changes that will affect the entire forest by implementing RODCs in locations without highly trusted administrators.

As you deal with the question of how many forests you need to deploy, you will need to balance the benefits of deploying a single forest with the ways in which a single forest requires a high level of integration between domains, OUs, and the business units that these objects represent.

Single or Multiple Forests

As mentioned earlier, the most significant question that you need to answer when creating your forest design is whether you will have a single forest or multiple forests. This decision should be made before deployment because it is very difficult to change after deployment. There is no one-step process to merge forests; rather, you must move whatever objects you want in the new forest from the old forest. Also, there is no easy way to split a single forest into two. You must create a separate forest and then move objects from one to the other.

The most common AD DS forest deployment is a single forest. For most companies, the benefits of a shared global catalog, built-in trusts, and a common configuration directory partition are more important than maintaining a complete separation of all administrative roles. As you work with designing AD DS, your first choice should always be to deploy a single forest. Assume that you will be deploying a single forest, but be prepared to be convinced to do otherwise.

Having said this, there are clearly situations where multiple forests are the best option:

■ Some companies deploy separate AD DS forests in perimeter networks (or DMZs). Most organizations deploy servers that need to be directly accessible from the Internet in a perimeter network to provide an extra level of security for the internal network. These servers can be deployed as stand-alone servers, but by deploying a separate AD DS forest in the perimeter network, you can take advantage of the computer and user management features provided by AD DS while still maintaining isolation from the internal AD DS forest.

- Some companies do not have a strong requirement for intracompany collaboration. In some companies, business units operate quite independently of each other, with little need to exchange information other than e-mail. These companies are not giving anything up by deploying multiple forests.

- Some companies require a complete separation of network information. For security or legal reasons, a company might be required to ensure that some network information not be accessible to anyone outside a business unit. By default, the information in one forest is not visible in any other forest.

- Some companies require incompatible schema configurations. If two parts of the organization require a unique schema because they are deploying applications that make incompatible changes to the schema, you must create separate forests.

- Some companies cannot agree on centralized administrative procedures. If business units in the company cannot agree on policies for forest or schema change control, or if they cannot agree on centralized administration, you will have to deploy separate forests.

- Some companies must limit the scope of trust relationships. Within a forest, all domains share a transitive trust, and there is no option to break these trusts. If your network environment requires a trust configuration where there cannot be a two-way transitive trust between all domains, you must use multiple forests.

For some companies, deploying multiple forests might be an appealing option. However, deploying multiple forests adds significant complexity to the network infrastructure. Some of these issues are:

- Increased administrative effort required to manage the network. At least one domain as well as the forest-level configuration must be managed in each forest.

- Decreased ability of users to collaborate. One example of this is searching for resources on the network. Users are no longer able to search the global catalog for resources in the other forest. Users must be trained in how to search for resources outside of the global catalog.

- Additional administrative effort required for users to access resources between forests. Administrators must configure the trusts rather than using the built-in trusts. If any information must be synchronized between the forests, this must also be configured.

Business Involvement and Forest Design

Few companies have purely technical reasons to deploy more than one forest. A forest can contain multiple domains, with each domain containing hundreds of thousands of objects. The domains can be deployed with multiple namespaces and with distinct administration for each domain.

> However, when you present decision makers in your organization with the list of forest requirements, such as centralized control, a common schema, or trusted administrators, you are sure to meet resistance. The most common reasons why companies deploy multiple forests is company politics or the inability of different departments or business units to work out how to deal with the centralized components of managing a single forest. In some cases, the company cannot agree on a forest modification or schema modification process. In other cases, the fact that a domain administrator in one domain can affect all other domains in the forest means that a single forest is not acceptable. This is especially true in the common scenario in which a number of formerly independent companies must now work together due to corporate takeovers or mergers.
>
> Separate forests might be the answer for some of these companies, but you must also alert the decision makers to what they will lose if they do insist on multiple forests. Implementing multiple forests enables autonomy between business units, but also means that it is much more difficult to share information and the environment will be much more costly to manage.

Designing Forests for AD DS Security

For some companies, the decision to deploy more than one forest will come down to whether the company requires administrative autonomy or administrative isolation between business units. In AD DS, there are many types of administrative activity including both the configuration of the directory services (forest configuration, domain controller placement, Domain Name System [DNS] configuration) and management of the data in the directory service (managing user or group objects, Group Policy objects, and so forth).

> ### Service and Data Owners and Administrators
>
> In large organizations, AD DS administrative roles are often divided into different categories. One way to describe the different categories is to distinguish between service owners and administrators and data owners and administrators:
>
> - Service owners and administrators are responsible for AD DS as a service. That is, they are responsible for the design and administration of the AD DS infrastructure. The service owners will make the decisions on how many forests, domains, and sites will be required to ensure that the AD DS service meets the company requirements. The service administrators have the required rights and permissions to create and manage these AD DS objects.
>
> - Data owners and administrators are responsible for the data that is stored in AD DS. The data owners set policies and processes for managing the data, and the data administrators have the rights and permissions to create the AD DS objects within the structure defined by the service owners and administrators.

As a best practice, an organization should have very few service administrators. That is, very few accounts should have the required permissions to change the AD DS structure. By default, the Domain Admins in the forest root domain, Enterprise Admins, and Schema Admins groups have service owner permissions. However, because data administrator permissions can be limited to specific containers within an OU, the organization may have significantly more data administrators. To configure data administrator accounts, you should create the required groups and accounts and assign permissions specific to the container where the data administrator requires access.

You need to consider both service administrators and data administrators when designing for administrative isolation or autonomy. Although a service administrator may have a higher level of permissions, a data administrator can still make changes to AD DS that will affect the entire forest. For example, when a data administrator creates a new user account, the global catalog for the entire organization is modified.

For a more detailed discussion on the role of service and data owners and administrators, see "Creating a Forest Design" at *http://technet2.microsoft.com/windowsserver/en/ library/ff92f142-66ea-498b-ad0f-a379c411eb6e1033.mspx?mfr=true*. This guide is based on deploying Windows Server 2003 forests. Many of the principles apply to Windows Server 2008. You should also check the Windows Server 2008 TechCenter site for an updated version of this guide.

Administrative autonomy means that you have complete administrative control over some component of the forest. You might have administrative autonomy at the forest level, domain level, or OU level. However, administrative autonomy does not mean that you have ultimate or exclusive control. For example, you might be able to completely administer your domain, but the Enterprise Admins group from the forest root domain also has administrative permissions to your domain.

Administrative isolation, on the other hand, means that you have exclusive control over a component of the directory. If you have administrative isolation, no one else has any control over your part of the forest, and no one else can modify the directory service configuration or modify the data in your part of the forest.

AD DS provides many ways to achieve administrative autonomy. Domain administrators can do anything they want in a domain. OU administrators can be given full rights to create and administer any types of objects in an OU. A single forest in AD DS is designed for administrative delegation and autonomy.

However, if you require administrative isolation, the only way to achieve this is through the creation of separate forests. Part of the reason for this is because of the way AD DS is designed. The Enterprise Admins group is automatically added to each domain's local Administrators group. The Domain Admins group has full administrative control over every object in the domain and is automatically added to the Administrators group on every computer in the domain. Although the default configuration can be modified and the groups removed from the lower-level administrative groups, the higher-level administrators can always regain control of lower-level objects. This means that no part of the forest is isolated administratively.

Another reason a separate forest is needed for administrative isolation is because of the possibility of malicious actions on the part of administrators in the domain. Anyone with administrative access to a domain controller can violate the administrative isolation of any other partition in the forest. An administrator might install software on the domain controller in one domain that modifies the directory information for every domain in the forest. The administrator might modify his or her own security identifier (SID) so that it appears that he or she is a member of the Enterprise Admins group and then use this access to make forest-wide changes.

All of the domain controllers and partitions in the forest are tightly integrated, and any change made on one writable domain controller will be replicated to all other domain controllers. There is no security check on the validity of replicated information; there is only a security check on making changes to the directory information. So, if a malicious administrator manages to make a change to the directory information, all other domain controllers will accept the replicated change without question. For these reasons, you must create separate forests if you require administrative isolation. In some cases, you might be required to guarantee complete isolation of a directory partition. If so, you must accept the added administrative effort and loss of collaboration that comes from deploying multiple forests.

Many companies, however, require administrative autonomy along with a reasonable assurance that administrators from other partitions in the forest will not act maliciously. This reasonable assurance can be addressed in most companies by doing the following:

- Putting only highly trusted administrators into groups that have administrative control over domain controllers. These groups include the Domain Admins group as well as the domain's local Administrators, Server Operators, and Backup Operators groups. Administrative tasks that do not require access to the domain controllers should be delegated to other groups.
- Physically securing the domain controllers with only highly trusted administrators given access to the servers.
- Auditing all actions performed by high-level administrators.

High-level administrators should log on using the administrative account only when necessary. These administrators should also have normal user accounts for day-to-day work.

Forest Design Models

At a high level, there are three common forest design models used when creating the forest design. Most organizations will require one of these forest design models, although you may need to use a combination of designs in some organizations.

Organizational Forest Model

In the organizational forest model, the forests are designed along some organizational criteria. For example, an organization with multiple business units or geographical locations, or an organization that was formed by acquisitions or mergers, may choose to use an organizational forest model. To enable access to resources between the organizational entities, you can configure forest trusts between forests or external trusts between specific domains in each forest. See Figure 5-4 for an illustration of the organization forest model.

 Note   If an organization has deployed only a single forest, it is using the organizational forest model.

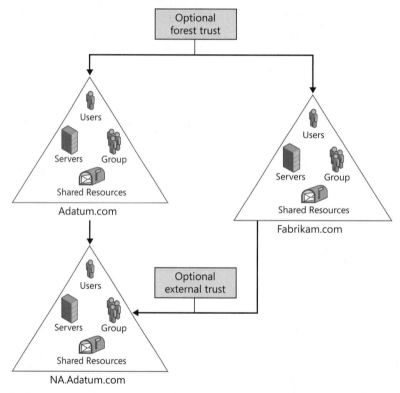

Figure 5-4   An organizational forest model.

In this model, all user accounts and shared resources related to each organizational entity are stored within the relevant forest. By creating separate forests, you can ensure administrative autonomy and isolation between the business units.

Resource Forest Model

In the resource forest model, user and group account management is isolated from resource management by creating separate forests for each function. All user and group accounts are stored in one or more account forests, and all shared resources are configured on servers in one or more resource forests. The resource forests do not contain user accounts other than administrative accounts and service accounts required by applications.

In the resource forest model, you must configure trusts between the two forests. In most cases, this will be a one-way forest trust configured so that users in the account forest can access the resources contained in the resource forest. You can enable two way trusts, external trusts, or forest trusts with selective authentication in this model. See Figure 5-5 for an illustration of the organization forest model.

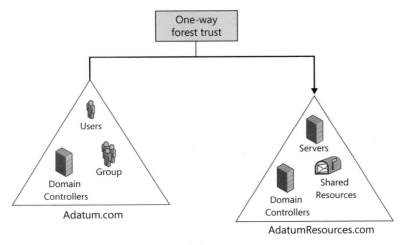

Figure 5-5   A resource forest model.

The resource forest model enables administrative autonomy and isolation for both the account and resource forests.

Restricted Access Forest Model

The restricted access forest model is a variation on the organizational forest model. In a restricted access forest model, a separate forest is created to contain user accounts and shared resources that must be isolated from the rest of the organization. The restricted access forest is different than the organizational forest in that no trusts are configured between the two domains.

The restricted access forest is designed to ensure administrative isolation. This means that no user account in a forest outside the restricted access forest can have any permissions or access to any data in the forest. If users in the organizational forest require access in the restricted access forest, they must have a separate user account created in this forest and must have two client computers, each joined to a different forest. See Figure 5-6 for an illustration of the restricted access forest model.

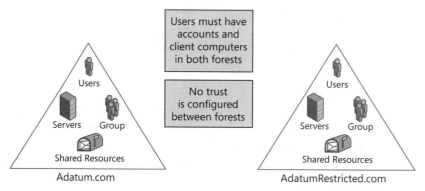

Figure 5-6   A restricted access forest model.

Defining Forest Ownership

Regardless of how many forests you deploy, you will need to identify the forest owners for each forest. In technical terms, it is easy to define who the forest owners are. The Schema Admins group, the Enterprise Admins group, and the Domain Admins group in the root domain can be considered the forest owners because they control what changes can be made to the forest. However, these roles are purely technical, and the people in these groups are almost never the final authority on whether or not modifications are actually made to the forest. For example, the Schema Admins group can change the schema, but a member of the Schema Admins group will usually not have the authority to decide whether a request for a schema change will be approved.

Forest owners should possess a combination of technical expertise and business awareness. They should be people who understand the overall business requirements of an organization, but who also understand the technical implications of fulfilling all these requirements. Forest owners might decide that an application that modifies the schema will be deployed because it brings significant business value to the company. The schema administrator is then given the task of modifying the schema as required.

In a company with multiple business units, the forest ownership group should be made up of representatives from all the business units. Although it is important that all business units be represented, this group must also be able to function efficiently. That is, a process must be in place so that the group can efficiently decide whether or not a forest-level change will be implemented. If implementing a global change takes an inordinate amount of time, individual business units might regret that they ever agreed to deploy a single forest.

Forest Change Control Policies

The first task for forest owners is to define a forest change control policy. The forest change control policy defines what changes can be made to the forest-level configuration and under what circumstances those changes can be made. Essentially there are two types of forest changes: schema changes and configuration directory partition changes (for example, add or remove domains or application directory partitions, or modify the site configuration).

The forest change control policy also defines the procedures for testing, approving, and implementing any forest change. This is especially significant for schema changes, because schema changes are not easily reversed, and any schema change must be compatible with all other schema changes. The forest change control policy should define the testing procedure for schema changes, and the forest owners should provide a test lab for testing these changes. The forest change control policy should require thorough testing of all forest-level changes, but should also ensure that the testing can be done expeditiously. If each change request takes a very long time to process, the frustration level for the users will keep increasing.

The forest change control policy should be in place before you deploy AD DS. In companies with diverse and separate business units, developing this policy might be difficult and time-consuming, but it will not be any easier after AD DS has been deployed. If business units cannot agree on a forest change control policy before deployment, you might need to make the decision to deploy multiple forests.

On the Disc   You can use the Forest Design Decisions tab in the ADDS_DesignDocument.xlsx spreadsheet on the CD to document your forest design decisions.

Designing the Integration of Multiple Forests

Organizations that need multiple forests may still require some integration between the forests. For example, in the organizational or resource forest model, users in one forest will require access to resources in another forest. Organizations that use separate forests but still want to enable some of the collaboration features available with Exchange Server will also need to design some means of integration between multiple forests.

There are two high-level options for enabling the integration of forests. If organizations only need to provide access to resources between forests, then they can configure inter-forest trusts. If organizations need to provide more advanced integration between forests, they can explore options for implementing some type of directory synchronization between forests.

Note   Active Directory Federated Services provides another alternative for providing access to applications in one forest to users in another forest. For more details, see Chapter 19, "Active Directory Federated Services."

Designing Inter-Forest Trusts

The easiest way to enable access to shared resources between forests is to configure trusts between the forests or between domains in each of the forests. When configuring trusts between forests, you can either configure forest trusts, which means that you establish transitive trusts between the forest root domains, or you can configure external trusts between any two domains in both forests.

> **Note**   Before configuring trusts between AD DS forests, you must ensure that domain controllers in either forest can resolve the DNS addresses for domain controllers in the other forest. The easiest way to enable name resolution between forests is to configure conditional forwarders in each forest. As well, both forests in a forest trust must be configured at least at the Windows Server 2003 functional level (or higher).

Designing Forest Trusts

When you create a forest trust, you are establishing a trust relationship between the forest root domains in the two forests. When you design the forest trust configuration, you will need to:

- Design the forest trust direction
- Design selective authentication
- Design SID filtering
- Design UPN suffix routing

Designing Forest Trust Direction   When you configure a forest trust, you can choose the trust direction. When creating the forest trust design, always plan on the least level of access while still meeting the business requirements. For example, in a resource forest scenario, you should be able to configure a one-way trust from the account forest to the resource forest. Enable two-way trusts only if users in both forests require access to resources in the other forest.

Designing Selective Authentication   The second option that you can configure when creating a forest trust is selective authentication. By enabling selective authentication, you have more control over which groups of users in a trusted forest can access shared resources in a trusting forest and which resources they can access. When forest-wide authentication is enabled, users who are authenticated over an inter-forest trust are automatically provided the Authenticated Users SID of the trusting forest. The Authenticated Users SID is used to grant many of the default rights for users in a forest. Because of this, after you set up an inter-forest trust, users from the trusted forest receive some default rights to all of the resources in the trusting forest that are accessible by the Authenticated Users group.

How It Works: Selective Authentication Across Windows Trusts

Selective authentication restricts the ability of users in trusted forests from accessing resources in the trusting forest. Essentially, the users must pass an additional, more granular, security check. This feature is only available in forests that are configured at the Windows 2003 forest functional level or higher.

Without selective authentication, users in a trusted forest function are almost like members of the trusting forest, because they are added to the Authenticated Users group in that forest. This permits access to any resource in the trusting forest where the Access Control List is configured to allow access to Authenticated Users group.

Selective authentication is configured on the outgoing portion of a cross-forest trust. After doing so, when users in the trusted forest try to access a resource in the trusting forest, they will receive the message, "Logon Failure: The machine you are logging onto is protected by an authentication firewall. The specified account is not allowed to authenticate to the machine." To grant users or groups in the trusted forest access to the appropriate resources, you must grant the user the "Allowed to Authenticate" permission on the appropriate computer that they need to reach. Now, when the user tries to access the resource, their access token will include the security principal called Other Organization, and they will be granted access.

Darol Timberlake

Senior Premier Field Engineer, Microsoft

Security Alert   As a best practice, if you are enabling forest-wide authentication on a forest trust, ensure that you remove the Authenticated Users group from all confidential resources in the trusted domain.

When you enable selective authentication, you can limit which groups of users can access resources across the trust, and you can limit which computers in the trusting domain can be accessed across the trust.

To implement selective authentication, you must configure the forest trust to use selective authentication rather than forest-wide authentication. You can enable this option when you create the trust, or after the trust has been created. After configuring the trust, you must access the computer account properties in AD DS, and grant groups or users from the trusted domain the Allowed to Authenticate permission on the computer object.

> **Note** To enable selective authentication on forest trusts, the trusting forest in which shared resources are located must have the forest functional level set to Windows Server 2003 or later. To enable selective authentication on external trusts, the trusting domain in which shared resources are located must have the domain functional level set to Windows 2000 native.

Controlling authentication in this way provides an extra layer of protection to shared resources by preventing them from being randomly accessed by any authenticated user working in a different organization. When you enable selective authentication, all authentication requests made over a trust to the trusting forest are verified by domain controllers in the trusting forest. If the user account does not have the Allowed to Authenticate permission assigned on the server that the user is trying to access, the domain controller will not provide the service ticket required to access the forest.

As a security best practice, you should enable selective authentication on all forest and external trusts. However, if many users in both forests require access to many resources in the other forest, managing selective authentication may become too cumbersome.

Designing SID Filtering SID filtering is used to prevent users from using the SIDs stored in the *SIDHistory* attribute when accessing resources in a separate forest. The *SIDHistory* attribute is typically used when migrating user and group accounts from one domain to another. During the migration, the SIDs assigned to the user or group in the source domain can be migrated to the user or group account in the destination domain and stored in the *SIDHistory* attribute. By retaining the SIDs, the user account can access resources in source domain during the migration of resources to the new domain. If SID filtering is not enabled, the SIDs in the *SIDHistory* attribute can be used to access resources in any trusted forest.

> **More Info** For more details on user and group migration and the use of *SIDHistory,* see Chapter 7, "Migrating to Active Directory Domain Services."

Enabling SID filtering poses a security threat because the *SIDHistory* attribute can be used to exploit the unprotected trust. A malicious user with administrative credentials can add administrator account SIDs from administrative accounts in the trusting forest to the *SIDHistory* attribute of a security principal in the trusted forest. The account could then be used to gain administrator access to the trusted forest.

You can use SID filtering to block the use of the *SIDHistory* attribute across the forest trust. If SID filtering is enabled, the domain controllers in the trusted domain compare the SID of the requesting security principal to the domain SID of the trusted domain. Any SIDs from domains other than the trusted domain are removed, or filtered. This means that even if the *SIDHistory* attribute includes the SIDs from highly trusted administrator accounts in the trusting domain, the SIDs will not be accepted across the trust.

SID filtering is enabled by default on all trusts created on Windows Server 2008 computers, and should be disabled only after careful consideration. If you are migrating user and group accounts from one forest to another, you may choose to disable SID filtering only during the migration. After the migration is complete, re-enable SID filtering.

Designing UPN Suffix Routing   A user principal name (UPN) is a logon name that includes the user principal name prefix and suffix. By default, the UPN prefix is the user logon name, and the suffix is the domain name in which the user account was created. You can use the other domains in the network, or additional suffixes that you created, to configure other suffixes for users. For example, you may want to configure a suffix to create user logon names that match users' e-mail addresses.

UPNs can be used in a multiple-domain or multiple-forest environment to simplify the user logon experience. For example, if users frequently travel between company locations and may be logging on to computers in several different domains, they can be told to just logon by using their UPN. The UPN must be unique in the forest, so the user will always be able to authenticate regardless of which domain they are in. If the UPN is the same as the user e-mail address, the user only has to remember as single user name to get access to both the network and e-mail.

When you design forest trusts, you need to consider how name suffix routing works between forests. *Name suffix routing* is a mechanism that provides name resolution across forests, based on the following criteria:

- When two Windows Server 2008 forests connect via forest trust, name suffix routing is enabled automatically. For example, if a forest trust is configured between the ADatum.com forest and the Contoso.com forest, a user with an account in the ADatum.com forest could use their UPN to log on to a computer in the Contoso.com forest. The authentication request would be routed automatically to the appropriate domain controller in the ADatum.com forest.

- If both forests have the same UPN suffix, users will not be able to use the UPN name with that suffix when logging on to a computer in a different forest. If both the ADatum.com and the Contoso.com organization used TreyResearch.com as a UPN suffix, for example, then users would not be able to log on in the other forest using this suffix.

UPN name suffix routing errors are identified when you configure forest trusts. If the forests share a UPN suffix, the New Trust Wizard detects and displays the conflict between the two UPN name suffixes when you attempt to configure the trust. If you add a conflicting UPN suffix to a domain with an existing forest trust, the UPN suffix will not be allowed to authenticate in the trusting domain.

Designing Directory Integration Between Forests

In some organizations, just creating trusts between forests does not provide the required functionality. These organizations may not have any requirement to enable resource access between different forests but may have a requirement to synchronize directory information between forests. In many organizations that have deployed multiple forests and multiple Exchange Server organizations, users in the separate organizations must be able to easily send e-mail to each other. To enable this, user accounts in both forests must be synchronized with the other forest to be available as message recipients within the messaging clients.

More Info In addition to directory synchronization, many other issues such as calendar availability, public folder replication, and message routing need to be addressed when designing Exchange Server deployments in complex organizations. For more information, see "Planning for a Complex Exchange Organization" at *http://technet.microsoft.com/en-us/ library/aa996010.aspx*.

The easiest way to enable directory synchronization between multiple forests is to use a tool such as Microsoft Identity Lifecycle Manager (ILM) 2007. One of the ILM components is Microsoft Identity Integration Server 2003 (MIIS). By using MIIS, or by using the Identity Integration Feature Pack for Microsoft Windows Server Active Directory (IIFP), you can automate the process of synchronizing the directory information between multiple forests. MIIS is a full-featured identity management solution that can be used to synchronize many different types of directories, whereas IIFP is a more limited version of MIIS that can be used to synchronize identity information between Microsoft directories.

When you configure directory synchronization using MIIS or IIFP, user accounts and mail-enabled groups in a source forest are usually represented as mail-enabled contacts in the destination forest. This means that the recipients appear in the global address list.

More Info Designing the integration of multiple forests is complicated and dependent on the level of integration required between the forests. For a detailed discussion on the integration options available and for guidance on how to implement the options, see the "Windows 2000/ 2003: Multiple Forests Considerations" white paper located at *http://www.microsoft.com/ downloads/details.aspx?familyid=b717bfcd-6c1c-4af6-8b2c-b604e60067ba&displaylang=en*.

Designing the Domain Structure

After the question of how many forests you will deploy has been settled, the next step is to determine the domain structure within each of the forests. Domains are used to partition a large forest into smaller components, primarily for administration or replication purposes. The following domain characteristics are important in AD DS design:

- **Replication boundaries** Domain boundaries are replication boundaries for the domain directory partition and for the domain information stored in the SYSVOL folder on all domain controllers. Whereas other directory partitions like schema, configuration, and the global catalog are replicated throughout the forest, the domain directory partition is replicated only within one domain.

■ **Resource access boundary**   Domain boundaries are also boundaries for resource access. By default, users in one domain cannot access resources in another domain unless a trust is in place and they are explicitly given the appropriate permissions.

■ **Security policy boundaries**   Some security policies, when applied at the domain level, will apply to all user accounts in the domain. These policies include password policies, account lockout policies, and Kerberos ticket policies.

Figure 5-7 shows the process for creating a domain design.

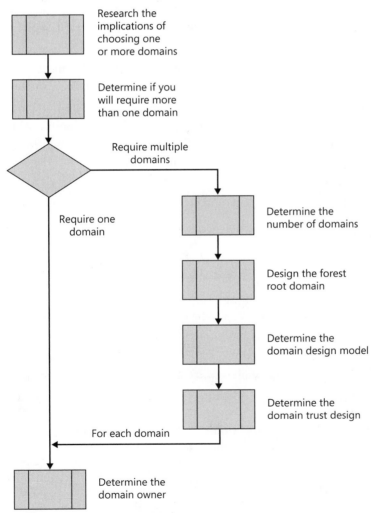

Figure 5-7   Creating a domain design.

Important   As discussed in the previous section on designing the forest structure, domain boundaries are not security boundaries.

Determining the Number of Domains

Although most companies will deploy a single forest, most large companies will deploy multiple domains within that forest. Ideally, a single domain is the easiest to manage and provides the users with the least complex environment. However, there are also several reasons why companies choose to deploy multiple domains.

Choosing a Single Domain

Most small-sized to medium-sized businesses should consider implementing a single domain because:

- The AD DS data store can easily contain over 1 million objects. This means that the total number of objects in AD DS is very rarely a reason to create multiple domains.

- If an organization requires administrative autonomy between different business units, you can use organizational units and delegate administrative tasks at the OU level. If the organization requires administrative isolation, you must deploy multiple forests, because domains are not an administrative security boundary.

- If your company frequently reorganizes, or if users move between business units, it is easy to move users between OUs in a domain. It is much more difficult to move users between domains.

- Single domains are easier to manage in that you need only be concerned with one set of domain-level administrators and one set of domain-level policies. Also, you need to administer only one set of domain controllers.

- The easiest scenario for managing group policies is in a single domain environment. Some Group Policy components are stored in the SYSVOL folder on each domain controller in a domain. If you only have one domain, the Group Policy objects are automatically replicated to all domain controllers.

- A single domain provides the easiest environment for which to design authentication and resource access. With a single domain, you do not need to be concerned about trusts or about assigning access to resources to users in other domains. Within a single domain it is also quite practical to use only a single group for assigning resource access rather than configuring both account and resource groups.

- In a single domain, all domain controllers can be global catalog servers because the infrastructure master restrictions do not apply. This means that you do not need to plan for global catalog placement.

Choosing Multiple Domains

Although a single domain might be an ideal configuration for many companies, most large companies deploy multiple domains. Separate domains are a good idea in these situations:

- Replication traffic must be limited. The domain directory partition, which is the largest and most frequently modified directory partition, is replicated to all domain controllers in a domain. As well, the SYSVOL folder is replicated to all domain controllers in the same domain. In some cases, this might cause too much replication traffic between company locations (even if multiple sites are configured). This might be the case if there are slow network connections between company locations or if there are large numbers of users in multiple company locations. The only way to limit this replication traffic is to create additional domains.

- Some locations use Simple Mail Transfer Protocol (SMTP) connectivity. Any company locations that have only SMTP connectivity must be configured as separate domains. The domain partition cannot be replicated through site links that use SMTP.

- Different password policies are required. The only way to have different password policies, account lockout policies, and Kerberos ticket policies is to deploy separate domains. Although you can configure fine-grained password policies to modify the password policies for some users in a single domain, managing different password policies for several groups of people in the same domain may require additional administrative effort.

- Access must be limited. If you need to be able to limit access to resources and restrict administrative permissions, you will want to deploy additional domains. For some companies, there might be legal reasons for creating separate administrative units.

- Different namespaces are required for different business units. When organizations amalgamate, it may be important for all business units to maintain a unique identity. By deploying multiple domains in different trees, you can maintain a unique namespace for each domain.

- The best migration path for the organization is to upgrade several of the current domains.

There are many good reasons for creating additional domains. However, each additional domain can add significant administrative and financial cost to an organization. Before choosing to create additional domains, consider the following:

- Each additional domain requires additional hardware and additional administrators. If you want to configure consistent administrative processes and auditing to all domains, you must configure the settings in each domain.

- Maintaining consistent Group Policy settings across all domains is difficult. You must configure the GPOs in each domain and copy files such as scripts and template files to domain controllers in each domain.

- In a multiple-domain environment, users will be accessing resources across trusts, which means greater complexity and potentially more points of failure.

- Users who travel between locations with different domains must authenticate to a domain controller in their home domain. If a network connection is not available to the home domain, the user will not be able to authenticate to the domain.

Because of these additional costs, the total number of domains should be kept as low as possible.

Designing the Forest Root Domain

Another important decision you will need to make when designing an AD DS solution with multiple domains is whether or not you should deploy a dedicated root domain (also called an empty root). A *dedicated root domain* is a domain that is dedicated to the role of operating as the forest root domain. That is, the only user accounts or resources in that domain are those needed to manage the forest. A forest with a dedicated root domain is shown in Figure 5-8.

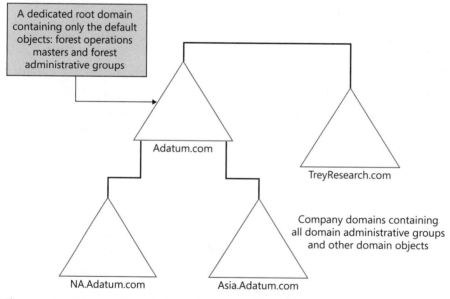

A dedicated root domain containing only the default objects: forest operations masters and forest administrative groups

Adatum.com

TreyResearch.com

NA.Adatum.com   Asia.Adatum.com

Company domains containing all domain administrative groups and other domain objects

Figure 5-8 A forest with a dedicated root domain.

For most companies deploying multiple domains, a dedicated root domain is highly recommended. The root domain is a crucial domain in AD DS structure. Deploying a dedicated root domain has the following benefits:

- The root domain contains the forest-level administrative groups (the Enterprise Admins and Schema Admins groups) and the forest-level operations master domain controllers (the domain naming master and the schema master). Using a dedicated root domain also makes it easier to limit the membership of the forest-level administrative groups.

Even if you strictly limit the number of administrators in the Schema Admins and Enterprise Admins groups, any member of the Domain Admins group in the forest root domain can modify the membership list for these groups.

■ A dedicated root domain is easily replicated to other sites. The forest root domain must always be available when users log on to domains other than their home domain or when users access resources in other domains. Because you will not need to make changes to the dedicated forest root domain data store very often, there is almost no replication traffic between root domain controllers, so you can locate domain controllers in several company locations to ensure redundancy. This also makes it easy to move the root domain to another location in a disaster recovery scenario.

■ A dedicated root domain is easier to manage than a root domain that contains many objects. Because the directory database will be small, it is easy to back up and restore the root domain controllers. The root domain cannot be replaced; if the root domain is destroyed and it cannot be recovered, you must rebuild the entire forest.

■ A dedicated root domain also never becomes obsolete, especially if the domain is given a generic name.

For these reasons, most companies that choose to deploy multiple domains should seriously consider deploying a dedicated root domain. Even some companies that plan to deploy only one domain should consider the advantages of deploying a dedicated root domain.

The dedicated root domain requires some configuration that might not be applied to the other domains in the forest. First of all, because the root domain contains the forest operations masters, the domain controllers for the root domain must be secured as much as possible. The forest domain also contains the groups that can modify the forest and schema. More than with any other domain, the members of the administrative groups in the root domain must be highly trusted. You probably will want to use the Restricted Group option in the Domain Security Policy to manage the membership of these groups. The DNS configuration of the root domain should also be as secure as possible. Because additional computers are not likely to be installed in the root domain, you should enable secure dynamic updates for the root domain DNS zone while the domain controllers are being installed and then disable dynamic updates for this zone.

Designing Domain Hierarchies

After the root domain design is in place, the next step is to determine how many additional domains you will need to deploy and how the rest of the domains will fit into the DNS namespace for the forest.

There are three high-level models for creating additional domains in an AD DS forest:

■ **Creating domains based on geographic location, or regional domains**   Regional domains are used primarily to reduce replication traffic across slow or expensive WAN links.

Regional domains are the preferred options for organizations with large numbers of users that are geographically dispersed. For example, organizations with offices in multiple continents may choose to implement regional domains to restrict replication traffic between continents. Regional domains are also the preferred option if the geographic divisions in the organization are well-established and not likely to change. The domain configuration is difficult to change after deployment.

> **Important**   The available bandwidth between company locations may be the most important criterion for creating additional domains in organizations with more than 10,000 users and with very limited bandwidth in WAN links between company locations. Because all changes in AD DS will be replicated to all domain controllers in a single domain, AD DS replication traffic may use up all of the available bandwidth. By creating separate domains on either side of a slow WAN link, you can significantly reduce the amount of network bandwidth used for replication. For a detailed analysis of the bandwidth requirements for replication, see "Determining Your Active Directory Design and Deployment Strategy" at *http://technet2.microsoft.com/windowsserver/en/library/ ff92f142-66ea-498b-ad0f-a379c411eb6e1033.mspx?mfr=true*. This guide is based on deploying Windows Server 2003 forests. Many of the principles apply to Windows Server 2008. You should also check the Windows Server 2008 TechCenter site for an updated version of this guide.

- **Creating domains based on business units**   Some organizations create additional domains based on business units. This design is the preferred option if the business units are quite autonomous, or if there is a business requirement to maintain a separate namespace for each business unit. Creating domains for business units is quite common in organizations that have a history of mergers and acquisitions.

- **Creating account and resource domains**   Some organizations create additional domains in order to separate account and resource domains. This enables domain administrators in the resource domain to have full control of all aspects of resource management without having any access to account management. Separating account domains and resource domains was common in organizations that deployed Windows NT 4.0, and some organizations have just migrated the Windows NT domains to Active Directory. Because you can delegate administrative access at the OU level in AD DS and because AD DS can contain millions of objects, the requirement for deploying account and resource domains is much less likely in Windows Server 2008 AD DS.

Domain Trees and Trusts

As you add more domains to the forest, you can add the domains in either a single-tree or multiple-tree configuration. If you add all of the domains in a single tree, all the domains will have a contiguous namespace (that is, they will fall under the root domain namespace). This is often the best design for a centralized corporation in which all of the business units are known by one name. However, if the corporation has several business units with distinct identities, there is likely to be considerable resistance to using another business unit's namespace. In this case, you will add domains in separate trees, thus creating several namespaces.

Default Trust Configuration

From a functional point of view, there is almost no difference between deploying a single tree or multiple trees. In either case, all the domains will share a transitive trust with all other domains, and they will also share the global catalog and configuration container. The primary complicating factor with multiple trees is designing the DNS namespace and configuring the DNS servers.

The default trust configuration between domains in an AD DS forest is either a parent-child trust or a tree-root trust. Each parent and child pair shares a two-way trust, and the roots of each tree share a two-way trust. Because the trusts are transitive, this means that all the domains in the forest trust each other. However, when a user logs on in a domain other than the home domain, the logon process might have to traverse the entire trust path. For example, a corporation might have a domain structure as illustrated in Figure 5-9. If a user with an account in the Asia.Fabrikam.com domain logs on in the Canada.NA.ADatum.com domain, the initial logon request would go to a domain controller in the Canada domain. The logon request would be referred up the trust path to the NA domain, then to the ADatum domain, then to the Fabrikam domain, and finally to the Asia domain.

Shortcut Trusts

If you deploy multiple domains, and if users frequently access resources in other domains or log on in domains other than their home domain, you might want to include shortcut trusts in your domain design. *Shortcut trusts* are used to improve performance for resource access or logon between domains. For example, if a shortcut trust is configured between the Canada domain and the Asia domain, the logon request could be forwarded directly to a domain controller in the Asia domain. The shortcut trust also optimizes accessing resources between the domains.

Note   Because shortcut trusts add more administrative overhead, they should be implemented only if necessary. They will be necessary only if the trust path includes more than four or five domains, and if users frequently log on or access resources in domains other than their own.

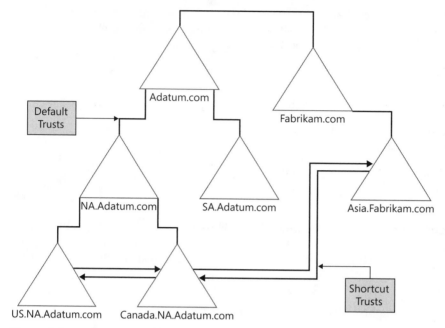

Figure 5-9   A shortcut trust can be used to optimize resource access between domains.

Changing the Domain Hierarchy After Deployment

Your domain plan should be completed before you begin deployment because it is difficult to change the domain configuration after deployment. With Windows Server 2003 or later, you can rename domains in a forest that is running at the Windows Server 2003 or Windows Server 2008 functional level. When you rename domains, you can move a domain from one tree to another within the forest, but you do not have the option of replacing the forest root domain. You also do not have the option of adding or removing domains from the forest by using the domain rename tool.

The domain rename process is complex and requires a great deal of care in planning and execution. In addition, the time that is required for a complete domain rename operation is directly proportional to the size of an Active Directory forest in terms of its number of domains, domain controllers, and member computers.

> **More Info**   For details on how to rename domains, see "Domain Rename Technical Reference" at *http://technet2.microsoft.com/windowsserver/en/library/35e63f1e-f097-4c9c-a788-efc840d781931033.mspx?mfr=true.*

Defining Domain Ownership

For each of the domains included in the AD DS design, you must assign a domain owner. In most cases domain owners are business unit administrators or the administrators in the geographical region where the domain has been defined.

> **Note**   If you are deploying a dedicated root domain, the domain owners of the domain are also the forest owners. The only real functions performed in a dedicated root domain are forest functions, so it makes sense that the forest owners also own the root domain.

The role of the domain owner is to manage the individual domain. Tasks include:

- **Creating the domain-level security policies**   These include the password policies, account lockout policies, and Kerberos ticket policies.

- **Designing the Group Policy configuration at the domain level**   The domain owner might design the Group Policy objects (GPOs) for the entire domain and delegate the right for OU-level administrators to link GPOs to OUs.

- **Creating the top-level OU structure in the domain**   After the top-level OU structure has been created, the task of creating subordinate OUs can be assigned to OU-level administrators.

- **Delegating administrative rights within the domain**   The domain owner should establish the administrative policies for the domain level (including policies on naming schemes, group design, etc.) and then delegate rights to OU-level administrators.

- **Managing the domain-level administrative groups**   As mentioned earlier, the administrators in each domain must be highly trusted because their actions can have forest-wide implications. The domain owner's role is to limit the membership of the domain-level administrative groups and delegate lower-level administrative rights whenever possible.

Designing Domain and Forest Functional Levels

As part of the AD DS design process, you will also need to choose which domain and forest functional level to implement.

Features Enabled at Domain Functional Levels

Table 5-1 shows which features are enabled at each domain functional level. It also shows the operating systems for domain controllers that are supported at each functional level.

Table 5-1   Domain Functional Levels

Domain Functional Level	Enabled Features	Supported Domain Controller Operating Systems
Windows 2000 native	All default Active Directory features and the following features: ■ Universal groups enabled for both distribution groups and security groups ■ Group nesting ■ Group conversion enabled ■ Security identifier (SID) history	Windows 2000 Windows Server 2003 Windows Server 2008

Table 5-1 Domain Functional Levels *(continued)*

Domain Functional Level	Enabled Features	Supported Domain Controller Operating Systems
Windows Server 2003	All default Active Directory features, all features from the Windows 2000 native domain functional level, and the following features:	Windows Server 2003 Windows Server 2008
	■ Domain rename	
	■ Update of the logon time stamp: the *lastLogonTimestamp* attribute will be updated with the last logon time of the user or computer	
	■ The ability to set the *userPassword* attribute as the effective password on *inetOrgPerson* and *User* objects	
	■ The ability to redirect Users and Computers containers	
	■ The ability to store Authorization Manager policies in AD DS	
	■ Constrained delegation so that applications can take advantage of the secure delegation of user credentials by means of the Kerberos authentication protocol	
	■ Selective authentication, through which it is possible to specify the users and groups from a trusted forest who are allowed to authenticate to resource servers in a trusting forest	
Windows Server 2008	All default Active Directory features, all features from the Windows Server 2003 domain functional level, and the following features:	Windows Server 2008
	■ Distributed File System Replication support for SYSVOL	
	■ Advanced Encryption Services (AES 128 and 256) support for the Kerberos protocol	
	■ Last Interactive Logon Information, which displays the time of the last successful interactive logon for a user, from what workstation, and the number of failed logon attempts since the last logon	
	■ Fine-grained password policies, which enable password and account lockout policies to be specified for users and global security groups in a domain	

Features Enabled at Forest Functional Levels

Table 5-2 shows which features are enabled at each forest functional level. It also shows the operating systems for domain controllers that are supported at each functional level.

Table 5-2   Forest Functional Levels

Forest Functional Level	Enabled Features	Supported Domain Controllers
Windows 2000	All default Active Directory features	Windows Server 2008 Windows Server 2003 Windows 2000
Windows Server 2003	All default Active Directory features, and the following features: ■ Forest trust ■ Domain rename ■ Linked-value replication (changes in group membership to store and replicate values for individual members instead of replicating the entire membership as a single unit) ■ The ability to deploy a read-only domain controller (RODC) that runs Windows Server 2008 ■ Improved Knowledge Consistency Checker (KCC) algorithms and scalability ■ The ability to create instances of the dynamic auxiliary class called *dynamicObject* in a domain directory partition ■ The ability to convert an *inetOrgPerson* object instance into a *User* object instance, and the reverse ■ Deactivation and redefinition of attributes and classes in the schema	Windows Server 2003 Windows Server 2008
Windows Server 2008	Provides all the features that are available at the Windows Server 2003 forest functional level, but no additional features; all domains that are subsequently added to the forest, however, will operate at the Windows Server 2008 domain functional level by default	Windows Server 2008

Implementing a Domain and Forest Functional Level

In most cases, you should plan to implement the highest domain and forest functional level that you can based on the domain controller operating systems that you have deployed or plan to deploy. If you are deploying a new Windows Server 2008 forest and do not plan on ever deploying Windows Server 2003 domain controllers in the forest, you should set the domain and forest functional levels at Windows Server 2008. If you are upgrading an existing domain, you should raise the domain level after you have removed the last domain controller running Windows 2000 or Windows Server 2003. After all domains have been upgraded to Windows Server 2008 functional level, you should raise the forest functional level to the same level.

On the Disc   You can use the Domain Design Decisions tab in the ADDS_DesignDocument.xlsx spreadsheet on the CD to document your domain design decisions and use the AD Domain Design tab to document the forest and domain designs.

Designing the DNS Infrastructure

After you have decided how many domains you will need to deploy and determined the domain hierarchy, the next step is to design the DNS infrastructure for your network. AD DS in Windows Server 2008 requires DNS, as each domain name is a part of the DNS namespace. A key design decision is to determine where to locate AD DS domains within that namespace. In addition to designing the namespace, you must also design the DNS server configuration. If the company already has a DNS infrastructure in place, you might have to design your namespace to fit into the current namespace and also configure the Windows Server 2008 DNS servers to interoperate with the existing DNS servers.

On the Disc   The first step in designing the DNS infrastructure is to examine the current DNS infrastructure. You can use the DNS Zone Configuration and DNS Server Configuration worksheets in the CurrentNetworkEnvironment.xslx to document the DNS zone configuration.

Namespace Design

After you have gathered the information on the current DNS infrastructure, you are ready to start designing your AD DS namespace.

Internal and External DNS Namespaces

One of the first questions that you must answer before beginning the namespace design is whether you want to use the same internal and external DNS namespace.

Using the Same Namespace Internally and Externally   Some companies might choose to use the same DNS name internally and externally. In this case, a company would have registered only one DNS name on the Internet. For example, as shown in Figure 5-10, A. Datum might decide to use ADatum.com both internally and externally.

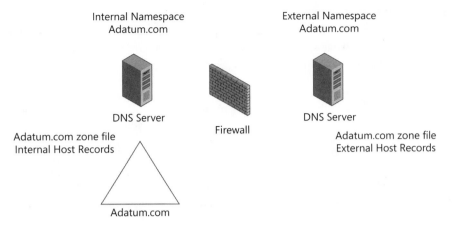

Figure 5-10   Using a single DNS namespace.

Security Alert   Regardless of whether you use the same or different internal and external namespaces, your internal DNS server should never be accessible to external clients. The internal DNS server will host all domain controller records as well as possibly the records for all computers on your network (if you have dynamic DNS enabled). The only records that should be accessible from the Internet are the records for resources that need to be accessible from the Internet. For most companies, the list of externally available resources consists of the addresses for the SMTP servers, Web servers, and possibly a few other servers. Using the same namespace does not mean that you should use one DNS server or zone file internally and externally.

The primary advantage of using the same namespace internally and externally is that it provides a consistent experience for the end user. The user always uses the same domain name for any connection to the corporate network. The user's SMTP address and the user principal name (UPN) will use the same domain name as the public Web site. When the user needs to access Web-based resources, he or she can use the same name both internally and externally (although he or she might not access the same server). Another advantage of using the same namespace is that only one DNS name needs to be registered.

The primary disadvantages of using the same namespace have to do with security and administrative effort. Many companies are concerned about exposing the internal DNS name to the Internet and see this as a potential security risk. Using the same namespace internally and externally can complicate DNS administration because the DNS administrators must now administer two different zones with the same domain name. Using the same name can also complicate some client configurations. For example, most Web proxy clients can be configured to interpret specified domain names as internal so that the client will connect to them directly without going through the proxy server. Using the same name can complicate this configuration.

Using a Different Namespace Internally and Externally   Most companies use a different namespace internally and externally. For example, a company might decide to use *ADatum.com* as the external namespace and a name like *ADatum.net* or *AD.ADatum.com* for the internal namespace. (See Figure 5-11.)

> **Note**   Any difference in the domain names means that you are using a different namespace internally. For example, if you are using *ADatum.com* as the external namespace, *ADatum.net*, *ADADatum.com*, and *AD.ADatum.com* are all different namespaces. *AD.ADatum.com* will require a different DNS configuration than the other two, but all three are unique.

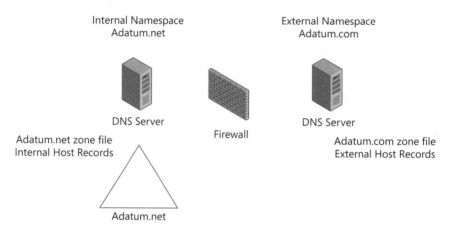

Figure 5-11   Using separate namespaces internally and externally.

Often the unique internal namespace is chosen for security reasons; that is, to prevent the internal namespace from being exposed to the Internet. Also, the DNS and proxy configurations are easier to manage with the unique namespace. The primary disadvantage to using a unique namespace is that the company might need to register additional DNS names with the Internet naming authorities. Although registering the internal DNS name with the Internet naming authorities is not a requirement, it is recommended. If you do not register the name and another company does register it, your users will not be able to locate Internet resources with the same domain name as the internal namespace.

Namespace Design Options

The actual names that you choose for your DNS namespace are flexible and will be determined largely by the current DNS infrastructure. If you do not have an existing DNS infrastructure in place and you have one or more second-level domain names already registered for your company, your DNS namespace design will be quite simple. In this case, you can choose the registered second-level domain name as the root domain name and then delegate child domain names for additional domains in the same tree, or additional second-level domain names for additional trees in the forest. Figure 5-12 shows an example.

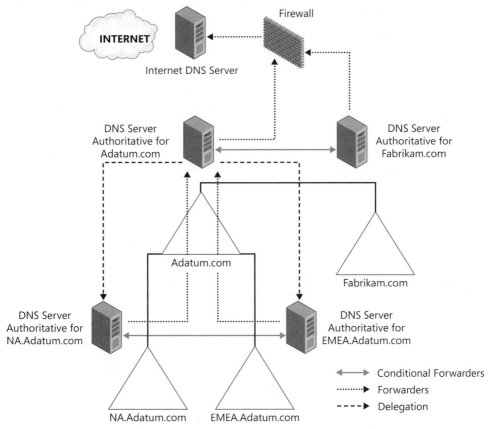

Figure 5-12   DNS namespace design with no existing DNS infrastructure.

Figure 5-12 also illustrates how the DNS servers would be configured in this scenario. The ADatum.com DNS server is authoritative for its domain and contains delegation records to NA.ADatum.com and EMEA.ADatum.com as well as conditional forwarders or stub zones for the Fabrikam.com domain. The Fabrikam.com DNS server is authoritative for its zone and contains conditional forwarders or stub zones for ADatum.com. To resolve Internet addresses, the tree root servers could be configured with a forwarder pointing to a server on the Internet, or they could be configured with the Internet root hints.

Internal and External Namespaces

The issue of using an internal namespace that is different than the external, public namespace can lead to a significant amount of discussion within the company. In some cases the best technical answer may be to use different namespaces internally and externally, but business decision makers might have strong resistance to using anything other than the Internet namespace. Often, the reason for this is name branding: some companies have spent years and millions of dollars creating a name brand that customers instantly recognize. The corporate Web sites and SMTP addresses for all users reflect this namespace. Some companies might even have multiple public identities, with several business units within the company, each with its own name branding. Most of the time, business users are resistant to showing any name other than their recognizable corporate name to the external world.

The good news is that you can use different namespaces internally and externally and still display only one namespace externally. For example, A. Datum might decide to use *ADatum.net* as the internal namespace and *ADatum.com* as the public namespace. The internal namespace can be almost completely hidden from everyone but network administrators. The SMTP addresses for all users can still be *alias@ADatum.com*, and all the Web servers can still use the ADatum.com Web suffix. If required, the UPN for all users can even be configured as *alias@ADatum.com* despite using a different internal namespace.

The DNS design can be slightly more complicated if you have an existing internal DNS infrastructure. In this case, you have at least three options for integrating with the current infrastructure. The first option is to use only the current DNS infrastructure, including the domain name, for AD DS. For example, A. Datum might be using *ADatum.net* as its internal namespace and using BIND DNS servers to provide the DNS service. The company could decide to use *ADatum.net* as the AD DS domain name and continue to use the current DNS servers (providing they support service locator [SRV] records). Alternatively, the company could decide to use the same domain name but move the DNS service to a DNS server running Windows Server 2008. In either case, very little reconfiguration of the DNS servers is required. The DNS servers can continue to use the same forwarders or root hints for Internet name resolution.

Note   When you configure the DNS servers for Internet name resolution, you have two options: you can use forwarders, or you can configure the DNS servers with root hints. The use of forwarders is generally more secure in that you can configure the internal DNS server to forward to one or two external DNS servers. This can simplify the configuration of the firewall. Using root hints might result in better redundancy because you remove the single point of failure. If one root hint server does not respond, the DNS server will simply contact another.

The second option with an existing DNS infrastructure is to choose a different DNS name for AD DS domains. For example, A. Datum might be using *ADatum.net* as the current internal DNS namespace and decide to deploy AD DS domains using *ADADatum.net* as the domain name. (See Figure 5-13.)

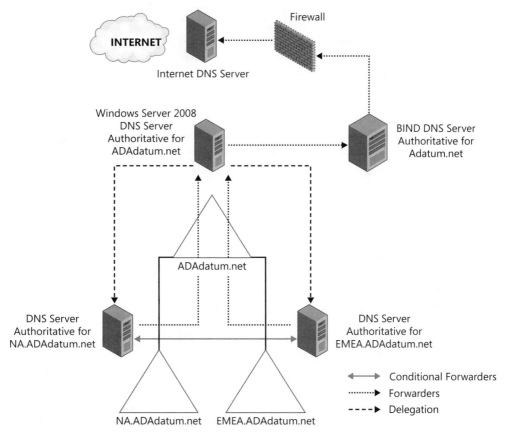

Figure 5-13   Configuring DNS to use a different internal namespace.

In this case, a DNS server can be deployed as the primary name server for ADADatum.net with delegation records for NA.ADADatum.net and EMEA.ADADatum.com. This DNS server might be the same DNS server as the authoritative server for ADatum.net, or you might choose to deploy an additional DNS server. If you do deploy an additional DNS server for the AD DS domain, you must configure the forwarders and root hints for this DNS server.

The third DNS design that you can use with an existing DNS infrastructure is one in which the AD DS domain(s) are child domains to the existing internal namespace. For example, A. Datum might decide to create a subdomain, AD.ADatum.net, as the AD DS domain. (See Figure 5-14.) In this case, the DNS server for the ADatum.net would be configured with a delegation record for the AD.ADatum.net domain. The AD.ADatum.net DNS server would then be configured with a forwarder record pointing to the ADatum.net DNS server.

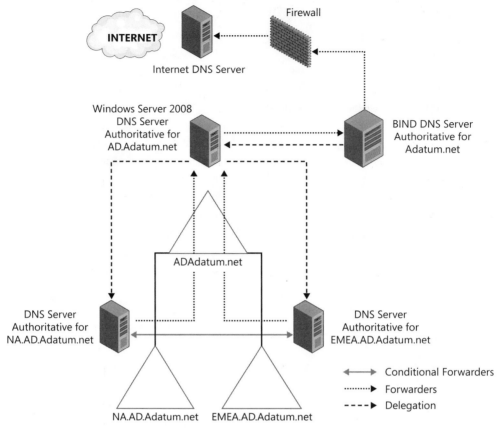

Figure 5-14   Configuring DNS by adding a subdomain to the existing internal namespace.

Integration with the Current DNS Infrastructure

Almost all large companies already have a DNS infrastructure in place. If the company has already deployed Active Directory, a DNS infrastructure will be in place to support the Active Directory. In addition, most large companies use DNS for name resolution to UNIX servers or to provide the DNS services that users need for Internet access. In many cases, the DNS services are provided by BIND DNS servers running on UNIX servers. Most companies with an existing BIND DNS infrastructure are not likely to just remove the current infrastructure and move everything to Windows Server 2008. This means that the DNS requirements for AD DS will have to interoperate with the current DNS infrastructure.

There are two options for integration if the current BIND DNS infrastructure is to be maintained. The first option is to use non-Microsoft DNS servers and host the required DNS zone information for AD DS on these servers. This is certainly a possibility. The only absolute requirement for integrating DNS and AD DS is that the server must support SRV records. In addition, you probably want to ensure that the DNS servers also support dynamic updates (especially if you are planning on registering all of the client IP addresses in DNS) and incremental zone transfers. If the current infrastructure uses BIND DNS servers, BIND 8.1.2 servers support SRV records and dynamic updates. In addition to the support provided by BIND 8.1.2, BIND 8.2.1 supports incremental zone transfers. As long as you are using one of these recent versions of BIND, you can continue using the BIND DNS servers.

Choosing Which DNS Server to Use

The question of whether to use DNS servers running Windows Server or use non-Microsoft DNS servers can lead to heated discussions with no satisfactory resolution. Large companies have been running BIND DNS servers for many years, and the DNS administrators are often very knowledgeable, experienced, and reluctant to give up the DNS services to a Microsoft platform. Often these administrators express concerns about the stability, reliability, and security of DNS on Microsoft servers.

One approach to this discussion is to take the position that it really does not matter how the DNS service is provided. As long as the DNS servers support SRV records, Windows Server 2008 AD DS can work with any DNS server. What is absolutely critical, however, is that the DNS service always be available. If the DNS service ever shuts down during working hours, no clients or servers will be able to find any AD DS domain controllers. So the crucial question becomes which DNS server will provide the reliability that AD DS needs.

Both UNIX servers and Windows Servers can be very reliable if configured correctly. However, even the discussions regarding the reliability of various servers seem to miss the mark. No single server can ever be completely reliable, so one question to ask is which DNS server provides the best options for eliminating a single point of failure and spreading the service availability across multiple servers. Windows Server 2008 provides excellent options for providing this reliability across multiple servers, especially if AD DS integrated zones are used. With AD DS integrated zones, every domain controller that is also a DNS server can have a writable copy of the DNS information. AD DS integrated zones also address the security concerns by implementing secure updates.

Many companies have decided to stay with the BIND DNS servers, and these servers have provided the required functionality without any problems. Some companies have decided to move the primary DNS to Microsoft DNS servers and to retain the BIND DNS servers as secondary name servers. Almost any configuration will work, and as long as the DNS servers are always available, it really does not matter which option a company uses.

The second option for integrating the Windows Server 2008 DNS with BIND is to deploy both types of DNS. Many companies use the BIND DNS server as the primary name server for the internal namespace. For example, A. Datum might be using BIND for name resolution for ADatum.com. If A. Datum decides to deploy AD DS and use DNS servers running

Windows Server 2008, the company has a number of options. If A. Datum wants to use ADatum.com as the AD DS DNS name, it can move the primary zone to the DNS server running Windows Server 2008 and maintain the BIND DNS server as a secondary name server. Or the DNS server running Windows Server 2008 could be the secondary name server to the BIND DNS server.

> **Note** You can use BIND DNS servers and Windows Server 2008 DNS servers for the same namespace. Both DNS servers can operate as either primary or secondary name servers for each other's zone information. However, if you are planning to use AD DS integrated zones, the BIND DNS zone must be configured as a secondary zone. An AD DS integrated zone cannot be a secondary zone.

A. Datum might also decide to deploy AD DS using a different domain name than that currently used on the BIND DNS servers. For example, the company might decide to use ADatum.net as the AD DS DNS name. In this case, the DNS servers running Windows Server 2008 can be configured as the authoritative servers for ADatum.net and the BIND servers as authoritative for ADatum.com. The DNS server running Windows Server 2008 can then be configured with a conditional forwarder to the BIND DNS server for ADatum.com.

> **Note** The earlier section in this chapter on planning the DNS namespace illustrated a number of possible scenarios for DNS namespace deployment. The DNS servers discussed in the namespace planning section are essentially interchangeable: any of the DNS servers could be BIND servers, and any of the DNS servers could be DNS servers running Windows Server. Theoretically, you could even use Windows Server 2008 DNS to host the external DNS name and use BIND DNS for AD DS domains.

Designing the Organizational Unit Structure

After the domain-level design is complete, the next step is to create an OU design for each domain. As described in Chapter 2, "Active Directory Domain Services Components," OUs are used to create a hierarchical structure within a domain. This hierarchy can then be used to delegate administrative tasks or to apply a set of Group Policy settings to a collection of objects.

Organizational Units and AD DS Design

When you design the OU structure, you are grouping a collection of objects together for the purpose of administering the objects in the same way. For example, you might want to configure a common set of desktop settings for all the users in a particular department. By grouping all of the users into an OU, you can assign a Group Policy to that OU that automatically configures the user desktop. You might also want to group objects together for the purpose of assigning an administrator for that group of objects. For example, if you have a remote office with a local administrator, you can create an OU, put all the user and computer objects in the remote office into that OU, and then delegate the administration of that OU to the local administrator.

OUs have several characteristics:

- OU design does not have any implications for DNS namespace design. OUs are given directory names within a DNS namespace. For example, an OU might have the distinguished name of OU=ManagersOU,DC=ADatum,DC=com. In this case, the DNS name is ADatum.com, and the OU names are LDAP names inside the DNS namespace.

- OUs can be created inside of other OUs. By default, administrative rights and Group Policy settings set at upper-level OUs are inherited by child OUs. This default behavior can be modified.

- OUs are transparent to end users. When a user searches AD DS for any object, the user's application will query the global catalog for the information. The user does not need to be aware of the OU structure to log on or to locate objects in AD DS.

- Compared to the other AD DS components, such as domains and forests, the OU structure is easy to modify after deployment. Also, moving objects between OUs is just a matter of right-clicking the object and selecting Move from the context menu.

Caution   Although it is easy to move objects between OUs and easy to change the OU structure, you still need to consider the implications of these changes. When you move a user from one OU to another, the Group Policy objects applied at the OU level will change. If you move OUs within the domain, you need to consider how inherited administrator permissions and Group Policy objects will apply to the moved OU.

Designing an OU Structure

In most companies, you have a considerable amount of flexibility when you create the OU design. However, as you create the OU design for each domain, there are a number of factors to consider.

Corporate Structures and OU Design

The first tendency when creating an OU structure might be to mimic the company's organization chart. This might work in some companies, but it could result in an ineffective OU structure in others. For example, the corporate organizational chart is usually based on business units with no regard for where users are actually located. Perhaps the members of the same business unit are scattered in multiple locations around the world. Grouping these users into a single OU could be quite inefficient.

However, examining the corporate structure and organizational model is often a good place to start with the OU design. For example, if the company is highly centralized and hierarchical, the OU structure will probably reflect that model. If the company structure gives a great deal of autonomy to business units or geographic locations, the OU design should reflect this approach. As you examine the corporate structure, also examine the information technology (IT) management structure. In some companies, separate business units are given a great deal of autonomy to manage the business as they want, but the IT management might still be strongly centralized. In this case, you will design the OU structure based on the IT management structure, not on the business management structure.

OU Design Based on Delegation of Administration

One of the reasons for creating an OU structure is to be able to delegate administrative tasks. Many companies with separate business units have deployed a single AD DS domain but still want to delegate the administrative tasks based on resources or business units. Some companies that have multiple locations with local network administrators at each site might want to delegate administration for each location. Other companies might want to be able to delegate a specific administrative task. For example, perhaps they want to give one or two people in each department the right to reset user passwords in the department and to modify user information for everyone in the department.

All of these options, and many more, are possible by creating an OU structure in AD DS and then delegating administrative access. You can grant almost any level of administrative access at an OU level. For example, if you create an OU for a remote office, you can grant the administrator in that remote office full control of all the objects in that office. This administrator can then perform any administrative task in that OU, including creating child OUs and delegating permissions to other administrators. If you create an OU for each department, you can grant very specific rights, such as the reset password right, to a few users in the department. You can even grant administrative rights based on the types of objects in an OU—the department administrators might be able to modify user accounts but not group objects or computer objects. Chapter 9, "Delegating the Administration of Active Directory Domain Services," goes into detail about delegating administration.

For most companies, the top-level OUs will be designed based on the requirement to delegate administration. The top-level OU will likely be based on geographic location or business departments. Often these OU boundaries will also be administrative boundaries.

OU Design Based on Group Policy Design

The second reason for creating OUs is to manage the assignment of Group Policy objects. Group Policy settings are used for change and configuration management of desktops. With Group Policy settings, you can provide users with a standard desktop configuration, including the automatic installation of a set of applications. Group Policy settings can also be used to control what changes users can make to their computers and to configure many of the security settings. Almost all of the Group Policy settings in AD DS will be assigned at an OU level, so the deployment of Group Policy settings will play an important part in the OU design. As you plan the OU structure, group together objects that require the same Group Policy settings. For example, if all the users in one department require the same set of applications, these can be installed using a Group Policy object. The users might also need a standard set of mapped drives. The logon scripts for the users can be assigned using a Group Policy object. Perhaps you want to apply a security template to all of the file servers in your organization. To do this, group all of the file servers into an OU and assign the security template using a Group Policy object.

In most companies, the lower levels of the OU design will be determined primarily by the need to apply Group Policy objects. By default, all Group Policy settings are inherited from parent OUs. This means that you can apply a Group Policy object to many departments high in the OU structure, and then apply more specific Group Policy objects at a lower level. If you want to modify the default inheritance of Group Policy settings, you can do so by creating an OU and blocking any policy inheritance at that OU level. This strong dependency on Group Policy for the OU design means that you must understand the Group Policy functionality and requirements for your organization. Chapter 11, "Introduction to Group Policy"; Chapter 12, "Using Group Policy to Manage User Desktops"; and Chapter 13, "Using Group Policy to Manage Security," discuss in detail what you can do with Group Policy.

Creating an OU Design

As you begin the OU design, you should begin with the top-level OUs first. Top-level OUs are harder to modify after deployment because of all of the OUs under them. This also means that the top-level OUs should be based on something static in the organization. Usually these OUs are based on geographic regions or business units.

A geographically based OU design is likely to be the most resistant to change. Some companies seem to reorganize frequently but rarely change their geographic configuration. An OU structure based on geographic locations also works well if the corporation uses a decentralized administrative model, especially when the administration is geographically based. If each geographic location (either a single office or a central office with several branch offices connected to it) has its own set of network administrators, the geographic OUs can be used to delegate administrative tasks to these administrators. A geographically based OU structure may not be the best choice if there are multiple business units in every geographic location. For example, if every department is represented in each office in the company, it might be more effective to use a business-unit-based OU structure at the top level.

The second most common top-level OU structure is one based on business units. In this model, a top-level OU is created for each business unit within the corporation. This type of configuration is most appropriate if a company has only one location or if many of the administrative tasks are delegated at a business-unit level. One of the problems with an OU structure based on business units is that the top-level OUs might need to be modified in the event of a corporate reorganization.

Most large corporations will actually use a combination of geographically based and business-unit–based OUs. One of the most common configurations is a top-level OU based on geographic regions, with the next level OUs within each region based on business units. Some companies might choose a top-level OU based on business units and then create a geographically based OU structure under these top-level OUs.

Figure 5-15 illustrates what an OU design might look like in one domain for a large company.

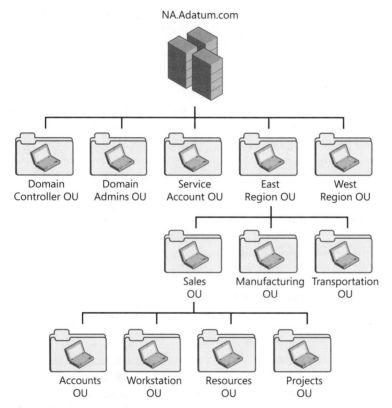

Figure 5-15   A sample OU structure.

In this example, the top-level OUs include the Domain Controllers OU (all domain controllers are located in this OU) and an OU for the domain-level administrators. Top-level OUs might also include a Service Account OU for all of the service accounts used in the domain. Creating an OU at the top level for special user accounts like service accounts simplifies the administration of these accounts. The top-level OUs might also include a Servers OU if all of the servers are centrally managed. In addition to these administrative OUs, there can be top-level OUs based on the geographic locations for the corporation. The geographically based OUs might be used primarily to delegate administrative tasks.

The second-level OUs in each geographic region are based on the business units in each region. The business-unit OUs might be used to delegate administration, but are also likely to be used to assign Group Policy objects. Under the business-unit OUs are OUs based on departments within the business units. At this level, the OUs will be used primarily to assign Group Policy objects or to assign specific administrative tasks such as the right to reset passwords. The department OUs might contain several other OUs:

- **Accounts OU**   This OU contains the user and group accounts for the department. In some cases, the accounts OUs might be further split up into OUs containing groups, user accounts, or remote users.

- **Workstations OU**   This OU contains all the user workstations and might include separate OUs for Windows NT workstations, Windows 2000 workstations, Microsoft Windows XP Professional workstations, and portable computers.

- **Resources OU**   This OU contains the resources linked to the OU. This could include objects like domain local groups, servers, printers, and shared folders.

- **Application or project-based OUs**   If a group of people and resources are working on a particular project or application that requires unique management, you can create an OU structure for those users and then group the users, resources, and computers needed for that project in this OU.

> **Note**   Theoretically, there is no limit to how many levels your OU structure can have. However, it is generally a best practice not to have more than 10 layers. For most companies, an OU structure that is four or five levels deep is all you will ever need.

As you work on creating the OU design, ensure that you document the design carefully. This design will include a diagram of OU structure, a list of all the OUs, and the purpose for each OU. Also, if you are using the OU to delegate administrative tasks, document the rights delegated at each OU level. As you deploy group policies linked to each OU, document the Group Policy configuration.

> **On the Disc**   You can use the AD Organizational Unit Design tab in the ADDS_ DesignDocument.xlsx spreadsheet on the CD to document your OU design.

Designing the Site Topology

All of the design topics discussed so far have dealt primarily with the logical aspects of AD DS design, with little regard for the actual network topology in the organization. Before you can deploy an AD DS design, you must deal with the issue of site design, which will be directly impacted by the network topology.

Figure 5-16 shows the process for creating a site design.

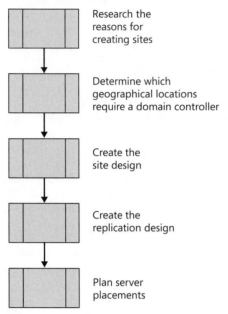

Figure 5-16   Creating a site design.

Sites and AD DS Design

In AD DS, sites are specific organizational entities and are used to manage network traffic. This is done in three primary ways:

■   Replication between sites is compressed so replication between sites uses less bandwidth than replication within a site. Further, replication can be scheduled to ensure it occurs when few other demands are being placed on the network.

■   Client logon traffic will remain within the site if the local domain controller is available.

■   AD DS–aware applications like Distributed File System (DFS) and Exchange Server 2007 can use sites to limit client access traffic or manage message routing based on the site configuration.

Creating a Site Design

Because site design is so dependent on the networking infrastructure, the first step in creating a site design is to document that infrastructure. After you have collected the information about the corporate network, you are ready to design the sites. To begin, examine each location where the computers are connected with a fast network connection. How many users are there in the location? Are there enough users in the location to require a domain controller in the location? What are the network connections from this location to other locations in the company?

> **Note**   The definition of a fast network connection will vary depending on factors such as the number of users in the location, the total number of objects in the domain, and the number of domains in the forest. You will also need to determine how much of the total bandwidth is available for replication. In most cases, the network connections within a site should have at least 512 kilobits per second (Kbps) of available bandwidth; in a large company, you might want to consider at least 10 megabits per second (Mbps) as the minimum network connection within a site.

If the reason for creating a site is to ensure that users can log on to AD DS, every site should have a domain controller, and most sites should also have a global catalog server. This means that if you are trying to decide whether or not to create a site for a company location with a small number of users and a slow network connection to other company locations, the question is really whether or not you want to put a domain controller into that site. One way to answer this question is to determine which option will result in the least network traffic across the network link. Which will create more traffic: the clients logging on to a domain controller in another location or the replication traffic between domain controllers?

In addition to determining which option results in the most network traffic, you also need to consider other factors. If you do not put a domain controller in the location, you need to consider the work disruption to the users if the network connection fails and the users cannot log on to the domain. You might also consider if a server is required in the location for other reasons. If you are deploying a server running Windows Server 2008 in the location anyway, can it also serve as a domain controller for the site?

One of the most critical factors when deciding whether to locate a domain controller in a company location is the physical security of the domain controller. If the physical security of the domain controller cannot be ensured, then you should not deploy a writable domain controller in the location. Deploying an RODC can address some of these security concerns, but you should still do as much as possible to ensure that RODCs are physically secure.

> **Note**   As you create an AD DS design for a company, the general rule of keeping things as simple as possible applies to everything but sites. When you are planning the forest, domain, or OU structure, simplicity should be one of your primary goals. However, creating additional sites for all of the company locations separated by slow network connections provides significant benefit without a significant increase in administration. So this might be the only time in the AD DS design process that the simplest solution might not be the best solution.

After you have determined how many AD DS sites you will require, the next step is to create the design for each site. Each site in AD DS is linked to one or more IP subnets, so as you create the design for each site, you should identify which subnets will be included in each site.

If you decide not to deploy a domain controller into a company location, you must determine which site this location will belong to and add that IP subnet to the appropriate site. This ensures that the clients in the remote location will connect to the domain controllers that are closest to them.

Direct from the Field: Subnet Definitions in Active Directory

Subnets are defined in Active Directory solely to define the sites in Active Directory to which a set of computers belongs. The subnet definitions do not correspond to the actual layer 3 routing within the organization. This is a key misunderstanding—the layer 3 routing design does not have to correspond to the subnet/site definitions in Active Directory at all. Second, Active Directory will match the most specific subnet. This means that if you have defined two subnet objects in Active Directory—10.1.0.0/16 and 10.1.2.0/24, and a client with an IP of 10.1.2.5, it will match the second subnet object.

One of the common events that fills up the event log on domain controllers in large organizations is NetLogon warning #5807. There are a couple of scenarios in which this happens. For example, one is when the Active Directory administrators simply don't define any subnets to go along with their site objects. The second example—and also the more common scenario—is one in which the team that runs Active Directory may not communicate well with the network administrators who provision subnets on the network. In large organizations, the subnet configuration may change frequently, and the Active Directory site specifications may not be maintained. The solution that I use and recommend is to define very broad-reaching supernets at my hub sites. For example, given a simple hub and spoke network design with one hub using private 10.0.0.0/8 IP addresses, I would associate 10.0.0.0/8 with the hub site. This guarantees me that any client coming from any 10.0.0.0 IP will match a subnet in Active Directory.

You can also apply this principal to organizations with multiple hub sites. Figure 5-17 shows an example.

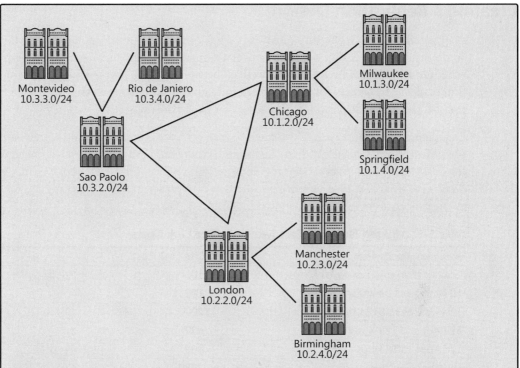

Figure 5-17   You can assign subnet objects with different subnet masks to hub sites and spoke sites.

In this scenario, it's easy to associate the 10.x.x.0 subnets with the spoke sites and then associate the 10.x.x.0/16 subnets with the hub sites. For example, I would create a subnet in Active Directory Sites and Services for the 10.3.0.0/16 subnet and assign that to São Paolo. I would then configure separate subnet objects for Montevideo and Rio de Janeiro using the 10.3.x.0/24 subnets. The advantage of using this approach is that if the IP address subnets at Montevideo or Rio de Janeiro are modified, or if an additional office is created and linked to the hub site, the clients in the site will use the closest hub site to locate a domain controller.

Another interesting option to apply when you configure subnets in Active Directory is to use defined host subnets by configuring subnets using /32 or 255.255.255.255 subnet masks. You can use this option to build a site within a site. For example, an organization may want to create a dedicated site for their Exchange environment but may not choose to create a provision for a dedicated subnet for the Exchange servers and associated domain controllers. By creating host subnets and grouping the subnets in a single site, you can associate the servers with a common site.

Brian Desmond

Microsoft MVP, Directory Services

www.briandesmond.com

Creating a Replication Design

After you have created the sites, the next step is to create the replication topology for the sites. To do this, you will design site links between company locations. For each site link, plan the schedule and replication interval as well as the site link cost. If you want to designate replication bridgehead servers for each site, identify all AD DS partitions that will be located in the site and designate a bridgehead server for each partition.

Calculating the cost for each of the site links can be complicated, especially if there are multiple possible routes between company locations. If there are multiple routes, you need to assign the costs for the site links so that the optimal route is used for AD DS replication. One way to determine what cost to assign to each site link is to create a table linking network bandwidth to site link cost. An example is shown in Table 5-3.

Table 5-3   Linking Network Bandwidth to Site Link Costs

Available Bandwidth	Site Link Cost
Greater than or equal to 10 Mbps	10
10 Mbps to 1.544 Mbps	100
1.544 Mbps to 512 Kbps	200
512 Kbps to 128 Kbps	400
128 Kbps to 56 Kbps	800
Less than 56 Kbps	2000

Using the information outlined in this table, you can assign a cost to each site link. Then calculate which route the replication traffic will take through the network if all links are available. Also calculate the effects of a network link failure. If there are redundant paths within the network, ensure that the site link costs are configured so that the optimal backup path will be selected in the event of link failure.

Direct from the Field: Costing Active Directory Site Links

There are a few things that you really have to consider when you're setting up your site links. Of these, the cost that you assign to the site links may be most important, but it can also be totally irrelevant. The cost of the link is used when computing the spanning tree where you have multiple network connections to a site. If you have a series of spokes off a hub that have a single link back to the hub, the cost is totally irrelevant when calculating the routing topology. On the other hand, if you have multiple paths from one site to another, the cost is used by the KCC to create the routing topology.

To assign a cost to a site link, I like to use a formula that relates the speed of the underlying transport to a numerical value that can then be assigned to the site link cost. I like to use the following formula:

$$\sqrt{\frac{\text{Reference Bandwidth}}{\text{Link Bandwidth}}}$$

The reference bandwidth is your maximum bandwidth, which will have a cost of 1, and the link bandwidth is the speed of the underlying transport. For example, if you have full 38.4 Gbps OC768 connection, it will have a cost of 1. If you have a T1 connection (1536 Kbps) connecting another location in your organization, the site link to the site at that location should have a cost of 158.

Assigning costs to your site links based on the underlying transport between the connected sites requires that you work closely with your WAN group to get all of the circuit information and make sure you're informed when they change a circuit. As well, you need to consider the available bandwidth for the connection when assigning the site link costs. For example, you might have a high bandwidth WAN connection that is significantly saturated most of the day and an alternative slower WAN link is not highly utilized. To ensure that the replication traffic is sent across the less-utilized WAN connection, you may need to increase the cost of the saturated link. You may also need to modify the cost of the site links if they use WAN links that have a monetary cost on a bytes transferred basis.

Brian Desmond

Microsoft MVP–Directory Services

www.briandesmond.com

Another option to manage AD DS replication is to turn off site link bridging. By default, site link bridging is enabled, which means that all site links become transitive. That means that if Site A has a site link to Site B, and Site B has a site link with Site C, Site A can replicate directly with Site C. In most cases, this is the desired behavior. However, there are exceptions when you might want to turn off site link bridging. For example, a company might have several hub sites throughout the world, with several smaller offices connecting to the hub sites using slow or medium network connections. (See Figure 5-18.) If the hub sites are connected with fast network connections, the automatic site link bridging is acceptable. However, if the network connections between the hub sites are fairly slow, or if most of the bandwidth is used for other applications, you might not want to have transitive connections.

In Figure 5-18, the network connection between Hub A and Hub B might have limited available bandwidth. If the default site link bridging is not modified, the bridgehead server in Hub A will replicate with the bridgehead server in Hub B, but also with the bridgehead servers in other sites connected to Hub B. This means that, potentially, the same replication traffic could cross the network connection five times. To modify this, you can turn off site link bridging and then create manual site link bridges for all of the site links between the hub sites and the smaller sites connecting to the hub sites. After this is configured, all replication from Hub A will flow to Hub B, and then it will be distributed to all the sites connected to Hub B.

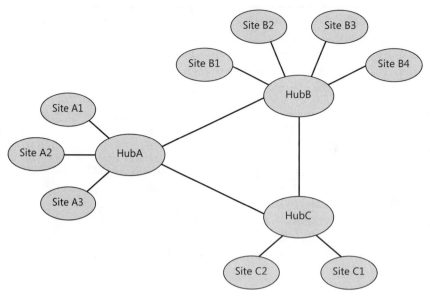

Figure 5-18 Configuring site link bridging.

On the Disc You can use the Site Design Decisions tab in the ADDS_DesignDocument.xlsx spreadsheet on the CD to document your site design decisions, and the AD Site Design and AD Site Link Design tabs to document your final site design.

Exchange Server 2007 and Site Design

One of the factors that you need to consider when creating a site design is whether or not your organization has deployed Exchange Server, and particularly whether or not the organization has or is planning to deploy Exchange Server 2007.

Exchange 2000 or later and messaging clients such as Outlook XP or later depend on the AD DS site configuration and on the domain controller and global catalog servers deployed in the sites. When Exchange Server services start, the server uses DNS to locate a domain controller in the same site as the Exchange Server and to read the Exchange Server configuration from AD DS. When the Exchange Server routes messages between recipients, the Exchange Server queries the global catalog for the recipient properties and queries a domain controller for information on how to route messages to the recipients. When Outlook clients access the global address list, the client is redirected by the Exchange Server to use a global catalog server to retrieve a listing of all users in the organization who are mail-enabled. In order for the Exchange Servers and message clients to respond quickly, a fast network connection is required to domain controllers and global catalog servers.

Exchange Server 2007 introduces several new dependencies on AD DS sites. In Exchange Server 2007, all messages must be routed through an Exchange Server running the Hub Transport server role. When a message is submitted to the server, the server queries Active Directory for information about where the message must be delivered. If the recipient's mailbox is on a Mailbox server in the same AD DS site as the Hub Transport server, it delivers the message directly to that mailbox. If the recipient's mailbox is on a Mailbox server in a different AD DS site, the message is relayed to a Hub Transport server in that site, which then delivers it to the Mailbox server. If the message is intended for a recipient outside the organization, the message is routed to an Exchange Server in an AD DS site with a connection to the Internet. If more than one route is available between AD DS sites, the Hub Transport server will use the site link costs to determine the most efficient route between sites. In other words, message routing in Exchange Server 2007 is dependent on the AD DS site design.

How clients access their mailboxes is also dependent on the site design. When users use any messaging client other than Outlook configured as a Messaging API (MAPI) client to connect to their mailbox, they must connect to an Exchange Server running the Client Access server role. The Client Access server role uses AD DS site information to provide efficient access to user mailboxes. When the Client Access server role receives a user connection request, it queries AD DS to determine which Mailbox server is hosting the user's mailbox and the server's site membership. If the Client Access server that received the initial user connection is not in the same site as the user's Mailbox server, the connection is redirected or proxied to a Client Access server in the same site as the Mailbox server.

This tight integration between Exchange Server 2007 and AD DS sites means that you should work on the Exchange Server design and the AD DS site design at the same time. When designing your AD DS sites to support Exchange Server 2007, consider the following:

- If you are deploying an Exchange Server 2007 in any company location, always deploy a domain controller and global catalog server in the same location. In addition, when planning the hardware requirements for the domain controller and global catalog server, consider the extra load that will be imposed on the server by the Exchange Servers and messaging clients.

- Consider deploying all Exchange Servers in a central site. You do not have to deploy Exchange Servers in each AD DS site. If high-bandwidth and reliable network connections link all of your organization's locations, regardless of the distance between offices, consider implementing a centralized messaging system in which all Exchange Servers are in one central location. Because all Exchange servers, and other required services such as domain controllers and DNS servers, are on the same fast network, this design will produce the best Exchange Server performance. However, if the requirements for user experience and availability cannot be met by connecting to a central location, you may have no choice but to position servers in the remote sites.

■ Consider creating a dedicated AD DS site for Exchange servers. If you use a centralized design for Exchange servers, or if you deploy several Exchange servers in a data center, consider creating a dedicated AD DS site that contains all of the Exchange servers in the location, as well as domain controllers and global catalog servers that are dedicated to providing directory services for the Exchange servers. This design enables more predictable Exchange Server performance because other clients are not using the domain controllers for authentication or directory lookups.

For additional information on designing AD DS to meet Exchange Server 2007 requirements, see "Guidance on Active Directory Design for Exchange Server 2007," located at *http://msexchangeteam.com/archive/2007/03/28/437313.aspx*; "Dedicated Active Directory Sites for Exchange," located at *http://msexchangeteam.com/archive/2006/08/28/428776.aspx*; and "Planning Active Directory," located at *http://technet.microsoft.com/en-us/library/bb123715.aspx*.

Designing Server Locations

As part of the site design, you will also need to determine where to locate DNS servers, domain controllers, global catalog servers, RODCs, and operation masters. In most cases, after you have completed the site design, locating the servers is not complicated.

Locating DNS Servers

As you know, DNS is a critical service in Windows Server 2008 AD DS. Without DNS, clients cannot locate AD DS domain controllers, and domain controllers cannot locate each other to replicate. This means that DNS should be deployed in every location in your organization, with the possible exception of very small offices with only a few users.

As a general rule, you should deploy at least one DNS server in every site that contains a domain controller. It is strongly recommended that you use AD DS integrated zones and deploy DNS on the domain controller. For small offices where you choose to locate a domain controller, consider deploying an RODC with DNS installed.

Site Design for Branch Offices

One of the special cases for site design is when a company has several hundred small locations with domain controllers in each location. This scenario complicates AD DS design and deployment in a number of ways. One example is the time that it takes for the Knowledge Consistency Checker (KCC) to calculate the replication topology. With every extra site, it takes longer to calculate the routing topology. While KCC is running on a domain controller, it can use 100 percent of the CPU time on the server. With a large number of sites, the domain controller running Inter-Site Topology Generator (ISTG) at the central office might run at 100 percent CPU utilization constantly and still never complete the calculation. Another complication has to do with the replication window. If the site connector is configured with a schedule to replicate for only six hours every night, you might find that you must deploy multiple bridgehead servers to complete the replication to all remote locations every night. Even setting up domain controllers for each site is complicated in this scenario. If the network connection is very slow and you simply install a domain controller in the site and then populate the directory by replication, the initial replication for a large directory may take hours.

Windows Server 2003 and Windows Server 2008 provide several significant enhancements that make the deployment of AD DS in this scenario easier than it was in Windows 2000. Enhancements to the calculation algorithm used by the ISTG process greatly reduce the amount of time required to calculate the intersite replication topology. The option to build a domain controller and populate AD DS from backup media means that building a domain controller in a remote office does not create as much replication traffic.

Despite these enhancements, designing and deploying AD DS sites in a company with hundreds of sites is still a special case. If you are dealing with this type of environment, the best resource available is the *Windows Server 2003 Active Directory Branch Office Guide*, available for download at *http://www.microsoft.com/downloads/details.aspx? FamilyId=9353A4F6-A8A8-40BB-9FA7-3A95C9540112&displaylang=en*. Though this guide was prepared for the Windows Server 2003 environment, many of the concepts are still applicable to Windows Server 2008.

How It Works: KCC Improvements in Windows Server 2008

Windows Server 2008 includes Knowledge Consistency Checker (KCC) improvements for RODCs that help to automatically balance the replication workload on domain controllers in a data center with multiple RODCs in sites connected to the site containing the data center.

A typical deployment scenario for RODC is the branch office. The Active Directory replication topology most commonly deployed in this scenario is based on a hub-and-spoke design, where branch domain controllers in multiple sites replicate with a small number of bridgehead servers in a hub site.

One administrative challenge highlighted by the hub-and-spoke topology on previous Windows Server operating system versions is that after adding a new bridgehead domain controller in the hub, there is no automatic mechanism to redistribute the replication connections between the branch domain controllers and the hub domain controllers to take advantage of the new hub domain controller.

In Windows Server 2008, normal Knowledge Consistency Checker (KCC) provides some rebalancing. When the KCC on an RODC detects a new bridgehead server candidate that it can replicate from, it determines whether to switch replication partners to that new bridgehead. The decision is based on an algorithm that provides probabilistic load balancing.

For example, a hub site could have four bridgehead servers and 100 RODCs that perform inbound replication from the four bridgehead servers—a 25:1 ratio. When another bridgehead server is added to the hub site, each RODC will detect the new bridgehead server when it replicates the Configuration partition from a bridgehead server. Then on the next KCC run, the RODC determines if it should switch its replication connection to the new bridgehead server. In this example, there is a 1-in-5 chance (a 20 percent probability) that an RODC will switch its replication connection. After all 100 RODCs have performed this operation, approximately 20 of them will have switched to replicate from the new bridgehead server.

The new functionality is enabled by default. You can disable it by adding the following registry key setting on the RODC:

HKEY_LOCAL_MACHINE\SYSTEM\CurrentControlSet\Services\NTDS\Parameters

"Random BH Loadbalancing Allowed"

1 = Enabled (default), 0 = Disabled

Rob Lane

Microsoft Escalation Engineer IV

Locating Domain Controllers

In most cases, a domain controller should be located in company locations where there are a significant number of users. There are at least two reasons for putting a domain controller in a particular geographical location. First, if the network fails, the users can still log on to the network. Second, locating a domain controller in an office ensures that the client logon traffic does not cross the WAN connection to a different location. If your business requirements state that users must be able to log on in the event of a network and single server failure, you should put two domain controllers in each location. In a small branch office, you may choose to deploy a single domain controller to limit the total number of domain controllers. If you do deploy a domain controller in a company location, then you should also create a site for that geographical location so that all logon traffic stays within the site.

There are two reasons why you might decide not to put a domain controller in a single site. If the replication traffic to the domain controller in the location would be higher than the client logon traffic, you could simply configure the domain controller location so that the clients can attempt to use a domain controller in an adjacent site for logon. Also, if there are no means of physically securing the servers, you should not put a writable domain controller in the site.

If you do decide not to deploy a domain controller in a site, you can still control which domain controllers the clients will log on to. One option is to configure a site for the branch office location and include all IP subnets for the office in the site. Then, configure a site link to one or more of the existing sites. Through automatic site coverage, AD DS will choose the domain controllers in the site connected by the lowest cost site link to cover the site that does not have a domain controller. A second method for controlling which domain controller will be used to authenticate users is to create IP subnet objects for the office without a domain controller and then add the IP subnet object to an existing site.

Another issue that you need to plan for if you are deploying multiple domains is the forest root domain controller locations. These domain controllers are required whenever a user accesses a resource in another domain tree or when a user logs on to a domain in a domain tree other than their own. Because of this, you should locate forest root domain controllers in any offices where there are a large number of users or where a significant amount of traffic will be directed to the root domain controllers. If your company has a network topology that includes regional hub offices, consider deploying a root domain controller in each of the hub offices.

> **Caution**   Because of the importance of the root domain and the impact to the forest if the root domain is ever lost, the forest root domain controllers should be geographically distributed. Even if there is no good reason to put a root domain controller in offices outside of the head office, consider doing so just to provide geographic redundancy. Like all domain controllers, however, the root domain controllers should never be located in an office where they cannot be physically secured.

Locating Global Catalog Servers

Global catalog servers are required for users to log on to AD DS domains, or when a user searches AD DS for directory information. In general, this means that you should put a global catalog server in every site. However, this ideal must be balanced with the replication traffic created by putting a global catalog server in every site. If you have a very large enterprise, with several large domains, the global catalog replication traffic will be significant.

One of the enhancements to Windows Server 2003 Active Directory and Windows Server 2008 AD DS is the fact that it does support logons to a domain without access to a global catalog server by supporting *universal group membership caching*. When universal group membership caching is enabled, domain controllers can cache the universal group member- ships for users in the domain. The first time the user logs on to the site, the user's universal group membership must be retrieved from a global catalog server. After the first logon, however, the domain controller will cache the user's universal group membership indefi- nitely. The universal group membership cache on the domain controller is updated every eight hours by contacting a designated global catalog server. To enable universal group membership caching, open the AD DS Sites And Services administrative tool and expand the site object for the site where you want to enable this setting. Right-click the *NTDS Site Settings* object and select Properties. On the Site Settings tab, select the Enable Universal Group Membership Caching option and, in the Refresh Cache From drop-down list, select the site where the closest global catalog server is located.

Designing Read-Only Domain Controller Deployments

One of the important new features in Windows Server 2008 is the option to deploy RODCs. RODCs provide all of the functionality required by clients to authenticate while providing additional security for domain controllers deployed in offices where the physical security of the domain controllers cannot be ensured. When designing your RODC deployment, you need to be concerned with the RODC placement as well as how user account passwords will be cached on the server, and how to configure delegated administrative permissions for the domain controller.

Designing RODC Placement   RODCs are designed to be placed in locations where you would like to deploy a domain controller, but where you have concerns about the domain controller security. You might also consider deploying RODCs in offices where there are no administrators who need to make changes to AD DS. In most cases, RODCs will be deployed in branch offices, but they can also be used to run applications that must run a domain controller.

When choosing whether to deploy an RODC in a branch office, use the same considerations as for deploying a domain controller with less emphasis on physical security. As a general rule, an RODC should be deployed as the only domain controller for its domain in a site. There are two additional considerations when designing RODC placements:

- Each RODC requires a writable domain controller running Windows Server 2008 for the same domain from which the RODC can directly replicate. RODCs can replicate changes to the schema, configuration, and application partitions from a Windows Server 2003 domain controller but can only replicate changes to the domain partition from a Windows Server 2008 domain controller. This means that a writable domain controller running Windows Server 2008 should be placed in the nearest site in the topology. If you have not disabled site link bridging, this is not an absolute requirement, but it is still strongly recommended.

- Domain controllers running Windows Server 2003 will perform automatic site coverage for sites with RODCs. Automatic site coverage is used to ensure that clients in domains without domain controllers will authenticate to the closest possible domain controller. Domain controllers running Windows Server 2003 do not consider RODCs when they evaluate site coverage requirements. As a result, they perform automatic site coverage for any site that includes only an RODC for the same domain. This means that Windows Server 2003 domain controllers will register site-specific SRV records for the site and potentially cause client computers to authenticate to the domain controllers outside the site rather than the local RODC. To prevent this from happening, you can:

- ❑ Ensure that all domain controllers in the site closest to the site containing the RODC are running Windows Server 2008 and ensure that at least one of those servers is a global catalog server.

- ❑ Disable automatic site coverage on domain controllers running Windows Server 2003. You can do this by editing the registry.

- ❑ Increase the weight the DNS SRV resource records registered by the RODC or decrease the priority of SRV records registered by Windows Server 2003 so that client computers are more likely to authenticate to the RODC that to a Windows Server 2003 domain controller.

- ❑ Use Group Policy to configure domain controller DNS Locator records. You can assign different weights to the DNS locator records by using Group Policy.

More Info   For details on how to configure these options, see "Step-by-Step Guide for Read-Only Domain Controller in Windows Server 2008" at *http://technet2.microsoft.com/windowsserver2008/en/library/ea8d253e-0646-490c-93d3-b78c5e1d9db71033.mspx?mfr=true.*

Designing RODC Administration   When designing the RODCs deployment, you also need to plan for delegated administration for the RODCs. One of the benefits of deploying an RODC is that you can configure a delegated local administrator for the RODC without granting any domain-level permissions. The delegated administrator can log on to an RODC to perform maintenance work on the server such as upgrading a driver. However, the delegated administrator would not be able to log on to any other domain controller or perform any other administrative task in the domain.

Consider delegating administrative permissions on the RODC if the domain controller is located in a branch office that does not have any domain administrators onsite. Although you may be able to perform most administrative tasks remotely, the local administrator will be available if the WAN link is not available (if you have configured credential caching for the local administrator). When you delegate local administrator permissions, the user account is not added to any extra security group. Instead, the user or group name is kept in an attribute in the RODC computer object in AD DS, which is used when that user tries to log on to the RODC.

The delegated local administrator credentials are not cached by default on the RODC. This means that the delegated local administrator will not be able to log on to the RODC if a writable domain controller is not available. If you are planning to use the delegated administrator primarily as a backup in case of WAN failure, you will need to enable credential caching for the administrator account. In addition, you need to ensure that the administrator has been authenticated by the RODC, or the credential cache has been prepopulated for this user account.

Designing Password Replication Policies   Another design option that you will need to consider for RODCs is credential caching. By default, no credentials other than the RODC computer account and a special krbtgt account are stored on the RODC. This means that the RODC must have an available connection to a writable domain controller whenever a user or computer authenticates to the RODC. When the RODC receives the authentication request, it forwards the request to a writable domain controller.

If you modify the Password Replication Policy, passwords will be cached on the RODC after the next successful logon of a security principal identified in the policy. After an account is successfully authenticated, the RODC attempts to contact a writable domain controller at the hub site and requests a copy of the appropriate credentials. The writable domain controller recognizes that the request is coming from an RODC and consults the Password Replication Policy in effect for that RODC. If the Password Replication Policy allows it, the writable domain controller replicates the credentials to the RODC, and the RODC caches them. After the credentials are cached on the RODC, the RODC can directly service that user's logon requests until the credentials change or until the Password Replication Policy changes.

When implementing a password replication policy, you must balance user convenience with security concerns. By default, no passwords are cached on the RODC. In addition, the policy explicitly denies credential caching for all domain administrative groups. If you do not change the default, users will not be able to logon to the RODC if a connection to the Windows Server 2008 writable domain controller is not available. If you enable password caching for all accounts, the impact of a security breach on the RODC is increased.

> **Note**   If the security of an RODC is compromised, you should remove the RODC computer account from Active Directory and reset the passwords for all user accounts that are cached on the server. When you delete the RODC account, you are given the opportunity to export a list of all accounts with cached credentials on the RODC. In addition, if the RODC is compromised, you should perform a security check on all workstations in the site to ensure that they have not been compromised as well.

When implementing a password replication policy, you have three high-level options:

- **Accept the default configuration so that no credentials are cached on the server.**   This option is feasible if the server security is most critical, and the WAN connection between the site containing the RODC and a site containing a writable domain controller is highly available. Although this option will not significantly improve the logon experience for users in the remote site, the RODC can still be used for DNS and global catalog lookups (if these features are installed on the RODC).

- **Explicitly allow or deny caching of user or computer credentials on the server.**   To do this, access the RODC computer account properties in Active Directory Users and Computers and add users, groups, or computer accounts to the appropriate list. By choosing this option, you can enable credential caching for those users and computers that are located in the RODC's site. When you access the RODC computer properties in Active Directory Users and Computers, you can identify which users and computers have authenticated to the RODC. You can then add these accounts to the password replication policy and also prepopulate the passwords on the RODC. This option provides a reasonable balance between user experience and security concerns in most organizations. If the RODC is compromised, only a limited number of credentials will be stored on the RODC.

- **Configure the RODC replication groups to configure credential caching.**   AD DS has two groups designed for RODCs to manage credential caching:

  - ❑ The Allowed RODC Password Replication Group includes all accounts whose credentials can be cached on all RODCs in the domain. When you add a user or group to this list, their credentials can be cached on all RODCs in the domain. By default, this group does not have any members.

  - ❑ The Denied RODC Password Replication Group includes all accounts whose credentials are explicitly denied from being cached on all RODCs in the domain. By default, this group contains all administrator accounts and all domain controller accounts. The Denied Password Replication Group has prevalence over the Allowed group; this means that if a user or computer is in both allowed and denied groups, the credentials will not be allowed to get cached on the RODC.

Choose this option if you want to apply a consistent password replication policy to all RODCs in the domain. For example, if you have a group of users that travel frequently to all of the remote sites that contain RODCs, you may choose to add the group to the Allowed RODC Password Replication Group. You can still enable password caching for local users by adding local groups directly to the password replication policy.

> **Caution**   Another factor that you may need to consider when deploying RODCs is application compatibility. Most applications that use AD DS will continue to function even if they connect to a read-only version of the data store, but applications that require write access to the AD DS may not work. For details on applications that do work with RODCs and for suggestions on how to test third-party compatibility with RODCs, see "Application Compatibility with Read-Only Domain Controllers," located at *http://technet2.microsoft.com/windowsserver2008/en/library/f1b06c27-0f6a-4932-afe6-a70749f8ab2f1033.mspx*.

Locating Operations Master Servers

The most important operations master for day-to-day operations is the primary domain controller (PDC) emulator. This server is especially important if your organization includes Windows NT or Window 9x down-level clients, as these clients must connect to the PDC emulator to change their passwords. Even if your organization does not have these older clients, the PDC emulator still receives priority updates of user password changes. As a result, the placement of the PDC emulator is significant. The PDC emulator should be placed in a central location where the maximum number of clients can connect to the server.

The placement of the other operations masters is not as crucial because the impact of these servers not being available for a short time is minimal. When deciding where to locate the operations masters, use the following guidelines:

- If possible, the schema master, domain naming master, and the relative identifier (RID) master should be located in a site with another domain controller as a direct replication partner. This is for disaster recovery purposes. If one of these servers fails, you might have to seize the operations master role to another domain controller. Ideally, you would like to seize the role to another domain controller that is fully replicated with the original operations master. This is more likely to be the case if the two domain controllers are in the same site and are configured as direct replication partners.

- The RID master must be accessible to all domain controllers through a remote procedure call (RPC) connection. When a domain controller requires more RIDs, it will use an RPC connection to request them from the RID master.

- The infrastructure master should not be located on a global catalog server if you have more than one domain. The infrastructure master's role is to update object display name references between domains. For example, if a user account is renamed and the user is a member of a universal group, the infrastructure master updates the user name. If the infrastructure master is located on a global catalog server, it will not function because the global catalog is constantly updated with the most recent global information. As a result, the infrastructure master will never detect any out-of-date information and thus never update the cross-domain information.

As a general rule, if an organization has a central location where most of the users are located, all the operations masters should be put in that site.

Summary

AD DS design is a topic that could take up an entire book by itself. As described in this chapter, AD DS design consists of understanding the organization's requirements for the AD DS design, designing the top-level components first, and then moving to lower-level components to meet those designs. This means that the first step in AD DS design is to create the forest design. This is followed by the domain design, then the DNS design, and finally the OU design. As you create the AD DS logical structure, you also need to design the physical AD DS components by designing the sites and domain controller placements.

Best Practices

- When creating a forest design, always start with the expectation that you will implement only a single forest. This is the easiest option to deploy and manage and automatically enables collaboration features such as the global catalog searching and Exchange Server features. However, be prepared to be convinced that additional forests are needed for administrative isolation.

- In any organization that has more than one domain, creating a dedicated root domain is strongly recommended. This design makes it easy to provide geographic redundancy for the root domain and isolates forest administrators from domain administrators.

- Never expose the DNS servers hosting your AD DS domain records to the Internet. If you are using the same namespace internally and externally, implement a split DNS in which two different servers host the internal and external zones.

- Implement AD DS integrated zones for AD DS domains even if you retain a DNS server infrastructure for other DNS functionality in your organization. AD DS integrated zones provide a high level of redundancy by enabling all DNS servers to have writable copies of the zone files.

- If you decide that you need to install a domain controller in an office, create a site for the office. If you cannot ensure the physical security of the domain controller, deploy an RODC.

Additional Resources

Related Information

- Chapter 4, "Active Directory Domain Services Replication," provides details on how to configure AD DS sites and replication.

- Chapter 6, "Installing Active Directory Domain Services," provides details on how to install AD DS domain controllers, including how to configure RODC settings.

- Chapter 9, "Delegating the Administration of Active Directory Domain Services," and Chapter 11, "Introduction to Group Policy," should be read before creating an OU design, as the topics covered in these chapters are critical when creating the design.

- "Multiple Forest Considerations in Windows 2000 and Windows Server 2003" at *http///technet2.microsoft.com/windowsserver/en/library/bda0d769-a663-42f4-879f-f548b19a8c7e1033.mspx?mfr=true*

- "Windows 2000/2003: Multiple Forests Considerations" white paper at *http://www.microsoft.com/downloads/details.aspx?familyid=b717bfcd-6c1c-4af6-8b2c-b604e60067ba&displaylang=en*

- "Domain Rename Technical Reference" at *http://technet2.microsoft.com/windowsserver/en/library/35e63f1e-f097-4c9c-a788-efc840d781931033.mspx?mfr=true*

- "Windows Server 2003 Active Directory Branch Office Guide" at *http://www.microsoft.com/downloads/details.aspx?FamilyId=9353A4F6-A8A8-40BB-9FA7-3A95C9540112&displaylang=en*

- "Creating a Forest Design" at *http://technet2.microsoft.com/windowsserver/en/library/ff92f142-66ea-498b-ad0f-a379c411eb6e1033.mspx?mfr=true*

- "Determining the Number of Domains Required" at *http://technet2.microsoft.com/ windowsserver/en/library/d390f147-22bc-4ce3-8967-e65d969bc40b1033.mspx?mfr=true*

- The following articles all discuss the impact of deploying Exchange Server 2007 has on creating an AD DS design:

  - "Planning for a Complex Exchange Organization" at *http://technet.microsoft.com/ en-us/library/aa996010.aspx*

  - "Guidance on Active Directory Design for Exchange Server 2007" at *http://msexchangeteam.com/archive/2007/03/28/437313.aspx*

  - "Dedicated Active Directory Sites for Exchange" at *http://msexchangeteam.com/ archive/2006/08/28/428776.aspx*

  - "Planning Active Directory" at *http://technet.microsoft.com/en-us/library/ bb123715.aspx*

- "Application Compatibility with Read-Only Domain Controllers" at *http://technet2.microsoft.com/windowsserver2008/en/library/f1b06c27-0f6a-4932-afe6- a70749f8ab2f1033.mspx*

Resources on the CD

- ListDomainControllers.ps1 is a Windows PowerShell script that lists all of the domain controllers in your domain and global catalog servers in your forest.

- ListFSMOs.ps1 is a Windows PowerShell script that lists all of the operations master servers in your forest and domain.

- ListADDSDomains.ps1 is a Windows PowerShell script that lists information about all of the domains in your forest.

- ListADDSSites.ps1 is a Windows PowerShell script that lists information about all of the sites in your forest.

- CurrentDirectoryEnvironment.xlsx and CurrentNetworkEnvironment.xlsx are spread- sheets that can be used to document the current directory and network environments at your organization.

- The CD contains several Microsoft Office Visio templates that can be used to diagram LAN and WAN configurations as well as a sample WAN diagram, WANDiagram_Sample.vsd.

- ADDS_DesignDocument.xlsx is a spreadsheet that can be used to document AD DS design decisions and the AD DS design.

Chapter 6

Installing Active Directory Domain Services

The process of installing Active Directory Domain Services (AD DS) on a server running Windows Server 2008 is a straightforward procedure. This is due to the well-designed Active Directory Domain Services Installation Wizard, the user interface used to install the service. When AD DS is installed on a computer running Windows Server 2008, the computer becomes a domain controller (DC). This process is also called *promotion*; a member server is promoted to a DC. If the promoted server is the first domain controller in a new domain and forest, a pristine directory database is created, ready to store the directory service objects. If this is an additional domain controller in an existing domain, the replication process is used to propagate all of the directory service objects of this domain to this new domain controller.

This chapter will present the information necessary for you to successfully navigate through the Active Directory Domain Services Installation Wizard, as well as discuss the unattended installation and installing from media (IFM). This chapter also covers the process for installing a Read-Only Domain Controller (RODC). Finally, it will present the process of removing AD DS from a domain controller.

Prerequisites for Installing AD DS

Any server running Windows Server 2008 that meets the prerequisites described in the following section can host AD DS and become a domain controller. In fact, every new domain controller begins as a stand-alone server until the AD DS installation process is complete. This process will accomplish two important goals. The first is to create or populate the directory database, and the second is to start AD DS so that the server is responding to domain logon attempts and to Lightweight Directory Access Protocol (LDAP) requests.

After AD DS is installed, the directory database is stored on the hard disk of the domain controller as the Ntds.dit file. During the installation of Windows Server 2008, the necessary packages are copied to the computer to install AD DS. Then, during installation of AD DS, the Ntds.dit database is created and copied to a location identified during the installation process, or to the default folder %systemroot%\NTDS if no other location is specified. The installation process will also install all of the necessary tools and DLLs required to operate the directory service.

The following sections explain the prerequisites for installing AD DS on a computer running Windows Server 2008.

Hard Disk Space Requirements

The amount of hard disk space required to host Active Directory will ultimately depend on the number of objects in the domain, and in a multiple domain environment, whether or not the domain controller is configured as a global catalog (GC) server. Windows Server 2008 has the following hard disk space requirements for installation:

- Minimum: 10 gigabytes (GB)
- Recommended: 40 GB or more

> **Note**   A Server Core installation requires only approximately 1 GB of disk space to install and approximately 2 GB for operations after the installation.

To perform an install of AD DS on a clean server running Windows Server 2008, the following minimum hard disk requirements should be met:

- 15 megabytes (MB) of available space required on the system install partition
- 250 MB of available space for the AD DS database Ntds.dit
- 50 MB of available space for the extensible storage engine (ESENT) transaction log files. ESENT is a transacted database system that uses log files to support rollback semantics to ensure that transactions are committed to the database.

For domain controllers running Windows Server 2003 that are being upgraded to Windows Server 2008, there are additional disk space considerations. You must plan for the necessary disk space for the following resources:

- Application Data (%AppData%)
- Program Files (%ProgramFiles%)

- Users Data (%SystemDrive%\Documents and Settings)
- Windows Directory (%WinDir%)

AD DS installation in an upgrade scenario requires free disk space equal to or greater than the disk space used for the four resources in this list (and their subordinate folders). In a default Active Directory installation, both the NTDS database and the log files are stored in the %WinDir%/NTDS folder, so they must be included in the total disk space calculation required for the upgrade. During the upgrade, these resources, including the NTDS database and the log files, will be copied to a quarantine location and then copied back after the upgrade is complete. All of the disk space that was reserved for the copying of the Active Directory files will be returned to the file system as available space.

In addition to the hard disk requirements listed here, at least one logical drive must be formatted with the NTFS file system to support the installation of the SYSVOL folder. In the upgrade scenario, unlike the Ntds.dit database and log files, the SYSVOL folder is moved, not copied, so no additional free disk space is required for that resource.

Before you create a new Windows Server 2008 domain in a Windows 2000 Server or Windows Server 2003 forest, you must prepare the existing environment for Windows Server 2008 by extending the schema. Running Adprep.exe will ensure that the existing Active Directory schema is prepared to interoperate with AD DS installed on a computer running Windows Server 2008. Adprep is covered in greater detail in Chapter 7, "Migrating to Active Directory Domain Services."

Network Connectivity

After installing Windows Server 2008 and before installing AD DS, verify that the server is properly configured for network connectivity. To do this, attempt to connect to another computer on the network, either by typing the UNC path or the IP address of the target computer into the Address line of Windows Explorer, or by using the Ping utility (for example, from the command line, type **ping 192.168.1.1**). In addition to ensuring network connectivity, you will have already determined that there is sufficient bandwidth on the network segment to support domain controller-based network traffic during the design phase of the AD DS implementation. For more information on planning for domain controller placement, see Chapter 5, "Designing the Active Directory Domain Services Structure."

Before installing AD DS, you should also configure the Internet Protocol (TCP/IP) settings on the Local Area Connection Properties sheet. To access this dialog box, right-click the Local Area Connection object in the Network Connections folder, select Manage Network Connections in the Network Sharing Center in Control Panel, and select Properties. On the Local Area Connection Properties sheet, select Internet Protocol Version 4 (TCP/IPv4) and/or Internet

Protocol Version 6 (TCP/IPv6); then click the Properties button. On the Internet Protocol (TCP/IP) Properties sheet, do the following:

- On the General tab, configure the computer with a static IP address.

- On the General tab, if the domain controller you are installing is *not* going to serve as a DNS server, configure the DNS server address with the IP address of the DNS server that is authoritative for the domain. See the following section for more information on configuring DNS for AD DS installation.

- For the IP v4 stack, on the Advanced TCP/IP Settings page, click Advanced on the General tab of the Internet Protocol Version 4 (TCP/IPv4) Properties sheet, click the WINS tab, and configure the server with the IP address of the Windows Internet Naming Service (WINS) server that the domain controller will use. (There is no WINS setting for the IP v6 stack.)

DNS

AD DS requires DNS as its resource locator service. Client computers rely on DNS to locate the domain controllers so that they can authenticate themselves and the users who log on to the network as well as to query the directory to locate published resources. Furthermore, the DNS service must support service locator (SRV) resource records, and it is recommended that it also support dynamic updates. If DNS has not been previously installed on the network, the Active Directory Domain Services Installation Wizard will install and configure DNS at the same time as AD DS.

Note   In Windows Server 2003, DNS server installation is offered, if it is needed. In Windows Server 2008, DNS installation and configuration is automatic, if it is needed. When you install DNS on the first domain controller in a new child domain in Windows Server 2008, a delegation for the new domain is created automatically in DNS. However, if you prefer to install and configure DNS manually, this is also possible.

Administrative Permissions

To install or remove AD DS, you must supply account credentials with administrative permissions. The type of account permissions you must have in order to install an AD DS domain depends on the installation scenario: installing a new Windows Server 2008 forest, installing a new Windows Server 2008 domain in an existing forest, or installing a new Windows Server 2008 domain controller in an existing domain. The Active Directory Domain Services Installation Wizard checks account permissions before installing the directory service. If you are not logged on with an account with administrative permissions, the wizard prompts you to provide the appropriate account credentials.

When you choose to create a new forest root domain, you must be logged on as a local administrator, but you are not required to provide network credentials. When you choose to create either a new tree-root domain or a new child domain in an existing tree, you must supply network credentials to install the domain. To create a new tree-root domain, you must provide account credentials from a member of the Enterprise Admins group. To install an additional domain controller in an existing domain, you must be a member of the Domain Admins global group.

Operating System Compatibility

Domain controllers running Windows Server 2008 are more secure than those running previous versions of the Windows Server operating system, and the Active Directory Domain Services Installation Wizard provides information on how this security affects client logon. The default security policy for domain controllers running Windows Server 2008 requires two levels of domain controller communication security: Server Message Block (SMB) signing and encryption and signing of secure channel network traffic.

These domain controller security features can present a problem for down-level client computers when logging on, as well as for some third-party applications. This will impact down-level client operating systems that reside in a mixed Windows Server 2008 and pre-Windows Server 2008 domain controller environment; they may experience intermittent failures when Windows Server 2008 domain controllers service authentication requests and requests to join the domain.

Windows Server 2008 domain controllers are configured with a "policy" that prohibits Windows and third-party clients that use weak cryptography methods from establishing secure channels with such DCs.

To fix this problem, update incompatible clients to use cryptography methods that are compatible with the secure default in Windows Server 2008. This may require getting updated software from the vendor in question.

If incompatible clients cannot be upgraded without causing a service outage, perform the following steps:

1. Log into the console of a Windows Server 2008 domain controller.

2. Start the Group Policy Management console.

3. Edit the default domain controllers policy.

4. Locate the following path in Group Policy Editor: Computer Configuration|Policies|Administrative Templates|System|Net Logon

5. Set Allow Cryptography Algorithms Compatible With Windows NT 4.0 to Enabled.

> **Note**   Allow Cryptography Algorithms Compatible With Windows NT 4.0 defaults to "not configured" in the default domain policy, default domain controllers policy, and local policy—but the default behavior for Windows Server 2008 domain controllers is to programmatically disallow connections using NT 4.0 style cryptography algorithms. As a result, tools that enumerate effective policy settings on a member computer or domain controller will not detect the existence of Allow Cryptography Algorithms Compatible With Windows NT 4.0 unless explicitly enabled or disabled in a policy.
>
> Windows 2000 and Windows Server 2003 domain controllers will not apply Allow Cryptography Algorithms Compatible With Windows NT 4.0 in their effective policy. Therefore, pre-Windows Server 2008 domain controllers will continue to service secure channel requests from computers using NT 4.0 style cryptography methods. This may cause inconsistent results if secure channel requests are intermittently serviced by Windows Server 2008 domain controllers.

6. Install corrective fixes or retire incompatible clients.

7. After less secure clients and devices have been upgraded or removed from the domain, set the option Allow Cryptography Algorithms Compatible With Windows NT 4.0 to Disabled.

Understanding AD DS Installation Options

You can start the installation of AD DS by using one of several graphical interfaces, or you can start it directly from the command line or the Run command. The graphical interfaces will install and configure the directory service as well as create and initialize the directory data store. Since AD DS requires a DNS implementation to be authoritative for the planned domain, the installation process will install and configure the DNS Server service if an authoritative DNS server is not already in place.

There are several methods for starting the installation of Active Directory:

- Initial Configuration Tasks Wizard and Add Roles Wizard
- Active Directory Domain Services Installation Wizard (Dcpromo.exe)
- Unattended installation

Installation Configuration Tasks and the Add Roles Wizard

When you first install Windows Server 2008, the Initial Configuration Tasks Wizard will appear. From this interface you can set the time zone, configure networking, and name the computer. In addition, you can also choose to add server roles—including AD DS, AD CS, AD FS, AD LDS, and AD RMS. Adding the AD DS role to the computer will install the necessary files and prepare the computer for running the Active Directory Domain Services

Installation Wizard. Figure 6-1 shows the Add Roles Wizard interface with AD DS server role selected.

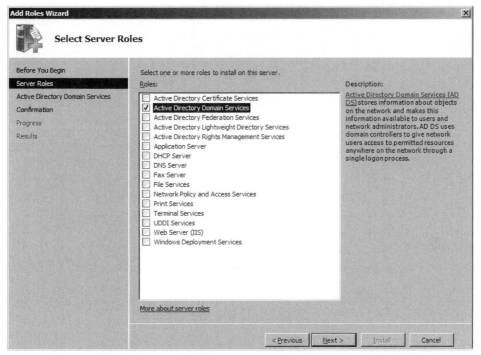

Figure 6-1   The Add Roles Wizard interface with the AD DS server role selected.

After the AD DS role is added to the server, you can launch the Active Directory Domain Services Installation Wizard (Dcpromo.exe) from the Add Roles Wizard interface, or you can continue to add additional server roles and run Dcpromo.exe at a later time.

Server Manager

Server Manager is a new feature that is included in Windows Server 2008, which is designed to guide administrators through the process of installing, configuring, and managing server roles and features that are part of the Windows Server 2008 release. Server Manager is launched automatically after the administrator closes the Initial Configuration Tasks Wizard. If the Initial Configuration Tasks Wizard has been closed, Server Manager is launched automatically when an administrator logs on to the server. From Server Manager, you can choose to add server roles to the server, including AD DS. You may want to use this interface to add server roles to the computer after you have closed the Initial Configuration Tasks interface. Figure 6-2 shows the Server Manager interface with the AD DS server role installed.

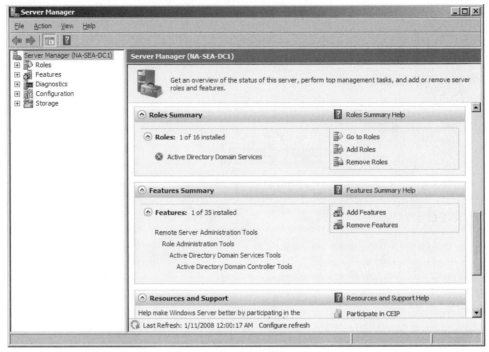

Figure 6-2   Server Manager with the AD DS server role installed.

After the AD DS server role is added, you will launch the Active Directory Domain Services Installation Wizard, either from the Run command, from the command prompt, or directly from a link within Server Manger. The installation wizard is covered in the next section.

Active Directory Domain Services Installation

The Active Directory Domain Services Installation Wizard can be started by typing **dcpromo.exe** in the Run dialog box or at the command prompt. Several command-line parameters are available for use with Dcpromo.exe:

- The /*adv* parameter is used to start the Active Directory Domain Services Installation Wizard in Advanced mode. In Windows Server 2008, the option to run Dcpromo in Advanced mode is now available from the Welcome page of the AD DS Installation Wizard. Use the Advanced mode when the domain controller will be created from restored backup files (also known as Installed From Media, or IFM), or when you are setting the Password Replication Policy for an RODC. When you add the /*adv* parameter, you will be prompted for the path to the restored backup files during the installation process.

- The /*unattend*:[unattendfile] parameter is used to perform an unattended installation of AD DS, on either a full install of Windows Server 2008 or a Server Core installation.

(The Server Core installation is a new installation option for Windows Server 2008 that does not provide graphical user interface options, such as the Active Directory Domain Services Installation Wizard.)

■ The */CreateDCAccount* parameter is used to create a Read-Only Domain Controller (RODC) account.

■ The */UseExistingAccount:Attach* parameter attaches the server to an RODC account.

The */CreateDCAccount* and */UseExistingAccount:Attach* options are mutually exclusive.

Detailed information on the key decision points is provided in the section titled "Using the Active Directory Domain Services Installation Wizard" later in this chapter.

Unattended Installation

In addition to the graphical user interface for installing Active Directory Domain Services, the installation process can be run in an unattended, or silent, mode by typing **dcpromo.exe /unattend:*unattendfile***, where *unattendfile* represents the filename of the unattend file that you have created. The unattended installation script file passes values for all of the user-input fields that you would ordinarily complete when using the Active Directory Domain Services Installation Wizard. For any key that is not defined in the unattend file, either the default value will be used for that key, or an error will be returned by Dcpromo indicating that the unattend file is incomplete. In Windows Server 2008, creating the unattend file for unattended installations has been greatly simplified from previous versions of AD DS and will be covered later in this chapter.

Using the Active Directory Domain Services Installation Wizard

The Active Directory Domain Services Installation Wizard is a straightforward user interface that prompts you for all of the options and variables in the AD DS installation process. Instead of walking you through this otherwise self-explanatory process, this section will discuss the key decision points you will encounter when installing AD DS.

To start the Active Directory Domain Services Installation Wizard, type **dcpromo** in the Run dialog box or at the command prompt. The Active Directory Domain Services Installation Wizard Welcome page appears. On the Welcome page, you can select to run Dcpromo in Advanced mode, which includes additional wizard pages for all but the most common installation scenarios. The selection of Advanced Mode in the Active Directory Domain Services Installation Wizard interface is illustrated in Figure 6-3.

Figure 6-3   The Active Directory Domain Services Installation Wizard Welcome page.

Deployment Configuration

The first decision you must make in the installation process is what type of domain controller you want to create. You must select either to create a domain controller in an existing forest or to create a new domain in a new forest, as illustrated in Figure 6-4. If you choose to add a domain controller to an existing domain or to create a new domain in an existing forest, be aware that all local accounts that exist on the server will be deleted, along with any cryptographic keys that are stored on the computer. You will also be prompted to decrypt any encrypted data, because it will be inaccessible after AD DS is installed.

If you are creating a new domain, you must choose whether to create a root domain in a new forest, a child domain in an existing domain, or a new domain tree in an existing forest. Consult your AD DS design documentation (see Chapter 5) to determine the nature of the domain you are creating. To create either a child domain in an existing domain or a new domain tree in an existing forest, you must supply the appropriate network credentials to continue with the installation process. No network credentials are required to create a new forest root domain.

> **Note**   The option to install a new domain tree appears only if you run the Active Directory Domain Services Installation Wizard in Advanced mode.

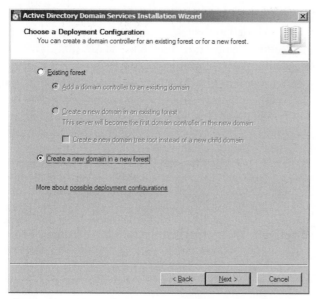

Figure 6-4   The Choose A Deployment Configuration page.

Naming the Domain

When creating a new domain controller for a new forest, you must provide the fully qualified domain name (FQDN) of the new forest root domain. Figure 6-5 shows the first stage of this process. You must follow specific rules when creating these names.

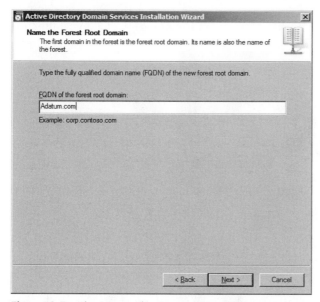

Figure 6-5   The Name The Forest Root Domain page.

The FQDN must contain a unique name for the new domain, and, if you are creating a child domain, the parent domain must be included in the DNS name and the parent domain must be available. For example, if you are creating the new domain NA in the ADatum.com domain tree, the FQDN that you must provide would be NA.ADatum.com. When naming the domain, available characters include the case-insensitive letters *A* through *Z*, numerals *0* through *9*, and the hyphen (-). Each component (label) of the FQDN (the sections separated by the dot [.]) cannot be longer than 63 bytes. (Internationalized domain names can encode Unicode characters into the byte strings within the FQDN character set, extending the available character and length support.)

> **Caution**   It is recommended that you do not use single-label DNS names when naming your AD DS domain. DNS names that do not contain a suffix such as .com, .corp, .net, .org, or companyname are considered to be single-label DNS names. For example, "host" is a single-label DNS name. Most Internet registrars do not allow the registration of single-label DNS names. It is also recommended that you do not create DNS names that end with .local. For more information on this best practice, see the article "Information About Configuring Windows for Domains with Single-Label DNS Names" located at *http://support.microsoft.com/kb/300684*.

Setting the Windows Server 2008 Functional Levels

Windows Server 2008 Domain and Functional Level settings determine the AD DS features that are enabled in a domain or in a forest and which version of Windows Server can be installed as domain controllers in the domain or forest. Forest and Domain Functional Levels are named after the Windows Server operating system that represents the features support for that version of Active Directory: Windows 2000, Windows Server 2003, and Windows Server 2008. Figure 6-6 shows the Set Forest Functional Level page in the Active Directory Domain Services Installation Wizard, and Table 6-1 lists the available features for each forest functional level.

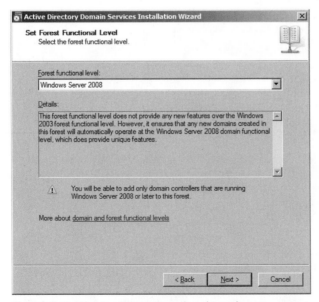

Figure 6-6   The Set Forest Functional Level page.

Table 6-1   Forest Functional Levels in Windows Server 2008

Forest Functional Level	Available Features	Supported Domain Controllers
Windows 2000 native	All of the default AD DS features are available.	Windows Server 2008, Windows Server 2003, Windows 2000
Windows Server 2003	All of the default AD DS features, as well as the following features, are available: ■ Forest trust/ ■ Domain rename/ ■ Linked-value replication/ ■ The ability to deploy a Read-Only Domain Controller (RODC) ■ Improved Knowledge Consistency Checker (KCC) algorithms and scalability ■ An improved ISTG algorithm ■ The ability to create instances of the dynamic auxiliary class named *dynamicObject* in a domain directory partition ■ The ability to convert an *inetOrgPerson* object instance into a *User* object instance and to complete the conversion in the opposite direction ■ The ability to create instances of new group types to support role-based authorization ■ Deactivation and redefinition of attributes and classes in the schema	Windows Server 2003, Windows Server 2008
Windows Server 2008	All of the features that are available at the Windows Server 2003 forest functional level, but no additional features are available. All domains that are subsequently added to the forest, however, operate at the Windows Server 2008 domain functional level by default.	Windows Server 2008

Table 6-2 lists the available features for each domain functional level.

Table 6-2 Domain Functional Levels in Windows Server 2008

Domain Functional Level	Available Features	Supported Domain Controllers
Windows 2000 native	All of the default AD DS features and the following directory features are available: ■ Universal groups for both distribution and security groups. ■ Group nesting. ■ Group conversion, which allows conversion between security and distribution groups. ■ Security identifier (SID) history.	Windows Server 2008, Windows Server 2003, Windows 2000
Windows Server 2003	All the default AD DS features, all the features that are available at the Windows 2000 native domain functional level, and the following features are available: ■ The domain management tool, Netdom.exe, which makes it possible for you to rename domain controllers. ■ Logon time stamp updates. ■ The *lastLogonTimestamp* attribute is updated with the last logon time of the user or computer. This attribute is replicated within the domain. ■ The ability to set the *userPassword* attribute as the effective password on inetOrgPerson and user objects. ■ The ability to redirect Users and Computers containers. ■ By default, two well-known containers are provided for housing computer and user accounts, namely, cn=Computers,<domain root> and cn=Users,<domain root>. This feature allows the definition of a new, well-known location for these accounts. ■ The ability for Authorization Manager to store its authorization policies in AD DS. ■ Constrained delegation. ■ Constrained delegation makes it possible for applications to take advantage of the secure delegation of user credentials by means of Kerberos-based authentication.	Windows Server 2003, Windows Server 2008

Table 6-2   Domain Functional Levels in Windows Server 2008 *(continued)*

Domain Functional Level	Available Features	Supported Domain Controllers
	■ You can restrict delegation to specific destination services only. ■ Selective authentication. ■ Selective authentication makes it is possible for you to specify the users and groups from a trusted forest who are allowed to authenticate to resource servers in a trusting forest.	
Windows Server 2008	All of the default AD DS features, all of the features from the Windows Server 2003 domain functional level, and the following features are available: ■ Distributed File System (DFS) replication support for the Windows Server 2003 System Volume (SYSVOL). ■ DFS replication support provides more robust and detailed replication of SYSVOL contents. ■ Advanced Encryption Standard (AES 128 and AES 256) support for the Kerberos protocol. ■ Last Interactive Logon Information. Last Interactive Logon Information displays the following information: ■ The time of the last successful interactive logon for a user. ■ The name of the workstation that the used logged on from. ■ The number of failed logon attempts since the last logon. ■ Fine-grained password policies. Fine-grained password policies make it possible for you to specify password and account lockout policies for users and global security groups in a domain.	Windows Server 2008

When you are setting the Forest Functional Level and Domain Functional Level, in general, set the domain and forest functional levels to the highest value that your environment can support. This way, you can use as many AD DS features as possible. However, if you may be adding Windows Server 2003 domain controllers to your environment, you should select the Windows Server 2003 functional level during Dcpromo. You can raise the functional level at a later time, once you have removed any down-level domain controllers from your environment. This procedure is covered in Chapter 7.

> **Important**   You cannot go back to a lower functional level after raising the domain or forest functional level or setting the domain or forest functional level to Windows Server 2008 during Dcpromo.

Additional Domain Controller Options

AD DS requires DNS to be installed on the network so that client computers can locate domain controllers for authentication. The DNS implementation must also support SRV records to achieve this end. It is recommended that the DNS implementation support dynamic updates.

If the computer on which you are installing AD DS is not a DNS server, or if the Active Directory Domain Services Installation Wizard can not verify that a DNS server is properly configured for the new domain, the DNS Server service can be installed during the AD DS installation. If a DNS implementation is located on the network but is not configured properly, the Active Directory Domain Services Installation Wizard provides a detailed report of the configuration error. At this point, you should make any necessary changes to the DNS configuration and retry the DNS diagnostic routine. If you select the default option to install and configure the DNS server, the DNS server and the DNS Server service will be installed during the installation of AD DS. The primary DNS zone will match the name of the new AD DS domain, and it will be configured to accept dynamic updates. The Preferred DNS server setting (on the TCP/IP properties sheet) will be updated to point to the local DNS server. Forwarders and root hints are also configured to ensure that the DNS server service is functioning properly.

> **More Info**   When the DNS Server service is installed by the Active Directory Domain Services Installation Wizard, the DNS zone is created as an AD DS integrated zone. For more information on configuring AD DS integrated zones, see Chapter 3, "Active Directory Domain Services and Domain Name System."

If you are creating the first domain controller in a new forest, the DC must be configured as a global catalog server. The first DC in the forest cannot be configured as an RODC. In the Dcpromo interface (as illustrated in Figure 6-7), the Global catalog option is selected by default and cannot be cleared, and the RODC option is unavailable. These options become configurable when you are installing additional domain controllers in the domain.

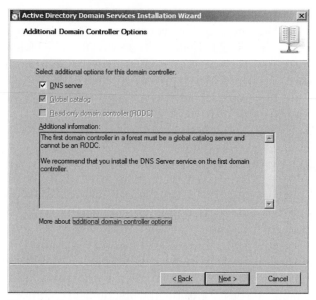

Figure 6-7   The Additional Domain Controller Options page.

File Locations

The Active Directory Domain Services Installation Wizard prompts you to select a location to store the AD DS database file (Ntds.dit), the AD DS log files, and the SYSVOL folder. You can either select the default locations or specify the locations for these folders. Figure 6-8 shows this interface.

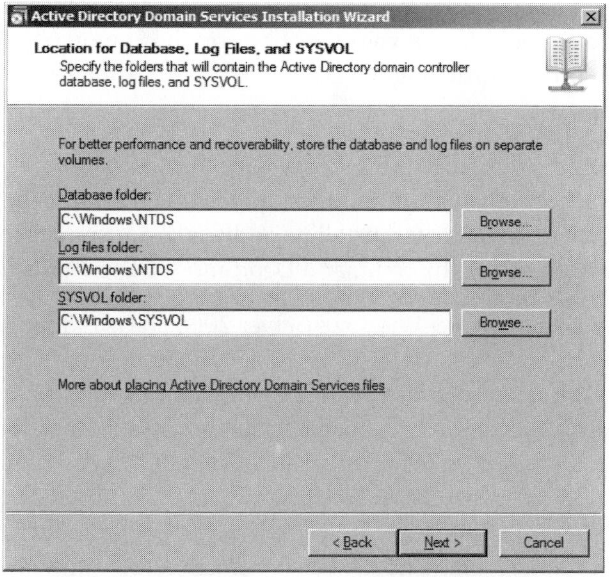

Figure 6-8   The Location For Database, Log Files, And SYSVOL page.

The default location for both the directory database and the log files is the %systemroot%\ NTDS folder. However, for best performance, you should configure AD DS to store the database file and the log files on separate physical hard disks. The SYSVOL shared folder default location is %systemroot%\sysvol. The only restriction on selecting the location for the shared SYSVOL folder is that it be stored on an NTFS v5 volume. The SYSVOL folder stores all of the files that must be accessible to all clients across an AD DS domain. For example, logon scripts or group policy objects must be accessible to all clients upon logging on to the domain, and they are stored in the SYSVOL folder.

Completing the Installation

The final pages of the Active Directory Domain Services Installation Wizard are straightforward. They involve setting the Directory Services Restore Mode password and reviewing the Summary page.

The Directory Services Restore Mode (DSRM) password is used for authenticating to the registry-based security accounts manager (SAM) database when the domain controller is started in this special recovery mode. If you are creating the first domain controller in the forest, the password policy in effect on the local server is enforced for the DSRM Administrator password. For all other installations, the Active Directory Domain Services Installation Wizard enforces the password policy in effect on the domain controller that is used as the installation partner. This means that the DSRM password that you specify must meet the minimum password length, history, and complexity requirements for the domain that contains the installation partner. By default, a strong password that contains a combination of uppercase and lowercase letters, numbers, and symbols must be provided.

The Summary page reports all of the options selected during the Active Directory Domain Services Installation Wizard. You should review your selections on the Summary page before completing the installation wizard and installing AD DS, and go back to previous pages if necessary.

You can select the Export Settings button on the Summary page to create an unattended file containing all of the options you selected in the Active Directory Domain Services Installation Wizard. You can then use the unattended file for installing additional domain controllers when you initiate the install process using the command Dcpromo /unattend:[*unattendfile*].

When you select Next on the Summary page, Windows Server 2008 starts the process of installing and configuring AD DS on the server. If this is the first domain controller in a new domain, this process is relatively quick because only the default domain objects are created and the directory partitions are quickly created. If you are installing an additional domain controller for an existing domain, all of the directory partitions must be fully synchronized after the domain controller is created. To allow you to delay this full replication process until after the computer restarts, a Finish Replication Later button appears at the beginning of the initial replication process. Although it is not recommended as a best practice, this option enables the normal replication process to synchronize the directory partitions on this domain controller at a later time.

Since the initial replication of the directory partition data can be time-consuming, especially across slow network links, you can choose to install an additional domain controller from restored backup files. This feature is discussed in detail later in this chapter in the section titled "Installing from Media."

Verifying Installation of AD DS

After you install AD DS, you should open the Active Directory Users and Computers (ADUC) and verify that all of the Builtin security principals were created, such as the Administrator user account and the Domain Admins and Enterprise Admins security groups. You should also verify the creation of the *special identities* such as Authenticated Users and Interactive. Special identities are commonly known as groups, but you cannot view their membership. Instead, users will automatically be joined to these groups as they log on or access particular resources. These special identities, however, are not displayed in the ADUC by default. To view these objects, select View and then select Advanced Features.

This will display additional components in the tool that are not visible by default. When you open the Foreign Security Principals container, you will find the objects *S-1-5-11* and *S-1-5-4*, which are the *Authenticated Users SID* and the *Interactive SID*, respectively. Double-click these objects to view their properties and default permissions.

In addition to the verification steps in ADUC, perform the following steps to verify the installation of AD DS:

- Check the Directory Service log in Event Viewer and resolve any errors.
- Ensure that the SYSVOL folder is accessible to clients.
- If you installed DNS during the installation of Active Directory Domain Services, verify that the service installed properly:
    1. Open DNS Manager.
    2. Click Start, click Server Manager, and then navigate to the DNS Server page.
    3. Navigate to the Forward Lookup Zones page to verify that the _msdcs.forest_root_domain and forest_root_domain zones were created.
    4. Expand the forest root_domain node to verify that the DomainDnsZones and ForestDnsZones application directory partitions were created.
- Verify that AD DS replication is working properly using the Domain Controller Diagnostics tool, Dcdiag.exe:
    1. Open a Command Prompt.
    2. Type the following command and then press Enter:

       dcdiag /test:replication

3. To verify that the proper permissions are set for replication, type the following command and then press Enter:

dcdiag /test:netlogons

Messages indicate that the connectivity and netlogons tests passed.

Performing an Unattended Installation

To install AD DS without user interaction, you can use the /*unattend*:[unattendfile] parameter with the Dcpromo.exe command. With this parameter, you must include the filename for the unattended installation (or *answer*) file. The answer file contains all of the data that is normally required during the installation process. It can be automatically generated by selecting the Export Settings option during a previous running of Dcpromo.

> **Note**   In addition to running Dcpromo in the unattended mode on an installed Windows Server 2008 computer, you can also install AD DS while installing Windows Server 2008 in unattended mode. In this scenario, you will use the <media_drive>\I386\winnt32 /unattend:[*unattend.txt*] command, where *unattend.txt* is the name of the answer file used for the full Windows Server 2008 installation. Specifically, Unattend.txt must contain the [DCInstall] section to be able to install the AD DS role during the unattended installation of Windows Server 2008.

To perform an unattended installation of AD DS after the Windows Server 2008 operating system has been installed, create an answer file that contains all of the information necessary to install AD DS. To execute this unattended installation, at the command prompt or in the Run dialog box, type **dcpromo /unattend:unattendfile.** The unattended file is an ASCII text file that contains all of the information required to complete the pages of the Active Directory Domain Services Installation Wizard. To create a new domain in a new tree in a new forest with the DNS Server service automatically configured, the contents of the unattended file would look like this:

```
[DCInstall]
InstallDNS=yes
NewDomain=forest
NewDomainDNSName=Adatum.com
DomainNetBiosName=Adatum
ReplicaOrNewDomain=domain
ForestLevel=3
DomainLevel=3
DatabasePath="C:\Windows\NTDS"
LogPath="C:\Windows\NTDS"
RebootOnCompletion=yes
SYSVOLPath="C:\Windows\SYSVOL"
SafeModeAdminPassword=Pa$$w0rd
```

Keys and Appropriate Values in Unattended Installations

During an unattended installation, for keys with no values set or omitted keys, the default value will be used. The required keys for the answer file will change depending on the type of domain to be created (new or existing forest, new or existing tree). An additional key that can be used for promoting a domain controller using a restore from backup media is *ReplicationSourcePath*. To use this key, assign the value of the location of the restored backup files that will be used to populate the directory database for the first time. (This is the same as the path to the restored backup files that is selected when using this feature through the Active Directory Domain Services Installation Wizard.) See the following section, "Installing from Media," for more information on this feature.

For more information regarding keys and appropriate values, see the Appendix of Unattended Installation Parameters in the Step-by-Step Guide for Windows Server 2008 Active Directory Domain Services Installation and Removal at *http://technet2 .microsoft.com/windowsserver2008/en/library/f349e1e7-c3ce-4850-9e50- d8886c866b521033.mspx?mfr=true.*

Installing from Media

You can use the install from media (IFM) option to install an additional domain controller in an existing domain and use restored backup files to populate the AD DS database. This will minimize replication traffic during the installation, and the option is well suited for deployments with limited bandwidth to other replication partners (such as a branch office scenario). You can create the installation media by using the Windows Server Backup tool in Windows Server 2008. In this case, you need to use the Wbadmin command-line tool option to restore system state data to an alternate location.

Windows Server 2008 includes an improved version of Ntdsutil.exe that you can also use to create the installation media. Using Ntdsutil.exe is recommended, because Windows Server Backup can back up only the set of critical volumes, which occupies much more space than is required for AD DS installation data. Ntdsutil.exe can create the four types of installation media, for both writable domain controllers and for RODCs.

 Note   For RODC installation media, Ntdsutil removes any cached secrets, such as passwords.

To create installation media using Ntdsutil.exe, follow these steps:

1. Click Start, right-click Command Prompt, and then click Run As Administrator to open an elevated command prompt.

2. Type **ntdsutil** and then press Enter.

3.   At the ntdsutil prompt, type **activate instance ntds** and then press Enter.

4.   At the ntdsutil prompt, type **ifm** and then press Enter.

5.   At the ifm prompt, type the command for the type of installation media that you want to create and then press Enter. For example, to create RODC installation media that does not include SYSVOL data, type the following command:

     Create rodc *filepath*

     where *filepath* is the path to the folder where you want the installation media to be created. You can save the installation media to a local drive, shared network folder, or to any other type of removable media.

The four different types of installation media are listed in Table 6-3.

Table 6-3   IFM Types

Parameter	Type of Installation Media
Create Full	Full (or writable) domain controller
Create RODC	Read-only domain controller
Create Sysvol Full	Full (or writable) domain controller without SYSVOL data
Create Sysvol RODC	Read-only domain controller without SYSVOL data

To populate the AD DS database when installing additional domain controllers, you will provide the location of the shared folder or removable media where you store the installation media on the Install From Media page in the Active Directory Domain Services Installation Wizard. During an unattended installation, you will use the */ReplicationSourcePath* parameter to point to the installation media.

Deploying Read-Only Domain Controllers

Windows Server 2008 provides a new way for you to install a domain controller in a branch office scenario. This installation process lets you deploy a Read-Only Domain Controller (RODC) to a branch office in two stages. First, you create an account (or slot) for the RODC. When you create the account, you will designate the user account that will install and administer the RODC. The delegated RODC administrator can complete the installation by attaching a server to the RODC account you created for it. This eliminates the need to use a staging site for building branch office domain controllers or to use domain administrator credentials to build the RODC in the branch office.

When you install an RODC, keep the following considerations in mind:

■   Before installing an RODC in your forest, you have to prepare it by running adprep /rodcprep (available from the Windows Server 2008 installation media).

■   The first DC installed in a new forest must be a Global Catalog server (GC) and cannot be an RODC.

- The RODC must replicate domain data from a writable domain controller that runs Windows Server 2008.

- By default, the RODC does not cache the passwords of any domain users. You must modify the default password replication policy for the RODC to allow the RODC to authenticate users and their computers when the WAN link to the hub site is offline.

Server Core Installation Window Server 2008

The best practice is to deploy an RODC on a Server Core installation of Windows Server 2008. A Server Core installation provides a minimal environment for running specific server roles, which enhances network security by reducing the attack surface for those server roles. In this sense, *minimal* refers to the low use of memory and disk space by the Server Core installation. In addition, a Server Core installation does not provide any graphical UI (GUI).

To install AD DS on a Server Core installation of Windows Server 2008, perform an unattended installation. A Server Core installation supports the following server roles:

- AD DS Domain Services (AD DS)
- AD DS Lightweight Directory Services (AD LDS)
- DHCP Server
- DNS Server
- File Services
- Print Services
- Web Services (IIS)
- Hyper-V

Deploying the RODC

You can perform a staged installation of an RODC. In this case, different designated users run the installation wizard at different times, and most likely in different locations. First, a member of the Domain Admins group creates an RODC account by using the Active Directory Users And Computers snap-in in Microsoft Management Console (MMC). Either right-click the Domain Controllers container or click the Domain Controllers container, click Action, and then click Pre-create Read-only Domain Controller account to start the wizard and create the account. The pre-creation of the RODC account can also be done by using the command-line parameter *dcpromo /ReplicaDomainDNSName:<domain_name> /createDCaccount*. When you create the RODC account, you can delegate the installation and administration of the RODC to a user or, preferably, to a security group.

On the server that will become the RODC, the delegated RODC administrator runs the Active Directory Domain Services Installation Wizard by typing **dcpromo /UseExistingAccount: Attach** at a command prompt to start the wizard.

Removing AD DS

AD DS is removed from a domain controller using the same command that is used to install it—Dcpromo.exe. When you run this command on a computer that is already a domain controller, the Active Directory Domain Services Installation Wizard notifies you that it will uninstall AD DS if you choose to proceed. This section will discuss the removal of AD DS from both the last domain controller and an additional domain controller in a Windows Server 2008 domain.

When you remove AD DS on a domain controller, the directory database is deleted, all of the services required for AD DS are stopped and removed, the local SAM database is created, and the computer is demoted to a member server. More specifically, what happens will depend on whether the domain controller is an additional domain controller or the last domain controller in the domain or forest.

To remove AD DS from a domain controller, type **dcpromo** at the command prompt or in the Run dialog box. Your first decision is to determine whether or not the domain controller is the last domain controller in the domain. See Figure 6-9 for an illustration of the wizard page that prompts you for that decision.

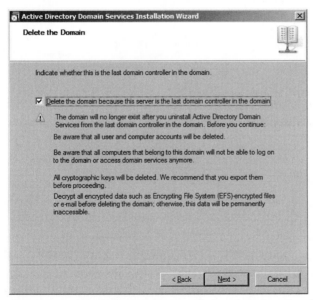

Figure 6-9   The option to remove the last domain controller.

Next, the Active Directory Domain Services Installation Wizard displays a list of all of the application directory partitions found on the domain controller. If this is the last domain controller in the domain, then this is the last source for this application data. You may want to back up or otherwise protect this data before continuing to use Active Directory Domain Services Installation Wizard, which will delete these directory partitions. If the domain controller from which you are removing AD DS is also a DNS server, there will be at least two application directory partitions to store the zone data. See Figure 6-10 for an example of DNS application directory partitions found while uninstalling AD DS.

Figure 6-10   Removing the DNS application directory partitions.

After you confirm the removal of the application directory partitions, you are prompted to enter a new password for the local Administrator account. Finally, review the Summary page and complete the removal of AD DS. You must restart the computer to complete the process. After the computer restarts, it will hold the role either of member server or stand-alone server.

Removing Additional Domain Controllers

Removing AD DS from additional domain controllers is not as intricate as removing AD DS from the last domain controller in a domain or forest. This is because replicas of the directory partitions are stored on the other domain controllers, so no directory data is actually lost. However, data in application partitions will be deleted during removal, so you should make sure that you either do not need the application after AD DS is removed, or that you choose another DC in the domain to be a replica for the application partition. A number of changes do occur on the domain controller as AD DS is uninstalled:

- All operations master roles are transferred to other domain controllers in the domain. However, to better control the placement of FSMO roles in your environment, you should transfer the FSMO roles manually before demotion.

- The SYSVOL folder and all of its contents are removed from the domain controller.

- The *NTDS Settings* object and cross-references are removed.

- DNS is updated to remove the domain controller SRV records.

- The local SAM database is created to handle local security policy.

- All Active Directory–related services that start when AD DS is installed (such as Net Logon) are stopped.

Finally, the computer account type is changed from domain controller to member server, and the computer account is moved from the Domain Controllers container to the Computers container. To remove AD DS from an additional domain controller, you must be logged on as either a member of the Domain Admins or the Enterprise Admins group.

> **Note**   When removing AD DS from an additional domain controller, make sure that there are other GCs available in the domain. GCs are required for user logon, and unlike the operations master roles, this role is not automatically transferred.

Removing the Last Domain Controller

In addition to all of the interesting things that occur when an additional domain controller is removed, specific events occur when the last domain controller in a domain is removed. Most importantly, of course, the removal of the last domain controller in a domain serves to remove the domain itself. Likewise, if the domain controller is the last in a forest, the forest is also removed. Among the events associated with the removal of the last domain controller in a domain are these:

- Active Directory Domain Services Installation Wizard verifies that no child domains exist. Removal of AD DS is blocked if child domains are found.

- If the domain to be removed is a child domain, a domain controller in the parent domain is contacted and changes are replicated.

- All objects related to this domain are removed from the forest.

- Any trust objects on the parent domain controllers are removed.

Finally, after AD DS is removed, the computer account type is changed from a domain controller to a member server. The server is then placed in a workgroup called *Workgroup*.

To remove the last domain controller in a child domain or in a tree-root domain, you must either be logged on as a member of the Enterprise Admins group or provide enterprise administrator credentials during the running of the Active Directory Domain Services Installation Wizard. If you are removing AD DS from the last domain controller in the forest, you must be logged on either as Administrator or as a member of the Domain Admins group.

Unattended Removal of AD DS

Removal of AD DS can be automated in a fashion similar to the unattended installation previously discussed. In fact, the same command line is used to remove AD DS as is used to install it. The only difference is the content of the answer file.

To perform an unattended removal of AD DS, at the command line or in the Run dialog box, type **dcpromo /unattend:***answerfile* (where *answerfile* is the filename of the answer file that you create). The answer file contains the key values that represent the decisions discussed earlier for using the Active Directory Domain Services Installation Wizard to uninstall AD DS. A key value of note is *IsLastDCInDomain*, which can have the value of *Yes* or *No*. If you set the value of this key to *Yes*, then you have indicated that you are removing AD DS from the last domain controller in the domain, and the domain itself will be removed. A sample answer file for removing an additional domain controller is reproduced below:

```
[DCInstall]
RebootOnSuccess=Yes
IsLastDCInDomain=No
AdministratorPassword=password
Password=DomainAdminPassword
UserName=Administrator
```

Forced Removal of a Windows Server 2008 Domain Controller

There is a new feature in Windows Server 2008 to forcefully remove a domain controller, even when it is started in Directory Services Restore Mode. This feature is specifically useful if the domain controller has no connectivity with other domain controllers. Because the domain controller cannot contact other domain controllers during the operation, the AD DS forest metadata is not automatically updated as it is when a domain controller is removed normally. Instead, you must manually update the forest metadata after you remove the domain controller.

> **More Info**   For more information about performing metadata cleanup, see article 216498 in the Microsoft Knowledge Base at *http://go.microsoft.com/fwlink/?LinkId=80481*.

You can forcefully remove a domain controller at a command line or by using an answer file. To force the removal a Windows Server 2008 domain controller using the graphical user interface, perform the following steps:

1. At a command prompt, type **dcpromo /forceremoval** and then press Enter.

2. If the domain controller hosts any FSMO roles, or if it is a DNS server or a global catalog server, warning messages appear that explain how the forced removal will affect the rest of the environment. After you read each warning, click Yes.

> **Note**   To suppress the warnings in advance of the removal operation, type **/demotefsmo:yes** at the command line.

3. On the Welcome to the Active Directory Domain Services Installation Wizard page, click Next.

4. On the Force The Removal Of Active Directory Domain Services page, review the information about forcing the removal of AD DS and metadata cleanup requirements and then click Next.

5. On the Administrator Password page, type and confirm a secure password for the local Administrator account and then click Next.

6. On the Summary page, review your selections in the wizard. Click Back to make any necessary changes, if necessary.

7. Click Next to remove AD DS.

8. Select the Reboot On Completion check box to have the server restart automatically, or you can restart the server to complete the AD DS removal when you are prompted to do so.

Summary

In this chapter, you were introduced to the major decisions you must make during a Windows Server 2008 AD DS installation. Although the mechanics of installing AD DS are straightforward, the decisions that you will make should be carefully planned and must fit into your AD DS design plan. The ability to deploy RODCs in your remote sites is a powerful new feature of Windows Server 2008, and this chapter covered how that deployment is performed first by creating the DC slot and role delegation, and next by installing the DC in the remote site and replicating the attributes you have determined safe to store at that remote site. Removal of AD DS is also a simple procedure, but you must consider the impact on the rest of your directory services infrastructure caused by removing a domain controller. This chapter also introduced a new AD DS installation feature: installing an additional, or replica, domain controller from restored backup files. This feature will greatly reduce the amount of time it takes to install an additional domain controller due to the time it takes to synchronize the directory partitions.

Additional Resources

The following resources contain additional information and tools related to this chapter.

Related Information

You can refer to these additional resources for more information on installing AD DS on a computer running Windows Server 2008.

■ For more information about planning your DNS namespace and designing the AD DS structure, see Chapter 5, "Designing the Active Directory Domain Services Structure."

■ For more information about installing and removing AD DS, see "Step-by-Step Guide for Windows Server 2008 Active Directory Domain Services Installation and Removal" at *http://go.microsoft.com/fwlink/?LinkId=100492.*

- For more information about deploying AD DS, see "Planning an Active Directory Domain Services Deployment" at *http://go.microsoft.com/fwlink/?LinkId=100493*.

- For more information about assessing the hardware requirements of domain controllers in a Windows Server 2008 domain, see "Planning Domain Controller Capacity" at *http://go.microsoft.com/fwlink/?LinkId=89027*.

- For more information about AD DS functional levels, see "Enabling Windows Server 2008 Advanced Features for Active Directory Domain Services" at *http://go.microsoft.com/fwlink/?LinkId=89030*.

- For more information about deploying AD DS regional domains, see "Deploying Windows Server 2008 Regional Domains" at *http://go.microsoft.com/fwlink/?LinkId=89029*.

- For more information about installing and configuring a DNS server, see "Deploying Domain Name System (DNS)" at *http://go.microsoft.com/fwlink/?LinkId=93656*.

- For more information about additional methods of installing a new Windows Server 2008 forest, see "Installing a New Windows Server 2008 Forest" at *http://go.microsoft.com/fwlink/?LinkId=101704*.

- For more information about tests that you can perform by using Dcdiag.exe, see "Dcdiag Overview" at *http://go.microsoft.com/fwlink/?LinkId=93660*.

- For more information about verification tasks that can be performed on a computer on which Active Directory has been newly installed, see "Verifying Active Directory Installation" at *http://go.microsoft.com/fwlink/?LinkId=68736*.

- For more information about configuring and deploying the Windows Time Service, see "Administering the Windows Time Service" at *http://go.microsoft.com/fwlink/?LinkId=93658*.

- For more information about DNS server forwarders, see "Using Forwarders to Manage DNS Servers" at *http://go.microsoft.com/fwlink/?LinkId=93659*.

- For information about using media to install the domain controller, see "Installing AD DS from Media" at *http://go.microsoft.com/fwlink/?LinkId=93104*.

- For more information about alternate methods of installing additional Windows Server 2008 domain controllers in an existing forest, see "Installing an Additional Windows Server 2008 Domain Controller" at *http://go.microsoft.com/fwlink/?LinkId=92692*.

- For more information about configuring DNS Client services, see "Configuring and Managing DNS Clients" at *http://go.microsoft.com/fwlink/?LinkId=93662*.

- For a procedure to help you transfer operations master roles, see "Transfer Operations Master Roles" at *http://go.microsoft.com/fwlink/?LinkId=93664*.

- For more information about operations master role placement, see "Planning Operations Master Role Placement" at *http://go.microsoft.com/fwlink/?LinkId=93665*.

Related Tools

■ To determine if the network segment where you will place the domain controller has sufficient bandwidth to support domain controller traffic, you can use a network frame analysis tool, such as Network Monitor. The current version, 3.1, is available on the Microsoft Download Center at *http://www.microsoft.com/downloads/details.aspx? FamilyID=18b1d59d-f4d8-4213-8d17-2f6dde7d7aac&DisplayLang=en.*

■ For more information on Network Monitor, see the blog Network Monitor at *http:// blogs.technet.com/netmon.* Also see the Network Monitor page on Microsoft Technet at *http://technet2.microsoft.com/WindowsServer/en/library/ad2b59d1-0fb8-45e3-9055-a5aeba8817a91033.mspx?mfr=true.*

Chapter 7
Migrating to Active Directory Domain Services

Chapter 6, "Installing Active Directory Domain Services," covered the key decisions you will have to make when installing AD DS on a computer running Windows Server 2008. For ease of understanding, that chapter assumed a "green field" environment—one with no preexisting directory service infrastructure in place. Chapter 6 emphasized the importance of the AD DS namespace and the Domain Name System (DNS) namespace. Most likely, the organization that is moving (or *migrating*) to AD DS and Windows Server 2008 will be coming from some preexisting directory services environment, including previous versions of AD DS. This chapter examines the migration to Windows Server 2008 AD DS from an existing Microsoft directory services environment—specifically from either a Windows 2000 Server or Windows Server 2003 Active Directory platform. Migration scenarios from non-Microsoft directory services technologies, such as Novell Directory Services (NDS) or UNIX-based directory services implementations, are outside the scope of this chapter.

 More Info The Microsoft Web site hosts many useful resources for migrating to AD DS from other directory service platforms. For more information on migrating from a UNIX or Linux environment, see the "UNIX Migration Project Guide" available from the Microsoft Download Center.

This chapter begins with a discussion of different upgrade and migration path options when moving to Windows Server 2008 and AD DS. It then looks at the key points of each path and the procedures required for performing the upgrade or migration.

Migration Paths

A directory services migration can be described as getting from the *source domain* (Point A) to the *target domain* (Point B), where the source domain is your current directory services infrastructure and the target domain is your desired Windows Server 2008 AD DS structure. The first decision you need to make when planning to migrate to AD DS is how to get to the target domain. Not surprisingly, there are several ways to get from the source domain to the target domain on what are called *migration paths*. Your migration path will be the fundamental component in the overall plan that is your *migration strategy*. Your migration strategy includes how you intend to migrate, which directory services objects you will move, and the order in which you will move them. A best practice for any directory services migration project is to document every detail of the migration strategy into an actionable document called the *migration plan*.

There are three migration paths from which to choose:

- Domain upgrade
- Domain restructure
- Upgrade-then-restructure

A domain upgrade migration path is achieved by upgrading the operating system on a down-level domain controller to Windows Server 2008, or by installing Windows Server 2008 domain controllers into a Windows 2000 Server or Windows Server 2003 domain. After you have upgraded the domain to Windows Server 2008, the original domain environment (Point A in our scenario) ceases to exist. The domain upgrade migration path is the least complex migration method. For this reason, you might consider it the default migration option.

The second option is the domain restructure migration path. During a domain restructure, directory services objects are copied from the existing directory services platform (source domain) to AD DS (target domain). This process is also referred to as *cloning*. In a domain restructure, the source and target domain coexist. When all of the directory services objects are migrated from the source to the target, and all clients and computers have been configured to use AD DS, source domain domain controllers (DCs) can either be demoted or retired. If your specific conditions indicate that a domain restructure is the appropriate migration path, there are several additional considerations to take into account as compared to a domain upgrade migration path. These factors are discussed in the sections that follow.

There is a third migration path: the upgrade-then-restructure migration path, also known as the *two-phase migration*. In short, the upgrade-then-restructure path is achieved by first upgrading the source domain or domains and then migrating the accounts into new or existing Windows Server 2008 domains. This method combines the short-term benefits of the domain upgrade path and the long-term benefits of the domain restructure.

The next few sections outline the advantages and disadvantages of each of these paths.

The Domain Upgrade Migration Path

A domain upgrade, also known as an *in-place* domain upgrade, is the most straightforward of the three migration choices. In a domain upgrade, the existing domain environment is converted to AD DS, either at the same time that the domain controller is upgraded to Windows Server 2008, or when new Windows Server 2008 domain controllers are installed into the source domain. One reason that a domain upgrade is a straightforward procedure is because you do not have the opportunity to modify the domain structure during the upgrade. For example, if you are the administrator for the NA domain of ADatum.com, a Windows 2000 Server–based domain environment, then by definition you will be the administrator of the NA domain in Windows Server 2008 after the upgrade. In a domain upgrade, you do not have the opportunity to change the domain structure, or even the domain name, of the source domain at the time of the upgrade.

Windows NT 4.0 Upgrade

Windows Server 2008 does not support direct server upgrades from Windows NT 4.0, and you cannot run NT 4.0 domain controllers in a Windows Server 2008 network, or vice versa. If you are interested in upgrading your Windows NT 4.0 source domain structure to Windows Server 2008 AD DS, you must first upgrade your Windows NT 4.0 domain environment to Windows 2000 Server or Windows Server 2003. After your domain migration to Windows 2000 Server or Windows Server 2003 is complete, you can then upgrade the source domain to Windows Server 2008. This chapter will focus exclusively on the Windows 2000 Server and Windows Server 2003 domain migration scenarios.

Using the Active Directory Migration Tool (ADMT v. 3.1) for Windows Server 2008, you can *attempt* to perform migration operations involving Windows NT 4.0 domain controllers (with Service Pack 4 or higher installed). However, since Windows NT 4.0 is not a currently supported product, this is an unsupported scenario.

Domain Upgrade

An even more straightforward migration path is available for current AD users who are planning to upgrade to Windows Server 2008. Many of the directory service's architectural changes were most likely implemented either when customers created their existing network environment or when they upgraded from Windows NT Server 4. The customer migrating to Windows Server 2008 AD DS from Windows 2000 or Windows Server 2003 is most likely planning to capitalize on the new AD DS features available in Windows Server 2008.

The domain upgrade migration path is accomplished in one of two ways. The first is by upgrading the operating system on the domain controllers from either Windows 2000 Server or Windows Server 2003 to Windows Server 2008. After the upgrade is complete, you can begin to take advantage of the desirable new features in AD DS.

> **More Info**   For more information on the new features available in Windows Server 2008 Active Directory, see Chapter 1, "What's New in Active Directory for Windows Server 2008."

The second method is to install new Windows Server 2008 domain controllers (DCs) into a Windows 2000 Server or Windows 2003 Server source domain environment. The directory service objects will replicate to the Windows Server 2008 domain controllers, and either immediately or over time, you can decommission the down-level DCs.

There are two premigration steps you must perform when you upgrade to Windows Server 2008. You must first prepare the forest and then prepare the domain for Windows Server 2008. These tasks are both completed using the Adprep.exe tool. The procedures for preparing the forest and domain prior to upgrading are covered later in this chapter in the section titled "Upgrading the Domain."

Domain Restructuring

In domain restructuring, a new Windows Server 2008 domain is created and AD DS objects are migrated into this new environment. One advantage of this migration path is that the original Active Directory environment is unaffected during the creation of the target environment. Another benefit is that domain restructuring is a selective process. Unlike a domain upgrade, you get to choose what objects you want to migrate to the new domain. A domain upgrade is an all-or-nothing proposition—every object in the domain is upgraded to Windows Server 2008 and AD DS. A domain restructuring event is a perfect time to eliminate any duplicate, nonactive, test, or otherwise defunct user, group, service, and computer accounts. They will disappear when you migrate to the new domain model and either flatten and repurpose, or simply retire, the old domain controllers.

User, group, service, and computer accounts, also called *security principals*, are migrated from NTDS database to the new AD DS database. This migration can be performed in two ways; accounts can be either *moved* or *copied*. Moving an object removes the original security principal in the source domain during the migration process. *Moving* is a destructive process, and it does not preserve the source domain objects for the purposes of rollback (disaster recovery). *Copying* is the process of creating a new, identical security principal in the target domain based on the object in the source domain. The preferred method of transferring the security principals into the Windows Server 2008 pristine forest is copying. Moving security principals is more commonly performed when doing an intraforest migration between two Windows Server 2008 domains, or between a Windows 2000/Windows

Server 2003 forest and a Windows Server 2008 domain, where copying of security principals is not an option.

How It Works: Using SID History to Preserve Resource Access

When you migrate user accounts from one domain to another, how do those user accounts maintain access to resources, such as printers and shared folders?

Consider the following example: During a domain restructure operation, you migrate a batch of user accounts from a Windows Server 2003 domain to a Windows Server 2008 domain. Upon completion of the account migration, you instruct the users to log on to the new domain and reset their passwords. User X successfully logs on to the target domain and then attempts to access a preexisting shared folder on a file server running Windows Server 2003—one that she has been accessing for several months. Will User X be able to access the folder?

The answer is *yes*, because of the *sIDHistory* attribute.

The *sIDHistory* attribute of AD DS security principals (such as User accounts and Group accounts) is used to store the former security identifiers (SIDs) of that object. So, for example, if User X in the previous example had the SID of S-1-5-21-2127521184-1604012920-1887927527-324294 in the Windows Server 2003 domain, that same value would now appear in the *sIDHistory* attribute field for the newly created Windows Server 2008 account object. As groups are migrated from the Windows Server 2003 domain to the AD DS domain, the SID from the Windows Server 2003 domain is also retained in the *sIDHistory* attribute for the group. As users and groups are migrated, the migrated user accounts are automatically assigned to the migrated groups in the Windows Server 2008 domain. This means that the access assigned to the groups in the Windows Server 2003 domain is retained during the migration process. During the migration process, the SID from the source domain is moved to the *sIDHistory* attribute. The new SID generated by the target domain controller is placed in the *objectSID* attribute of the migrated account.

How does this preserve access to resources following a migration? When User X attempts to access the shared folder on the Windows Server 2003 file server, the security subsystem checks her access token to ensure that she has the necessary permissions to the folder. The access token not only contains User X's SID and the SIDs of all the groups that User X belongs to, but all the SID history entries for both the user and group accounts as well. When a match is found between the discretionary access control list (DACL) on the folder's security descriptor and the previous SID (now included in the access token by way of the *sIDHistory* attribute), permission is granted and the folder is accessed.

> Ensuring access to secure resources is the most troublesome area of user account migration. By understanding how permissions are maintained following a migration, you, as the administrator, can effectively troubleshoot resource access issues. During the migration, you might need to take additional steps to ensure that the *sIDHistory* attribute is populated. You will learn more about this when examining the account migration utility: the Active Directory Migration Tool (ADMT).
>
> SID history does not come into play in the domain upgrade scenario. During a domain upgrade, the SID is maintained with the user and group accounts. User X will be able to access resources as normal.

Determining Your Migration Path

Keep in mind when deciding on a migration path that it is a per-domain decision and that it is completely legitimate to use different migration paths for different domains within your organization. If your existing domain model is geographically oriented, you might upgrade one or two of the larger domains and then restructure the smaller domains into these larger ones, preserving their administrative autonomy through organizational units (OUs). This is an example of *domain consolidation*.

Now that you have learned the basics of the different migration paths, let's take a look at the decision criteria used to choose among these paths.

The following questions are relevant in determining the most appropriate migration path for your organization:

- **Are you satisfied with your current domain model—does it meet your current organizational and business needs?**   If there are no major changes desired of the domain model as part of the upgrade to Windows Server 2008, the domain upgrade will provide the easiest migration path. The name of the domain will remain the same, as will the existence of all user and group accounts. A domain upgrade is an "all or nothing" proposition—you will simply be creating a Windows Server 2008 version of your current directory services implementation.

- **How much risk can you tolerate in migrating to a new domain model?**   In addition to offering the easiest migration path, a domain upgrade is also the lowest risk method. The process is carried out automatically when you upgrade the operating system on down-level domain controllers. Without user interaction, there are few opportunities for error. The disaster recovery methodology for a domain upgrade is relatively straightforward as well. If the upgrade fails, turn off the upgraded domain controller, address the errors in the upgrade process, and start again.

- **How much time do you have available to perform the migration?**   While the migration timeline is not often the most decisive factor in selecting a migration path, it can be a significant consideration for smaller organizations with limited resources to dedicate to the migration project. Because there are far fewer steps involved in a domain upgrade than in a domain restructure, it takes less time to complete overall. In comparison, a domain restructure requires sufficient time to create and test the target domain infrastructure and to migrate all of the accounts from the source to the domain. Very large organizations might not be able to migrate all of the objects at one time, so it is not uncommon for a domain restructure to occur in several phases over a period of time. In contrast, a domain upgrade is a linear process and must be completed once begun.

■ **How much system downtime is acceptable during the course of the migration project?** Another timeline consideration is the amount of directory services uptime needed during the migration process. During a domain upgrade, the account objects (users, groups, computers) are themselves upgraded into Windows Server 2008 AD DS objects. As a result, these account objects are not available during the upgrade itself. A domain upgrade impacts access to network resources for the period of time necessary for the NOS upgrade to complete. Depending upon the size of your down-level domain and the number of verification steps you put in place, this can certainly take the better part of a day (if all goes according to plan). So, an organization that chooses a domain upgrade migration path will need to accommodate some amount of network downtime.

■ **What resources are available to complete the migration?**   Because the domain upgrade is a less complex operation (or at least a highly automated one) it will require fewer resources to perform this migration path. Organizations that are not able to staff the more complex tasks of a domain restructure might choose this path.

■ **What is the migration project budget?**   A domain upgrade is a less expensive proposition than a domain restructure because you can use the existing server hardware. However, an NOS upgrade is an advantageous time to upgrade the hardware for domain controllers and other mission-critical servers (e-mail, Web servers, etc.). If your current server hardware is able to run Windows Server 2008, you can spend less money performing a domain upgrade. Initially, you will avoid the need to purchase the additional servers required to create the pristine forest environment required of a domain restructure. Other contributing budgetary factors will be the lower resources required (including minimized contract spending and lost-opportunity costs for full-time resources) as well as the reduced test spending (as there are fewer migration tasks to test).

■ **How many down-level servers will be required to run server-based applications after the migration?**   A domain upgrade is a good choice if the domain controllers you want to upgrade are not running a network service or line-of-business application that requires the down-level network operating system. These applications can include a fax or communication application, an accounting application, or any other server-based application that does not get upgraded very often. If these services and applications exist in your organization, it is well worth your time to test all of your line-of-business applications on a Windows Server 2008 computer and determine that the applications are functioning properly. If you determine that you have applications that will not run on Windows Server 2008, you have several choices: you can postpone the upgrade until a compatible version of the application is available or a suitable substitute is found;

you can transfer the application off the domain controller onto a member server in the domain (if possible); or you can elect not to upgrade that down-level server until the new version becomes available. Keep in mind that a down-level server can coexist indefinitely on your Windows Server 2008–based network.

Imagine the possible answers to these questions on a spectrum from low to high, with domain upgrade aligning with the low end of the spectrum and domain restructure aligning with the high end, as shown in Figure 7-1.

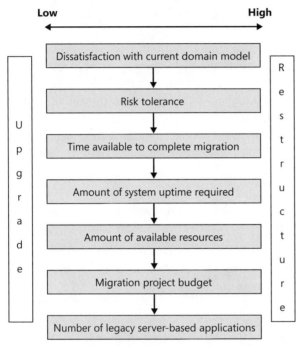

Figure 7-1 The domain migration path decision criteria spectrum.

Upgrading the Domain

Upgrading the domain to AD DS is the second stage of the process of upgrading to Windows Server 2008. (The first stage is the upgrade of the NOS.) When upgrading a domain controller running either Windows 2000 Server or Windows Server 2003, after the NOS upgrade is complete and the computer restarts, the Active Directory Domain Services Installation Wizard begins. You should complete the fields in the Active Directory Domain Services Installation Wizard according to your AD DS design document. After the wizard is complete, the directory service is updated to AD DS for Windows Server 2008.

More Info For more information on designing your Active Directory structure, see Chapter 5, "Designing the Active Directory Domain Services Structure." For more information on using the Active Directory Domain Services Installation Wizard, see Chapter 6.

There are several steps you must perform during an upgrade, depending on what version of Windows Server you are upgrading from. This next section describes the processes of upgrading the domain from Windows 2000 Server and then from Windows Server 2003.

Upgrading from Windows 2000 Server and Windows Server 2003

The process of upgrading the domain from Windows 2000 Server and Windows Server 2003 Active Directory to Windows Server 2008 AD DS is a straightforward one. Windows 2000 Server and Windows Server 2003–based networks are already using Active Directory for directory services, so this is more of a pure upgrade scenario than a migration. There are a few unique steps to a down-level upgrade that you will need to be aware of before starting the upgrade. (For the purpose of this section, *down-level* includes both Windows 2000 Server and Windows Server 2003, but not Windows NT 4.0 or previous versions of the Windows network operating system.)

Specifically, you will need to "prepare" the Windows 2000 Active Directory domain and forest for an upgrade to Windows Server 2008 AD DS. These processes will update the existing domain and forest structures to be compatible with the new features of Windows Server 2008 Active Directory.

Preparing the Forest

To prepare the Active Directory forest for an upgrade to Windows Server 2008 AD DS, you will use an administrative tool, Adprep.exe, to make the necessary changes to the Active Directory schema. Remember, this process is completed *before* the upgrade to Windows Server 2008 is initiated on the down-level domain controller.

To prepare the forest for an upgrade of the first down-level domain controller to Windows Server 2008, perform the following steps:

1. Locate the server that is the schema operations master. To do this, open the Active Directory Schema Microsoft Management Console (MMC) snap-in, right-click the Active Directory Schema node, and then click Operations Master. In the Change Schema Master dialog box, note the name of the current schema operations master.

2. Back up the schema operations master. You might need to restore this image if the forest preparation is not successful.

3. Disconnect the schema operations master from the network. Do not reestablish the connection until step 8 in this procedure.

4. On the schema operations master, insert the Windows Server 2008 DVD.

5. Open a command prompt, change to the DVD drive, and open the \I386 folder.

6. Type **adprep /forestprep**. To run *adprep /forestprep*, you must be a member of the Enterprise Admins group and the Schema Admins group in Active Directory, or you must have been delegated the appropriate authority.

7. To verify that the command has run without errors, open the Event Viewer and check the system log for errors or unexpected events. If you identify error messages related to the forest preparation process, address those errors before continuing with the next step. If you are unable to troubleshoot the errors, use the Active Directory Diagnostic tool (by typing **dcdiag** in the Run dialog box) to test the functionality of the domain controller. If you are unable to resolve these errors, restore the schema operations master from backup and investigate the corrective steps so that the forest preparation can be completed successfully.

8. If *adprep /forestprep* has run without errors, reconnect the schema operations master to the network.

This completes the forest preparation for a domain upgrade from Windows 2000 Server or Windows Server 2003 to Windows Server 2008. The next step is to prepare the domain.

> **Note**   Before you begin your domain preparation, wait for the changes made to the schema master to replicate to the infrastructure master. Remember that if the servers are in different sites, you will need to wait longer for the replication to complete. If you try to perform the domain preparation process before the changes have replicated, an error message will notify you that more time is needed.

Preparing the Domain

Domain preparation is similar to forest preparation, and there is a slight variation for the Windows 2000 Server upgrade scenario. To complete this task, you will identify and prepare the infrastructure master role holder instead of the schema master, as in the previous process.

To prepare each domain for an upgrade of the first down-level domain controller in a domain to Windows Server 2008, perform the following steps:

1. Locate the server that is the infrastructure operations master. To do this, open the Active Directory Users And Computers administrative tool, right-click the domain node, and then click Operations Masters. On the Infrastructure tab of the Operations Masters sheet, note the name of the current infrastructure operations master.

2. On the server functioning as the infrastructure operations master, insert the Windows Server 2008 DVD.

3. Open a command prompt, change to the DVD drive and open the \I386 folder.

4. For Windows 2000 Server domain controllers, type **adprep /domainprep /gpprep**. To run *adprep /domainprep /gpprep*, you must be a member of the Domain Admins group or the Enterprise Admins group in Active Directory, or you must have been delegated the appropriate authority. For Windows Server 2003 domain controllers, type **adprep / domainprep**. As previously, you must be a member of the Domain Admins group or the Enterprise Admins group in Active Directory, or you must have been delegated the appropriate authority.

If you prepare a Windows Server 2003 domain by running adprep /domainprep / gpprep, you can safely disregard the error message that indicates that domain updates were not necessary.

5. To verify that the *adprep /domainprep* command has run without errors, open the Event Viewer and check the system log for errors or unexpected events. If *adprep /domainprep* ran without errors, you have successfully prepared the domain for an upgrade to Windows Server 2008.

Once again, you should wait until the changes made to the infrastructure master replicate to the other domain controllers in the forest before upgrading any of the other domain controllers. If you begin to upgrade one of the domain controllers before the changes have replicated, an error message will notify you that more time is needed.

Now that the domain and forest are prepared for the upgrade to Windows Server 2008 and AD DS, you can begin the upgrade process.

Restructuring the Domain

The domain restructure migration path is most often chosen by organizations that want or need to change their Active Directory structure. To perform a domain restructure, you will first create the desired forest and domain structure and then migrate the existing AD DS objects into this new structure. At the time of its creation, the new structure is also known as the *pristine forest*.

There are two primary types of domain migration strategies:

- **Interforest migration** User, group, and computer accounts are migrated between two separate AD DS forests, including forests that are hosted on different versions of the Windows Server operating system.

- **Intraforest migration** User, group, and computer accounts are migrated between two domains in the same AD DS forest.

The job of migrating the Active Directory objects (which includes user, group, and computer accounts, as well as trusts and service accounts) is made easier through the use of domain migration tools. There are a number of tools available for this task, both from Microsoft and from third-party software vendors. This next section will cover domain restructuring using the Active Directory Migration Tool (ADMT).

The Active Directory Migration Tool simplifies the process of restructuring your directory services environment to meet the needs of your organization. You can use ADMT to migrate users, groups, and computers from down-level domains to AD DS domains; between Active Directory domains in different forests (interforest migration); and between Active Directory domains in the same forest (intraforest migration). ADMT also performs security translation from source to target domains and between AD DS domains in different forests.

> **Note**   At the time of the release of Windows Server 2008, the latest version of the ADMT is version 3.0, which will install on Windows Server 2003 only. An update is planned for the ADMT specifically for Windows Server 2008 (v3.1). Be sure to select the version of the tool that supports migrations to AD DS in Windows Server 2008. The latest version for the ADMT will be available from the Microsoft Download Center at *http://www.microsoft.com/download*.

Interforest Migration

Restructuring the domain by performing an interforest migration will move or copy the AD DS objects from the source domain to the target domain. Unlike a domain upgrade, users will have access to the source domain shared resources during the migration event and will suffer very little downtime as a result. In this section, the following tasks and considerations will be explained:

- Creating the pristine forest
- Creating the migration accounts
- Creating the trusts
- Installing the Active Directory migration tool
- Enabling auditing in the source and target domains
- Migrating global group and domain local group accounts
- Migrating user accounts
- Identifying service accounts
- Migrating computer accounts
- Migrating service accounts
- Decommissioning the source domains

The first step in an interforest migration is to create the optimal Point B to which you are going to migrate accounts.

Creating the Pristine Forest

The pristine forest includes the Widows Server 2008 target domain into which you will be migrating your existing accounts—your Point B on the journey from A to B. With a domain restructure migration path, you have the opportunity to create the optimal domain environment for your organization. Hopefully, this step comes at the end of a complete AD DS design process, and all components of your AD DS structure are clearly defined in your design document. For more information on the design process, see Chapter 5. After you have implemented your target domain structure, there are several steps you must take to prepare for the migration of accounts.

Creating the Migration Accounts

The first user account you might choose to create in your pristine forest is the one necessary to perform the migration. By creating a specific user account for the migration, you can ensure that the account meets all of the security requirements necessary to perform the tasks involved with a domain restructure. Additionally, you exercise the security best practice of not logging in using the Administrator account. For example, you can create a new user account (such as Migrator) or several accounts (Migrator1, Migrator2, etc.) if you plan to have several trusted administrators performing the migration. This way, you can track the events performed by each account holder and avoid having a shared account with administrative privileges.

For migrating user, group, and service accounts, the account must be a member of the Domain Admins group in the target domain if you are using SID history to preserve access to resources. The account should also be a member of the Administrators group in the down-level source domain.

Creating the Trusts

Because the migration process requires the granting of administrative permissions to accounts from a different domain, you will have to create several trusts to be able to migrate accounts from the source domain (or domains) to the target domain. In the Windows Server 2008 target domain and the down-level source domains, create a one-way trust from each of the source domains (trusting) to the target domain (trusted).

After you create these trusts, validate them using the Active Directory Domains And Trusts administrative tool in both the Windows Server 2008 target domain and the down-level source domain.

Installing the Active Directory Migration Tool

ADMT can perform both *interforest* migrations (moving accounts from one forest to another) and *intraforest* migrations (moving accounts within a forest). ADMT provides both a graphical user interface (GUI) and a scripting interface, and it should be installed on the Windows Server 2008 target domain controller.

ADMT supports the following tasks for completing your domain migration:

- User account migration
- Group account migration
- Computer account migration
- Service account migration
- Trust migration
- Exchange directory migration
- Security translation on migrated computer accounts

- Reporting to view the results of the migration events

- Functionality to undo last migration and retry last migration

After the ADMT is installed, it can be started from the Administrative Tools folder on the Start menu. The ADMT starts as an MMC snap-in, with all of the wizards available from the Action menu.

Enabling Auditing in the Target and Source Domains

The domain restructuring process requires that auditing must be enabled for the success or failure of account management operations in both the source and the target domains.

To enable auditing on the Windows Server 2008 target domain and the down-level source domain, perform the following steps:

1. Open the Active Directory Users And Computers administrative tool, right-click the Domain Controllers container, and select Properties.

2. On the Domain Controllers Properties sheet, select the Group Policy tab.

3. Select the Default Domain Controllers Policy and click Edit.

4. Expand Default DomainControllers Policy\Computer Configuration\Policies\ Windows Settings\Security Settings\Local Policies\Audit Policy, double-click Audit Account Management, and then select both the Success and the Failure options.

5. Force replication of this change to all domain controllers in the domain, or wait for the change to replicate automatically.

Migrating Global Group and Domain Local Group Accounts

The order of operations for migrating accounts is global groups first, then users. This pre-serves group membership when user accounts are later migrated to the target domain, and it preserves access to resources. When you migrate global groups from down-level domains to Windows Server 2008, a new SID is created for the new global group. The SID from the source domain is added to the *sIDHistory* attribute for each new group object. You will recall that by preserving the SID from the source domain in the *sIDHistory* field, users can continue to access resources on the not-yet-migrated source domains.

By copying the global groups (using ADMT), you will create in the target domain the skeletal group structure as defined in your Active Directory design. As user accounts are later migrated, they will automatically join the groups of which they were members in the source domain.

The process of migrating global groups from the source to the target domain using the ADMT Group Account Migration Wizard is a straightforward one. To migrate global groups using the ADMT Group Account Migration Wizard, perform the following steps:

1. Identify the source and target domains. If the domain names do not appear in the drop-down list, you can type them in.

2. Select the source domain global groups that you want to migrate to Windows Server 2008.

3. Select the OU to which you want to add the global groups in the target domain.

> **Note**   ADMT only enables you to select a single OU as the destination container of the migrated global group accounts. Keep this in mind as you plan the migration of your global groups. Rather than selecting *all* of the source global groups, you might want to select all of the groups that will be migrated to a specific OU. Then you can rerun the Group Account Migration Wizard to migrate the groups that are to be stored in another OU.

4. Select the desired group options. This includes whether or not to copy the group members (that is, the user accounts) at the same time as copying the groups. The default is not to copy group members. Copying group members at the time you migrate the group might be an expeditious choice if yours is a smaller organization and migrating by groups is an acceptable staged approach. In larger organizations, however, top-level global groups (such as Employees) contain too large a body of users to migrate at one time.

> **Note**   After all batches have been migrated, perform a final global group remigration to ensure that any late changes made to global group membership in the source domain are reflected in the target domain. You can remigrate global groups by using the Active Directory Migration Tool console, by using the ADMT command-line option, or by using a script.

After the global group, you can migrate the domain local groups using the Group Account Migration Wizard. After all of the groups are migrated over to Windows Server 2008, it is time to start migrating the user accounts.

Migrating User Accounts

The migration of user accounts does not have to be done all at once. In fact, it is a good idea to carefully plan the order and timing of migrating the users. Because you will be preserving access to the down-level source domain-based resources during the migration, this process can be stretched out over days, weeks, or months.

The first step in migrating user accounts is to determine the sets of users to migrate and when to perform the migration. The actual migration of user accounts is procedurally very similar to the migration of global group accounts.

To migrate user accounts using the ADMT User Account Migration Wizard, perform the following steps:

1. Select the source and target domains.

2. Select the down-level source domain user accounts you want to migrate.

3. Select the destination OU in the Windows Server 2008 target domain.

4. Select whether or not you want to migrate user account passwords. Using ADMT, you have the choice to do one of the following:

❏ **Create new, complex password** In this case, a text document (comma-separated value [.csv] format) is created that maps user names to the new passwords. You then have the task of communicating the password to the migrated users.

❏ **Set password same as user name** In this case, the password is set to the username value. Since both this option and the previous one pose a security risk, the *User Must Change Password At Next Logon* attribute is set for the migrated user in the target domain.

❏ **Migrate passwords** This option migrates the user passwords from the source domain to the target domain. Selecting this option requires you to identify the password migration source domain controller.

> **Note** The *password migration source domain controller* is a domain controller in the source domain that is configured as the Password Export Server (PES) by installing the password migration DLL. Password migration is a separate component of ADMT and can be installed on any domain controller in the source domain. To install the password migration DLL on the source domain controller, open the \%systemroot%\windows\ ADMT\PWDMIG folder and double-click the Pwdmig.msi file. The PES maintains a database of the source domain user passwords and creates a secure communication channel to the target domain for the purpose of migrating these passwords.

5. Manage the account state with account transition options. With the help of ADMT, you can manage the transition from the source account to the target account on the Account Transition Options page. This enables you to control the state of the target domain account (enabled, disabled, or same as source) and the source domain account (disabled, or enabled for a configurable number of days).

A common scenario is to migrate batches of user accounts but not activate (enable) the accounts until you complete the migration. At that time, you can programmatically activate all of the user accounts and cut over to the target domain. For security reasons, it is not a good idea to have an account active in both the source and the target domains. If your plan is to have users log on to the Windows Server 2008 domain immediately after their accounts are migrated, use ADMT to disable the source domain account during the migration. Alternatively, if you want to allow users to have the source domain to fall back on during the migration, use ADMT to disable the source domain account some number of days after ADMT runs.

Identifying Service Accounts

Service accounts are special user accounts that are used to operate services on computers running Windows 2000 Server, Windows Server 2003, and Windows Server 2008. Most services operate under the Local System Authority (LSA) account. When you migrate the source domain, you must first identify all of the services that are configured not to run under the LSA.

Migrating service accounts is a two-stage process. First, you must identify the service accounts. Then, after the computers running the down-level operating system are migrated to the Windows Server 2008 target domain, the identified service accounts can be migrated.

To identify the service accounts operating in the source domain using ADMT, perform the following steps:

1.   Open the Service Account Migration Wizard.

2.   Select the source and target domains.

3.   In the source domain, select all of the computers on which you want to search for service accounts. To complete this task, you will need to consult your premigration documentation of the existing domain environment.

4.   Finish the Service Account Migration Wizard.

At this point, the wizard has identified all the service accounts running on the computers you identified. This information is stored in the ADMT database until it is needed later for the actual migration of these accounts. Migration of the service accounts occurs after the migration of the computer accounts themselves.

Migrating Computer Accounts

The computer accounts that reside in source domain include all of the down-level member servers, as well as all of the computers running Windows 2000 Professional, Windows XP Professional, and Windows Vista Business edition and higher. Migrating computer accounts will clone all of the computer accounts from the source domain to an OU in the target domain.

To migrate computer accounts using ADMT, complete the following steps:

1.   Open the Computer Migration Wizard.

2.   Select the source and target domains.

3.   From the source domain, select the computer accounts you want to migrate.

4.   Select the OU in the target domain into which you want to migrate the computer accounts.

5.   Select any computer objects for which you want to translate security for accounts previously migrated from the source domain to the target domain. This process updates the discretionary access control lists (DACLs) for the resources on the migrated computers with the new target domain SIDs of the migrated group and user accounts. The available objects include:

    ❏   Files and folders

    ❏   Local groups

    ❏   Printers

    ❏   Registry

    ❏   Shares

❑ User profiles

❑ User rights

Note If you choose not to translate security for these listed objects during the running of the Computer Migration Wizard, you can do it later using the Security Translation Wizard in ADMT. The integral component of the Security Translation Wizard is the same as the Translate Objects page in Computer Migration Wizard. The first page in the Security Translation Wizard queries whether or not you want to translate security for previously migrated objects. If you run the Security Translation Wizard after you have migrated computer accounts, select the Previously Migrated Objects option.

6. Configure the restart of the migrated computer. To move a computer account from one domain to another, ADMT dispatches an agent to make the change on the computer itself. To complete the computer account migration process, the computer being migrated must be restarted. ADMT enables you to configure the amount of time after the wizard completes before the computer restarts.

7. Complete the Computer Migration Wizard. When the wizard is finished, click on View Dispatch Log to verify the success of the *dispatch agent*. This is the component that updates the domain membership of the computer and then restarts the computer. The dispatch log is very useful for troubleshooting failed computer account migrations.

Migrating Service Accounts

Now that the computer accounts are migrated to the target domain, you can complete the second phase of the service account migration process. You will recall that before the computer accounts were migrated, you *identified* the service accounts that were used to operate services on member servers. At this point in the process, you will migrate those service accounts from the source domain to the Windows Server 2008 target domain. This procedure will ensure that all of the services not running under the LSA will continue to start the required services after the member server is migrated to the target domain.

To migrate the service account using ADMT, complete the following steps:

1. Open the User Account Migration Wizard.

2. Select the source and target domains.

3. Select the service accounts that you want to migrate.

Note If you do not recall the account name of the previously identified service accounts, you can review the contents of the dispatch agent log file, Dctlog.txt, which is located in the %userprofile%\Temp folder. For example, if you are logged on to the Windows Server 2008 computer as Migrator1, you will find this file in C:\Users\Migrator1\Temp.

4. Select the OU in the target domain into which you want to migrate the service accounts.

5. Complex password generation will be used for service account migration. Regardless of which password migration option you choose on the Password Options page, ADMT will always use the complex password option. ADMT recognizes that the user account you are migrating is a service account, and it will grant the account the right to log on as a service.

> **Note** If the service accounts that you are migrating have local rights inherited only from membership in a local group (such as "log on as a service" as a member of the local administrators group), you must fix these rights by running the Security Translation Wizard. If this is the case, on the Translate Objects page of the Security Translation Wizard, select the *Local Groups* and the *User Rights* objects for the migrated member server that contained the local group through which the rights were inherited. This is the computer on which the security translation will take place.

Decommissioning the Source Domains

After all of the source domains have been migrated to Windows Server 2008 and AD DS, you can decommission the down-level source domains. At this point, the only computers left in the source domains are the domain controllers. If your migration plan calls for moving these domain controllers to the Windows Server 2008 target domain, you can move these computers to the target domain. The most straightforward approach to do this is to ensure that all necessary data has been moved off of these servers and to then perform a New Installation of the Windows Server 2008 operating system.

The final task is to remove all of the trusts that were created to perform the migration. Using the Active Directory Domains And Trusts administration tool, select each of the trusts to the now-defunct down-level source domains and click Remove.

Intraforest Migration

The third migration path to examine is the upgrade-then-restructure path, or the intraforest migration. Recall from earlier in this chapter that the upgrade-then-restructure approach first involves an upgrade of the down-level domain controllers to Windows Server 2008 (which preserves the original domain hierarchy), followed by a domain restructuring in which AD DS objects are migrated from the upgraded source domains to the target domain (or domains). Having read the sections of this chapter on domain upgrades and domain restructuring, you already are familiar with the tasks necessary to complete an upgrade-then-restructure migration to Windows Server 2008 AD DS. Due to Windows Server 2008 security requirements, however, you will see that account migration works differently in an intraforest scenario than in an interforest scenario.

The process of restructuring the domain after an upgrade to Windows Server 2008 does not necessarily have to occur immediately following the upgrade. Domain restructuring can simply be considered a domain management skill, so that your AD DS structure can change as your business changes. This section will focus on how an intraforest migration is different from what you have already learned about the interforest migration path. This section does not discuss a specific tool, as these technical differences will apply to any domain migration tool that you choose.

An intraforest migration differs from an interforest migration in the following ways:

- In an intraforest migration, to preserve access to resources using SID history, accounts must be moved instead of cloned. However, moving account objects in the intraforest scenario is a destructive process, and in that process, the user, group, and computer accounts from the source domain are deleted as the new accounts are created in the target domain. As a result, you will not be able to maintain the "parallel environment" that offered a convenient fall-back environment in the interforest restructure scenario.

- In an intraforest migration, to maintain group membership rules, you must move user accounts and the groups to which they belong at the same time. This is called a *closed set*. ADMT does not calculate a complete closed set, however, so you must be very careful when migrating users who are members of global groups. If you migrate a group whose membership includes a user account that is a member of another global group, and if that global group is not recursively a member of any groups being migrated at this time, it will break the membership between that user account and the global group that is not included. Other group types (such as universal groups) do not have this issue because they can contain members outside of their domains.

Configuring Interforest Trusts

As an alternative to performing a domain restructure, you can use interforest trusts, or *forest trusts*, from one Windows Server 2008 forest in order to access resources in another disjoined Windows Server 2008 forest.

One of the significant enhancements that occurred in Windows Server 2003 Active Directory was the option to create trusts between AD DS forests. In Windows 2000 Active Directory, you can only create a trust between a single domain in one forest and a single domain in another forest. In Windows Server 2003 and Windows Server 2008, you can configure a trust between the forest root domains. This trust can be a one-way or a two-way trust. After the trust is created, you can use global groups or universal groups from one forest to grant permissions to resources in another forest.

> **Note**   Creating a trust between the two forests only enables the sharing of resources between the forests. All of the other forest-level distinctions still apply after the trust is created. For example, creating the trust does not mean that the forests will share a global catalog (GC) or a common schema. When you create a forest trust in Active Directory, the trust automatically

enables name suffix routing between the two forests. With name suffix routing, users can use their user principal names (UPNs) when logging on to any domain in either forest. For example, if you create a forest trust between the ADatum.com forest and the TreyResearch.com forest, users from the TreyResearch.com forest can log on to a workstation in the ADatum.com forest using their *username*@treyresearch.com UPN. Name suffix routing is applied by default to all first-level domain names available in the forest. This includes both the default UPN suffixes and any alternative suffixes configured in the forest. The only time the name suffix routing does not work between forests is if the same UPN suffix is configured in both forests. If the TreyResearch.com UPN suffix is configured in the ADatum.com forest, users from the TreyReserch.com forest will not be able to log on to the ADatum.com forest using their UPN.

When you first enable the forest trust, all of the first-level domain suffixes are automatically routed in the UPN trust. All child domain suffixes are routed implicitly through the parent domain suffix. If you add another UPN suffix to a forest after the trust is created, you must enable name suffix routing for the new suffix. You can do this by verifying the trust between the domains or by manually adding the new suffix to the Name Suffix Routing tab on the trust's Properties sheet.

To create a forest trust, the forest must be running at Windows Server 2003 or Windows Server 2008 forest functional level. Only members of the Enterprise Admins group in a forest have permission to create forest trusts.

To create a forest trust, use the following procedure:

1. Start the Active Directory Domains And Trusts administrative tool. Right-click the name of the forest root domain and select Properties. Select the Trusts tab.

2. Click New Trust. The New Trust Wizard starts. Type in the domain name of the forest root domain in the other forest.

3. You are then given a choice of what type of trust you want to configure. You can create the following types of trusts:

    ❑ External domain trust

    ❑ NT 4.0 trust

    ❑ Kerberos (v5) realm trust

    ❑ Forest trust

    An external trust is a nontransitive trust, whereas a forest trust is always transitive. Select Forest Trust.

4. Select the direction for the trust. The choices are:

    ❑ **Two-way**   Users in this domain can be authenticated in the specified domain, realm, or forest, and users in the specified domain, realm, or forest can be authenticated in this domain.

❑ **One-way, incoming**   Users in this domain can be authenticated in the specified domain, realm, or forest.

❑ **One-way, outgoing**   Users in the specified domain, realm, or forest can be authenticated in this domain.

5. You are then given a choice of whether to create the trust only for this domain or for the other domain as well. (These two domains are the forest root domains in each forest.) The forest trust can only be configured between the forest root domains. If you chose to configure both sides of the trust at one time, you have to type in the name and password for the Enterprise Admins account that exists in the other forest. If you chose to set up the trust for this domain only, you are asked to type in a password that will be used to configure the initial trust. You must then use this password to configure the trust in the forest root domain from the other forest.

6. You are then given the choice of the level of authentication to be granted for both the outgoing trust and the incoming trust. This option allows you to carefully control access to resources between the forests. If you choose to apply forest-wide authentication, the users from one forest will have access to all servers and resources in the other forest. This is the same configuration as the trusts between the domains within a forest. Users from one domain in a forest can access resources in any other domain in either forest, provided that they have been given permission to access the resource. You can also apply selective authentication for the forest trust. In this case, you must explicitly give the users or groups from one forest permission to access servers in another forest. You can do this by granting the users or groups the Allowed To Authenticate right in Active Directory.

7. After configuring the trust, you are given the option to automatically verify the trust.

With the two-way, transitive forest trust in place, users can now access shared resources in the trusted forest.

Summary

This chapter explored the different migration paths to go from either a Windows 2000 Server or Windows Server 2003 Active Directory to Windows Server 2008 AD DS. The three primary migration paths—upgrade, restructure, and upgrade-then-restructure—were described. There are several criteria you can use to determine which migration path is right for your organization. For organizations that are satisfied with the current domain structure, the upgrade migration path is the least complicated, least risky means to upgrade the directory service from Windows 2000 Server or Windows Server 2003 to Windows Server 2008. If your domain structure is not in line with your current business or organizational model, you will need to restructure your domain. Regardless of the chosen path, careful planning, testing, and piloting of your migration plan is critical to the success of your migration project.

This chapter also examined the key decision points for performing an in-place upgrade to Windows Server 2008. Next, the process of domain restructuring using ADMT was discussed. Then the upgrade-then-restructure migration path, also known as an intraforest migration, was distinguished from a domain restructure. A discussion of the interforest trust feature of Windows Server 2008 completed this chapter.

Best Practices

The following best practices will ensure success in migrating to Windows Server 2008.

- **Applying Service Packs to Windows 2000 Server DCs**   Before preparing the domain (and the forest in which it is located) for migrating, you should apply Windows 2000 Server Service Pack 4 (SP4) or later to all domain controllers running Windows 2000 Server. You can download the latest service packs for Windows 2000 Server from the Microsoft Web site at *http://technet.microsoft.com/en-us/windowsserver/2000/bb735341.aspx*.

- **Migrating Computer Accounts on Virtual Private Networks**   For Virtual Private Network (VPN) clients, when migrating computer accounts using ADMT, you will need to ensure that the dispatch agent is able to be installed across the VPN connection. To do this, configure the VPN to allow connecting directly to the dial-up client. ADMT will attempt to install the dispatch agent service on the to-be-migrated computer, so if Server Message Block (SMB) server traffic is blocked by the firewall or proxy server, this will fail. Configure the firewall settings to allow this traffic before migrating computer accounts that connect via the VPN.

- **Migrating Domain Controllers**   You cannot migrate domain controller computer accounts using the ADMT. Domain controllers must be moved to the Windows Server 2008 domain rather than migrated. To move a DC from the source to the target domain, you should demote it (uninstall Active Directory), join the server to the target domain, and then promote it to a Windows Server 2008 domain controller.

Additional Resources

The following resources will provide additional information you will need to migrate to Windows Server 2008 AD DS.

Related Information

- For more information about the new features available in Windows Server 2008 Active Directory, see Chapter 1, "What's New in Active Directory for Windows Server 2008."

- For more information about designing your Active Directory structure, see Chapter 5, "Designing the Active Directory Domain Services Structure."

- For more information about using the Active Directory Domain Services Installation Wizard, see Chapter 6, "Installing Active Directory Domain Services."

- Before you begin your migration to Windows Server 2008 and AD DS, you should carefully plan and design your infrastructure. Please read the article "Planning an Active Directory Domain Services Deployment" at *http://technet2.microsoft.com/windowsserver2008/en/library/f349e1e7-c3ce-4850-9e50-d8886c866b521033.mspx?mfr=true* to plan for your deployment.

- The Step-by-Step Guide for Windows Server 2008 Active Directory Domain Services Installation and Removal is available at *http://technet2.microsoft.com/windowsserver2008/en/library/f349e1e7-c3ce-4850-9e50-d8886c866b521033.mspx?mfr=true*.

- For more information about deploying AD DS, see "Planning an Active Directory Domain Services Deployment" at *http://go.microsoft.com/fwlink/?LinkId=100493*.

- For more information about assessing the hardware requirements of domain controllers in a Windows Server 2008 domain, see "Planning Domain Controller Capacity" at *http://go.microsoft.com/fwlink/?LinkId=89027*.

- For more information about deploying AD DS regional domains, see "Deploying Windows Server 2008 Regional Domains" at *http://go.microsoft.com/fwlink/?LinkId=89029*.

- For more information about upgrading Active Directory domains to Windows Server 2008, see "Upgrading AD DS Domains to Windows Server 2008" at *http://go.microsoft.com/fwlink/?LinkId=89032*.

- For more information about restructuring AD DS domains within and between forests, see "Active Directory Migration Tool Version 3.1 Migration Guide" at *http://go.microsoft.com/fwlink/?LinkId=82740*.

- For more information about additional methods of installing a new Windows Server 2008 forest, see "Installing a New Windows Server 2008 Forest" at *http://go.microsoft.com/fwlink/?LinkId=101704*.

- For more information about tests that you can perform by using Dcdiag.exe, see "Dcdiag Overview" at *http://go.microsoft.com/fwlink/?LinkId=93660*.

- For information about using media to install the domain controller, see "Installing AD DS from Media" at *http://go.microsoft.com/fwlink/?LinkId=93104*.

- For a procedure to help you transfer operations master roles, see "Transfer Operations Master Roles" at *http://go.microsoft.com/fwlink/?LinkId=93664*.

- For more information about Operations Master Role placement, see "Planning Operations Master Role Placement" at *http://go.microsoft.com/fwlink/?LinkId=93665*.

Related Tools

- Active Directory Migration Tool v.3.1, available at *http://go.microsoft.com/fwlink/?LinkId=82740*

Part III
Administering Windows Server 2008 Active Directory

Chapter 8
Active Directory Domain Services Security

One of the primary reasons for deploying a directory service like Active Directory Domain Services (AD DS) is to provide security on the corporate network. Every company stores business-critical information on file servers on the network. E-mail has become one of the primary means for exchanging business information. Intranet or Internet sites may contain confidential information, and access to the sites may need to be restricted to specific users. Managing secure access to these types of information is critical to ensure that only properly authorized users have access to the data. Microsoft Windows Server 2008 AD DS provides the directory service that enables security in these and many other scenarios.

This chapter begins by introducing the basics of AD DS security. AD DS uses several basic building blocks and concepts to provide security on a Windows Server 2008 network. After an introduction to the security basics, this chapter will focus on the authentication and authorization functions used by AD DS to ensure that users are who they say they are (authentication) and to provide access to the resources to which the user should have access (authorization). Windows Server 2008, like Microsoft Windows 2000 and Windows Server 2003, uses Kerberos as the primary authentication protocol, so much of the first part of this chapter will focus on understanding the role of Kerberos in authentication.

After discussing authentication and authorization, this chapter moves on to consider AD DS domain controller security and developing secure administrative practices. This is an essential second component in creating a secure AD DS environment.

> **More Info**   This chapter provides a basis for understanding and implementing security in a Windows Server 2008 network. Later chapters, such as Chapter 9, "Delegating the Administration of Active Directory Domain Services," and Chapter 13, "Using Group Policy to Manage Security," expand on the concepts discussed in this chapter.

AD DS Security Basics

There are some basic concepts needed to understand how AD DS security works on a Windows Server 2008 network. Essentially, AD DS security consists of two types of objects and the interaction between the two objects. The first object is a *security principal,* or an object that represents a user, group, or computer that needs access to some resource on the network. The second object is the resource itself, which is the object to which the security principal needs access. To provide the proper level of security, AD DS must have some way of determining the identity of the security principal and then giving the right level of access to the resources.

Security Principals

Security principals are the only objects in AD DS that can be granted permission to access resources on the network. Every security principal is assigned a security identifier (SID) when the object is created. The SID is made up of two parts. The first part is a domain identifier, and all security principals in a domain have the same domain identifier. The second part of the SID is the relative identifier (RID), which is unique for each security principal in an AD DS domain.

The SID is an essential component when configuring security for resources on a Windows Server 2008 network. When you grant permission to a resource, you use the security principal's display name, but Windows Server 2008 actually uses the SID to manage access to the resource. When a user tries to access a resource on a server in the domain, the operating system grants permission to the user's SID, rather than the person's name. This means that if a user's display name is changed, the permissions granted to the user do not change. However, if a user object is deleted and then re-created with the same name, the user will not be able to access the same resources, because the SID will be different.

Direct from the Field: Security IDs

A security identifier, or SID, is a numerical representation that uniquely identifies a security principal. SIDs are made up of three components: Revision Level, Identifier Authority, and Subauthority or Relative Identifier (RID).

SIDS use the following syntax:

```
S-R-I-S-S
```

The letter *S* indicates that the information following is a SID. The letter *R* indicates the Revision Level of the security identifier. The letter *I* represents the Identifier Authority, and the next *S* is for the Subauthority or RID. There can be more than one Subauthority/RID value:

- **Revision Level**   The Revision Level represents the revision Level of the SID Structure. The current Revision Level is 1.

- **Identifier Authority**   The Identifier Authority is a 48-bit value that identifies the authority that issued the SID.

- **Subauthority/Relative Identifier**   Subauthority/RIDs are used to uniquely identify the security principal relative to the authority that issued the SID. Subauthority/RIDS are used to ensure that no two SIDS are identical. This is accomplished by not allowing any SID-issuing authority to assign a RID more than once.

Windows creates security identifiers using the identifier authority of 5 and a subauthority of 21. Therefore, SIDs created on Windows start with S-1-5-21. The next subauthority is derived from either the domain or the local computer. This depends on whether the new security principal is a domain or local security principal. The remaining three subauthorities derive from the relative identifier. Each domain controller is allocated a pool of relative identifies from the RID manager FSMO role. The domain controller that creates the new security principal assigns a relative identifier, from its RID pool, to the new security principal. This creates the full security identifier:

S-1-5-21-3093361465-529454648-2942243305-1007

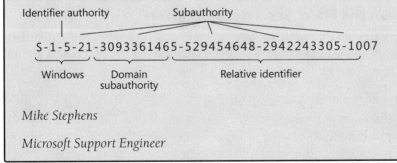

Mike Stephens

Microsoft Support Engineer

Access Control Lists

The other component that is included in AD DS security is the object that a security principal needs to access. This object may be an AD DS organizational unit (OU), printer object, or even a security principal. The object may also be a resource such as a file on a server running Windows Server 2008 or a mailbox on a server running Microsoft Exchange Server 2007.

The permissions that have been granted to these objects are located in an access control list (ACL). Every object in AD DS or on an NTFS file system partition has a security descriptor. The security descriptor includes the SID of the security principal that owns the object as well as the SID for the object's primary group. In addition, every object has two separate ACLs: a discretionary access control list (DACL) and a system access control list (SACL). The DACL lists the security principals or trustees that have been assigned permission to the object, as well as the level of permissions that have been assigned to each security principal. The DACL is made up of a series of access control entries (ACEs). Each ACE lists one SID and then identifies the level of access that the SID has to the object. The ACE can include an entry for all types of security principals. For example, a user account might have Read permissions to a file and a security group might have Full Control. The DACL for the file will have (at least) two ACEs, one granting the user Read permission and another granting the group Full Control.

The SACL lists the security principals whose access to the resource needs to be audited. The list of ACEs in the SACL indicates whose access is to be audited and the level of auditing required.

> **Note**   The DACL can contain ACEs that grant access to a resource as well as ACEs that deny access. The ACEs that deny access should be listed first in the ACL, so they are evaluated first by the security subsystem. If an ACE denies access to the resource, the security subsystem does not evaluate any other ACEs. This means that an ACE that denies permission to a resource always overrides any ACE that grants access to a specific SID. For more information on how security descriptors are used to grant access to AD DS objects, see Chapter 9.

Direct from the Field: Security Descriptors

Windows uses security descriptors to protect and audit resources. A security descriptor is comprised of an owner, a primary group, a discretionary access control list, and a system access control list.

Owner and Primary Group

The owner and primary group fields are security identifiers. The owner is the security principal that owns the object. The resource owner has full permissions to the object, including the ability to add or remove permissions within the security descriptor.

The primary group remains in the security descriptor for compatibility with the POSIX subsystem. Windows does not rely on this part of the security descriptor unless you are using utilities that require POSIX interoperability. By default, the security principal that created the object will write its default primary group to the security descriptor. Windows' default primary group is Domain Users.

The primary group is an implied group membership. When a user logs on, the operating system inserts the SID for this group in the user's token. The *memberOf* attribute does not have the primary group listed. The *memberOf* attribute includes only group memberships that are explicitly assigned.

Discretionary and System Access Control Lists

Access control lists (ACLs) include two parts. The first part of the access control list is named control flags. These settings control how Windows applies permissions within the access control list and the rules of inheritance. The second part of the access control list is the list itself. The access control list contains one or more access control entries (ACEs).

Access control flags determine how Windows applies the access control entries contained within the access control list. Windows primarily uses the protected and automatic flags. The protected flag prevents the access control list from being modified by any inherited access control lists. This flag is equivalent to clearing the "Allow inheritable permissions from parent to propagate to this object" check box. The automatic flag is equivalent to selecting the "Allow inheritable permissions from parent to propagate to this object" option. This flag automatically allows access control entries in the access control lists to propagate to child objects.

Access Control Entries

Access control lists include one or more access control entries. Windows categorizes access control entries into two types: Allow and Deny. Each ACE type has a subtype object and nonobject subtypes. Allow and Deny access control entries designate the level of access the authorization subsystem provides based on the requested right by the security principal. Object access control entries are exclusive for objects in AD DS because they provide additional fields for object inheritance. Windows uses nonobject access control entries for most of the remaining resources such as file system and registry resources. Nonobject ACEs provide container inheritance—where an object residing in a container inherits the access control entry of the container. This is similar to files inheriting permissions from their parent folders. Each access control entry type has a rights field and a trustee field. The rights fields are usually comprised of predefined numbers that represent a specific action that a security principal can request. An example of a right would be a user requesting to read or write to a file. In this example, Read and Write are two separate rights. The trustee field is a security identifier that is allowed or denied the specified right. An example of a trustee would be user or group that is allowed or denied the action specified in the right field.

Mike Stephens

Microsoft Support Engineer

Access Tokens

The connecting point between the security principal's SID and the ACL is the *access token*. When Windows authenticates the user by using Kerberos, the user is assigned an access token on the local computer during the logon process. This token includes the user's primary SID, the SIDs for any groups to which the user belongs, and the user's privileges and rights.

> **Note**   The access token may also include additional SIDs in the SIDHistory attribute. These SIDs can be populated when you move user accounts from one domain to another. For a detailed discussion on SIDHistory, see Chapter 7, "Migrating to Active Directory Domain Services."

The access token is used by the security subsystem whenever a user tries to access a resource. When the user tries to access a local resource, the token is presented by the client workstation to any thread or application that requests security information before allowing access to a resource. The access token is never transmitted across the network to another computer; rather, a local access token is created on each server where the user tries to access a resource. For example, when a user tries to access a mailbox on a server running Exchange Server 2007, an access token is created on the server. In this case, the security subsystem on the server running Exchange Server 2007 will compare the SIDs in the access token to the permissions granted in the mailbox ACL. If the permissions granted to the SID allow it, the user will be able to open the mailbox.

Authentication

In order for the security processes, including their use of SIDs and ACLs, to work, there must be some way for a user to gain access to the network. Essentially, users must be able to prove that they are who they say they are so that they can retrieve their access token from the domain controller. This process is called *authentication*.

Authentication occurs during the initial client logon process on a computer that is a member of an AD DS domain. The exact steps vary depending on the operating system that the client is logging on to. When the user sits down at a Windows 2000, Microsoft Windows XP Professional, or Windows Server 2003 computer and enters Ctrl+Alt+Del, which is known as a secure attention sequence (SAS), the Winlogon service on the local computer switches to the logon screen and loads the Graphic Identification and Authentication (GINA) dynamic-link library (DLL). By default, this is the Msgina.dll. However, third parties can build alternative GINAs (for example, the NetWare client uses the Nwgina.dll). After the user has typed in the user name and password and has selected a domain, GINA passes the entered credentials back to the Winlogon process. The Winlogon service passes the information to the Local Security Authority (LSA).

Windows Vista and Windows Server 2008 do not use the GINA dll. Windows Vista and Windows Server 2008 introduce a new authentication model in which LogonUI and Winlogon communicate directly with each other. This means that when the users provide their credentials in these operating systems, the credentials are passed directly by the LogonUI component to the Winlogon service, which passes the information to the LSA. In order to authenticate to other directories, a third party can create a credential provider, which is a module that plugs into the LogonUI, to describe the UI and to gather the credential and pass it on to WinLogon. Credential providers are completely transparent to WinLogon.

In either case, the LSA immediately applies a one-way hash to the user's password and deletes the clear text password that the user typed in. The LSA then calls the appropriate Security Support Provider (SSP) through the Security Support Provider Interface (SSPI). Windows Server 2008 provides two primary SSPs for network authentication, the Kerberos SSP and the NT LAN Manager (NTLM) SSP. If Windows 2000 (or later) clients are logging on to a Windows Server 2008 network, the Kerberos SSP is selected and the information is passed to the SSP. The SSP then communicates with the domain controller to authenticate the user. The Kerberos authentication process will be covered in detail later in this chapter.

If authentication succeeds, the user is authenticated and granted access to the network. If the user has logged on to a domain, and if all the resources that the user needs to access are in the same forest, the user will be asked for authentication credentials only once. Until the user logs off, all the permissions the user gets on the network are based on the initial authentication. Although the user account is authenticated again each time the user accesses resources on a server to which the user has not authenticated, this authentication is transparent to the user.

Authorization

Authorization is the second step in the process of gaining access to network resources, and it takes place after authentication. During authentication, you are proving your identity by typing in the correct user name and password. During authorization, you are given access to resources on the network. Another way to think about this is to say that during authentication, the access token is created for you. During authorization, an access token is presented to a server and requests access to a resource. If the SIDs in your access token matches the SIDs in the DACL, then you are allowed or denied access, based on the access control entry on the resource.

Authorization, also known as *access control*, is the process of determining the level of access that is allowed or denied to an Active Directory object or file system object. After the Key Distribution Center (KDC) confirms the identity of the user, the security system on the authenticating domain controller generates authorization data in the form of the user's primary SID, plus SIDs for groups to which the user belongs that are recognized by all the resources on the Windows network. The authorization data is used by the computer that manages the network resource to generate an access token. The access token is used to determine the level of access that the user has to the network resource.

The access token contains the following:

- The list of SIDs that represent the user (including SIDs stored in SIDHistory)

- All groups (including nested groups) of which the user is a member

- The user's privileges (also called *user rights*) on the local computer

All objects or resources that are secured have a discretionary access control list (DACL) assigned to them that specifies the access rights of users and groups on that resource. Access to one of these objects or resources is controlled by an access check, in which the security system determines whether the requested access should be granted or denied by evaluating the contents of the access token of the requestor against the DACL on the resource.

Kerberos Security

So far this chapter has covered the basics of AD DS security without discussing the actual mechanism that implements the security. The primary mechanism for delivering authentication in AD DS is the Kerberos protocol. This protocol was first developed by engineers at the Massachusetts Institute of Technology (MIT) in the late 1980s. The current version of Kerberos is version 5 (Kerberos 5), which is described in RFC 1510, "The Kerberos Network Authentication Service (V5)." The Windows Server 2008 implementation of Kerberos is fully RFC-1510 compliant, with some extensions for public key authentication.

Kerberos is the default authentication protocol for Windows 2000 and Windows Server 2003 Active Directory, and for Windows Server 2008 AD DS. Whenever a Windows 2000 or later client authenticates to Active Directory or AD DS, the client will always try to use Kerberos. The other protocol that can be used to authenticate to AD DS is NTLM, which is supported primarily for backward compatibility for older clients. Kerberos has a number of advantages over NTLM:

- **Mutual authentication**   With NTLM, authentication is only one-way; that is, the server authenticates the client. With Kerberos, the client can also authenticate the server, ensuring that the server that is responding to the client request is the correct server.

- **More efficient access to resources**   When a user tries to access a network resource on an NTLM-based network (such as Microsoft Windows NT 4), the server where the resource is located has to contact a domain controller to check the user's access permissions. On a Kerberos-based network, the client connects to the domain controller and acquires a service ticket to connect to the resource server. This means that the resource server does not need to connect to the domain controller.

- **Improved trust management**   NTLM trusts are always one-way, nontransitive, and manually configured. Kerberos trusts are automatically configured and maintained between all the domains in a forest and are transitive and two-way. In addition, Kerberos trusts can be configured between forests and between Windows Server 2008 Kerberos domains and other Kerberos implementations.

- **Delegated authentication**   When a client connects to a server using NTLM authentication, the server can use the client credentials to access resources only on the local server. With Kerberos authentication, the server can use the client credentials to access resources on another server.

> **Note**   Windows Server 2008 also supports authentication through Secure Sockets Layer/Transport Layer Security (SSL/TLS), Digest authentication, and Passport authentication. Since these authentication services are primarily used in an Internet environment for authentication to Microsoft Internet Information Services (IIS) 7.0, these authentication options will not be discussed.

Introduction to Kerberos

There are three components in a Kerberos-based system. The first is the client who needs to gain access to network resources. The second is the server that manages the network resources and ensures that only properly authenticated and authorized users can gain access to the resource. The third component is a Key Distribution Center (KDC), which serves as a central location to store user information and as a central service to authenticate users.

The Kerberos protocol defines how these three components interact. This interaction is based on two key principles. First of all, Kerberos operates on the assumption that authentication traffic between a workstation and server crosses an insecure network. This means that no confidential authentication traffic is ever sent across the network in clear text. A practical example of this is that the user password is never sent across the network, not even in an encrypted form. The second principle is that Kerberos operates based on a shared secret authentication model. In a shared secret authentication model, the client and the authenticating server share a secret that is not known by anyone else. In most cases, when users are authenticating to the network, this shared secret is the user password. When the user logs on to a network secured by Kerberos, a hash of the user's password is used to encrypt a packet of information. When the KDC receives the packet, it decrypts the information using the stored user password hash that is stored in AD DS. If the decryption is successful, then the authenticating server knows that the user knows the shared secret and access is granted.

> **Note**   When the user logs on, he or she will usually type in a password. The domain controller checks to see if that password is accurate. However, because Kerberos operates with the assumption that the network is insecure, this checking is done without sending the password across the network.

One of the problems with a shared secret authentication model is that the user and the server managing the network resource must have some way of sharing the secret. If one user is trying to access a resource on one server, a user account can be created on the server with a password that only the user knows. When the user tries to access the resources on the server, that user can present the shared secret (password) and gain access to the resource. However, in a corporate environment, there may be thousands of users and hundreds of servers. Managing distinct shared secrets for all of these users would be impractical. Kerberos deals with this issue by using a Key Distribution Center (KDC). The KDC runs as a service on a domain controller on the network and manages the shared secrets for all users on the network. The KDC has one central database of all user accounts on the network, and it stores the shared secret for each user (in the form of a one-way hash of the user's password). In an AD DS environment, these shared secrets are stored in the AD DS data store. When a user needs access to the network and resources on the network, the KDC confirms that the user knows the shared secret and then authenticates the user. The KDC also stores shared secrets for computers that are members of the AD DS domain, which are used to authenticate computers that are used to access network resources.

> **Note**   In Kerberos terminology, this central server that manages user accounts is a KDC, as discussed previously. In the Windows Server 2008 implementation of Kerberos, this server is called a domain controller. Every AD DS domain controller, including read-only domain controllers, is a KDC. In Kerberos, the boundary defined by the user database on one KDC is called a *realm*. In Windows Server 2008 terminology, this boundary is called a *domain*.

Each KDC (which runs as the Kerberos Key Distribution Center service in Windows Server 2008) is made up of two separate services: the Authentication Service (AS) and the Ticket-Granting Service (TGS). The AS is responsible for the initial client logon and issues a Ticket-Granting Ticket (TGT) to the client. The TGS is responsible for all service tickets that are used to access resources on the Windows Server 2008 network.

The KDC stores the account database used for Kerberos authentication. In the Windows Server 2008 implementation of Kerberos, the database is managed by the directory system agent (DSA), which runs within the LSA process on each domain controller. Clients and applications are never given direct access to the account database; all requests must go through the DSA, using one of the AD DS interfaces. Every object within the account database (in fact, every attribute on every object) is protected with an ACL. The DSA ensures that any attempts to access the account database are properly authorized.

> **Note**   When AD DS is installed on the first domain controller in the domain, a special account named *krbtgt* is created in the domain. The account cannot be deleted or renamed and should never be enabled or moved from the Users container. The account is assigned a password when it is created, and the password is automatically changed on a regular basis. This password is used to create a secret key that is used to encrypt and decrypt the TGTs issued by all the domain controllers (KDCs) in the domain. Each read-only domain controller is issued a unique krbtgt account when the computer is promoted. This provides cryptographic isolation between KDCs in different branches, which prevents a compromised RODC from issuing service tickets to resources in other branches or a hub site.

Kerberos Authentication

Kerberos authentication begins when the Kerberos security provider is called by the LSA on a Windows Vista workstation or a Windows Server 2008 computer. When a user logs on by typing a user name and password, the client computer applies a one-way hash to the user's password to create a secret key, which is cached in secure memory on the workstation. A one-way hash means that the password cannot be derived from the hash. This hash is also consistent—each time the hash is applied to the same password, the result will always be the same.

> **Note**   This process also applies to computers running Windows 2000 Professional or later client operating systems, and to Windows 2000 Server or later server operating systems.

To perform a client logon process, the client and server systems follow these steps:

1. The Kerberos SSP on the workstation sends an authentication message to the KDC. (See Figure 8-1.) The message includes:

   ❑   The user name

   ❑   The user realm (domain name)

   ❑   A request for a TGT

   ❑   Preauthentication data, which includes a time stamp, plus possibly other data

   The preauthentication data is encrypted using the secret key derived from the user password.

2. When the message arrives at the KDC, the server examines the user name and then checks the directory database for its copy of the secret key associated with the user's account. The server decrypts the encrypted data in the message with the secret key and checks the time stamp. If the decryption is successful and the time stamp is recorded as being within five minutes of the current time on the server, the server prepares to authenticate the user. If the decryption fails, the user must have entered the wrong password, and the authentication fails. If the time stamp is more than five minutes off the current time on the server, the authentication will also fail. The reason for the small time difference is to prevent someone from capturing the authentication packets and then replaying them at a later time. The default maximum allowable time difference of *5 minutes* can be configured on the domain security policies.

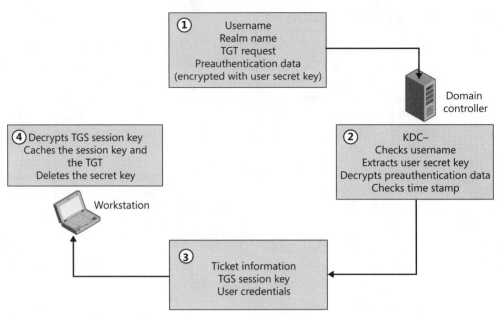

Figure 8-1   Getting a Kerberos TGT.

3. After the user is authenticated, the server sends the client a message that includes a Ticket Granting Service (TGS) *session key* and a *TGT*. (See Figure 8-1.) The session key is an encryption key that is used to interact with the KDC instead of using the client's secret key. The TGT grants the user access to the TGS. For the lifetime of the TGT, the client will present the TGT to the TGS whenever the client needs access to resources on the network. All access tokens for the principal (including the user SID and security group SIDs) are also included in the TGT. This information is known as the Privilege Attribute Certificate (PAC). The TGS session key is encrypted using the user's secret key. In addition, the TGT is encrypted using the KDC's (krbrgt) long-term secret key.

4. When the packet arrives at the client computer, the user's secret key is used to decrypt the TGS session key. If the decryption is successful and the time stamp is valid, the user's computer assumes that the KDC is authentic because it knew the user's secret key. The TGS session key is then cached on the local computer until it expires or until the user logs off the workstation. This TGS session key will be used to encrypt all future connections to the KDC. This means that the client no longer needs to remember the secret key, which is deleted from the workstation cache. The TGT is stored in an encrypted form in the workstation cache.

Note   The Kerberos protocol includes the Authentication Service (AS) Exchange, which is the subprotocol used to perform the initial authentication for the user. The process just described uses the AS Exchange subprotocol. The initial message sent by the client to the KDC is called a KRB_AS_REQ message. The server response to the client is called a KRB_AS_REP message.

5. At this point, the user has been authenticated, but the user still does not have access to resources on the network. The TGT grants access to the Ticket Granting Service, but to gain access to any other resources on the network, the user must acquire a service ticket from the TGS. (See Figure 8-2.) The client workstation sends a service ticket request to the TGS. The request includes the name of the target computer, the domain of the target computer, the TGT granted during authentication, the service principal name (SPN) that the user principal(UPN) wants access to , and a time stamp that is encrypted using the TGS session key that was acquired during the AS Exchange process.

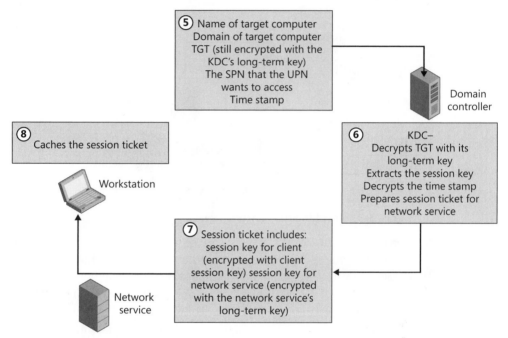

Figure 8-2   Acquiring a Kerberos session ticket for a network resource.

6. The KDC decrypts the TGT using its long-term key. It then extracts the TGS session key from the TGT and decrypts the time stamp to ensure that the client is using the correct session key and that the time stamp is valid. If the session key and time stamp are acceptable, the KDC then does an LDAP query to find the account that has the service principal registered on it. After this is done, it prepares a service ticket for the requested service.

7. The response includes two copies of a service session key. The first copy of the service session key is encrypted using the TGS session key the client obtained during the initial logon. The second copy of the service session key is intended for the service principal hosting the requested service and includes the user's access information—a service ticket. The service ticket is encrypted using the secret key of the service principal hosting the network service, which is unknown to the client workstation but known to both the KDC and the service principal, because the service principal is located in the KDC realm or a trusted Kerberos realm.

8. The client workstation caches both parts of the session ticket in memory.

> **Note** The process described in steps 5 through 8 uses the Ticket-Granting Service
> (TGS) Exchange subprotocol. The session ticket request sent by the client is called a
> KRB_TGS_REQ message; the server response is a KRB_TGS_REP message.

9. The client now presents the service ticket to the network service to gain access.
   (See Figure 8-3.)

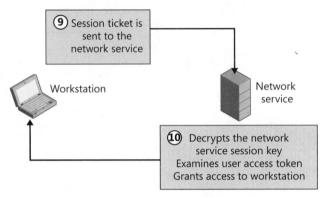

Figure 8-3   Accessing the network service.

10. The network service decrypts the service ticket using its secret key. Using the service
    session key, the service then decrypts the time stamp included in the request. If both
    decryptions are successful and the time stamp is within five minutes of the hosting
    computers time, the service trusts that the ticket comes from the KDC. The network
    service then determines if the client requested mutual authentication. If the client
    requests mutual authentication, the service encrypts the time stamp it received in the
    request, using the service session key and replies back to the client.

    The service sends a reply back to the client when the client requests mutual authentica-
    tion. If this occurs, the client decrypts the time stamp using the service session key.
    The client then compares the time stamp it received in the reply with the time stamp it
    sent in the original request. If the time stamps match, the client then trusts the service.

    After Kerberos authentication completes, the service principal hosting the requested
    service passes the service ticket to LSA. LSA then decrypts the service ticket and extracts
    the authorization data. The authorization data includes the user SID and the SIDs of
    groups of which the user is a member. LSA uses this data to create an access token. The
    authorization data is known as Privilege Attribute Certificate or PAC.

> **Note** The process described in steps 9 and 10 uses the Client/Server (CS) Exchange
> subprotocol. The client request is called a KRB_AP_REQ message.

Direct from the Field: Service Principal Names

You can assign service principal names (SPN) to user or computer accounts. Service principal names are stored in a multivalued Active Directory attribute on the user or computer account, which allow each user or computer to have more than one SPN. SPNs *must* be unique across the entire Active Directory forest.

An example of a service principal name attribute on an Active Directory object looks like this:

Host /DC1

Host/DC1.contoso.com

You read this example SPN as follows—the service name of **host** on security principal **DC1.** The next service principal name describes the same service but uses a different security principal, **DC1.contoso.com**. Kerberos authentication relies on names. If your clients connect by both NetBIOS and FQDN names, then you want to ensure that you register the requested service using both names, as shown in the example.

The following is an example of a service principal name for a user account under which the SQL service runs. Windows starts the SQL service using a domain user account (also called a service account). You must register the SQL service principal name on the user account, because that is the account to which you are delegating authentication. A common configuration error is to register the SPN on the computer account that hosts the SQL service.

MSSQLSvc/sqlsrvr.contoso.com:1433

MSSQLSvc/sqlsrvr:1433

Kerberos-enabled services use a preconfigured service identifier in their SPN. In this example, the Microsoft SQL service uses MSSQLSvc. This is how you read this service principal name. The Microsoft SQL service (**MSSQLSvc**) is hosted on the computer **sqlsrvr.contoso.com,** and this instance of SQL is listening on port **1433**. Again, we include both the FQDN and NetBIOS names for the server to ensure that authentication works when connecting to either name. Remember, these service principal names *must* be unique to the Active Directory forest.

Microsoft provides several utilities that you can use to view service principal names. These utilities include LDP, LDIFDE, ADSIEdit, and SETSPN.

Robert Greene

Microsoft Support Escalation Engineer

Assuming the authentication and authorization are successful, the client is given access to the server resources. If the client needs subsequent use of the same resource or service, the session ticket is pulled from the client's ticket cache and is reissued to the target resource server. If the session ticket has expired, the client has to return to the KDC to obtain a new ticket.

> **Note**   You can view the contents of the client cache by using two tools. KList.exe, which is installed on Windows Server 2008 computers, provides a command-line interface to view and delete the Kerberos tickets. The Kerberos Tray tool (Kerbtray.exe) provides a graphical user interface (GUI) for viewing the tickets. Figure 8-4 shows an example of the information provided by the Kerberos Tray tool. The Kerberos Tray tool is available as part of the Windows Server 2003 Resource Kit tools, which can be downloaded at *https://www.microsoft.com/downloads/details.aspx?FamilyID=9d467a69-57ff-4ae7-96ee-b18c4790cffd&displaylang=en*.

Figure 8-4   Viewing Kerberos tickets using the Kerberos Tray tool.

How It Works: Kerberos Ticket Flags

Ticket flags are configured within all tickets and are used to identify the ticket purpose and/or constraints. You can view these flags when you use the Kerberos Tray utility. Kerberos tickets use the following ticket flags:

- *Forwardable*   Only valid for a TGT. Instructs the Ticket Granting Server that it can issue a new TGT with a different network address based on the TGT that is presented. A forwardable ticket can be used in Kerberos delegation.

- *Forwarded*   Indicates that the TGT has been forwarded or that a ticket was issued from a forwardable TGT. The middle-tier application in Kerberos delegation should have this type of ticket.

- *Proxiable*   A proxiable ticket is a ticket (generally only a TGT) that allows you to get a ticket for a service with IP addresses other than the ones in the TGT. This is different than aforwardable ticket in that you cannot proxy a new TGT from your current TGT; you can only proxy non-TGT service tickets.

- *Proxy*   This ticket flag indicates that the service ticket was obtained from a proxiable TGT.

- *Renewable*   Indicates if the ticket can be renewed. This is used in combination with the EndTime and Renew-Till Fields to cause tickets to be renewed at the KDC periodically.

- *Initial*   Indicates that this is a Ticket Granting Ticket (TGT).

Other flags include *May Postdate, Invalid, HW Auth, OK As Delegate,* and others. Postdated tickets may be requested in advance for batch processing and so on, but they are flagged invalid until the time that they become effective. A KDC must validate the ticket and remove the Invalid flag at that time.

Robert Greene

Microsoft Support Escalation Engineer

This process of gaining access to a resource on the network means that the KDC is only involved during the initial client logon and the first time the client tries to access a specific resource on a specific server. When the user first logs on, that user is given a TGT that gives the client access to the KDC during the lifetime of the ticket. When the client tries to connect to a network resource, the client contacts the KDC again and gets a service ticket to access that resource. This service ticket includes the authorization data for the user. After successful authentication, the Local Security subsystem uses this data to create an access token on the computer hosting the service or resource so the server can determine the level of resource access the user should have.

Authenticating Across Domain Boundaries

The same authentication process applies when a user authenticates across domain boundaries. For example, a company may have a three-domain forest, as shown in Figure 8-5.

If a user with an account in TreyResearch.com travels to the NA.ADatum.com domain location and tries to log on to the network on a machine in the NA.ADatum.com domain, the client workstation must be able to connect to a domain controller (KDC) in the TreyResearch.com as well as NA.ADatum.com and ADatum.com domain. In this case, the client computer sends the initial logon request to the NA.ADatum.com domain controller. The domain controller determines that the user account is located in the TreyResearch.com domain, so it needs to refer the client workstation to that domain. If all of the domains were configured with shortcut trusts with each other, the domain controller could directly refer the client computer to a domain controller in the TreyResearch.com domain. However, if no shortcut trusts have been created, there is no direct trust between NA.ADatum.com and TreyResearch.com. In this case, the NA domain controller will refer the client computer to a domain controller in the ADatum.com domain. The referral includes a TGT for ADatum.com that is encrypted with an inter-realm session key, which is shared by both ADatum.com and NA.Adatum.com. This TGT allows access to KDC service on the domain controller in the Adatum.com domain. The inter-realm session key was created when the NA domain was added to the Adatum.com forest and the initial trust was created between the two domains. The inter-realm session key guarantees that the logon request is coming from a trusted domain. The client computer then sends an authentication request to the ADatum.com domain. The client is then referred to a domain controller in the TreyResearch.com domain. Again, this referral includes TGT for TreyResearch.com that has an inter-realm session key to access the KDC services on the domain controller in TreyResearch.com. The client computer then sends a TGT request to the home domain controller in TreyResearch.com.

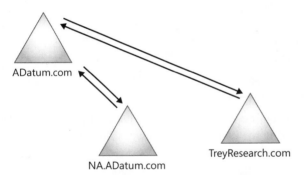

ADatum.com

NA.ADatum.com

TreyResearch.com

Figure 8-5   Authentication across domain boundaries.

A similar process is followed when a client tries to gain access to a resource on a domain other than the user's home domain. In this case, the client needs to acquire a service ticket from a domain controller in the domain where the resource is located, so the client will be referred through the same process until it can connect to the right domain controller.

This authentication process has implications for forest design, especially if users frequently log on to domains other than their home domain or access resources in domains other than the home domain. If you are designing a forest with multiple domains, the client may have to traverse the entire trust path between the domains. If this happens often, you may want to put domain controllers for the root domains in locations close to the users. You can also use shortcut trusts so that the domain controller referrals can be sent directly to the appropriate domains.

Delegation of Authentication

One of the issues that can complicate accessing network services is that the network service may be distributed across multiple servers. For example, the client might connect to a front-end server that must connect to a back-end database server to collect some information. In this environment, the user's credentials (rather than the front-end server's credentials) should be used to access the back-end server so that the user will only get access to authorized information. In Windows 2000, Kerberos provides this functionality in two ways: using proxy tickets and using forwarded tickets. If proxy tickets are enabled, the client will send a session ticket request to the KDC requesting access to the back-end server. The KDC grants the session ticket and sets the *Proxiable* flag on the ticket. The client then presents the session ticket to the front-end server, which uses the ticket to access information on the back-end server. The main problem with proxy tickets is that the client must know the identity of the back-end server. The other option is to use forwarded tickets. If these tickets are enabled, the client will send an AS Exchange request to the KDC requesting a TGT that the front-end server will be able to use to access back-end servers. The KDC creates a TGT and sends it to the client. The client sends the TGT to the front-end server, which then uses the TGT to acquire a session ticket to access the back-end server on behalf of the client.

There are two significant concerns with the way delegation of authentication is implemented in Windows 2000. The first concern is that delegation of authentication can only be used if the client is authenticated using Kerberos. This means that no Windows NT, Microsoft Windows 95, or Windows 98 client can use delegation of authentication. The second Windows 2000–related concern is related to the security of the delegation. In Windows 2000, after the front-end server obtains the forwarded ticket from the KDC, it can use the ticket to access any network service on behalf of the client. Windows Server 2003 and Windows Server 2008 provide the option for constrained delegation, which means you can configure the account so it is delegated for only specific services on the network (based on service principal names). Constrained delegation is available only when the domain is set to Windows Server 2003 or Windows Server 2008 functional level.

In order for the delegation of authentication to be successful, you must ensure that both the user account and the service or computer account are configured to support delegation of authentication. To configure this on a user account, access the user's Properties sheet through the Active Directory Users and Computers administrative tool, select the Account tab; then scroll through the Account Options list and make sure that the Account Is Sensitive And Cannot Be Delegated option is not selected. (This is not selected by default.) To configure the service account for delegation, you must first determine whether the logon account used by the service is a normal user account or whether it is the LocalSystem account. If the service runs under a normal user account, first ensure that you have added an SPN to the user account. Then access the user's Account tab and make sure the Account Is Sensitive And Cannot Be Delegated option is not selected. (This is not selected by default.) Also check the appropriate level of delegation on the delegation tab of the user account. (Figure 8-6 shows the interface.)

If the service runs under a LocalSystem account, the delegation must be configured on the computer account's Properties sheet. To implement the Windows 2000 level of authentication, select the Trust This Computer For Delegation To Any Service (Kerberos Only) option. To implement the Windows Server 2003 or Windows Server 2008 enhancements, select the Trust This Computer For Delegation To Specified Services Only option. You can then select whether the client must authenticate using Kerberos only or can use any protocol and then select the services (based on service principal names registered in AD DS) to which the computer can present delegated credentials.

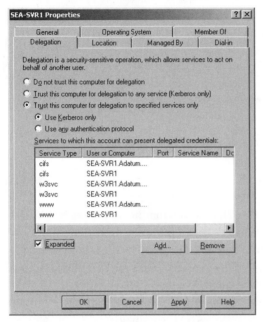

Figure 8-6 Configuring constrained delegation on a computer account.

Direct from the Field: Delegated Authentication

Delegated authentication is becoming more frequent in customer environments because of the need to limit user access to confidential data as well as a need to be able to audit what data users are accessing on a day-to-day basis. Today's applications are typically multi-tier solutions, which increases the complexity of authentication. For example, delegated authentication is required when a Web-based application must request data from a SQL database using the credentials of the user who authenticated to the Web site. Following are the most common problems that cause delegated authentication to fail:

■ The client application is not configured to use Kerberos. In the example given, the Web browser is the client application that you must configure to support Kerberos authentication.

■ SPNs are not registered on the correct service account. In the example, the service account that runs the Web application must have the proper SPNs registered for the name that users use to connect to the Web application. If users connect using both NetBIOS and FQDN names, then you must register both names on the service account (http/webapp1 and http/webapp1.contoso.com). Also, the correct service account in the example is the service account used to run the Web application pool, which includes the Web application that connects to SQL. Lastly, no SPN registration is required if the Web application pool is running as the network service.

- Duplicate SPNs can also cause delegated authentication to fail. Each SPN in the domain must be unique. Two security principals, each having the same SPN, causes the delegation to fail.

- There is an incorrect configuration on the IIS server. You must configure IIS to use Kerberos authentication. Ensure that the Web application is configured for Integrated authentication. Also, make sure the Negotiate authentication provider has not been disabled. For more information, see the Microsoft Knowledge Base article 215383, "How to Configure IIS to Support Both the Kerberos Protocol and the NTLM Protocol for Network Authentication" available at *http://support.microsoft.com/kb/215383*.

Robert Greene

Microsoft Support Escalation Engineer

Configuring Kerberos in Windows Server 2008

As mentioned earlier, Kerberos is the default authentication protocol for clients using Windows 2000 or later to log on to AD DS. You can configure several Kerberos properties through the domain security policy. To access the Kerberos policy settings, open the Group Policy Management console and edit the Default Domain Policy. Under Computer Configuration, first expand Security settings and then expand the Account Policies folder. (The interface is shown in Figure 8-7.)

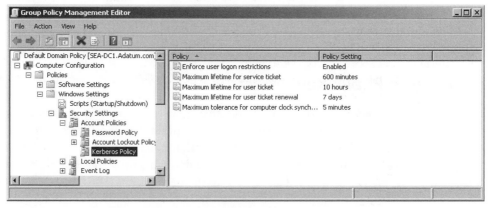

Figure 8-7   Configuring the Kerberos settings through Domain Security Policy.

- **Enforce User Logon Restrictions**   This policy sets the option for the KDC to validate every request for a session ticket against the user rights setting on the target computer. If this policy is enabled, the user requesting the session ticket must have either the Allow Log On Locally right, if they are logging on interactively, or the Access This Computer From The Network right on the target computer. The Allow Log On Locally right and the Access This Computer From The Network right are assigned under Local Policies\User Rights Assignment in the Domain Security Policy. By default, this policy is enabled.

- **Maximum Lifetime For Service Ticket**   This policy sets the maximum amount of time (in minutes) that a service ticket can be used to access a specific service. If the setting is *zero minutes*, the ticket will never expire. If the setting is not *zero*, the setting must be *greater than 10 minutes* and *less than, or equal to, the setting for Maximum Lifetime For User Ticket*. By default, the setting is *600 minutes (10 hours)*.

- **Maximum Lifetime For User Ticket**   This policy sets the maximum amount of time (in hours) that a user's TGT can be used. After the TGT expires, a new one must be requested from the KDC or the existing ticket must be renewed. By default, the setting is *10 hours.*

- **Maximum Lifetime For User Ticket Renewal**   This policy sets the amount of time (in days) that a TGT can be renewed (as opposed to having to get a new TGT). By default, the setting is *7 days.*

- **Maximum Tolerance For Computer Clock Synchronization**   This policy sets the maximum time difference (in minutes) that Kerberos will tolerate between the time on a client computer and the time on the domain controller that provides Kerberos authentication. If the time difference between the two computers is greater than this tolerance level, all Kerberos tickets will be refused. By default, the setting is *5 minutes*. Be aware that if this setting is changed, it will revert to the default when the computer is restarted.

In most cases, the default Kerberos settings are appropriate. In high security environments, you can decrease the settings for ticket lifetimes. However, as these settings are decreased, the clients will need to connect to the KDC more often, creating additional network traffic and additional load on the domain controllers. As a best practice, it is recommended that these settings should always be defined within one Group Policy object and the GPO should be linked at the domain level.

Integration with Public Key Infrastructure

As mentioned earlier, Kerberos is based on a shared-secret authentication model. This provides excellent security but imposes one important limitation on providing access to a Windows Server 2008 network. This limitation is that every user who accesses the network must have a user account in the KDC account database. If a user does not exist in the database, he or she cannot be granted any access to the network.

This works well for a company in which all users who log on to the network are known, and a user account can be created for each user. However, many companies are expanding the list of users who require access to network resources to include users who are not employees. A company may enter into a short-term partnership with another company and be required to provide access to network resources to employees from the partner organization. Or a company may want to provide specified customers with access to resources on the company network. In these scenarios, the list of people requiring access to the network might be very long, so creating a user account for each of the users would be impractical.

Public Key Infrastructure (PKI) moves away from a shared-secret authentication model and replaces it with a certificate-based authentication model. In PKI, users are not authenticated based on the fact that they know the correct password, but they are authenticated based on the fact that they hold the right certificate. PKI is based on three essential concepts: public and private keys, digital certificates, and certificate authorities (CAs). PKI begins with the concept that every user or computer involved in the information exchange has two keys: a private key and a public key. The private key is known only to one user. It can be stored on the computer's hard drive, as part of a roaming profile, or on a different device, such as a smart card. The public key, on the other hand, is made available to anyone who asks for it. The private and public keys are mathematically related, but there is no way to derive a private key from a public key. These public and private keys are used in a variety of ways.

One way that public and private keys are used is to encrypt information as it is sent across the network. A user's public key is used to encrypt the message. Because the public key is made available to anyone who requests it, anyone can send a message encrypted with a user's public key. However, the only key that can decrypt the message is the user's private key. That means that the only person who can decrypt a message that is encrypted using a public key is the person holding the private key. Anyone else capturing this packet on the network does not have the correct private key and therefore cannot read the message.

Another way that public and private keys are used is to digitally sign messages sent between two users. A digital signature is used to ensure the identity of the sender of the message and also to ensure the integrity of the message. To create a digital signature, the entire message is sent through a mathematical hash. This hash creates a message digest, which is encrypted using the message sender's private key. The encrypted hash is sent with the message as a digital signature. When the message recipient gets the message, the same hash is applied to the message, creating a second message digest. Then the sender's public key is used to decrypt the digital signature. If the recipient's message digest is identical to the result of the decrypted signature, the integrity and authenticity of the message are confirmed.

The second component of PKI is the digital certificate. The purpose of a certificate is to identify the certificate holder. When a person or company applies for a certificate from a certificate authority (CA), the CA confirms the identity of the person or company requesting the certificate. When you create the certificate request, the private key is created and stored on the local computer. When the certificate is assigned, the user is also given the associated public key. The certificate is also digitally signed by the certificate authority, thus adding the certificate authority's stamp of authenticity to the certificate. The current standard for these certificates is X.509 v3. The certificate includes information about the person, computer, or service to which the certificate has been issued, information about the certificate itself, such as the expiration date, and information about the CA that issued the certificate.

The certificates required for PKI are issued by CAs, which are network servers that manage the granting and revoking of certificates. Because of the importance of PKI for the Internet, a wide variety of CAs is currently available, including popular commercial CAs such as Verisign and Thawte. Most Internet clients like Microsoft Internet Explorer are automatically configured to trust certificates issued by these commercial CAs. You can also set up your own CA using Windows Server 2008. The Active Directory Certificate Services (AD CS) role included with Windows Server 2008 is a full-featured CA that can be used to issue certificates to people within your company or to people in partner organizations.

> **Note**   One of the benefits of using AD CS is that you can deploy the CA as an Enterprise CA. The Enterprise CA is tightly integrated with AD DS, which means that you can configure policies to automatically issue and manage certificates to users and computers. Chapter 17, "Active Directory Certificate Services," provides details on planning and implementing AD CS.

One reason for using certificates is to allow users who may not have an account in AD DS to gain access to resources on the Windows Server 2008 network. For example, you may want to set up a secure Web site so that partner organizations or customers can get access to some confidential information on your network. However, in Windows Server 2008, permission to access network resources can only be granted to security principals. There is no option to assign permissions based solely on certificates. However, you can provide access to resources for users who have certificates, but not AD DS user accounts, by mapping a certificate to a user account and then using the account to assign permissions.

Windows Server 2008 provides two different ways that a certificate can be mapped to a user account:

- **One-to-one mapping**   In this case, a single certificate is mapped to a single Windows Server 2008 user account. With a one-to-one mapping, you must assign a certificate as well as create a user account for each user. This may be a good solution if you want remote employees of the company to access secure resources through a secure Web site. However, it does not simplify your administration. Nonetheless, with one-to-one name mapping you can control the level of access for each user.

- **Many-to-one mapping**   In this case, many certificates are mapped to one AD DS account name. For example, if you are creating a partner relationship with another company and the employees of the company need access to a secure Web site, you can create one user account. Then you can link as many certificates as you want to that one user account. For example, if that company has its own CA, you can create a rule that maps all certificates issued by that CA to one user account in your domain. Then you can assign permissions to network resources using that one account.

> **Note**   You can map certificates to user accounts through the Active Directory Users And Computers administrative tool or through the Microsoft Internet Information Server (IIS) Manager. In the Active Directory Users And Computers administrative tool, enable Advanced Features on the View menu and then use the Name Mappings option that is available when you right-click a user account.

Integration with Smart Cards

Smart cards provide another option for integrating PKI with Kerberos authentication. When Kerberos is used without PKI, the shared secret between the client and the KDC is used to encrypt the initial logon exchange with the authentication service. This key is derived from the user's password, and the same key is used to encrypt and decrypt the information. Smart cards use a PKI model in which both a public key and a private key are used to encrypt and decrypt the logon information.

A smart card contains the user's public and private keys, plus an X.509 v3 certificate. All of these components are used when the user uses the smart card to authenticate to AD DS. The logon process begins when the user inserts a smart card into the smart card reader and enters his or her personal identification number (PIN). The insertion of the smart card into the reader is interpreted as a Ctrl+Alt+Del sequence by the LSA on the computer, and the logon process begins.

The PIN is used to read the user's certificate and public and private keys from the smart card. The client then sends a regular TGT request to the KDC. However, rather than sending the preauthorization data (time stamp) encrypted with the user's secret key derived from the password, the client sends the public key and the certificate to the KDC. The TGT request still includes the preauthorization data, but it is digitally signed with the user's private key.

When the message arrives at the KDC, it checks the client certificate to ensure that it is valid and that the CA that issued the certificate is trusted. The KDC also checks the digital signature of the preauthorization data to ensure the authenticity of the message sender and the integrity of the message. If both of these checks come back positive, the KDC uses the user principal name (UPN) included on the client certificate to look up the account name in AD DS. If the user account is valid, the KDC authenticates the user and sends a TGT including a session key back to the client. The session key is encrypted using the client's public key, and the client uses its private key to decrypt the information. This session key is then used for all connections to the KDC.

Note It takes a considerable amount of work to set up smart card logon for your network. First of all, you will have to deploy a CA to issue the certificates. Then you will have to set up smart card enrollment stations where users can get their smart cards, and the certificates and keys can be assigned to the cards. After the initial deployment, you will have to handle the administrative tasks of dealing with lost or forgotten cards. Smart cards provide excellent additional security on your network, but this additional security comes with considerable administrative effort. In many organizations, smart cards are used only to secure administrative accounts and to enable remote access security.

Interoperability with Other Kerberos Systems

Because Kerberos is based on an open standard, it provides excellent opportunities for interoperability with other Kerberos-based systems. Any of the components that are part of the Windows Server 2008 Kerberos implementation can be replaced by a non-Windows equivalent. These three components are:

- The Kerberos client
- The Kerberos Key Distribution Center
- The network resource that is using Kerberos for authorization

There are four possible scenarios for interoperability:

- A Windows 2000 or Windows XP Professional client may be logging on to a domain controller running Windows Server 2008 and accessing resources on either a server running Windows Server 2008 or on another Kerberos-based service.

- A Windows client may be logging on to a non-Windows KDC and accessing resources on either a server running Windows Server 2008 or on another Kerberos-based service.

Note Windows Server 2008 provides the command-line tool Ksetup.exe, which can be used to configure Windows clients to communicate with non-Windows KDCs.

- A non-Windows Kerberos client may be logging on to a Windows Server 2008 KDC and accessing resources on a server running Windows Server 2008 or on another Kerberos-based service.

- A non-Windows Kerberos client may be logging on to a non-Windows Kerberos implementation and accessing resources on a server running Windows Server 2008 or on another Kerberos-based service.

Windows Server 2008 can be configured to participate in any of these configurations. The easiest option is a homogenous solution in which either the entire environment is based on Windows Server 2008 Kerberos or on a non–Windows-based Kerberos implementation.

However, the Windows Server 2008 implementation of Kerberos also makes it fairly easy to interoperate with other Kerberos implementations. The easiest way to implement this is to create cross-realm trusts between the Windows Server 2008 domain and the non-Windows Kerberos realm. These realm trusts can be configured as transitive or nontransitive and as one-way or two-way. To configure a trust with another realm, open the Active Directory Domains And Trusts administrative tool and access the Properties sheet for the domain where you want to create a trust. On the Trusts tab, click New Trust, and the New Trust Wizard will start. Using this wizard, you can create the Windows Server 2008 side of the trust with another Kerberos realm.

> **More Info**   Microsoft provides a step-by-step guide to configuring Kerberos cross-realm trusts. This guide, titled "Step-by-Step Guide to Kerberos 5 (krb5 1.0) Interoperability," is available on the Microsoft Web site at *http://technet.microsoft.com/en-us/library/Bb742433.aspx*.

Troubleshooting Kerberos

If your organization has deployed only Windows 2000 or later clients and servers, all users in your organization will use Kerberos as the authentication protocol. Because all client access to network resources is based on a successful authentication, any authentication failure will significantly disrupt user interaction with the network. This means that you need to be prepared to troubleshoot Kerberos authentication.

TCP/IP Network Connectivity Requirements

For Kerberos authentication to succeed, client computers must be able to communicate with domain controllers. If firewalls are deployed between the client computers and domain controllers, ensure that the ports listed in Table 8-1 are open.

Table 8-1   Ports Required for Kerberos Authentication

Port	Service	Description
53/TCP 53/UDP	DNS service	The internal DNS server needs to be accessible to all clients for the location of KDC computers.
88/TCP 88/UDP	Kerberos ticket-granting service	All clients need to be able to connect to this port on the KDC servers.
123/TCP 123/UDP	Time service	All clients need to be able to connect to this port for time synchronization, either to an internal time server or to an external time source.
464/TCP	Microsoft Windows 2000 Kerberos change password protocol	This port is also used by the kpasswd protocol. This port should only be open if clients use the kpasswd protocol.

> **Note**   Although not required for Kerberos authentication, you should ensure that client computers can also communicate with domain controllers using LDAP (Port 389) and Global Catalog LDAP (Port 3268) in order to perform directory lookups.

Troubleshooting Authentication

When users cannot log on to the domain, the problem may be related to Kerberos authentication. In particular, if the system event log on domain controllers or client computers shows errors from any services that provide authentication such as Kerberos, KDC, LsaSrv, or Netlogon, you should approach the troubleshooting as a Kerberos error. You should also check the security event log for failure audits that may provide hints as to why authentication failed.

As a first step in troubleshooting authentication failures, use the Windows network troubleshooting tools to verify server and client availability and configuration. For example, you can use Dcdiag to check the health status of the services supporting the authentication services on the domain controllers. On the client side, check the IP address configuration and clear the name cache. You can also run the Nltest command to verify that the domain controller with which the client has established the secure channel is the expected one. You can also use Nslookup and Portquery to eliminate name resolution or port blocking issues.

If you suspect that the authentication error is due to a Kerberos problem, take the following steps to further identify the cause of the error:

1. Use Kerberos Tray or Kerberos List to verify that you have a service ticket for the server you are attempting to connect to. These tools will list all of the service tickets active on the workstation. If you have a service ticket for the server and you are still getting an error message when trying to access a resource, the problem may be a service principal name error or an authorization error.

2. If you do not have a service ticket, then use Kerberos Tray or Kerberos List to confirm that you have a TGT. The TGT is granted by the KDC service on a domain controller when the user logs on. If you have a TGT but no service ticket, examine the system event log. Errors logged in the system log will help you determine why you cannot get a ticket for the service.

> **Note**   By default, detailed Kerberos event logging is not enabled. To enable Kerberos logging, add a LogLevel value of REG_DWORD type to the HKEY_LOCAL_MACHINE\ SYSTEM\CurrentControlSet\Control\Lsa\Kerberos\Parameters registry key. Set the value to **0x1**.

3. If Kerberos authentication is failing, check the system event log or captured data in a network trace, which should contain the Kerberos error code that was returned by the KDC or the Kerberos SSP.

> **More Info**   For a complete listing of error codes that relate to Kerberos authentication, see the "Troubleshooting Kerberos Errors" article at *http://www.microsoft.com/technet/ prodtechnol/windowsserver2003/technologies/security/tkerberr.mspx*.

Some common reasons for Kerberos authentication errors are:

■ The time difference between the client computer and domain controllers is more than five minutes. When a Kerberos client authenticates, it includes a time stamp inside the authentication packet sent to the KDC. In addition, all tickets issued by the KDC have an expiration time. This means that Kerberos authentication relies on the date and time that are set on the KDC and the client. If there is too great a time difference between the KDC and a client requesting tickets, the KDC cannot determine whether the request is legitimate or a replay. Therefore, it is vital that the time on all of the computers on a network be synchronized in order for Kerberos authentication to function properly. This means that all of the domains and forest in a network must use the same time source. An AD DS domain controller will act as an authoritative time server for its domain, which guarantees that an entire domain will have the same time. However, multiple domains might not have their times synchronized. It is recommended that you use either an external time source or a single time source within the network to synchronize all computers.

■ AD DS replication may be failing or delayed. The Kerberos ticketing process leverages account password hashes, so if the user or computer has recently changed their password and this new password has not replicated throughout the environment, the KDC may encrypt a service ticket with the wrong secret. When this happens, Kerberos authentication will fail.

■ UDP packets may be fragmented between the client computer and domain controllers. By default, Kerberos authentication uses UDP to transmit its data. However, UDP provides no guarantee that a packet sent along the network will reach its destination intact. Thus, in environments with a high amount of network congestion, it is common for packets to get lost or fragmented on the way to their destination. You can diagnose UDP fragmentation by reviewing Network Monitor captured data. If network congestion is causing UDP fragmentation, you should consider configuring the Kerberos authentication service to use TCP instead of UDP. TCP provides a guarantee that a packet that is sent will reach its destination intact and can therefore be used in any network environment. In order to force Kerberos authentication to use TCP, see "How to Force Kerberos to Use TCP Instead of UDP" in the Microsoft Knowledge Base at *http://support.microsoft.com/kb/244474*.

■ Users may be members of too many groups. After the user has successfully authenticated, the KDC will transmit Privilege Attribute Certificate (PAC) data in the TGT. The PAC contains various types of authorization data including groups that the user is a member of, rights the user has, and what policies apply to the user. When the client receives a ticket, the information contained in the PAC is used to generate the user's access token. In order to optimize performance, the buffer size for the PAC is preallocated. The preallocated buffer size is usually adequate to hold all the required authorization data. However, if a user has a very high group membership—from over 70 to over 120, depending on what groups—the size of the PAC might exceed the preallocated buffer size. In such a case, the system will generate a memory allocation error, PAC creation will fail, and the Kerberos ticket-granting service will either fail to generate a valid ticket or will generate a ticket with an empty PAC. You can use the Tokensz.exe tool to verify that this is the problem. If this is the problem, you can reduce the number of groups that the user is a member of or modify the registry to increase the MaxTokenSize value for domain workstations. See "New Resolution for Problems with Kerberos Authentication When Users Belong to Many Groups" in the Microsoft Knowledge Base at *http://support.microsoft.com/kb/327825*.

■ The service principal name for the requested server may not be available. Service principal names (SPNs) are unique identifiers for services running on servers. Each service that will use Kerberos authentication needs to have an SPN set for it so that clients can identify the service on the network. It is registered in AD DS under a user or computer account as an attribute called *service-Principal-Name*. The SPN is assigned to the account under which the service or application is running. Any service can look up the SPN for another service. When a service authenticates to another service, it uses that service's SPN to differentiate it from other services running on the same computer. In general, SPNs should be set when you create a computer account. If an SPN is not set for a service, then the KDC will have no way of locating that service. Because multiple services can run simultaneously under the same account, setting an SPN requires four pieces of information that will make the SPN unique:

   ❑ The service class, which allows you to differentiate between multiple services running under the same account

   ❑ The account under which the service is running

   ❑ The computer on which the service is running, including any aliases that point to that computer

   ❑ The port on which the service is running

These four pieces of information uniquely identify any service running on a network and can be used to mutually authenticate to any service. If the SPN for a service is not registered in AD DS, use the Setspn.exe utility to configure the SPN. For details, see the "Service Logons Fail Due to Incorrectly Set SPNs" article at *http://technet2.microsoft.com/windowsserver/en/library/579246c8-2e32-4282-bce7-3209d1ea8bf11033.mspx?mfr=true*.

Service principal names must be unique. Another common problem related to service principal names is that multiple accounts (user or computer) have the same SPN defined on them. The best way to test for this is to do an LDAP query to search for the existence of accounts that have duplicate SPNs. For details, see the "Event ID 11 in the System Log of Domain Controllers" article at *http://support.microsoft.com/kb/321044.*

NTLM Authentication

The second option for authenticating to a Windows Server 2008 domain controller is to use NTLM authentication. NTLM authentication is supported primarily for backward compatibility with client computers running Windows NT 4.0, Windows 95, and Windows 98. This protocol is used in the following situations:

- When a computer running Windows 95, Windows 98, or Windows NT authenticates to a Windows Server 2008 domain controller. The Active Directory Client Extension must be installed on computers running Windows 95 and Windows 98, or these operating systems can only authenticate using the LAN Manager protocol.

- When a computer running Windows XP Professional or Windows Server 2008 authenticates to a server running Windows NT 4.

- When any client accesses a stand-alone server running Windows Server 2008.

- When a client running Windows XP Professional or Windows 2000 tries to log on to a Windows Server 2008 domain controller but is unable to authenticate by using the Kerberos protocol. In this instance, NTLM authentication can be used as an alternative protocol.

> **More Info**   The Active Directory Client Extension is available for download from "How to Install the Active Directory Client Extension" at *http://support.microsoft.com/kb/288358.*

The NTLM protocol is significantly less secure than Kerberos. With Windows NT 4 Service Pack 4, Microsoft introduced a new version of the NTLM protocol called NTLMv2. This new version includes additional security, such as creating a unique session key each time a new connection is established, as well as an advanced key-exchange process to protect the session keys.

NTLM uses a challenge-response mechanism to authenticate users and computers. With this format, the user is prompted (the challenge) to provide some personal information (the response). Windows Server 2008 supports the following three methods of challenge-response authentication:

- **LAN Manager (LM)**   LM authentication is the least-secure form of challenge-response authentication. You can use LM authentication to provide compatibility with older operating systems, including Windows 95 and Windows 98, without the Active Directory Client Extension installed. There are also earlier applications that might rely on this authentication mechanism. However, LM authentication is the weakest protocol, because when a password is created by the user and stored for use with LM, the password is converted to all uppercase. The password is limited to 14 characters, which are stored on the computer in two seven-character hashes.

- **NTLM version 1**   This is a more secure form of challenge-response authentication than LM. It is used for connecting to servers running Microsoft Windows NT with Service Pack 3 or earlier. NTLMv1 uses 56-bit encryption to secure the protocol.

- **NTLM version 2**   This is the most secure form of challenge-response authentication. This version includes a secure channel to protect the authentication process. It is used for connecting to servers running Windows 2000, Windows XP, and Windows NT with Service Pack 4 or higher. NTLMv2 uses 128-bit encryption to secure the protocol.

Domain controllers running Windows Server 2008 can accept all types of authentication protocols, including LM, NTLMv1 and NTLMv2, and Kerberos, to ensure compatibility with earlier operating systems. To ensure that computers in your organization accept only the most secure authentication protocols, you can configure Group Policy to support only the more secure protocols, such as NTLMv2 and Kerberos.

Windows Server 2008 provides the following two options for enhancing authentication security by using Group Policy. Both of these options are available in the Computer Configuration\Policies\Windows Settings\Security Settings\Local Policies\Security Options section.

- **Network Security: Do Not Store LAN Manager Hash Value On Next Password Change**   By default, this option is enabled in a Windows Server 2008 domain and is enforced by the default domain policy. This means that the policy applies to all member servers as well as domain controllers. When this option is enabled, the server will not create a copy of the LAN Manager password hash the next time a user changes their password.

Security Alert   If you store LAN Manager password hash values, anyone gaining access to the AD DS data store file will be able to extract the user passwords from the file. As a best practice, you should never disable this option in a Windows Server 2008 domain. If you have this option disabled, identify if there are any applications or client operating systems that require this option to be disabled. If there are specific servers that require this option, move the servers to a separate OU and disable the option for just that OU. If you change this setting from *disabled* to *enabled*, you should force all users to change their passwords so that all LAN Manager hashes are deleted from the AD DS data store.

- **Network Security: LAN Manager Authentication Level**   This setting specifies the minimum level of authentication that must be supported by all clients on the network. The configuration options are listed in Table 8-2.

Table 8-2   LAN Manager Authentication Settings

Level	Setting	Result
0	Send LM & NTLM responses	Clients use LM and NTLM authentication and never use NTLMv2 session security; domain controllers accept LM, NTLM, and NTLMv2 authentication.
1	Send LM & NTLM—use NTLMv2 session security if negotiated	Clients use LM and NTLM authentication and use NTLMv2 session security if the server supports it; domain controllers accept LM, NTLM, and NTLMv2 authentication.
2	Send NTLM response only	Clients use NTLM authentication only and use NTLMv2 session security if the server supports it; domain controllers accept LM, NTLM, and NTLMv2 authentication.
3	Send NTLMv2 response only	Clients use NTLMv2 authentication only and use NTLMv2 session security if the server supports it; domain controllers accept LM, NTLM, and NTLMv2 authentication.
4	Send NTLMv2 response only/refuse LM	Clients use NTLMv2 authentication only and use NTLMv2 session security if the server supports it. Domain controllers refuse LM and accept only NTLM and NTLMv2 authentication.
5	Send NTLMv2 response only/refuse LM & NTLM	Clients use NTLMv2 authentication only and use NTLMv2 session security if the server supports it; domain controllers refuse LM and NTLM (they accept only NTLMv2 authentication).

By default, this setting is configured at Level 3, Send NTLMv2 response only for the Default Domain Controller Policy in Windows Server 2008. It is recommended that you set the authentication level to Level 4 or higher to ensure that the domain controller will not accept LM authentication. Doing so might cause some applications that rely on earlier authentication methods to fail.

More Info   For a detailed explanation of the issues you may experience if you increase the security settings for LM authentication, as well as other security settings, see "Client, Service, and Program Incompatibilities That May Occur When You Modify Security Settings and User Rights Assignments" at *http://support.microsoft.com/kb/823659/en-us*.

Implementing Security for Domain Controllers

In addition to configuring AD DS security by configuring the authentication settings, you should also take additional steps to secure your domain controllers. Because the domain controllers store all of the AD DS data, securing your domain controllers is a critical step in increasing the security of your AD DS deployment.

Note   Two key components when planning domain security are configuring secure domain boundaries and planning for the physical security of your domain controllers. See Chapter 5, "Designing the Active Directory Domain Services Structure," for details on designing administrative isolation and autonomy, and for planning considerations for deploying read only domain controllers in locations where you cannot ensure the physical security of the domain controllers.

Decrease the Domain Controller Attack Surface

The first step in securing domain controllers is to reduce the attack surface on the domain controller. When you reduce the attack surface, you are reducing the number of options available to an attacker to gain access to the domain controller. Usually this means that you remove all applications and disable all services that are not required on the domain controller.

One of the best tools available for reducing the attack surface of a domain controller is the Security Configuration Wizard (SCW). When you run the SCW, the SCW examines the actual configuration for the target server. Based on the information gathered during the examination, the SCW identifies which server roles, client features, and other components are installed and enabled on the computer. The SCW then uses a security configuration database to identify which services and settings need to be enabled on the server. The SCW uses this information and the decisions that you make when you create an SCW policy to:

- Disable services that are not required. The SCW policy will disable any services that are not required on the server based on the server roles installed. You can also configure the SCW to disable or not modify the service startup settings for any services not included in the Security Configuration Database.

- Configure Windows Firewall. When you apply an SCW policy, it will block access to the server for all ports other than those ports required to provide the server role functionality. You can also configure the policy to apply further address or security restrictions for ports that are left open. For example, you can configure Windows Firewall to only accept connections from a local subnet, or only accept connections for certain protocols when the connection is secured by IPSec.

- Prohibit unnecessary IIS Web extensions. If IIS is installed on the server, the SCW policy can be used to disable IIS Web extensions that are not required.

- Reduce protocol exposure to server message block (SMB), LanMan, and Lightweight Directory Access Protocol (LDAP).

- When you run the SCW, you can choose which types of clients and servers you have on your network. Based on the decisions you make, the SCW can configure the servers to only accept encrypted SMB or LDAP connections and to disable LAN Manager connections.

- Configure an audit policy. When you run the SCW, you can also configure an audit policy for the server.

SCW guides you through the process of creating, editing, applying, or rolling back a security policy based on the selected roles of the server. The SCW is made up of three components:

- **SCW user interface**   The SCW guides you through the process of creating a security policy, based on the roles performed by a given server. After a policy is created, it can be edited or applied to one or more similarly configured servers. Applied policies can be rolled back in order to undo changes that have caused problems.

■ **Scwcmd command-line tool**   SCW includes the Scwcmd.exe command-line tool. You can use Scwcmd for the following tasks:

❑ Configure one or many servers with an SCW-generated policy.

❑ Analyze one or many servers with an SCW-generated policy.

❑ View analysis results in HTML format.

❑ Roll back SCW policies.

❑ Transform an SCW-generated policy into native files that are supported by Group Policy.

❑ Register a Security Configuration Database extension with SCW.

> **Note**   When you use Scwcmd to configure, analyze, or roll back a policy on a remote server, SCW is required to be installed on the remote server.

■ **Security Configuration Database**   The Security Configuration Database consists of a set of XML documents that list services and ports that are required for each server role that is supported by SCW. These files are installed in %Systemroot%\Security\Msscw\KBs. When you run the SCW, it uses the Security Configuration Database to determine:

❑ Which roles are installed on the server

❑ Which roles are likely being performed by the server

❑ Which services are installed but are not part of the Security Configuration Database

❑ The IP addresses and subnets that are configured for the server

SCW combines this server-specific information into a single XML file named Main.XML. The Security Configuration Wizard displays Main.XML if you click View Security Configuration Database on the Processing Security Configuration Database page. Figure 8-8 shows the information that is displayed for the domain controller role on a server running Windows Server 2008.

> **On the Disc**   For an example of an SCW policy configured for a domain controller, see the SampleDC_SCWPolicy.xml file on the CD. You can open this file in Internet Explorer, or open it in SCW.

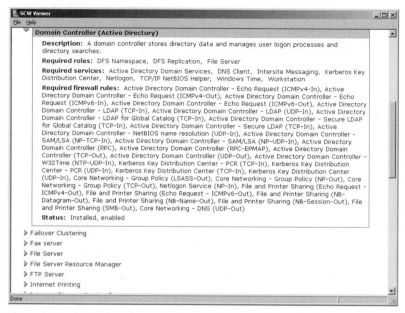

Figure 8-8   SCW domain controller services and firewall rules.

After configuring an SCW policy, you can apply the policy to the server where you configured the policy. You can also apply that SCW policy to other computers with the same configuration by running use the Scwcmd tool to either directly apply the policy or to transform the policy into a Group Policy Object that can then be linked to the Domain Controllers OU. For details on how to do this, see Chapter 13.

> **Caution**   Be careful when applying an SCW policy that was configured on one computer to other computers. The SCW policy is specific to the computer where it was created, so if the other computers have a different configuration (for example, they are running other server roles or applications), the SCW policy may disable services or block firewall ports. Ensure that all servers have the same configuration before applying the SCW policy.

Configuring the Default Domain Controllers Policy

In addition to reducing the domain controller attack surface, you can also use Group Policy to increase the security of your domain controller deployment. When you deploy a Windows Server 2008 domain, the following two default GPOs are created and applied to the domain and to the Domain Controllers OU:

- Default Domain Policy, which is linked to the domain object and affects all users and computers in the domain (including computers that are domain controllers) through policy inheritance.

- Default Domain Controllers Policy, which is linked to the Domain Controllers OU. This policy generally affects only domain controllers, because by default, computer accounts for domain controllers are kept in the Domain Controllers OU.

You can configure security policies using both the Default Domain Policy and the Default Domain Controller Policy. By default, all polices defined at the domain level are inherited by OUs in the domain unless the policy inheritance is blocked or a policy linked to the OU contains settings that override the domain policies. By applying domain controllers specific security settings in the Default Domain Controller Policy, or in another GPO linked to the Domain Controllers OU, you can apply security policy settings that are specific to domain controllers, but not to all users, groups, and computers in the domain.

Note   This chapter is primarily concerned with domain controller security, so this chapter will focus on settings available in the Default Domain Controllers Policy. For details on configuring the security settings in the Default Domain Policy, see Chapter 13. For details on configuring Group Policy, including configuring Group Policy links and inheritance, see Chapter 11, "Introduction to Group Policy."

Configuring Domain Controller Audit Policy Settings

One of the key components in a domain controller security policy is auditing changes made on the domain controllers. By auditing changes made on domain controllers, you can identify who is responsible for directory changes and when the changes were made.

Windows Server 2008 introduces some important changes to the auditing on domain controllers. In Windows 2000 Server and Windows Server 2003, there was one audit policy, Audit Directory Service Access, that controlled whether auditing for directory service events was enabled or disabled. In Windows Server 2008, this policy is divided into four subcategories:

- Directory Service Access
- Directory Service Changes
- Directory Service Replication
- Detailed Directory Service Replication

Note   These subcategories are not visible through Group Policy Management Editor. To view and configure the subcategories, use the Auditpol.exe command-line tool. To view the current directory service access audit settings, type **Auditpol /get /category:"ds access"**.

From a security auditing perspective, the most important new feature is the Directory Service Changes subcategory. This new subcategory adds the following functionality:

- When you change an attribute on an object, AD DS logs the previous and current values of the attribute. If the attribute has more than one value, only the values that change as a result of the modify operation are logged.

- When you create a new object, values of the attributes that are populated at the time of creation are logged. If the user adds attributes during the create operation, those new attribute values are logged. In most cases, AD DS assigns default values to attributes (such as *samAccountName*). The values of such system attributes are not logged.

- If an object is moved, the previous and new location (distinguished name) is logged for moves within the domain. When an object is moved to a different domain, a create event is generated on the domain controller in the target domain.

- If an object is undeleted, the location where the object is moved to is logged. In addition, if the user adds, modifies, or deletes attributes while performing an undelete operation, the values of those attributes are logged.

By default, the Audit directory service access audit category is not enabled in the Default Domain Controllers OU, but the Directory Service Access subcategory is enabled. This audit policy logs when administrators access objects in AD DS, but the changes to those objects are not logged. To enable the Directory Services Changes auditing, you can choose to enable the Audit directory service access option in the Default Domain Controllers Policy audit policy. When you enable this option, all subcategories are also enabled.

To enable just the Directory Service Changes subcategory, you must use the Auditpol.exe command-line tool and run the following command:

```
auditpol /set /subcategory:"directory service changes" /success:enable
```

Windows Server 2008 also introduces subcategories under the other audit categories. The categories, subcategories, and default settings for AD DS specific audit settings are listed in Table 8-3. To view these audit settings, type **Auditpol /get /category:*** at a command prompt.

Table 8-3   Configuring Domain Controller Audit Policy Settings

Category	Subcategory	Default Setting
Audit logon events	Logon	Success and Failure
Audit logon events	Logoff	Success
	Account Lockout	Success
Audit logon events	IPSec Main Mode, IPSec Extended Mode, IPSec Quick Mode	No Auditing
Audit logon events	Special Logon	Success
Audit logon events	Other Logon/Logoff events	No Auditing
Audit logon events	Network Policy Server	Success and Failure

Table 8-3   Configuring Domain Controller Audit Policy Settings *(continued)*

Category	Subcategory	Default Setting
Audit policy change	Audit Policy Change	Success
Audit policy change	Authentication Policy Change	Success
Audit policy change	Authorization Policy Change, MPSSVC Rule-Level Policy Change, Filtering Platform Policy Change, Other Policy Change Events	No Auditing
Audit account management	User Account Management	Success
Audit account management	Computer Account Management	Success
Audit account management	Security Group Management	Success
Audit account management	Distribution Group Management, Application Group Management, Other Account Management Events	No Auditing
Audit account logon events	Kerberos Service Ticket Operations	Success
Audit account logon events	Other Account Logon Events	No Auditing
Audit account logon events	Kerberos Authentication Service	Success
Audit account logon events	Credential Validation	Success

In most cases, if the goal of your audit policy is to audit administrator activity in AD DS, you should accept the default domain controller audit settings. If you are using the audit policy for other purposes, such as intrusion detection, you may want to also audit the failure of events such as logon events or account management events. By default, if you enable auditing for any of the categories, auditing will also be enabled for all subcategories.

> **Note**   Configuring the audit policy is only the first step in enabling AD DS auditing. After configuring the audit policy, you must configure the System Access Control List (SACL) on each object to enable auditing. To do this, enable auditing for the domain or OU object in Active Directory Users and Computers.

Configuring Domain Controller Event Log Policy Settings

When you configure the audit settings for domain controllers, you should also consider changing the event log settings on the domain controllers. In particular, you should increase the maximum size of the security log to accommodate the increased number of audited events that might be generated. Table 8-4 lists the changes that are recommended for the Event Log settings on the Default Domain Controller Policy.

Table 8-4   Recommended Domain Controller Event Log Policy Settings

Policy	Default Setting	Recommended Setting	Comments
Maximum security log size	Not defined; by default, maximum log size is *128 MB*	131,072 KB	Increased to accommodate security auditing that is enabled in the default domain controller Audit Policy
Prevent local guests group from accessing application log	Not defined	Enabled	Prevents members of the built-in group Guests from reading the application log events
Prevent local guests group from accessing security log	Not defined	Enabled	Prevents members of the built-in group Guests from reading the security log events
Prevent local guests group from accessing system log	Not defined	Enabled	Prevents members of the built-in group Guests from reading the system log events
Retain security log	Not defined	(No change)	Specifies the number of days the events are retained if the retention method for this log is By Days
Retain system log	Not defined	(No change)	
Retention method for security log	Not defined	Overwrite events as needed	Overwrites the security log when the maximum log size is reached to ensure that the log contains the most recent security events and to ensure that logging continues
Retention method for system log	Not defined	Overwrite events as needed	Overwrites the system log when the maximum log size is reached to ensure that the log contains the most recent security events and to ensure that logging continues

Security Alert   To ensure that you retain the audit information, you must archive the system and security logs regularly, and before they fill up. If you accept the recommended settings for the retention method, the oldest events will be overwritten when the log files fill up. If you use a retention method of Do Not Overwrite Events, new events will not be written to the log file when it has reached its maximum size.

Configuring Domain Controller User Rights Assignment Policy Settings

User rights define what types of administrative or operations tasks users can perform on domain controllers. In order to ensure domain controller security, you should configure the user rights assignment to limit which users can log on to and perform administrative tasks on domain controllers.

> **Important**   Most of the default settings for the domain controller user rights and security options are configured for optimal security. Although most of the settings are configured as Not Defined in the Default Domain Controller Policy, almost all of the settings do have a default value which meets security requirements. To review the default value, access the setting properties and click on the Explain tab.
>
> Because the default settings are configured to be secure, you do not necessarily need to enable or disable most of the settings. However, if you do modify any of these settings at the domain level, they will be inherited by domain controllers in the Domain Controllers OU. Before making any changes to the security settings at the domain level, you should configure the security settings in the Default Domain Controllers Policy to match the default setting or block policy inheritance at the Domain Controllers OU.

Table 8-5 lists the default and recommended policy settings for domain controller user rights assignment policies.

Table 8-5   Default and Recommended Domain Controller User Rights Assignment Policy Settings

Policy	Default Setting	Recommended Setting	Comments
Allow log on locally	Account Operators Administrators Backup Operators Print Operators Server Operators	Administrators Backup Operators Server Operators	Printers should not be installed on domain controllers, so Print Operators should not need to log on to domain controllers. Account Operators should have the administration tools installed on their workstations rather than logging on to domain controllers.
Shut down the system	Administrators Backup Operators Print Operators Server Operators	Administrators Backup Operators Server Operators	See above.
Load and unload device drivers	Administrators Print Operators	Administrators	If no printers are installed on the domain controller, Print Operators should not be allowed modify device driver settings.

**Table 8-5   Default and Recommended Domain Controller User Rights Assignment
Policy Settings** *(continued)*

Policy	Default Setting	Recommended Setting	Comments
Manage auditing and security log	Administrators	Depends on company requirements	In some organizations, users other than administrators may need to access and manage the security logs. Create a group for this specific purpose and assign this right to that group.

Configuring Domain Controller Security Options Policy Settings

The Default Domain Controllers Policy includes a large number of security settings that affect a wide variety of domain controller, network, file system, and user logon security configuration settings. Although some of these settings will only affect domain controllers, other settings can also affect network connectivity for client computers.

> **Important**   Like the user rights settings, most of the security settings are configured as Not Defined in the Default Domain Controller Policy. However, almost all of the settings do have a default value.

Table 8-6 lists the security setting categories available in the policy.

Table 8-6   Security Setting Categories

Category	Description
Accounts	Use these settings to enable, disable, or rename the Administrator and Guest accounts, or to restrict access to the local accounts with blank passwords.
Audit	Use to configure global audit settings. This category contains two settings that require some consideration: ■ Force audit policy subcategory settings (Windows Vista or later). If you enable this option, you force all audit settings to be made at the subcategory level rather than have the subcategory inherit the category settings. ■ Shut down system immediately if unable to log security audits. Enabling this option means that the domain controller will be shut down if a security audit cannot be logged. In most cases, you should disable this setting to avoid domain controller shut downs.
DCOM	Use to enable or disable users from launching DCOM applications remotely or locally.

Table 8-6   Security Setting Categories *(continued)*

Category	Description
Devices	Use to configure access to devices such as CD-ROMs or floppy disks or to restrict users from installing print drivers on print servers.
Domain controller	Use to set restrictions on server operators scheduling tasks using the AT command, configure LDAP signing, and configure the domain controller to refuse password changes from member computers.
Domain member	Use to configure network security settings and configure settings for setting computer passwords.
Interactive logon	Use to set restrictions on the interactive logon process on the domain controllers. Options include: ■ Clearing the last user logon name ■ Configuring logon messages when users log on to the domain ■ Configuring smart card requirements
Microsoft network client	Use to configure requirements for digitally signing network communications for client computers.
Microsoft network server	Use to configure settings for digitally signing network communications and for disconnecting users when their logon hours expire.
Network access	Use to configure a wide variety of network access settings including whether to allow anonymous enumeration of SAM accounts and configuring options for connecting to shares.
Recovery console	Use to define who can access the recovery console, and if floppy drives and other drives are accessible from the recovery console.
Shutdown	Use to configure if users can shutdown the computer without logging on and if the virtual memory pagefile should be cleared at shut down.
System cryptography	Use to enforce security requirements for keys stored on computers, and for algorithms used to create secure keys.
System objects	Use to set security requirements for Windows system objects.
System settings	Use to configure additional subsystems, such as POSIX, and to enable certificate rules for software restriction policies.
User Account Control	Use to configure how user account control settings will be applied to Windows Vista client computers.

More Info   For details on all of the security settings available in Windows Server 2008, download the Group Policy Settings Reference Windows Vista spreadsheet located at *http://www.microsoft.com/downloads/details.aspx?FamilyID=41dc179b-3328-4350-ade1-c0d9289f09ef&displaylang=en.*

Implementing SMB Signing

Windows Server 2008 supports SMB signing as a means to ensure that all file share access on domain controllers is encrypted. Computers in the same domain as the domain controller access file shares during the user logon process to access logon scripts and profiles in the Netlogon share. Group Policy objects are accessed through the SYSVOL share. For these reasons, all domain controllers should take advantage of SMB signing to improve security.

Table 8-7 describes the Security Options policy settings for SMB signing.

Table 8-7   Security Options Policy Settings for SMB Packet Signing

SMB Setting	Explanation
Microsoft network client: Digitally sign communications (always)	The domain controller requires SMB signing when initiating SMB requests with other domain controllers, member servers, or workstations. The domain controller refuses to communicate with other systems that do not support SMB signing. For enhanced security, enable this Group Policy setting.
Microsoft network client: Digitally sign communications (if server agrees)	The domain controller negotiates SMB signing when initiating SMB requests with other domain controllers, member servers, or workstations. The domain controller requests SMB signing, but it will communicate with other systems that do not support SMB signing. Enable this option only if you have Windows 95 and earlier operating systems.
Microsoft network server: Digitally sign communications (always)	The domain controller requires SMB signing when receiving SMB requests from other domain controllers, member servers, or workstations. The domain controller refuses to communicate with other systems that do not support SMB signing. For enhanced security, enable this Group Policy setting. This option is enabled by default in the Default Domain Controllers Policy.
Microsoft network server: Digitally sign communications (if client agrees)	The domain controller negotiates SMB signing when receiving SMB requests with other domain controllers, member servers, or workstations. The domain controller requests SMB signing, but it will communicate with other systems that do not support SMB signing. This option is enabled by default in the Default Domain Controllers Policy.

Note   You can also enforce these options by applying an SCW policy to the domain controllers. When you run the SCW, you have the option of configuring registry settings on the server to enforce SMB security. Figure 8-9 shows the interface. If you select both options, SMB signing will be enforced on the server.

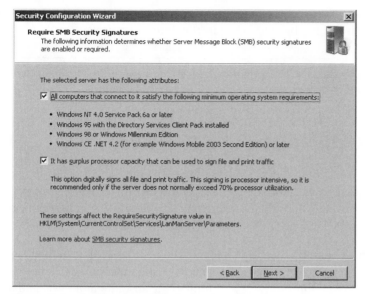

Figure 8-9   Configuring SMB signing by using the SCW.

Configuring SYSKEY

By default, the AD DS data store is encrypted when it is stored on the domain controller hard disk. This provides a level of security if an attacker gains access to the physical hard disk on which the data store is located. The data is encrypted by using the system key (SYSKEY) in Windows Server 2008.

You can use the SYSKEY tool to provide an extra level of security when domain controllers start up. SYSKEY gives you three options for configuring the startup key:

- **Store Startup Key Locally**   This option creates a machine-generated random key stored on the local system by using a complex encryption algorithm. This is the default configuration of Syskey.exe, and it provides strong encryption of password information in the registry. Because the System Key is stored on the local system, this method allows for unattended system restarts.

- **Password Startup**   This option requires an administrator-chosen password to derive the System Key. If you select this option, an administrator must enter System Key password during system startup.

- **Store Startup Key on Floppy Disk**   This option creates a machine-generated random key that stored on a floppy disk. The floppy disk with the System Key must be inserted into the floppy drive to start the domain controller.

Configuring SYSKEY to use a password or floppy disk to start may provide an additional level of security for domain controllers that are not physically secure. However, this option also requires that an administrator who knows the password be present or that the floppy disk be available when the domain controller is restarted. If you do store the SYSKEY on a floppy disk and the disk is lost, you will not be able to restart the domain controller.

> **Note** Consider using an RODC in situations where the domain controller cannot be physically secured, rather than implementing SYSKEY security settings.

Designing Secure Administrative Practices

One of the most important components in designing AD DS security is designing secure administrative practices. Because administrators have full control of the AD DS environment, they can circumvent or modify even the best security design. When creating your administrative practices, consider the following suggestions:

- Limit the number of enterprise and domain administrator accounts to highly trusted personnel. This is particularly important for service administrator accounts. Keep the membership of service administrator accounts to the absolute minimum and assign only reliable, trusted users who fully understand the implications of any changes made to the directory. Do not use service administrator accounts for day-to-day administrative tasks.

- Implement a change control process. All changes made in an AD DS environment should be subject to a change control process. This is particularly important for changes that have an impact on the entire directory service environment. For example, schema changes should be implemented only after careful planning and testing and after approval from the forest owners.

- Limit the Schema Admins group to temporary members. Most organizations will change the schema very rarely, so no one needs to be logged on as a schema administrator on a regular basis. To secure the schema change process, keep the membership of the Schema Admins group empty. Add a trusted user to the group only when an administrative task must be performed on the schema. Remove that user after the task is completed.

- Use a Restricted Group policy to restrict the membership for the critical domain and forest accounts. When you implement a Restricted Group policy, the group membership is monitored by the domain controllers and any users that are not included in the Restricted Group Policy are automatically removed.

- Ensure that administrators have and use two different accounts. For users who fill administrative roles, create two accounts: one regular user account to be used for normal, day-to-day tasks and one administrative account to be used only for performing administrative tasks. The administrative account should not be mail-enabled or used for running applications that are used every day, such as Microsoft Office, or for browsing the Internet.

- Apply the principal of least privileges for all administrative groups. Carefully define the permissions that are actually required for each administrative group and then assign only those permissions. For example, if an administrator needs to manage only specific users accounts or computer accounts, or manage only some settings for these accounts, create an OU to contain these accounts, and then delegate permissions to the administrative account. Also avoid using the Account Operators group to assign permission to configure user and group accounts. The default directory permissions give this group the ability to modify the computer accounts of domain controllers, including deleting them. By default, there are no members of the Account Operators group, and its membership should be left empty.

- Hide the domain administrator account. Every installation of AD DS has an account named Administrator in each domain. This is the default administrative account, which is created during domain setup, that you use to access and administer the directory service. This is a special account that the system protects to help ensure that it is available when needed. This account cannot be disabled or locked out. You should rename it to something other than Administrator. When you rename the account, make sure that you also change the text in the Description for the account. In addition, you should create a decoy user account called Administrator that has no special permissions or user rights and monitor for event IDs 528, 529, and 534 in connection with both the renamed and decoy accounts.

- Never share administrator accounts. In some organizations, all senior administrators know the password for the default Administrator account, and all of them use this account to perform administrative tasks. Sharing administrator accounts makes it impossible to accurately audit who made the changes to the directory, so this practice is strongly discouraged. Sharing administrator accounts and passwords can also create a security problem as administrators leave the team or company.

- Secure the Administrative logon process. To minimize the chances of someone misusing or compromising an administrator account, consider taking these steps to enforce strong administrative credentials:

  - Require smart cards for administrative logon. Have service administrators use smart cards for their interactive logons. In addition to forcing the administrative users to have physical possession of the cards to log on, smart cards also ensure the use of randomly generated, cryptographically strong passwords on the user accounts. These strong passwords help to protect against the theft of weak passwords to gain administrative access. You can enforce the use of smart cards by enabling the Interactive logon: Require smart card security option for each administrative account.

  - Split the logon credentials for sensitive administrative accounts. For each account that is a member of the Enterprise Admins and Domain Admins groups in the forest root domain, assign two users to share that account, so that both users must be present to log on successfully with that account. You can split the logon credentials by using either split passwords (where each administrator only knows part of the password) or split smart cards plus personal identification numbers (PINs).

■ Secure service administrator workstations. In addition to configuring administrator account security, you should also ensure the security of the administrator workstations. To do this, consider implementing the following processes:

❏ Restrict which workstations service administrators can log on to. Each administrative account can be restricted so that it is allowed to log on only to specific workstations. If one of your administrative accounts is compromised, limiting the possible workstations limits the number of locations where that account can be used.

❏ Apply a special security policy to the administrator workstations. Consider moving all of the service administrator workstations into a dedicated OU and then apply a highly secure policy for the workstations. For example, you might limit the Allow Log On Locally user right to the service administrator accounts.

❏ Ensure that administrative workstations have all security updates installed and the antivirus software on the workstations is current.

❏ Encourage administrators to use Remote Desktop to perform administrative tasks. You can enable Remote Desktop on any Windows Server 2008 server and configure the security settings so that only specified administrators can connect to the server through Remote Desktop. If you install the Remote Desktop 6 client on Windows XP clients or use a Windows Vista client, you can enforce network encryption for all Remote Desktop connections.

■ Secure backup media. When you back up the domain controllers in your organization, the entire directory store is copied to the backup media. Although the data is encrypted, an attacker who gains access to the tapes will have unlimited time to decrypt and gain access to the data. You can help prevent unauthorized users from gaining physical access to backup media by doing the following:

❏ Store backup media that is used on-site in a secure location where access is audited.

❏ Store archival backup media securely off-site.

❏ Establish secure processes for transporting backup media.

■ Set object ownership quotas. On domain controllers that are running Windows Server 2008, you can set quotas that limit the number of objects that a security principal (user, group, computer, or service) can own in a domain, configuration, or application directory partition. By default, the security principal that creates an object is the object owner, although ownership can be transferred. AD DS quotas eliminate the ability to create unlimited numbers of objects in a directory partition, which can be used for denial-of-service attacks. By default, quotas are not set; therefore, there are no limits to the number of objects that any security principal can own. To set quotas, use the Dsmod Quota command.

Summary

This chapter provided a brief overview of the basic concepts of Windows Server 2008 AD DS security, including the security principals, access control lists, authentication, and authorization. The first part of this chapter focused on the primary means of providing authentication and authorization in AD DS through the Kerberos protocol. Kerberos provides a secure mechanism for users to authenticate to AD DS and to gain access to network resources.

The second component to providing AD DS security is to secure domain controllers and implement secure administrative practices. The second part of this chapter provided details on how to implement this type of security.

Best Practices

- If possible, upgrade all servers and workstations to at least Windows Server 2000 with the latest service packs. By doing this, you can ensure that Kerberos is used for all authentication requests, and you can configure security features like SMB signing on domain controllers.

- Implement dedicated domain controllers. In other words, do not run applications or services that are not required on domain controllers. Doing so makes it easier to reduce the attack surface of the domain controllers and also makes it easier to create one SCW policy that can be applied to all domain controllers.

- Implement a complex password policy and encourage administrators to configure extremely complex passwords. Suggest that administrators use pass phrases rather than just passwords.

- Assign the least permissions possible to all administrator accounts. Ensure that all administrators only have permission to perform the tasks required for their jobs.

Additional Resources

These resources contain additional information related to this topic:

Related Information

- Chapter 5, "Designing the Active Directory Domain Services Structure," goes into detail on designing secure AD DS boundaries.

- Chapter 9, "Delegating the Administration of Active Directory Domain Services," explains how to delegate administrative permissions within AD DS. This is useful when applying the least permission standard.

- Chapter 11, "Introduction to Group Policy," goes into detail about how to configure Group Policy, including how to enable and block Group Policy inheritance. You may want to block Group Policy inheritance at the Domain Controllers OU to prevent domain level security settings from being applied to domain controllers.

- Chapter 13, "Using Group Policy to Manage Security," provides information on additional Group Policy settings that are available to configure security.

- "The Kerberos Network Authentication Service (V5)," available at *http://www.ietf.org/rfc/rfc1510.txt,* describes the current Kerberos standard.

- "Kerberos Authentication Technical Reference," available at *http://technet2.microsoft.com/windowsserver/en/library/74d58697-970a-45db-9139-ebcd3db051181033.mspx?mfr=true*

- "Authorization and Access Control Technologies," available at *http://technet2.microsoft.com/windowsserver/en/library/74d58697-970a-45db-9139-ebcd3db051181033.mspx?mfr=true*

- "Troubleshooting Kerberos," available at *http://technet2.microsoft.com/windowsserver/en/library/26ce2e7f-52d6-4425-88cc-1573bc5e646d1033.mspx?mfr=true*

- "Troubleshooting Kerberos Errors," available at *http://www.microsoft.com/technet/prodtechnol/windowsserver2003/technologies/security/tkerberr.mspx*

Related Tools

Windows Server 2008 provides several tools that can be used when troubleshooting Kerberos authentication. Table 8-8 lists some of these tools and when you would use each of the tools.

Table 8-8 Kerberos Troubleshooting Tools

Tool Name	Description and Use
Klist.exe: Kerberos List	This tool is installed on Windows Server 2008 domain controllers and is available for download as part of the Windows Server 2003 Resource Kit tools.
	Kerberos List is a command-line tool that is used to view and delete Kerberos tickets granted to the current logon session. To use Kerberos List to view tickets, you must run the tool on a computer that is a member of a Kerberos realm.
Kerbtray.exe: Kerberos Tray	Kerberos Tray is available for download as part of the Windows Server 2003 Resource Kit tools.
	Kerberos Tray is a graphical user interface tool that displays ticket information for a computer running Microsoft's implementation of the Kerberos version 5 authentication protocol. You can view and purge the ticket cache by using the Kerberos Tray tool icon located in the notification area of the desktop. By positioning the cursor over the icon, you can view the time left until the initial TGT expires. The icon also changes in the hour before the Local Security Authority (LSA) renews the ticket.

Table 8-8   **Kerberos Troubleshooting Tools** *(continued)*

Tool Name	Description and Use
Tokensz.exe Kerberos Token Size	Kerberos Token Size is available for download from the Microsoft download center.
	You can use Kerberos Token Size to verify if the source of the Kerberos errors stems from a maximum token size issue. The tool will simulate an authentication request and report the size of the resulting Kerberos token. The tool will also report the maximum supported size for the token.
Setspn.exe	The Setspn utility is installed on Windows Server 2008 domain controllers and is included in the Windows Server 2003 Support Tools.
	The Setspn utility allows you to read, modify, and delete the Service Principal Names (SPN) directory property for an Active Directory service account. Because SPNs are security-sensitive, you can only set SPNs for service accounts if you have domain administrator privileges.
Ksetup.exe	The Ksetup utility is installed on Windows Server 2008 domain controllers and is included in the Windows Server 2003 Support Tools.
	The Ksetup utility configures a client connected to a server running Windows Server 2008 to use a server running Kerberos V5. The client then uses a Kerberos V5 realm instead of a Windows Server 2008 domain.
Ktpass.exe	The Ktpass utility is installed on Windows Server 2008 domain controllers and is included in the Windows Server 2003 Support Tools.
	The Ktpass utility is used to configure a non–Windows Server Kerberos service as a security principal in the Windows Server 2008 AD DS.
W32tm.exe: Windows Time	This tool is included in Microsoft Windows server and client operating systems.
	W32tm.exe is used to configure Windows Time service settings. It can also be used to diagnose problems with the time service.

Resources on the CD

- SampleDC_SCWPolicy.xml. This is a sample Security Configuration Wizard file that configures the services, Windows Firewall, and registry settings for a Windows Server 2008 domain controller.

Related Help Topics

- Security Configuration Wizard help

Chapter 9

Delegating the Administration of Active Directory Domain Services

Active Directory Domain Services (AD DS) is typically deployed as a common directory service shared between various business divisions within an organization. Using a common directory service helps reduce the costs associated with maintaining the infrastructure, but introduces a number of other considerations:

- How to manage users and resources independently between divisions when decentralized administration is required

- Ensuring that administrators or users can only perform permitted tasks within their own business division

- Ensuring that specific objects or information stored within the directory is only available to administrators with the appropriate permissions

These considerations can be addressed by a thorough understanding of how to delegate administrative tasks. Delegation involves a higher-level administrator granting permissions to other users to perform specific administrative tasks within the Active Directory structure. The Active Directory structure provides a hierarchical view of the directory service: first at the site and domain level, and then at the organizational unit (OU) level within a domain. This hierarchy provides powerful options for managing permissions and delegating administrative tasks at various levels throughout the logical infrastructure.

This chapter describes administrative delegation, starting with a discussion of the various types of tasks that might be delegated within an enterprise. Then it describes object access, the types of permissions that can be assigned to objects residing within the directory, and how to use these permissions for delegation of administration. Finally, the chapter provides information about auditing changes to objects residing within AD DS.

Active Directory Administration Tasks

Active Directory administration tasks typically fall into one of two categories—data management or service management. Data management tasks relate to the management of content that is stored within the Active Directory database. Service management tasks relate to the management of all aspects that are required to ensure a reliable and efficient delivery of the directory service throughout the enterprise.

Table 9-1 describes some of the tasks that are related to each of these categories.

Table 9-1   Active Directory Administration

Category	Tasks
Data management	■ **Account management**—includes creating, maintaining, and removing user accounts
	■ **Security group management**—includes creating security groups, provisioning security groups to grant access to network resources, managing memberships of security groups, and removing security groups
	■ **Resource management**—includes all aspects of managing network resources such as end-user workstations, servers, and resources hosted on servers such as file shares or applications
	■ **Group Policy management**—includes all aspects of creating, assigning, and removing Group Policy objects within the Active Directory structure
	■ **Application-specific data management**—includes all aspects of managing Active Directory-integrated or enabled applications such as Microsoft Exchange Server
Service management	■ **Installation and trust management**—includes aspects such as the creation and deletion of domains, the deployment of domain controllers, and the configuration of appropriate Active Directory functional levels
	■ **Domain controller and directory database management**—includes aspects related to the management of domain controller hardware, database maintenance, and the application of service packs and security updates
	■ **Schema management**—includes the extension or modification of the schema to support the deployment of Active Directory-enabled applications

Table 9-1 Active Directory Administration *(continued)*

Category	Tasks
	■ **Operations master roles management**—includes tasks that ensure the proper assignment and configuration of operations master roles
	■ **Backup and restore management**—includes all tasks related to performing regular backups of the directory database and restore procedures when required
	■ **Replication management**—includes all tasks related to the creation, maintenance, and monitoring of the replication topology
	■ **Security policy management**—includes all tasks related to the management of the default domain controller security policy and managing the password, account lockout, and Kerberos account policies

More Info   For more information about the tasks related to data management and service management, refer to "Best Practices for Delegating Active Directory Administration" found at *http://www.microsoft.com/technet/prodtechnol/windowsserver2003/technologies/directory/activedirectory/actdid1.mspx.*

Delegating data and service management tasks within an organization requires an understanding of the administrative needs of all business units. This understanding ensures the most effective delegation model used to provide a more effective, efficient, and secure networking environment. To deploy the delegation model, you need to understand Active Directory object permissions, delegation methods, and auditing. These concepts are discussed in the next few sections.

Accessing Active Directory Objects

To effectively delegate administrative tasks, you need to know how Active Directory controls access to objects stored within the directory service. Access control involves the following:

- Credentials of the security principle attempting to perform the task or access the resource

- Authorization data used to protect the resource or authorize the task being performed

- An access check that compares the credentials against the authorization data to determine if the security principle is permitted to access the resource or perform the task

When a user logs on to an AD DS domain, authentication takes place and the user receives an access token. An access token includes the security identifier (SID) for the user account, SIDs for each security group of which the user is a member, and a list of privileges held by the user and the user's security groups. The access token helps to provide the security context and credentials needed to manage network resources, perform administrative tasks, or access objects residing in Active Directory.

Security is applied to a network resource or an Active Directory object by authorization data that is stored in the *Security Descriptor* of each object. The Security Descriptor consists of the following components:

- **Object owner**   The SID for the current owner of the object. The owner is typically the creator of the object or a security principal that has taken over ownership of an object.

- **Primary group**   The SID for current owner's primary group. This information is only used by the Portable Operating System Interface for UNIX (POSIX) subsystem.

- **Discretionary access control list (DACL)**   A list of access control entries (ACEs) that define the permissions each security principle has to an object. Each security principal that is added to the access control list obtains a set of permissions that specify the extent to which that user or group can manipulate the object. If a user does not appear in an ACE, either individually or as a member of a group, that user has no access to the object.

- **System access control list (SACL)**   Defines the audit setting on an object including which security principle is to be audited and the operations that are to be audited.

Figure 9-1 illustrates the architecture of a user's access token and an object's security descriptor. When a user tries to access a network resource or an Active Directory object, an access check is performed and each ACE is examined until a User or Group SID match is found. Access is then determined by the permissions configured on the ACE.

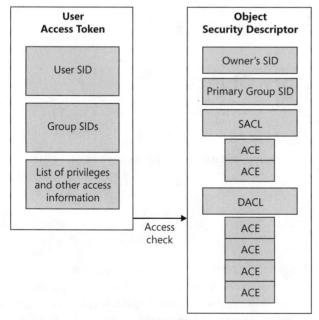

Figure 9-1   Access check between a user's access token and an object's security descriptor.

Evaluating Deny and Allow ACEs in a DACL

ACEs are listed within a DACL in a specific order, which has a direct affect on the outcome of the access check. During an access check, ACEs are evaluated in sequence. The evaluation sequence is listed as follows:

- ACEs that have been explicitly assigned are evaluated before inherited ACEs.

- For each set of explicit or inherited ACEs, Deny ACEs are always evaluated before Allow ACEs.

Figure 9-2 illustrates how Allow and Deny permissions are evaluated for both explicit and inherited ACEs.

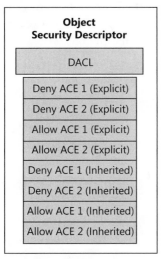

Figure 9-2   Evaluating Allow and Deny ACEs.

Active Directory Object Permissions

Every object in Active Directory has an access control list (ACL), which means that you can modify the permissions on that object. This includes objects visible through the Active Directory Users And Computers administrative console as well as objects visible through the Active Directory Sites and Services administrative console, ADSI Edit, or Ldp.exe. The most common tool used to modify Active Directory object access is Active Directory Users And Computers. However, each of the previously mentioned tools can be used to perform the common task of managing object access within the directory service.

Access control permissions on an Active Directory object are separated into two categories: *standard permissions* and *special permissions*. Special permissions are granular options that can be applied to an object. A standard permission is made up of a group of special permissions to allow or deny a specific function. For example, the Read standard permission is made up of the Read permissions, List contents, and Read all properties special permission entries.

Standard Permissions

To view the standard permissions for any Active Directory object in the domain directory partition, access the Security page for that object's Properties sheet in the Active Directory Users And Computers administrative console.

> **Note**   If the Security page is not visible, select Advanced Features on the View menu and then reselect the object and open its Properties sheet.

The Security page displays the group or user names that are assigned permissions to the object. As you select a group or user entry, the associated allow or deny permissions for that entry are shown. Figure 9-3 illustrates the permissions for the Domain Admins group on the Sales organizational unit. Notice that, by default, the Allow box is checked for each permission to provide the Domain Admins group full control over the Sales OU.

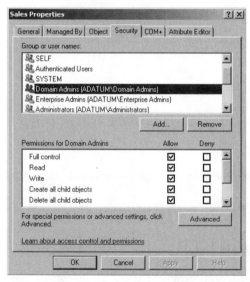

Figure 9-3   Viewing the Security page on an Organizational Unit object.

Depending on the type of object being secured, you will notice that different permissions may be visible on the security page. For example, the following standard permissions are common with all objects:

- Full control
- Read
- Write
- Create all child objects
- Delete all child objects

Some Active Directory objects also have standard permissions that are applied to grouped sets of properties. For example, a user object has several read-and-write property sets such as General Information, Personal Information, Phone And Mail Options, and Web Information. Each of these property sets refers to a set of object attributes, so granting access to a single property set provides access to a set of attributes. For example, the Personal Information property set includes attributes such as *homePhone*, *homePostalAddress*, and *streetAddress*. Using the property sets to assign access to groups of attributes simplifies the process of assigning permissions without having to modify at the granular attribute level.

Note   The Active Directory schema defines which attributes are part of each property set by using the *rightsGuid* value for the property category (in the Configuration directory partition) and the *attributeSecurityGUID* for the *schema* object. For example, the *rightsGuid* value for cn=Personal-Information, cn=Extended-Rights, cn=configuration, dc=*forestname* is equivalent to the *attributeSecurityGUID* for cn=Telephone-Number, cn=Schema, cn=Configuration, dc=*forestname*. This means that the telephone number is included in the Personal Information property set.

In addition to the standard permissions, the Security page may also show extended rights related to the object being secured. Depending on the object, these rights include options such as Allowed To Authenticate, Generate Resultant Set Of Policy, Receive As, Send As, Send To, Change Password, and Reset Password.

Special Permissions

One of the entries in the permissions list on the Security page is Special Permissions. In addition to being able to grant standard permissions, you can also grant special permissions to Active Directory objects.

Note   You can determine if special permissions are applied to an object by viewing the Allow or Deny check boxes located next to the Special Permissions entry. If a check mark is visible, special permissions have been assigned.

As mentioned previously, special permissions are much more granular and specific than standard permissions. To simplify management, you would typically use standard permissions on an object; however, there may be specific needs that require you to modify the special permission entries.

To get access to special permissions, click Advanced on the Security page and then ensure that the Permissions page is selected. Figure 9-4 shows the interface. Table 9-2 explains the options available on the Permissions page.

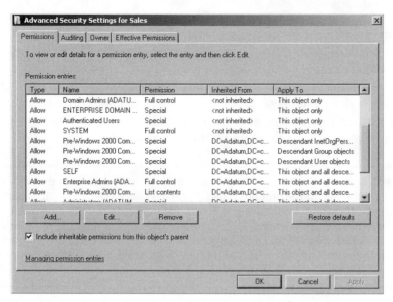

Figure 9-4 Viewing the Advanced Security Settings for an object.

Table 9-2 Special Permissions Configuration

Option	Explanation
Type	This value is set to either *Allow* or *Deny*. Normally, the interface sorts the permissions so that all Deny permissions are listed first, but the sort order can be changed by clicking any column header. Regardless of the order of appearance in this column, the Deny permissions are always evaluated first.
Name	This is the name of the security principal to which each ACE applies.
Permission	This column lists the level of permission granted for the security principal. Levels of permission can be standard rights, such as Full Control; special permissions such as Create/Delete User Objects; or just Special. The types of permissions available depend on the type of object and how granular the permission entry is.
Inherited From	This column lists the location where this permission is set and if the permission is inherited from a parent container.
Apply To	This column specifies the depth to which this permission applies. It has a variety of settings, including This Object Only, This Object And All Descendant Objects, All Descendant Objects, as well as many others.
Include Inheritable Permissions From This Object's Parent	This option allows you to specify if parent permission entries are to be applied to the object.
Add/Edit/Remove buttons	These buttons allow you to add new ACEs, remove existing ACEs, or edit a specific ACE to provide more granular permission settings.

> **Note**   The Restore Defaults button on the Permissions page resets the permissions on the object to the default permission settings as indicated in the Default Security settings of the object class in the Active Directory Schema.

In many cases, the same security principals may be listed in multiple ACEs. For example, the Account Operators group has multiple Create/Delete entries for Computer objects, Group objects, User objects, Printer objects, and InetOrgPerson objects in separate ACEs. This happens whenever you specify a combination of permissions that cannot be stored within a single ACE. In this example, each ACE can only contain focus on one type of object (Computer, User, etc.), and cannot be combined into a single ACE.

If you add or edit the permissions granted to a security principal, you are provided two different options for applying permissions. Figure 9-5 shows the first option, which is applying permissions to the object.

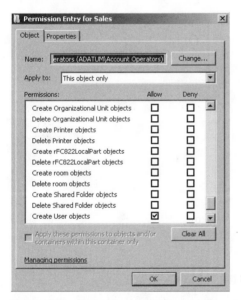

Figure 9-5   Assigning special permissions to Active Directory objects.

The Object tab is used to apply permissions to various object scopes:

- **This object only**   Permissions only apply to the object being secured or modified.
- **This object and all descendant objects**   Permissions will apply to both the object being secured and all child objects within the object.
- **All descendant objects**   Permissions will only apply to child objects within the object being modified.

■ **Individual descendant objects**   Windows Server 2008 provides a large selection of individual descendant objects that can be granularly secured. For example, if you are assigning permissions at the OU level, you may choose to only apply permissions to computer objects within the Sales OU. These options provide the capability to delegate permissions at a granular object level.

The second option for applying permissions is to control access to the object properties. Figure 9-6 shows the interface.

The Properties page is used to apply permissions for the security principal listed in the Name field to the individual properties for the object. For example, if you are applying permissions to a user object, you are given the option of assigning Read and Write permissions to each attribute available on the object class, such as *general information, group membership,* and *personal information.*

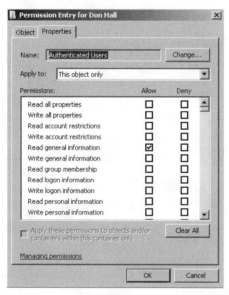

Figure 9-6   Configuring an object's property permissions.

How It Works: Viewing the ACE Using Ldp.exe

Ldp.exe is a graphical user interface (GUI) tool that is used to perform operations such as connect, bind, search, modify, add, or delete against any LDAP-compatible directory service. LDP can be used to view advanced Active Directory metadata such as security descriptors and replication metadata.

To view the ACL using Ldp.exe:

1. Open the Run dialog box, type **ldp**, and then press **Enter**.

2. Click the Connection menu and then click Connect.

If you leave the server box empty, the server will connect to the local computer. You can also type in the server name.

3.   After you are connected to the server, click the Connection menu and then click Bind. If you are not logged in with a user account that has administrative rights, type in alternate credentials. Otherwise, leave the logon information blank.

4.   After binding to the domain, click the View menu and then click Tree.

5.   To view the entire domain, click OK. The domain OU structure will be listed in the left pane.

To view the ACL for any object, locate the object in the tree view in the left pane. Right-click the object, point to Advanced, click Security Descriptor, and finally, click OK.

As shown in Figure 9-7, a number of advanced options are available such as modifying DACL and SACL rights and modifying the security descriptor controls such as DACL and SACL protection.

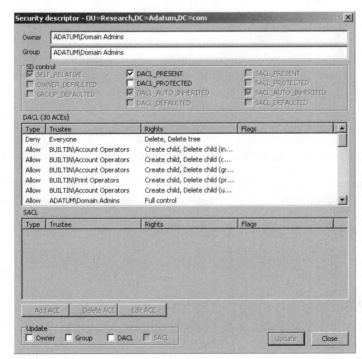

Figure 9-7   Using Ldp.exe to modify the security descriptor.

When you add or edit an ACE using Ldp.exe, you are able to modify specific permissions and ACE flags on various object types and specify object inheritance. Figure 9-8 shows an illustration of the ACE editor provided with Ldp.exe.

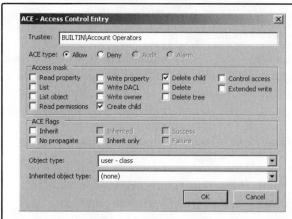

Figure 9-8   Modifying an ACE using Ldp.exe.

Permissions Inheritance

AD DS uses a static permissions inheritance model. That is, when permissions are changed on a container object in the Active Directory structure, the changes are calculated and applied to the security descriptor for all objects in that container. Consequently, if permissions are changed higher in the Active Directory structure and these permissions are applied to all descendant objects, calculating the new ACL for each object can be a processor-intensive process. However, this initial effort means that the permissions do not need to be recalculated when a user or process tries to access the object.

There are two primary methods that are used to control inheritance of permissions:

- **Configuring inheritable permissions on the object**   By default, when an object is created in Active Directory, inheritable permissions are included from the object's parent. You can determine if a permission entry is inherited by looking to see whether the check box on the Security page is shaded or not, or by viewing the Inherited From column of the Advanced Security Settings box.

- **Configuring the scope of how permissions are applied**   As described previously, another way to control inheritance is to specify how permissions apply to descendant objects when security is applied to an object. By default, when a new group or user name is manually added to the ACE, the entry has permissions that apply to *this object only*. To force inheritance to a child object, you need to modify the scope to apply to descendant objects in addition to the current object.

> **Note**   If you use the Delegation Of Control Wizard, inheritance will automatically be set to This Object And All Descendant Objects. More information about the Delegation Of Control Wizard is provided in the "Delegating Administrative Tasks" section later in this chapter.

If you have designed your OU structure with the goal of delegated administration, you will have created an OU structure in which top-level administrators that require permissions to all Active Directory objects are granted permissions high in the hierarchy with delegated permissions to all descendant objects. As you move further down the hierarchy, you may be delegating permissions to other administrators who should only have control over a smaller part of the domain. For example, Figure 9-9 shows the Sales OU. Within the Sales OU are two child OUs called Eastern Sales and Western Sales. The manager who is in charge of the entire Sales division may be delegated permissions to the entire Sales OU object and all descendant objects, whereas the Eastern Sales or Western Sales managers may be delegated permissions to their own specific OU only.

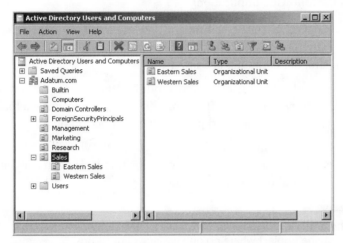

Figure 9-9   Delegating management of the Sales OU.

In some cases, however, you may want to block higher-level administrators from having any administrative permissions to a specific child OU. For example, if you create a child OU for a branch office in your company, you may assign a local administrative group full control of the OU. However, you may not want those local administrators to have access to any executive user accounts in the OU. To limit their access, you can create an Executives OU within the branch office OU and then remove the option to include inheritable permissions from the object's parent. This, in effect, blocks permissions inheritance at the Executives OU level.

To block the inheritance of permissions on an Active Directory object, access the Advanced Security Settings dialog box for the object (shown in Figure 9-4). Then clear the Include Inheritable Permissions From This Object's Parent option. When you clear this option, you are presented with the choice to copy the existing permissions or remove all permissions before explicitly assigning new permissions, as shown in Figure 9-10.

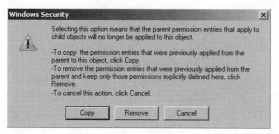

Figure 9-10   Selecting the option to copy or remove permissions when blocking permissions inheritance.

Blocking inheritance has the following implications:

■ The permissions are blocked for the object and any descendant objects. This means that you cannot block the permissions inheritance at a container level and then reapply the inheritance from a higher container at a lower level.

■ Even if you decide to copy the permissions before modification, permissions inheritance begins where you block the permissions. If you modify the permissions at a higher level, the permissions will not be inherited past the blocked permissions.

■ You cannot be selective about which permissions are blocked. When you block permissions, all inherited permissions are blocked. Permissions that have been explicitly assigned to the object or child objects are not blocked.

> **Note**   One of the possible concerns with blocking inherited permissions is that you might create an orphaned object where no one has any permissions. For example, you can create an OU, block all permissions inheritance to that OU, and assign the permissions to only one administrative group. You can even remove the Domain Admins group from the ACL of the OU so that the Domain Admins does not have any permissions under normal circumstances. If that administrative group gets deleted, the OU would have no group with administrative control. In this case, the Domain Admins group would have to take ownership of the object and reassign permissions.

Direct from the Source: Delegating Control of an OU Model

There are many schools of thought on how one should design an OU model and perform delegation within the model. The most common OU model starting points are based on business function, geography, or a hybrid of the two. A delegation model can be centralized, decentralized, or centralized with decentralized execution, but ultimately its design is a result of how a customer wants to provide operational support.

Anyone considering delegation is at one of two points in the Active Directory life cycle—either he or she is considering migrating to Active Directory, or else he or she has migrated to Active Directory and has the opportunity to revisit earlier decisions to provide a more effective and efficient environment.

For those considering migrating to Active Directory, the lesson learned is to engage early and often in discussions with the customers. Understanding how customers run their business is critical in developing an infrastructure that will work for them. If you are an employee of a company and have been tasked with migrating the environment to Active Directory, the same advice stands—talk early and often to upper management to gain a better understanding of how they want to run the business. When deciding on how to architect the solution, keep in mind that Active Directory can provide infinite granularity (depth) as well as infinite scope (breadth) because of the flexible nature of the product. One could conceivably define groups for every imaginable role (depth) and groups to cover every scope (breadth), resulting in an environment that would be difficult to manage and maintain. There is balance point between depth and breadth, and that point may be different for every customer. Factors such as number of sites and support personnel are critical in designing an effective delegation model. This is why it is critical, as an architect, to have thorough planning and design sessions with the customer or upper management from the beginning of the design process, so that there is a clear understanding of how operational support will be provided.

For those who already have an established Active Directory environment and have the ability to revisit the existing delegation model, I would recommend looking at the way you are currently maintaining operational support. You may be able to streamline your operations by scaling back the depth and breadth of your current model. It has been my experience that sometimes less is more when dealing with operational support.

Finally, communication is critical to be truly effective and meet customer or upper management expectations. I have been involved in many customer discussions in which IT professionals are discussing a topic such as delegation within Active Directory with the customer or upper management, and the terminology used has caused frustration for both sides. Before engaging in technical discussions, you should consider the following topics:

- **Who is my audience?** Your audience may differ depending on whether it is a meeting or if you are writing a white paper or proposal.

- **How do I make my audience more knowledgeable?** Take a few minutes to go through your delivery strategy. Are there words, phrases, or topics that may have a different meaning or connotation, depending on your audience?

- **Consider developing two or three different strategies for discussion.** Using analogies is a great method for removing the technical nature from a discussion and placing the subject in a context that most non-IT professionals can understand.

Barry Hartman

Senior Consultant

Microsoft Consulting Services

Effective Permissions

As discussed so far in this chapter, a user can obtain permissions to a specific object in Active Directory in several ways:

- The user account may be granted explicit permissions to an object.

- One or more groups that the user belongs to may be granted explicit permissions to an object.

- The user account or one or more groups that the user belongs to may be given permissions at a container-object level and permissions inherited by lower-level objects.

All of these permissions are cumulative; that is, the user is granted the highest level of permissions from any of these configurations. For example, if a user is explicitly given Read permission to an object, the user belongs to a group that is explicitly given Modify permissions, and the user belongs to a group that is given Full Control at the container level, the user will have Full Control. When a user attempts to access an object, the security subsystem examines all of the ACEs that are attached to the object. All of the ACEs that apply to the security principal (based on user account or group SIDs) are evaluated and the highest level of permission is set. However, in addition to ACEs that grant permissions, Active Directory also supports Deny permissions. Deny permissions can be applied at two levels:

- The user object or one or more of the groups that the user belongs to may be explicitly denied permission to an object.

- The user object or one or more groups that the user belongs to may be denied permissions at a container level, and this denial of permission may be inherited to lower-level objects.

Deny permissions almost always override Allow permissions. For example, if a user is a member of a group that is given Modify permissions to an Active Directory object, and the user is explicitly denied Modify permissions to the object, the user will not be able to modify the object. This is because the ACEs that deny permissions are evaluated before the ACEs that allow permissions. If one of the ACEs denies permission to the security principal, no other ACEs are evaluated for the object.

The one situation in which Allow permissions do override Deny permissions is when the Deny permissions are inherited and the Allow permissions are explicitly assigned. For example, you can deny a user the permission to modify any user accounts in a container. But, if you explicitly allow Modify permissions to an object within the container, the user account will have Modify permissions on that object.

Deny Permissions: Use Carefully

Using the Deny option to deny permissions can make your Active Directory security design very difficult to manage. There are a number of different scenarios in which you may think about using the Deny permission. One is a situation in which you may want to use the Deny option to remove some permissions that are being inherited. For example, you may grant Modify permissions at a container level but may want to change that to Read-Only farther down the hierarchy. In this case, you could deny the Write permission on any objects or properties farther down the hierarchy.

Another scenario in which you may think of using the Deny option is when you want to create a container that requires higher security. For example, you may have a container for all of the executives, and you may want to make sure that a normal user cannot read the executive account properties. You may choose to deny Read permissions on the container using the Domain Users group. Unfortunately, this denies everyone the right to read the directory objects, including all administrators. Because of the complications that can result from using the Deny option, you should use it with care.

In most cases, rather than denying permissions, you can just ensure that a user or group has not been given permissions. If a user has not been granted any permissions and is not a member of any group that has been granted permissions, the user will not have any access and will be implicitly denied. You do not need to explicitly apply the Deny permission to prevent users from accessing objects in Active Directory.

One of the few scenarios in which it can be beneficial to use the Deny option is if you have a case where a group should be given permissions, but one or more users in the same group should have a lower level of permissions. For example, you may have a group called Account Admins that is responsible for managing all user accounts in the domain. Some members of this group may be temporary employees who need to be able to manage all user accounts in the domain, but who should not be able to modify any properties on executive accounts. In this case, you could assign the Account Admins group permission to manage all user accounts in the domain. Next, create an OU for the executive accounts, and create a group for the temporary members of the Account Admins group. Then, deny the temporary users the right to modify any user accounts in the Executive OU.

As you can see, configuring security on Active Directory objects can involve managing a large number of interrelated variables. Many companies may start out with a fairly simple security design in which a small group of administrators are given all the permissions in Active Directory. Most of the time, the initial Active Directory security configuration is clearly documented. However, as time goes by, this simple initial configuration often becomes much messier. Sometimes another group of administrators is given a set of permissions for a specific task and for a specific period of time. Granting the permissions is easy to do, but often the permissions are never removed. Often these security modifications made after the initial deployment are also not clearly documented.

For any Active Directory structure that has been deployed for some time, the current security configuration is likely more complex than was initially designed. Sometimes this results in users having more permissions than they should have. Fortunately, Windows Server 2008 provides a tool that can be used to easily determine the effective permissions a security principal has to any object in Active Directory.

To determine the effective permissions that a security principal has on an Active Directory object, access that object's properties through the appropriate Active Directory administrative tool. Click the Security page, click Advanced, and then click the Effective Permissions page. To determine the effective permissions for a specific user or group account, click Select and then search for the user or group name. After you have selected the name, click OK. The Effective Permissions page displays all of the permissions the security principal has to the Active Directory object. Figure 9-11 shows the interface for the Active Directory Users And Computers administrative tool. Notice that the Effective Permissions page for the Sales OU displays the overall permissions assigned to the *Don Hall* user object.

> **Note**   This tool has some limitations that may affect the effective permissions displayed. The tool determines the effective permissions based on inherited and explicitly defined permissions for the user account and the user's group memberships. However, the user may also get some permissions based on how the user logs on and connects to the object. For example, in Windows Server 2008, you can assign permissions to the interactive group (that is, anyone logged on to the computer) or the network login group (that is, anyone accessing the information across the network). This Active Directory administrative tool cannot determine the permissions granted to a user based on these types of groups. Also, the tool can only determine permissions by using the permissions of the person running the tool. For example, if the user running the tool does not have permission to read the membership of some of the groups that the evaluated user object belongs to, the tool will not be able to determine the permissions accurately.

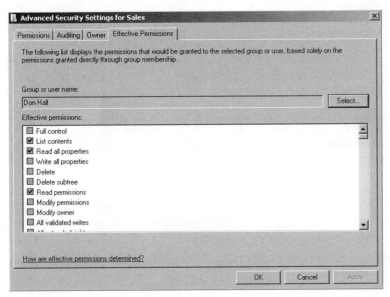

Figure 9-11   Displaying the effective permissions for an Active Directory object.

Ownership of Active Directory Objects

Every object in Active Directory has an owner. By default, the user who created an object is the owner. The owner of an object has the right to modify permissions on the object, which means that, even if the owner does not have full control of an object, the owner can always modify the permissions on the object. In most cases, the owner of an object is a specific user account rather than a group account. One exception to this is when an object is created by a member of the Domain Admins group; the ownership of the object is then assigned to the Domain Admins group. If the owner of the object is a member of the local Administrators group but not a part of the Domain Admins group, the ownership of the object is assigned to the Administrators group.

To determine the owner of an Active Directory object, access that object's properties using the appropriate Active Directory administrative tool. Select the Security page, click Advanced, and then select the Owner page. Figure 9-12 shows the interface for the Active Directory Users And Computers administrative tool.

If you have the Modify owner permission to the object, you can use this interface to modify the owner of the object. You can chose either to take ownership for your own account or to assign the ownership to another user or group. This last option is unique in Windows Server 2003 And Windows Server 2008 Active Directory. In Microsoft Windows 2000 Active Directory, you could only take ownership of an object; you could not assign the ownership to another security principal.

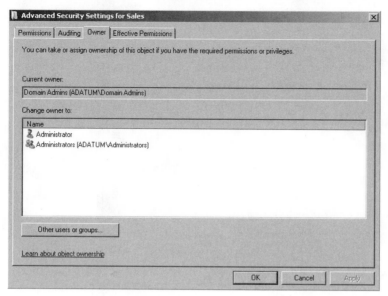

Figure 9-12   Viewing the ownership of an Active Directory object.

Administrative Privileges

The administrative permissions discussed so far have to do with specific permissions on Active Directory objects and define what actions the administrator can perform on those objects. In addition to these permissions, a user may also be able to perform some tasks in Active Directory because of the privileges assigned to him or her. The permissions discussed so far are based on the ACLs that are attached to each Active Directory object. User privileges are different because user privileges are applied to user accounts. User privileges are something that the user has because of who he or she is, not because he or she has permission to modify a particular Active Directory object. For example, there are two ways that you can give a user or group the right to add workstations to the domain. One option is to give the user or group permission to Create Computer Objects either at an OU level or at the Computers container level. This allows the user to add as many workstations as needed to the domain in the specified container.

Another way to allow a user to add workstations to the domain is to ensure that the user has the *Add workstations to domain* privilege. This user right is a part of the Default Domain Controllers Policy. Any user who has this privilege can add up to 10 workstations to the domain. By default, the Authenticated Users group is granted this permission.

Delegating Administrative Tasks

This chapter has thus far discussed how to ensure the security of Active Directory objects. This has been in preparation for this section, which applies the security options to delegate administrative tasks. Because every object in Active Directory has an ACL, you can control administrative access down to any property on any object. This means that you can grant other Active Directory administrators very precise permissions so that they can perform only the tasks they need to do.

Although you can get extremely specific about delegating administrative permissions, you should maintain a balance between keeping things as simple as possible and meeting your security requirements. In most cases, delegating administrative permissions in Active Directory falls under one of the following scenarios:

- **Assigning full control of one OU**   This is a fairly common scenario when a company has multiple offices with local administrators in each office who need to manage all objects in the local office. This option also may be used for companies that have merged multiple resource domains into OUs in a single Active Directory domain. The former resource domain administrators can be given full control of all objects in their specific OU. Using this option means that you can almost completely decentralize the administration of your organization while still maintaining a single domain.

- **Assigning full control of specific objects in an OU**   This is a variation on the first scenario. In some cases, a company may have multiple offices, but local administrators should have permission to manage only specific objects in the office OU. For example, you may want to allow a local administrator to manage all user and group objects, but not computer objects. In a situation in which resource domains have become OUs, you may want OU administrators to manage all computer accounts and domain-local groups in their OU, but not to manage any user objects.

- **Assigning full control of specific objects in the entire domain**   Some companies have highly centralized user and group administration, in which only one group has permission to add and delete user and group accounts. In this scenario, this group can be given full control of user and group objects regardless of where the objects are located within the domain. This is also a fairly common scenario for a company with a centralized desktop and server administration group. The desktop team may be given full control of all computer objects in the domain.

- **Assigning rights to modify only some properties for objects**   In some cases, you may want to give an administrative group permission to manage a subset of properties on an object. For example, you may want to give an administrative group permission to reset passwords on all user accounts, but not to have any other administrative permissions. Or the Human Resources department may be given permission to modify the personal and public information on all user accounts in the domain, but not permission to create or delete user accounts.

It is possible to use all of these options, and any combination of these options, with Windows Server 2008 AD DS. As mentioned previously, one way to configure delegated permissions is by directly accessing the ACL for an object and configuring the permissions. The problem with this option is that it can get quite complex because of the number of options available and the real possibility of making a mistake.

Direct from the Source: Delegating Control

When delegating control to create users and groups, it is imperative to maintain a tracking system for changes that are made. This will make not only daily administration easier, but will be of great use when troubleshooting access issues.

Greg Robb

Microsoft Premier Field Engineer

To make this task easier, AD DS includes the Delegation Of Control Wizard. To use the Delegation Of Control Wizard, follow these steps:

1. Open the Active Directory Users And Computers administrative console and identify the parent object where you want to delegate control. In most cases, you will be delegating control at an OU level, but you can also delegate control at the domain or container level (for example, the Computers or Users container). Right-click the parent object and click Delegate Control. Click Next.

2. On the Users Or Groups page, add the users or groups to which you want to delegate control. Click Add to search Active Directory for the appropriate users or groups.

3. Next, select the tasks that you want to delegate. The interface (shown in Figure 9-13) enables you to select from a list of common tasks or to create a custom task to delegate.

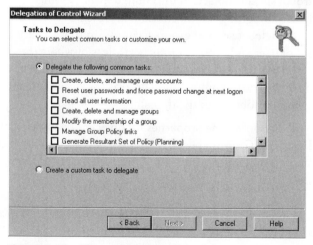

Figure 9-13   Using the Delegation Of Control Wizard to select a common task or create a custom task to delegate.

4. If you choose to create a custom task, you can choose the type or types of objects to which you want to delegate administrative permissions. (Figure 9-14 shows the interface.)

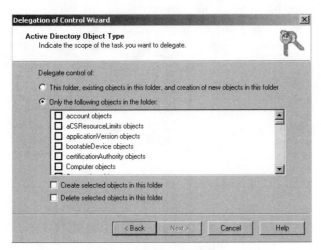

Figure 9-14   Selecting the type of object or objects to which permissions will be delegated.

5. After you have selected the type of object to which to delegate permissions, you can choose what levels of permissions you want to apply to the object. You can choose full control over the object, or you can delegate permissions to specific properties. (The interface is shown in Figure 9-15.)

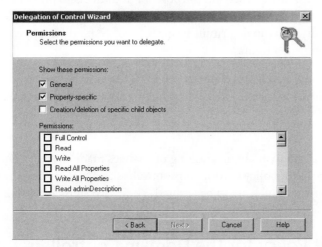

Figure 9-15   Selecting the specific permissions to delegate.

The Delegation Of Control Wizard makes it much easier to delegate control in a consistent manner than when configuring permissions through the ACL. However, the effect of either method is the same; that is, the ACL on the objects is modified to provide the appropriate level of access.

> ### Direct from the Source: The Delegation Of Control Wizard
>
> You are able to use the Delegation Of Control Wizard to delegate many common tasks by giving control to individual users or to groups. These tasks can be set to certain predefined items such as Create, Delete, And Manage User Accounts and Reset User Passwords And Force Password Change At Next Logon. In addition to the predefined items, it is possible to delegate custom tasks using very granular choices, such as account objects, computer objects, or group objects. This makes the Delegation Of Control Wizard a very powerful tool for enabling the share of control throughout Active Directory.
>
> *Greg Robb*
>
> *Microsoft Premier Field Engineer*

Auditing the Use of Administrative Permissions

Delegating administrative tasks in AD DS results in the need to be able to monitor and audit the use of administrative permissions throughout the directory structure. Auditing serves at least two primary purposes. First of all, it provides evidence for changes that have been made to the directory. If a change has been made to the directory, you may need to track down who has made the change. This is especially important if an incorrect or malicious change has been made to the domain information. A second purpose for auditing is to provide an additional check on the administrative permissions being exercised throughout the domain. By examining audit logs occasionally, you can determine if someone who should not have administrative rights is in fact exercising such rights.

When AD DS events are audited, entries are written to the Security log on the domain controller. You can then use the Event Viewer to view events that Windows Server 2008 logs in the Security log. You can also save events to an event file that can be used to archive and track trends over time.

There are two steps involved in enabling auditing of changes made to Active Directory objects—configuring the audit policy for domain controllers and configuring the SACL on specific Active Directory objects which are to be audited. These two steps are discussed in the following sections.

Configuring the Audit Policy for the Domain Controllers

Your first step for enabling auditing is to configure the audit policy for the domain controllers. This can be configured on the Default Domain Controllers Policy found within the Group Policy Management console. When you open the Group Policy Management console, browse to the Group Policy Objects container. In the details pane, you can right-click Default

Domain Controllers Policy and then click Edit to open the Group Policy Management Editor. From the Group Policy Management Editor, you can browse to Computer Configuration\ Policies\Windows Settings\Security Settings\Local Policies and then click Audit Policy. Figure 9-16 shows the default auditing configuration in Windows Server 2008 AD DS.

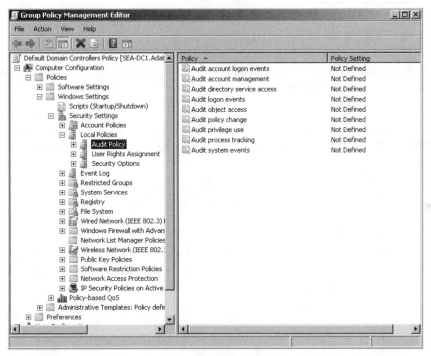

Figure 9-16   Configuring auditing on the Default Domain Controllers OU.

To audit changes to Active Directory objects, you need to enable and configure the Audit Directory Service Access policy. When this policy is enabled and configured, all modifications made to Active Directory objects are reported in the Security log. You can audit both successful changes to Active Directory objects and failed attempts at modifying Active Directory objects.

In Windows 2000 Server and Windows Server 2003, the Audit Directory Service Access policy was the primary option used to audit directory service events. Windows Server 2008 divides this policy into four subcategories:

- Directory Service Access

- Directory Service Changes

- Directory Service Replication

- Detailed Directory Service Replication

Dividing the Audit Directory Service Access policy into four subcategories provides more granular control on what is or is not audited in relation to directory service events. Enabling the Audit Directory Service Access policy enables all the directory service policy subcategories. To modify the subcategories, you cannot use the Group Policy Object Editor. You can only view and modify the subcategories with the command-line tool Auditpol.exe. For example, if you want to view all of the possible categories and subcategories, type the following line at the command prompt, and then press Enter:

auditpol /list /subcategory:*

> **Note**   For a list of commands that can be used with Auditpol.exe, open a command prompt and type the following: **Auditpol.exe /?**

Auditing Changes to Objects Using the Directory Service Changes Subcategory

The Directory Services Changes subcategory provides the ability to audit changes to objects in AD DS. This subcategory audits the following types of changes:

■ When a modify operation is successfully performed on an attribute, AD DS logs both the previous and current values of the attribute.

■ When a new object is created, all values of the attributes that are populated during the creation are logged. Note that any default values to attributes that are assigned by AD DS are not logged.

■ When an object is moved within the domain, both the previous and new location is logged.

■ If you undelete an object, the location where the object is moved to is logged as well as any additions or modifications to attributes while performing the undelete operation.

To enable the Directory Service Changes audit subcategory, you can type the following line at the command prompt, and then press Enter:

auditpol /set /subcategory:"directory service changes" /success:enable

When you enable the Directory Services Changes audit subcategory, AD DS logs various types of events in the Security event log, as shown in Table 9-3.

Table 9-3   Directory Services Changes Events

Event ID	Type	Description
5136	Modify	Logged when a modification is made to an attribute in AD DS.
5137	Create	Logged when a new object is created in AD DS.
5138	Undelete	Logged when an object is undeleted in AD DS.
5139	Move	Logged when an object is moved within the domain.

Configuring Auditing on Active Directory Objects

The second step to configuring Active Directory object auditing is to enable auditing directly on the SACL of each Active Directory object to be audited. To enable Active Directory object auditing, access the object's Properties sheet through the appropriate Active Directory administrative tool. Then, click the Security page, click Advanced, and click the Auditing page. Figure 9-17 shows the interface for the Active Directory Users And Computers administrative console and the default audit setting for an OU in Active Directory.

To add additional auditing entries, click Add and select which users or groups and what actions you want to audit. In most cases, you should select the Everyone group so that modifications made by anyone can be audited. Then you can select which activities you want to audit. You can audit all modifications made to any object in the container, to specific types of objects, or to specific properties. You can enable the auditing of all successful modifications, of all failed attempts to make modifications, or both. If you audit all successful modifications, you will have an audit trail for all changes made to the directory. If you enable failed attempts, you will be able to monitor any illicit attempts to modify directory information. After auditing is enabled, all of the audit events are recorded in the Security log accessible through the Event Viewer.

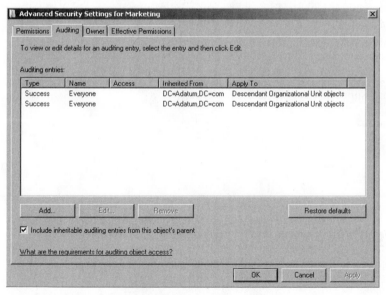

Figure 9-17   Configuring auditing on Active Directory objects.

Enabling auditing is easy. Managing auditing is much more difficult. If you enable the auditing of all directory modifications at the domain controller OU level, the Security log will grow very rapidly. Almost all of the events will be legitimate changes and thus of no interest to you except as an audit trail. However, interspersed among the legitimate changes may be a small number of changes that you need to be aware of. The problem is finding the few interesting audit events among the large number of routine events. In some companies, one administrator may be given the task of reviewing the event logs every day. A better way to deal with this is to create some automated way of centralizing and analyzing the event logs. Another way is to use a tool such as Microsoft System Center Operations Manager (a separate product available for purchase) to filter the events and raise alerts only on the interesting events.

> **More Info**   If you want to find out more about Microsoft System Center Operations Manager, you can go to the following Web site: *http://www.microsoft.com/systemcenter/ opsmgr/default.mspx*. Operations Manager provides a great deal of functionality that goes far beyond just monitoring Security logs.

Direct from the Source: Consider Event Log Settings Carefully

Always think through the ramifications of enabling an option that will increase the amount of information being sent to the event logs. Many customers will customize the event logs to meet their specific security requirements but never revisit the settings to determine if the additional logging will cause them problems. I have seen many instances in which auditing was enabled and the policy setting Audit: Shut Down System Immediately If Unable To Log Security Audits was also enabled, resulting in a denial of service attack. Another setting that many IT professionals change is the maximum log size. Before changing event log sizes to high values, do some preliminary analysis to determine if the system on which you are enabling this setting has enough memory available. Information about the event log and memory constraint can be found at *http://support.microsoft.com/kb/183097*.

Barry Hartman

Senior Consultant

Microsoft Consulting Services

Tools for Delegated Administration

AD DS provides powerful options for delegating administrative tasks and assigning only the precise permissions that users need to have to perform specific tasks. To complement this delegation, Windows Server 2008 also makes it easy to develop administrative tools that fit the user's task. For example, if you delegate the right to reset passwords for a single OU, you can also provide a very simple administrative tool that can only be used to reset passwords in the specified OU. Windows Server 2008 provides the ability to create a customized view of the Microsoft Management Console (MMC) administrative snap-in in order to allow delegated administrators effective tools to complete their tasks.

Direct from the Source: Working with Third-Party Delegation Tools

Many customers use third-party products to perform delegation. These products usually provide a Web interface and allow administrators to develop custom Web views for daily administrative functions versus creating customized MMCs. When working with customers dealing with branch office scenarios, make sure you understand the business and branch office operational requirements in the event of an extended communications outage. If a customer has highly reliable communication links to the branch office, then this topic isn't as much of a concern; however, for those customers who don't have highly reliable communications, it is a subject that needs to be addressed.

In the event of a communications outage, you must understand what the branch office requires to continue to function. In the case of delegation, if the branch office needs to continue to function and system administrative actions still need to occur, but the Web interface required to perform some of these functions is unavailable because it is hosted from headquarters, how will the people at the branch office perform their jobs? If the third-party product instantiated the delegation model natively into Active Directory Users and Computers, then the same restrictions that applied through the Web interface would apply when using native tools. It is important that you, the trusted advisor, have an understanding of how third-party products interface and interact with Active Directory. Having this type of knowledge will allow you to advise and prepare your customers so they are still able to maintain operations when situations such as a communications outage occur.

Barry Hartman

Senior Consultant

Microsoft Consulting Services

Customizing the Microsoft Management Console

One option for developing an administrative tool is to create a customized MMC using one of the default snap-ins and then modify what the user can see in the MMC.

Caution   Simply creating the customized MMC does not grant or limit the user's rights to perform administrative tasks. Before creating the customized administrative interface, you must first delegate the correct level of permissions. For example, if you give a user the right to create user accounts at a domain level, and then you create an MMC that only allows the user to view one OU, the user can still create user accounts in any OU in the domain. If the user loads the regular Active Directory Users And Computers administrative tool or sits down at another desk with a different MMC, the user will be able to create the account anywhere.

To create the customized MMC, open the Run dialog box and type **mmc**. This opens an empty MMC. From the File menu, add the appropriate Active Directory administrative tool snap-in. If you create a custom MMC using the Active Directory Users And Computers snap-in, you would then expand the domain and locate the container object where you have delegated permissions. In the left pane, right-click on the container object and select New Window From Here.

This opens a new window with just the container object and all child objects visible. You can then switch back to the window that displays the entire domain and close the window. Finally, save the administrative tool and provide it to the users, who will administer only the part of the domain that is visible in the MMC. The MMC can be provided to the user in a number of ways. For example, you may install the MMC on his or her desktop, or you may create a shortcut to the administrative tool on a network share.

To make sure that the administrators do not modify the custom MMC after you have given it to them, you can modify the MMC options by selecting Options from the File menu. You can configure the MMC to be saved in User Mode and modify the permissions on the MMC so that the end user cannot save any changes to the MMC. Figure 9-18 shows the interface. For full details on how to create customized MMCs, see Windows Help And Support.

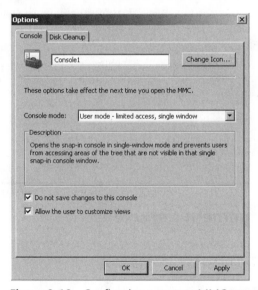

Figure 9-18 Configuring a custom MMC to prevent changes to the MMC.

Planning for the Delegation of Administration

As shown in this chapter, Windows Server 2008 AD DS provides the tools you need to delegate administrative permissions in your domain. However, with all of the positive things you can do in delegating permissions, you also take the risk of assigning incorrect permissions. Incorrect permissions may result in allowing users to do things in Active Directory that they should not be able to do. Incorrect permissions can also mean assigning too few permissions, so that users cannot do the work they need to do. Creating a delegation structure that will provide users with the precise permissions they need requires a significant amount of planning. The following are several suggestions to help with your administrative delegation planning:

- Carefully document the administrative requirements for all potential administrators. In most companies, you will find that there are various users and groups that need some administrative permissions in the domain. Many of these users could be members of the Domain Admins group. As you document the administrative tasks that users need to perform, you will usually find that they really need a much lower level of access. Often the only way to document the level of administrative permissions each group needs is to document all of the administrative work they do every day. By documenting the activities they have to perform, you can design the precise permissions they need to have.

- Before making any changes to the production environment, test all security modifications in a test environment. Making a wrong security configuration can have serious implications for your network. Use the test lab to ensure that the modifications meet the permission requirements but do not give any additional permissions that are not needed.

- Use the Effective Permissions page in the Advanced Security Settings window to monitor and test the users' permissions. The Effective Permissions page can be used to determine the precise permissions a user or group has in AD DS. Use the tool in the test environment to ensure that your configuration is accurate and use it again in the production environment to make sure that your implementation followed the plan.

- Document all the permissions that you assign. Of all the tasks assigned to network administrators, documenting changes made to the network appears to be the most disliked because it can be very tedious and not seem important. As a result, documentation is often incomplete or out of date. The only way to effectively manage the security configuration on your network is to document the initial configuration and then to make a commitment to keep the documentation updated whenever one of the original settings is modified.

Summary

The option to delegate administrative permissions in Windows Server 2008 AD DS provides a great deal of flexibility in how your domain can be administered. The delegation of administrative rights is based on the Active Directory security model, in which every object and every attribute on every object has an ACL that controls what permissions security principals have to a specific object. According to the security model, all permissions are, by default, inherited from container objects to objects within the container. These two basic features of the security model mean that you can assign almost any level of permission to any Active Directory object. This flexibility can also mean a great deal of complexity if the security for Active Directory is not kept as simple as possible. This chapter provided an overview of security permissions, Active Directory object access, delegation of administration, and auditing changes made in Active Directory.

Additional Resources

The following resources contain additional information and tools related to this chapter.

Related Information

- Chapter 5, "Designing the Active Directory Domain Services Structure," provides details on planning the structure of Active Directory such as site, domain, organizational unit, and forest designs.

- Chapter 6, "Installing Active Directory Domain Services," provides details on delegating administration for Read-Only Domain Controllers.

- Chapter 8, "Active Directory Domain Services Security," provides additional details on Active Directory security basics and authentication.

- "Best Practices for Delegating Active Directory Administration" located at *http://www.microsoft.com/technet/prodtechnol/windowsserver2003/technologies/ directory/activedirectory/actdid1.mspx.*

- "Best Practices for Delegating Active Directory Administration Appendices" located at *http://www.microsoft.com/downloads/details.aspx?FamilyID=29dbae88-a216-45f9-9739-cb1fb22a0642&DisplayLang=en.*

- "Delegating Authority in Active Directory" located at *http://www.microsoft.com/technet/ technetmag/issues/2007/02/ActiveDirectory/default.aspx.*

- "Using Scripts to Manage Active Directory Security" located at *http:// www.microsoft.com/technet/scriptcenter/topics/security/exrights.mspx.*

- "Sample Scripts to Manage Active Directory Delegation and Security" located at *http://www.microsoft.com/technet/scriptcenter/scripts/security/ad/default.mspx?mfr=true.*

- "Step-by-Step Guide to Using the Delegation Of Control Wizard" located at *http://www.microsoft.com/technet/prodtechnol/windowsserver2003/technologies/ directory/activedirectory/stepbystep/ctrlwiz.mspx.*

- "Default Security Concerns in Active Directory Delegation" located at *http://support.microsoft.com/?kbid=235531.*

Chapter 10

Managing Active Directory Objects

The most common tasks that you will perform using Windows Server 2008 Active Directory Domain Services (AD DS) will involve the management of Active Directory objects such as users and groups. Most companies create an Active Directory design and implement it once. After the deployment, few changes are made to most Active Directory objects. However, user objects and group objects are a significant exception to this rule. As employees join or leave the company, the administrator spends time managing users and groups. Printer objects, computer objects, and shared folder objects are other Active Directory objects that may require frequent administration.

This chapter discusses the concepts and procedures that you will use to manage Active Directory objects. It discusses the types of objects that can be stored in Active Directory and explains how to manage those objects. This chapter specifically covers tools that you can use to manage Active Directory objects, including using VBScript and Windows PowerShell to automate changes.

Managing Users

Windows Server 2008 Active Directory makes available three different objects that are used to represent individual users in the directory. Two of these, the user object and the inetOrgPerson object, are security principals that can be used to assign access to resources on your network. The third object, the contact object, is not a security principal and is used primarily for e-mail.

User Objects

One of the most common objects in any Active Directory database is a user object. A user object, like any other Active Directory class object, is a collection of attributes. A user object can have over 250 attributes created by the system and even more created by your organization. In this way, Windows Server 2008 Active Directory is very different than the more limited local security databases found on member servers, Windows workstations, and some Linux computers. In local security databases, user objects have very few attributes, such as *password* and *home directory*. Because Active Directory can provide additional attributes for objects, Active Directory is useful as a directory service in addition to simply being a database for storing authentication information. For example, Active Directory can become the primary location for most user information in your company. The directory can become the place where all user information, such as telephone numbers, addresses, and organizational information is stored. When users learn how to search Active Directory, they will be able to find almost any information about other users that they are given permission to view.

When you create a user object, some attributes are mandatory and others are optional. As shown in Figure 10-1, only six attributes are mandatory. These six must be configured when you create a user account. Of these six, the *cn* and the *sAMAccountName* attributes are configured based directly on the data you provide when you create the account by using Active Directory Users And Computers. All other mandatory attributes, including the *security identifier* (SID), are automatically populated. When users are created programmatically with scripts and the *sAMAccountName* attribute is not provided, it will also be randomly generated.

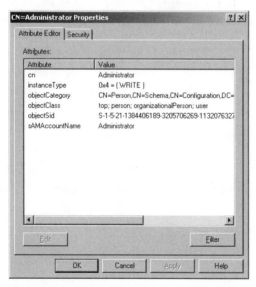

Figure 10-1   Mandatory attributes for a user account viewed in Adsiedit.msc.

When you create a user account, you can assign a value to many of the other user object attributes. Some of these attributes are not visible through the user interface (UI) in any of the standard administrative tools, such as Active Directory Users And Computers. For example, each user object has an attribute called *Assistant* that is not visible through a UI. You can still populate this attribute by using a script or a tool like Adsiedit.msc that directly accesses the attribute. You can also populate attributes unavailable in a GUI during a bulk import of directory information using either the Csvde or the Ldifde command-line utility (covered later in this chapter).

Attributes that are not visible in a UI can be used by applications to store additional user information. In most cases, hidden attributes are available through the Find dialog box in Active Directory Users And Computers. For example, in the Active Directory Users And Computers administrative tool, to search for all users that have the same *Assistant* attribute, use the Advanced tab on the Find dialog box to create a query based on the *Assistant* attribute. Figure 10-2 shows the Advanced tab in the Find dialog box. In this interface, click Field, select User, and then select the attribute you want to search for. Many of the hidden attributes can be found from this interface.

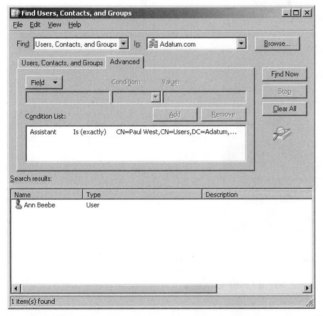

Figure 10-2   Searching for a user account based on an attribute that is not visible in the UI.

Note   You can view and modify any attribute on a user object using a tool like Adsiedit.msc or Ldp.exe. If you need to modify many objects, a more efficient way to modify these attributes is to use scripts. Active Directory is written to allow and encourage the use of scripts. You will find more information about using scripts to automate Active Directory management tasks later in this chapter.

You can manage most regular user administration tasks by using the Active Directory Users And Computers administrative tool. To create a user object in the Active Directory Users And Computers administrative tool, locate the container where you want to create the object, right-click, point to New, and click User. When you create the user, you must provide at least the user's *Full Name* and *User Logon Name. The Full Name* data is used to populate the *cn* attribute for the user, whereas the *User Logon Name* data becomes the *sAMAccountName* value. After you have created the user, you can access the object properties to fill in additional attributes for the user. Most of the attributes for the user object are easy to understand. The most important tab for administering a user account is the Account tab (shown in Figure 10-3). The user settings available on the Account tab are described in Table 10-1.

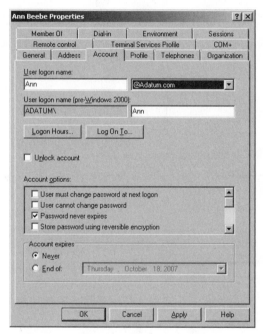

Figure 10-3   The Account tab for a user object.

Table 10-1   Account Properties for a User Object

Account Setting	Explanation
User Logon Name	Identifies the user principal name (UPN) for this user.
User Logon Name (pre-Windows 2000)	Identifies the pre-Microsoft Windows 2000 logon name using the domain\username format.
Logon Hours	Defines the hours when a user can log on to the domain. By default users are disconnected when their logon hours expire. Behavior can be configured in Group Policy by using the *Computer Configuration\Windows Settings\Security Settings\Local Policies\Security Options\Network security: Force logoff when hours expire* setting.

Table 10-1   Account Properties for a User Object *(continued)*

Account Setting	Explanation
Log On To	Lists the computers where the user is allowed to log on. These can be NetBIOS or DNS names.
Unlock Account	Used to unlock the account (allow logon) when the account has been locked out after too many failed logon attempts. This is different from enabling and disabling a user account that is controlled by an administrator.
Account Options	Provides several options for settings, such as password policies and authentication requirements.
Account Expires	Specifies when the account will expire. Typically used when a user requires temporary access to domain resources.

Sometimes it is useful to know when a user has last logged on to the network. The Windows Server 2003 domain functional level introduced the *lastLogonTimestamp* attribute for users that shows when a user last logged on to the network. However, this attribute is not visible in Active Directory Users And Computers. You must use scripting to access it. If the domain is at the Windows Server 2008 functional level, then the Last Interactive Logon Information is enhanced to include the time of the last successful interactive logon, the workstation used for logon, and the number of failed logon attempts since the last logon.

Naming User Objects in Active Directory

Although every object in Active Directory must have a unique name, this simple concept can become quite complicated when discussing user objects, because a user object actually has a number of names that can be used for identification. Table 10-2 lists all of the names that can be associated with a user name and the scope within which that name must be unique.

Table 10-2   User Name Uniqueness Requirements

User Name	Uniqueness Requirement
First name, initials, last name	No uniqueness requirement
Display name—The *Display name* is shown in most Active Directory administrative tools such as Active Directory Users And Computers. By default, the *Display name* is generated by using the *First name, Initials,* and *Last name* fields in the New Object–User dialog box.	No uniqueness requirement
Full name—The *Full name* is used to populate the *cn* attribute on the user account. This value is set equal to the *Display name*. However, the *Full name* and *Display* can be edited independently after creation.	Must be unique within the container that the user is located in

Table 10-2   User Name Uniqueness Requirements *(continued)*

User Name	Uniqueness Requirement
User principal name (UPN)—The UPN is made up of the logon name and the domain DNS name, or an alternative UPN if additional UPN suffixes have been configured for the forest.	Must be unique within the forest
User logon name (pre-Windows 2000)	Must be unique within the domain

Modifying the Default Display Name

During user creation, the default *Display name* is generated by using the *First name*, *Initials*, and *Last name* fields in the New Object–User dialog box. You can override the default by typing in an alternate Display name. You can also modify how the default Display name is generated by using Adsiedit.msc:

1. Open Adsiedit.msc and open the Configuration Container naming context.

2. Browse to CN=409,CN=DisplaySpecifiers,CN=Configuration,*DomainName*, where *DomainName* is the name of your domain.

    Note that the 409 Locale ID is for U.S. English. If you are using other languages, you may need to edit additional code pages. For more information about code pages, see the International Telecommunication Union (ITU) and International Organization for Standardization Web sites.

3. Open the properties of CN=user-Display.

4. Edit the attribute *createDialog*. The value of this attribute can include text and the variables %<sn>, %<givenName>, and %<initials>. The names of these variables are case-sensitive.

The most common reason to modify the Display name format is to control the format of names listed in the Exchange Server global address lists. It is common to change the default Display name to *Last name, First name*. This is done by setting the value of the *createDialog* attribute to %<sn>, %<givenName>.

Changing the value of the *createDialog* attribute does not affect existing users. It only affects the default Display name created for new users created by using Active Directory Users And Computers. In most cases, you will use a script, Csvde, or Ldifde to modify batches of existing users rather than editing each user with a tool such as Adsiedit.msc.

User Principal Names

The UPN can simplify the logon process for a user. A user can go to any domain in the forest and log on using his or her UPN rather than selecting his or her home domain when logging on. By default, the UPN suffix is the Domain Name System (DNS) name for the domain. However, you can modify the UPN suffix. For example, you may be using a different DNS name internally than the one that is visible to the external

Internet. In most cases, the Simple Mail Transfer Protocol (SMTP) e-mail address for all users would match the external DNS name. Your users may want to be able to log on to the domain using their SMTP addresses. You can enable this option by adding an alternative UPN suffix to the forest and then assigning this suffix to all user accounts. To create an additional UPN suffix, open the Active Directory Domains And Trusts administrative tool, right-click the Active Directory Domains And Trusts entry at the top of the left pane, and select Properties. Figure 10-4 shows the interface. Type in any alternative UPN suffixes that you want to use.

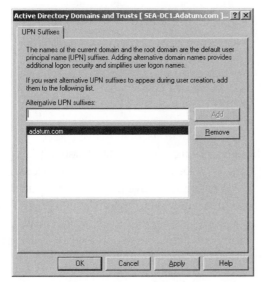

Figure 10-4   Adding alternative UPN suffixes to your forest.

inetOrgPerson Objects

One of the new objects available starting in Windows Server 2003 Active Directory is the inetOrgPerson object. This object is the primary user account used by other Lightweight Directory Access Protocol (LDAP) and X.500 directories that are Request for Comments (RFC) 2798-compliant. By enabling the inetOrgPerson object, Microsoft has made it easier to integrate Active Directory with other directories. This will also simplify migration from other directories to Active Directory.

Note   If you are upgrading a Windows 2000 forest to Windows Server 2008, the inetOrg-Person object is created in the schema when you run the *Adprep.exe* command with the */forestprep* switch. Adprep.exe is found in the \sources\adprep folder on the Windows Server 2008 DVD.

The inetOrgPerson object can be created using the Active Directory Users And Computers administrative tool. To create an inetOrgPerson object in the Active Directory Users And Computers administrative tool, locate the container where you want to create the object, right-click, point to New, and click InetOrgPerson. You must provide at least the user logon name and the full name when creating the inetOrgPerson object. The inetOrgPerson object is a subclass of the user object, which means that it has all of the characteristics of the user class, including acting as a security principal. The inetOrgPerson objects can be managed and used in all ways that you would use any user object.

The domain functional level of at least Windows Server 2003 is required to allow the *userPassword* attribute to be used as an effective password for authentication for inetOrgPerson objects and user objects. This is useful for programmers using Active Directory as an LDAP directory. The forest functional level of at least Windows Server 2003 is required to convert an inetOrgPerson object into a user object, or the reverse.

Contact Objects

The third type of object that can be used to represent users in Active Directory is the contact object. Contact objects are different from user objects and inetOrgPerson objects in that contact objects cannot be security principals. Usually, contact objects are used for informational purposes only. To create a contact object in the Active Directory Users And Computers administrative tool, locate the container where you want to create the object, right-click, point to New, and click Contact. You must provide at least the full name when creating the contact object. In addition, when you create a contact object, you can populate a number of attributes for the object, including telephone numbers and addresses.

Note   You can modify the default Display name for contacts by using Adsiedit.msc, just as you can for user objects. For contacts, modify the *createDialog* attribute of the CN=*contact-Display* object instead of the CN=*user-Display* object.

Contacts are useful in several scenarios. One way you can use contacts is if you have a user who cannot be a security principal in your domain, but whose contact information needs to be accessible. For example, you may have consultants working in your office who cannot log on to the network, but whose contact information must be stored where it is easily located by anyone in the company. You can also use contacts to share information between forests. Your company may have merged with another company that has already deployed Active Directory. You can create cross-forest trusts between the two forests so that you can share network resources, but the global catalog (GC) in each forest will still only contain accounts for that single forest. You may want all or some of the accounts from both forests to be visible to the users. To enable this, you can use a tool like Microsoft Identity Integration Server (MIIS) 2003 or Microsoft Identity Lifecycle Manager (ILM) 2007 to create a contact object for every user account from the other forest and populate the contact object with the appropriate contact information.

More Info   For more information about ILM 2007, see the Microsoft Identity Lifecycle Manager 2007 Web page at *http://www.microsoft.com/windowsserver/ilm2007/default.mspx.*

The most common use for contact objects is integration into the global address list of Microsoft Exchange Server. When you mail-enable a contact object, you assign an e-mail address to the account. The assigned e-mail address is for an external e-mail system, such as an Internet service provider or another organization. This mail-enabled contact is visible in the Exchange Server global address list. When you send mail to the contact, the mail is delivered to the e-mail address specified in the contact.

Service Accounts

Services are computer programs that run in the background on Windows servers. Because services are designed to run without a user interface and without any users being logged on at the console, a logon account must be provided for the service. When the service starts, it authenticates as the logon account and has the same rights to resources as the logon account. When specifying a logon account on a domain controller (DC), you can specify a specific user account in Active Directory or a local user. You would then assign the necessary rights to the specified user account for the service to run properly.

Windows Server 2008 includes some local accounts that are designed to be used specifically for running services. These accounts have the most commonly required sets of rights that services need to run. Passwords cannot be configured for these accounts. Table 10-3 lists commonly used service accounts.

Table 10-3   Commonly Used Service Accounts

Local Account Name	Description
SYSTEM	This account has full access to the computer and can access network resources with the rights of the computer account. On a DC, this account has access to the entire domain. Use of this account should be avoided whenever possible.
LOCAL SERVICE	This account has the same level of access as the built-in Users group. Access to network resources is performed as a null session (anonymous). This is the preferred account for running services when possible because it has limited rights.
NETWORK SERVICE	This account has the same access to local resources as the LOCAL SERVICE account. However, for accessing network resources, the permissions of the computer account determine which resources can be accessed.

Managing Groups

One of the primary functions of a directory service like Active Directory is to provide authorization for access to network resources. Ultimately, all access to network resources is based on the individual user accounts. However, in most cases, you do not want to administer access to resources by using individual user accounts. In a large company, this would result in a great deal of administrative effort. Also, the access control lists (ACLs) on network resources would soon be unmanageable if you assigned permissions using individual user accounts. Because managing access to network resources using individual user accounts is unmanageable, you create group objects to manage large collections of users at one time.

Group Types

Windows Server 2008 provides four different types of groups. *Distribution groups* and *security groups* are the group types typically used by administrators. *Application basic groups* and *LDAP query groups* are used by Authorization Manager applications. When you create a new group object by using Active Directory Users And Computers, you are given the choice of creating a *distribution group* or a *security group*. Figure 10-5 shows the interface.

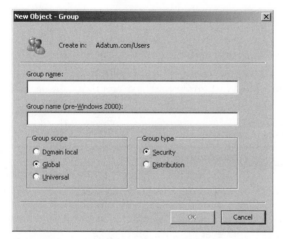

Figure 10-5   Creating a new group in the Active Directory Users And Computers administrative tool.

The most commonly used type of group in Active Directory is the security group. A security group is a security principal and can be used to assign permissions to network resources. A distribution group cannot be a security principal. Because it cannot be used to assign access to resources, the distribution group has a very limited usefulness. It is most commonly used when Microsoft Exchange Server is installed and users need to be grouped so that e-mail can be sent to the entire group. If you have installed Microsoft Exchange Server, you can mail-enable a distribution group and then add mail-enabled users and contacts to the group. You can then send mail to the whole group of users at one time.

You can convert distribution groups to security groups and back as long as your domain is running at least Windows 2000 native functional level. The membership of a group is maintained after conversion.

Authorization Manager Application Groups

Authorization Manager was introduced in Windows Server 2003 as a new way to grant role-based authorization within applications. This system is used by application developers to control access to application data and functionality. It is not used by network administrators to control access to network resources. Authorization Manager supports the use of Active Directory, Active Directory Lightweight Directory Server, or XML files for data storage. To use Active Directory as the storage location for Authorization Manager, the domain must be at the Windows Server 2003 functional level. The two types of Authorization manager groups are *application basic groups* and *LDAP query groups*.

Applications basic groups are a collection of security principals with a member list and a nonmember list. The nonmember list is used as an alternative to deny permissions. Verification of membership for application basic groups is performed when the resource is accessed rather than when the user logs on. This results in higher load on the server, but allows group membership changes to take effect without logging off.

LDAP query groups have a dynamic membership list based on an LDAP query. The query can be based on any user attribute available in Active Directory. This provides the benefit of automatically updating the membership of the group when user characteristics change. Verification of membership for LDAP query groups is performed when the resource is accessed.

More Info   For more information about Authorization Manager, see "Role-Based Access Control for Multi-tier Applications Using Authorization Manager" at *http://technet2.microsoft.com/windowsserver/en/library/72b55950-86cc-4c7f-8fbf-3063276cd0b61033.mspx.*

Note   Because distribution groups have limited use in Active Directory, the rest of this chapter will focus on security groups.

Group Scope

In Windows Server 2008 Active Directory, you can create groups with three different scopes: domain local, global, and universal. Table 10-4 lists the characteristics of each group scope.

> **Note**   Universal groups are available only if the domain is set to at least Windows 2000 native functional level. *Nested groups* are groups that are members of other groups. The options for nesting groups depend on the domain functional level. For example, you can nest a global group in a domain local group at any functional level, but you can nest a global group inside another global group only if the domain functional level is Windows 2000 native or higher.

Domain local groups are fully functional only when the domain has been elevated to at least the Windows 2000 native functional level. If the domain is running in a Windows 2000 mixed functional level, domain local groups operate just like local groups on domain controllers in Windows NT 4. The group can be used to assign permissions to resources on the domain controllers but not on any other computers in the domain. If the domain has been switched to at least Windows 2000 native functional level, domain local groups can be used to grant permissions to resources on any Windows server in the domain.

Table 10-4   Active Directory Group Scopes

Group Scope	Group Membership Can Include	Can Be Used
Domain local	■ User accounts from any domain in the forest ■ Global groups or universal groups from any domain in the forest ■ User accounts or global or universal groups from any domain in a trusted forest ■ Nested domain local groups from the local domain	■ To assign access to resources only in the local domain ■ On all servers in the domain running Windows 2000, Windows Server 2003, or Windows Server 2008
Global	■ User accounts from the domain where the group is created ■ Nested global groups from the same domain	■ To assign access to resources in all domains in the forest, or between trusted forests ■ On any member server running Windows, including member servers running Windows NT

Table 10-4   Active Directory Group Scopes *(continued)*

Group Scope	Group Membership Can Include	Can Be Used
Universal	■ User accounts from any domain in the forest ■ Global groups from any domain in the forest ■ Nested universal groups from any domain in the forest	■ To assign access to resources in all domains in the forest or between trusted forests ■ On all servers in the domain running Windows 2000, Windows Server 2003, or Windows Server 2008

Note   How you use groups will vary depending on what servers you have deployed in your environment. If your domain contains only servers running Windows 2000 and Windows Server 2003, you can use domain local groups to assign permissions to all resources on these servers. However, you can also still use local groups on the member servers. Note that you will still have to use local groups on servers running Windows NT. In either case, the local groups can contain global groups from any domain in the forest. If you create the local groups on a server running Windows 2000 or Windows Server 2003, the groups can also contain universal groups from any domain in the forest or trusted forest.

Global group functionality has remained consistent in Windows Server 2008 Active Directory from Windows 2000 Active Directory. If the domain has been switched to at least Windows 2000 native functional level, you can nest global groups from the same domain inside other global groups. Nesting groups is useful for avoiding multiple group memberships. For example, your company may have several unique business units, each with a group of managers and executives. You may decide to create a Managers global group for each business unit and then nest these global groups in a company-wide Managers group.

Note   If your domain is still at the Windows 2000 native or Windows 2000 mixed mode functional level, you should limit group membership to 5,000 users or less to avoid potential replication issues. Nesting of groups can be used to alleviate this problem. This problem is resolved by an updated process for linked value replication when the domain is raised to Windows Server 2003 functional level.

Universal groups are the most flexible groups in Active Directory, but this flexibility comes with a cost. Universal groups can contain members from any domain in the forest and can be used to assign permissions to resources in any domain in the forest. To make this possible, the membership list for all universal groups is stored in the global catalog (GC). The membership list is stored as a single attribute in the GC. This means that if your domain is running at the Windows 2000 native functional level, every time a member is added to the universal group, the entire membership list must be replicated to all other global catalog servers. If the universal group contains thousands of members, this can result in a great deal of replication. This problem is resolved by linked-value replication if the domain has been switched to at least the Windows Server 2003 functional level.

Linked-value replication reduces the replication traffic for multivalued linked attributes. Group membership lists are an example of a multivalued linked attribute. Each member of the group is a value in the member attribute for the group. When linked-value replication is used, only changes to a multivalued linked attribute are replicated. In the case of group membership changes, this means that only updates to the group membership are replicated, rather than the entire group membership list.

Universal Groups also affect the logon process if the domain is at the Windows 2000 native mode or higher. During authentication, the DC performing authentication communicates with a global catalog server to confirm user membership in universal groups. This is required because a DC does not hold the membership list of universal groups located in other domains. If the DC is running Windows 2000 Server and cannot contact a GC, then the DC will not authenticate the user and cached credentials from the workstation are used. If there are no cached credentials on the workstation, the user is unable to log on to the domain.

If a DC is running Windows Server 2008 or Windows Server 2003, then the DC can perform Universal Group Membership Caching. When Universal Group Membership Caching is enabled, the DC caches universal group SIDs and global group SIDs in the *msDS-Cached-Membership* attribute of user and computer objects. Caching occurs the first time the user logs on. After the initial logon, cached information is used during authentication and no lookup on a GC is performed. If a GC is unavailable, the logon process is unaffected. If a user has not logged on to the domain previously and a GC is unavailable, then the user is unable to log on to the domain.

Note   Universal Group Membership Caching is not dependent on a specific domain functional level. However, this feature must be enabled for each Active Directory site by using the Active Directory Sites and Services tool.

Cached group membership information is refreshed every eight hours by default. Consequently, changes to universal or global group membership may not be effective for up to eight hours. For an individual user, you can force cache information to be updated at next logon by using ADSI edit to clear the *msDS-Cached-Membership* and *msDS-Cached-Membership-Timestamp* attributes.

Caution   If the Universal Group Membership cache information cannot be refreshed for seven days, then the cached information is considered stale and will not be used. In such a case, the logon process proceeds as if there is no information cached, and a GC is required during the logon process.

Rebooting a domain controller forces the cache to restart the cache refresh interval and refreshes all cached group memberships. However, this can affect a variety of services on your network and should be avoided whenever possible. To refresh the cached group membership information without rebooting a domain controller, you can set the *updateCachedmemberships* operational attribute on the *rootDSE* object to a value of *1* by using Ldp.exe. Both of these methods must be performed on all domain controllers in an Active Directory site to get consistent results.

> **More Info** For more information about Universal Group Membership Caching, including registry entries that can be used to modify default refresh behavior, see "How the Global Catalog Works" at *http://technet2.microsoft.com/windowsserver/en/library/440e44ab-ea05-4bd8-a68c-12cf8fb1af501033.mspx?mfr=true.*

Default Groups in Active Directory

Windows Server 2003 Active Directory contains a large number of default groups, both in the Users container and in the Builtin container. These groups have a wide variety of purposes and default permissions within the domain. Groups in the Builtin container are equivalent to the local builtin groups that exist on member servers. On member servers, these groups give members rights to the local server. In Active Directory, these groups give members right to all domain controllers in the domain. Table 10-5 lists the built-in groups for Active Directory.

Table 10-5   Active Directory Built-in Groups

Group	Description
Account Operators	Members can administer domain user, group, and computer accounts in the domain. However, they cannot modify the Administrators or Domain Admins groups, the Administrator account, or computer accounts in the domain controllers OU.
Administrators	Members have unrestricted access to the domain.
Backup Operators	Members are able to backup and restore files on DCs regardless of their security permissions.
Certificate Service DCOM Access	Members can connect to Certification Authorities in the domain.
Cryptographic Operators	Members can perform cryptographic operations.
Distributed COM Users	Members can launch, use, and activate DCOM objects on DCs in the domain.
Event Log Readers	Members can read event logs on DCs in the domain.
Guests	Members have equivalent access to the users groups. However, the Guest account is limited by being a member of the Everyone group but not the Authenticated users group.
IIS_IUSRS	Used by IIS to apply permissions for anonymous access.

Table 10-5   Active Directory Built-in Groups *(continued)*

Group	Description
Incoming Forest Trust Builders	Members can create incoming one-way forest trusts for this forest.
Network Configuration Operators	Members can configure some networking features on DCs in the domain.
Performance Log Users	Members can log data from performance counters, enable trace providers, and collect event traces on DCs in the domain.
Performance Monitor Users	Members can view performance counter data on DCs in the domain.
Pre-Windows 2000 Compatible Access	Members have read access to all users and groups in the domain. Used for backward compatibility with Windows NT servers.
Print Operators	Members can administer printers on DCs in the domain.
Remote Desktop Users	Members can log on to DCs in the domain by using Remote Desktop.
Replicator	Used to support file replication in the domain.
Server Operators	Members can administer DCs in the domain.
Terminal Server License Servers	Used to support tracking of Terminal Server Per User CAL usage.
Users	Members can run most applications, but cannot perform most system-wide changes on DCs in the domain.
Windows Authorization Access Group	Members have access to the *tokenGroupsGlobalAndUniversal* attribute on user objects.

The default groups in the Users container are used to assign rights and permissions to Active Directory and domain resources. The default groups in the Users container are listed in Table 10-6.

Table 10-6   Active Directory Default Groups in the Users Container

Group	Description
Allowed RODC Password Replication Group	Members can have their passwords replicated to read-only DCs.
Cert Publishers	Members can publish certificates in Active Directory.
Denied RODC Password Replication Group	Members do not have their passwords replicated to read-only DCs.
DnsAdmins	Members can administer DNS objects in the domain.
DnsUpdateProxy	Members can perform dynamic DNS updates on behalf of other clients. Members are typically DHCP servers.

Table 10-6   Active Directory Default Groups in the Users Container *(continued)*

Group	Description
Domain Admins	Members can administer domain objects in Active Directory and can manage all DCs and computers joined to the domain. This group is a member of all local Administrators groups in the domain.
Domain Computers	All workstations and member servers in the domain.
Domain Controllers	All DCs in the domain.
Domain Guests	This group is a member of all local Guests groups in the domain.
Domain Users	This group is a member of all local Users groups in the domain.
Enterprise Admins	Members have administrative rights to the entire Active Directory forest.
Enterprise Read-Only Domain Controllers	All Read-Only DCs in the forest.
Group Policy Creator Owners	Members can create and modify Group Policy objects in the domain.
RAS and IAS Servers	Servers in this group can read the remote access properties of users.
Read-Only Domain Controllers	All Read-Only DCs in the domain.
Schema Admins	Members can make changes to the schema for the forest.

There are very few groups that contain any users when you create a new domain. The domain Administrator account is a member of the Administrators domain local group and the Domain Admins global group. If the domain is the first domain in the forest, the Administrator account is also added to the Enterprise Admins global group and the Schema Admins global group. The Guest account is disabled, but it is a member of the Domain Guests global group. All new users are automatically added to the Domain Users group.

> **More Info**   For a detailed list of the user rights granted to each default group, see "Default Groups" at *http://technet2.microsoft.com/windowsserver/en/library/1631acad-ef34-4f77-9c2e-94a62f8846cf1033.mspx?mfr=true*.

Special Identities

Special identities are groups with dynamic membership based on the circumstances of the user. Membership in these groups is maintained automatically by the system and you cannot modify them. You can assign rights and permission to these groups. The concept of group scope does not apply to special identities. Some of the special identities are listed in Table 10-7.

Table 10-7   Special Identities

Special Identity	Definition
ANONYMOUS LOGON	Users or services that are not logged on with an account name
Authenticated Users	All users from the local domain and remote domains, except the guest account
Everyone	All users from the local domain, other domains, and guests; does not include members of ANONYMOUS LOGON
NETWORK	All users that are accessing the computer over the network
INTERACTIVE	All users that are logged on locally to the computer
TERMINAL SERVER USER	All users that are logged on over the network by using Remote Desktop

Creating a Security Group Design

One of the detailed design components for Active Directory implementation is the security group design. Creating a security group design can be very detailed and painstaking work, especially in a large organization. This section will provide general principles for creating the security group design for your organization.

The first step in creating the security group design is to determine which of the group scopes to use. In many companies, there is a great deal of discussion about how to use the various groups. The use of groups in Active Directory is very flexible. For example, in a single domain, users can be added to a group of any scope in the domain, and the groups can be used to assign permissions to any resource in the domain. In a multidomain environment, there are several options for using universal groups, global groups, and domain local groups.

For most companies, the best way to use the various group scopes is to implement the following steps:

1.   Add users to global or universal groups.

2.   Add the global or universal groups to domain local groups.

3.   Assign access to resources using the domain local groups.

In some companies, there is significant resistance to creating both a domain local group and a global or universal group when one group will do, but there are also important reasons why using two groups is the best approach.

If the approach of using global or universal groups and domain local groups is followed, global or universal groups can be created based on the need to collect users who have something in common. In most cases, global or universal groups are based on a business department or on a functional purpose. For example, all members of the Sales department usually have more in common with each other than they do with members of other departments. Users may all require access to the same resources, or they may all need the same software installed. Group membership is also frequently organized on a functional basis. All managers may need to be grouped together, regardless of which business unit they are part of. All members of a project team will likely need access to the same project resources.

Domain local groups are usually used to assign permissions to resources. In many cases, the permissions may be closely linked to business departments or functions. For example, all members of the Sales department may require access to the same Sales shared folder. All project team members usually require access to the same project information. In other cases, access to resources may cross the regular business or functional boundaries. For example, the company may use a shared folder to which everyone in the company has Read-Only access. Or several departments and project teams may require access to the same shared folder. By creating a domain local group that is specific to a particular resource, you can easily manage access to the resource. You can then add the appropriate global or universal groups to the domain local group.

Often, users require different levels of access to shared folders. For example, a company might have a Human Resource shared folder where all employee policy information is stored. All users may need to be able to read the information in the folders, but only members of the Human Resources department should be able to modify the information in the folder. In this case, you would create two domain local groups for the shared folder. One group can be given Read-Only permission, while the other group is given Full Control or Modify permissions. The Human Resources global group can then be added to the domain local group that has been assigned Full Control, and all other global groups that only need Read-Only access can be added to the Read-Only domain local group.

Using global groups and domain local groups in this way means that you can split the ownership of the global groups and domain local groups. An important security concern in any large corporation is ensuring that only the right users have access to any shared information. One step to ensuring this is to make sure that every group has an owner, also known as an authorizer. Only the owner can authorize any modification to the group configuration. The owner of the global group is usually a department administrator. The owner of a project-based global group is probably the project manager. These owners are the only people who can authorize any change to the membership list.

The owner of a domain local group is usually the data, or resource, owner. If every resource in your company has an owner who is the only person who can authorize any modifications to permissions to the shared resource, that person also becomes the owner of the domain local group that is associated with the resource. Before any global or universal group can be added to the domain local group, this owner must approve the modification.

Using the two levels of groups is particularly important in scenarios where you have multiple domains and users from each domain need access to a shared resource in one domain. As illustrated in Figure 10-6, you can create a global group in each domain and then add that global group to a domain local group in the domain where the resource is located.

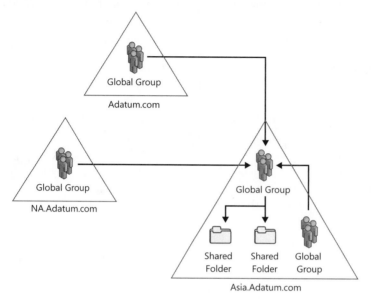

Figure 10-6 Configuring resource access using global groups and domain local groups with multiple domains.

Note Windows NT uses global groups and local groups, but does not have the option of using domain local groups. If you have Windows NT member servers in your domain, you will still need to use local groups on each server. If you have servers running Windows 2000, Windows Server 2003, or Windows Server 2008, and your domain is running in at least Windows 2000 native functional level, you should use domain local groups whenever possible. If you do, you can use the domain local groups across multiple servers. In addition, if you use domain local groups rather than local groups, you can move a resource between servers and use the same domain local group to assign permissions.

One of the questions that must be asked when creating the security group design is when to use global groups and when to use universal groups. In some cases, you do not have any option. For example, mail-enabled groups for Exchange 2000 Server and Exchange Server 2003 that contain members from multiple domains cannot be properly processed unless they are universal groups. Exchange Server 2007 creates all new mail-enabled groups as universal groups.

In most cases, the best practice when creating the universal group design in Windows 2000 Active Directory was to minimize the use of universal groups, especially if you had any sites that were separated by slow network connections. This was because of replication issues with the GC. This recommendation is still valid if your forest is running in Windows 2000 functional level. However, if your forest has been switched to the Windows Server 2003 or

Windows Server 2003 interim functional level, this replication issue is no longer relevant because linked-value replication has been implemented. Also, the option to enable Universal Group Membership Caching reduces the need to deploy a GC server in every site. Because of these enhancements, the decision of when to use universal groups or global groups is not so critical in Windows Server 2008 Active Directory. In most cases, you will be able to use global groups and universal groups almost interchangeably.

Managing Computers

Another type of object in Active Directory is the computer object. Computer objects are used to represent domain controllers, member servers, and workstations. Computers authenticate to the domain by using the computer object just as users authenticate to the domain by using user objects. Computer accounts automatically change their password every 30 days as a background process.

> **Note**   All computers running Windows NT, Windows 2000, Microsoft Windows XP Professional, Windows Server 2003, Windows Vista, and Windows Server 2008 must have a computer account in the domain. Computers running Microsoft Windows 95 or Microsoft Windows 98 cannot have accounts in the domain.

You will rarely manage the computer objects in Active Directory directly. If you right-click a computer account in Active Directory, you will see that there are very few management options. One option available is to reset the computer account. Use this option with caution, because when you reset a computer account, you break that computer's connection to the domain, and the computer must then be rejoined to the domain. Verify that the computer account is not disabled before resetting the computer account. When a computer account is disabled, the computer will not be able to log on to the domain.

The option to reset a computer account is useful when a computer is unable to properly communicate with the domain. This occurs if the computer account and computer do not have the same password. This can occur because of communication errors or after disaster recovery. If you reset the computer account and then rejoin the computer to the domain, the password is synchronized again. This process is not valid for DCs because DCs cannot rejoin a domain. A simpler process that works for member servers and DCs is to use the Netdom.exe utility. The Netdom.exe utility can reset the password on the local computer and on the computer object at the same time. This avoids the need to rejoin the domain. For a domain controller, the Kerberos Key Distribution Center service must be stopped first. Then, at a command line, enter **netdom resetpwd /s:***DomainController* **/ud:***domainname***\Administrator /pd:***. When resetting a domain controller computer account, the domain controller used by Netdom must be another domain controller in the same domain. When prompted, enter the password for the Administrator account. After you run the command, the computer must be restarted.

More Info   For more information about using Netdom.exe to reset the password of a computer account, see "How to Use Netdom.exe to Reset Machine Account Passwords of a Windows Server 2003 Domain Controller" at *http://support.microsoft.com/kb/325850*.

An option that is very useful from an administrative point of view is the option to access the Computer Management application for any computer from Active Directory. Locate a computer in the Active Directory Users And Computers administrative tool, right-click the icon for the workstation or server you want, and choose Manage. The Computer Management Microsoft Management Console (MMC) opens focused on the workstation or server that you selected.

In most cases, computer objects are created when the computer joins the domain. The computer objects for member servers and workstations are created in the Computers container. When a member server is promoted to a domain controller, the computer object for the domain controller is moved to the Domain Controllers OU.

Caution   You can move the computer objects for domain controllers out of the Domain Controllers OU, but this is not recommended. Many of the domain controller security settings are configured on the Domain Controllers OU, and moving the computer object for a domain controller out of this container will effectively modify the security settings for any moved domain controllers.

In most cases, you will move the computer objects from the Computers container into specific OUs. The reason for doing this is so you can manage the computers differently. For example, you will probably want to manage the member servers in your company differently from the workstations, so you will need to create two separate OUs. Often, workstations can be split up into smaller groupings. All the workstations in the Sales department will require different applications than the workstations in the Engineering department, for example. By creating two OUs and moving the workstations into the appropriate OUs, you can manage the two types of workstations differently.

Note   Group Policy cannot be applied directly to the Computers container because it is not an OU.

You can redirect the default location for computer objects during creation when joining the domain. If your domain is at least at the Windows Server 2003 functional level, then you can use the Redircmp.exe utility to set a new location. Open a command prompt and then enter **redircmp ou=*OUforComputers*,dc=*DomainName*,dc=*com***.

> **Note**   The *Rediruser.exe* command can be used to change the default location for new user objects.

To avoid moving computer objects after creation, you can create computer objects in the desired OU before the computers join the domain. If a computer object already exists that matches the name of the computer, it will use the existing computer object. This also avoids the need to delegate administrative rights to join computers to the domain.

The Authenticated Users group is assigned the Add Workstations To A Domain right. This allows all users to add workstations to a domain and create up to 10 computer accounts. If users need to create more than 10 computer accounts, then the users can be delegated the Create Computer Objects permission in Active Directory. This permission can be delegated for only specific OUs if desired. Alternatively, users can be given the Add Workstations To A Domain right in a Group Policy that will allow users to create computer objects in the domain. In addition, members of the Account Operators group, Domain Admins group, and Enterprise Admins group can create computer objects. Account operators cannot create computer objects in the Domain Controllers OU.

When creating new computer objects, you can use command-line tools to script the process. The Dsadd.exe utility allows you to specify the specific location of a computer object during creation. The Netdom.exe utility can also be used to join a computer to the domain and specify the OU for the new computer object.

> **Note**   The fact that you will not likely perform a great deal of administration on the computer objects in Active Directory certainly does not mean that you will not be using Active Directory to manage computers. Chapter 11, "Introduction to Group Policy"; Chapter 12, "Using Group Policy to Manage User Desktops"; and Chapter 13, "Using Group Policy to Manage Security," deal with Group Policy, which provides powerful tools for managing computers.

Managing Printer Objects

A third group of objects in Active Directory consists of printer objects. You can create a printer object by publishing the printer in Active Directory. When you publish a printer in Active Directory, a printer object is created that stores printer attributes, such as printer location, but also printer features such as printing speed, color printing capabilities, and other printer-specific functionality. The primary reason for publishing printer objects in Active Directory is to make it easier for users to locate and connect to network printers.

Publishing Printers in Active Directory

By default, any printer that is installed and shared on a computer running Windows 2000 Server and Windows Server 2003 in an Active Directory domain is automatically published in Active Directory. If you want a shared printer on a computer running Windows Server 2008 to be automatically published in Active Directory, you can select the option List in the directory on the Sharing tab in the properties of the printer.

> **Note**   Printer objects that are added to Active Directory automatically are stored under the computer object. To view these objects by using Active Directory Users And Computers, you must enable the option Users, Groups, And Computers As Containers in the View menu.

If a shared printer is located on a server running Windows NT or another non–Windows-based server operating system, you must manually publish the printer in Active Directory. To do so, locate the container object where you want to publish the printer object, and then right-click, point to New, and click Printer. Then type the Universal Naming Convention (UNC) path to the shared computer. Printer objects that are added to Active Directory manually are not automatically updated with changes to printer information and appear in the container where you create them.

Windows Server 2008 includes the script Pubprn.vbs to automatically add shared printers from Windows NT to Active Directory. This script is not used for printers shared on computers running Windows 2000 Server, Windows Server 2003, or Windows Server 2008. The Pubprn.vbs script is located in %WINDIR%\System32\Printing_Admin_Scripts\<language>.

> **More Info**   For detailed information about the syntax for Pubprn.vbs, see the Pubprn.vbs Web page in the Windows Server 2008 Technical Library at *http://technet2.microsoft.com/windowsserver2008/en/library/0bc7f7e3-84e1-4359-b477-7b1a1a0bd6391033.mspx?mfr=true*.

Publishing a printer in Active Directory allows users to search Active Directory for printer objects. When a printer is published in Active Directory, information about the printer is populated in the printer object. This can be very useful information for a user who is looking for a specific printer. For example, the user may be looking for a color printer that also prints at least six pages per minute. If this information is stored in Active Directory, the client can use Find Printers dialog box to locate any printers that meet these requirements. Figure 10-7 shows the interface on a Windows Vista workstation. After the network printer has been located, the user can right-click on the printer and select Connect to install the printer on the client machine.

If the printer objects are published in Active Directory, you can use Group Policy to manage the printer objects. Figure 10-8 shows the options for managing printer settings.

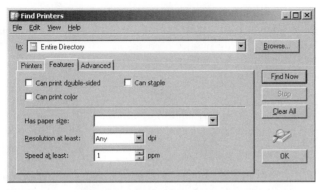

Figure 10-7   Searching for printers in Active Directory.

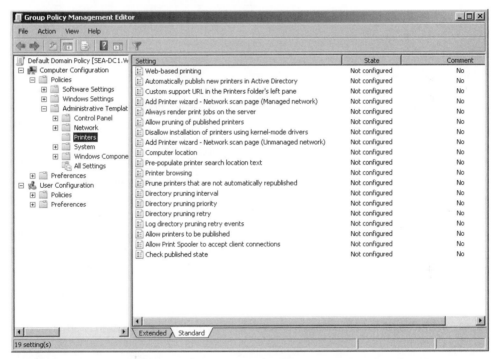

Figure 10-8   Configuring printer settings using the Group Policy Object Editor.

Some of the options that you can configure using Group Policy manage printer pruning. The pruning service on a domain controller automatically deletes printer objects from Active Directory if the printer objects become obsolete. For example, if a printer is removed from a print server, or if the printer is no longer shared on the server, printer pruning will remove the printer object. By default, the pruning service on one of the Active Directory domain controllers tries to contact each print server every eight hours to confirm the validity of the printer information. If the print server does not respond, the printer object is deleted from Active Directory. Each time a print server running Windows 2000 or later restarts, it automatically republishes the shared printers on the server in Active Directory. You can configure the printer pruning parameters by using the Group Policy Object Editor. Table 10-8 describes Group Policy settings for managing printer objects.

Table 10-8   Printer Object Management GPO Settings

GPO Setting	Description
Automatically publish new printers in Active Directory	When this option is enabled, shared printers are automatically published in Active Directory.
Allow pruning of published printers	When this option is enabled, printer objects in Active Directory are removed by the pruning service on a domain controller when the computer that published the printer does not respond to contact requests.
Prune printers that are not automatically republished	This option applies only to printers that were not created automatically (published), such as those created with Pubprn.vbs or manually created by using Active Directory Users And Computers. This can be configured for *Never, Only if print server is found,* or *Whenever printer is not found.*
Directory pruning interval	Specifies how often the pruning service on a domain controller verifies that printers are operational. This option is only relevant if pruning of printers is enabled. The default pruning interval is *eight hours.*
Directory pruning priority	Specifies the priority of the thread that performs directory pruning on domain controllers. The default priority is *normal.*
Directory pruning retry	Specifies how many additional attempts are made to contact a printer before it is pruned. The default value is *two retries.*
Log directory pruning retry events	When this option is enabled, attempts to contact printers by the pruning thread are recorded in the event log.
Allow printers to be published	When this option is enabled, the option List in directory is available on the Sharing tab in a printer's properties. When this option is disabled, then the computer cannot publish printers. This setting overrides *Automatically publish new printers* in Active Directory.
Check published state	Specifies how often a computer verifies that its published printers are in Active Directory. By default, printers are checked only at startup.

Printer Location Tracking

One of the most interesting options in Active Directory for managing printer objects is the option to automatically pre-populate the printer location setting for users when they browse for a printer. Many companies with multiple locations have employees who travel between company locations. Most companies have meeting rooms that are in different parts of the building. Whenever users move from one part of the company to another, they usually need to be able to print, regardless of their location. If users are unfamiliar with where the printers are in their current location, it can often take some time to find the closest printer.

You can simplify this search for printers by assigning each printer a location in Active Directory and then using the user's location to present a list of printers that are close to the user. This functionality is based on the site configuration in Active Directory.

To enable printer location tracking, perform the following steps:

1. Open the Active Directory Sites And Services administrative tool and locate the *subnet* object where you will enable printer tracking. Right-click the *subnet* object and select Properties. Click the Location tab and enter the *location* value for this subnet. The location entry should be in the location/sublocation format (for example, HeadOffice/ 3rdFloor).

2. Use the Group Policy Object Editor to enable the Pre-Populate Printer Search Location Text policy for a selected container. In most cases, you will do this at the domain level.

3. On your print server, access the Properties sheet for each printer. On the General tab, you can fill in the printer location. If you have completed the first two steps of this procedure, you can click Browse to locate the printer location. You can add more details to the printer location so that the printer location is more specific (for example, HeadOffice/3rdFloor/Outside Meeting Room 5).

After you have enabled printer location tracking, users can easily locate the printer closest to them. When the user starts the Add Printer Wizard and searches for a printer in Active Directory, the *Location* attribute is filled in based on the user's current subnet. Figure 10-9 shows the interface on a Windows Vista client. The user can then click Browse for a more specific printer location.

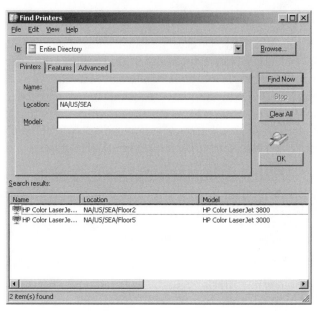

Figure 10-9 Searching for printer objects in Active Directory using the *Location* attribute.

You can configure printer location tracking parameters by using the Group Policy Object Editor. Table 10-9 describes Group Policy settings for managing printer location tracking.

Table 10-9 Printer Location Tracking GPO Settings

GPO Setting	Description
Computer location	Used to override the default location value used when searching for printers. The default value is defined in the *subnet* object for the site in Active Directory.
Pre-populate printer search location text	Configures the Add Printer Wizard to search for printers based on the location defined in the local Active Directory *subnet* object. Users are also able to browse for printers by location. By default, the Add Printer Wizard locates printers based on IP address and subnet mask of the client.

Managing Published Shared Folders

Another object that you can publish to Active Directory is a shared folder object. To publish a shared folder on Active Directory, locate the Active Directory container where you want to publish the shared folder. Right-click the container, point to New, and click Shared Folder. Then type a name for the Active Directory object as well as the UNC for the shared folder. After you create the shared folder object in Active Directory, users can browse for the shared folder or search Active Directory for the object. After the users locate the object in Active Directory, they can right-click on the object and map a drive to the shared folder.

The primary advantage of publishing a shared folder to Active Directory is so that users can search for shares in Active Directory based on a variety of properties. When you create a shared folder object, you can provide a description for the shared folder. Figure 10-10 shows the interface. After creating the shared folder, you can open its Properties sheet to provide keywords associated with the shared folder. When clients need to locate the shared folder, they can search Active Directory using an argument based on the object name, keywords, or description.

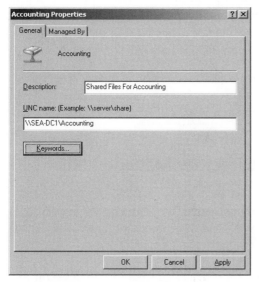

Figure 10-10   Publishing a shared folder in Active Directory.

The most significant limitation with publishing shared folders in Active Directory is that if you ever move the shared folder to another server, any client with a drive permanently mapped to that shared folder will find that the mapping no longer works. This is because when you map a drive to a shared folder in Active Directory, the drive mapping on the client is still based on the UNC path to the share. For example, you may create and publish a shared folder called SalesInfo that points to \\SEA-SRV1\SalesInfo. When a user browses to that shared folder in Active Directory and maps a drive, the drive mapping uses the \\SEA-SRV1\SalesInfo syntax. If you ever move the folder to another server, the drive mapping will fail even if you change the Active Directory object to point to the new location.

This limitation of publishing shared folders can be overcome if you use Distributed File System (DFS). DFS can provide a namespace (UNC path) that is fault tolerant and allows data to be moved from server to server without clients losing connectivity.

Automating Active Directory Object Management

Windows Server 2008 includes graphical utilities, such as Active Directory Users And Computers, for managing Active Directory objects. Graphical utilities make it easy to create and edit Active Directory objects by providing wizards and structure for object creation. For example, when creating a new user object by using Active Directory Users And Computers, the wizard asks you for all the necessary information such as full first name, last name, and user logon name. This avoids the need for you to remember details such as the property names.

Graphical utilities have limited support for making bulk changes to Active Directory objects. For example, you can modify only a few user properties when multiple users are selected in Active Directory Users And Computers. As well, graphical utilities typically do not have the ability to automate management of Active Directory objects. For example, an application cannot use Active Directory Users And Computers to create new user objects.

To make bulk changes to Active Directory objects and automate management of Active Directory objects, you must use tools that are designed for that purpose. The tools included in Windows Server 2008 include command-line tools, LDIFDE, CSVDE, VBScript support, and Windows PowerShell.

Command-Line Tools for Active Directory Management

The Windows Support tools for Windows 2000 Server and Windows Server 2003 included a number of command-line tools for managing Active Directory objects. In Windows Server 2008, these tools are installed when the AD DS role is added rather than as a separate downloadable component.

Command-line tools for managing Active Directory are most useful in batch files. A batch file is a text file with the BAT file extension (.bat). Each line in the batch file is a command. The contents of the batch file are interpreted by Cmd.exe. Consequently, you can use any command in a batch file that you could at a command prompt. Batch files also offer the ability to do more complex processing such as displaying menus.

You can use batch files to automate processes that are performed on many objects at a time. For example, you could create a batch file that modifies the address information for all users in an OU when the department changes locations. You can also automate tasks that need to be performed on a regular basis by running the batch file as a scheduled task. Table 10-10 lists the command line tools available for managing Active Directory objects in Windows Server 2008.

Table 10-10   **Command-Line Tools for Active Directory Management**

Tool	Description
Dsadd	Used to add objects to Active Directory. You can add computer objects, contacts, groups, OUs, and users. You can also add a quota specification to an Active Directory partition. A quota specification limits the number of objects a security principal, such as a user, can own in the partition.
Dsmod	Used to modify objects in Active Directory. You can modify computer objects, contacts, groups, OUs, users, and quota specifications. You can also modify the properties of a domain controller or Active Directory partition. You can pipe output from the *Dsquery* command as input to this command.
Dsmove	Used to move and rename objects in Active Directory. This utility can only move objects within a domain.
Dsrm	Used to remove objects from Active Directory. In addition to removing individual objects, you can remove a container and its contents.
Dsquery	Used to find objects in Active Directory with specific properties. For commonly used object types, there are options you can use at a command line for certain properties. Dsquery can also be used to perform LDAP queries, which allow you to find any object type and any object attribute. The results of a *Dsquery* command can be piped to other commands, such as *Dsmod, Dsget, Dsmove,* and *Dsrm*.
Dsget	Used to view the properties of an object in Active Directory. By default, the properties are displayed on screen, but they can be redirected to a file for further evaluation.

Note   Use the /? option with each command-line tool to view additional information about how to use each tool and the syntax for each tool.

Using LDIFDE and CSVDE

Windows Server 2008 includes LDIFDE and CSVDE to perform bulk imports and exports of information from Active Directory. Each tool reads information from a data file and then creates or modifies Active Directory objects as dictated by the data file. The main difference between the two tools is the format of the data. CSVDE uses data in a comma-separated values (CSV) file, whereas LDIFDE uses data in LDAP directory interchange format (LDIF).

The tool you select to use will be based on the format of your data. For example, if an organization has a human resources application that exports data about new hires in LDIF format, then LDIFDE should be used. However, if a school has a list of new students in a Microsoft Office Excel spreadsheet that can be easily saved as a CSV file, then CSVDE should be used to create the new students.

LDIFDE

LDIF is a proposed standard data format as defined in RFC 2849. It is commonly used for importing and exporting data from directories, including Active Directory and other Lightweight Directory Access Protocol (LDAP) directories.

The data in an LDIF file contains multiple entries separated by a blank line. Each entry has multiple lines with specific information. *Dn* is used to specify the object being modified. *Changetype* is used to specify the action being taken. Valid values for changetype are *add*, *modify*, and *delete*. A "-" is used to separate multiple attributes for a single object and is also required at the end of each entry when the changetype is set to *modify*. The following LDIF file modifies two attributes of the *Paul West* user object:

```
dn: CN=Paul West,OU=Accounting,DC=Adatum,DC=com
changetype: modify
replace: physicalDeliveryOfficeName
physicalDeliveryOfficeName: 315
-
replace: title
title: HR Manager
-
```

LDIFDE can be useful in a number of scenarios:

- **Bulk modification of user accounts**   To do this, export the selected user accounts to an LDIF file, modify the LDIF as necessary for importing, and then import the LDIF file. Modification of the LDIF file after export requires more than a simple search and replace of the attribute value you want to modify. The *changetype* value is set to *add* during an export, and this must be modified to *change* after the export is complete and before the import is performed. The attribute values must also be modified to the format necessary for import.

- **Moving user accounts to a new domain**   User accounts in one domain can be exported to an LDIF file and then imported into a new domain. The users will not maintain existing security identifiers (SIDs). However, users can be added to appropriate groups as part of the import process.

- **Bulk creation of new users**   In addition to the *dn* and *changetype* lines, the minimum attributes that must be provided when creating a new user are cn=*displayname* and objectClass=*user*. The samAccountName=*logonname* attribute should also be included, but will be randomly generated if not included. Newly created users are disabled. You can also set a password for new users with the *unicodePwd* attribute if your connection to the server is encrypted by using SSL.

You should limit the export of user information to only those objects and attributes you want to modify. For example, if the accounting department has moved to a new location, export only user objects in the Accounting OU and only the address attributes that are being modified. As part of the export process, you can define a filter that lets you limit the Active

Directory objects that are exported to certain objects classes and objects with specific attribute values. You can also specify a RootDN that defines which OU the LDAP query applies to. Only objects within the RootDN will be returned. A scope defines how many levels within the RootDN are searched.

More Info   For more information about using LDIFDE to perform bulk operations, see the "Step-by-Step Guide to Bulk Import and Export to Active Directory" on the Technet Web site at *http://technet.microsoft.com/en-us/library/Bb727091.aspx.*

CSVDE

CSVDE is useful in cases in which data is not readily available in LDIF format. Many applications are able to export data as a CSV file, but not as an LDIF file. Each line in the CSV file used by CSVDE is an individual entry that will be processed by CSVDE. This line is a list of the attribute values to be added or modified. No action is defined in the file, since unlike LDIFDE, CSVDE always creates a new object for each line in the CSV file. The first line in the CSV file is a header that defines which attribute corresponds with each value in the lines below.

When using CSVDE to export data, the same options for filtering data exist as for LDIFDE. You can filter output based on object class and attributes. You can perform an export without any filtering of attributes to create a CSV file that shows you the proper names for all of the attributes in the header of the CSV file. CSVDE will export only attributes that have a value in at least one object.

More Info   For more information about CSVDE syntax and options, see "CSVDE" on the Technet Web site at *http://technet2.microsoft.com/windowsserver/en/library/1050686f-3464-41af-b7e4-016ab0c4db261033.mspx?mfr=true* or use the /? option to view CSVDE help.

Using VBScript to Manage Active Directory Objects

Batch files are a simple implementation of scripting that can be used in Windows Server 2008. However, if you create scripts using a scripting language such as VBScript, then you can perform much more complex tasks. Some benefits of using scripting to manage Active Directory objects are:

- Running a script is typically faster than performing the same task in a graphical tool.

- Scripts are reusable. The initial development of a script takes longer than a graphical tool, but after the script is completed, it can be reused many times with slight modifications to suit new circumstances.

- Scripts can reduce or eliminate human error. By reusing a single tested script, you can avoid errors that may be introduced when repetitive processes are performed manually. Scripts can also validate information that is entered.

■ Scripts can manipulate all available object attributes. Graphical tools allow you to modify only certain object attributes. A script has no such limitations.

■ Scripts can be scheduled. Scheduling a script to run is useful for performing routine maintenance. For example, you can move all disabled user accounts to a specific OU each week.

Active Directory Scripting Components

Scripting in Windows Server 2008 is supported by Windows Script Host (WSH). There are two run-time environments for WSH: *Wscript.exe* is a Windows-based run time for graphical applications and *Cscript.exe* is a command-line based run time that writes output to a command prompt. *Wscript.exe* is the default run time used when you double-click a script.

Windows Script Host supports using both VBScript and JScript as scripting languages. In most cases, those with less scripting experience prefer to use VBScript. Most scripting examples available on the Microsoft Web site also use VBScript. VBScripts typically end in the .vbs file extension. However, the .vbe file extension is also used for VBScripts. Files with the .wsf file extension are a generic Windows Script Host file that can contain a combination of VBScript and JScript.

A scripting interface is an abstract layer that allows you to access information from a data source. Active Directory Service Interfaces (ADSI) is the most commonly used scripting interface to access Active Directory objects. By using ADSI, you can create, modify, and delete Active Directory objects. ActiveX Data Objects (ADO) can also be used to access Active Directory objects. However, ADO can only be used to query Active Directory objects, not modify them. When performing a query, the primary difference between ADSI and ADO is that the result set from an ADO query is flat. A list of users is returned as a single list rather than hierarchically organized by domain or OU.

Windows Management Instrumentation (WMI) is a scripting interface that is the Microsoft implementation of Web-Based Enterprise Management (WBEM) initiative, which is a standardized way to manage network and computer resources. In addition to manipulating Active Directory objects, WMI enables you to query, change, and monitor configuration settings on desktop and server systems, applications, networks, and other enterprise components.

Creating and Running a VBScript

When you create a VBScript, only a simple text editor such as Notepad is required. The only requirement is to save the script with the .vbs or .vbe file extension. However, there are script editors that can simplify the process of creating a script. A script editor is able to verify syntax in the script so that you can correct errors during the writing process instead of having to address errors only after you run the script. Script editors also typically provide code completion and syntax coloring.

Binding to an Object   The first step for manipulating an Active Directory object in a VBScript is binding to an Active Directory object. "Binding to an object" is another way of saying connecting to an object. If you are creating a new object, you bind to the container the object will be created in. If you are modifying an existing object, you bind to the object you are modifying. When you bind to an object, it is stored in a local cache on the computer where the script is running.

VBScript is an object-based scripting language. This allows you to work with objects in Active Directory as a single unit and perform actions on an entire object as well as on object properties. When you bind to an Active Directory object, that object is placed into a variable that represents the object. You then manipulate the variable rather than the object.

The following code is an example of binding to an Active Directory OU. The variable *acctOU* is set as an in-memory instance of the Accounting OU. Notice that the Accounting OU is defined by an LDAP path:

```
Set acctOU = GetObject("LDAP://OU=Accounting,dc=adatum,dc=com")
```

Creating an Object   Creating a new object requires that a new variable be created with the information about the new object. The new object is created by using the *Create* method on the variable for the container. *Methods* are actions that an object can perform. Table 10-11 lists some commonly used methods available for Active Directory objects through the ADSI interface.

Table 10-11   VBScript Methods for Managing Active Directory Objects

Method	Description
Create	Used to create new objects.
Get	Used to retrieve the value of an object attribute.
GetEx	Used to retrieve values as an array. Typically used for multivalued attributes.
Put	Used to place a new value in an object attribute.
PutEx	Use to place a new value in an object attribute with advanced options. This method allows you to manage the values of a multivalued attribute.
SetInfo	Used to save the changes to a new or modified object.

The following code is an example of creating a new user in the Accounting OU. The variable *newUser* is set equal to the new user object *Paul West*. Then the *sAMAccountName* attribute of the *newUser* variable is set to be *Paul*:

```
Set newUser = acctOU.create("User","cn=Paul West")
newUser.Put "sAMAccountName","Paul"
```

When you create a new object, you must define all of the mandatory attributes for that object class. In this case, defining *cn* and *sAMAccountName* are sufficient to create a new user object. Other necessary attributes such as the SID are generated automatically by the system.

Saving Changes   When you manipulate objects by using a script, the changes are made only to the locally cached version of that object. These changes must be saved to Active Directory by using the following code:

```
newUser.SetInfo
```

The *SetInfo* method saves changes only for a single object. If you have modified multiple objects in your script, then you must use the *SetInfo* method for each object. In some cases, you must use SetInfo for one object before modifying another. For example, you use SetInfo for a newly created user before you can add that user to a group, because the user does not exist in the directory and therefore cannot be referenced by the group until SetInfo is used to create the user in Active Directory.

Modifying an Existing Object   The following code demonstrates how to modify the properties of a user account. The variable *modUser* is set equal to the *Paul West* user object and then the *givenName*, *sn,* and *displayName* attributes of the objects are modified. Finally, the modifications in cache are saved to Active Directory.

```
Set modUser = GetObject("LDAP://cn=Paul West,OU=Accounting,DC=Adatum,DC=com")
modUser.Put "givenName","Paul"
modUser.Put "sn","West"
modUser.Put "displayName","Paul West"
modUser.SetInfo
```

> **More Info**   For more information about using VBScript to manage Active Directory objects, visit the Getting Started page of the TechNet Script Center at *http://www.microsoft.com/ technet/scriptcenter/hubs/start.mspx*. For more examples of VBScripts that can be used to manage Active Directory objects, visit the Active Directory page of the Script Repository at *http://www.microsoft.com/technet/scriptcenter/scripts/default.mspx?mfr=true*.

Using Windows PowerShell to Manage Active Directory Objects

Windows PowerShell is a new scripting and command-line environment included in Windows Server 2008 that you can use for administering Windows systems. You must install Windows PowerShell as a feature; it is not installed by default. Windows PowerShell can also be downloaded for Windows XP SP2, Windows Vista, and Windows Server 2003.

The Windows PowerShell commands can be used directly from a command prompt or in a script. The command shell PowerShell.exe provides the environment for running Windows PowerShell commands in the same way that Cmd.exe provides the environment for running traditional command-line utilities. Windows PowerShell scripts are text files with Windows PowerShell commands in the same way that batch files are text files with commands that can be run from a command line. Windows PowerShell scripts have the .ps1 file extension.

Some Microsoft Management Console (MMC) snap-ins use Windows PowerShell to perform tasks. For example, the Exchange Management Console for managing Microsoft Exchange Server 2007 requires Windows PowerShell.

> **More Info**   For more information about Windows PowerShell, visit the Windows PowerShell page on the Microsoft Web site at *http://www.microsoft.com/windowsserver2003/technologies/management/powershell/default.mspx.*

Cmdlet Syntax

A *cmdlet* is a command used in Windows PowerShell. Each cmdlet is composed of a verb-noun pair separated by a dash. The verb describes the action to be taken and the noun describes what the action is to be taken on. Some of the common verbs used in cmdlets are *Get, Set, New*, and *Remove*. In most cases, additional parameters are added to the cmdlet to provide additional information. The parameters are preceded by a dash. The following example shows the syntax for using a cmdlet:

```
Verb-noun –parametername parametervalue –parametername
```

The following example shows a command that uses the Get-Help cmdlet to display help information for the Get-Service cmdlet. The *-Name* parameter is used to indicate the name of the cmdlet that information is desired for. The *-Detailed* parameter is used to indicate that a detailed listing of information is desired rather than a summary:

```
Get-Help –Name Get-Service -Detailed
```

Accessing Active Directory Objects

Windows PowerShell does not include any cmdlets that are specific to managing Active Directory objects. However, there are two interfaces that can be used to access Active Directory objects for manipulation. System.DirectoryServices.DirectoryEntry is a class object in the Microsoft .Net Framework that can be used to access all possible Active Directory functions from within Windows PowerShell. [ADSI] is a type accelerator to System.DirectoryServices.DirectoryEntry that simplifies access to Active Directory. The use of [ADSI] is similar to how Active Directory objects are accessed and modified by using VBScript. Both of these methods can be used in combination. For example, you can connect to an object by using [ADSI] and then use DirectoryEntry commands to manipulate it. The remainder of this section will use [ADSI] because it is simpler to use and understand.

> **More Info**   For more information about using the DirectoryEntry object and how it compares to [ADSI], see "Benp's Basic Guide to Managing Active Directory Objects with PowerShell" on the Technet Blogs Web site at *http://blogs.technet.com/benp/archive/2007/03/05/benp-s-basic-guide-to-managing-active-directory-objects-with-powershell.aspx.*

The process for accessing Active Directory objects in Windows PowerShell is approximately the same as when using VBScript, but with slightly different syntax. First, you must bind the selected Active Directory objects, make the changes you desire, and then commit the changes. The most common methods used by [ADSI] are *Create()*, *Get() Put()*, *Delete()*, and *SetInfo()*.

The following example creates a new user in the Accounting OU. The variable *$acctOU* is used to create a binding with the Accounting OU. The *$newUser* variable is used to create the new user *Paul West*. Notice that the *SetInfo* method must be used to commit the new user before the *sAMAccoutName* attribute is defined and committed. This is different than the process used in the VBScript example.

```
$acctOU = [ADSI] 'LDAP://OU=Accounting,DC=Adatum,DC=com'
$newUser = $acctOU.create('User','CN=Paul West')
$newUser.setinfo()
$newUser.sAMAccountName = 'Paul'
$newUser.setinfo()
```

Using CSV Files

You can use the Import-Csv cmdlet to load data from CSV file into a variable. The most likely scenario for using this is the bulk creation of objects in Active Directory. The CSV file must have a header row that describes each column of data, but unlike a data file for the CSVDE utility, the header row descriptions do not need to match the name of the object attributes exactly. The header row descriptions are used only to reference the data that is imported. For example, the header row could use the description *LoginName* for the data that is eventually used as the *sAMAccountName* attribute.

If you do not want to use all data in a CSV file, you can filter the data by using the Where-Object cmdlet. This cmdlet allows you to specify a filter based on the data in the CSV file. The following example filters the contents of Users.csv to use only rows where the department is Accounting. More complex queries can be created by adding additional criteria to the filter. After the specified rows are stored in the *$users* variable, then the data can be used to create new users or further manipulated.

```
$users = Import-Csv C:\Users.csv | Where-Object {$_.department -eq "Accounting"}
```

Exchange Management Shell Commands

The Exchange Management Shell is an extension to Windows PowerShell that is included with Microsoft Exchange Server 2007. It includes some cmdlets that can be used to manage Active Directory users and groups. Some of the cmdlets for managing Active Directory objects are listed in Table 10-12. There are additional cmdlets that are specific to mailbox-enabled users, mail-enabled users, mail-enabled contacts, and distribution groups. For example, the New-Mailbox cmdlet can be used to create new users with an Exchange mailbox.

Table 10-12   **Exchange Management Shell Cmdlets**

Cmdlet	Description
Get-User	Retrieves a list of users matching specified criteria. Several parameters are included for filtering users based on organizational unit, company name, or department. There is also a generic filter parameter that allows you to use a wide variety of other user attributes as filters.
Set-User	Modifies characteristics of the specified user. Lists of users retrieved by the Get-User cmdlet can be piped to this cmdlet.
Get-Group	Retrieves a list of groups matching specified criteria.
Set-Group	Modifies a limited number of characteristics for the specified group.
Get-Contact	Retrieves a list of contacts matching specified criteria.
Set-Contact	Modifies characteristics of the specified contacts. Lists of contacts retrieved by the Get-Contact cmdlet can be piped to this cmdlet.

Summary

This chapter provided an overview of the most common Windows Server 2008 Active Directory objects and procedures for administering Active Directory objects. A great deal of your administrative effort will be spent administering these objects. In particular, you will be administering group and user accounts as employees join and leave your company, or as you create new groups to secure network resources. Determining an effective strategy for group types and scopes is essential. You will also spend your time administering objects such as computer objects, printer objects, or shared folder objects.

Windows Server 2008 provides many opportunities to automate the management of Active Directory objects. These include command-line tools, CSVDE, and LDIFDE. For more advanced tasks, you can use either VBScript or Windows PowerShell.

Best Practices

- Use Ldp.exe and Adsiedit.msc to modify object attributes that are not visible standard administrative tools such as Active Directory Users And Computers. Use caution when directly editing objects.

- Use UPNs to simplify logon in multidomain environments. Users can log on at any computer without selecting the appropriate domain in the logon box.

- When selecting a service account, use the account with the least permissions possible. The LOCAL SERVICE account has the least permissions. The NETWORK SERVICE can access network resources as the local computer account. SYSTEM has full access to the local computer and can access network resources as the local computer account.

■ Organize groups into a hierarchy for easier application. Add users to global or universal groups to organize them. Assign domain local groups permissions to resources and then make the appropriate global and universal groups members of the domain local groups.

■ When organizing groups between trusted forests, users should be placed into global groups, which are then placed into universal groups in the same forest. Domain local groups should be assigned permissions to resources and then make the appropriate universal groups members of the domain local groups.

■ Use Netdom.exe to reset the password on a computer account to avoid the need to rejoin a domain when the trust between a computer account and the domain is broken.

■ Use printer location tracking and publish printer objects in Active Directory to make it easier for users to locate printers.

■ Use command-line tools and scripting when performing bulk actions on Active Directory objects. Initial testing may take longer, but implementation is much faster, particularly if the task is performed regularly.

■ Use LDIFDE to modify objects rather than CSVDE. CSVDE cannot modify existing objects; it can only create new objects.

■ In Windows PowerShell, use System.DirectoryServices.DirectoryEntry to access Active Directory objects when [ADSI] does not provide the functionality that you require.

■ Remember to use SetInfo in both VBScripts and PowerShell scripts to save changes from the local cache to Active Directory.

■ Use Exchange Management Shell commands when possible to provide a simple way to perform basic creation and manipulation of user and group objects.

Additional Resources

The following resources contain additional information and tools related to this chapter.

Related Information

■ "Microsoft Identity Lifecycle Manager 2007" Web page at *http://www.microsoft.com/windowsserver/ilm2007/default.mspx*

■ "Role-Based Access Control for Multi-tier Applications Using Authorization Manager" at *http://technet2.microsoft.com/windowsserver/en/library/72b55950-86cc-4c7f-8fbf-3063276cd0b61033.mspx*

■ "How the Global Catalog Works" at *http://technet2.microsoft.com/windowsserver/en/library/440e44ab-ea05-4bd8-a68c-12cf8fb1af501033.mspx?mfr=true*

■ "Default Groups" at *http://technet2.microsoft.com/windowsserver/en/library/1631acad-ef34-4f77-9c2e-94a62f8846cf1033.mspx?mfr=true*

- "How to Use Netdom.exe to Reset Machine Account Passwords of a Windows Server 2003 Domain Controller" at *http://support.microsoft.com/kb/325850*.

- "Pubprn.vbs" at *http://technet2.microsoft.com/windowsserver2008/en/library/0bc7f7e3-84e1-4359-b477-7b1a1a0bd6391033.mspx?mfr=true*

- "Step-by-Step Guide to Bulk Import and Export to Active Directory" on the Technet Web site at *http://technet.microsoft.com/en-us/library/Bb727091.aspx*

- "CSVDE" on the Technet Web site at *http://technet2.microsoft.com/windowsserver/en/library/1050686f-3464-41af-b7e4-016ab0c4db261033.mspx?mfr=true*

- The Getting Started page of the TechNet Script Center at *http://www.microsoft.com/technet/scriptcenter/hubs/start.mspx*

- The Active Directory page of the Script Repository at *http://www.microsoft.com/technet/scriptcenter/scripts/default.mspx?mfr=true*

- The PowerShell page on the Microsoft Web site at *http://www.microsoft.com/windowsserver2003/technologies/management/powershell/default.mspx*

Related Tools

- Ldp.exe is a tool that uses LDAP to access Active Directory. This tool can view and modify object properties that standard administrative tools such as Active Directory Users And Computers cannot.

- Adsiedit.msc is a tool that uses ADSI to access Active Directory. This tool can view and modify object properties that standard administrative tools such as Active Directory Users And Computers cannot.

Resources on the CD

The CD includes a number of sample VBScript and PowerShell scripts. These scripts are fully commented so that you can modify them for use in your own environment.

- CreateUser.vbs is a VBScript that shows the basic steps required to create a user.

- CreateUser.ps1 is a PowerShell script that shows the basic steps required to create a user.

- CreateUserFromCSV.vbs is a VBScript that shows how to create users based on data read from a csv file. This is useful for bulk creation of users.

- CreateUserFromCSV.ps1 is a PowerShell script that shows how to create users based on data read from a csv file. This is useful for bulk creation of users.

- SearchforUserFromCSV.vbs is a VBScript that searches for users that match those listed in a csv file. This is useful for verifying uniqueness before bulk creation of accounts from the same csv file.

- SearchforUserFromCSV.ps1 is a PowerShell script that searches for users that match those listed in a csv file. This is useful for verifying uniqueness before bulk creation of accounts from the same csv file.

- FindAndModifyUsers.vbs is a VBScript that shows how to find users with a specific attribute value and then modify those users. This is useful for bulk modification of user accounts.

- FindAndModifyUsers.ps1 is a PowerShell script that shows how to find users with a specific attribute value and then modify those users. This is useful for bulk modification of user accounts.

- CreateGroupAndAddMembers.vbs is a VBScript that shows the basic process for creating and group and adding members to that group.

- CreateGroupAndAddMembers.ps1 is a PowerShell script that shows the basic process for creating and group and adding members to that group.

Chapter 11
Introduction to Group Policy

Ever since the early days of Active Directory, Group Policy has played a major role in the goal of moving towards a more highly managed computing environment. Many organizations realize that the initial purchase or lease price of a computer is only a small part of the entire cost associated with managing and maintaining the computer over its lifetime. The primary cost is the expense of the people managing those computers. If all client computers must be manually administered, the cost of owning those computers can very quickly grow to an unacceptable level. To address this issue, organizations need to move away from manual processes and establish a more automated and centrally administered form of change and configuration management for user and computer settings within the environment.

Group Policy in Windows Server 2008 provides many of the features needed to lower the cost of managing computer systems. Change and configuration management is enhanced with Group Policy by grouping together user and computer-based policy settings that can then be applied throughout various levels of the Active Directory hierarchy. When you apply a configuration setting using Group Policy, this setting (or group of settings) can be applied to some or all of the computers and users within your organization.

This chapter introduces Group Policy and explains how it can be configured to be applied throughout the Active Directory structure. It also describes some of the new Group Policy features and enhancements provided by Windows Server 2008.

> **Note**   Group Policy settings are effective only for computers running Microsoft Windows 2000 or later. You can use policy settings to manage servers running Windows 2000, Windows Server 2003, and Windows Server 2008. You can manage client computers running Windows 2000, Windows XP Professional, and most editions of Windows Vista; however, you cannot use Group Policy to manage client computers running Windows NT, Windows 95, Windows 98, or Windows Millennium. Windows Server 2008 contains a superset of all policy settings from previous operating system versions. However, settings will only apply to operating systems supported by the specific setting. Any setting that is not supported by a specific operating system will be ignored and not processed on the computer system.

Group Policy Overview

Group Policy in Windows Server 2008 provides powerful capabilities to manage configuration settings related to computers and users within your Active Directory environment. As shown in Table 11-1, there are a number of things you can do with Group Policy.

Table 11-1   Group Policy Configuration Features

Feature	Explanation
Software installation and management	For Active Directory-based Group Policy, you can deploy software and software upgrades to users and computers. You can also remove software or control software deployments based on the location of user or computer objects within the Active Directory structure.
Scripts	You can run computer startup and shutdown scripts as well as user logon and logoff scripts.
Security settings	You can configure a large number of security settings for both computer and user objects. Computer-based security settings include Account Policies, Local Policies, Event Log settings, and settings related to Restricted Groups, System Services, Windows Firewall, and Network Access Protection. User-based security settings include Public Key Policies and Software Restriction Policies.
Folder redirection	You can redirect some parts of the user's work environment, such as the Documents folder, the Start Menu, or Desktop, to a network share where it can always be available to the user and can be backed up with the organization's standard backup procedures. This redirection is transparent to the user. Windows 2008 and Windows Vista provide additional functionality to redirect more folders such as the Contacts, Downloads, Favorites, Links, Music, Saved Games, Searches, and Videos folders.
Policy-based Quality of Service (QoS)	You can use Group Policy to apply settings to prioritize and throttle outbound network traffic. A QoS policy can assign outbound network traffic a specific Differentiated Services Code Point (DSCP) value and control which applications, IP addresses, or protocol and port numbers are to be prioritized and controlled throughout the network.

Table 11-1   **Group Policy Configuration Features** *(continued)*

Feature	Explanation
Internet Explorer settings	You can use Group Policy to manage the Browser menus and toolbars, Connection settings, URL favorites, Security features, and default Internet settings. Extensive Internet Explorer settings can now be configured under Administrative Templates\Windows Components\Internet Explorer.
Administrative templates	You can use Administrative templates to manage a large number of graphical user interface (GUI) elements such as the Control Panel settings, Desktop settings, and Start Menu and Taskbar settings. These settings configure registry values that limit the modifications that users can perform on their computers.
Preferences	Preferences provide the ability to manage a large number of options related to Windows settings or Control Panel settings including drive mappings, environment variables, network shares, local users and groups, services, devices, and many more.
Printers	Administrators now have the ability to delegate permission for users to install printer drivers (as well as other device drivers) by using Group Policy. For more information about this feature, see "New Categories of Policy Management" at *http://technet2.microsoft.com/WindowsVista/en/library/ 0077cf9d-b06c-4264-99ff-1beb569dd3d21033.mspx*.
Blocking device installation	You can centrally restrict devices from being installed on computers in your organization. You can create policy settings to control access to devices such as USB drives, CD-RW drives, DVD-RW drives, and other removable media. Device installation settings are located under Computer Configuration\ Policies\Administrative Templates\System\Device Installation.
Power management settings	All power management settings have been Group Policy-enabled, providing a potentially significant cost savings. You can modify specific power settings through individual Group Policy settings or build a custom power plan that is deployable by using Group Policy. Power management settings are located under Computer Configuration\Policies\Administrative Templates\ System\Power Management.

How Group Policy Works

Each of the features described in Table 11-1 consists of a large number of policy settings that can be configured to affect either a user or computer. Policy settings are configured as Group Policy objects (GPOs) and linked to various levels of the Active Directory structure, such as the site, domain, or organizational unit (OU). The Active Directory hierarchy provides the ability for Group Policy settings linked at higher-level containers (such as the domain or first-level OU containers) to be inherited by lower-level containers. This inheritability provides an efficient and effective method for applying Group Policy settings throughout your entire environment.

When an Active Directory domain is first created, two GPOs are created and linked within Active Directory: the Default Domain Policy and the Default Domain Controllers Policy. The

Default Domain Policy is linked at the domain level and is used to set the default security and password policies for the entire domain. The Default Domain Controllers Policy is linked at the Domain Controllers OU and is used to configure security settings for domain controllers. In addition to these default GPOs, you can create as many additional GPOs as you want and link them to different locations throughout your Active Directory structure.

> **Note**   It is considered a best practice to not edit or modify the Default Domain or Default Domain Controllers Policy. Always create new GPOs to apply custom policy settings and ensure that the default GPOs are at the top of the priority list.

In addition to Active Directory-based Group Policy, local or stand-alone computer environments also use what is called a Local Group Policy object (LGPO). Computers running Windows 2000, Windows XP, and Windows Server 2003 only contain one LGPO, which affects all users that log on to the local computer. Windows Vista and Windows Server 2008 also, by default, contain a single LGPO but do have the ability to use multiple-user LGPOs for added administration and security capabilities of stand-alone computers or computers located in a workgroup.

> **Note**   There is always a single LGPO applying to the computer, which is also processed on all computers that belong to Active Directory. However, the LGPO has the least precedence and is the first policy applied; the Active Directory–based Group Policy settings will often override the LGPO settings. You can disable LGPO processing for domain-based computers by using the Group Policy Management console and enabling the Turn Off Local Group Policy Objects Processing policy found under Computer Configuration\Policies\Administrative Templates\System\Group Policy. This will only affect Windows Vista and Windows Server 2008 computers.

Figure 11-1 illustrates how Group Policy is applied from the LGPO throughout the various levels of Active Directory:

1. If enabled, the LGPO is always processed first for both stand-alone computers and computers that are a member of an Active Directory domain.

2. Group Policy objects applied at the Site level are processed next. In the illustration, GPO1 will be applied to all users and computers that reside in domains and OUs that belong to the specific site. If there are any conflicting settings with the LGPO, the settings configured in GPO1 will override those specific settings.

3. The next step is to process any GPOs assigned at the domain level. GPOs assigned at the Domain level will affect only users and computers of that specific domain. If there are conflicting settings from the Site or LGPO, the domain-based settings will take precedence. Any nonconflicting settings will be inherited from the higher-level GPOs.

4. The final step is to process any GPOs assigned at the OU levels. GPOs assigned at an OU level will typically affect users and computers within that OU and will also be inherited by any child OUs. If there are conflicting settings from the Domain, Site, or LGPO, the OU-based settings closest to the computer and user will take precedence. Any nonconflicting settings will be inherited from the higher-level GPOs.

> **Note**   The earlier description provides the default behavior of Group Policy processing. Override, block from above, and loopback are other mechanisms that can be used to change the processing order to meet the needs of the administrator.

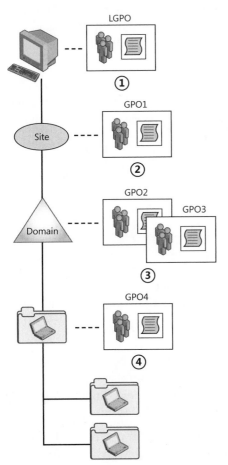

Figure 11-1   Applying Group Policy objects throughout Active Directory.

What's New in Windows Server 2008 Group Policy?

Windows Server 2008 introduces significant feature updates and enhancements to help with the processing and administration of Group Policy. These new enhancements include the following:

- **Integration of the Group Policy Management console**   Group Policy is no longer managed from the Active Directory Users and Computers console. The Group Policy Management console (GPMC), which previously had to be downloaded as a separate add-on component from the Microsoft Download Center, is now an integrated feature within Windows Server 2008. The GPMC can be installed using the Add Features Wizard or installed automatically when a server is assigned the Active Directory Domain Services server role. The GPMC has also been enhanced to support the new ADMX file template and incorporates new filtering capabilities and the ability to provide comments related to specific policy settings.

- **The Group Policy client service**   The Group Policy engine and client-side extensions are no longer managed by the Winlogon process. Group Policy now runs as a service (gpsvc) that provides a more efficient and secure processing environment for applying Group Policy settings.

- **Network Location Awareness**   Group Policy no longer relies on the ICMP protocol (PING) to determine effective network bandwidth. In Windows Server 2008, Group Policy now uses the Network Location Awareness service (NlaSvc) to determine changing network conditions that may affect the application of policy settings.

- **New XML-based Administrative templates**   Group Policy has traditionally used a unique file format known as an ADM file. This file contains the language used to describe registry-based settings that may be applied to network clients using Group Policy. Windows Server 2008 introduces a new XML-based file format known as ADMX files. This new file format provides easier management of Administrative templates within multilingual environments and provides the ability to incorporate change management processes.

- **The Group Policy central store**   ADMX template files can be stored within a centralized repository located on the SYSVOL share on domain controllers. This central store allows administrators to access the same set of ADMX files when editing Group Policy object settings and ensures a consistent management experience throughout the domain.

- **Improved Group Policy logging**   Previous versions of Group Policy relied on logging being enabled for the userenv.dll component. In Windows Server 2008, a stand-alone service runs under the Svchost process. Related event messages now appear in the system log with an event source of Microsoft-Windows-GroupPolicy. Also a new Group Policy Operational log replaces Userenv.dll logging; this provides improved event messages related to Group Policy processing.

- **Support for multiple Local Group Policy objects**   Windows Server 2008 and Windows Vista both support the use of multiple Local Group Policy objects on a single computer. This provides enhanced capabilities for controlling environments that involve shared computing on a single computer (such as a library), or computers placed within a workgroup. Multiple Local Group Policy settings may be assigned to individual local users or applied to local users who are members of either the local Administrators or local Users (Non-Administrators) built-in groups. Typically, this feature would be used for stand-alone workstations located in a workgroup, but LGPOs will also work with domain-based Group Policy. This feature can also be disabled through a Group Policy setting.

- **New Group Policy settings**   Windows Server 2008 now includes over 2600 Administrative template policy settings, including categories related to deploying power management settings, assigning printers based on location, blocking device installation (such as USB, DVD, and other removable drives), and many others. A number of new client-side extensions (CSE) called *Preferences* are also introduced; they provide enhanced control over various Windows and Control Panel settings with the ability to target individual registry settings outside the policy hive to apply only to selected users or groups (similar to the way many organizations currently use logon scripts). The main benefit of the Preferences feature is that it will allow these individual registry settings to be treated as policy settings and to be removed when no longer in scope.

Group Policy Components

An Active Directory-based Group Policy object actually consists of two main components that represent the logical and physical structure of the object. The logical component is stored within the Active Directory database and is called the Group Policy container (GPC). The physical component is stored within the replicated SYSVOL folder located on every domain controller and is called the Group Policy template (GPT).

Overview of the Group Policy Container

The Group Policy container is created in the Active Directory database when you create a new GPO. You can view the container object using the Active Directory Users And Computers console and browsing to the System\Policies container. If you do not see the System container, select Advanced Features from the View menu. Figure 11-2 illustrates the System\Policies container with several GPCs.

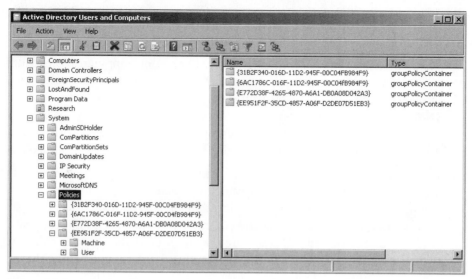

Figure 11-2   Locating GPCs in Active Directory.

As shown in Figure 11-2, the GPC is created in Active Directory as a *groupPolicyContainer* object type and displays a globally unique identifier (GUID) for the Name. The GPC contains attributes that describe various types of information about the GPO:

- **Name of the GPO**   The *displayName* attribute provides the name of the GPO.

- **Path to the GPT**   The *gPCFileSysPath* attribute provides the path to the location of the corresponding Group Policy template which is identified using the same GUID name as the GPC.

- **List of machine and user extensions**   The *gPCMachineExtensionNames* and *gPCUser-ExtensionNames* attributes provide a list of which client side extensions will be used to process the GPO. The following format is used to provide the list:

    [{GUID of CSE}{GUID of MMC extension}{GUID of second MMC extension if appropriate}][GUIDs of next CSE and MMC extensions as configured]

- **Version number**   The *versionNumber* attribute provides the version associated with the GPC portion of the GPO. A version number is maintained by both the GPC and GPT and is used to make sure that the two objects are synchronized.

- **Group Policy object state**   The *flags* attribute illustrates the state of the GPO. If the value is set to *0*, the GPO is enabled; if the value is set to *1*, the User Configuration portion of the GPO is disabled; if the value is set to *2*, the Computer Configuration portion of the GPO is disabled; if the value is set to *3*, the entire GPO is disabled.

- **Access control list**   The access control list displays the users or groups that have permission to manage the settings for the GPO as well as which users or groups should have the GPO settings applied.

These details of the GPC object can be viewed by using Active Directory Users And Computers or a tool such as ADSI Edit. Figure 11-3 shows the Attribute Editor tab from the GPC Properties dialog box within Active Directory Users and Computers. The Attribute Editor is a new Active Directory Users and Computers enhancement available in Windows Server 2008.

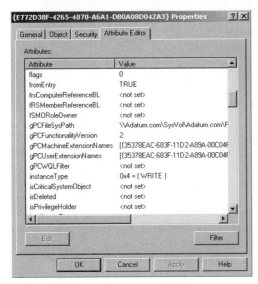

Figure 11-3   Viewing GPC attributes.

Caution   Modifying the access control list or corresponding attributes directly on the GPC is not recommended, unless you are troubleshooting. Group Policy should always be managed using the Group Policy Management console (GPMC). This tool will ensure that both the GPC and GPT are modified appropriately.

Components of the Group Policy Template

When a new GPO is configured, the associated GPT is created and stored in the %System-Root%\SYSVOL folder on each domain controller within the domain. Figure 11-4 illustrates examples of several GPTs stored within the shared SYSVOL folder (\SYSVOL\sysvol\ Adatum.com\Policies). Notice that each GPT is named with the same corresponding GUID number that is stored with the Active Directory-based GPC.

Note   The folder with the same name as the domain within the shared SYSVOL folder is not a folder, but a file junction. File junctions look and behave like file system folders, but contain a link pointing to an actual folder. You can view the target of a junction using the DIR command in a console window. The word <JUNCTION> appears before the name of the junction, followed by the name of the target folder enclosed in brackets ([ ]). Group Policy management tools read and write GPTs through the domain junction (Adatum.com) on the SYSVOL share. However, Windows actually stores the GPTs at %SYSTEMROOT%\SYSVOL\domain\policies. This gives the appearance that there are two copies of Group Policy templates.

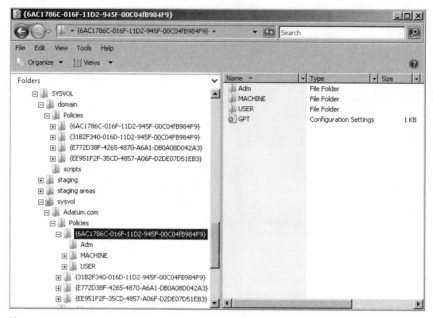

Figure 11-4 Viewing GPT locations on domain controllers.

The Group Policy template contains most of the actual settings for the GPO and contains a number of folders and configuration files, as described in Table 11-2.

Table 11-2 Components of a Group Policy Template

Component	Description
Adm	If you use Windows Vista or Windows Server 2008, this folder will not be used. However, if the Group Policy Object Editor from previous Windows versions is used, this folder will contain a copy of all the Administrative template (.adm) files from the %SystemRoot%\inf folder of the computer that was used to create the GPO.
USER	Contains all of the settings for the User configuration. Depending on what has been configured, this folder may contain the following: ■ Registry.pol—contains the registry settings for any Administrative template configurations. ■ \Applications—contains information that is used for Group Policy software installation. ■ \Documents & Settings—contains information about folder redirection policies configured in the GPO. ■ \Microsoft\IEAK—contains information about Internet Explorer settings configured in the GPO. ■ \Scripts\Logon—contains the actual files used for logon scripts defined in the GPO. ■ \Scripts\Logoff—contains the actual files used for logoff scripts defined in the GPO.

Table 11-2   **Components of a Group Policy Template** *(continued)*

Component	Description
MACHINE	Contains all of the settings for the computer configuration. Depending on what has been configured, this folder may contain the following: ■ Registry.pol—contains the registry settings for any Administrative template configurations. ■ \Applications—contains information that is used for Group Policy software installation. ■ \Microsoft\Windows NT\SecEdit—contains a file called GptTmpl.inf that is used to define various security settings as configured in the Security Settings portion of the GPO. ■ \Scripts\Shutdown—contains the actual files used for shutdown scripts defined in the GPO. ■ \Scripts\Startup—contains the actual files used for computer startup scripts defined in the GPO.
Gpt.ini	The Gpt.ini file is used to store the version number of the GPT and the display name of the associated GPO. The version number provides the ability for client-side extensions to check if the client is up to date with the last processing of the policy settings.

Replication of the Group Policy Object Components

Most Active Directory domain environments contain more than one domain controller. When you create or modify a GPO, the modifications need to replicate from one domain controller to another. It is important to understand that that the components that make up a GPO (mainly the Group Policy container and Group Policy template) rely on different mechanisms to replicate throughout the domain. The GPC is replicated as part of the regular Active Directory replication. The replication of the GPT depends on the domain functional level configured for the domain. If your domain is configured at the Windows Server 2008 functional level, the GPT is replicated by the Distributed File System Replication service (DFS-R). Domains configured at the Windows Server 2003 domain functional level or lower will use the File Replication service (FRS) that has been typically used in previous versions of Windows server.

Group Policy Processing

The Group Policy infrastructure is a client-server architecture that incorporates both server and client components used to apply policy settings to network clients. The server-side extensions (SSEs) are Microsoft Management Console (MMC) snap-ins that you use to administer and configure Group Policy settings using the Group Policy Management console. The client-side extensions (CSEs) interpret the Group Policy settings configured on the server and apply them to the client computer. Figure 11-5 illustrates the interaction between the server and client Group Policy architecture.

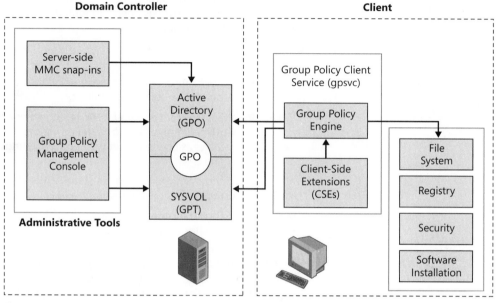

Figure 11-5   Group Policy interaction between the server and client.

How Clients Process GPOs

As shown in Figure 11-5, Windows Vista and Windows Server 2008 computers contain a new service called the Group Policy Client Service (gpsvc). This service takes over the Group Policy processing tasks that used to be part of the Winlogon service in previous versions of Windows.

> ## Direct from the Source: The Group Policy Service
>
> Group Policy now runs as its own service and not within the Winlogon process. This change improves Group Policy reliability by running the Group Policy service as a hosted service under Svchost. Benefits from this change include improved network detection, more efficient Group Policy processing, and reduced memory consumption for each process using Group Policy. Microsoft client-side extensions run within the same process space. However, third-party client-side extensions run under a separate process to improve reliability.
>
> *Mike Stephens*
>
> *Group Policy Technical Writer*
>
> *Management and Solutions Division UA*

Any Windows operating system that is Group Policy-aware contains the client-side extension (CSE) components installed and registered as part of its installation. These extensions consist of a number of Dynamic Link Libraries (DLLs) that are called by the Group Policy engine, which then uses the information provided by both the GPT and GPC to determine which policy settings to apply to the user or computer.

> **Note** The CSE DLLs are stored in the %WinDir%\System32 folder. Other third-party application vendors can also write and provide additional extensions to provide Group Policy management of their applications.

Each CSE DLL uses CSE registration settings that are listed under the following registry key:

```
HKEY_LOCAL_MACHINE\Software\Microsoft\Windows
NT\CurrentVersion\Winlogon\GPExtensions
```

You can view the list of CSEs on a client computer using the Registry Editor (Regedit.exe) as shown in Figure 11-6.

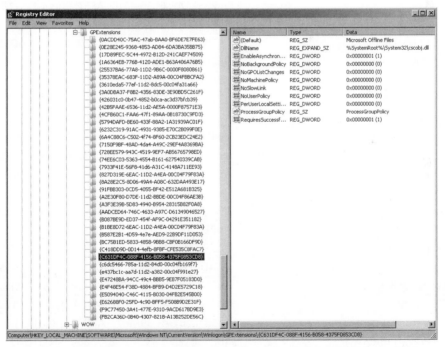

Figure 11-6 Viewing the client-side extensions registered on a Windows client.

In Figure 11-6, you will notice that each CSE is associated with a GUID. These are the GUIDs that are referenced in the GPC object within Active Directory. Each extension has a number of attributes that determine various processing configurations such as whether the user or machine part of the policy is processed (as per the *NoMachinePolicy* and *NoUserPolicy* keys) or if the policy is processed over a slow link (as per the *NoSlowLink* key). You can also determine the associated DLL by viewing the value listed for the *Dllname* key.

A summary of the default client-side extensions and associated GUIDs are provided in Table 11-3.

Table 11-3   Default Client-Side Extensions

Client-Side Extension	GUID
Wireless Group Policy	{0ACDD40C-75AC-47ab-BAA0-BF6DE7E7FE63}
Group Policy Environment	{0E28E245-9368-4853-AD84-6DA3BA35BB75}
Group Policy Local Users and Groups	{17D89FEC-5C44-4972-B12D-241CAEF74509}
Group Policy Device Settings	{1A6364EB-776B-4120-ADE1-B63A406A76B5}
Folder Redirection	{25537BA6-77A8-11D2-9B6C-0000F8080861}
Administrative Templates	{35378EAC-683F-11D2-A89A-00C04FBBCFA2}
Microsoft Disk Quota	{3610eda5-77ef-11d2-8dc5-00c04fa31a66}
Group Policy Network Options	{3A0DBA37-F8B2-4356-83DE-3E90BD5C261F}
QoS Packet Scheduler	{426031c0-0b47-4852-b0ca-ac3d37bfcb39}
Scripts	{42B5FAAE-6536-11d2-AE5A-0000F87571E3}
Internet Explorer Zone Mapping	{4CFB60C1-FAA6-47f1-89AA-0B18730C9FD3}
Group Policy Drive Maps	{5794DAFD-BE60-433f-88A2-1A31939AC01F}
Group Policy Folders	{6232C319-91AC-4931-9385-E70C2B099F0E}
Group Policy Network Shares	{6A4C88C6-C502-4f74-8F60-2CB23EDC24E2}
Group Policy Files	{7150F9BF-48AD-4da4-A49C-29EF4A8369BA}
Group Policy Data Sources	{728EE579-943C-4519-9EF7-AB56765798ED}
Group Policy Ini Files	{74EE6C03-5363-4554-B161-627540339CAB}
Windows Search Group Policy Extension	{7933F41E-56F8-41d6-A31C-4148A711EE93}
Security	{827D319E-6EAC-11D2-A4EA-00C04F79F83A}
Deployed Printer Connections	{8A28E2C5-8D06-49A4-A08C-632DAA493E17}
Group Policy Services	{91FBB303-0CD9-4055-BF42-E512A681B325}
Internet Explorer Branding	{A2E30F80-D7DE-11d2-BBDE-00C04F86AE3B}
Group Policy Folder Options	{A3F3E39B-5D83-4940-B954-28315B82F0A8}
Group Policy Scheduled Tasks	{AADCED64-746C-4633-A97C-D61349046527}
Group Policy Registry	{B087BE9D-ED37-454f-AF9C-04291E351182}
EFS Recovery	{B1BE8D72-6EAC-11D2-A4EA-00C04F79F83A}
802.3 Group Policy	{B587E2B1-4D59-4e7e-AED9-22B9DF11D053}
Group Policy Printers	{BC75B1ED-5833-4858-9BB8-CBF0B166DF9D}
Group Policy Shortcuts	{C418DD9D-0D14-4efb-8FBF-CFE535C8FAC7}
Microsoft Offline Files	{C631DF4C-088F-4156-B058-4375F0853CD8}
Software Installation	{c6dc5466-785a-11d2-84d0-00c04fb169f7}
IP Security	{e437bc1c-aa7d-11d2-a382-00c04f991e27}

Table 11-3   Default Client-Side Extensions *(continued)*

Client-Side Extension	GUID
Group Policy Internet Settings	{E47248BA-94CC-49c4-BBB5-9EB7F05183D0}
Group Policy Start Menu Settings	{E4F48E54-F38D-4884-BFB9-D4D2E5729C18}
Group Policy Regional Options	{E5094040-C46C-4115-B030-04FB2E545B00}
Group Policy Power Options	{E6288F0-25FD-4c90-BFF5-F508B9D2E31F}
Group Policy Applications	{F9C77450-3A41-477E-9310-9ACD617BD9E3}
Enterprise QoS	{FB2CA36D-0B40-4307-821B-A13B252DE56C}

Initial GPO Processing

Whenever a new GPO is created or modified, the policy settings within the GPO are only processed on client computers when specifically requested by the client. This request takes place at various times and may depend upon specific conditions:

- The type of operating system used
- Whether the computer is part of a domain or not
- The location of the computer in Active Directory
- The quality or type of the network connection (such as a slow dial-up or VPN connection)
- Background refresh settings (default refresh times are *5 minutes* for a DC and *90 minutes* + a random variation that can be up to 30 minutes for domain members. *Note:* This is plus only—not minus.)

Group Policy settings are requested and applied to users and computers at various intervals. When a computer starts up, the computer policy settings are applied. When a user logs on to the computer, the user policy settings are then applied. Depending on the type of operating system used, this can take place using synchronous or asynchronous processing methods.

Direct from the Source: Synchronous and Asynchronous Group Policy Processing

Windows Server 2008 provides synchronous and asynchronous Group Policy processing. Asynchronous Group Policy processing (also known as background processing) is the default Group Policy processing mode for Windows Server 2008, Windows Vista, Windows Server 2003, and Windows XP. In this mode, computer and user Group Policy processing takes place in the background, while the computer starts up or the user logs on. This behavior improves logon time, because the computer or user does not wait for Group Policy processing to complete. However, Folder Redirection and Software installation apply only during synchronous Group Policy processing, because applying these policy settings asynchronously (in the background) could result in computer instability or loss of user data. Also, users configured with a roaming profile, home directory, or user logon script do not use asynchronous processing and default to synchronous Group Policy processing.

Unlike asynchronous processing, synchronous Group Policy processing occurs during computer startup and user logon, and must complete before progressing to the next step of the logon process. Computer Group Policy processing must complete before Windows allows a user logon. User Group Policy must complete before Windows provides the user desktop. Periodic Group Policy refreshes always process asynchronously regardless of the Group Policy processing mode.

You can use Group Policy to change the Group Policy processing mode on computers and users by enabling the **Always wait for network at computer startup and logon** policy setting located under Computer Configuration\Policies\Administrative Templates\System\Logon.

Mike Stephens

Group Policy Technical Writer

Management and Solutions

To improve logon times, Windows XP Professional and Windows Vista clients are configured to use the Fast Logon Optimization feature. This feature enables asynchronous processing of Group Policy settings for both computer startup and user logon tasks. As a result, users can start up and log on to a computer faster, while Group Policy settings are applied in the background.

Note   You can modify the Fast Logon Optimization setting by using the Group Policy Management console and configuring the **Always wait for the network at computer startup and logon** policy setting found under Computer Configuration\Policies\Administrative Templates\System\Logon.

It is important to note that Fast Logon Optimization does not take effect under the following conditions and will result in synchronous processing of the Group Policy settings:

- When a user logs on to a new or different computer for the first time
- When a user is configured to use synchronous logon scripts
- When a user is configured to use a roaming user profile or home directory for logon purposes
- When applying software installation policy settings

> **Note**   By default, Windows 2000 and all versions of Windows Server use synchronous processing for applying Group Policy settings and do not support fast logon optimization.

> **Note**   Software Installation and Folder Redirection policies only apply during synchronous policy processing. If you have asynchronous processing enabled, these extensions will take two logons to apply the policy settings. The first logon sets the synchronous processing flag, and then the second logon completes the task.

Background GPO Refreshes

You may decide to make changes to an existing GPO or apply new policy settings after users are already logged on to their computers. To ensure that all new or modified GPO changes are applied, Group Policy uses a background refresh interval.

The background processing interval depends on the operating system used, as explained in the following points:

- For member servers and client workstations, background processing takes place, by default, every *90 minutes* with a random offset of *plus 0 to 30 minutes*. The random offset is in place to ensure that computers do not attempt to refresh their policy settings all at the same time. As a result, any change to a Group Policy setting may take as little as 90 minutes, or as long as 120 minutes, to take effect on users and computers already logged on to the network.

- For domain controllers, by default, Group Policy settings are refreshed every *5 minutes*.

> **Note**   On all operating systems, Security processing follows the same rules as other policy settings; however, security settings are also refreshed every 16 hours on nondomain controllers and every 5 minutes on domain controllers, regardless of whether or not the GPO settings have been changed. This ensures that any security related policy setting is always refreshed with the latest configuration.

It is important to note that the background refresh interval is applied separately for the user and computer parts of the GPO. You can modify the processing interval and the random offset interval by using the Group Policy Management console and configuring the following Group Policy settings:

- *Group Policy refresh interval for computers* found under Computer Configuration\Policies\Administrative Templates\System\Group Policy

- *Group Policy refresh interval for domain controllers* found under Computer Configuration\Policies\Administrative Templates\System\Group Policy

■ *Group Policy refresh interval for users* found under User Configuration\Policies\
Administrative Templates\System\Group Policy

> **Note** Software Installation or Folder Redirection only occurs during computer
> startup or user logon and do not perform a background refresh interval. Also, script files
> referred to in the Scripts CSE and disk quotas do not perform a background refresh.
> Even though the Scripts CSE performs background processing to set up registry pointers,
> the actual script files referred to in the CSE only run at their configured time (such as
> during startup, shutdown, logon, or logoff). Disk quotas only take effect after the
> computer has been restarted.

How GPO History Relates to Group Policy Refresh

Each computer that processes Group Policy settings maintains processing history in the local
registry. This history information is one of the main methods used to determine if a GPO
has changed since its last processing interval. Stored history data includes the associated
GUID of any CSEs that have been processed, a numerical list of GPOs that use the specific
CSE, the display name for each GPO, the path to the GPC and GPT for each GPO, and the
version number of each GPO when it was last processed.

In order for a specific CSE to perform a background refresh, the version number of the
GPO being processed must be larger than the version number registered in the history data. If
the version number between the GPO and the history data is the same, the CSE will not
refresh for that specific GPO.

You can view the Group Policy history data on a computer by using the Registry Editor and
accessing the following registry key:

```
HKEY_LOCAL_MACHINE\SOFTWARE\Microsoft\Windows\CurrentVersion\Group Policy\History
```

Figure 11-7 illustrates the history data stored in the registry of a typical network client. Notice
that the {827D319E-6EAC-11D2-A4EA-00C04F79F83A} CSE has been previously processed
using two GPOs. The one that is highlighted is the Default Domain Controller Policy, which
has a version number of 0x00010001. In order for processing to take place during the next
refresh interval, the version number of the machine or user portions of the GPO must be
larger than the current number. If it is not, then the background refresh will not take place for
that specific portion of the GPO.

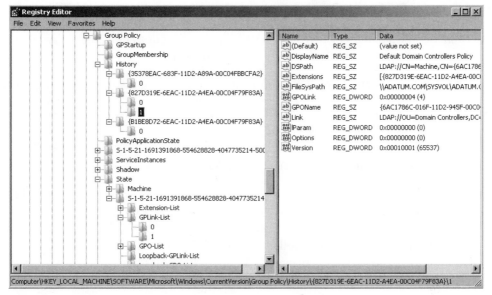

Figure 11-7   Viewing Group Policy processing history data.

How It Works: How GPO Version Numbers Work

The GPO version number in the GPT.INI file of a GPO represents machine and user version numbers combined in one number. The machine version number is always the lower half of the number. The user version number is always the upper half of the number. When converted to a hexadecimal number, the machine version will be displayed in the first four hexadecimal characters. The user version number will be the remaining top hexadecimal characters past the lower four hexadecimal numbers. Located on the companion CD are two scripts that can be used to display user and computer version numbers of a local GPO, as an illustration of how to break these apart using masking. See DisplayMachineVersionLGPO.vbs and DisplayUserVersionLGPO.vbs.

Judith Herman, Group Policy Programming Writer

Windows Enterprise Management Division UA

History information is also used to determine when a GPO has been deleted. During GPO processing, if it has been determined that a specific GPO has been deleted or no longer applies, the policy settings will be removed and in most cases set back to default settings on the network client.

Exceptions to Default Background Processing Interval Times

There may be situations where Group Policy processing does not necessarily follow the default intervals discussed previously. Exceptions include times when:

- The background refresh of Group Policy is triggered on demand from the client.

- Group Policy detects a slow link.

- Loopback processing takes place.

Forcing a Background Refresh of Group Policy

After creating or modifying a GPO, you may want the policy settings to apply right away. To force client machines to request a refresh of Group Policy settings, you use a command-line tool called Gpupdate. You can use Gpupdate to immediately receive any updates to the GPO, assuming that the domain controller used by the client has received the updated GPC and GCT contents and version information. Table 11-4 outlines the syntax and parameters for using the Gpupdate tool.

Table 11-4   Gpupdate Syntax and Parameters

gpupdate [/*target:*{computer | user}] [/*force*] [/*wait:Value*] [/*logoff*] [/*boot*]	
/*target:*{computer | user}	Refreshes only the changes to the Computer settings or the User settings. If you do not provide the computer or user switch, both settings are processed.
/*force*	Refreshes all GPO settings whether they have been changed or not.
/*wait:Value*	Number of seconds that policy processing waits to finish. The default is *600 seconds*. 0 equals *no wait*, and *–1* equals *wait indefinitely*.
/*logoff*	Logs off after the policy refresh has completed. This is re-quired for those client-side extensions that do not process on a background refresh cycle but that do process when the user logs on, such as user Software Installation and Folder Redirection. This option has no effect if there are no extensions called that require the user to log off.
/*boot*	Restarts the computer after the refresh has completed. This is required for those client-side extensions that do not process on a background refresh cycle but that do process when the computer starts up, such as computer Software Installation. This option has no effect if there are no extensions called that require the computer to be restarted.
/?	Displays Gpupdate help.

> **Note**   Gpupdate supersedes the *secedit /refreshpolicy* command that was used in Windows 2000. For Windows 2000, you still need to use secedit to refresh policy settings.

Processing GPOs over Changing Network Conditions

Windows Server 2008 and Windows Vista both introduce a new method to respond to changing network conditions. Network Location Awareness has been incorporated to help compatible applications be aware of and respond to changes to network conditions and resource availability. Network Location Awareness provides several benefits for Group Policy:

- The ability to determine if the network adapter is disabled or disconnected. This provides more efficient startup times and shortens the wait in determining if the network is available.

- Immediately refreshing policy settings whenever domain controller availability returns. For example, computers recovering from hibernation or standby mode will not wait until the next refresh interval to process policy settings. As soon as domain controller availability is detected, policy settings will start a refresh cycle. Group Policy processing will also be triggered by establishing VPN or wireless sessions, successfully exiting quarantine, and docking a laptop into a network-connected docking station. This can potentially increase the level of security on workstations by applying Group Policy changes more quickly.

- The ability to determine bandwidth conditions for GPO processing and removing the reliance on the ICMP protocol (PING). This benefit allows organizations to secure their networks with firewalls and filter the ICMP protocol, while still being able to apply Group Policy.

By default, as long as Group Policy determines that the network bandwidth is 500 kilobits (Kbps) per second or greater, all policy processing will take place as expected. If network conditions are determined to be less than 500 Kbps, only CSEs that are considered to be critical are processed. You can modify this behavior by configuring the **Group Policy slow link detection** policy setting found under Computer Configuration\Policies\Administrative Templates\System\Group Policy or User Configuration\Policies\Administrative Templates\System\Group Policy. Figure 11-8 shows the Properties dialog box of the Group Policy slow link detection policy. If this setting is disabled or not configured, the default *500 Kbps* value is used. You can also disable slow link detection by configuring the connection speed to be *0*.

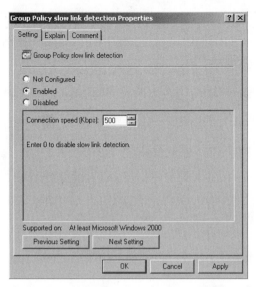

Figure 11-8   Configuring the **Group Policy slow link detection** policy setting.

How It Works: Group Policy Slow Link Detection

The Group Policy service determines link speed by using the Network Location Awareness (NLA) service to sample the current TCP traffic between the client and the domain controller. This sampling occurs during the preprocessing phase of Group Policy, when the Group Policy service relies on communicating with a domain controller to retrieve computer- and user-specific information and Group Policy objects within scope of the computer or user. The Group Policy service asks the NLA service to start sampling TCP bandwidth on the network interface that hosts the domain controller soon after the Group Policy service discovers a domain controller. The Group Policy service continues through the preprocessing phase by communicating with the domain controller to discover the role of the current computer (member or domain controller), the logged on user, and Group Policy objects within scope of the computer or user. Then, the Group Policy service requests the NLA service to stop sampling the TCP traffic and provide an estimated bandwidth between the computer and the domain controller, based on the sampling. Group Policy considers a link slow when the NLA service sampling is lower than 500 Kbps. Administrators can use a policy setting to define a slow link for the purpose of applying Group Policy.

Mike Stephens

Group Policy Technical Writer

Management and Solutions Division UA

For troubleshooting purposes, it is important to understand how each CSE is affected by slow link detection. Table 11-5 provides a summary for each CSE.

Table 11-5   Slow Link Processing Defaults

Client -Side Extension	Default Slow Link Behavior
Administrative Templates	Processed (cannot be disabled)
Software Installation	Not processed
Security	Processed (cannot be disabled)
Folder Redirection	Not processed
Scripts	Not processed
IP Security	Processed (cannot be disabled)
Internet Explorer Maintenance and Zone Mapping	Processed
Microsoft Disk Quota	Not processed (however currently cached quota settings are enforced)
EFS Recovery	Processed (cannot be disabled)
Windows Search Group Policy Extension	Processed
QoS Packet Scheduler and Enterprise QoS	Processed (cannot be disabled)
Wireless Group Policy	Processed
Deployed Printer Connections	Not processed
802.3 Group Policy	Processed
Microsoft Offline Files	Processed
Software Restriction Policies	Processed
Group Policy Preferences	Processed

Note   You can change the default slow link processing behavior for many of the CSEs listed in Table 11-5 by modifying the appropriate policy setting located at Computer Configuration\Policies\Administrative Templates\System\Group Policy. For example, Figure 11-9 shows the Internet Explorer Maintenance policy processing CSE enabled to allow processing over a slow network connection.

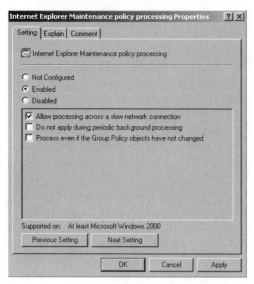

Figure 11-9 Configuring Group Policy slow link processing behavior.

Group Policy Loopback Processing

Typically, when a user logs on to any computer, policy settings applicable to that user are applied. However, there may be situations in which you do not want this to happen. When you enable loopback processing, the computer settings will remain the same no matter who logs on to the machine.

Loopback processing can be configured using the User Group Policy Loopback Processing Mode option in the Computer Configuration\Policies\Administrative Templates\System\Group Policy container. Figure 11-10 shows the configuration options.

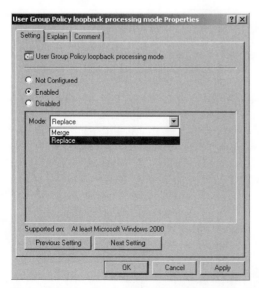

Figure 11-10 Configuring Group Policy loopback processing.

When loopback processing is enabled, you have two configuration options. First, the Merge mode gathers the list of GPOs for the user during the logon process. Next, the GPOs for the computer account are gathered. Finally, the list of GPOs from the computer account is appended to the list of GPOs for the user, causing the computer's GPOs to have a higher precedence than the user's GPOs.

The Replace mode does not gather the GPOs for the user account. Only the list of GPOs based on the computer object is processed. The User Configuration settings within this list are applied to the user.

Group Policy loopback processing is useful in a number of scenarios. One of the most common is when you need to lock down a computer that is located in a public place. For example, you might have a computer in a public reception area and allow customers to log on to the computer. Because the computer is publicly accessible, you might want to ensure that the computer is always locked down, regardless of who logs on to the computer. You can enable lockdown by placing the public computers into an appropriate organizational unit (OU) and configuring a restrictive group policy for that OU. You can then configure loopback processing for that OU. Now when a user logs on to the computer, the user will get the restrictive desktop defined for the public computer through the use of Administrative templates and loopback processing.

Implementing Group Policy

Windows Server 2008 introduces a number of changes to the way Group Policy is implemented in Active Directory. A major change to note is that Group Policy is no longer managed using the Active Directory Users And Computers console. The standard tool for managing Group Policy is the Group Policy Management console (GPMC), which is now available as an installable feature within the Windows Server 2008 operating system and Windows Vista SP1. The GPMC provides a single tool for deploying, managing, editing, and reporting on Group Policy settings throughout the entire enterprise.

When the Active Directory Domain Services (AD DS) server role is installed, the Group Policy Management feature is automatically included, which provides access to the GPMC. You can also install the Group Policy Management feature on any member server by using the Add Features Wizard found in the Server Manager console.

> **Note** Windows Vista includes the GPMC installed with the operating system, which is accessed by typing **gpmc.msc** at the Start Search box or command prompt. Note that if you install Windows Vista SP1, the GPMC is removed. It can then be installed with the Remote Server Administration Tools (RSAT) package available from the Microsoft Download Center.

After the GPMC is installed, it can be accessed by clicking the Start button, pointing to Administrative Tools, and then clicking Group Policy Management. You can also start the GPMC by typing **gpmc.msc** at the Run dialog box or command line. Figure 11-11 shows the interface for the GPMC.

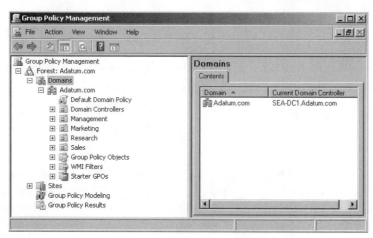

Figure 11-11   Managing Group Policy using the GPMC.

GPMC Overview

As shown in Figure 11-11, the GPMC consists of a number of nodes that provide various levels of functionality. The first-level node indicates the forest that is currently in focus for Group Policy management. If you plan on managing Group Policy settings for multiple forests, you can add additional forest nodes by right-clicking the *Group Policy Management* node and then clicking Add Forest. The Add Forest dialog box provides a field to enter the name of a domain in the forest that you want to add. As long as a trust relationship is in place to the new domain, the connection will be established along with forest information to be displayed in the GPMC.

When the *Forest* node is expanded, four additional nodes are displayed. The following list provides an explanation about each node:

- **Domains**   The *Domains* node provides a list of domains that are being administered for Group Policy. By default, only your logon domain is shown; however, you can add additional domains by right-clicking the *Domains* node and then clicking Show Domains. The Show Domains dialog box provides the ability to select or remove domains from the GPMC.

- **Sites**   The *Sites* node provides a list of sites associated with the Active Directory forest. By default, *Sites* are hidden from the console, but can be added by right-clicking the *Sites* node and then clicking Show Sites. The Show Sites dialog box provides the ability to select or remove sites from the GPMC.

 Note   To actually create sites for specific subnets, you will need to use the Active Directory Sites And Services tool.

- **Group Policy Modeling**   The *Group Policy Modeling* node provides the ability to use the Group Policy Modeling Wizard to create and save simulated scenarios related to the application and processing of Group Policy within your environment. You can also use this to evaluate "What if?" scenarios, such as moving computers or users to different containers and applying different filtering options, such as security groups and Windows Management Instrumentation (WMI) filters. *Note:* The modeling tool doesn't take into account any local policy settings on a machine. So your results may differ from the actual machine results after deployment if you've deployed LGPOs in your environment.

■ **Group Policy Results**   The *Group Policy Results* node provides the ability to use the Group Policy Results Wizard to determine current results of policy processing on users and computers within the Active Directory environment.

When the GPMC is started, by default all administration takes place on the domain controller that holds the primary domain controller (PDC) emulator role. In most cases, you should accept this default to reduce the possibility of multiple administrators making incompatible changes to the Group Policy settings. However, if the PDC emulator is not available when you want to make a change, you are provided with a choice of which domain controller to connect to. If you have to work over a slow link to get to the PDC emulator, you can repoint to a local domain controller. However, there may be a lag in seeing newly created containers or objects when doing this. Another workaround is to use remote desktop to terminal into the domain controller hosting the PDC emulator role and configure Group Policy settings directly on the domain controller.

As Figure 11-11 illustrates, you can verify which domain controller is in focus by viewing the Current Domain Controller column on the Contents tab of the *Domains* node. You can also modify which domain controller the GPMC is focused upon by right-clicking the domain name and then clicking Change Domain Controller. Figure 11-12 shows the choices that are available in the Change Domain Controller dialog box.

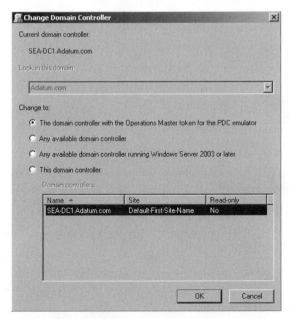

Figure 11-12   Changing the domain controller focus in the GPMC.

Using the GPMC to Create and Link GPOs

Creating a Group Policy object technically consists of two separate tasks. The GPO must be created and configured with appropriate policy settings, and then it must be linked to the domain, site, or OU container within Active Directory.

> **Note**   A single GPO can be linked to multiple containers at various levels throughout Active Directory in a forest. However, due to potential performance issues, it is generally not recommended to cross-link GPOs to other domains.

Your IT management strategy or personal preference will dictate how you create and link GPOs throughout your Active Directory environment. One method is to first create all required GPOs in the Group Policy Objects container without actually linking them to any domain, site, or OU location. The main advantage to this method is that you can have one group of administrators in charge of planning and creating GPOs for a given domain, while a second delegated group may be in charge of actually linking the configured GPOs to specific locations throughout Active Directory. You can create and link the GPOs using separate tasks as outlined in the following steps:

1. Expand the *Forest* node and the *Domains* node. You will also have to expand the node that represents your domain name.

2. Select the Group Policy Objects container. Notice that all GPOs that have been created in the domain are listed in the details pane.

3. Right-click the Group Policy Objects container and click New.

4. In the New GPO dialog box, type the name for the GPO. You can also specify a Source Starter GPO. A Starter GPO is a preconfigured GPO that contains policy settings that you can use as a starter template for your new GPO. Figure 11-13 shows the New GPO dialog box.

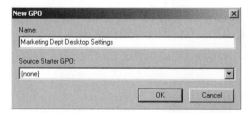

Figure 11-13   Creating a new GPO.

5. Click OK to close the New GPO dialog box. Notice that the new GPO is now listed in the Group Policy Objects container.

6. To link the GPO to the domain, a site, or a specific OU, right-click the target container and then click Link an Existing GPO. The Select GPO dialog box opens as shown in Figure 11-14.

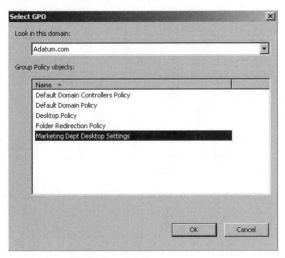

Figure 11-14   Linking a GPO.

7. Select the GPO to be linked and then click OK.

8. Select the container to which you linked the GPO. The details pane provides information about the linked GPO, such as the link order, whether or not the link is enforced, and the status of the link and GPO.

A second method is to create a GPO for a selected domain, site, or OU, and have it automatically linked to that specific location. The main advantage to this method is that both the creation and linking is completed in one step that provides immediate application of the policy settings to the target location. To create a linked GPO, right-click the target location (domain, site, OU) and then click Create A GPO In This Domain, And Link It Here. You can specify a name and source starter GPO with the additional benefit of having the GPO automatically linked to the target location.

> **Note**   The Create A GPO In This Domain, And Link It Here option is not available for sites. You must precreate the GPO and then use the Link An Existing GPO option for sites.

Modifying the Scope of GPO Processing

The scope of management of a GPO can be can be modified by configuring a number of settings, such as:

- Modifying the Link order
- Disabling the GPO or GPO link

- Enforcing or blocking a GPO link
- Filtering the application of a GPO using security groups or Windows Management Instrumentation (WMI) filters

Modifying the Link Order of GPO Links

As mentioned previously, Group Policy settings are, by default, inherited from top-level containers to lower-level containers. Recall that as a computer starts up, or a user logs on, policy settings are applied in the following order:

1. **Local group policy**   The first policy setting to be applied is always the local group policy located on the local computer.

2. **GPOs assigned at the site level**   The second policy setting to be applied is any GPO linked to the site object in Active Directory.

3. **GPOs assigned at the domain level**   The next policy setting to be processed is any GPO assigned to the domain object in Active Directory.

4. **GPOs assigned at the OU level**   Finally, if the domain contains multiple levels of OUs, the Group Policy settings for the higher-level OUs are applied first and the Group Policy settings linked to lower-level OUs are applied next.

Quite often you may have more than one GPO linked to any of the Active Directory levels. In this case, the link order determines the order in which the GPOs are applied. You can view and modify the link order for a specific container, as shown in Figure 11-15. The point to remember here is that GPOs are processed from the bottom of the list to the top. In other words, a higher-numbered link order will process first, followed by lower-numbered link orders. For example, Figure 11-15 shows three GPOs linked to the Sales OU. In this case, the Scripts Policy would be applied first, followed by the Folder Redirection Policy, and then the Desktop Policy. Any conflicting policy settings will be overwritten by settings configured in a GPO configured at a lower link order (in this case the Desktop Policy). You can modify the Link order by selecting the GPO link and then clicking the arrows located on the left side of the details pane.

To gain a better understanding of how multiple GPOs will process policy settings, you can also click the Group Policy Inheritance tab. The Precedence column shows the order that GPOs will be processed for a given site, domain, or OU, as shown in Figure 11-16. A higher-numbered GPO will be processed before lower-numbered GPOs, which means the lower-numbered GPOs will have precedence over conflicting settings.

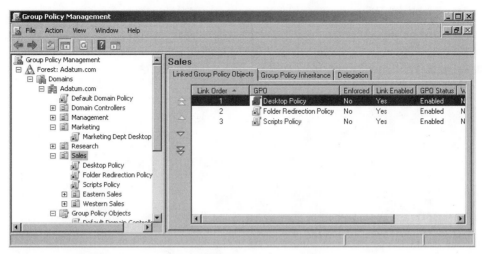

Figure 11-15   Modifying GPO link order.

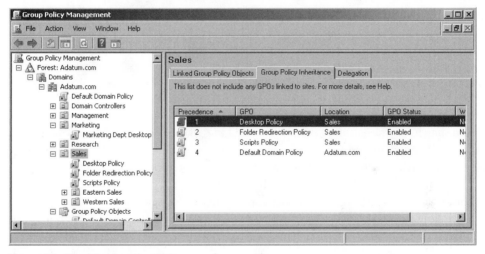

Figure 11-16   Viewing the GPO precedence order.

Enabling and Disabling Policy Processing

Group Policy objects can be enabled or disabled by modifying the GPO Status located on the Details tab of a specific GPO. Figure 11-17 shows the options available for changing the GPO status, and the options and their uses are listed here:

- **All settings disabled**   This option disables the GPO and stops processing any configured policy settings.

- **Computer configuration settings disabled**   This option only disables the computer settings of the GPO. You may want to disable this section if there are no settings to be processed related to the computer configuration within the GPO.

■ **Enabled**   This option enables the processing of the entire GPO.

■ **User configuration settings disabled**   This option disables only the user settings of the GPO. You may want to disable this section if there are no settings to be processed related to the computer configuration within the GPO.

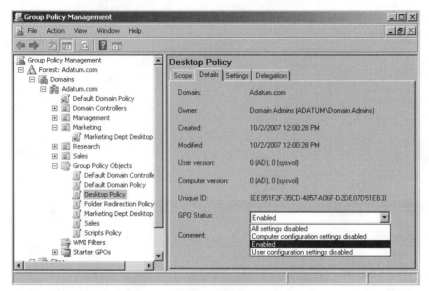

Figure 11-17   Modifying the GPO status.

You may have a situation in which you need to disable GPO processing for a specific OU; however, you cannot disable the entire GPO itself, because it is linked to other containers within Active Directory. In this situation, you have the option to just disable the GPO link associated with the OU. You can do this by right-clicking the GPO link associated with the container (OU, domain, site) and then removing the check mark next to Link Enabled. Removing the check mark disables the link for only the selected container; all other GPO links to other containers still process as expected.

Blocking and Enforcing GPO Processing

There may be times that you will want to block inheritance so that no policy settings are applied from higher levels of Active Directory. For example, you may have a domain-based policy setting that removes the *Run* command from all computers. By default, this policy setting will apply to all computers within the domain. However, there may be some users that require the *Run* command, such as the IT administrators or Help Desk groups. To override the domain-based policy, you can ensure that these groups are contained within their own OUs. You can then block policy inheritance by right-clicking the OU and then selecting Block Inheritance. When Block Inheritance is enabled, only policy settings linked directly to the container will apply.

> **Note**   When an OU is configured to block inheritance, a blue circle with an exclamation point is placed on top of the container to remind you that block inheritance is enabled from that point. If the container has any child containers, inheritance will continue from that point unless otherwise configured.

Figure 11-18 illustrates the Marketing OU with Block Inheritance enabled.

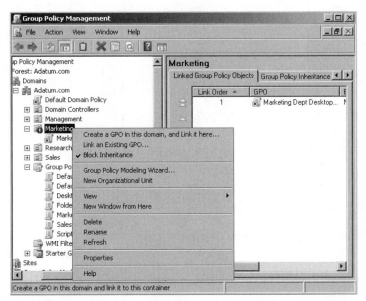

Figure 11-18   Blocking Group Policy inheritance.

On the other hand, you may also have mandatory policy settings that must be applied to every user or computer within the Active Directory structure. To prevent administrators from blocking mandatory inherited policies, you can enforce inheritance. When a GPO link is enforced, all policy settings configured in the enforced GPO will be applied regardless of the Block Inheritance setting. To enforce GPO processing, right-click the GPO link associated with the container from which you want to start the enforcement from and then click Enforced. When a GPO link is configured to be enforced, a lock icon will appear to remind you that the link is enforced. You can also view the Group Policy Inheritance tab on child container objects to verify an enforced GPO link. Figure 11-19 shows the Marketing OU's Group Policy Inheritance tab. Notice that the Default Domain Policy has been enforced even though Block Inheritance has been enabled (as illustrated by the exclamation mark).

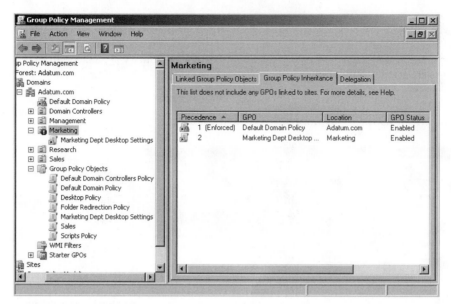

Figure 11-19 Viewing Group Policy enforcement.

Filtering GPO Processing Using Security Groups and WMI

Another way to modify the scope of GPO processing is to filter the application of Group Policy settings. This can be accomplished by implementing Security Filtering or linking a WMI filter to a GPO.

Overview of Security Filtering   By default, when you create a GPO, the policy settings are applied to all authenticated users. You can view this setting by selecting a Group Policy object and then clicking the Scope tab. As you can see in Figure 11-20, the Security Filtering Section shows that the policy settings in the Desktop Policy GPO will apply to any member of the Authenticated Users group (which includes standard users, computers, and administrators).

You can use Security Filtering to target specific GPO processing to specific security groups, users, or computers.

You can specify which users or computers will be affected by the GPO by modifying which accounts are listed in the Security Filtering list. To configure this setting, first remove the Authenticated Users group from the list. Then add the appropriate accounts to the list by clicking the Add button. Although you can add any security principal, it is a best practice to always use Active Directory security groups rather than individual user or computer accounts.

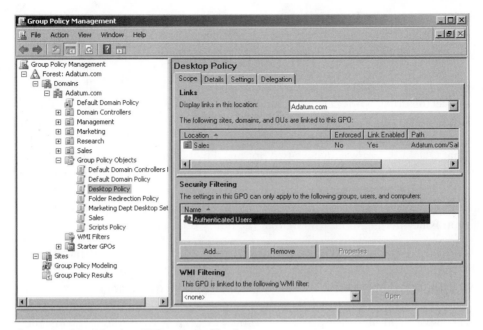

Figure 11-20   Viewing GPO security filtering.

 Note   You can view the actual Access Control List by clicking the Delegation tab and then clicking the Advanced button. On the Access Control List, you will notice that each security principle that you add to the Security Filtering list will be assigned the Allow Read and Allow Apply group policy permissions for the GPO. Figure 11-21 shows the Marketing Dept with Read and Apply group policy permissions.

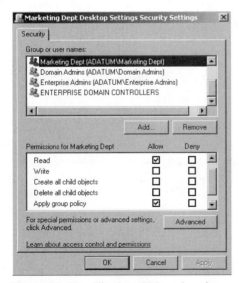

Figure 11-21   Filtering GPOs using the access control list.

The option to apply Group Policy settings to a selective security group is useful in a number of different scenarios. For example, you might need to install a particular software package for users who belong to a common security group, but whose user accounts are scattered in a variety of OUs throughout the domain. To install this application using Group Policy, you can link the GPO to a parent container object that incorporates all of the user accounts (such as the domain object) and then modify the security filter of the GPO so that the policy applies only to the specified group that should receive the software package. In another scenario, you might have a GPO linked to an OU that you do not want to apply to all users in that OU. In this case, you have two options. First, you can create a group that contains all the user accounts that require the Group Policy settings and configure the Apply Group Policy permission for that group only. Second, you can create a group that contains all the user accounts that do not require the Group Policy settings and use the Deny setting on the Apply Group Policy permission to ensure that the policy does not apply to these users.

Using WMI Filters with GPOs   Windows Server 2008 also provides the option to filter the application of Group Policy settings based on Windows Management Instrumentation (WMI) filters. The WMI filters, which are written in WMI query language (WQL), can be used to more precisely specify which computers should receive Group Policy settings. For example, you can use WMI filters to specify that a software package should only be installed on a computer with more than 200 MB of available disk space or on a computer with more than 512 MB of RAM. WMI Filters are supported on Windows XP, Windows Server 2003, Windows Vista, and Windows Server 2008. WMI filters are ignored on earlier versions of Windows. This means that on earlier operating systems, all GPOs with WMI filters will always be applied regardless of the WMI query assigned.

The first step in using WMI filters is to create or obtain a WQL query that meets your requirements for the GPO. For example, you may want to deploy a new application using Group Policy software installation only to computers that have at least 100 MB free on the C: drive. The following syntax provides the WQL query that can be used for this scenario:

```
Select * from Win32_LogicalDisk where FreeSpace > 104857600 AND Caption = "C:"
```

Scriptomatic.exe is a tool used for creating WQL queries, which can then be copy and pasted into a WMI filter for Group Policy. Refer to the "Additional Resources" section of this chapter for links to information about this utility.

The second step is to create the WMI filter using the GPMC. To do this, right-click the *WMI Filters* node and then click New. You can then provide a Name, Description, and the associated query for the new WMI filter, as shown in Figure 11-22.

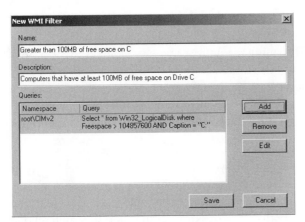

Figure 11-22 Filtering GPOs using WMI Filters.

The final step is to associate the WMI filter with a Group Policy object. To do so, select the Group Policy object that is to be filtered and then configure the WMI filter at the bottom of the Scope tab as shown in Figure 11-23.

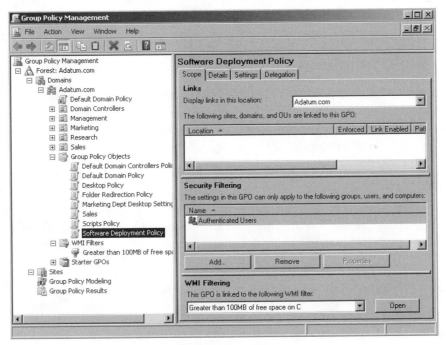

Figure 11-23 Associating a WMI filter with a GPO.

Group Policy and OU Design

As discussed in Chapter 5, "Designing the Active Directory Domain Services Structure," one of the factors in creating the OU design is the consideration of Group Policy processing. Such consideration is especially important at the lower-level OUs, where the Group Policy requirements are probably the most important factor influencing the design. In most cases, the design should take advantage of the default inheritance of the policy settings.

Even if using default inheritance is one of your design goals, most large enterprises are simply too complex to allow its use in every situation. For example, you might create an OU design based on business units or departments because most users in the same business unit are likely to require the same desktop settings and the same set of applications. However, some of the users in each business unit are also likely to be part of a team that crosses department lines, either permanently or for specific projects. The other departments might have different software requirements, so the user might need access to both applications. Because these types of complex configurations are common in most enterprises, Windows Server 2008 provides the options described in this section for modifying the default application of Group Policy settings.

Delegating the Administration of GPOs

As discussed in Chapter 9, "Delegating the Administration of Active Directory Domain Services," one of the biggest advantages of Active Directory is the option to delegate many of the administrative tasks within the organization. The management of Group Policy is no exception; you can also delegate the management of this important administrative tool.

There are three options for delegating the administration of Group Policy. First, you can delegate permission to create, delete, and modify the GPOs. By default, only the Domain Admins group, Group Policy Creator Owners group, and the System account have this right. The Group Policy Creator Owners group has an additional restriction in that the members of this group have permission to modify the settings only on GPOs that they actually create.

You can grant the right to create and delete GPOs to any other group or user by selecting the Delegation tab on the Group Policy Objects container and then clicking Add. Figure 11-24 shows the Group Policy Objects Delegation tab.

The second option for delegating the administration of Group Policy is to delegate the right to manage Group Policy links. This option does not give the administrators permission to modify any GPO, but it does give them the right to add or remove GPO links for a container object. The easiest way to grant this level of permission is to use the Delegation Of Control Wizard. In the Active Directory Users And Computers console, right-click the object that you want another user or group to control and then click Delegate Control to start the wizard.

When you start the wizard at an OU level, one of the standard tasks that can be delegated is the permission to Manage Group Policy links. Figure 11-25 shows the interface.

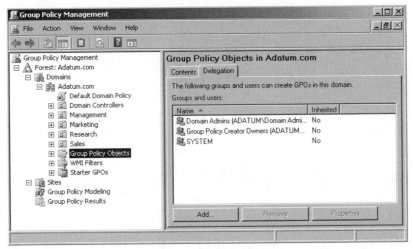

Figure 11-24   Delegating the permission to manage Group Policy objects.

The third way to delegate the administration of Group Policy is to give users the right to generate Resultant Set of Policy (RSoP) information. Again, you can use the Delegation Of Control Wizard to grant the right to generate the RSoP tool in either logging or planning mode. Figure 11-25 also shows this delegation option.

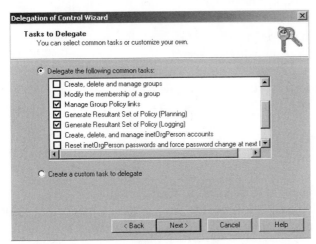

Figure 11-25   Delegating the permission to manage Group Policy links and RSoP.

You can also use the GPMC to delegate the right to manage GPO links, Group Policy Modeling, and Group Policy results. The Delegation tab located on the domain or OU containers provide the ability to add or remove users and groups and apply specific permission, as shown in Figure 11-26.

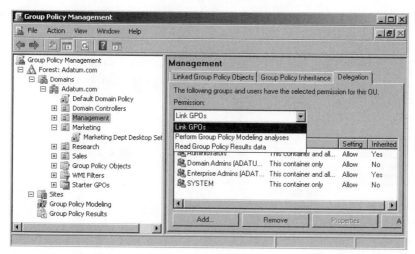

Figure 11-26 Using the GPMC to delegate permission to manage Group Policy links and RSoP.

Implementing Group Policy Between Domains and Forests

You can use Group Policy to enforce policy settings between domains and even between trusted forests. In both cases, there are some significant limitations and issues that you need to deal with before implementing such policy settings.

After creating a GPO in a Windows Server 2008 Active Directory, you can link that GPO to any site, domain, or OU in the forest. The primary limitation with linking GPOs between domains is that the GPOs are stored only on the domain controllers in the domain where they are created. If you choose to link a GPO to a container in a different domain, you might need to deal with significant network bandwidth and security issues. For example, if a GPO is linked to an OU in a different domain than the one where the GPO was created, all the computers in the OU must be able to connect to a domain controller in the GPO's source domain to download the Group Policy. If one of these domain controllers is in the same site as the client computers, network bandwidth will not be significantly impacted. However, if all domain controllers that have a copy of the GPO are in a different site across a slow wide area network (WAN) connection, the application of the policy settings can be very slow and can seriously impact the available bandwidth. In addition, if the users from one domain must apply a GPO from another domain, the users and computers from the destination domain must have Read access to both the GPC in Active Directory and the GPT in the SYSVOL folder. In most cases, it is better practice to create GPOs for each domain rather than share one GPO across multiple domains.

These issues also apply when using Group Policy between trusted forests. Windows Server 2008 Active Directory provides the option to share GPOs between trusted forests. This option can be useful when users travel between company locations that are in separate forests. In this scenario, users logging on to a computer in another forest can still have Group Policy settings from their home domain applied. Other functionality that is available between forests includes the following:

- The shares used for software distribution can be in a separate forest.
- Logon scripts can be located and read from a domain controller in another forest.
- Redirected folders and roaming user profile files can be located on a computer in another forest.

In each case, the network bandwidth and security issues might mean that you would rather implement separate GPOs in each forest than between forests.

Managing Group Policy Objects

The GPMC provides a number of tasks that can be performed to manage and maintain your Group Policy infrastructure. Some of these tasks include:

- Backing up and restoring Group Policy objects
- Copying Group Policy objects
- Importing settings from a Group Policy object
- Modeling and reporting Group Policy results

Backing Up and Restoring GPOs

The security and management of your Active Directory infrastructure relies heavily on Group Policy. Because of this, it is critical that you plan for and maintain a backup strategy for the Group Policy objects within your environment. The GPMC provides a backup feature that allows you to backup individual GPOs or the entire set of GPOs configured within your domain. The backup function can also be used to export GPOs to be migrated or imported into other domains or Active Directory Forests.

The GPMC backup feature backs up GPOs into a folder location specified during the backup process. In order to perform the backup, you must have Read permissions on the GPO and Write permissions on the folder that the GPO backup will use as a target location.

Important   It is recommended that the target folder be secured and only allow authorized administrators to access the backed-up GPOs.

Use the following steps to back up an individual GPO or all GPOs within the domain:

1. In the GPMC, navigate to the Group Policy Objects container.
2. To back up all of the GPOs in the domain, right-click Group Policy Objects and then click Back Up All. To only back up a single GPO, right-click the GPO and then click Back Up. Both methods result in the dialog box shown in Figure 11-27.

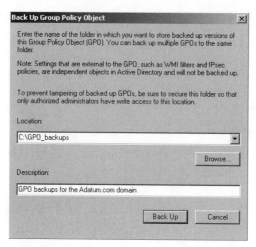

Figure 11-27   Using the GPMC to back up GPOs.

3.   In the Location field, enter the path to the folder that will store the GPO backup. You can also provide a description related to the backup task.

4.   Click the Back Up button to start the backup process.

The GPMC also allows you to manage and restore backed up GPOs. Technically, each GPO is backed up separately with version information containing a backup time stamp and description. This allows you to restore either the most recent version of a specific GPO or previous versions if necessary. In order to restore a GPO, you must have privileges to create GPOs in the domain and Read permissions on the folder that contains the backed-up GPOs.

Use the following steps to restore GPOs within the domain:

1.   In the GPMC, navigate to the Group Policy Objects container.

2.   To manage the backed-up GPOs, right-click the Group Policy Objects container and then click Manage Backups. The Manage Backups dialog box opens, as shown in Figure 11-28.

3.   Select the GPO to be restored and then click the Restore button. You can also use the View Settings button to view a report on what settings have been configured within the GPO.

> **Note**   You can also right-click an individual GPO and then click Restore from Backup. This will start the Restore Group Policy Object Wizard. The only difference is that the wizard will only restore the GPO that you had selected and will not show the Manage Backups dialog box.

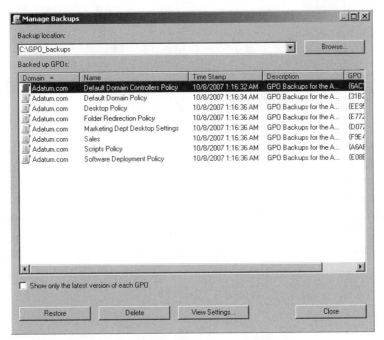

Figure 11-28   Using the GPMC to manage GPO backups.

Copying Group Policy Objects

The Copy feature built into the GPMC provides an easy way to migrate Group Policy settings from one domain to another. In order to perform copy operations, you need to have Read permissions on the GPO in the source domain and Write permissions in the target domain to create the new GPO. To copy a GPO, just right-click the GPO and then click Copy. You can then navigate to the destination domain, right-click the Group Policy Objects container, and then click Paste. The cross-domain copying wizard will appear to assist in the copy process. The wizard may ask for the configuration of a migration table to complete the copy process to another domain. A migration table is used to translate specific GPO information that may not be suitable in the new domain. For example, you may have a GPO that is configured to provide folder redirection for users in the source domain. When you attempt to copy the GPO to a new target domain, a migration table can be used to specify new URL information specific to the folder redirection needs in the new domain.

Importing Group Policy Object Settings

In some situations, you may need to copy Group Policy object configurations between two disconnected locations. For example, to test Group Policy in a lab environment, you may be required to implement the approved GPO configurations into your production environment. Your first step is to create a backup of the GPOs, as described in "Backing Up and Restoring GPOs" earlier in this chapter. You can then copy the backup files to a removable drive or shared network location. The final step is to create a new GPO or overwrite an existing GPO by importing the backed-up GPO settings from the removable drive or network location. In this scenario, a migration table may also have to be used to specify domain-specific settings such as security groups and UNC paths.

Modeling and Reporting Group Policy Results

Windows Server 2008 collects Group Policy processing data and stores the information in a WMI database on the local computer. This information contains the list, content, and logging information for each GPO processed and can be used to determine how policy settings are applied to users and computers. Architecturally, this feature is called the Resultant Set of Policy (RSoP). RSoP can be run in two modes—logging mode and planning mode. *Logging mode* provides information on the overall results of policy settings applied to an existing user or computer. *Planning mode* provides a method to simulate the results of policy settings that may be applied to a user or computer based on specific variables.

The GPMC integrates the logging and planning modes of RSoP. Planning mode is referred to as Group Policy Modeling, and logging mode is referred to as Group Policy Results.

Group Policy Modeling

Group Policy Modeling provides the ability to perform what-if scenarios based upon your current Group Policy infrastructure. For example, you may have a user that is transferring to a different department within your organization. You may want to proactively determine what may happen to the user object when it is moved from its current OU to the new departmental OU. The Group Policy Modeling Wizard can be used to simulate and report on the policy setting results without you having to perform the actual move to the real account.

To use Group Policy Modeling, you must have the Generate resultant set of policy permission on the domain or OU that contains the objects on which you want to run the query. A domain controller with at least Windows Server 2003 must also be present within the environment in order to provide the appropriate information for the query.

You can start a modeling scenario using two methods. The first method is to use Active Directory Users And Computers by right-clicking the domain or OU, pointing to All Tasks, and then clicking Resultant Set of Policy (Planning). The second method is to use the GPMC. You can access the wizard by right-clicking Group Policy Modeling and then clicking Group Policy Modeling Wizard. Either method will result in an initial dialog box that allows you to provide the user and computer information that will take part in the simulation. Figure 11-29 shows that the user ADatum\Don and the computer ADatum\SEA-CL1 will take part in the modeling simulation.

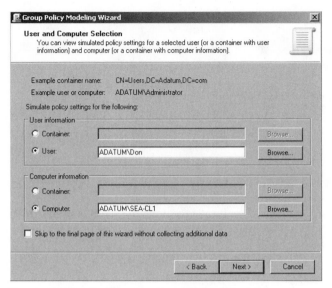

Figure 11-29   Configuring Group Policy Modeling.

As you work through the modeling scenario, the wizard will ask for a number of variables, such as:

- Do you want to simulate a slow network connection?

- Do you want to enable loopback processing?

- The new location to be simulated for both the user and computer accounts

- Changes to the user's security group memberships

- Changes to the computer's security group memberships

- WMI filters to be linked for users and computers

The results of the Group Policy Modeling scenario are displayed in an extensive report format, as shown in Figure 11-30.

The Group Policy Modeling report contains three tabs that together present detailed information about the results of the scenario. The Summary tab provides general details for the Computer configuration and User configuration, including the applied GPO and denied GPO based upon the simulation. The Settings tab provides a list of all settings that have been applied by the simulated GPOs. The Query tab provides statistical information such as when the query was last run, which domain controller processed the simulation, and the criteria used for the simulation.

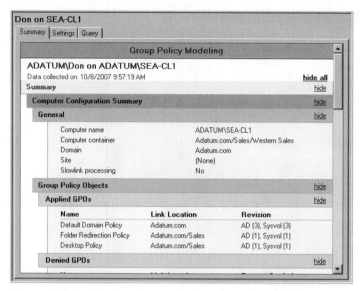

Figure 11-30 Viewing the results of Group Policy Modeling.

Group Policy Results

Group Policy Results provides a useful method for troubleshooting the application of policy settings for a specific user or computer. For example, if the wrong policy settings are continually being applied to a user, Group Policy Results can help determine which policy settings are being applied and the order of application.

Group Policy Results can be started from either the Active Directory Users And Computers console or the GPMC. You can use Active Directory Users And Computers by right-clicking a specific computer or user object, pointing to All Tasks, and then clicking Resultant Set of Policy (Logging). In the GPMC, you can access the wizard by right-clicking Group Policy Results and then clicking Group Policy Results Wizard. When you start the wizard, you indicate which computer (local or remote) to query. You will then be provided with a list of user accounts that are cached on the machine for which you can obtain policy settings.

> **Caution** The preferred way to check for the resultant set of policy settings is to use the GPMC. The tool available within Active Directory Users And Computers may not show all results for all extensions.

The Group Policy Results report contains three tabs related to the GPO processing results. The Summary tab provides general summary about which GPOs were applied and denied for the user and computer being tested. The Settings tab provides a list of all settings that have been applied with Group Policy. The Policy Events tab provides event information related to Group Policy that has been reported on the target machine.

To successfully obtain Group Policy result information, consider the following requirements:

- You must have Read Group Policy Results data permission on the domain or OU that contains the computer or user, or you must be a member of a local administrator's group on the target computer.

- The computer being queried must be Windows XP, Windows Vista, Windows 2003, or Windows Server 2008.

- The computer being queried must be turned on and connected to the network.

- The Windows Management Instrumentation service must be turned on.

- To perform remote generation of Group Policy results, the Remote Administration exception must be enabled on the target computer's Windows Firewall settings.

- The user that you are troubleshooting or performing a query about must have logged on to the target computer at least once.

Note   You can save the results for both Group Policy Modeling and Group Policy Results as a stand-alone interactive Web-based report. This provides an easy way to distribute modeling or processing information to others within your organization. The only requirement is that Microsoft Internet Explorer 6 or later be used for viewing the saved reports.

Note   Group Policy results can also be obtained based on a local or remote computer using a command-line tool called Gpresult. For more information, type **gpresult** at the command prompt.

How It Works: Gpresult.exe

Gpresult.exe displays Group Policy settings and Resultant Set of Policy (RSoP) for a user or a computer. Use the following syntax on a local computer:

```
gpresult [/s computer [/u domain\user [/p password]]] [/scope {user|computer}]
[/user TargetUserName] [/r | /v | /z] [/x | /h filename [/f]]
```

Parameters:

Parameter	Description
/s <computer>	Specifies the name or IP address of a remote computer. Do not use backslashes. The default is the local computer.
/u <domain\user>	Runs the command using the account permissions of the user that is specified by User or Domain\User. The default is the permissions of the current logged-on user on the computer that issues the command.
/p <password>	Specifies the password of the user account that is specified in the /u parameter.
/scope {user|computer}	Displays either user or computer results. Valid values for the /scope parameter are user or computer. If you omit the /scope parameter, Gpresult displays both user and computer settings.
/user <TargetUserName>	Specifies the user name of the user whose RSoP data is to be displayed.
/r	Displays RSoP summary data.
/v	Specifies that the output display verbose policy information.
/z	Specifies that the output display all available information about Group Policy. Because this parameter produces more information than the /v parameter, redirect output to a text file when you use this parameter (for example, gpresult /z >policy.txt).
/x <filename>	Saves the report in XML format at the location and with the filename specified by the <filename> parameter (valid in Windows Server 2008 and Windows Vista with Service Pack 1).
/h <filename>	Saves the report in HTML format at the location and with the filename specified by the <filename> parameter (valid in Windows Server 2008 and Windows Vista with Service Pack 1).
/f	Forces Gpresult to overwrite the filename specified in the /x or /h parameter.
/?	Displays help at the command prompt.

Examples

The following examples show how you can use Gpresult.exe:

```
gpresult /user targetusername /scope computer
gpresult /s srvmain /u maindom\hiropln /p p@ssw23 /user targetusername /scope USER
gpresult /s srvmain /u maindom\hiropln /p p@ssw23 /user targetusername /z >policy.txt
gpresult /h gpresult.html /f
```

Judith Herman, Group Policy Programming Writer

Windows Enterprise Management Division UA

Scripting Group Policy Management

The GPMC provides a set of COM interfaces that allows for the use of various scripting technologies or programming languages such as Jscript, VBScript, Visual Basic, and VC++. This capability provides a way for automating many of the standard Group Policy management tasks:

- Creating/deleting/renaming GPOs
- Linking/unlinking GPOs and WMI filters
- Delegating security
- Generating reports of GPO settings
- Generating reports of RSoP data
- Backing up or restoring/importing GPOs
- Copying and pasting GPOs
- Searching for GPOs, WMI filters, and backups

Note   You can only script management tasks based on entire GPOs, you cannot use scripting to modify policy settings within GPOs.

On the Disc   The CD provided with this book contains a file called GPMCSample-Scripts.msi. This executable file contains a number of sample scripts that you can use to manage Group Policy.

The sample scripts included in GPMCSampleScripts.msi on the CD accompanying this book should be tested in a test environment before implementing them within your production environment. Table 11-6 provides a summary of the sample scripts included.

Table 11-6   Sample Scripts in GPMCSampleScripts.msi

Administrative Task	Script Name	Description
Back up a GPO	BackupGPO.wsf	Backs up all GPOs in a domain to the specified backup directory.
Back up all GPOs in a domain	BackupAllGPOs.wsf	Given a GPO name or a GUID, backs up the GPO to a specified backup directory.
Create a GPO with default options	CreateGPO.wsf	Creates a GPO with the specified name, in the current domain, using the default options.

Table 11-6   Sample Scripts in GPMCSampleScripts.msi *(continued)*

Administrative Task	Script Name	Description
Create a migration table	CreateMigrationTable.wsf	Populates the entries of a migration table with security principals and UNC paths that are referenced in a GPO or backup.
Copy a GPO	CopyGPO.wsf	Creates a new GPO and copies the settings from the source GPO into the new destination GPO, given a source GPO name or GUID and a new destination GPO name.
Create a policy environment using an XML representation	CreateEnvironmentFromXML.wsf	Reads an XML file that specifies a policy environment, for example, OUs, GPOs, links, and security groups. The script can either create the environment in a domain by creating the objects or can delete the environment by deleting objects specified in the XML file.
Create an XML representation of a policy environment	CreateXMLFromEnvironment.wsf	Reads an existing policy environment and creates an XML file representing that environment. The XML file captures information about OUs, GPOs and GPO links, and security on GPOs. You can use this script in conjunction with the CreateEnvironmentFromXML.wsf script to create a replica of domain for staging purposes.
Delete a GPO	DeleteGPO.wsf	Deletes the specified GPO when given a GPO name or GUID. By default, the script deletes links to that GPO within the same domain.
Grant permissions for all GPOs in a domain	GrantPermissionOnAllGPOs.wsf	Grants a user or group the specified level of permission for all GPOs in the specified domain.
Generate a report for a GPO	GetReportsForGPO.wsf	Creates an HTML and XML report for a given GPO at a given location in the file system.
Generate a report for all GPOs in the domain	GetReportsForAllGPOs.wsf	Creates HTML and XML reports for all GPOs in the domain, at a given location in the file system.
Import settings into a GPO	ImportGPO.wsf	Imports the settings from the specified backup to the existing destination GPO in the domain.

Table 11-6   Sample Scripts in GPMCSampleScripts.msi *(continued)*

Administrative Task	Script Name	Description
Import multiple GPOs into a domain	ImportAllGPOs.wsf	Creates a new GPO and imports settings into that GPO for each backed-up GPO stored at a specific file system location.
Restore a GPO	RestoreGPO.wsf	Restores a backed-up GPO.
Restore all GPOs	RestoreAllGPOs.wsf	Restores all GPOs that are stored at a given file system location.
Grant permissions for GPOs linked to a domain, OU, or site	SetGPOSecurityBySOM.wsf	Grants a user or group the specified permission type for all GPOs that are linked to a specified domain, OU, or site. You can specify *Read, Apply, Edit, FullEdit,* or *None* for the permission type.
Set GPO permissions	SetGPOPermissions.wsf	Sets the permission level for a security principal on a given GPO. You can specify *Read, Apply, Edit, FullEdit,* or *None* for the permission type.
Set permissions to create GPOs	SetGPOCreationPermissions.wsf	Grants or removes the ability to create GPOs in a domain for a given security principal.
Set policy-related permissions on a given site, domain, or OU	SetSOMPermissions.wsf	Sets policy-related permissions on a given scope of management (SOM). A SOM is any site, domain, or OU.
List all GPOs in a domain	ListAllGPOs.wsf	Prints all GPOs in the specified domain.
List disabled GPOs	FindDisabledGPOs.wsf	Prints all GPOs in the specified domain that are disabled or partially disabled.
List GPO information	DumpGPOInfo.wsf	Prints the information for a specific GPO, including creation time, modification time, owner, status, version number, links, security groups that filter the GPO, and security groups that have full control, edit, read, or custom permissions.
List scope of management information	DumpSOMInfo.wsf	Prints all information for a specific Scope of Management (SOM), including GPO links and policy-related permissions on the SOM.

Table 11-6   Sample Scripts in GPMCSampleScripts.msi *(continued)*

Administrative Task	Script Name	Description
List GPO by policy extension	FindGPOsByPolicyExtension.wsf	Prints all GPOs in the specified domain for which a specific policy extension is configured; for example, find all GPOs that contain the Software Installation or Folder Redirection policy settings.
List GPOs by security group	FindGPOsBySecurityGroup.wsf	Prints all GPOs that for which a given security principal has the specified permission on that GPO. You can specify *Read, Apply, Edit,* or *Fulledit* for the permission type.
List GPOs with duplicate names	FindDuplicateNamedGPOs.wsf	Prints all GPOs in the specified domain that have duplicate names.
List GPOs without Apply permission	GPOsWithNoSecurityFiltering.wsf	Prints all GPOs in the specified domain that do not apply to anyone because Apply permission is not set on the GPO.
List GPOs Orphaned in SYSVOL	FindOrphanedGPOsInSYSVOL.wsf	Finds and prints all GPOs in SYSVOL with no corresponding component in Active Directory.
List domains and OUs with external GPO links	FindSOMsWithExternalGPOLinks.wsf	Prints all domains and OUs in the specified domain that link to a GPO in a different domain.
List unlinked GPOs in a domain	FindUnlinkedGPOs.wsf	Prints all GPOs in the specified domain that have no links. Links outside the domain, including site links, are not checked.
Print the scope of management policy tree	ListSOMPolicyTree.wsf	Prints all SOMs in the specified domain with the list of GPOs that are linked to the domain and each OU.
List GPO backups in a given file system location	QueryBackupLocation.wsf	Prints information about all backed up GPOs at the file system location specified by the user.

Planning a Group Policy Implementation

Group Policy is a powerful tool for managing computer configurations on your network. Implementing Group Policy can also be very complicated, and if implemented incorrectly, can greatly impact the work environment for all users in your organization. This section describes a few best practices for designing the Group Policy implementation on your network.

More Info   To find out more about using Group Policy to manage computer configurations, see Chapter 12, "Using Group Policy to Manage User Desktops," and Chapter 13, "Using Group Policy to Manage Security," which describe additional best practices for using this powerful tool.

One of the important issues you will run into when designing your Group Policy strategy is how many GPOs you will implement. Because all policy settings are available in every GPO, you could theoretically configure all the required settings in a single GPO. Or you could deploy a separate GPO for every setting that you want to configure. In almost every case, the optimum number of GPOs will fall between these two extremes, and no one solution is right for all situations. When the client computer starts and the user logs on, all the applicable GPOs must be processed and applied to the local computer. Therefore, having fewer GPOs usually enhances the startup and logon performance for the client. However, having only a few GPOs that do a number of different tasks can become much more difficult to document and manage. Also, if you have GPOs that have only a few settings, it is much easier to reuse them across multiple OUs. In general, it is a good practice to use GPOs to configure only one group of settings. For example, you might use one GPO to set the security configuration, another to set the Administrative templates, and another to install a software package.

Another design issue has to do with where you want to deploy the policy objects. Usually you have a choice of deploying GPOs high in the OU structure and then possibly using security filtering and/or blocking to make sure that the policy settings are applied to the appropriate computers or users. Or you might choose to link most of the GPOs lower in the hierarchy so that you can apply each policy at the right point in the hierarchy and avoid any complicated inheritance configuration. In most cases, a combination is probably the right answer. If you have some policy settings that need to be applied to all users in your domain, set those policies as high as possible. As you go down the hierarchy, policy settings will become much more specific.

Troubleshooting Group Policy

Windows Server 2008 and Windows Vista both introduce new methods to troubleshoot the application of Group Policy settings. One notable feature is the use of the Group Policy Operational log for event reporting. The Group Policy Operational log replaces the userenv logging that was used in previous versions of Windows.

You can view the Group Policy Operational log by opening the Event Viewer and browsing to Applications and Services Logs\Microsoft\Windows\GroupPolicy and then selecting Operational. Figure 11-31 shows the Event Viewer with the Group Policy Operational log selected.

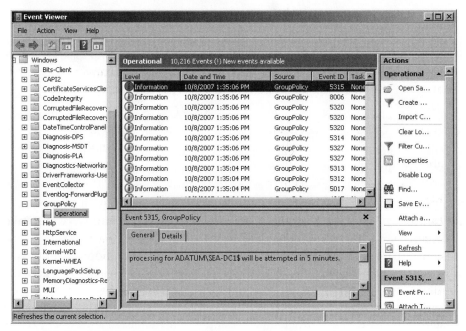

Figure 11-31   Viewing the Group Policy Operational log.

GPLogView.msi is a troubleshooting tool to be used with Windows Vista that can create an output file for Group Policy–related events logged in the System event log and the Group Policy Operational event log. You can download the tool from *http://go.microsoft.com/fwlink/ ?LinkId=75004*.

Troubleshooting specific Group Policy issues can be quite difficult because of the sheer number of components included in the process. However, most issues can be related to the following points, which may direct you to the cause of the problem:

- **Status of the GPO and GPO link**   Make sure that the GPO or GPO link is not disabled and that a link exists to the appropriate site, domain, or OU container. Also recall that only changed GPOs are actually processed during refreshes.

- **Location of the user or computer object**   Make sure that the user or computer object is in the container to which the GPO is linked.

- **Replication issue**   If the GPO has just been created, it is possible that some domain controllers have not yet received the replicated GPT and GPC information. You may also have to troubleshoot DFS or FRS replication issues if you notice that the SYSVOL information is not being replicated as expected.

- **GPO inheritance**   You can use Group Policy Results to verify how Group Policy settings are being inherited for a specific user. Be sure to double-check block inheritance and enforcement, as well as the link order, to ensure that GPOs are being processed as expected.

- **Security filtering**   Double-check security filtering on the GPO. Recall that by default authenticated users are added to the filter, which includes standard users, computers, and administrators. You may need to modify the user or groups on the filter to ensure proper processing.

- **Slow link or loopback processing**   You may need to determine if the client computer having issues thinks it is on a slow network link. Recall that not all Group Policy CSEs are processed over slow links. Also, it is important to determine if the computer is in a loopback processing mode. Both of these can be identified by running the Group Policy Results tool focused on the computer displaying the issue.

- **Network connections**   In order to obtain the GPO list and process Group Policy settings correctly, all computers need to be able to contact the Active Directory domain controller. In order to find a domain controller, DNS has to be functional within the network environment. Ensure that your network infrastructure is working as expected; also ensure that the time is synchronized between all computers, which may be the root cause of Group Policy processing issues (as well as many other problems associated with network connectivity).

Summary

This chapter has provided the framework for the next two chapters by explaining the architecture and configuration options for Group Policy in Windows Server 2008. This chapter described how to create and manage Group Policy objects using the Group Policy Management console. This chapter also discussed how policy settings are inherited and applied to user and computer objects within the Active Directory structure. You also read that you can modify the default inheritance of policy processing by blocking or filtering the inheritance. Chapters 12 and 13 focus on what you can actually do with Group Policy settings. Chapter 12 deals with how you can use Group Policy to manage client computers, and Chapter 13 discusses how you can use Group Policy to manage security throughout the Active Directory environment.

Additional Resources

The following resources contain additional information and tools related to this chapter.

Related Information

- Chapter 5, "Designing the Active Directory Domain Services Structure," provides details on planning the structure of Active Directory such as site, domain, organizational unit, and forest designs.

- Chapter 9, "Delegating the Administration of Active Directory Domain Services," provides additional details on using the Delegation Of Control Wizard to delegate administrative tasks in Active Directory.

- "Windows Server Group Policy" at *http://technet.microsoft.com/en-us/windowsserver/grouppolicy/default.aspx*

- "Loopback Processing of Group Policy" at *http://support.microsoft.com/?id=231287*

- "Group Policy Wiki" at *http://grouppolicy.editme.com/*

- "Group Policy Team Blog" at *http://blogs.technet.com/GroupPolicy/*

- "HOWTO: Leverage Group Policies with WMI Filters" at *http://support.microsoft.com/kb/555253*

- "WMI Filters" at *http://technet2.microsoft.com/windowsserver/en/library/dfba1dc6-6848-4ed8-96da-f4241c1acfbd1033.mspx?mfr=true*

- "Scriptomatic Tool" at *http://www.microsoft.com/technet/scriptcenter/tools/wmimatic.mspx*

- "Writing WMI Scripts Using the Scriptomatic Utility" at *http://www.microsoft.com/downloads/details.aspx?displaylang=en&familyid=9ef05cbd-c1c5-41e7-9da8-212c414a7ab0*

- "Troubleshooting Group Policy Using Event Logs" at *http://technet2.microsoft.com/WindowsVista/en/library/7e940882-33b7-43db-b097-f3752c84f67f1033.mspx?mfr=true*

- "Group Policy Script Center" at *http://www.microsoft.com/technet/scriptcenter/hubs/gp.mspx*

- "Introduction to Group Policy in Windows Server 2003" at *http://www.microsoft.com/windowsserver2003/techinfo/overview/gpintro.mspx*

- "Microsoft IT Showcase: Group Policy Object Infrastructure Management" at *http://www.microsoft.com/downloads/details.aspx?FamilyID=43090fae-e22a-4b6f-abc7-487a58b303a5&DisplayLang=en*

- "Administering Group Policy with Group Policy Management Console" at *http://www.microsoft.com/downloads/details.aspx?familyid=D8291B79-922A-439C-88E9-54041A2953DD&displaylang=en*

- "Migrating GPOs Across Domains with GPMC" at *http://www.microsoft.com/windowsserver2003/gpmc/migrgpo.mspx*

Chapter 12
Using Group Policy to Manage User Desktops

One of the primary benefits of Group Policy is the ability to centrally manage desktops within your Active Directory environment. Traditionally, Group Policy has been used to simplify administration tasks such as managing the configuration of Windows components, implementing security, controlling user settings and data access, and deploying and maintaining software. Windows Server 2008 expands upon these capabilities and provides even more manageability and administration options by introducing new user profile formats, new XML-based Administrative template files, a number of new and updated policy settings, and a new Group Policy feature called Group Policy preferences.

This chapter describes how you can use Group Policy to help manage desktop configuration settings. This chapter also introduces new features related to Group Policy management and functionality.

Note Group Policy settings can be applied to both user desktops and servers. However, this chapter will focus on managing the user desktops within your Active Directory environment.

Individual Control vs. Centralized Control of Computer Desktops

Managing user desktops requires a critical balance between strict centralized control of computers and users who want complete control to customize their own desktop. If you were to implement all of the policy settings available in Group Policy, you could lock down user desktops very tightly and ensure that users do not make any unauthorized changes. Many administrators think that providing users with any ability to modify settings only means that they will configure things incorrectly, leading to more work for the administrators. Many users, on the other hand, see any attempt to control their desktops as an invasion of their space. From the user's point of view, the workstation is part of one's individual work environment, and any attempt to manage that work environment is strongly resisted.

Deciding the right balance between centralized desktop control and end-user control is different for every organization. Some may already have a history of using Group Policy in Windows 2000 or Windows 2003 Active Directory environments, where the end users are already accustomed to some level of desktop control. In these organizations, you might be able to implement new restrictions without too much concern. However, others may not have implemented any restrictions. For these organizations, the first attempt at implementing restrictions might be met with great resistance.

The best approach to implementing desktop control is to start slowly and create a positive first impression. Creating a positive first impression usually means that you use Group Policy to help address specific issues. If you can show the end users that desktop management will actually make their jobs easier, they are much more likely to accept additional management. On the other hand, if you try to implement desktop control and the first attempt results in hundreds of service desk calls, you will lose all support for implementing any desktop management. Another important ingredient to a successful implementation of Group Policy is support from management. In most organizations, management will support any effort that decreases the cost of managing workstations. If you can show that decreased cost is the end result of implementing desktop management, you are almost certain to have management support in dealing with the complaints from those end users who don't want you managing their desktops.

Desktop Management Using Group Policy

A large part of effective desktop management is to adopt a standard policy on how desktops are configured within your Active Directory environment. Standardization can then be implemented using the various features available with Group Policy. You can view the various features and components that can be managed within a Group Policy object (GPO) by using the Group Policy Management console (GPMC). When you choose to edit a GPO, the Group Policy Management Editor window opens. As shown in Figure 12-1, the Group Policy Management Editor window is divided into various components related to computer or user-based policy and preference settings.

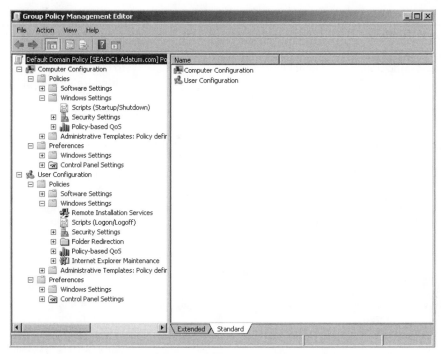

Figure 12-1   Viewing the Group Policy Management components.

Table 12-1 briefly explains the top-level containers displayed in the Group Policy Management Editor window.

Table 12-1   Group Policy Containers

Top-Level Container	Child Containers	Contents
Computer Configuration and User Configuration	Policies	Contains Software Settings, Windows Settings, and Administrative Templates containers used for configuring standard Group Policy settings.
Computer Configuration and User Configuration	Policies\Software Settings	Contains the configuration for software packages used for software distribution.
Computer Configuration and User Configuration	Policies\Windows Settings\ Scripts	Contains the startup and shutdown scripts for computers and the logon and logoff scripts for users.
Computer Configuration and User Configuration	Policies\Windows Settings\Security Settings	Contains the settings used to configure computer security. Some settings are specific to the domain level, and some can be set at the container level. Most security settings are configured under Computer Configuration.

Table 12-1 Group Policy Containers *(continued)*

Top-Level Container	Child Containers	Contents
Computer Configuration and User Configuration	Policies\Windows Settings\ Policy-based QoS	Contains the settings used to configure user- or computer-based traffic prioritization and throttling for specific applications, IP Addresses, protocols, or ports.
User Configuration	Policies\Windows Settings\Folder Redirection	Contains settings that redirect user folders, such as the Documents folder, to a network share.
User Configuration	Policies\Windows Settings\Remote Installation Services	Contains a single configuration option for Remote Installation Services (RIS).
User Configuration	Policies\Windows Settings\Internet Explorer Maintenance	Contains settings for managing the Microsoft Internet Explorer configuration on user desktops.
Computer Configuration and User Configuration	Policies\Administrative Templates	Contains a large number of configuration settings that can be used to configure the registry on target computers.
Computer Configuration and User Configuration	Preferences	Contains preferences related to Windows and Control Panel settings.
Computer Configuration and User Configuration	Preferences\Windows Settings	Contains preference settings that relate to Windows configurations such as Environment variables, Shortcuts, Registry and Ini files, Drive Maps (User only), and Application settings (User only), as well as many other settings.
Computer Configuration and User Configuration	Preferences\Control Panel Settings	Contains preference settings related to the Windows Control Panel, such as controlling Local Users and Groups, Power Options, Printers, Folder Options, and many other settings.

The rest of this chapter provides details on many of these high-level containers.

Managing User Data and Profile Settings

An often-challenging task for many network administrators is the management of user data and profile settings. End users typically expect that their computing environment looks the same, no matter how or when they log on to the network. Users also expect that data is available when they need it, again no matter how or when they log on to the network.

The information that users work with is often business-critical and must be properly secured and managed. In most cases, company data is centrally stored on shared network folders and regularly backed up. Users are encouraged to store all company data in those shared folders; however, with increases in the mobile workforce, many users also store data locally on their portable computers to provide access to the files when they are not connected to the network.

The management of user profiles is often of more concern to end users than it is to administrators. Some users spend a considerable amount of time configuring their applications and desktop to suit their own preferences. For these users, their personal settings are important, and they want the same desktop configuration to appear regardless of which computer they log on to. To provide this functionality, many organizations have implemented roaming user profiles, in which the user profile is stored on a network share and is accessible from any computer in the domain. To maintain standardized desktop configurations, some organizations impose restrictions on their user profiles by implementing mandatory profiles. With mandatory profiles, an administrator can create a standard profile for a user or a group of users and then configure the profile so that users cannot save changes to the profile. This ensures that the computing environment stays consistent for all users who are assigned this specific profile.

Roaming and mandatory user profiles can be implemented using Active Directory, and some of the settings for controlling roaming and mandatory user profiles can be configured through Group Policy. In addition to user profiles, however, Active Directory also provides folder redirection and offline files functionality to help manage user data and settings. Folder redirection provides some significant benefits for managing the size and availability of specific folders usually found in user profiles, whereas offline files can provide benefits for mobile users disconnected from the network.

Managing User Profiles

Windows Server 2008 and Windows Vista have both introduced significant changes to the structure of user profiles. These changes require careful consideration when deploying roaming user profiles throughout a mixed environment containing Windows Server 2008, Windows Vista, and previous versions of Windows.

A user profile contains information that maps to the HKEY_CURRENT_USER hive in the registry and is stored at the root of the user's profile folder as NTUSER.DAT. This file helps to maintain various types of information such as application settings and desktop configuration settings. A user profile also contains a number of visible and hidden folders that store information such as application settings, the Start Menu and Desktop configuration, and various types of personal data folders. Figure 12-2 shows the contents of a user profile on a server running Windows Server 2008.

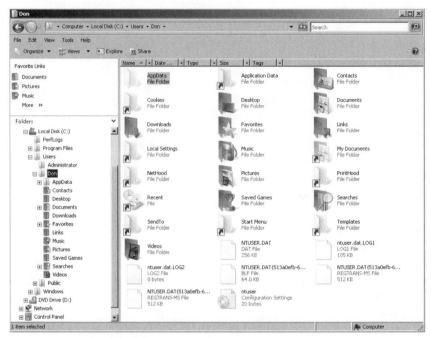

Figure 12-2   The user profile contains all user desktop settings and folders for user data.

In previous versions of Windows, user profiles were stored under the Documents and Settings folder. In Windows Server 2008, this location has changed to a folder named Users. Within the user's profile folder, many of the names and locations of specific profile-related folders have also changed. Table 12-2 outlines the differences between previous versions of Windows and Windows Server 2008.

> **Note**   Windows Vista also contains the same profile changes as discussed for Windows Server 2008.

Table 12-2   Comparing Profile Folders Between Windows Versions

Windows Server 2008/Vista	Windows 2003/XP	Description
AppData	N/A	This is a hidden folder and is used as the default location for user application data. It also contains the following folders:
		Local—Stores computer-specific and user-specific application settings that should not roam with a user when roaming profiles are implemented.
		Roaming—Stores application data and settings that must roam with the user when roaming profiles are implemented.
		LocalLow—Stores application data and settings for low integrity processes, such as protected-mode in Internet Explorer. This data will not roam with a user when roaming profiles are implemented.
Contacts	N/A	This is the default location for user contacts.
Desktop	Desktop	This stores items that appear on the desktop, such as shortcuts and files.
Documents	My Documents	This is the default location for all documents created by the user.
Downloads	N/A	This is the default location for all files downloaded by the user.
Favorites	N/A	Internet Explorer Favorites.
Links	N/A	Internet Explorer Favorite Links.
Music	My Music	Default location for Music files saved by the user.
Pictures	My Pictures	Default location for Picture files saved by the user.
Saved Games	N/A	Default location for games saved by the user.
Searches	N/A	Default location for saved searches.
Videos	My Videos	Default location for videos saved by the user.

In addition to the standard profile folders, there are also a number of hidden folders that contain shortcut arrows as shown in Figure 12-2. These folders, called junction points, are used by legacy applications to resolve the location of the common folders used in previous Windows versions. These junction points are described in Table 12-3.

Table 12-3   Windows Server 2008 Junction Points

Junction Point	Points to New Location in Windows Server 2008/Vista
Application Data	.. \AppData\Roaming
Cookies	.. \AppData\Roaming\Microsoft\Windows\Cookies
Local Settings	...\AppData\Local
	...\AppData\Local\Microsoft\Windows\History
	...\AppData\Local\Temp
	...\AppData\Local\Microsoft\Windows\Temporary Internet Files
My Documents	...\Documents

Table 12-3   Windows Server 2008 Junction Points *(continued)*

Junction Point	Points to New Location in Windows Server 2008/Vista
NetHood	…\AppData\Roaming\Microsoft\Windows\Network Shortcuts
PrintHood	…\AppData\Roaming\Microsoft\Windows\Printer Shortcuts
Recent	…\AppData\Roaming\Microsoft\Windows\Recent
SendTo	…\AppData\Roaming\Microsoft\Windows\Send To
Start Menu	…\AppData\Roaming\Microsoft\Windows\Start Menu
Templates	…\AppData\Roaming\Microsoft\Windows\Templates

The new folder structure provides a more organized and logical format that clearly displays the intended use and function of each folder. The new structure also enhances the functionality of folder redirection tasks to help minimize the amount of data transferred with roaming profiles.

How It Works: Junction Points and Their Targets

The new roaming version two (v2) user profile folder structure included in Windows Server 2008 and Windows Vista has a more streamlined approach for locating user data. However, applications created before Windows Server 2008 and Windows Vista may have hardcoded the names in the folder structure used prior to Windows Server 2008 and Windows Vista. Profile developers planned ahead and tried to mitigate application compatibility problems between v1 and v2 user profiles by creating junction points that share the names of user data folders found in earlier versions of Windows.

Junction points look like folders when viewed with Windows Explorer. But they actually contain a link that redirects the file request to another portion of the disk. Junction points allow applications that use earlier user data folder names to write data to folders that use the new user data names found in v2 user profiles. For example, Windows Server 2003 and Windows XP both used v1 user profiles. The My Documents folder is one of the user data folders present in the v1 user profile. However, Windows Server 2008 and Windows Vista (v2 user profiles) use the Documents folder as the equivalent user data folder to My Documents. Windows Server 2008 creates a hidden junction point in the v2 user profiles with the name My Documents. The target of the My Documents junction point is the location of the new user data folder named Documents. An application written specifically to write data to the My Documents folder would fail on Windows Vista if it were not for the junction point redirecting the file operation to the correct user data folder.

You can view the junction points in the v2 user profiles from the command prompt using the Dir command. To do so, start a command prompt. The command prompt window opens into the user profile folder of the currently logged on user. Type **Dir /al** and then press Enter. Windows displays the list of hidden junction points within the user profile folder and the target locations to which they point.

Mike Stephens

Support Escalation Engineer

How Local Profiles Work

By default, a local profile is created on each computer the first time that a user logs on to the computer. The initial profile is based on the hidden profile named *Default*, which is stored under the %SystemDrive%\Users folder. If a computer is joined to a domain, it will first check to see if there is a network version of the default user profile, which is located on the NETLOGON share of domain controllers.

When the user logs off, the user's profile, including any changes made to the profile, is saved in a folder with the same name as the user's logon name in the Users folder. When the user logs on again to the same computer, the profile is retrieved to present the user with the same desktop that was saved when logoff took place. User profiles are associated with the user's security ID. Therefore, two users with the same logon name will not load the same profile. Each user is assigned their own profile.

The main advantage of a local profile is that each user who logs on to the computer will maintain unique personal settings. However, users who roam between multiple workstations will have to maintain multiple profiles stored distinctly on each individual workstation. To help address this problem, many organizations implement roaming user profiles.

How Roaming Profiles Work

Roaming user profiles are stored on a network share so that the profile is available as the user moves between multiple workstations. With the changes to the profile folder structure in Windows Server 2008 and Windows Vista, careful consideration has to be given to implementing roaming profiles in a mixed environment. Any roaming profile created for a Windows Vista or Windows Server 2008 client is not compatible with roaming profiles created for Windows XP or Windows Server 2003.

Note   Windows Vista and Windows Server 2008 also cannot read Windows XP and Windows 2003 (v1) user profiles. This is a significant change from the past, when the former operating system could read the previous operating system's roaming profile and simple upgrades were made possible. This is no longer the case with v2 profiles.

When a user who is configured with a Windows Server 2008/Windows Vista roaming user profile logs on to a computer for the first time, the default profile is generated from one of two places and applied to the computer:

- **A preconfigured user profile found in the NETLOGON share**   If you want to have a default user profile that is already preconfigured with specific settings, you can use a Windows Server 2008 or Windows Vista computer to modify a user profile with unique user settings such as background colors, screen saver, and desktop settings. You can then copy this profile to a folder called Default User.v2 located in the NETLOGON share of a domain controller. The v2 suffix indicates that this is a version 2 profile used by Windows Vista and Windows Server 2008.

- ■ **The local default profile**   If the Default User.v2 folder does not exist in the NETLOGON share or the computer is not joined to a domain, the local Default profile is used as the initial profile settings for the user.

When the user logs off, the changes made to the user profile are evaluated and copied back to the NETLOGON network share. By default, a copy of the profile is also cached on the local workstation. If a user has logged on to a workstation before, the time stamp for the profile on the local workstation is compared to the time stamp for the profile stored on the NETLOGON network share. The time stamp on individual files is used to determine which files in the profile are newer. If the profile on the server is newer than the local profile, the entire profile is copied from the server to the local workstation.

Configuring Roaming Profiles

To configure roaming profiles, you need to configure a network location to store each of the individual user profiles. Next, you have to configure each user account to map to the network location to retrieve and save changes to its associated profile. To configure roaming user profiles, follow these steps:

1. Create a shared folder on a file or profile server used to store the roaming profiles. Many organizations name the folder Profiles.

2. Share the folder so that the Authenticated Users group has Full Control to the share. This ensures that both computers and users can access this share to create profile folders as needed. You will also need to ensure that Allow Modify permissions are set on the local (NTFS) permissions for the Users group.

3. Optionally, create a default network profile and store it on the NETLOGON share of a domain controller. The folder used to contain the custom profile must be named Default User.v2. The Everyone group should have full access to the default network profile. If you do not create a default network profile, the %SystemRoot%\Users\Default profile will be used instead.

4. Use Active Directory Users and Computers to configure the profile path for each user that should use the roaming profile. As shown in Figure 12-3, you must specify the server and shared folder that stores the profiles. You can also use the %UserName% environment variable as a placeholder for the logon name used in the profile path. After the user logs on, the profile folder will then be automatically created in the username.v2 format and the appropriate permissions will be automatically assigned.

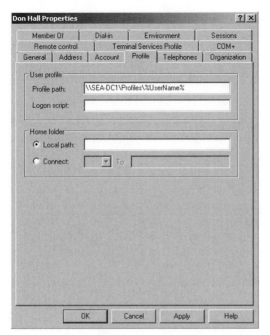

Figure 12-3   Configuring a roaming user profile.

Mandatory and Super Mandatory Profiles

Mandatory profiles are used in combination with roaming profiles to create a locked-down standard desktop configuration for a group of users. For example, you might have a group of users who all perform the same functions and require a very limited desktop configuration. You can create one standard desktop for this group of users and use mandatory profiles to prevent the users from changing the configuration. To enable mandatory profiles, you must first create the standard roaming user profile and use the Profiles tab of the Computer Properties dialog box to copy the profile to the NETLOGON share and assign the appropriate permissions for profile usage. You then have to rename the NTUSER.DAT file to NTUSER.MAN and configure the file as read-only. Finally, you configure all of the required users to use this profile as their roaming user profile. When a user configured with the mandatory profile logs on to the network, the profile will be applied, and because it is configured as a mandatory profile, changes to the profile will not be saved to the profile server when the user logs off.

> **Note**   Folders dedicated to storing mandatory profiles should have the share permissions to allow the Authenticated Users group Read permission and allow the Administrators group Full Control permission.

Normally, if a roaming or mandatory user profile is not available because of network problems, Windows will create a temporary profile for the user based on the Default network or local profile. This temporary profile is then deleted when the user logs off. However, when circumstances require that mandatory profiles always be used, then, if the profiles are not available, logon is not allowed. To accomplish this goal, you can create a super mandatory profile. Super mandatory profiles do not allow users to log on to a workstation if the roaming profile is not available. This can add an additional layer of security for the workstation but can also require additional troubleshooting and result in loss of user productivity in the event that a user cannot access the roaming profile.

To configure super mandatory roaming user profiles, follow these steps:

1.   Create a mandatory user profile as described previously.

2.   Connect to the network share storing the user profile folder. Rename the user folder that is to become a super mandatory user profile with .man.v2 at the end of the folder name.

3.   Use Active Directory Users And Computers to configure the profile path for each user that should use the super mandatory roaming profile. Add .man to the end of the profile path. For example, the path shown in Figure 12-3 would be \\SEA-DC1\ Profiles\Don.man.

Any user configured with a super mandatory user profile will not be able to save settings back to the profile server. In addition, Windows will not allow the user to log on to the computer if the mandatory user profile fails to load.

Using Group Policy to Manage Roaming User Profiles

You can use Group Policy to manage many aspects of user profiles. User profile settings can be found in the following locations when editing a domain-based Group Policy object:

■   Computer Configuration\Policies\Administrative Templates\System\User Profiles

■   User Configuration\Policies\Administrative Templates\System\User Profiles

Table 12-4 explains the configuration options available at these two locations.

Table 12-4   Configuring User Profiles Using Group Policy Settings

Policy Setting	Explanation
Add the Administrators security group to roaming user profiles	Use this option to add the Administrator security group to the roaming user's profile share and have Full Control permissions. If this setting is not configured or disabled, only the user is given full control of their user profile (which is the default setting). This setting must be enabled before a profile is created; if this setting is enabled after the profile is created, the setting will have no effect.
	Note: This setting has to be configured on the client computer, not on the profile server. The client computer sets the file share permissions for the roaming profile at creation time.

Table 12-4 Configuring User Profiles Using Group Policy Settings *(continued)*

Policy Setting	Explanation
Delete user profiles older than a specified number of days on system restart	This Windows Vista setting provides the ability to automatically delete Windows Vista client user profiles that have not been used for a specified number of days on system restart.
Do not check for user ownership of roaming profile folders	Use this option to configure what to do if a roaming user profile folder already exists and the workstations have been upgraded to Microsoft Windows 2000 Service Pack 4 or Microsoft Windows XP Professional Service Pack 1. These recent service packs increase the default security on the user profiles. Enabling this option means that the earlier security is maintained.
Delete cached copies of roaming profiles	Enable this option to delete the locally cached copy of the roaming user profile when the user logs off. Do not enable this option if you are using the slow link detection feature of Windows 2000 or Windows XP Professional, because that feature requires a locally cached copy of the user profile.
Do not forcefully unload the users registry at user logoff	By default, Windows Vista will always unload the user's registry when a user logs off. This policy setting can prevent Windows from forcefully unloading the user's registry. This setting should only be used to address application compatibility issues related to this default behavior.
Do not detect slow network connections	Enable this option to prevent the computer from using slow link detection to configure how to manage roaming user profiles. If you enable this option, roaming user profiles will always be downloaded, regardless of network speed.
Prompt user when a slow network connection is detected	Enable this option to provide the user with a prompt indicating that a slow network connection has been detected and providing the user with a choice about whether to load the local profile or the server profile. If you do not enable this option, the local profile is loaded without advising the user.
Leave Windows Installer and Group Policy Software Installation data	By default, when you delete a user profile, all information related to the profile, such as user's settings, data, Windows Installer information, and Group Policy Software Installation data, is removed. As a result, if a user logs on to the machine whose profile was previously deleted, all applications installed through Group Policy will need to be reinstalled. If you enable this policy setting, Windows will not delete Windows Installer or Group Policy Software Installation data when a roaming user profile is deleted. This will improve performance and logon time if the user subsequently logs on to the machine at a later time.
Only allow local user profiles	Enable this option to configure whether or not roaming user profiles are available on a specific computer. If you enable this option, the roaming user profile will not be applied and only the local profile will be used.

Table 12-4 **Configuring User Profiles Using Group Policy Settings** *(continued)*

Policy Setting	Explanation
Set roaming profile path for all users logging onto this computer	Use this policy setting to specify a network path to access roaming profiles for all users logging onto a specific computer. The path should be in the form of \\Computername\ShareName\%USERNAME%. It is important to note that there are four ways to configure a roaming profile for a user, which is evaluated in the following order and uses the first configured setting: 1. Terminal services roaming profile path specified by a Terminal Services policy setting 2. Terminal services roaming profile path specified in the properties of the user object 3. A per-computer roaming profile path specified in this policy setting 4. A per-user roaming profile path specified in the properties of the user object
Timeout for dialog boxes	Use this option to configure how long the system will wait after prompting the user that a slow network connection has been detected. If the timeout is allowed to expire, the dialog box's default value or action is applied.
Do not log users on with temporary profiles	This policy setting automatically logs off users when Windows cannot load their profile. By default, if Windows cannot access the user profile folder, or the profile cannot be found, Windows allows the user to log on using a temporary user profile.
Maximum retries to unload and update user profile	Use this setting to configure how many times the system tries to update the NTUSER.DAT file when the user logs off and the update fails. By default, the system will try to update the file once per second for 60 seconds.
Prevent roaming profile changes from propagating to the server	Use this option to configure what happens when the user logs off the computer. If this option is enabled, the roaming profile on the server is not updated when the user logs off.
Wait for remote user profile	Enable this option to always load the roaming user profile from the server. If you enable this option, the workstation will load the user profile even if a slow network connection is detected.
Slow network connection timeout for user profiles	Enable this option to define a slow network connection. If you enable this option, the default definition of a slow network connection is *less than 500 Kbps*, or for non-IP computers, *if the server takes more than 120 milliseconds to respond*.

Table 12-4   Configuring User Profiles Using Group Policy Settings *(continued)*

Policy Setting	Explanation
Set maximum wait time for the network if a user has a roaming user profile or remote home directory	If a user has a roaming user profile or remote home directory, and the network is unavailable, Windows will wait 30 seconds for the network to become available. If the network is unavailable after the maximum wait time, the user will be logged on without a network connection. You can modify the default wait time using this policy. This may be useful for slower connections such as wireless connections.
Connect home directory to root of the share (under User Configuration)	If you enable this option, the home drive for all users will be the network share where the user home folders are located. If you disable this option (the default), the home drives are mapped to the user-specific folder rather than to the higher-level share.
Network directories to sync at logon/Logoff time only (under User Configuration)	You can use this policy setting to specify which network directories will be synchronized only at logon and logoff using Offline files.
Exclude directories in roaming profile (under User Configuration)	Use this option to prevent specified user directories from being included in the roaming user profile.
Limit profile size (under User Configuration)	Use this option to limit how large a user's roaming profile can be. You can also use this option to configure how the user will be prompted if his or her profile space is exceeded.

Folder Redirection

With a roaming profile, a user's work environment is the same regardless of where the user logs on. However, roaming user profiles also have some limitations. In most cases, the biggest problem is that the user profile can become very large. For example, the user might store a large amount of data in the Documents folder. The user might also store large files on the desktop. Often, files located in the Music or Videos folders can grow to be many megabytes in size. All of these files are stored in the user profile. The problem with large roaming profiles is that the entire profile must be copied to the local workstation whenever the user logs on and the computer detects that the profile on the server is newer than the profile on the local workstation. If the user makes changes to any of the profile data, when the user logs off, the profile must be copied back to the server. This process can create a significant amount of network traffic and cause extended logon times.

Group Policy provides folder redirection as a way to get some of the benefits of using roaming profiles while minimizing concerns related to network bandwidth and logon performance. When you enable folder redirection, folders that are normally part of the local user profile are redirected out of the profile and stored on a network share. For example, one of the most common folders for folder redirection is the Documents folder. This is a logical folder to redirect because it is the default location where most users save files. When you configure folder redirection, you can direct the Documents folder located on a computer to a network share where it can be centrally backed up. This folder redirection is almost completely transparent to the end-user—the only way you can tell that the folder has been redirected is by looking at the properties to determine the path of the Documents folder.

Another reason to use folder redirection is that you can use this option to deploy a standard desktop environment rather than use mandatory user profiles. For example, you can redirect folders such as the Start Menu and Desktop folders to a network share. Then, you can configure a group of users to all use the same folder. By giving all the users only Read permissions to these folders, you can configure a standard mandatory desktop for a group of users.

As shown in Figure 12-4, Windows Server 2008 and Windows Vista provide a large number of folders that can be redirected out of the user profile.

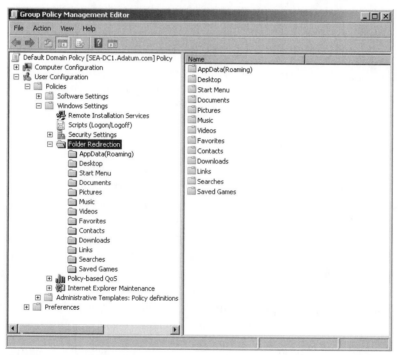

Figure 12-4 Folders available for folder redirection.

Configuring Folder Redirection

Folder redirection is configured in a domain-based Group Policy object under User Configuration\Windows Settings\ Folder Redirection.

To configure a specific folder for redirection, right-click the folder and then click Properties. The first page of the object's Properties sheet is the Target page, which contains the following options:

- **Not configured**   By default, the Setting option is set to Not Configured, which means that the folder is not redirected to a network share.

- **Basic—Redirect everyone's folder to the same location**   This setting is used if you want to create one location where all folders will be redirected. For example, you might want the folders for all users affected by this policy to be located on a *servername**sharename* network share.

- **Advanced—Specify locations for various user groups**   This setting is used to configure alternate locations for the redirected folder depending on which Active Directory security group the user belongs to. If you choose this option, you can assign an alternate target folder location for each security group.

Configuring Basic Redirection   When you select the Basic option, you can then configure the target folder location. You have several options for where you can store the folder:

- **Redirect to the user's home directory**   This setting is used to redirect the Documents folder to the user's home directory as specified on the user account properties. Use this option only if you have already configured the home directory on the user object. If the home directory has not been created, configuring this option will not create the home directory. This option is only available for the My Documents folder.

- **Create a folder for each user under the root path**   This setting is used to specify a root path where the folders will be stored. When you choose this option, a folder will be created under the root path for each user. The folder name is based on the %username% logon variable.

- **Redirect to the following location**   This setting is used to specify a root path and folder location for each user. You can use a Universal Naming Convention (UNC) path or a local drive location. You can use the %username% variable to create individual folders. This option can also be used to redirect several users to the same folder. For example, if you wanted to configure a standard Start Menu for a group of users, you would point them all to the same file.

- **Redirect to the local userprofile location**   This setting is the default configuration if no policies are enabled. If you set this option, the folders are not redirected to a network share.

Figure 12-5 shows an example of the Documents folder with the Basic option selected.

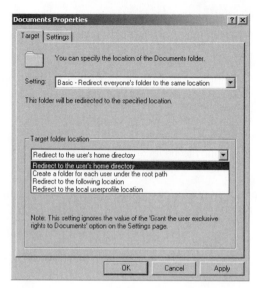

Figure 12-5   Configuring basic folder redirection.

In addition to configuring the target location for the redirected folders, you can also configure additional settings for the redirected folders. To do so, click the Settings tab on the object's Properties sheet. Figure 12-6 shows the interface.

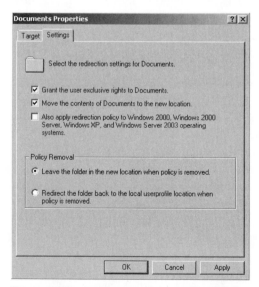

Figure 12-6   Configuring folder redirection settings.

The Settings tab provides several configuration options:

- **Grant the user exclusive rights to *foldername***   This setting grants the user and the system account full permission to the folder. Administrator accounts will not have any access. If you clear the check box, the folder permissions will be configured based on the inherited permissions.

> **Note**   This setting controls the permissions on newly created folders. If the target folder does not exist, Folder Redirection will create the folder and set the permissions, allowing only the user and Local System to have Full Control permissions. The administrator and other user will not have permission to the folder. If the target folder does exist, Folder Redirection will verify the ownership of the folder. If another user owns the folder, Folder Redirection will fail redirection for the specified folder. Folder Redirection will not check ownership of the folder when you clear this check box.

- **Move the contents of *foldername* to the new location**   This setting moves the current contents of the redirected folder to the target location. If you do not select this option, the current folder contents will not be copied to the target location.

- **Also apply redirection policy to Windows 2000, Windows 2000 Server, Windows XP, and Widows Server 2003 operating systems**   This option provides the ability to redirect folders known by previous versions of Windows, such as the Documents, Pictures, Desktop, Start Menu, and Application Data. If you select this option, previous versions of Windows will be able to redirect these known folders.

- **Policy Removal**   This setting is used to define what should happen if the policy is removed. If you accept the Leave The Folder In The New Location When Policy Is Removed default setting, the redirected folder contents will not be moved to the local user profile if the policy is removed. Choosing the Redirect The Folder Back To The Local Userprofile Location When Policy Is Removed option will move the folder contents when the policy is removed.

Configuring Advanced Redirection   When you select the Advanced option, you can then configure the target folder location based upon security group memberships, as shown in Figure 12-7.

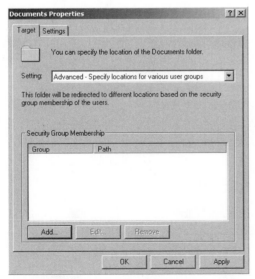

Figure 12-7   Configuring advanced folder redirection.

When you click the Add button, you can then select the security group and configure the Target Folder Location, as described previously. Figure 12-8 shows the interface.

Figure 12-8 Selecting security group memberships and target folder locations.

Managing Offline Files for Folder Redirection

When you implement Folder Redirection, all redirected folders are available offline by default. After Folder Redirection has been implemented and a user logs on to a Windows Vista computer, a message appears in the notification area from the Sync Center indicating that Offline files have been configured for synchronization. Double-clicking the notification icon opens the Sync Center, which provides additional features such as configuring synchronization options and viewing synchronization results. Figure 12-9 illustrates the Windows Vista Sync Center.

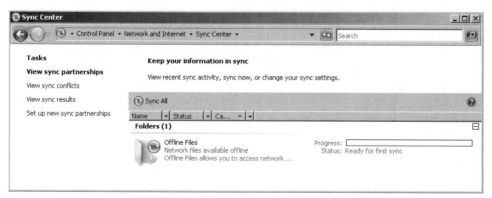

Figure 12-9 Viewing the Windows Vista Sync Center after enabling Folder Redirection.

When a redirected folder is opened on a Windows Vista client, information and synchronization indicators show the status and availability of the data within the folder. You can also force synchronization and switch between offline and online mode, as shown in Figure 12-10.

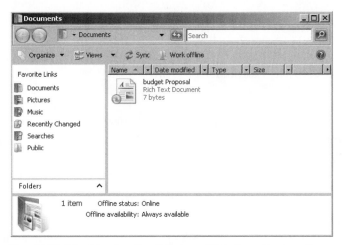

Figure 12-10   Viewing the Windows Vista Sync Center after enabling Folder Redirection.

Group Policy Settings for Folder Redirection

Windows Server 2008 provides additional Group Policy settings related to Folder Redirection, as described in Table 12-5. These can be found at the following location in the Group Policy Management Editor:

- Computer Configuration\Policies\Administrative Templates\System\Folder Redirection

- User Configuration\Policies\Administrative Templates\System\Folder Redirection

Table 12-5   Folder Redirection Policy Settings

Policy Setting	Explanation
Use localized subfolder names when redirecting Start and My Documents	This Windows Vista–based policy provides the ability to define if Folder Redirection should use localized names for the All Programs, Startup, My Music, My Pictures, and My Videos subfolders when redirecting the parent Start menu and legacy My Documents folders.
	If you disable or do not configure this setting, standard English names will be used for these subfolders.
Do not automatically make redirected folders available offline (under User Configuration)	This setting provides the ability to not allow the redirected folders to be available for offline use automatically. However, users can still choose to make the files and folders available offline manually.

Direct from the Source: Using Folder Redirection for User Profile Interoperability

Windows Server 2008 introduced version two (v2) user profiles. It also introduced some challenges for keeping user data available to users who may have to temporarily interoperate between v2 user profiles and v1 user profiles (Windows Server 2003). You can mitigate some of these challenges by using Windows Server 2008 Group Policy Folder Redirection to redirect user data folders into the v1 user profile.

Application Data

Use the Redirect To The Following Location option and redirect Application Data to \\ServerName\ShareName\%username%\Application Data, where \\Server-Name\ShareName\%username% is the central location of the user's v1 user profiles. If you've already redirected the Application Data folder, then make certain the path entered matches that of your existing redirected Application Data folder.

Desktop

Use the Redirect To The Following Location option and redirect the Desktop folder to \\ServerName\ShareName\%username%\Desktop, where \\ServerName\Share-Name\%username% is the central location of the user's version on user profile. If you've already redirected the Desktop folder, then make certain the path entered matches that of your existing redirected Desktop folder. Also, be sure to select the Also Apply Redirection Policy To Windows 2000, Windows 2000 Server, Windows XP, And Windows Server 2003 Operating Systems check box.

Documents

Use the Redirect To The Following Location option and redirect the Documents folder to a central location that does *not* reside in the v1 user profile. If you've already redirected the Documents folder, then make certain the path entered matches that of your existing redirected Documents folder. Also, be sure to select the Also Apply Redirection Policy To Windows 2000, Windows 2000 Server, Windows XP, And Windows Server 2003 Operating Systems check box.

Favorites

Use the Redirect To The Following Location option and redirect Application Data to \\ServerName\ShareName\%username%\Favorites, where \\ServerName\ShareName\%username% is the central location of the user's v1 user profile.

Music

Use the Follow The Documents folder option to ensure that you redirect the Music folder as a folder under the Documents folder.

Pictures

Use the Follow The Documents folder option to ensure that you redirect the Pictures folder as a folder under the Documents folder. If you've already redirected the Pictures folder, then make certain the path entered matches that of your existing redirected Pictures folder.

Start Menu

Use the Redirect To The Following Location option and redirect the Start Menu folder to \\ServerName\ShareName\%username%\Start Menu, where \\ServerName\ ShareName\%username% is the central location of the user's v1 user profile. If you've already redirected the Start Menu folder, then make certain the path entered matches that of your existing redirected Start Menu folder.

Videos

Use the Follow The Documents folder option to ensure you redirect the Videos folder as a folder under the Documents folder.

Redirecting v2 user data folders into v1 user profiles provides some level of interoperability; however, it does have some limitations. For example, Windows downloads roaming user profiles on logon and reconciles the files at logoff. Data modified while logged on using the v1 user profile is not available through redirection until Windows reconciles the v1 profile at logoff.

For more information about profile interoperability, you can read the "Managing Roaming User Data Deployment Guide" found at *http://go.microsoft.com/fwlink/? LinkId=73760.*

Mike Stephens

Support Escalation Engineer

Administrative Templates

The Administrative Templates node consists of over 1,300 registry-based policy settings that are used to manage various components such as the Control Panel, Desktop, Network settings, Printer settings, the Start menu, and the taskbar, as well as many others. For a complete list of each policy setting, see the Group Policy settings reference spreadsheet found at *http://www.microsoft.com/downloads/details.aspx?familyid=2043b94e-66cd-4b91-9e0f-68363245c495&displaylang=en.*

The Group Policy settings reference spreadsheet describes policy settings that relate to Windows Server 2008, Windows Vista, Windows Server 2003, Windows XP Professional, and Windows 2000. It also includes an explanation for most of the categories found under the Security Settings node.

When an Administrative template–based Group Policy setting is applied, the changes are written into special subkeys in the registry. Any changes made to the User Configuration are written to HKEY_CURRENT_USER and saved under either \Software\Policies or \Software\Microsoft\Windows\CurrentVersion\Policies. Changes made to the Computer Configuration are saved under the same subkeys under HKEY_LOCAL_MACHINE. When the computer boots up or the user logs on, all the normal registry settings are loaded and these keys are then examined for any additional settings. If these locations contain additional settings, they are loaded into the registry, overwriting existing entries, if applicable. If the Administrative template is removed or if the computer or user is moved to another container where the template does not apply, the information in the corresponding Policies keys is deleted. This removal of the Policies key information means that the Administrative templates are not applied anymore, but the normal registry settings still apply.

Understanding Administrative Template Files

Administrative template files are used to provide the policy setting information for each item that appears under the Administrative Templates node. Previous versions of Microsoft Windows use several ADM files to expose various registry-based configuration settings. By default, these files are located in the %SystemRoot%\Inf folder. Table 12-6 lists the Administrative template files that are installed and used by default with Windows Server 2003.

Table 12-6   Default Templates Loaded in Windows Server 2003

Administrative Template	Configuration Settings
System.adm	System settings
Inetres.adm	Internet Explorer settings
Wmplayer.adm	Microsoft Windows Media Player settings
Conf.adm	Microsoft NetMeeting settings
Wuau.adm	Windows Update settings

The Administrative template files are made up of a series of entries defining the options available through the template. Each entry in the ADM file looks similar to the example shown in Figure 12-11.

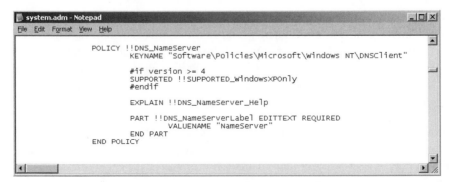

Figure 12-11   Viewing the make-up of an ADM template file.

Table 12-7 explains the makeup of a typical ADM template.

Table 12-7   Components of a Template Option

Template Component	Explanation
Policy	Identifies the policy name.
Keyname	Identifies the registry key modified by this setting.
Supported	Identifies the supported workstations or the required software version for this setting. Examples include Windows XP Professional, Windows 2000, Windows 2000 with a specified service pack, and Microsoft Windows Media Player version 9.
Explain	Identifies the text that explains the policy setting. The actual text is listed later in the ADM file.
Part	Identifies the entries that can be configured for this policy.
Valuename	Identifies the registry value that will be populated with the information from this setting.

Windows Server 2008 and Windows Vista have both introduced new XML-based ADMX templates that replace the ADM templates used in previous versions of Windows. ADMX templates provide improvements related to template management and development, as well as new language localization capabilities.

ADMX templates actually consist of two main components used to display registry settings in the Group Policy Management Editor:

- **ADMX files**   ADMX files are the primary language-neutral files used to provide access to the registry-based policy settings from the GPMC. These files are found under the %SystemRoot%\PolicyDefinitions folder.

- **ADML files**   ADML files are language-specific files used to provide the ability for Group Policy Management tools to adjust the localized language of the GUI interface based on the administrator's configured language. Each ADMX file may have one or more associated ADML files for each language required by the Group Policy administrators. ADML files are found under the %SystemRoot%\PolicyDefinitions\[MUIculture] folder.

Figure 12-12 illustrates the PolicyDefinitions folder on a Windows Server 2008 computer. Notice that there are specific ADMX files for many of the Windows components. Also, take note of the en-US folder that contains the corresponding English-based ADML files.

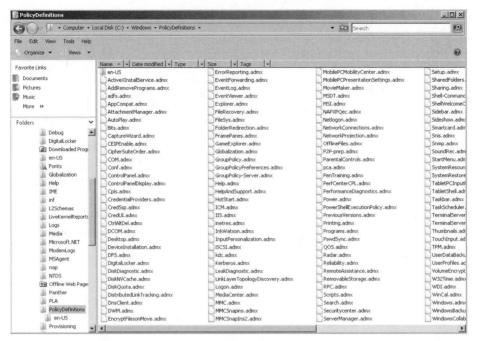

Figure 12-12 Viewing the PolicyDefinitions folder.

When you edit a domain-based GPO using GPMC on either a Windows Server 2008 or Windows Vista machine, the editor will automatically read all ADMX files stored in the local PolicyDefinitions folder and then display the policy categories and settings under the Policies\Administrative Templates node for both the Computer and User Configuration sections of the Policy. As you can see in Figure 12-13, the Group Policy Management Editor provides an indication that the Policy definitions (ADMX files) are currently being retrieved from the local machine.

Note Windows Vista RTM has GPMC; however, Windows Vista SP1 removes GPMC. You must install RSAT on Windows Vista SP1 to get GPMC.

Also, be aware that Windows Vista RTM GPMC and RSAT GPMC are different. Windows Vista RTM GPMC does not have filters, comments, Starter GPOs, or Preferences.

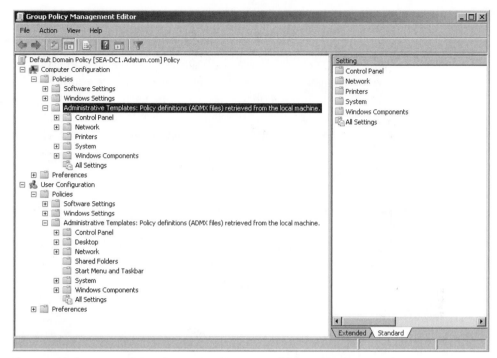

Figure 12-13   Determining the retrieval location of the ADMX files.

Windows Server 2008 does not include any legacy ADM files; however, the Windows Server 2008 and Windows Vista versions of the Group Policy Object Editor can still be used to manage all previous operating systems that support Group Policy, including Windows 2000, Windows Server 2003, and Windows XP. You can also add or remove custom ADM files to a GPO using the Add/Remove Templates option. However, there is no user interface for adding or removing ADMX files; custom ADMX files can be copied manually to the %SystemRoot%\PolicyDefinitions folder where they will be automatically recognized when the GPMC is restarted.

Managing Domain-based Template Files

Most large organizations have more than one individual in charge of configuring and deploying Group Policy settings throughout the Active Directory environment. In order to ensure that all administrators access the same set of ADMX files, you can create a central store in the SYSVOL directory of a domain controller for each domain in your organization. The central store will then be replicated to all domain controllers within each domain.

> **Note**   It is recommended that you create the central store on the domain controller containing the Primary Domain Controller (PDC) emulator role. The Group Policy Management console connects to the PDC emulator by default, which provides the ability to read the ADMX files more quickly without having to wait for replication tasks to complete.

To configure an ADMX central store, follow these steps:

1. On a domain controller, create the root folder for the central store at %SystemRoot%\ sysvol\domain\policies\PolicyDefinitions.

2. In the PolicyDefinitions folder on the domain controller, create a subfolder for each language required by your Group Policy administrators. Each subfolder must be named after the ISO-style language name. For example, the subfolder for United States English is %SystemRoot%\sysvol\domain\policies\PolicyDefinitions\EN-US.

3. From your Windows Vista administrative workstation, copy all ADMX files to the PolicyDefinitions folder on the domain controller using the following command:

```
copy %systemroot%\PolicyDefinitions\*
%logonserver%\sysvol\%userdnsdomain%\policies\
PolicyDefinitions\
```

4. From your Windows Vista administrative workstation, copy all ADML files to the language subfolder on the domain controller using the following command:

```
copy %systemroot%\PolicyDefinitions\[MUIculture]\*
%logonserver%\sysvol\%userdnsdomain%\policies\
PolicyDefinitions\[MUIculture]\
```

When an administrator opens the GPMC on a Windows Vista or Windows Server 2008 machine, it will automatically read all ADMX files stored in the central store and display all policy settings in the appropriate language of the workstation. After a central store is configured in the Sysvol folder, the Group Policy Management tools will only read the ADMX files from the central store and will ignore any ADMX files stored locally on the administrative workstation.

Best Practices for Managing ADMX Template Files

Consider the following recommendations when using ADMX Template files to deploy Group Policy settings:

■ Only use the Windows Vista SP1 (RSAT) or Windows Server 2008 versions of the Group Policy Management console to configure domain-based Group Policy settings. This will ensure that all settings are visible and available to be used in GPOs. This will also help reduce the size of each GPO folder created in the SYSVOL folder. For example, if you create a new GPO from a Windows Vista SP1 computer using GPMC from the Remote Server Administrator Tools and then edit the same GPO using a previous version of Windows, the ADM template files found in the %Windir%\inf folder are copied to the GPO folder and replicated to all domain controllers within the domain. This can increase the size of each GPO folder by approximately 4 MB per GPO.

- Many applications still contain ADM files for managing application settings using Group Policy. You can still import these files into the %Windir%\inf folder on administrative workstation using the Add/Remove Templates command. You can download Office 2003 ADM templates from the following location: *http://www.microsoft.com/downloads/details.aspx?FamilyID=BA8BC720-EDC2-479B-B115-5ABB70B3F490&displaylang=en.*

- If you need to manage Group Policy settings for the 2007 Microsoft Office system, you can download ADM or ADMX template files from the following location: *http://www.microsoft.com/downloads/details.aspx?FamilyID=92d8519a-e143-4aee-8f7a-e4bbaeba13e7&DisplayLang=en.*

- You can convert custom ADM files to the new ADMX format by using the ADMX Migrator. You can also use the ADMX Migrator as an editor with a graphical user interface to assist in the creation and editing of custom Administrative templates. You can download the ADMX Migrator from the following location: *http://www.microsoft.com/downloads/details.aspx?familyid=0F1EEC3D-10C4-4B5F-9625-97C2F731090C&displaylang=en.*

Direct from the Source: Managing ADMX/ADM Files in a Mixed Operating Systems Environment

The GPMC automatically reads and displays Administrative Template policy settings from ADMX files that are stored either locally or in the ADMX central store. If you have developed custom ADM files, the GPMC will automatically read and display Administrative Template policy settings from custom ADM files stored in the GPO. All Group Policy settings currently in ADM files delivered by the Windows Server 2003, Windows XP, and Windows 2000 will also be available in Windows Vista and Windows Server 2008 ADMX files.

New Windows Vista–based or Windows Server 2008–based policy settings can be managed only from Windows Vista–based or Windows Server 2008–based administrative machines running the GPMC. Such policy settings are defined only in ADMX files and, as such, are not exposed on the Windows Server 2003, Windows XP, or Windows 2000 versions of these tools.

The Windows Vista or Windows Server 2008 versions of the GPMC can be used to manage all operating systems that support Group Policy (Windows Vista, Windows Server 2008, Windows Server 2003, Windows XP, and Windows 2000).

The Windows Vista or Windows Server 2008 versions of Group Policy Object Editor and Group Policy Management Console support interoperability with versions of these tools on Windows Server 2003, and Windows XP. For example, custom ADM files stored in GPOs will be consumed by Group Policy Object Editor and GPMC on Windows Vista, Windows Server 2008, Windows Server 2003, and Windows XP.

> The Windows Vista or Windows Server 2008 versions of Group Policy Object Editor support interoperability with versions of Group Policy Object Editor on Windows Server 2000. For example, custom ADM files stored in GPOs will be consumed by Group Policy Object Editor on Windows Vista, Windows Server 2008, and Windows 2000. (GPMC does not run on Windows 2000.)
>
> *Christiane Soumahoro*
>
> *Microsoft Consulting Services*

Using Scripts to Manage the User Environment

Ever since the early days of networking, administrators have used logon scripts to help configure and manage the user environment. Typically, the most common use for scripts has been to create a simpler work environment for the user, such as providing mapped network drives or mapped printers. Windows Server 2008 provides the following capabilities related to using scripts with Group Policy settings:

- **Ability to assign startup and shutdown scripts**   Using Group Policy, you can assign scripts to run when computers start up and shut down. These scripts run in the security context of the LocalSystem account.

- **Ability to assign user logon and logoff scripts**   Windows Server 2008 allows you to assign both user logon and user logoff scripts.

- **Ability to assign scripts to containers rather than to individuals**   One of the biggest advantages of using domain-based Group Policy to assign scripts is that you can assign a script to a container object such as an Organizational Unit. When you assign a script to a container in Active Directory, the script applies to all users or computers inside the container.

- **Availability of native support for Windows Script Host scripts**   Most Windows clients provide native support for Windows Script Host (WSH) scripts. WSH scripts are much more flexible and powerful for configuring user desktops through scripts. With WSH, the scripts can be used for much more than just mapping network drives.

Windows Server 2008 Active Directory Domain Services still supports the personal logon scripts that are assigned to the individual user accounts. If you still have individual logon scripts assigned to user accounts, they are run after the user logon scripts assigned by Group Policy.

To deploy Group Policy-based scripts, you must create the scripts using a supported scripting language such as batch files (.cmd), Microsoft Jscript, or VBScript, and then copy the scripts to the domain controllers. You can store the scripts in any location on the server as long as they are accessible to the clients. A common place to store a script is in the %SystemRoot%\

SYSVOL\sysvol*domainname**GlobalPolicyGUID*\Machine\Scripts folder or the %System-Root%\SYSVOL\sysvol*domainname**GlobalPolicyGUID*\User\Scripts folder. You can also store the logon scripts in the %SystemRoot%\SYSVOL\sysvol*domainname*\scripts folder. This folder is shared with a share name of NETLOGON, which is the default location where down-level clients search for logon scripts. After copying the script files to the server, create or modify the GPO and locate the Scripts (Startup/Shutdown) folder under the Computer Configuration\Policies\Windows Settings folder or the Scripts (Logon/Logoff) folder under the User Configuration\Policies\Windows Settings folder.

For example, to create an entry for a startup script, expand the Scripts (Startup/Shutdown) folder and double-click Startup. You can then add any startup scripts to the GPO.

Windows Server 2008 provides a number of Administrative templates that can be used to configure how the scripts will be processed on client workstations. Most of these settings are located by selecting Computer Configuration\Policies\Administrative Templates\System\Scripts, and a few are accessible also by selecting User Configuration\Policies\Administrative Templates\System\Scripts. The configuration options include whether or not to run the startup scripts asynchronously. If you choose the asynchronous option, multiple startup scripts can run at one time. You can also choose to run logon scripts synchronously, which means that all the startup scripts must complete before the Windows desktop will appear for the user. You can also configure a maximum wait time for all the scripts to finish running. And, finally, you can configure whether the scripts will run in the background and be invisible or whether the scripts should be visible when they run.

> **Note**   Windows Server 2008 includes a new feature called Group Policy preferences that can be used to perform tasks that traditionally have been part of logon scripts. The preferences feature may help you remove or simplify your requirements for logon scripts. Group Policy preferences are discussed later in this chapter.

Deploying Software Using Group Policy

Managing the software on user desktops can be a very labor-intensive task if an administrator must visit each desktop every time a new software package needs to be installed or upgraded. Group Policy Software Installation can significantly reduce the effort required to manage user desktops. In fact, one of the biggest cost savings to be gained from deploying Active Directory Domain Services and Group Policy is in the area of software management.

Managing software in a corporate environment consists of much more than simply deploying the software. Many companies have a clearly defined software life-cycle management process that includes purchasing or building and testing the application, piloting the application to a small group of users, widescale deployment of the application, maintenance of the application after deployment, and finally, the removal of the application. Group Policy Software Installation can make many of these tasks more efficient.

Windows Installer Technology

In most cases, software management through Group Policy relies on the Microsoft Windows Installer technology. Windows Installer technology is used to install, manage, and remove software on Windows workstations. Windows Installer technology consists of two components:

- **A software installation package file (.msi file)**   The .msi package file contains a database of information that contains all the instructions required to install and remove applications.

- **The Windows Installer service (Msiexec. exe)**   This service manages the actual installation of software on the workstation. The service uses a dynamic link library (DLL) named Msi.dll to read the .msi package files. Based on the content of the software installation package file, the service then copies application files to the local hard disk, creates shortcuts, modifies registry entries, and performs all the tasks listed in the .msi file.

Windows Installer technology has a number of benefits. One of the most important benefits is that any application can be largely self-healing. Because the .msi file contains all the information needed to install the application, the same file can be used to repair an application that has failed. For example, if an application fails because a critical file has been deleted, the application will fail to start the next time the user selects the application. If the application has been installed using Windows Installer, the same .msi file that was used to install the application will be used to repair the application by reinstalling the missing file. The .msi file also enables a more efficient uninstall process for applications that you need to remove from a client workstation.

Most software manufacturers now provide an .msi software installation package file with all new software. This is known as a *native Windows Installer file*. If the software includes an .msi file, you can use that file to install the software. If you do not have a native Windows Installer file, you can obtain a software packaging tool and use it to create an .msi file to be used for deployment using Group Policy.

Deploying Applications

Group Policy Software Installation provides a means to advertise or make an application available for installation to computers or users. After you configure the software installation policy setting, the fact that the new software package is available is advertised to the computer the next time the computer boots up or the next time the user logs on. The application is then ready to be installed on that computer.

Before you can advertise an application to users on the network, you must copy the software installation files, including the .msi file, to a network share that is accessible to all users. When you create the network share, you must ensure that all users or computers have appropriate access to the share. If you are assigning applications to computers, the computer accounts must have Read access. If you are assigning or publishing applications to users, the users must have Read access.

After creating the network share and copying the installation files to the share, you are ready to implement the Group Policy object (GPO) that will advertise the application to the clients. You can create a new GPO or modify an existing GPO. The first choice that you have to make when configuring the GPO is whether you want to advertise the application to computers or to users. If you decide to advertise the application to computers, you will use the Computer Configuration\Policies\Software Settings container in the Group Policy Management Editor, and the application will be installed on the workstation the next time the workstation is rebooted. If you decide to advertise the application to users, you will use the User Configuration\Policies\Software Settings container in the Group Policy Management Editor, and the application will be available to the user the next time the user logs on.

When you use Group Policy Software Installation to deploy applications, you have two choices for how the application will be advertised to the client. The first option is to *assign* the application, which can target either a computer or a user. The second option is to *publish*, which makes an application available, but only to user accounts.

When you assign an application to a computer, the application is completely installed the next time the computer is rebooted, which means that the application is installed for all users of a computer the next time they log on to that computer.

When you assign an application to a user, the application is advertised the next time the user logs on to the network. You can configure how the application is advertised, but most of the time, the application is added to the Start menu. The application is also added to the Get Programs list in the Programs and Features application found in Windows Vista and Windows Server 2008. By default, the application is not installed when the user logs on, but will be installed when the user activates the application from the Start menu or chooses to install the application through Programs and Features. You can also configure the install logic so that an application can be installed when the user tries to open a file with a file extension that is associated with the application. For example, if Microsoft Word is not currently installed on the user's computer, when the user double-clicks a file with a .doc extension, Word will automatically be installed. This process is often referred to as *extension activation*.

One feature that is available in Windows Server 2003 and Windows Server 2008, but not in Windows 2000, is the option to completely install the software application when the user logs on rather than after user activation. Choosing this option means that the logon process will take longer to allow the application to be installed, but the application is then available to the client for use. This option is available only when the application is assigned to a user. Published applications cannot be completely installed until they are installed through Add Or Remove Programs (called Get Programs in Windows Vista) or through extension activation. This option is also not applicable when the application is assigned to computers because the application is completely installed the next time the computer is rebooted.

When you publish an application to a user, the application is advertised the next time the user logs on to the network. In this case, however, the application is only advertised in the Add Or Remove Programs control panel. To install the application, the user must choose that option in Add Or Remove Programs. By default, published applications are also installed through extension activation.

In most cases, publishing an application is the best option if only some of the users require the application. For example, you might have a graphics application such as Microsoft Visio that only the network architects require all the time. However, some other users might need Visio. By publishing the application to the users, you are not installing the application on their desktops or adding it to their shortcuts, but you are making the application available for those who need it.

To advertise an application using Group Policy, use the following procedure:

1. Copy the software installation files to a network share. Configure the permissions on the share to ensure that all required users and computers have Read access to the installation files.

2. Using the Group Policy Management console, create a new GPO or modify an existing GPO. Link the GPO as required.

3. If you are advertising the application to users, expand the User Configuration\Policies\Software Settings container in the Group Policy Management Editor, right-click Software installation, click New, and then click Package. If you are advertising the application to computer accounts, expand the Computer Configuration\Policies\Software Settings container in the GPO, right-click Software installation, click New, and then click Package.

4. Browse to the network location or type in the network path where the installation files are located. You must use a network location and not a local drive letter on the server because the network location is advertised to the client computers. Select the appropriate .msi file.

> **Note** If you do select the wrong network location or if you choose to modify the network location after deployment, you must re-create the software package. There is no means to modify the installation path for the software package.

5. When you select the .msi file, you are given a choice of how you want to advertise the software package. Figure 12-14 shows the options if you are advertising the application to user accounts. If you are advertising the application to computers, you can only assign the application.

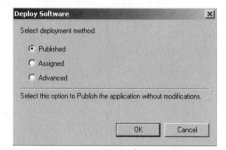

Figure 12-14   Options for advertising the software package.

6. If you chose to assign or publish the application, click OK. If you choose the Advanced option, you are presented with the Properties sheet for the package. This Properties sheet is discussed in the section "Configuring Software Package Properties" later in this chapter.

After the GPO is configured and linked to an appropriate container, the application will be advertised to all clients in the container object. By default, the software installation component of a GPO is applied only when the user logs on (if the policy is applied to user accounts) or when the computer reboots (if the policy is applied to computer accounts). The GPUpdate command-line tool can force a logoff or a reboot as part of the Group Policy update on the workstation. To force a logoff or a reboot, use the command *gpupdate /force /logoff* or *gpupdate /force /boot*.

Software Distribution and Network Bandwidth

One of the most difficult aspects of managing software distribution using Group Policy is network utilization management. If you assign a large multi-megabyte application to a large group of users and all of those users install the application at the same time, the installation might take hours because of the significant increase in the volume of network traffic. There are a number of options for managing the network bandwidth. One option is to assign applications to computers and ask users to reboot the computers at the end of the day. You can also force a reboot of the workstation by using the GPUpdate command. If you apply this command to only a few workstations at a time, the impact on the network can be minimized.

Another option is to assign applications to small groups of users at one time. In most cases, you might also want to avoid assigning applications that will be completely installed when the user logs on. If you advertise an application but allow the user to initiate the installation, you will be able to at least spread out the software installation over some time. Although none of these options is ideal, you can use them to at least manage the bandwidth to some extent.

Another way to manage network utilization if you have multiple sites is to use the Distributed File System (DFS). With DFS, you can create a logical directory structure that is independent of where the files are actually stored on the network. For example, you might create a DFS root named \\server1\softinst and then create subdirectories for all applications underneath that share point. With DFS, you can locate the subdirectories on multiple servers and configure multiple physical links to the same logical directories. If you use DFS Replication, you can even configure automatic replication of the folder contents between copies of the same directory. DFS is a site-aware application, which means that if you have multiple sites, the client computers will always connect to a copy of a DFS folder in their own site rather than cross a wide area network (WAN) link to access the folder on another site.

It is difficult to predict exactly what the effect of a network installation will be. One of the advantages of using Group Policy to install software is that you can easily perform a test to see the likely effect. For example, you can configure a GPO that includes the software package but make sure that the GPO is not linked to any organizational unit (OU). You can then create a temporary OU, add a few user or computer accounts to the OU, and link the GPO to the OU. This configuration can be used to test how long it takes to install the applications to a small group of users. You can also pilot the software distribution by linking the GPO to a production OU and then using Group Policy filtering to limit which users or computers will apply the GPO.

Regardless of the efforts you take to minimize the effect on the network, deploying a large application to a large number of users will always have some impact on the network. Since this is the case, you will probably have to plan on completing the installation over several days.

Using Group Policy to Distribute Non–Windows Installer Applications

In some cases, you might not want to go through the effort of creating an .msi file to install an application, but you might still want to use Group Policy to distribute an application. For example, you might have a simple application that must be installed on several workstations but that does not require any customization and is not likely to be upgraded. You can create and use a Zero Administration for Windows (ZAW) down-level applications package (.zap) file to install this application.

A *.zap file* is a text file that contains the setup instructions for installing an application. In most cases, the .zap file will contain only the following lines:

```
[Application]
FriendlyName = "applicationname"
SetupCommand = ""\\servername\sharename\installapplication.exe""
```

The *FriendlyName* value is the name that will be displayed in the Add Or Remove Programs control panel on the client computer. The *SetupCommand* value is the path to the installation file for the application. You can use a Universal Naming Convention (UNC) path or a mapped drive for the *SetupCommand* value. If the application provides a means to customize the installation by using setup parameters, you can include the parameters in the *SetupCommand* value, following the setup path's closing double quotation marks. For example, the value might be as follows:

```
SetupCommand = "\\servername\sharename\setup.exe" /parameter
```

Note that if the command line includes a parameter, the setup path uses a single set of double quotation marks instead of the two sets of double quotation marks required in the earlier example.

After you have created the .zap file and copied the application installation files to a network share, you can publish the application to users. The application is added to the list of available applications in the Add Or Remove Programs control panel. Users can then select the application to install. Applications that are distributed through .zap files cannot be assigned to either computers or users, and they will not install using extension activation.

Using a .zap file has several important limitations compared to using Windows Installer files. First, the installation of the application using the .zap file runs the normal installation program for the application, which means that you cannot customize the installation unless the application provides setup parameters to customize the installation. Further, the installation using .zap files cannot run with elevated permissions during the installation, which means that a user might need to be a local Administrator to install the application. Applications installed using .zap files are also not self-healing. If the application fails because a file has been previously corrupted or deleted, the user might have to run the original installation procedure again manually to reinstall the application. An application that has been installed using a .zap file also cannot be easily upgraded or patched. Because of these drawbacks, this software installation technology has limited usefulness and should be used only when you are installing a simple application that is not likely to be upgraded.

Configuring Software Package Properties

After you create the software package, you can modify the package properties. To access the package properties, right-click the package and select Properties. Figure 12-15 shows the Deployment tab. Table 12-8 describes the options available on this Properties sheet.

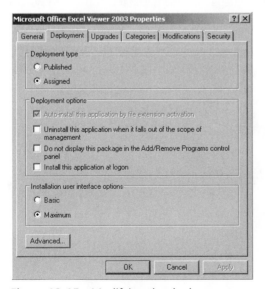

Figure 12-15   Modifying the deployment properties for a software package.

Table 12-8 Deployment Options for a Software Package

Setting	Explanation
Deployment type	Use this option to specify how the application will be advertised to clients.
Auto-install this application by file extension activation	Use this option to enable or disable the option to install software when the user opens a file of a selected extension. This option is not available if you assign an application.
Uninstall this application when it falls out of the scope of management	Use this option to control what occurs when the Group Policy no longer applies to the user or computer. For example, if the Group Policy is linked to user accounts in an OU, choosing this option means that the application will be uninstalled if the user account is moved out of the OU.
Do not display this package in the Add Or Remove Programs control panel	Use this option to control whether or not the application will be displayed in the Add Or Remove Programs control panel.
Install this application at logon	Use this option to completely install an application when the user logs on rather than wait for the user to initiate the installation. This option is not available when the application is published.
Installation user interface options	Use this option to control what is displayed for the user when the software is being installed. Selecting Basic means that only error messages and completion messages will be displayed. Selecting Maximum means that all software setup screens will be displayed.
Advanced	Use this option to configure additional settings for the software package. Options include installing 32-bit applications on 64-bit operating systems, installing the application even if it uses a different language than the destination operating system, and including Component Object Model (COM) components with the package so that the client can install the components from Active Directory. Figure 12-16 shows the interface.

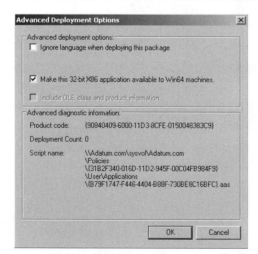

Figure 12-16 Using the Advanced Deployment Options page to configure Group Policy Software Installation.

Setting the Default Software Installation Properties

When you prepare to deploy software using Group Policy, you can configure the default settings for all software packages that are deployed using a specific GPO. You can access this interface by right-clicking the Software Installation container and selecting Properties. Figure 12-17 shows the interface.

Figure 12-17   Configuring the default software installation settings.

You can use this procedure to set the options that will be displayed when you create a new software package in this GPO. You can also set the default location for the software installation files and configure the installation's user-interface (UI) settings.

Installing Customized Software Packages

There may be situations that require you to customize the installation of a Windows Installer software package. For example, you might need to create a custom installation of your word-processing application to include custom dictionaries or templates. Or you might need to customize the installation of Microsoft Office to install only Microsoft Word and Microsoft Excel on every desktop, while deploying the full Office suite to only selected users. If you work for an international company, you might need to deploy the same application in multiple languages.

You can customize the installation of a software package by creating or obtaining a transform (.mst) file. The transform file contains instructions, in addition to the .msi file, that are used to customize the installation. The easiest way to create an .mst file is to use a software packaging application or a custom application provided by the software vendor. For example, Microsoft includes a Custom Installation wizard with the Resource Kit tools for most versions of Microsoft Office (prior to Office 2007). When you start this wizard, you select an .msi file, a name, and a location for the .mst file. Then the wizard presents all the options for customizing the default installation of the software. You can customize almost every aspect of the installation, including removing previous versions of Office, customizing which components will be installed, and deciding where those components will be installed. You can migrate user settings if the installation is an upgrade of existing software, or you can custom-configure personal settings and security settings. You can add additional files to the installation (such as custom templates), add or remove registry keys, add or remove shortcuts to Office applications, and configure e-mail client settings.

After creating the transform file, you must create a new software package to deploy the custom installation. When you create the new software package, select the Advanced option when choosing the deployment method so that you can add the transform file before the package is completed. From the software package's Properties sheet, select the Modifications tab and then add the transform files. Figure 12-18 shows the Modifications tab.

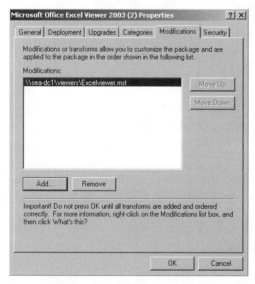

Figure 12-18   Adding transform files to a software package.

When you apply the transform file to the software package, all clients within the scope of the GPO that install the application will install the customized version. You can include more than one transform file with the software package. If you do, the transform files are applied starting from the top of the list, which means that transform files that are applied later in the installation process might overwrite earlier modifications.

Updating an Existing Software Package

Another useful feature that is available when Group Policy is used to deploy software is the option to update existing software packages. There are basically two ways to update existing software packages: updating or installing a service pack on an existing application and upgrading an application to a new version.

The two different methods for updating software require different procedures. If you are applying updates or a service pack to an existing application, you must first obtain an .msi file or a patch (.msp) file for the updated application. (Ideally, this file will come from the software manufacturer, but you can also create your own.) Copy the new .msi file and the other new software installation files into the same folder as the original .msi file, overwriting any duplicate files. Then redeploy the application. To do so, right-click the software package in the Group Policy Management Editor, select All Tasks, and then select Redeploy Application. The software package will be redeployed to all users and computers linked to the GPO.

If you are upgrading an existing application to a new version of the software, you will take a different approach. In this case, you must create a new software package to deploy the application. Then you can access the software package properties for the new application and select the Upgrades tab. Using the settings on this tab, you can create a link between the new software distribution package and an existing package. When you click Add from the Upgrades tab, you can choose which software package will be upgraded by this package. You can also configure whether or not the old application must first be uninstalled before the new application is installed. Figure 12-19 shows an example of upgrading Microsoft Office Excel Viewer 2003.

When you create the upgrade link, the Upgrades tab shows the new information. Figure 12-20 shows the interface. You can also use the Upgrades tab to make this a required upgrade. If you choose to make it a required upgrade, all software distributed by the previous GPO will be upgraded the next time the computer reboots or the user logs on. If you do not make it a required upgrade, the user can choose when to install the new application, either by activating the application from the Start menu or through the Programs And Features control panel. If you are using the same GPO for the upgrade software package that you used for the initial application, the original software package will show that the new package is upgrading it.

Figure 12-19   Upgrading an existing software package.

Figure 12-20   The Upgrades tab on a software package's Properties sheet.

Note   The fact that it is so easy to upgrade an application through Group Policy does not mean that upgrading should be taken lightly. Before deploying the upgrade, you should test the upgrade to ensure that it will not create problems with existing applications. You should also test the upgrade process to make sure that it will work smoothly in your organization. After you have ensured that the upgrade will work, you still have to manage the deployment. If the application that you are upgrading has been deployed to several thousand users and you decide to make the upgrade a required upgrade, the users might have to wait a long time for the installation to be completed. You must still manage the deployment of the upgrade to minimize the impact on the network bandwidth.

Configuring File Extension Activation

One of the means by which a user can initiate the installation of an application is through file extension activation. In most cases, you will have only one application that is linked to any specific file extension. However, in some cases, you might have more than one. For example, you might be upgrading Word 2000 to Word 2003, and for several months you might have both versions of the software available for installation. In this case, you can configure which of the application versions will be installed when a user initiates the install through file extension activation.

To configure this option, in the Group Policy Management Editor, access the Software Installation Properties sheet under Computer Configuration or User Configuration. Select the File Extensions tab. Figure 12-21 shows the interface. The application that is listed first will be installed when the file extension is activated.

Figure 12-21   Configuring file extension activation.

> **More Info**   There are a number of important issues to consider if you plan to use Group Policy Software Installation to deploy the 2007 Office Release. For more information, read "Use Group Policy Software Installation to Deploy the 2007 Office System," found at *http://technet2.microsoft.com/Office/en-us/library/efd0ee45-9605-42d3-9798-3b698fff3e081033.mspx?mfr=true.*

Removing Software Deployed by Group Policy

Group Policy Software Installation can be used to deploy applications and to remove previously installed applications. There are three options for removing software using Group Policy:

- Removing software as a preliminary step to installing a newer version of the software
- Removing software when the user or computer is moved outside the scope of management
- Removing software when you remove the software package

The first two options have been discussed earlier in the chapter. The last option requires some explanation. When you remove a software package from a GPO, you have a choice of how to manage the software that was installed by the GPO. Right-click the software package in the Software Installation listing, select All Tasks, and then select Remove. Figure 12-22 shows the dialog box that appears when you choose to remove a software installation package. If you choose Immediately Uninstall The Software From Users And Computers, the software will be uninstalled the next time the computer reboots or the user logs on. If you choose Allow Users To Continue To Use The Software, But Prevent New Installations, the application will continue to be available on the workstations, but new users will no longer be able to install the application using this GPO.

Figure 12-22   Configuring the removal of software when removing a software package.

Using Group Policy to Configure Windows Installer

Because most of the applications that you will install using Group Policy Software Installation use the Windows Installer technology, you might also need to configure how Windows Installer applications are installed. Several policy settings are used to configure how Windows Installer applications will be installed. Most of these settings can be configured at the following locations:

■ Computer Configuration\Policies\Administrative Templates\Windows Components\Windows Installer

■ User Configuration\Policies\Administrative Templates\Windows Components\Windows Installer

Table 12-9 explains the options that can be configured in both locations.

Table 12-9   Group Policy Setting Options for Windows Installer

Setting	Explanation
Enable user to browse for source while elevated (Computer Configuration only)	Use this option to browse for alternate installation sources if the application is being installed with elevated permissions.
Enable user to use media source while elevated (Computer Configuration only)	Use this option to allow the user to use removable media as the installation source if the application is being installed with elevated permissions.
Enable user to patch elevated products (Computer Configuration only)	Use this option to allow the user to install patches when the installation is running with elevated permissions.
Allow admin to install from terminal services session (Computer Configuration only)	Use this option to allow Terminal Services administrators to install and configure software using a Terminal Services session.
Always install with elevated privileges (Computer and User Configuration)	Use this option to allow users to install applications that require access to directories or registry keys that the user would normally not be able to access. Enabling this option means that Windows Installer will use the system permissions to install software.

Table 12-9 Group Policy Setting Options for Windows Installer *(continued)*

Setting	Explanation
Disable Windows Installer (Computer Configuration only)	Use this option to enable or disable the installation of software using Windows Installer. If you enable the policy, you can then disable Windows Installer completely, enable Windows Installer for all applications, or disable Windows Installer for those applications that are not distributed through group policies.
Prohibit rollback (Computer and User Configuration)	Use this option to disable the default Windows Installer behavior of creating files that can be used to roll back an incomplete installation.
Remove Browse Dialog Box For New Source (Computer Configuration only)	Use this option to disable the Browse button when the user wants to install a new feature using Windows Installer. Enabling this option disables the Browse button, which means that the user can install features only from administrator-configured sources.
Prohibit Patching (Computer Configuration only)	Use this option to prohibit the user from installing patches to programs using Windows Installer. Enabling this option provides enhanced security because it prevents the user from installing patches that might modify system files.
Disable IE Security Prompt For Windows Installer Scripts (Computer Configuration only)	Use this option to turn off the warning that the client receives when installing software through a browser interface, such as Microsoft Internet Explorer. You might want to use this option if most of your software is distributed through a Web site.
Enable User Control Over Installs (Computer Configuration only)	Use this option to give the user more control over the application installation. If you enable this option, the installation process will stop at each installation screen so that the user can modify the settings.
Cache Transforms In Secure Location On Workstation (Computer Configuration only)	Use this option to cache the transform files used to install a customized application on the local workstation. This transform file is required to repair or repeat the software installation.
Logging (Computer Configuration only)	Use this option to configure Windows Installer to increase the default level of logging for the software installation.
Prohibit User Installs (Computer Configuration only)	Use this option to manage whether or not the applications assigned to a user will be installed. If you enable this option, you can configure the setting so that only computer assigned applications will be installed. This setting can be useful if the computer is a kiosk or a shared computer. This option only applies to clients with Windows Installer v2.0 (or later) installed.

Table 12-9   Group Policy Setting Options for Windows Installer *(continued)*

Setting	Explanation
Turn Off Creation Of System Restore Checkpoints (Computer Configuration only)	Use this option to modify the default behavior on computers running Windows XP Professional, where a System Restore checkpoint is automatically created before any application is installed.
Search Order (User Configuration only)	Use this option to modify the default search order in which Windows Installer searches for installation files. By default, Windows Installer will first search the network, then removable media, and then an Internet URL.
Prevent Removable Media Source For Any Install (User Configuration only)	Use this option to prevent users from using Windows Installer to install any application from removable media.

Planning for Group Policy Software Installation

Using Group Policy to deploy and manage software installations can greatly decrease the amount of effort required to distribute and maintain software on client computers. However, taking advantage of this tool can be complicated, especially in a large company with many different software configurations for user desktops. Using Group Policy to manage software most effectively requires careful planning. This section outlines some of the things you should consider when planning for Group Policy Software Installation.

One of the factors that you must consider when deploying applications is whether or not to advertise the application to users or computers. In general, if most computers are shared computers, and every user requires a particular software package, you should assign the policy to computers. By assigning the policy to computers, the software is completely installed on the workstation the next time the workstation reboots and the software becomes available to all users. Assigning the software package to computers can also provide more options for managing network bandwidth. By using this option, you can configure a software installation GPO during the day and then ask users (or use a remote tool) to reboot the workstations after regular working hours.

If only a few users require a software package, it is usually more efficient to assign or publish the application to user accounts. In some cases, a software package must be distributed to users in multiple OUs. The best way to distribute the software in such cases is to assign a GPO high in the Active Directory hierarchy and then filter the application of the GPO by using security groups.

Another important decision to make when planning for software distribution is how many GPOs to use. At one extreme, you could use one GPO to distribute all software for a particular container, which will improve the client logon performance but could result in large and complicated GPO configurations. At the other extreme, you might choose to use many GPOs, with each GPO distributing a single application. In this case, the client logon performance might be affected because the computer has to read many GPOs. Organizations use a variety of approaches to deal with this problem. One fairly common approach is to create one GPO to install a standard set of applications that everyone needs and that is rarely modified. Additional GPOs are created for applications that are frequently updated (such as antivirus software) and for applications that are used by small groups of users.

You might also need to plan for software distribution across slow network links. Many companies have remote offices or remote users who connect to Active Directory using slow network connections. By default, the software distribution component of Group Policy is not applied when the client connects across a network connection that is less than 500 Kbps (kilobits per second). If the workstations on your network normally connect on a local area network (LAN) and only occasionally connect across a slow network connection, this default is probably acceptable. However, if you have network clients that almost always connect to the network across a slow network connection, you will need to prepare for these clients through some additional configuration.

One option is to leave the default software distribution as is, but force a complete installation of the software when the user does connect to the LAN. You can use this option if the clients occasionally do connect to your LAN. If you have clients that never connect to the LAN, you might need to use means outside of Active Directory to distribute software. For example, you might choose to distribute software using removable media or through a secure Web site if the clients have a fast Internet connection and normally connect to Active Directory through a slow virtual private network (VPN) connection.

Most large companies have some form of automated process for building workstations. Companies can use disk cloning technology or Windows Deployment Services (WDS) to rapidly build a standard desktop for a user. You can use this technology in combination with Group Policy to greatly optimize the distribution of software. For example, if you are using a disk cloning tool to build client workstations, you can build the client computer and then use a GPO to install a standard set of applications on each workstation. When this image is deployed to workstations, these applications can be managed using Group Policy. If you use WDS to install client machines, you can include the managed application in the WDS image for each department.

Perhaps the most important step in preparing to use a GPO to deploy software is to thoroughly test every software distribution before you deploy it. Most companies that use Group Policy to distribute software maintain a distribution test lab that contains workstations that are representative of the workstations in the production environment. You can easily create a test OU in Active Directory and move these computer accounts and some test user accounts into this OU. Then use this test environment to test every software distribution.

Limitations to Using Group Policy to Manage Software

Although Group Policy provides powerful tools for managing software on client computers, there are still some limitations with the technology. These limitations are particularly apparent when compared to software management tools such as Microsoft Systems Management Server (SMS) or System Center Configuration Manager (SCCM).

One of the most important limitations for many companies is that Group Policy can be used only to distribute software to Active Directory–aware Windows operating systems. Although this limitation is becoming less significant as more companies move to the latest operating systems, many large corporations still have Windows NT Workstation, Windows 95, or Windows 98 clients. If companies with these client computers want to use Group Policy to distribute software to newer clients, they must still maintain an alternative method for older clients.

A more significant limitation for companies that have the required clients is the lack of flexibility for scheduling a software installation. Applications are not advertised to the workstation until the user logs on again or until the computer reboots. The full-featured software distribution tools such as SCCM provide other options. For example, you can configure SCCM to start up a computer during the night using wake-on-LAN technology, install the software, and shut the computer down again. Or the software distribution can be scheduled at any time during the day, and the user does not need to log off or necessarily even be aware that the software distribution is occurring.

Another limitation with using Group Policy to distribute software is that it does not support the network's multicasting capabilities. Most network traffic is unicast traffic, that is, traffic that flows between two specific computers. With multicasting, a server can send out one stream of network traffic and multiple client computers can receive the same data. Because each software distribution is initiated by a client action, software distribution using a Group Policy cannot use multicasting. Using multicasting can save a great deal of bandwidth. For example, if you have several thousand clients in your company and you must distribute an urgent antivirus update, you will use up all the bandwidth on even the fastest network if you use a unicast solution. With multicasting, the software package is sent out only once and all the clients on the network will receive the update.

Using a GPO to distribute software also has a limitation in that it cannot discriminate which clients should receive a software package other than through the assignment of the GPO at the container level or through filtering based on groups. More full-featured software distribution tools such as SCCM create an inventory of all client computers. This inventory includes computer attributes such as hard disk space, CPUs, and RAM, as well as software installed on the computers. You can then use this inventory to discriminate which client computers will get a specific software package. For example, you might choose to install the latest version of Office only on the workstations that have adequate hard disk space and RAM.

Another important software distribution issue for some companies is dealing with disconnected clients. Some companies have large numbers of client computers that connect to the corporate network only occasionally, and then only through a dial-up or VPN connection. A full-featured software distribution tool can deal with these clients in a number of ways. One option is to provide a Web site that can be used to install the software and manage the software after installation. Another option is to provide very intelligent management of the software distribution when the client is connected. For example, you can distribute software to all dial-up clients, but strictly limit the amount of bandwidth the software distribution process can use. The software distribution process can also detect when the network connection is broken and restart the software distribution at the point where the connection was broken the next time the user connects to the network.

As can be seen from this list of limitations, using Group Policy to manage software does not provide all the functionality that you might want in a software distribution tool. However, for a small- to medium-sized company, Group Policy can solve many software distribution issues. For many companies, the price of using Group Policy is certainly right—especially when compared to the fairly expensive client licensing costs of using one of the other tools.

Overview of Group Policy Preferences

Group Policy preferences are a set of new client-side extensions included in Windows Server 2008 that provide the ability to centrally configure and manage operating system and application settings. Many of the settings that are configured as a preference have traditionally not been configurable using Group Policy and had to be applied by other methods, such as logon scripts. For example, if you wanted to configure a drive mapping to a network share or assign specific environment variables to a workstation, you had to create, test, and then assign logon scripts directly to user accounts or link a scripting GPO to an Active Directory container. The main disadvantage to scripting is that most organizations end up with complex logon scripts that require constant modifications or troubleshooting. Most organizations also only have one or two individuals who even know what the scripts do, and they have very minimal (if any) documentation describing the script actions. Group Policy preferences will most likely provide a way to remove or at least simplify the need for logon scripts within your organization.

Group Policy Preferences vs. Policy Settings

In order to effectively determine whether to use Preferences or Policy Settings to manage a client computer, it is important to understand the differences between these two technologies. In comparison, Preferences and Policy Settings differ in two main areas:

- **Enforcement**   When you configure a Group Policy setting, it is enforced on any user or computer assigned to the GPO. Typically, any Group Policy–aware application or operating system feature will disable the user interface so that users are prevented from changing any of the managed settings. This enforcement is also refreshed at a regular interval. On the other hand, if you configure a Group Policy preference, the configuration is not strictly enforced and allows users to change settings as they see fit. You can configure preferences to apply only once, or you can configure a preference setting to reapply during the standard Group Policy refresh interval.

- **Targeting**   One of the limitations of Group Policy settings is that you cannot filter individual policy settings within a GPO. Your only option is to create specific GPOs per policy setting and then apply the GPO using Windows Management Instrumentation (WMI) filtering or Security Group Filtering. However, the Preferences feature provides the ability to assign item-level targeting. For example, you may have a preference setting to apply drive mappings to two separate departments. You can target one preference setting to one department and then configure a second preference setting to a second department, all within a single GPO.

Table 12-10 provides a summary on the differences between Policy Settings and Preferences.

Table 12-10   Comparison Between Policy Settings and Preferences

Functionality	Policy Settings	Preferences
Enforcement	■ Settings are enforced ■ User interface is disabled ■ Settings are refreshed ■ Requires Group Policy–aware features and applications	■ Settings are not enforced ■ User interface is not disabled ■ Can be configured to apply only once or to be refreshed at regular intervals ■ Does not require Group Policy–aware features and applications
Local Group Policy Support	Supports Local Group Policy	Does not support Local Group Policy
Targeting and Filtering	Only supports filtering at the GPO level (via WMI or security group filtering)	Supports item-level targeting

Group Policy Preferences Settings

Group Policy preferences are organized to provide Windows Settings and Control Panel Settings. Windows Settings consist of many options that have typically been configured using scripts, such as drive maps, registry settings, and environment variables. Control Panel Settings are options that are typically configured from within the Control Panel on a Windows computer, such as Folder Options, Power Options, Local Users And Groups, and Start Menu settings.

Windows Settings

Table 12-11 and Figure 12-23 both provide a description and illustration of the preferences available under Windows Settings.

Table 12-11   Preferences Available for Windows Settings

Preference Setting	Description
Environment	Allows you to create user or system environment variables and modify or replace existing environment variables.
Files	Allows you to copy files to a new location and configure attributes. You can also modify or delete existing files and file attributes.

Table 12-11   Preferences Available for Windows Settings *(continued)*

Preference Setting	Description
Folders	Allows you to create, modify, or delete folders and folder attributes. You can also configure this preference to delete all files within a specific folder without deleting the folder (useful for maintaining the temporary files folder).
Ini Files	Allows you to add, replace, or delete sections or properties within specific .ini or .inf files. You can also delete an entire .ini or .inf file using this preference.
Registry	This preference allows you to copy, create, replace, or delete registry keys or values.
Network Shares (only under Computer Configuration)	This preference setting allows you to create, modify, or specify settings such as user limits, access-based enumeration, and comments for network shares.
Shortcuts	Allows you to create, modify, or delete shortcuts on a user's computer. Shortcuts can include traditional shortcut links, URLs, or shortcuts to shell objects such as the Control Panel.
Applications (only under User Configuration)	Allows you to configure settings for applications. This preference requires an application plug-in provided by the application vendor or developed by your software developer.
Drive Maps (only under User Configuration)	Provides the ability to create, modify, or delete drive mappings.

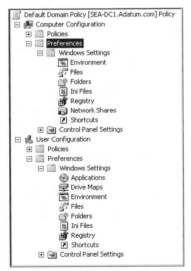

Figure 12-23   Viewing Windows Settings Preferences.

Control Panel Settings

Table 12-12 and Figure 12-24 show the preferences available under Control Panel Settings.

Table 12-12   Preferences Available for Control Panel Settings

Preference Setting	Description
Data Sources	Provides the ability to centrally configure Open Database Connectivity (ODBC) data source names for users or computers.
Devices	Provides the ability to enable or disable specific types of hardware devices, such as USB ports or floppy drives.
Folder Options	Provides the ability to configure various Windows Explorer settings, such as file associations and folder view options.
Internet Settings (User Configuration only)	Provides the ability to configure initial settings for Internet Explorer.
Local Users and Groups	Provides the ability to centrally manage local users and the members of local groups on domain member computers.
Network Options	Provides the ability to configure VPN and dial-up networking connection settings.
Power Options	Provides the ability to configure Windows Server 2003 and Windows XP power settings.
Printers	Allows you to create, configure, and delete local, shared, or network-based printers.
Regional Options (User Configuration only)	Provides the ability to configure how applications format regional settings such as numbers, currencies, dates, and times.
Scheduled Tasks	Provides the ability to create, modify, or delete a scheduled task. You can also specify that a command should be run immediately upon the next Group Policy refresh interval or at every refresh cycle.
Start Menu (User Configuration only)	Provides the ability to configure Start menu settings for both Windows XP and Windows Vista computers.
Services (Computer Configuration only)	Provides the ability to configure and manage services available on the computer.

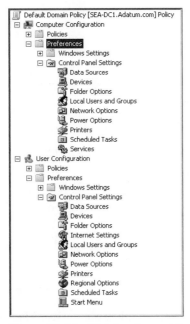

Figure 12-24 Viewing Control Panel Settings Preferences.

Group Policy Preferences Options

Many of the Group Policy preferences contain common actions and options related to how the preferences item is processed. For example, you can create preferences items that perform one of the following actions when processed during the Group Policy refresh cycle:

- **Create** A new item or setting is created and applied.
- **Replace** Remove an existing item and then replace it with the configured preference item.
- **Update** Modify an existing preference item and create it if it does not exist.
- **Delete** Remove an existing item or setting.

Each preference item also has a Common tab that contains a number of processing options, as shown in Figure 12-25.

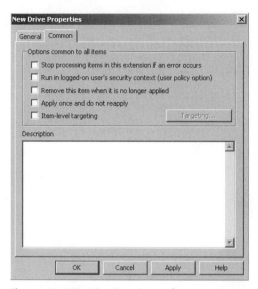

Figure 12-25 Viewing the preferences Common tab.

Table 12-13 describes the options available on the Common tab, which is included for each preference item.

Table 12-13 Common Options for Group Policy Preferences

Option	Description
Stop processing items in this extension if an error occurs	This option will stop processing this specific extension if an error occurs within the GPO itself. By default, if a specific extension fails to process, all other extensions will continue to be processed as configured.
Run in logged-on user's security context (user policy option)	By default, the local System account is used as the security context for GPO processing. If you need to access user environment variables and network resources, you must enable this option to run in the logged-on user's security context.
Remove this item when it is no longer applied	By default, preferences are not removed when a GPO no longer applies to the user or computer. Choosing this option changes this behavior.
Apply once and do not reapply	By default, Group Policy is refreshed every *90 minutes*. As a result, all policy settings and preferences are reapplied during the refresh cycle. If you select this option, the preferences item will only apply during the initial policy refresh cycle and will not then be reapplied. This allows end users to change the setting as they see fit.

Table 12-13   Common Options for Group Policy Preferences *(continued)*

Option	Description
Item-level targeting	Item-level targeting provides the ability to create filters based on various attributes such as *user name, disk space,* and *operating system.* Figure 12-26 provides an example of an item targeted for any computer that has free space greater than or equal to 80 GB on the C drive.

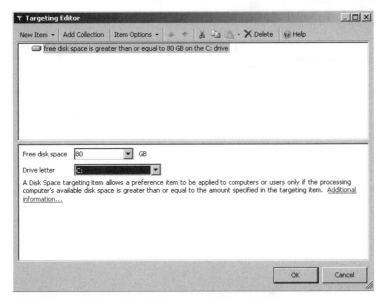

Figure 12-26   Configuring item-level targeting.

 Note   You must deploy the Group Policy preferences client-side extensions to any computer that you want to use preferences on. The CSE is already included with Windows Server 2008 but requires a separate download from Microsoft for Windows XP with SP2, Windows Vista, and Windows Server 2003 with SP1.

 Note   Many fields within Group Policy preferences can use environment variables. You can display a master list of available variables by placing your cursor in a field and then pressing F3. The Select A Variable dialog box opens, as shown in Figure 12-27.

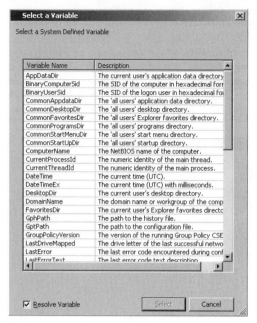

Figure 12-27   Selecting system defined variables.

Summary

Windows Server 2008 provides many updated and improved features for managing user desktops. Group Policy can be used to manage user data and profiles to provide users with a familiar work environment while still allowing centralized administration. Group Policy also provides powerful tools for deploying and managing software on workstations. Using Group Policy and Windows Installer technology, you can deploy software to workstations and then manage that software throughout the software life cycle. Group Policy preferences provide an easy way to configure operating system or application settings that previously had to be applied using logon scripts. This chapter provided an overview of how you can implement these options to manage user desktops.

Additional Resources

The following resources contain additional information and tools related to this chapter.

Related Information

- Chapter 11, "Introduction to Group Policy," provides details on the architecture and configuration of Group Policy objects.

- "Managing Group Policy ADMX Files Step-by-Step Guide," available at *http://go.microsoft.com/fwlink/?LinkId=75124*

- "Group Policy Preferences Overview," available at *http://www.microsoft.com/downloads/details.aspx?familyid=42E30E3F-6F01-4610-9D6E-F6E0FB7A0790&displaylang=en*

- "Group Policy Wiki," available at *http://grouppolicy.editme.com/*

- "Group Policy Team Blog," available at *http://blogs.technet.com/GroupPolicy/*

- "Deploying a Managed Software Environment," available at *http://technet2.microsoft.com/windowsserver/en/library/3ddda5bf-cf67-4408-b68c-7e1fcb5e47ee1033.mspx?mfr=true*

- "Use Group Policy Software Installation to Deploy the 2007 Office System," available at *http://technet2.microsoft.com/Office/en-us/library/efd0ee45-9605-42d3-9798-3b698fff3e081033.mspx?mfr=true*

- "Managing Roaming User Data Deployment Guide," available at *http://www.microsoft.com/downloads/details.aspx?\1displaylang=en&familyid=311f4be8-9983-4ab0-9685-f1bfec1e7d62&displaylang=en*

- "Windows Server Group Policy," available at *http://technet.microsoft.com/en-us/windowsserver/grouppolicy/default.aspx*

- "ADMX Migrator," available at *http://www.microsoft.com/downloads/details.aspx?FamilyId=0F1EEC3D-10C4-4B5F-9625-97C2F731090C&displaylang=en*

On the Companion CD

- LonghornGPSettings.xls, which contains all of the Group Policy settings available as of Windows Server 2008 Beta 3

Chapter 13

Using Group Policy to Manage Security

One of the most important administrative tasks related to desktop and server management is configuring and maintaining security. Maintaining a consistent security configuration across thousands of computers within an organization is almost impossible without some type of central management. Group Policy can be used to provide that central management to secure domain-level settings, server-based security settings, and network communication security settings.

This chapter describes how you can use Group Policy to configure and deploy domain-based security settings such as account and password policies. It begins with a description of the Default Domain Policy and the Default Domain Controllers policy and then continues with a discussion on how to increase security and manageability using fine-grained password policies. This chapter also describes additional Group Policy-based security scenarios such as securing wired and wireless networks and configuring Windows Firewall and IPsec security features. Finally, this chapter provides information for configuring and deploying Security Templates to assist in the management of security settings throughout your network environment.

Configuring Domain Security with Group Policy

During the installation of Active Directory Domain Services, two default Group Policy objects (GPOs) are created to deploy the initial security configurations for the domain and domain controllers within the environment. The next two sections describe the security settings configured within these default Group Policy objects.

Overview of the Default Domain Policy

The Default Domain Policy GPO provides the initial security settings for the entire domain. These initial security settings relate specifically to the Account Policies and Local Policies nodes found under Computer Configuration\Policies\Windows Settings\Security Settings. Figure 13-1 displays the settings contained within these two nodes.

Figure 13-1   Viewing the Account Policies and Local Policies nodes.

Account Policies

The Account Policies section includes three categories: Password Policy, Account Lockout Policy, and Kerberos Policy. These policies, with the exception of the Kerberos Policy, apply to all users in the domain, regardless of what type of workstation the users are logging on from. Kerberos Policy settings are applied only to those computers in the domain that are running Windows 2000, Windows XP Professional, Windows Server 2003/2008, and Business and Enterprise versions of Windows Vista.

Password Policy   The Password Policy configuration options contain domain-wide settings for password history, age, length, and complexity. Table 13-1 describes each setting.

Table 13-1   Password Policy

Configuration Setting	Description	Default
Enforce password history	Defines the number of new passwords that have to be unique before a user can reuse an old password. Possible values: *0* to *24*	*24* passwords remembered for domain controllers and domain-member computers; *0* for stand-alone servers.
Maximum password age	Defines the number of days that a password can be used before the user is required to change it. To configure passwords to never expire, set the number of days to *0*. Possible values: *0* to *999*	*42* days

Table 13-1   Password Policy *(continued)*

Configuration Setting	Description	Default
Minimum password age	Defines the number of days that a password *must* be used before a user is allowed to change it. To allow immediate changes, set to *0*. Possible values: *0* to *998*	*1* day for domain controllers and domain-member computers; *0* for stand-alone servers.
Minimum password length	Defines the least number of characters required in a password. If no password is required, set the value to *0*. Possible values: *0* to *14*	*7* characters for domain controllers and domain-member computers; *0* for stand-alone servers.
Passwords must meet complexity requirements	Increases password complexity by enforcing that passwords do not contain any part of the user's account name or parts of the user's full name that exceed two consecutive characters, are at least 6 characters in length, and contain characters from three of the four following categories: Uppercase letters (*A-Z*) Lowercase letters (*a-z*) Base-10 digits (*0-9*) Special characters (such as: *!, $, #, %*) Requirements are enforced when passwords are created or changed.	Enabled for domain controllers and domain-member computers; Disabled for stand-alone servers.
Store password using reversible encryption	Using this setting is the same as storing passwords in clear text. This policy provides support for applications that use protocols that require access to the user passwords for authentication. This setting is typically used when implementing Challenge-Handshake Authentication Protocol (CHAP) through remote access or Internet Authentication Services and is also required if you are using Digest Authentication in Internet Information Services (IIS).	Disabled

> **Direct from the Source: Using Custom Password Filters**
>
> You can use custom developed password filters to define what constitutes a complex password. For example, you can block certain keywords (such as a company's name or location) from being included in the passwords. You can also increase or lower the complexity levels that define a complex password. These password filters work with the newly introduced fine-grained password policies in Windows Server 2008. The platform's SDK has a sample custom password DLL. For more information, see the article located at *http://msdn2.microsoft.com/en-us/library/ms721884.aspx*.
>
> *Gautam Anand*
>
> *Technical Lead–Directory Services*
>
> *Premier Enterprise Platforms Support*

Account Lockout Policy   The Account Lockout Policy configuration options contain settings for the password lockout duration and threshold, as well as for account lockout counter reset. Table 13-2 describes each setting.

Table 13-2   Account Lockout Policy

Configuration Setting	Description	Default
Account lockout duration	Defines the number of minutes that a locked-out account remains locked out. After the specified number of minutes, the account will automatically become unlocked. To specify that an administrator must unlock the account, set the value to *0*. Any nonzero value should be equal to or greater than the value for Reset Account Lockout Counter After. Possible values: *0* to *99,999*	Not Defined Set to *30* minutes if Account Lockout Threshold is set to *1* or greater.
Account lockout threshold	Determines the number of failed logon attempts allowed before a user account will be locked out. A value of *0* means that the account will never be locked out. Possible values: *0* to *999*	*0* invalid logon attempts
Reset account lockout counter after	Determines the number of minutes that must elapse after a failed logon attempt before the bad logon counter is reset to *0*. Any nonzero value should be equal to or less than the value for Account Lockout Duration Possible values: *1* to *99,999*	Not Defined Set to *30* minutes if Account Lockout Threshold is set to *1* or greater.

Kerberos Policy   The Kerberos Policy configuration options contain settings for the Kerberos Ticket-Granting Ticket (TGT) and session ticket lifetimes and time-stamp settings. Table 13-3 describes each setting.

Table 13-3   Kerberos Policies

Configuration Setting	Description	Default
Enforce user logon restrictions	Requires the Key Distribution Center (KDC) to validate every request for a session ticket against the User Rights policy of the target computer.	Enabled
Maximum lifetime for service ticket	Determines the maximum amount of time, in minutes, that a service ticket is valid to access a resource. Possible values: greater than *10* minutes up to a value less than or equal to the value (expressed in minutes) of the Maximum Lifetime For User Ticket setting, but not exceeding *99,999*. A value of *0* can be set and will cause the ticket to never expire, the Maximum Lifetime For User Ticket value to be set to *1*, and the Maximum Lifetime For User Ticket Renewal to be set to *23*.	*600* minutes (10 hours)
Maximum lifetime for user ticket	Determines the maximum amount of time, in hours, that a TGT can be used. When this expires, the workstation must obtain a new TGT. Possible values: *0* to *99,999* A value of *0* indicates that the ticket will not expire and sets Maximum Lifetime For User Ticket Renewal to Not Defined.	*10* hours
Maximum lifetime for user ticket renewal	Determines the amount of time, in days, that a user's TGT can be renewed. During this time period, a TGT can be renewed rather than requiring a new ticket. A value of *0* indicates that ticket renewal is disabled.	7 days
Maximum tolerance for computer clock synchronization	Determines the amount of time difference, in minutes, that Kerberos will tolerate between the client computer's clock and the time on the domain controller's clock. Note that this setting is reset to the default value each time the computer is restarted.	*5* minutes

Account Polices configured within the Default Domain Policy GPO affect all users and computers in the domain. It is possible to create a custom GPO configured with Account Policy settings and link it to an OU; however, the configured settings will not affect anyone logging on to the domain. If you do configure the account policy settings in a specific GPO and link it to an OU, the settings will only affect the local security database for the computers in the OU. When account policy settings are configured at an OU level, they are applied only when a user logs on locally to a computer. When a user logs on to the domain, the Default Domain Policy GPO always overrides the local policy settings.

Local Policies

The Local Policies section controls the local security settings for computers that are within scope of the GPO. These security settings include the following:

- **Audit Policy**   This node is used to configure audit settings. You can set audit policies for options such as account management activities, logon events, policy changes, privilege use, and system events.

- **User Rights Assignment**   This node is used to configure the rights that users will have on computers affected by this policy. You can set a variety of settings, including who can perform actions such as logging on locally, accessing the computer from the network, backing up files and folders, logging on as a service, and so on.

- **Security Options**   This node is used to configure security options for computers affected by this policy. You can configure options such as renaming the local Administrator or Guest accounts, managing who can install printer drivers, controlling whether unsigned drivers can be installed, and controlling how User Account Control is managed on computers.

The Default Domain Policy only has a small subset of settings defined within the Local Polices node. These default settings can be found in the Computer Configuration\Policies\Windows Settings\Security Settings\Local Policies\Security Options node. These settings include the following:

- **Network access: Allow anonymous SID/Name translation**   This setting is defined and disabled by default. If this policy is enabled, an anonymous user can then request SID information about another user and then use the SID to get the name of the user. This could become a security issue and reveal critical administrative account information.

- **Network security: Do not store LAN Manager hash value on next password change**   This setting is defined and enabled by default. This setting is enabled to increase security and not use the LM hash to store password information. Note that this setting can affect the ability to communicate with computers running Windows 95 and Windows 98.

- **Network security: Force logoff when logon hours expire**   This setting is defined and disabled by default. This setting is used to disconnect users who are connected to the local computer after their valid logon hours. If the policy is disabled (as it is by default), an established client session is allowed to be maintained after the logon hours have expired.

Remember that any settings configured at the domain level will affect all computers within the domain. Most organizations require various audit policies, user rights assignments, or security options depending on the role or type of computer. For this reason, the Local Policies are typically configured at an OU level in order to only affect specific computers within the domain. The next section will discuss how the Default Domain Controllers Policy has specific Local Policies configured to affect all domain controllers within the domain.

> **Note** It is recommended to only use the Default Domain Policy to provide the domain-based security settings. If you have a need to add additional policy settings at the domain level, create and link new task-level GPOs containing the required policy settings.

Overview of the Default Domain Controllers Policy

The Default Domain Controllers Policy GPO provides the initial security settings for all domain controllers residing in the Domain Controllers OU. Specifically, this GPO provides security settings related to the User Rights Assignment and Security Options nodes found under Computer Configuration\Policies\Windows Settings\Security Settings\Local Policies. Figure 13-2 provides an illustration of the Default Domain Controllers Policy with the User Rights Assignment node highlighted.

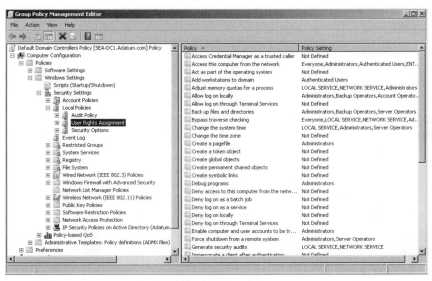

Figure 13-2   Viewing the User Rights Assignment for the Default Domain Controllers Policy.

User Rights Assignment

User Rights Assignments define which accounts can perform specific tasks on the computer. For example, if you want to provide the ability for a user or security group to be able to log on locally to domain controllers, you can configure that ability from within this node. Table 13-4 provides an overview of the policies available under User Rights Assignment and the default policy settings for the Default Domain Controllers Policy GPO.

Table 13-4 User Rights Assignment Policy Settings

Policy	Description	Default Setting for the Default Domain Controllers Policy GPO
Access Credential Manager as a trusted caller	Only used by Credential Manager for Backup and Restore procedures. No accounts should be provided with this user right.	Not Defined
Access this computer from the network	Specifies which users and groups are allowed to connect to this computer over the network. Note that Terminal Services is not affected by this user right.	Administrators Authenticated Users Enterprise Domain Controllers Everyone Pre-Windows 2000 Compatible Access
Act as part of the operating system	Allows a process to impersonate any user without authentication and gain access to local resources. Only used if your organization is running Windows NT or Windows 2000 servers that contain legacy applications.	Not Defined
Add workstations to domain	Determines which groups or users are allowed to add workstations to a domain. Note that this setting is only valid on domain controllers. Users will be able to create up to 10 computer accounts in the domain when provided with the user right.	Authenticated Users
Adjust memory quotas for a process	Specifies who can change the amount of memory that can be used by a process.	Administrators Local Service Network Service

Table 13-4   User Rights Assignment Policy Settings *(continued)*

Policy	Description	Default Setting for the Default Domain Controllers Policy GPO
Allow log on locally	Specifies which users can interactively log on to the server.	Account Operators Administrators Backup Operators Print Operators Server Operators
Allow logon through Terminal Services	Specifies which users or groups are able to log on as a Terminal Services client.	Not Defined
Back up files and directories	Specifies which users can bypass other object permissions for the purpose of backing up the system.	Administrators Backup Operators Server Operators
Bypass traverse checking	Specifies which users can access folders within a directory tree even though specific permissions may not be applied to parent folders within the tree.	Administrators Authenticated Users Everyone Local Service Network Service Pre-Windows 2000 Compatible Access
Change the system time	Specifies which user or group can change the system time on the server.	Administrators Local Service Server Operators
Change the time zone	Specifies which user or group can modify the time zone on the server.	Not Defined
Create a pagefile	Specifies which user or group can call an API to create a page file.	Administrators
Create a token object	Determines which accounts can be used by specific processes to create an access token object. Typically only used by the operating system.	Not Defined
Create global objects	Specifies which user or groups can create global objects during Terminal Services sessions.	Not Defined

Table 13-4   User Rights Assignment Policy Settings *(continued)*

Policy	Description	Default Setting for the Default Domain Controllers Policy GPO
Create permanent shared objects	Specifies which accounts can be used by processes to create a directory object. Typically only used by the operating system.	Not Defined
Create symbolic links	Specifies which user or groups can create a symbolic link from the computer the user is logged on to.	Not Defined
Debug programs	Specifies which users can attach a debugger to any process or to the kernel. This right provides complete access to critical operating system components and should be used with caution.	Administrators
Deny access to this computer from the network	Used to specify which users or computers are prevented from accessing the computer over the network.	Not Defined
Deny logon as a batch job	Used to specify which accounts are prevented from being able to log on as a batch job.	Not Defined
Deny logon as a service	Used to specify which accounts are prevented from being able to log on as a service.	Not Defined
Deny logon locally	Used to specify which accounts are prevented from being able to interactively log on to the computer.	Not Defined
Deny logon through Terminal Services	Used to specify which accounts are prevented from being able to log on as a Terminal Services client.	Not Defined
Enable computer and user accounts to be trusted for delegation	A process that is trusted for delegation can access resources on another computer using the credentials of a client.	Administrators

Table 13-4   User Rights Assignment Policy Settings *(continued)*

Policy	Description	Default Setting for the Default Domain Controllers Policy GPO
Force shutdown from a remote system	Specifies which user or group has the right to shut down a computer from a remote location over the network.	Administrators Server Operators
Generate security audits	Specifies which accounts can be used by a process to add entries to the security log.	Local Service Network Service
Impersonate a client after authentication	Specifies which accounts a program can use to impersonate a client. Use this right with caution, as it can be a security risk.	Not Defined
Increase a process working set	Specifies which user accounts can increase or decrease the size of the working set of a process, which is the set of memory pages currently visible in physical RAM.	Not Defined
Increase scheduling priority	Specifies which accounts can use a process with Write Property access to another process to increase the execution priority assigned to the other process. Changing the schedule priority is typically accomplished using the Task Manager.	Administrators
Load and unload device drivers	Specifies which accounts can dynamically load and unload device drivers in to the kernel mode. Note that this does not apply to Plug and Play device drivers.	Administrators Print Operators
Lock pages in memory	Specifies which accounts can use a process to keep data in the physical memory of the computer and prevent paging the data to virtual memory on disk.	Not Defined

Table 13-4   User Rights Assignment Policy Settings *(continued)*

Policy	Description	Default Setting for the Default Domain Controllers Policy GPO
Log on as a batch job	Provides the ability for a user to be logged on as a batch user rather than as an interactive user. Typically only used with older versions of Windows.	Administrators Backup Operators Performance Log Users
Log on as a service	Specifies which accounts can register a process as a service.	Not Defined
Manage auditing and security log	Specifies which users can configure object access auditing options as well as the ability to view and clear the security log.	Administrators
Modify an object label	Specifies which user account can modify the integrity label of objects such as files, registry keys, or processes owned by other users.	Not Defined
Modify firmware environment values	Specifies which accounts can modify firmware environment values such as settings stored in nonvolatile RAM.	Administrators
Perform volume maintenance tasks	Specifies which users or groups can run maintenance tasks such as remote defragmentation on a volume.	Not Defined
Profile single process	Specifies which accounts can use performance monitoring tools to monitor the performance of nonsystem processes.	Administrators
Profile system performance	Specifies which accounts can use performance monitoring tools to monitor the performance of system processes.	Administrators
Remove computer from docking station	Specifies which accounts are able to undock a computer from its docking station.	Administrators
Replace a process-level token	Specifies which account can call the CreateProcessAsUser() API so that one service can start another service.	Network Service Local Service

Table 13-4   User Rights Assignment Policy Settings *(continued)*

Policy	Description	Default Setting for the Default Domain Controllers Policy GPO
Restore files and directories	Specifies which accounts can bypass file and object permissions to perform restore tasks for backed-up information.	Administrators Backup Operators Server Operators
Shut down the system	Specifies which accounts are able to shut down the computer using the *Shut Down* command.	Administrators Backup Operators Print Operators Server Operators
Synchronize directory service data	Specifies which accounts have the right to perform Active Directory synchronization.	Not Defined
Take ownership of files or other objects	Specifies which accounts can take ownership of any securable object.	Administrators

Security Options

The Security Options node of the Default Domain Controllers Policy contains a number of defined default settings. Most of the default settings refer to how the domain controllers will apply network security and communication with clients. Table 13-5 lists the security options that are defined by default in the Default Domain Controllers Policy GPO.

Table 13-5   Security Options Defined in the Default Domain Controllers Policy

Security Option	Description	Default Setting
Domain controller: LDAP server signing requirements	Specifies whether or not an LDAP server requires signing negotiations with an LDAP client.	None
Domain member: Digitally encrypt or sign secure channel data (always)	Specifies whether or not all secure channel traffic initiated by the domain member must be signed or encrypted.	Enabled
Microsoft network server: Digitally sign communications (always)	Specifies whether or not packet signing is required by the server message block (SMB) component.	Enabled
Microsoft network server: Digitally sign communications (if client agrees)	Specifies whether or not packet signing will be negotiated if the client requests it.	Enabled
Network security: LAN Manager authentication level	Determines which challenge/response authentication protocol is used for network logons.	Send NTLMv2 response only

Recreating the Default GPOs for a Domain

If undocumented changes have been applied to the default GPOs and you need to revert back to the default settings, you have two choices. If you have used the backup feature from the Group Policy Management console to back up the Default Domain Policy and the Default Domain Controllers Policy, you can just restore the GPOs from backup. This is assuming that the backed-up versions contain the reverted settings that you need. The second option is to use a command-line tool called Dcgpofix. This command-line tool provides the ability to restore either the Default Domain Policy, Default Domain Controllers Policy, or both, back to the original settings. For example, you can restore the Default Domain Controllers Policy by typing the following command:

```
dcgpofix /Target: Domain
```

You can view more information about the Dcgpofix command by typing **dcgpofix /?** (as shown in Figure 13-3).

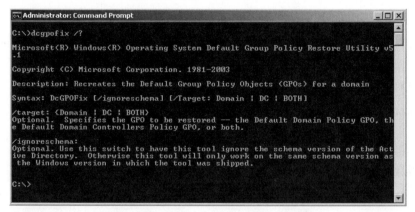

Figure 13-3 Viewing the Dcgpofix command-line options.

Direct from the Source: Impact of Using Dcgpofix

Be sure to back up your Default Domain Policy and your Default Domain Controllers Policy before running Dcgpofix. The following are some of the ways using Dcgopfix can have unintended effects:

- The EFS data recovery agent that is stored in the Default Domain Policy will be lost. The data recovery agent is specified in the following location of the group policy object: Computer Configuration\Policies\Security Settings\Public Key Policies\Encrypting File System.

  For more information, see "How to Back Up the Recovery Agent Encrypting File System (EFS) Private Key in Windows Server 2003, in Windows 2000, and in Windows XP" at *http://support.microsoft.com/kb/241201*.

In addition, you may lose any custom setting in Automatic Certificate Request Settings, Trusted Root Certification Authorities, Enterprise Trust, and Autoenrollment settings that are configured in the Default Domain Controllers Policy and/or the Default Domain Policy.

- Exchange 2000 and 2003 may be impacted by using Dcgpofix to recreate the Default Domain Controllers Policy. Exchange DomainPrep adds domain\exchange enterprise servers to the manage auditing and security log user right assignment for the Default Domain Controllers policy. If this is not present, the information store and MTA will not start on Exchange servers. You can resolve this by rerunning the Exchange setup /domainprep or by adding the entries back in manually after recreating the policy.

- Services installed on domain controllers that are running as domain users may not start. Applications such as IIS will create accounts on domain controllers and add user rights assignments for those accounts to run as service, access from network, and so on. If those entries are not present, the services may fail to start. This can happen in either the Default Domain or Default Domain Controllers policies.

- Audit settings and user rights will be changed. See Knowledge Base article 833783 at *http://support.microsoft.com/default.aspx?scid=kb;EN-US;833783* for more information about these changes.

Michael Hunter

Support Escalation Engineer

Directory Services Team

Fine-Grained Password Policies

In previous versions of Active Directory, domain-based Account Policies must be configured from within the Default Domain Policy GPO. As a result, every user within the domain is forced to have the same password policy and account lockout policies. For example, you may have a group of users (such as the domain administrators) that require a stricter password policy than normal domain users. Previous Active Directory implementations provided very minimal options for addressing this type of requirement.

Windows Server 2008 Active Directory Domain Services introduces a new enhancement called *fine-grained password policies*. You can use this feature to specify multiple password policies and account lockout settings to different users or security groups within a single domain. Now you are able to apply a stricter password policy for sensitive security groups or users without having to modify password or account lockout settings for standard users throughout the rest of your domain.

Planning for Fine-Grained Password Policies

In order to implement fine-grained password policies, it is important to be aware of a few considerations:

- Fine-grained password policies can only be applied to user objects and global security groups.

- You cannot apply a fine-grained password policy to an organizational unit (OU). However, it is a common practice to create a global security group that contains the same name and membership as a specific OU (commonly called a shadow group). You can then assign the fine-grained password policy to the security group.

- If you have custom password filters deployed within a domain, you can still continue to use those filters along with the additional security provided by fine-grained password policies.

- The domain functional level must be at the Windows Server 2008 level.

It is also important to develop a documented plan which addresses these questions:

- **How many different password policies are required?**   This is important for determining the additional security groups that may have to be created within your Active Directory environment as well as the preference order for when multiple password policies are evaluated for a specific user.

- **Which specific password and account lockout settings are required?**   As you configure the password policy, you will be prompted for various attributes as listed in Table 13-6.

- **Which security groups are going to be linked to the new password policies?**   You will need to create specific security groups that contain the users that require unique password policies.

Implementing Fine-Grained Password Policies

To support the fine-grained password policy feature, Windows Server 2008 Active Directory includes two additional object types:

- **Password Setting Container**   This container is created by default and can be viewed under the System container in the domain. It is used to store the Password Settings objects that you create and link to global security groups or users.

- **Password Settings Object**   Password Settings Objects (PSOs) are created by members of the Domain Admins group and are used to define the specific password and account lockout settings to be linked to a specific security group or user.

As shown in Figure 13-4, the Password Settings Container stores all custom password settings objects configured for the domain. In this example, the HR Managers are configured with specific password settings that vary from the rest of the domain.

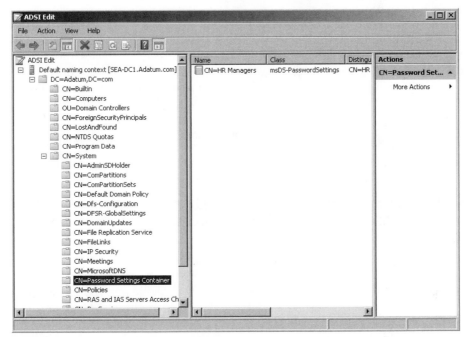

Figure 13-4 Viewing the Password Settings Container.

You can use the Active Directory Services Interfaces Editor (ADSI Edit) to provide a graphical interface in which to create the PSOs. You can also use the Ldifde command as a scriptable way to add multiple PSOs to the Password Setting Container.

> **More Info** For more information about using Ldifde to script the creation of PSOs, go to "Creating a PSO using Ldifde," at *http://technet2.microsoft.com/windowsserver2008/en/library/67dc7808-5fb4-42f8-8a48-7452f59672411033.mspx?mfr=true*.

To create and configure a PSO using ADSI Edit, follow these steps:

1. Open ADSI Edit and connect to the fully qualified domain name of the domain in which you want to create the PSO.

2. Browse to DC=<*domain_name*>\CN=System\CN=Password Setting Container.

3. Right-click CN=Password Settings Container, point to New, and then click Object.

4. In the Create Object box, ensure that msDS-PasswordSettings is selected and then click Next.

5. Fill in the appropriate values for each of the attributes, as described in Table 13-6.

Table 13-6   PSO Attributes

Attribute Name	Description	Value Range
Common-Name	Name for the new PSO.	Standard Unicode String
msDS-PasswordSettingsPrecedence	*Password Settings Precedence* used for when users are assigned multiple PSOs.	Any value greater than *10*. Lower values have greater precedence than higher values.
msDS-PasswordReversible EncryptionEnabled	Password reversible encryptions status for users.	*FALSE/TRUE* Recommended: *FALSE*
msDS-PasswordHistoryLength	Password history length for users.	*0–1024*
msDS-PasswordcomplexityEnabled	Password complexity status.	*FALSE/TRUE* Recommended: *TRUE*
msDS-MinimumPasswordLength	Minimum password length.	*0–255*
msDS-MinimumPasswordAge	Minimum password age before users can change the password. Note that this value must be smaller or equal to the value of *msDS-MaximumPasswordAge*.	(None) *00:00:00:00 through msDS-MaximumPasswordAge value* Example *1:00:00:00* (1 day)
msDS-MaximumPasswordAge	Maximum password age for when users must change the password. Note that this cannot be set to zero.	(Never) *msDS-MinimumPasswordAge value through (Never)* Example: *30:00:00:00* (30 days)
msDS-LockoutThreshold	Threshold value before a user is locked out.	*0–65535*
msDS-LockoutObservationWindow	Amount of time before the lockout threshold is reset. Note that this value cannot be smaller than the value of *msDS-LockoutDuration*.	(None) *00:00:00:01 through msDS-LockoutDuration value* Example *0:00:30:00* (30 minutes)
msDS-LockoutDuration	Amount of time that a user is locked out.	(None) (Never) *msDS-Lockout Observation-Window value* through (*Never*) Example*: 0:00:30:00* (30 minutes)
msDS-PSOAppliesTo	Used to link the PSO to security groups or users.	*0* or more distinguished names of users or global security groups.

> **Note**   When you use ADSI Edit to create PSOs, enter the values for *msDS-Maximum-PasswordAge*, *msDS-MinimumPasswordAge*, *msDS-LockoutObservationWindow*, and *msDS-LockoutDuration* in d:hh:mm:ss format.

6.   Modify properties by clicking the More Attributes button.

Understanding the Resultant PSO for a User

It is possible for a user or security group to have more than one PSO linked to it. This can happen if a user is a member of multiple security groups, which each have a PSO assigned, or a user object may have multiple PSOs directly assigned to it. In either case, it is important to understand that only one PSO can be applied as the effective password policy.

Recall that in Table 13-6 there is a PSO attribute called *msDS-PasswordSettingsPrecedence*. When multiple PSOs have been assigned to a user or group, this attribute helps to determine the resultant PSO. A PSO with a lower value takes precedence over a PSO with a higher value.

The following process describes how the resultant PSO is determined when multiple PSOs are linked to a user or group:

1.   Any PSO directly linked to a user object is the resultant PSO. If multiple PSOs are directly linked to the user object, the one with the lowest *msDSPasswordSettingsPrecedence* value will be the resultant PSO.

2.   If there are no PSOs directly linked to the user, the PSOs for all global security groups that contain the user are compared. The PSO with the lowest *msDSPasswordSettingsPrecedence* value will be the resultant PSO.

> **Note**   If multiple PSOs with the same *msDS-PasswordSettingsPrecedence* value are still evaluated after steps 1 and 2, then the PSO with the smallest Globally Unique Identifier (GUID) is applied.

3.   If the user does not have any PSOs directly or indirectly linked (through group membership), the Default Domain Policy is applied.

All user objects contain a new attribute called *msDS-ResultantPSO*. This attribute can be used to help you determine the distinguished name of the PSO that is applied to the user. If no PSO object is linked to the user, this attribute will not contain any value, and the Default Domain Policy GPO will contain the effective password policy.

You can use two methods to view the *msDS-ResultantPSO* attribute:

■   **The Windows Interface**   In Active Directory Users and Computers, ensure that Advanced Features is enabled from the View menu and then open the properties of a user account. You can view the *msDS-ResultantPSO* attribute from the Attribute Editor tab. You may need to enable the Show Read-Only Attributes\Constructed option on the Filter.

■ **The DSGET command-line tool**   Open a command prompt and then type the following command:

```
dsget user <User-DN> -effectivepso
```

Figure 13-5 shows the *msDS-ResultantPSO* attribute for *Don Hall.* Notice that the HR Managers PSO is the effective policy that has been applied for this user object.

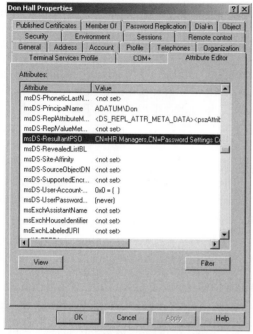

Figure 13-5   Viewing the Resultant PSO.

Hardening Server Security Using Group Policy

In addition to the domain-level security policies, Group Policy provides a large number of other settings to assist in hardening security settings for domain members. As with Account and Local Policies, many of these settings are configured by browsing to Computer Configuration\Policies\Windows Settings\Security Settings. Additional settings are configured by browsing to User Configuration\Policies\Windows Settings\Security Settings. Figure 13-6 illustrates the options under each of the Security Settings folders. Table 13-7 summarizes the configuration options under each heading.

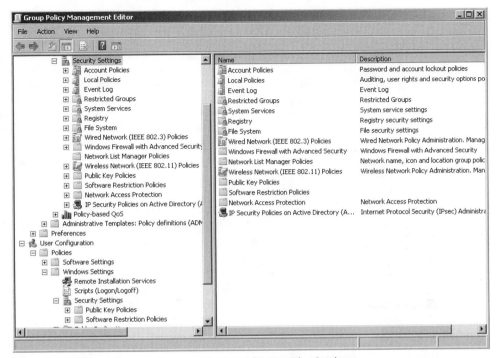

Figure 13-6   Additional policies available under Security Settings.

Using Group Policy to enforce the security settings for the computers on your network makes it much easier to create and maintain a secure networking environment. It is easier to configure security using Group Policy settings than to deal with each workstation individually. All you have to do is create the central security policies, configure them in a GPO, and link the GPO to an Active Directory container object. The next time the GPO is applied, the security will be configured on all the computers in the container. The use of Group Policy also makes it easy to continually manage the security settings for your computers. The security settings from the policy are continuously refreshed. Even if a user could modify the security configuration on a workstation, the policy would be reapplied at the next refresh cycle.

Table 13-7   Additional Security Hardening Settings in Group Policy

Configuration Option	Explanation
Local Policies\Audit Policy	Used to configure audit settings. You can set audit policies for options such as account management activities, logon events, policy changes, privilege use, and system events. For more information about configuring Audit Policy settings, read the Auditing the Use of Administrative Permissions section in Chapter 9, "Delegating the Administration of Active Directory Domain Services."
Event Log	Used to configure event log settings for all computers within the scope of management of the policy. You can configure options such as the maximum size for the event logs, who has permission to view the event logs, and whether or not to retain all event logs.

Table 13-7   Additional Security Hardening Settings in Group Policy *(continued)*

Configuration Option	Explanation
Restricted Groups	Used to limit the membership of local groups on computers affected by the policy. This is most commonly used to configure the membership of the local Administrators account on computers running Windows 2000 or later. If you use this option to configure the local group membership, all users or groups that are part of the local group but not on this policy's Members list will be removed the next time the policy is refreshed.
System Services	Used to manage services on computers. You can use this policy to define which services will automatically start on the computers or to disable services.
Registry	Used to configure security on registry keys. You can add any registry key to the policy and then apply specific security to that key.
File System	Used to configure security on files and folders. You can add any files or folders to the policy and then apply access control and auditing for those file system objects.
Software Restriction Policies (This setting is included in both the Computer Configuration and the User Configuration nodes)	Used to control which programs or files can run on a computer. More information about this policy setting is provided in the next section.

Direct from the Source: Group Policy Preferences

With Windows Server 2008, Microsoft introduces Group Policy preferences, which is basically an extension to the previously available Group Policy client-side extensions (CSE). With Group Policy preferences, you can further reduce the total cost of ownership (TCO) of your Windows servers by extending the reach of Group Policy manageability. Among the many settings available, a few are as follows:

- **Drive Maps**   Create, modify, or delete mapped drives and configure the visibility of all drives.
- **Environment**   Create, modify, or delete environment variables.
- **Network Shares**   Create, modify, or delete (unshared) shares.
- **Devices**   Enable or disable hardware devices or classes of devices.
- **Local Users and Groups**   Create, modify, or delete local users and groups.
- **Power Options**   Modify power options and create, modify, or delete power schemes.

There is a white paper available at *http://go.microsoft.com/fwlink/?LinkId=103735* if you are interested in learning more about Group Policy preferences.

Gautam Anand

Technical Lead–Directory Services

Premier Enterprise Platforms Support

Software Restriction Policies

One of the biggest security concerns in recent years has been users running unknown or untrusted software on their computers. In many cases, the users are running potentially unsafe software inadvertently. For example, millions of users have launched viruses or installed Trojan horse applications without any intent to run unsafe software. Software restriction policies are designed to prevent this from happening.

Software restriction policies protect your users from running unsafe software by defining which applications are allowed to run or not allowed to run on their workstations. When you set up a software restriction policy, you can define a policy that allows all software to run, except for software that you specifically block. Or you can define the software restriction policy to allow no software to run, except for software that you explicitly allow to run. Although the second option is more secure, the effort required to define all the applications that should be allowed to run in a complex enterprise environment might be too high. Most companies will opt for the less secure but more manageable option of allowing all software to run and blocking only selected software. However, if you are deploying a set of workstations in an environment that requires high security, you might want to deploy the more secure option.

When you create a software restriction policy, you can configure five types of rules that specify the applications affected by the policy:

- **Hash rules**   A *hash rule* is a cryptographic identifier that uniquely identifies a specific application file regardless of the filename or location. If the Unrestricted option has been selected as the default security level in the Security Levels folder and you want to restrict a particular application from running, you can create a hash rule using the software restriction policy. When a user tries to run the application, the workstation will check the hash and stop the application from running. If you have configured the software restriction policy to block all applications from running (by configuring the Disallowed security level), you can use the hash rule to enable a specific application.

- **Certificate rules**   You can create *certificate rules* so that the application selection criteria are based on the software publisher certificate. For example, if you have a custom application that you have developed, you can assign a certificate to that application and then configure the software restriction rule to trust the appropriate certificate.

- **Path rules**   You can create rules based on the path where the application's executable file is located. If you choose a folder, all the applications in the folder are affected by the rule. You can also use environmental variables (such as %systemroot%) to specify paths. You can also use wildcards in the path rule (such as *.vbs).

- **Registry path rules**   You can also create *rules based on the registry locations* that the application uses. Almost every application has a default location within the registry where it stores application-specific information that allows you to create a rule that blocks or enables an application based on these registry keys. No registry-specific option appears on the menu for creating registry path rules, but the New Path Rule option also allows you to create this unique set of rules. When you create a new software restriction policy, four default registry path rules are created. These rules configure an unrestricted software policy for applications in the system root folder and the default program files directory.

- **Network Zone rules**   The final rule type is based on the Internet zone from which the software was downloaded. For example, you might want to configure a rule to allow all applications downloaded from the Trusted sites zone to run or a rule that prevents all software downloaded from the Restricted Sites zone from running.

If you configure your default software restriction so that all applications should run except for specified applications, these rules define which applications will *not* run. If you have specified the more restrictive rule of disabling all applications, these rules specify which applications are allowed to run.

By default, no software restriction policies are configured with Active Directory. To define a policy, right-click the Software Restrictions Policies folder and select New Software Restrictions Policy. When you do, a default policy is created. Figure 13-7 shows the objects that are created.

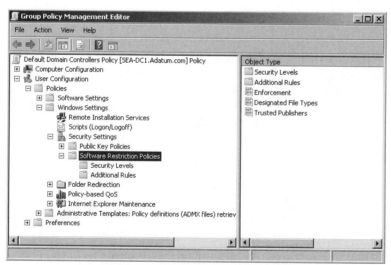

Figure 13-7   Creating a new software restriction policy.

The Security Levels folder is used to define the default security level. Inside the folder are three objects: *Disallowed, Basic User,* and *Unrestricted*. If you want to configure the security so that all applications can run except for the specified application, right-click the *Unrestricted* object and click Set As Default. If you want to prevent all software from running except for specified applications, right-click *Disallowed* and set it as the default. The Unrestricted security level is the default setting.

The Additional Rules folder is used to configure the software restrictions rules. To configure a rule, right-click the Additional Rules folder and select the type of rule you want to create. For example, if you want to create a new hash rule, select New Hash Rule. To create the new hash rule, click Browse and locate the file that you want to identify with the hash. When you select the file, the file hash is automatically created. Then you can configure whether this application will be Unrestricted, Disallowed, or run as a Basic User. The interface for reconfiguring an existing hash rule is shown in Figure 13-8.

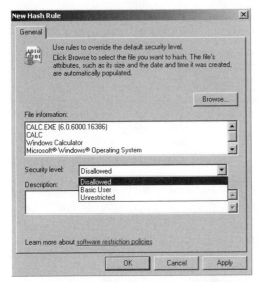

Figure 13-8   Configuring a hash rule.

The *Enforcement* object is used to define more specifically which applications are affected. You can configure the rules to apply to all applications or all applications except DLLs. You can also configure the rules to apply to all users or all users except local administrators.

The *Designated File Types* object defines all the file extensions that are considered to be executable code and therefore managed under this policy. You can add or remove file extensions from the list.

The *Trusted Publishers* object is used to define who can select whether a publisher is trusted or not. You can choose all users, only local administrators, or only enterprise administrators. You can also configure whether or not the workstation should check to see if an offered certificate has been revoked before running the application.

Configuring Network Security Using Group Policy

Group Policy implemented within a Windows Server 2008 Active Directory infrastructure provides a powerful way to centralize network security for your network clients. Table 13-8 provides a summary of policy settings that relate to network security.

Table 13-8   Network Security Settings in Group Policy

Configuration Option	Explanation
Wired Network (IEEE 802.3) Policies	Used to provide network connectivity and security settings for computers to connect to the network through an 802.1X-compatible switch.
Windows Firewall with Advanced Security	Used to centralize the configuration of the integrated features related to Windows Firewall and IPsec.
Network List Manager Policies	Used to specify the default location and user permissions for various network states such as when a network is being identified, identified networks, unidentified networks, and all networks.
Wireless Network (IEEE 802.11) Policies	Used to create wireless network policies. The policies can then be used to control the security requirements for computers using wireless network connections.
Public Key Policies (This setting is included in both Computer Configuration and User Configuration. The User Configuration includes a smaller subset of options.)	Used to configure several policies related to digital certificates and certificate management. You can also use these policies to create data recovery agents for recovering files that have been encrypted on local workstations using Encrypting File System (EFS).
Network Access Protection	Used to centrally configure NAP Client settings such as enabling and managing NAP enforcement clients, configuring user interface settings, and configuring settings for trusted server groups.
IP Security Policies On Active Directory (*domainname*)	Used to configure IP Security (IPSec) policies for previous versions of Windows (before Windows Vista and Windows Server 2008). You can configure policies that define precisely what type of network traffic must be protected with IPSec, as well as which computers must have the policy enforced. For Windows Vista and Windows Server 2008, it is recommended that you use the Windows Firewall with Advanced Security policy for IPsec-related settings.

Configuring Wired Network Security

Windows Server 2008 includes the new Wired Network (IEEE 802.3) Policies feature to provide automated configuration for Windows Vista or Windows Server 2008 computers connecting to a network using an 802.1X-compatible switch. Not only is this new feature an easy way to configure 802.1X-based connectivity, but it also provides additional security benefits by integrating with the new Network Access Protection (NAP) feature of Windows Server 2008.

To create a new Wired Network policy, right-click the Wired Network (IEEE 802.3) Policies node and then click Create A New Windows Vista Policy. As shown in Figure 13-9, you can then provide a Name and Description for the wired network policy.

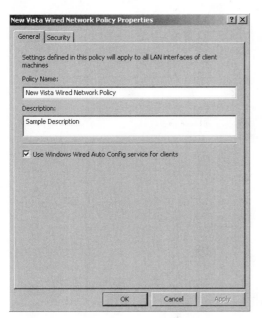

Figure 13-9 Configuring the Wired Network (IEEE 802.3) Policies feature.

The Use Windows Wired Auto Config Service For Clients option is an important feature that performs the actual configuration and connects clients to the 802.3 wired network. If you deselect this option, Windows will not control the wired LAN connection and the policy settings will not take affect.

Securing the Wired AutoConfig Service

Implementing wired network security settings using Group Policy relies on the Wired AutoConfig service (dot3svc). This service manages connections to Ethernet networks through 802.1X-compatible switches and also manages the profile used to configure a network client for authenticated network access. In order to ensure that proper authentication and security is maintained for your network clients, it is important that you prevent domain members from altering the startup mode of the Wired AutoConfig service. You can use Group Policy settings to specify the service startup type for the Wired AutoConfig service. To access this setting, browse to Computer Configuration/ Policies/Windows Settings/Security Settings/System Services. You can then configure the Security Policy Setting, as shown in Figure 13-10.

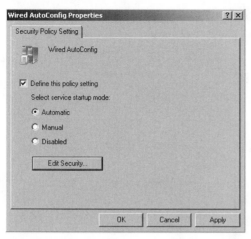

Figure 13-10 Configuring the Wired AutoConfig Properties.

The Security tab provides configuration settings for the authentication method and mode for the wired connection. Table 13-9 describes the options in more detail.

Table 13-9 Wired Network Policy Options

Item	Description
Enable use of IEEE 802.1X authentication for network access	Used to enable or disable the use of 802.1X authentication for network access. By default, it is enabled.
Select a network authentication method	Used to select the method used to authenticate network clients. Options include:
	Microsoft: Protected EAP (PEAP). The Properties box provides configuration settings related to the Authentication method used as well as the ability to enable Quarantine checks for use with NAP.
	Microsoft: Smart Card or other certificate. The Properties box provides configuration settings related to indicating which certificate to use when connecting as well as a list of Trusted Root Certification Authorities.
Authentication Mode	Used to specify how network authentication is performed. Options include:
	User re-authentication. This setting ensures that security credentials are evaluated based upon the current state of the computer. When no user is logged on, the computer credentials are authenticated. When a user logs on, the user credentials are evaluated. This is the recommended setting.
	Computer only. Authentication is only performed on the computer credentials.
	User authentication. This setting only enforces user authentication when the user connects to a new 802.1X-compliant device. Otherwise, authentication is mainly based on the computer credentials.
	Guest authentication. Allows connections based upon the Guest user account.

Configuring Wireless Network Security

Similar to the features provided with wired network security, Windows Server 2008 provides Group Policy settings to configure clients for securely connecting to 802.1X-compatible wireless access points. This feature prevents unauthorized and unauthenticated users and computers from connecting to your wireless network and supports computers running Windows XP, Windows Server 2003, Windows Vista, and Windows Server 2008.

To create a new Wireless Network policy, right-click the Wireless Network (IEEE 802.11) Policies node. You will notice that you can create two types of network policies. The Create A New Windows XP Policy is similar to the configuration methods and features available in previous versions of Windows. The Create A New Windows Vista Policy provides the ability to configure wireless network settings, security, and management settings that are only available in Windows Vista.

Windows Vista Wireless Network (IEEE 802.11) Policies provide many enhancements, including the following:

- Ability to configure multiple profiles specifying the same Service Set Identifier (SSID), but with different authentication methods

- Ability to configure allow and deny lists for wireless networks that are not controlled by the administrator

- Supports the latest in authentication options including Wi-Fi Protected Access 2 (WPA2)

- Integrates with Network Access Protection (NAP) to restrict wireless clients that do not meet specific configuration or health requirements

Configuring Windows Firewall and IPsec Security

Windows Server 2008 and Windows Vista both include a significant enhancement to how the Windows Firewall and IPsec policies are used to secure network communication. Windows Firewall with Advanced Security combines the functionality of a host firewall with the authentication and encryption capabilities of IPsec. This feature provides a stateful host firewall that can be used to inspect and filter incoming and outgoing IPv4 and IPv6 traffic. IPsec capabilities include the ability to request or require that computers authenticate to each other before communication and use data integrity or encryption when communicating with other network hosts.

Windows Firewall with Advanced Security provides three main components that can be configured and managed directly on the host computer, or centrally configured and applied to an Active Directory container using a Group Policy object. These components include:

- **Firewall rules**   Firewall rules can be created for both inbound and outbound traffic. You can create rules that determine specifically which computers, users, programs, services, ports, or protocols are able to connect with the protected computer. You can also specify which network connection the rule will be applied to, such as the local area network, wireless LAN, virtual private network, or all types.

■ **Connection Security rules**   Connection Security rules are used to configure IPsec connection settings between the host computer and other computers. Connection security is typically related to authentication between two computers before they begin exchanging information; however, you can also configure data integrity and data encryption to provide additional security.

■ **Profiles**   Depending on where the host computer is connecting from, a specific profile will be assigned to the computer in order to provide unique firewall and connection security rules. For Windows Vista and Windows Server 2008, there are three profiles that can be assigned firewall and connection security rules:

❑ *Domain* This profile is applied when a computer is connected to its corporate domain.

❑ *Private* This profile is applied when a computer is connected to a network in which the computers resident domain account does not reside (such as a home network). This setting should be more restrictive than the Domain Profile.

❑ *Public* This profile is applied when a computer is connected to a public location (such as an airport or coffee shop). It is important to ensure that this profile setting is as restrictive as possible.

As shown in Figure 13-11, the Windows Firewall with Advanced Security node in the Group Policy Management Editor provides a general overview of the current GPO configuration for each profile and provides a wizard-based method to configure both Connection Security Rules and Inbound\Outbound Rules.

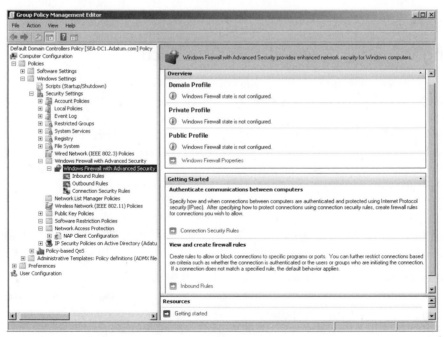

Figure 13-11   Configuring Windows Firewall with Advanced Security

You can configure the default state of each profile by right-clicking Windows Firewall with Advanced Security and then selecting Properties. As shown in Figure 13-12, each profile has specific settings related to Firewall state, Firewall settings, and Logging. The default IPsec settings, such as key exchange mode, data protection mode, and authentication mode, can also be configured to be applied to Group Policy-based clients.

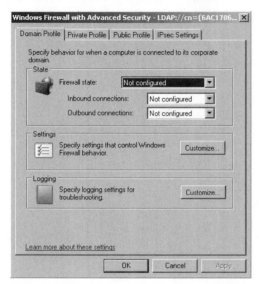

Figure 13-12   Configuring Profile and IPsec defaults.

More Info   For more information about creating firewall and connection security rules, read Introduction to Windows Firewall with Advanced Security found at *http://www.microsoft.com/ downloads/details.aspx?familyid=df192e1b-a92a-4075-9f69-c12b7c54b52b&displaylang=en.*

Configuring Security Settings Using Security Templates

As previously discussed, there are hundreds of options for configuring security using Group Policy. At first glance, the options can appear overwhelming; there are so many options that it is hard to know where to even start configuring the security options. Fortunately, Microsoft has provided the ability to create and apply security templates to make this task a little more manageable.

Note   Previous versions of Windows Server include samples of predefined security templates. Windows Server 2008 does not include any sample templates.

Security templates are predefined sets of security configurations that you can apply to computers on your network. Rather than having to go through every security setting discussed earlier in this chapter, you can choose a security template that is compatible with what you are trying to accomplish and then apply that template using Group Policy. For example, if you are deploying workstations in an environment where you want to set strict security settings, you can apply a security template that contains a number of high-security settings. If you are deploying workstations that need less security, you can apply another template with less security configured for those workstations. Security Templates can be modified to meet the specific needs and requirements for your organization.

Security templates do not include all security settings, but they do include the most common options that many organizations apply as standard settings. These options can be configured in a Security template:

- Account Policies
- Local Policies
- Event Log
- Restricted Groups
- System Services
- Registry
- File System

You can create your own security template or use a predefined template available from third-party sources. If you create a new template, you can save it as a text-based .INF file so that it can be imported into a Group Policy object to be applied to computers. To create a new security template, open an MMC console shell and add the Security Templates snap-in. You can then right-click the path node and select New Template. Figure 13-13 illustrates two custom templates created in the Security Templates console. Notice that each template can have unique settings for each configuration setting based on the requirements of the template.

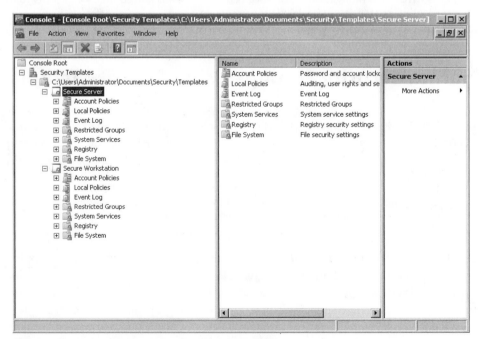

Figure 13-13   Creating a custom security template.

> **Note**   The *Windows Server 2008 Security Guide* provides specific guidance and sample templates for securing server roles using security templates. You can download the *Windows Server 2008 Security Guide* from *http://www.microsoft.com/downloads/details.aspx?familyid= FB8B981F-227C-4AF6-A44B-B115696A80AC&displaylang=en*.

Deploying Security Templates

After you have obtained or created a security template, you can deploy it using a number of different methods:

- Importing the security template into a Group Policy object
- Using the Security Configuration And Analysis tool
- Using the Secedit.exe command-line tool
- Using the Security Configuration Wizard

Using Group Policy to Deploy Security Templates

Group Policy provides a convenient way to deploy custom security templates to target OUs within Active Directory. The following steps outline how to use GPOs to deploy security templates:

1. From the Group Policy Management console, modify or create a new GPO.

2. Browse to Computer Configuration\Policies\Windows Settings\Security Settings.

3. Right-click Security Settings and then click Import Policy.

4. In the Import Policy From box, browse to and select the security policy that you want to import and then click Open.

5. Verify that the security settings are correct in the GPO and then close and link the GPO to the appropriate Active Directory container.

Using the Security Configuration And Analysis Tool to Apply Security Templates

The Security Configuration And Analysis tool can be used to create or modify existing security templates. A security template can be loaded into the Security Configuration And Analysis tool and used to analyze and compare a target computer. For example, you can load a preconfigured template and then analyze a computer to see what the differences would be between the template and the current computer configuration. Figure 13-14 shows an example of the result of this analysis.

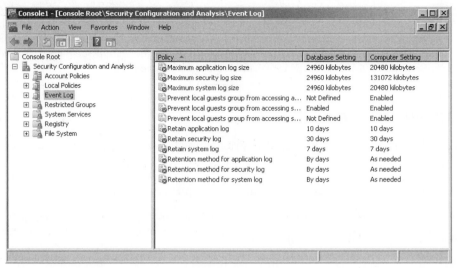

Figure 13-14   Analyzing a computer security configuration using the Security Configuration And Analysis tool.

You can also use this tool to apply the security template to the computer. If you decide that you want to apply the custom template to the computer, you can right-click Security Configuration And Analysis and select Configure Computer Now. All the security settings on the computer will then be modified to match the security template.

The Security Configuration And Analysis tool is not intended to be used with Group Policy. This tool can use the same predefined security templates as the Group Policy Management Editor, but it provides an alternative means to deploy the template. This tool is designed primarily to be used with stand-alone computers.

Using the Secedit.exe Tool to Apply Security Templates

The Secedit command-line tool provides functionality similar to the Security Configuration And Analysis tool. With Secedit, you can analyze the computer settings based on a template and then apply the settings. One of the useful features of the Secedit command-line tool is that you can use it to generate a rollback configuration before you apply a security template. This option provides an easy backout plan if the security template you apply is not appropriate. Like the Security Configuration And Analysis tool, Secedit is typically not used in an Active Directory environment, but rather for stand-alone configurations. However, you can use Secedit in logon or startup scripts to apply specific security-related settings to a workstation.

Integrating the Security Configuration Wizard with Security Templates and Group Policy

As described in Chapter 8, "Active Directory Domain Services Security," the Security Configuration Wizard (SCW) can be used to generate and configure XML-based policy files to help reduce the attack surface of a domain controller.

The SCW provides some additional features that can be used to integrate with security templates and Group Policy settings:

- Incorporating preconfigured security templates to the SCW-generated policy

- The ability to use the Scwcmd command-line tool to transform a SCW-generated policy into a Group Policy object

As you complete the configuration of a Security Policy using the SCW, you will need to provide a policy filename and a description of the policy and include preconfigured Security Templates. When you add security templates to the SCW policy, all configured settings will be applied along with the rest of the SCW policy. It is important to note that once applied, any security information related to the registry or file system objects defined in the security template cannot be removed using the SCW rollback feature. Figure 13-15 provides an example of including Security Templates in a Security Configuration Wizard policy.

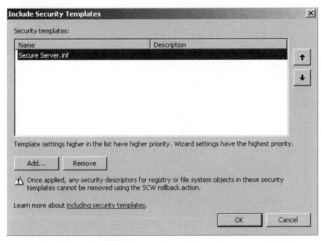

Figure 13-15   Including Security Templates in a SCW security policy.

The Security Configuration Wizard also provides the Scwcmd command-line tool, which can be used to convert a SCW-based policy into an unlinked Group Policy object. Use the following syntax to perform the conversion:

```
scwcmd transform /p:policyfile.xml /g:GPOdisplayname
```

The converted GPO is stored in the Group Policy object container and can be viewed and managed using the Group Policy Management console. You can then use the Group Policy Management console to link the GPO to target Active Directory containers.

Summary

Active Directory Domain Services relies on Group Policy to provide default security settings for both the domain and the domain controllers within the domain. One new feature that is sure to please domain administrators is the ability to implement fine-grained password policies. This allows for the implementation of different password settings (such as the password age or length), based on departments or roles within the organization. In addition to domain-based security settings, Group Policy also provides a centralized way to manage server security hardening and the configuration and security settings for wired and wireless network configurations. To assist in the management and deployment of specific security settings, security templates can be configured and either directly applied to a computer or imported into a Group Policy object to be applied to multiple computers.

Additional Resources

The following resources contain additional information and tools related to this chapter.

Related Information

- Chapter 8, "Active Directory Domain Services Security," provides details on securing Active Directory and additional information on domain controller security.

- Chapter 9, "Delegating the Administration of Active Directory Domain Services," provides details on auditing Active Directory objects.

- Chapter 11, "Introduction to Group Policy," provides details on the architecture and configuration of Group Policy objects.

- Chapter 12, "Using Group Policy to Manage User Desktops," provides details on various Group Policy settings.

- "Step-by-Step Guide for Fine-Grained Password and Account Lockout Policy Configuration," located at *http://technet2.microsoft.com/windowsserver2008/en/library/2199dcf7-68fd-4315-87cc-ade35f8978ea1033.mspx?mfr=true*

- "How To Use Software Restriction Policies in Windows Server 2003," located at *http://support.microsoft.com/kb/324036*

- "Introduction to Windows Firewall with Advanced Security," located at *http://www.microsoft.com/downloads/details.aspx?familyid=df192e1b-a92a-4075-9f69-c12b7c54b52b&displaylang=en*

- "Group Policy Wiki," located at *http://grouppolicy.editme.com/*

- "Group Policy Team Blog," located at *http://blogs.technet.com/GroupPolicy/*

- "Windows Server Group Policy," located at *http://technet.microsoft.com/en-ca/windowsserver/grouppolicy/default.aspx*

- "Windows Server 2008 Security Guide," located at *http://www.microsoft.com/downloads/details.aspx?familyid=FB8B981F-227C-4AF6-A44B-B115696A80AC&displaylang=en*

Part IV
Maintaining Windows Server 2008 Active Directory

In this part:

Chapter 14

Monitoring and Maintaining Active Directory

As part of any well designed, planned, and implemented Active Directory infrastructure, routine monitoring and maintenance is a must to optimize the performance and reliability of Active Directory. Active Directory Domain Services (AD DS) is a distributed network service that can be quite complex in larger organizations, and will be subject to thousands of changes every day, such as the creation or deletion of user accounts and the modification of object attributes, group memberships, and permissions. To ensure that these changes, as well as the ever-changing network and server environment on which the service is hosted, do not negatively affect the performance of Active Directory, you must take proactive measures accordingly. This chapter examines the two fundamental elements of supporting your AD DS infrastructure: monitoring domain controllers and maintaining the Active Directory database.

Monitoring Active Directory

To maintain a reliable directory service for your organization, it is essential to monitor the health of AD DS. Your users rely on the efficient running of the directory service—to log on to the network, to access shared resources, and to retrieve and send e-mail. The activities that your user community would rank as critical all depend on the health and availability of Active Directory.

Monitoring AD DS consists of a combination of tasks—all with the common goal of measuring the current state and performance of some key component (disk capacity, processor utilization, configuration, and so on) against a known good requirement (the *baseline*). Each component may consist of different indicators such as performance counters, system events and logs (also called *trace data*), and configuration information. With such a wide scope of information that may be collected, it is important to implement a monitoring solution that can bring all of these indicators together to provide you with information to proactively and efficiently assist you with your service level goals. Windows Server 2008 provides a much improved set of tools combined into what is called the *Windows Reliability And Performance Monitor*. This new monitoring console can be used to examine many different components related to your server's performance, both in real time and by collecting log data for analysis at a later time.

> **Note**   Many tool sets available on the market can bring the monitoring of these key indicators together in an easy-to-manage interface, and for large organizations, these tool sets might be essential, but they are also expensive, resource-hungry, and complex. Windows Reliability And Performance Monitor includes many essential features that can minimize the need for smaller organizations to purchase elaborate and sophisticated third-party monitoring solutions.

To fully understand Active Directory monitoring, you must know why monitoring is needed, how to monitor Active Directory, and exactly what to monitor within the Active Directory environment. To keep your directory service running at peak performance and reliably, you also need to know what to do in response to your monitoring efforts. The pages that follow will help you answer these questions and will assist in determining the best method for monitoring and maintaining your AD DS environment.

Direct from the Source: Monitoring Active Directory, Part 1

It is important to understand clearly what monitoring Active Directory means in a management context. Obviously, measuring the LDAP lookup performance, for instance, may be useful, but it can also be very incomplete. In this context, a successful LDAP lookup does not mean that the expected GPO can be applied or that you can locate the closest Active Directory Domain Controller to authenticate! The way Active Directory is used involves many functionalities spread all across the Windows system and closely coupled with the Active Directory content. For instance, an authentication request starts subsequent processes and leverages several features around and within Active Directory, such as DNS lookups, LDAP requests, Kerberos requests, GPO settings, network share access for the SYSVOL share, and HOME directories, to name just a few. Therefore, it is important that the monitoring of Active Directory is holistic and not component focused, even though it is the sum and the correlation of the monitored components that will bring the holistic monitoring and status of the Active Directory world as a whole. When the health of Active Directory is monitored holistically, it will give you a real sense of the availability and the reliability of your Active Directory world to support your entire business!

Alain Lissoir

Senior Program Manager

Active Directory–Connected System Division

Why Monitor Active Directory

The conventional reason given to monitor Active Directory is that monitoring identifies potential problems before they cause long periods of service disruption. A more business-oriented reason is that monitoring enables you to maintain your service-level agreement (SLA) to your customer (the network user). In either case, you should monitor the health of Active Directory to catch problems as soon as possible—before an interruption of service occurs.

> **Note**   An SLA is a contract between a service provider (you) and the user community that defines the responsibilities of each party and constitutes a commitment to provide a particular level of service to a specified degree of quality and quantity. In the context of Active Directory, an SLA between the Information Technology (IT) department and the user community would contain the maximum level of acceptable system downtime as well as other performance metrics, such as logon time and response time for support requests. In exchange for the service provider's commitment to meet certain performance and operational standards, the user community commits to a certain volume of usage; for example, having 10,000 or fewer users in the Active Directory forest.

Another reason to monitor the system health of Active Directory is to track changes to the infrastructure. Has the size of your Active Directory database grown since last year? Are all of your global catalog (GC) servers online? How long does it take for changes made on a domain controller in France to replicate to a domain controller in Australia? Knowing any of this information might not prevent an error from occurring today, but it will provide you with valuable data you can use to plan for the future.

Benefits of Monitoring Active Directory Domain Services

There are several benefits to monitoring Active Directory:

- Ability to maintain SLAs with users by avoiding service downtime
- Higher performance of Active Directory by eliminating otherwise undetected service bottlenecks
- Lower administrative costs through proactive system maintenance
- Increased ability to scale and plan for future infrastructure changes through in-depth knowledge of Active Directory components, capacity, and utilization
- Increased goodwill for the IT department through customer satisfaction

Costs of Active Directory Monitoring

Monitoring your Active Directory infrastructure is not without cost. The following are a few of the costs required to implement an effective monitoring solution:

- Man-hours are required to design, deploy, and manage a monitoring solution.

- Sufficient funds may be required to acquire the necessary management tools, training, and hardware required to implement service monitoring.

- A portion of your network bandwidth will be utilized to monitor the health of Active Directory on all the domain controllers in the enterprise.

- Memory and processor resources are used for running agent applications on target servers and on the central monitoring console computer.

It is worth noting that the initial cost of monitoring goes up quickly when you move to an enterprise-wide monitoring platform, such as Microsoft System Center Operations Manager. This type of solution adds additional software costs, requires operator training, and may use more system resources than many Windows Server 2008-native monitoring tools. However, enterprise monitoring systems are proven, integrated, and supported products that provide features that can lead to long-term cost savings and increase the operational efficiency of the management and monitoring environment.

The level of monitoring you select will depend on your cost-benefit analysis. In all cases, the amount of resources you dedicate to your monitoring solution should not exceed the projected costs you will save through monitoring. For this reason, larger organizations find it cost-effective to invest in enterprise monitoring solutions. Smaller organizations, more often, can justify using the monitoring tools built into Windows Server 2008.

Note   System Center Operations Manager incorporates event management, service monitoring and alerting, report generation, and trend analysis. It does so through a central console in which agents running on the managed nodes (monitored servers) send data to be analyzed, tracked, and displayed in a single management console. This centralization enables the network administrator to manage a large and disparate collection of servers from a single location with powerful management tools to remotely administer the server. Operations Manager uses management packs to extend the knowledge base of data for specific network services as well as server-based applications. Management packs are available for many services and applications including Active Directory, Domain Name System (DNS), Microsoft Internet Information Services (IIS), and Microsoft Exchange Server. For more information on Operations Manager, see *http://www.microsoft.com/systemcenter/opsmgr/default.mspx*.

Monitoring Server Reliability and Performance

Windows Server 2008 contains the *Reliability And Performance Monitor*, which is used to analyze system performance and provide detailed information on the reliability of various windows-related and application-related components. The Reliability And Performance Monitor is started from the Administrative Tools menu and consists of three monitoring tools that can be used to address specific monitoring and troubleshooting requirements: the Resource Overview, Performance Monitor, and the Reliability Monitor.

Resource Overview

The Resource Overview home page provides a summary of the usage and performance of the CPU, Disk, Network, and Memory for the server. Data is provided in real time and is displayed in four graphs. As shown in Figure 14-1, selecting the Root node of the Reliability And Performance Monitor displays the Resource Overview. You can also obtain additional information for each component by expanding its details section. For example, if you need to determine which processes are currently running and the average CPU utilization for the process, you can expand the CPU section, which will provide the information required.

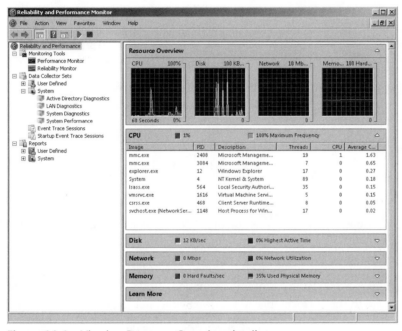

Figure 14-1   Viewing Resource Overview details.

> **Note**   You can open a stand-alone version of the Resource Monitor by typing **perfmon /res** in the Start Menu. If the Resource Overview does not display real-time data, be sure to start the monitor by clicking the green start button (Reliability And Performance console only), or by selecting Start from the Monitor menu (Resource Monitor view only).

Performance Monitor

The Performance Monitor (previously called System Monitor) can be used to view real-time performance data of a local computer or several remote computers. You can also use the Performance Monitor to view saved log files, which makes identifying performance trends a much easier task. The basic functionality of the Performance Monitor has not changed significantly from previous Windows versions and provides several useful options, such as the following:

■ To optimize the view of a particular counter, select the counter at the bottom of the details pane and select the Highlight button on the toolbar (or press Ctrl +H). Doing so will highlight the selected counter graph line, which is then easily viewed against the graph.

■ You can switch between the Line, Histogram, and Report view by selecting the appropriate button on the toolbar.

■ You can save Performance Monitor graph settings as an HTML page. To do so, configure a graph with the necessary counters, right-click the graph, and select Save Settings As. The graph will be saved as an HTML file that you can open in a browser. When you open the HTML version of the graph, the display is frozen. In the browser, click the Unfreeze Display button on the Performance toolbar to restart the monitoring.

■ You can import a saved graph back into System Monitor by dragging the HTML file onto the System Monitor window, which is a convenient way to save and reload frequently used performance graphs.

■ Two new security groups in Windows Server 2008 ensure that only trusted users can access and manipulate sensitive performance data: the Performance Log Users group and the Performance Monitor Users group.

 Note You can open a stand-alone version of the Performance Monitor by typing **perfmon /sys** in the Start Menu.

By default, the % Processor Time counter is preloaded into the Performance Monitor. To add additional counters to the Performance Monitor console, perform the following steps:

1. Right-click the Performance Monitor details pane and click Add Counters.

2. In the Add Counters dialog box, click <Local computer> to monitor the computer on which the monitoring console is run. To monitor a specific computer regardless of where the monitoring console is run, click Browse and specify a computer name.

3. Expand the desired Performance Object and then click the counter you want to add.

4. Click Add and then click OK.

Even though the basic functionality is the same, there are still some welcome enhancements to the Performance Monitor. Figure 14-2 illustrates some of these enhancements:

■ **Improved counter options** The Performance Monitor now provides more control over how counters are viewed within the details pane. For both the Line and Histogram bar graph types, you have the option to quickly hide or show selected counters by just selecting the check box located under the Show column. You can also easily scale selected counters in order to ensure that data remains visible within the graph. Figure 14-2 has the % Processor Time counter scaled at *10*.

- **Tool tips**   On Line graphs, you can a use your mouse pointer to determine exact performance counter data. Figure 14-2 shows how a tool tip can provide the counter name, value, and time for the data point that the mouse pointer is touching.

- **Zoom**   Performance Monitor provides the ability to view more granular detail for logged data by zooming into a specific time range. Note that you cannot use the zoom feature when capturing real-time data.

- **Comparison of multiple log files**   The stand-alone version of Performance Monitor includes a feature that helps you compare multiple log files to a base view using a transparent overlay. You can do this by opening multiple stand-alone Performance Monitor windows, adding the log file to be compared to each window, and then selecting the options found under the Compare menu.

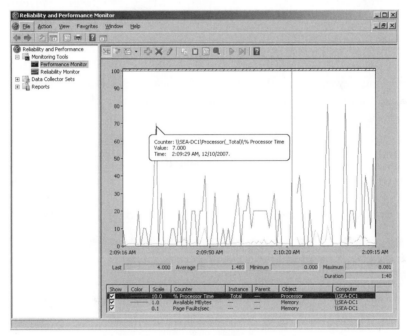

Figure 14-2   Viewing Performance Monitor data.

Reliability Monitor

The Reliability Monitor provides information on the overall stability of a server. A System Stability Index is calculated based on data collected as specific events occur within the server over a period of time. These events include:

- **Software installs and uninstalls**   This category includes applications installed or removed using an MSI installer package, driver installation and removal, software update installation and removal, and operating system updates such as service packs or hotfixes.

- **Application failures**   This category reports on events related to application hangs or crashes.

- **Hardware failures** This category reports on events related to hard disk and memory failures.

- **Windows failures** This category reports on boot failures, operating system crashes, and sleep failures.

- **Miscellaneous failures** This category reports on any unexpected shutdowns of the system.

- **System clock changes** This category reports on any changes to the system clock on the server. This category will not appear in the System Stability Report unless a day is selected on which a significant clock change occurred. An information icon will appear on the graph for any day that a significant clock change has taken place.

Note You can open a stand-alone version of the Reliability Monitor by typing **perfmon /rel** in the Start Menu.

Overall system stability can be determined by viewing either the System Stability Chart or by reviewing a variety of System Stability Reports. The System Stability Chart displays a daily stability index rating between *1* and *10*. A rating of *10* indicates a stable system; a rating of *1* indicates a very unstable system. As you highlight a specific day within the chart, you can view the average index and obtain detailed information from the reports located at the bottom of the details pane.

As shown in Figure 14-3, the highlighted date has an index of *8.81*, which indicates a less stable system when compared to previous days registered in the System Stability Chart. A warning indicator is displayed for the Software (Un)Installs category, and error indicators are displayed for the Application Failures and Miscellaneous Failures categories. The System Stability Report section shows the details related to the errors experienced on this specific day.

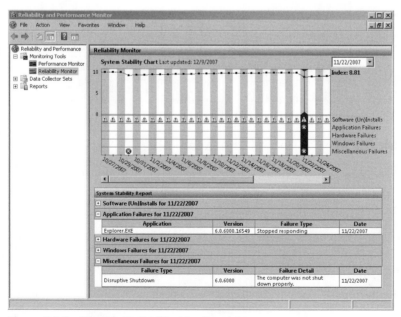

Figure 14-3 Viewing Reliability Monitor data.

Note   The Reliability Monitor needs to collect 24 hours of data before it calculates the System Stability index or generates information for the System Stability Report.

Overview of Data Collector Sets and Reports

Windows Server 2008 (as well as Windows Vista) introduces the concept of Data Collector Sets. A Data Collector Set may contain multiple data collection points (called *data collectors*) to form a single configurable component. This component can then be configured to provide settings such as scheduling for the entire data collection set, security for running or viewing the data collection set, and running specific tasks after the Data Collector Set stops gathering information.

A Data Collector Set can contain many different types of data collectors:

- **Performance counters**   Used to log data related to system performance. You can add the same counters that are used to display real-time data in the Performance Monitor.

- **Event trace data**   Used to log information based on system and application-based events. Event trace providers are typically installed with the operating system. They can also be provided by application vendors.

- **System configuration information**   Used to log information related to the configuration and changes to registry keys. You will need to know exactly which registry keys you want to include in the Data Collector Set to be monitored.

- **Performance counter alerts**   Used to configure an alert event for when a specific performance counter meets or exceeds a specified threshold. For example, you can configure an alert to perform an alert action or task whenever the % Free Space on a drive is below 20%. An alert action can be as simple as just logging an entry in the application event log, or it can start a subsequent Data Collector Set to provide additional monitoring or tracing capabilities. You may also configure an Alert Task to run a specific application when the alert is triggered, such as an e-mail notification or administrative utility. Note that this option is available when you manually create a Data Collector Set.

The Data Collector Sets node is located in the Reliability And Performance Monitor and consists of four containers used to store different types of Data Collector Sets:

- **User Defined**   This container allows you to create and store custom Data Collector Sets either manually or from predefined templates.

- **System**   Depending on the server roles added to the server, this container stores default system-based Data Collector Sets used to provide Active Directory Diagnostics, LAN Diagnostics, System Diagnostics, or System Performance. These cannot be modified directly, but they can be used as a template to create a new User Defined Data Collector Set.

- **Event Trace Sessions**   Used to store Data Collector Sets based on enabled event trace providers.

- **Startup Event Trace Sessions**   Used to store Data Collector Sets containing event trace providers used to monitor startup events.

Figure 14-4 provides an illustration of a User Defined Data Collector Set. This specific Data Collector Set contains two data collectors used to collect baseline performance for various counters and NT kernel trace data.

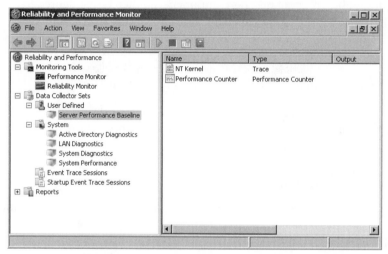

Figure 14-4   Viewing a User Defined Data Collector Set.

The following steps outline how to create a Data Collector Set:

1. From the Reliability And Performance Monitor, right-click User Defined, point to New, and then click Data Collector Set.

2. Provide a Name for the Data Collector Set and specify if you are going to create from a template or create the Data Collector Set manually.

3. If you choose to use a template, you can select a template based on the System Data Collector Sets, or you can click Browse and select a preconfigured XML-based template.

4. If you choose to create a new Data Collector Set manually, you can select which types of data logs you want to include (performance counter, event trace data, or system configuration information). You can also choose to create a Performance Counter Alert. Depending on which options you select, you will have specific configuration pages for each data log type.

5. Choose a location on where you would like to save the new Data Collector Set. By default, it is saved at %systemdrive%\PerfLogs\Admin\.

6. Specify the account to be used to run the Data Collector Set. By default, Data Collector Sets run as the System user.

7. Click Finish to return to the Reliability And Performance Monitor console.

8. Right-click the Data Collector Set and then click Properties to modify the settings for the entire collection. For example, you may want to specify a schedule or a stop condition to stop the data collection after a specific amount of time.

9. To start the Data Collector Set, right-click on the Data Collector Set and then click Start. The data collectors within the set begin to collect information as configured. When the data collection duration is complete, a report is also automatically generated and placed under the Reports node, as shown in Figure 14-5.

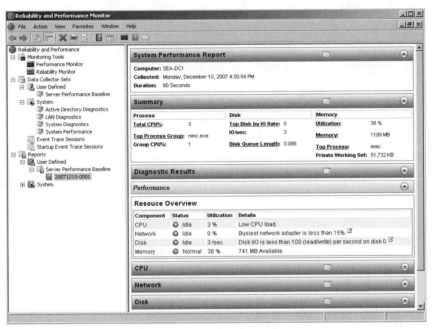

Figure 14-5 Report results of a data collection task.

How to Monitor Active Directory

Reliability And Performance Monitor exposes a variety of Active Directory counters and trace events that can be used to achieve effective system monitoring. The Active Directory monitoring process consists of tracking these key performance indicators and comparing them to a baseline condition that represents the service operating within normal parameters. The differences between the current monitoring results compared to the initial baseline values will help you determine current or potential issues related to your directory service.

As mentioned previously, a Data Collector Set can also contain Performance Counter Alerts. When a performance counter exceeds a specified performance threshold, an alert can be configured which notifies the network administration (or the monitoring operator, in the case of large organizations) of the condition. Exceeding the performance threshold can also initiate an automatic action configured within the Data Collector Set to remedy the problem or to minimize any further deterioration of performance or system health.

The following is a high-level outline of the Active Directory monitoring process:

1. Determine which data collectors you need to monitor and the metrics that are required within your organization. This will include performance counters, trace information, and registry settings. Your organization's SLA is a good start for providing information on expected metrics and thresholds for the performance indicators.

2. Create a Data Collector Set that includes all of the data collectors that are required.

3. Run the Data Collector Set to establish and document your baseline performance level.

4. Determine your thresholds for these performance indicators. (In other words, determine at what level you will need to take action to prevent a disruption of service.)

5. Design the necessary alert system to process a threshold hit. Your alert system should include:

   ❑ Operator notifications

   ❑ Automatic actions, if appropriate

   ❑ Operator-initiated actions

6. Design a reporting system to capture historical data on Active Directory system health. You can use the Reports node to contain reports based on the date that the Data Collector Set was run.

7. Implement your monitoring solution to measure performance of these key indicators on a schedule that reflects the variability of these indicators and the impact that each indicator has on Active Directory health.

The rest of this section examines the details of the monitoring process.

Establishing the Baselines and Thresholds

After you have identified which data collectors and performance counters you need to monitor, you should gather baseline data for these indicators by creating and running a baseline Data Collector Set. The baseline data collection set represents each type of data collector performing within normal limits of operation. The "normal limits" should include both the low and high values that are expected for a particular performance counter or trace event. To capture the most accurate baseline data, you should collect performance information over a sufficient period of time to reflect the range of values for a particular parameter during high and low activity. For example, if you are establishing the baseline for authentication request performance, be sure to monitor that indicator during the period when most of your users are logging on.

As you determine your baseline values, document this information and date the version of the document you create. In addition to being used for setting thresholds, these values will be useful for identifying performance trends over time. A spreadsheet formatted with columns for low, average, and high values for each counter, as well as thresholds for alerts, is well-suited for this purpose.

> **Note**   When your Active Directory environment changes (for example, if the number of users increases or hardware changes are made to domain controllers), reestablish your baselines. The baseline should always reflect the most current snapshot of Active Directory running within normal performance limits. An outdated baseline is not useful for analyzing current performance data.

After you have determined the baseline, next determine the threshold values that should generate an alert or event task. Apart from the recommendations made by Microsoft, there is no magic formula for determining threshold values. Because every situation is different, you will need to determine, based on your network infrastructure, what performance level indicates that a performance counter is trending toward service interruption. In establishing your thresholds, start conservatively. (Use values recommended by Microsoft or even lower values.) As a result, you will process a large number of alerts. As you gather more data about the counter, you can raise the threshold to reduce the number of alerts. This process might take several months, but it will eventually be fine-tuned for your particular implementation of Active Directory.

It is essential that you have a game plan in place for how you will respond to an alert. As you define your counters, baseline, and threshold values, be sure to document the remedial action you will perform to bring the indicator back within normal limits. This action might involve troubleshooting an error condition (for example, bringing a domain controller back online) or transferring an operations master role. If your system has reached its maximum capacity, you might have to add disk space or memory to correct the condition. Other alerts will trigger you to perform Active Directory maintenance, such as defragmenting the Active Directory database file. Such situations are discussed later in this chapter, in the section titled "Offline Defragmentation of the Active Directory Database."

Performance Counters and Thresholds

The following tables list key performance counters and threshold values that are helpful for monitoring and logging Active Directory performance. Keep in mind that every enterprise environment will have unique characteristics that will affect the applicability of these values. Consider these thresholds as a starting point and refine these values to reflect the needs and requirements for your environment.

Active Directory Performance   The performance counters listed in Table 14-1 monitor the core Active Directory functions and services. Thresholds are determined by baseline monitoring unless otherwise indicated. These counters can be added to the Performance Monitor to provide real-time data, or you can add a Performance Counter data collector or a Performance counter alert to a Data Collector Set to provide Active Directory performance logging and alert capabilities.

Table 14-1   Core Active Directory Functions and Services

Object	Counter	Interval	Why Counter Is Important
DirectoryServices/NTDS	DS Search sub-operations / sec	Every 15 minutes	Subtree search requests are very system-resource intensive. Any significant increase can indicate domain controller performance problems. Check to see if applications are incorrectly targeting this domain controller.
Process	% Processor Time (Instance=lsass)	Every 1 minute	This counter indicates the percentage of CPU time being used by the Active Directory service.
DirectoryServices/NTDS	LDAP Searches / sec	Every 15 minutes	This counter is a good indicator for the amount of overall use a domain controller is getting. Ideally, this counter should be fairly uniform across the domain controllers. An increase in this counter might indicate that a new application is targeting this domain controller or that more clients were added to the network.
DirectoryServices/NTDS	LDAP Client Sessions	Every 5 minutes	This counter indicates the number of clients currently connected to the domain controller. A significant increase might indicate that other machines are failing over to this domain controller. Trending this counter can also provide useful information as to what time of day people are connecting and the maximum number of clients connected per day.

Table 14-1   Core Active Directory Functions and Services *(continued)*

Object	Counter	Interval	Why Counter Is Important
Process	Private Bytes (Instance=lsass)	Every 15 minutes	This counter is good for trending memory needs by domain controllers. A continuously growing counter indicates either increased workstation demand, applications misbehaving (not closing handles), or increased number of workstations targeting this domain controller. When this counter significantly deviates from the normal value of other peer domain controllers, you should investigate the source of this demand.
Process	Handle Count (Instance=lsass)	Every 15 minutes	This trending statistic is useful for seeing if applications are misbehaving and not closing handles properly. This counter will increase linearly as client workstations are added.
Process	Virtual Bytes (Instance=lsass)	Every 15 minutes	This counter can be used to determine if Active Directory is running low on virtual memory address space, which might indicate a memory leak. Verify that you are running the latest service pack, and schedule a reboot during off hours to avoid a system outage. This counter can be used to determine if less than 2 gigabytes (GB) of virtual memory remains available.

Replication Performance Counters   The performance counters discussed in Table 14-2 monitor the quantity of replicated data. Thresholds are determined by the baselines you established earlier, unless otherwise indicated.

Table 14-2   Replication Performance Counters

Object	Counter	Recommended Interval	Why Counter Is Important
DirectoryServices/NTDS	DRA Inbound Bytes Compressed (Between Sites, After Compression) / sec	Every 15 minutes	Indicates the amount of replication data flowing to this site. A significant change in the counter indicates a replication topology change or that significant data was added or changed in Active Directory.
DirectoryServices/NTDS	DRA Outbound Bytes Compressed (Between Sites, After Compression) / sec	Every 15 minutes	Indicates the amount of replication data flowing out of this site. A significant change in the counter indicates a replication topology change or that significant data was added or changed in Active Directory.
DirectoryServices/NTDS	DRA Outbound Bytes Not Compressed	Every 15 minutes	Indicates the amount of replication data outbound from this domain controller, but to targets within the site.
DirectoryServices/NTDS	DRA Outbound Bytes Total / sec	Every 15 minutes	Indicates the amount of replication data outbound from this domain controller. A significant change in the counter indicates a replication topology change or that significant data was added or changed in Active Directory. This is a very important performance counter to watch.

Security Subsystem Performance   The performance counters listed in Table 14-3 monitor key security volumes. Thresholds are determined by baseline monitoring unless otherwise indicated.

Table 14-3   Key Security Volumes

Object	Counter	Recommended Interval	Why Counter Is Important
Security System-Wide Statistics	NTLM Authentications	Every 15 minutes	Indicates the number of clients per second authenticating against the domain controller using NTLM instead of Kerberos (pre–Windows 2000 clients or interforest authentications).
Security System-Wide Statistics	KDC AS Requests	Every 15 minutes	Indicates the number of session tickets per second being issued by the Key Distribution Center (KDC). This is a good indicator to use to observe the impact of changing the ticket lifetime.
Security System-Wide Statistics	Kerberos Authentications	Every 15 minutes	Indicates the amount of authentication load being put on the KDC. This is a very good indicator to use for trending purposes.
Security System-Wide Statistics	KDC TGS Requests	Every 15 minutes	Indicates the number of Ticket-Granting Tickets (TGTs) being issued by the KDC. This is a good indicator to use to observe the impact of changing the ticket lifetime.

Core Operating System Performance   The performance counters listed in Table 14-4 monitor core operating system indicators and have a direct impact on Active Directory performance.

Table 14-4   Core Operating System Indicators

Object	Counter	Interval	Threshold	Significance When the Threshold Value Is Exceeded
Memory	Page Faults / sec	Every 5 minutes	700 / second	High rate of page faults indicates insufficient physical memory.
PhysicalDisk	Current Disk Queue Length	Every 1 minute	2 Averaged over 3 intervals	Monitor volumes containing the Ntds.dit file and the .log files. This counter indicates that there is a backlog of disk I/O requests. Consider increasing disk and controller throughput.
Processor	% DPC Time (Instance=_Total)	Every 15 minutes	10	Indicates work that was deferred because the domain controller was too busy. Exceeding the threshold value indicates possible processor congestion.
System	Processor Queue Length	Every 1 minute	6 Averaged over 5 intervals	The CPU is not fast enough to process requests as they occur. If the replication topology is correct and the condition is not caused by failover from another domain controller, consider upgrading CPU.
Memory	Available MBytes	Every 15 minutes	4 megabytes (MB)	Indicates system has run out of available memory. Imminent service failure is likely.
Processor	% Processor Time (Instance=_Total)	Every 1 minute	85% Averaged over 3 intervals	Indicates CPU is overloaded. Determine if CPU load is being caused by Active Directory by examining the Process object, % Processor Time counter, lsass instance.

Table 14-4   Core Operating System Indicators *(continued)*

Object	Counter	Interval	Threshold	Significance When the Threshold Value Is Exceeded
System	Context Switches / sec	Every 15 minutes	70,000	Indicates excessive transitions. There might be too many applications or services running, or their load on the system is too high. Consider offloading a portion of this demand.
System	System Up Time	Every 15 minutes		Essential counter for measuring domain controller reliability.

Monitoring Active Directory with Event Viewer

In addition to using the Reliability And Performance Monitor to monitor Active Directory, you should also review the contents of the event logs by using the Event Viewer administrative tool. By default, the Event Viewer displays the following five logs:

- **Application**   Contains events logged by applications or programs.

- **Security**   Contains events such as valid and invalid logon attempts, as well as events related to resource use such as creating, opening, or deleting files or other objects.

- **Setup**   Contains events logged by the operating system and applications during setup.

- **System**   Contains events logged by Windows system components.

- **Forwarded Events**   Used to store events collected from other remote computers. In order to collect events from remote computers, you must configure a subscription.

In addition, for servers running Windows Server 2008 configured as domain controllers, the following event logs will be displayed under the Applications and Services Logs node of the Event Viewer:

- **Directory Service**   Contains events logged by Active Directory.

- **DFS Replication**   Contains events logged by the Distributed File System. This log will provide information related to SYSVOL replication.

If the Windows Server 2008 domain controller is a DNS server as well, the following log will also be displayed:

- **DNS Server**   Contains events logged by the DNS Server service.

To view the event logs, click Event Viewer from the Administrative Tools folder. Select the event log for the service you want to monitor. The left pane of Figure 14-6 shows all the event logs for a domain controller running Windows Server 2008 that is also a DNS server.

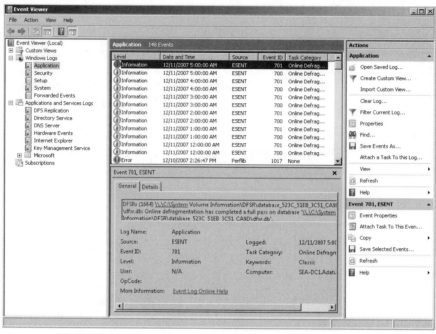

Figure 14-6   The Event Viewer administrative tool with event logs.

From the event log, review the event types for Errors and Warnings. To display the details of an event in the log, double-click the event. Figure 14-7 shows the details of a Warning event (*Event ID 2886*) from the Directory Service log.

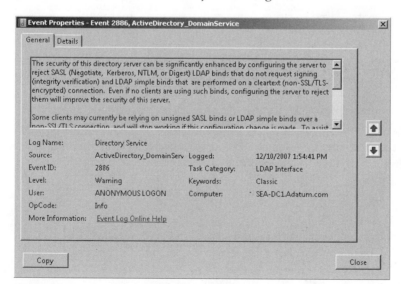

Figure 14-7   The Event Properties sheet for an event log entry.

What to Monitor

For monitoring the overall system health of Active Directory, you should monitor service-related performance and server-related performance indicators. You must ensure that Active Directory and the domain controllers on which it is running are performing optimally. When designing your monitoring solution, plan to monitor the following performance areas:

- **Active Directory service**   These performance indicators are monitored using the Directory Service counters and trace events in the Reliability And Performance Monitor.

- **Active Directory replication**   Replication performance is essential to ensuring that data integrity across the domain is being maintained.

- **Active Directory database storage**   The disk volumes that contain the Active Directory database file Ntds.dit and the .log files must have enough free space to allow normal growth and operation.

- **DNS performance and server health**   Because Active Directory relies on DNS as a service locator, the DNS server and service must be operating within normal limits for Active Directory to meet its service-level requirements.

- **File Replication Service (FRS) and the Distributed File System Replication (DFSR)**   The FRS must be running within normal limits to ensure that the shared system volume (SYSVOL) is replicating throughout the domain. If you are running in Windows Server 2008 functional mode, you can use DFSR for SYSVOL replication. This also has to be monitored to ensure proper performance.

- **Domain controller system health**   Monitoring for this area should cover overall server health, including memory counters, processor utilization, and paging. You must also ensure that the appropriate time and time zone settings are synchronized between all servers, which is critical for replication and proper authentication.

- **Forest health**   This area should be monitored to verify trusts and site availability.

- **Operations masters and global catalog roles**   For each Operations Master role, monitor to ensure server health. Also monitor to ensure global catalog availability to enable user logon and universal group-membership enumeration.

Direct from the Source: Monitoring Active Directory, Part II

Monitoring Active Directory can be a vast subject to investigate. As explained previously, monitoring Active Directory in a holistic way is critical. Therefore, even though in this chapter we focus on the Active Directory exposed information, there is a collection of things in Windows that are peripheral to Active Directory that are worth monitoring as well. In doing so, you will be able to track the general health state of the Active Directory ecosystem. For instance, this includes time synchronization to avoid time lags more than five minutes between Domain Controllers (if it is more than five minutes, the discrepancy can invalidate the Kerberos ticket and prevent Domain Controllers—and users—from being able to authenticate). You may also want to monitor Active Directory essential services such as NTFRS, DFSR, and KDC W32Time. These services all provide support to or depend on Active Directory, and they are critical in the overall health of the Active Directory ecosystem. Other more general aspects such as the disk space on the system disk and the Active Directory database size are also good things to track.

Something that people often do not monitor, but which can be useful in some circumstances—especially with very large Active Directory infrastructures—is the KCC CPU utilization. The KCC is the Knowledge Consistency Checker, and it is in charge of validating and building the Active Directory topology by creating the required connection objects. Although the performance of the KCC has been dramatically improved since Windows 2000, it could be interesting to monitor the CPU usage of the KCC on your domain controllers, especially the ones located in the hubs of your Active Directory infrastructure.

You can detect the KCC activity simply by changing the KCC diagnostic level to 3. To do this, set the "1 Knowledge Consistency Checker" registry key value to 3. The registry key is located in the HKLM\ SYSTEM\CurrentControlSet\Services\NTDS\Diagnostics registry hive. After it is set to 3, the KCC creates Event Log entries in the Directory Service Event Log each time it triggers. Events 1009 and 1013 with the NTDS KCC source name show the KCC start time and stop time, respectively. Then you can track the CPU usage at the same time and see how the KCC impacts the CPU during its execution. This can be useful to split the load between servers calculating the topology and the ones handling authentication requests, for instance.

In conclusion, when monitoring Active Directory, think about the big picture. This will avoid a lot of side effects and surprises, because you will become accustomed to working with the Active Directory ecosystem as a whole, and not with one software component at the time.

Alain Lissoir

Senior Program Manager

Active Directory–Connected System Division

Monitoring Replication

If you have more than one domain controller in your organization, one of the most critical components that you need to monitor is Active Directory replication. Replication between domain controllers is most commonly monitored with administrative tools such as Repadmin.exe, Dcdiag.exe, and the Directory Service log (described earlier with the Event Viewer).

Repadmin is a command-line tool that reports failures on a replication link between two replication partners. The following command displays the replication partners and any replication link failures for the DC1 domain controller in the Contoso.com domain:

```
repadmin /showrepl dc1.contoso.com
```

Dcdiag is a command-line tool that can check the DNS registration of a domain controller, check to see that the security identifiers (SIDs) on the naming context (NC) heads have appropriate permissions for replication, analyze the state of domain controllers in a forest or enterprise, and more. For a complete list of Dcdiag options, type **dcdiag /?**. The following command checks for any replication errors between domain controllers:

```
dcdiag /test:replications
```

Finally, the Directory Service log reports replication errors that occur after a replication link has been established. In particular, you should review the Directory Service log for any replication event where the event type is an Error or a Warning. The following are two examples of common replication errors as they are displayed in the Directory Service log:

- **Event ID 1311**   The replication configuration information in the Active Directory Sites And Services administrative tool does not accurately reflect the physical topology of the network. This error indicates that either one or more domain controllers or bridgehead servers are offline, or that the bridgehead servers do not host the required NCs.

- **Event ID 1265 (Access denied)**   This error can occur if the local domain controller failed to authenticate against its replication partner when creating the replication link or when trying to replicate over an existing link. This error typically happens when the domain controller has been disconnected from the rest of the network for a long time and its computer account password is not synchronized with the computer account password stored in the directory of its replication partner.

Direct from the Source: Monitoring Active Directory Replication

Monitoring Active Directory replication can be achieved in several ways. As described in this section, you can validate the configuration to ensure that Active Directory meets all required conditions to replicate properly. As described, you can determine this by using tools like Dcdiag. This would be more a proactive verification in which you would monitor before encountering any trouble. However, you can also monitor the Active Directory replication "after the fact" by checking any faults in the replication activities. You can achieve the latter type of monitoring by verifying reported events in the event log or specific replication failures with REPADMIN.

One additional way to validate the Active Directory replication is by reading some shared settings in an Active Directory domain controller, such as the FSMO roles. If everything looks fine, the FSMO roles reported for a given domain in a given forest should always be the same for all domain controllers within that given domain and forest. If you collect this information at the level of each domain controller and report it centrally (i.e., by dumping the collected results in a share), the FSMO role reported by all domain controllers can easily be compared. Any inconsistency in the FSMO role reported will surface a replication issue for the domain controller reporting different results.

Last but not least, a good way to monitor the Active Directory replication can be based on change injection. This technique involves updating a given and dedicated AD object for the purpose of the replication monitoring. For example, you can write an ADSI-based script that modifies an AD object in a selected domain controller. (The script could be executed regularly within the context of the Task Scheduler.) The modification may simply consist of a write operation of a date and a time in a string attribute like the *description* of a user object, for example. Because Active Directory replicates this type of change automatically, it is expected to see this information refreshed in all other Active Directory domain controllers at some point. Meanwhile, all these other domain controllers could regularly run a complementary script that reads this same object and compare the *description* attribute date/time with the value of the *whenChanged* attribute.

In doing so, this last script can determine two things: First, it can determine that the last change expected is successfully replicated (*description* attribute containing an updated date/time). Next, it can calculate the time it took for this replication change to occur by determining the time difference between the *description* attribute containing the original date/time write and the date/time contained in the *whenChanged* attribute. This will allow you to determine what is called the replication latency of the directory. More than confirming that replication works, the replication latency will tell you if your Active Directory design and infrastructure meet your expectation in terms of replication change speed, which is something you usually express during the Active Directory design time as a requirement. Therefore, it is also a good way to validate your design choices and maybe take some actions to meet your replication SLA.

Of course, this monitoring requires some scripting. You can refer to the white paper section of my Web site at *http://www.lissware.net* to acquire some ADSI script-based samples to create your own scripts to achieve this.

In addition, the Microsoft Active Directory Management Pack for Microsoft Operations Manager (MOM) 2005 and Operations Manager 2007 implements exactly this logic and leverages MOM to consolidate and compare the results collected across all domain controllers in your forest to determine the replication latency.

Alain Lissoir

Senior Program Manager

Active Directory–Connected System Division

Active Directory Database Maintenance

One of the important components of managing Active Directory is maintaining the Active Directory database. Under normal circumstances, you will rarely manage the Active Directory database directly, because regular automatic database management will maintain the health of your database in all but exceptional situations. These automatic processes include an online defragmentation of the Active Directory database as well as a garbage collection process to clean up deleted items. For those rare occasions when you do need to directly manage the Active Directory database, Windows Server 2008 provides the Ntdsutil tool.

Garbage Collection

One of the automatic processes used to maintain the Active Directory database is garbage collection. Garbage collection is a process that runs on every domain controller every 12 hours. During the garbage collection process, free space within the Active Directory database is reclaimed.

The garbage collection process starts by first removing tombstones from the database. *Tombstones* are the remains of objects that have been deleted from Active Directory. When an object such as a user account is deleted, the object is not immediately deleted. Rather, the *isDeleted* attribute on the object is set to *true*, the object is marked as a tombstone, and most of the attributes for the object are removed from the object. Only a few attributes required to identify the object are retained, such as the *globally unique identifier* (GUID), the *SID*, the *update sequence number* (USN), and the *distinguished name*. This tombstone is then replicated to other domain controllers in the domain. Each domain controller maintains a copy of the tombstoned object until the tombstone lifetime expires. By default, the tombstone lifetime is set to *180 days*. The next time the garbage collection process runs after the tombstone has expired, the object is deleted from the database.

After deleting the tombstones, the garbage collection process deletes any unnecessary transaction log files. Whenever a change is made to the Active Directory database, it is first written to a transaction log and then committed to the database. The garbage collection process removes all transaction logs that do not contain any uncommitted transactions.

As mentioned, the garbage collection process runs on every domain controller at 12-hour intervals. You can modify this interval by changing the *garbageCollPeriod* attribute. To modify this setting, you can use Adsiedit.msc. Open ADSI Edit from the Administrative Tools menu and then connect to the Configuration naming context. You can then expand CN=Configuration, expand CN=Services, expand CN=Windows NT, and then select CN=Directory Service. Right-click CN=Directory Service and then locate the *garbageCollPeriod* attribute and configure the value to meet your requirements. In most cases, you should not have to modify this setting. Figure 14-8 shows this attribute in ADSI Edit.

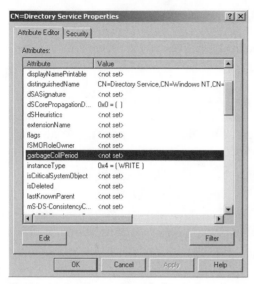

Figure 14-8   The *garbageCollPeriod* attribute in ADSI Edit.

Online Defragmentation

The final step in the garbage collection process is an online defragmentation of the Active Directory database. This online defragmentation frees up space within the database and rearranges the storage of Active Directory objects within the database to improve the efficiency of the database. The online defragmentation is necessary because of the process Active Directory uses when manipulating objects in the database.

During normal operation, the database system for Active Directory is optimized to be able to make changes to the Active Directory database as quickly as possible. When an object is deleted from Active Directory, the database page where the object is stored is loaded into the computer memory and the object is deleted from the page. As objects are added to Active Directory, they are written to database pages without consideration for optimizing the storage of that information for later retrieval. After several hours of committing changes to the database as fast as possible, the storage of the data in the database might not be optimized. For example, the database might contain empty pages where objects have been deleted, there might be many pages with some deleted items, or Active Directory objects that should logically be stored together might be stored on many different pages throughout the database.

The online defragmentation process cleans up the database and returns the database to a more optimized state. If some of the entries on a database page have been deleted, entries from other pages might be moved onto the page to optimize the storage and retrieval of information. Objects that should logically be stored together because they will be displayed together are moved onto the same database page or onto adjacent pages. One of the limitations of the online defragmentation process is that it does not shrink the size of the Active Directory database. If you have deleted a large number of objects from Active Directory, the online defragmentation process might create many empty pages in the database as it moves objects around in the database. However, the online defragmentation process cannot remove these empty pages from the database. To remove these pages, you must use an offline defragmentation process.

The online defragmentation process runs every 12 hours as part of the garbage collection process. When the online defragmentation process is complete, an event is written into the Directory Service log indicating that the process has completed successfully. Figure 14-9 shows an example of this event log message.

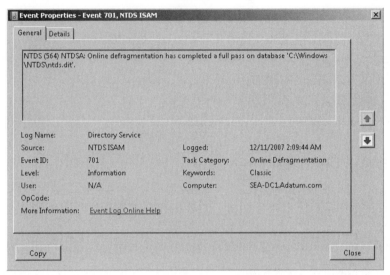

Figure 14-9   A Directory Service log message indicating a successful online defragmentation.

Offline Defragmentation of the Active Directory Database

As mentioned previously, the online defragmentation process does not shrink the size of the Active Directory database. Under normal circumstances, this is not a problem because the database pages that are cleaned up during the online defragmentation are just reused as new objects are added to Active Directory. However, in some cases, you might want to use offline defragmentation to shrink the overall size of the database. For example, if you remove the global catalog from a domain controller, you should run an offline defragmentation on the database to clean up the space used in the database to store the GC information. This need for an offline defragmentation is especially true in a multiple-domain environment where the GC can become very large. You might also want to use offline defragmentation if you have removed a large number of objects from the Active Directory domain.

To run offline defragmentation, perform the following steps:

1. Back up the Active Directory information on the domain controller. This process is described in Chapter 15, "Active Directory Disaster Recovery."

2. For Windows Server 2008 Domain Controllers, open the Services console and stop the **Active Directory Domain Services** service and all related services as prompted (or type **net stop ntds** at a command prompt).

> **Note**   For Windows Server 2000/2003, reboot the domain controller. As the server reboots, press **F8** to display the **Advanced Boot Options** and then choose **Directory Services Restore Mode**. After the server reboots, log on using the local Administrator account. Use the password that you entered as the Directory Services Restore Mode password when you promoted the domain controller.

3. Open a command prompt and type **ntdsutil**.

4. From the Ntdsutil prompt, type **Activate Instance NTDS**.

5. From the Ntdsutil prompt, type **files**.

6. From the File Maintenance prompt, type **info**. This option displays current information about the path and size of the Active Directory database and its log files.

7. Type **compact to** *drive:\directory*. Select a drive and directory that have enough space to store the entire database. If the directory path name contains any spaces, the path must be enclosed by quotation marks.

8. The offline defragmentation process creates a new database named Ntds.dit in the path you specified. As the database is copied to the new location, it is defragmented.

9. When the defragmentation is done, type **quit** twice to return to the command prompt.

10. Copy the defragmented Ntds.dit file over the old Ntds.dit file in the Active Directory database path and delete the old log files.

11. Restart the domain controller.

> **Note**   If you are defragmenting the database because you have deleted a large number of objects from Active Directory, you must repeat this procedure on all domain controllers.

Managing the Active Directory Database Using Ntdsutil

In addition to using Ntdsutil to defragment your Active Directory database while offline, you can use it to manage the Active Directory database in several other ways. The Ntdsutil tool can be used to perform several low-level Active Directory database recovery tasks. The database recovery options are all nondestructive—that is, the recovery tools will try to correct a problem with the Active Directory database, but they will never do so at the expense of deleting data.

Recovering the Transaction Logs

Recovering the transaction logs means forcing the domain controller to rerun the transaction logs. This option is automatically performed by the domain controller when the domain controller restarts from a forced shutdown. You can also force the soft recovery using the Ntdsutil tool.

> **More Info**   Chapter 15 describes in detail how transaction logs are used in Active Directory.

To perform a recovery of the transaction logs, perform the following steps:

1. Reboot the server and select the option to boot into Directory Services Restore Mode. As an option, you can also stop the Active Directory Domain Services service for Windows Server 2008 domain controllers. All of the Ntdsutil database operations require that AD DS be stopped.

2. Open a command prompt and type **ntdsutil**.

3. From the Ntdsutil prompt, type **Activate Instance NTDS**.

4. From the Ntdsutil prompt, type **files**.

5. From the File Maintenance prompt, type **recover**.

The recover option should always be the first step in any database recovery because it ensures that the database is consistent with the transaction logs. After this is complete, you can run the other database options if needed.

Checking the Database for Integrity

Checking the database for integrity means that the database is checked at a low (binary) level to look for database corruption. The process also checks the database headers and checks all the tables for consistency. Because every byte of the database is checked during this process, it will take a long time to run on a large database. To run the integrity check, type **integrity** at the File Maintenance prompt in Ntdsutil.

Semantic Database Analysis

The semantic database analysis is different from the integrity check in that it does not examine the database at a binary level. Rather, the semantic analysis checks the database consistency against the Active Directory semantics. The semantic database analysis examines each object in the database to ensure that each object has a GUID, a proper SID, and the correct replication metadata.

To perform the semantic database analysis, perform the following steps:

1. Open a command prompt and type **ntdsutil**.

2. From the Ntdsutil prompt, type **Activate Instance NTDS.**

3. At the Ntdsutil prompt, type **semantic database analysis**.

4. At the semantic checker prompt, type **verbose on**. This setting configures Ntdsutil to write additional information to the screen when the semantic checker is running.

5. At the semantic checker prompt, type **go**.

Moving Database and Transaction Log Locations

The Ntdsutil tool can also be used to move the Active Directory database and transaction logs. For example, if the transaction logs and the database are all on the same hard disk, you might want to move one of the components to a different hard disk. If the hard disk containing the database file fills up, you will have to move the database.

To move the database and transaction log to new locations with the server in Directory Services Restore Mode (or with the Active Directory Domain Services service stopped), perform the following steps:

1. Open a command prompt and type **ntdsutil**.

2. From the Ntdsutil prompt, type **Activate Instance NTDS.**

3. From the Ntdsutil prompt, type **files**.

4. To see where the files are currently located, at the Ntdsutil prompt, type **info**. This command lists the file locations for the database and all logs.

5. To move the database file, at the file maintenance prompt, type **move db to** *directory*, where *directory* is the destination location for the files. This command moves the database to the specified location and reconfigures the registry to access the file in the correct location.

6. To move the transaction logs, at the file maintenance prompt, type **move logs to** *directory*.

Summary

This chapter introduced the processes and some of the tools necessary to monitor Active Directory and the system health of domain controllers. By implementing a regular monitoring solution, you will be able to identify potentially disruptive and costly system bottlenecks and other performance issues before they occur. Effective monitoring of Active Directory will also provide you with valuable performance trend data so that you can prepare for future system improvements. Monitoring is one way to trigger the necessary support tasks that you must perform to keep your Active Directory infrastructure running in top condition. In the absence of event log errors and alert notifications, you must still implement a regular database maintenance program to keep the Active Directory database functioning efficiently. This chapter described the online and offline defragmentation process as well as the garbage collection process for removing deleted (tombstoned) Active Directory objects.

Additional Resources

The following resources contain additional information and tools related to this chapter.

Related Information

- Chapter 15, "Active Directory Disaster Recovery" provides details on Active Directory data storage and backing up and restoring the Active Directory database.

- "Windows Reliability And Performance Monitor," article located at *http://technet2.microsoft.com/windowsserver2008/en/library/ec5b5e7b-5d5c-4d04-98ad-55d9a09677101033.mspx?mfr=true*

- "AD DS: Restartable Active Directory Domain Services," article located at *http://technet2.microsoft.com/windowsserver2008/en/library/822ff47d-bd55-4c08-abc1-2d66336e33e51033.mspx?mfr=true*

- "Windows Vista: Reliability and Performance," article located at *http://technet.microsoft.com/en-us/windowsvista/aa905077.aspx*

- "Active Directory Directory Services Maintenance Utility (Ntdsutil.exe)," article located at *http://technet2.microsoft.com/windowsserver/en/library/819bea8b-3889-4479-850f-1f031087693d1033.mspx?mfr=true*

- "Relocating Active Directory Database Files," article located at *http://technet2.microsoft.com/windowsserver/en/library/af6646aa-2360-46e4-81ca-d51707bf01eb1033.mspx?mfr=true*

- "Relocating SYSVOL Manually," article located at *http://technet2.microsoft.com/windowsserver/en/library/300796c6-8148-49af-a327-b5dca853ac4f1033.mspx?mfr=true*

- "Best Practices for SYSVOL Maintenance," article located at *http://support.microsoft.com/kb/324175*

- "Microsoft Active Directory Management Pack Guide," article located at *http://www.microsoft.com/downloads/details.aspx?familyid=2B9D3613-5516-4F44-8550-B21E054F5047&displaylang=en*

- "Monitoring Active Directory with MOM," article located at *http://download.microsoft.com/documents/uk/technet/downloads/technetmagazine/issue4/36_monitoring_ad_with_mom.pdf*

Chapter 15

Active Directory Disaster Recovery

Active Directory Domain Services (AD DS) is perhaps the most critical network service that you will deploy on your network. If the Active Directory infrastructure fails, users on your network will be extremely limited in what they can do. Almost all network services on a Windows Server 2008 network depend on users authenticating to Active Directory before they access any network resource. Because Active Directory is critical, you must apply at least the same level of preparation to Active Directory disaster prevention and recovery as you do to any other network resource. When you deploy Windows Server 2008 Active Directory, it is essential that you prepare for the protection of the Active Directory database and put into place a plan for recovering the database in the event of a critical failure.

This chapter begins by discussing some basic practices that you can implement to provide redundancy and protection for Active Directory. It then discusses the components of the Active Directory database and the optimal configuration of these components to ensure disaster recovery functionality. The main part of this chapter discusses options and procedures for backing up and restoring the Active Directory database.

More Info This chapter does not address restoring an entire Active Directory forest from backup, just individual domain controllers and Active Directory objects in a domain. For information about recovering an entire Active Directory forest, see "Planning for Active Directory Forest Recovery" in the Microsoft Download Center at *http://www.microsoft.com/downloads/ details.aspx?FamilyID=AFE436FA-8E8A-443A-9027-C522DEE35D85&displaylang=en.*

Planning for a Disaster

The first steps in disaster recovery must take place long before the disaster strikes. In fact, if you haven't done the proper planning for a potential disaster, a problem such as a hardware component failure on a domain controller might turn into a real catastrophe rather than just a minor inconvenience.

Planning for disaster includes considering all the elements that make up the normal network infrastructure, as well as some Active Directory–specific planning. The following procedures are critical:

- **Develop a consistent backup and restore regimen for the domain controllers.** The first step in any recovery plan is to install the appropriate backup hardware and software to back up the domain controllers. You should then create and test a backup and restore plan. You should also back up Active Directory before every major state change such as a schema update or bulk import.

- **Test your backup plan before you deploy Active Directory and frequently after you deploy.** After you have deployed Active Directory, your users will require that it be available all the time. You should also repeatedly test the restore plan. Many of the best-managed network environments have a consistent restore testing procedure, in which every week some component of the restore procedure is tested. If you actually have a disaster, you will be under a great deal of pressure to get Active Directory back up and running as quickly as possible—a crisis should not be the first time that you are using the Active Directory restore procedure.

- **Test changes to Active Directory in a lab environment.** This minimizes the risk that major updates to Active Directory will cause problems in the production environment. After the update is successfully performed in the lab environment, it can be implemented in the production environment.

- **Deploy Active Directory domain controllers with hardware redundancy.** Most servers can be ordered with some level of hardware redundancy at little additional cost. For example, a server with dual power supplies, redundant network cards, and a hardware-based redundant hard disk system should be standard equipment for the domain controllers. If this redundancy saves you even one all-night effort restoring a domain controller, it will be one of the best investments you have ever made. In many large environments, this hardware redundancy is taken to another level where each domain controller is connected to a different power circuit and connected to a different Ethernet switch or network segment.

- **In all but the smallest networks, you should deploy at least two domain controllers.** Active Directory uses circular logging for its log files, and this default cannot be modified. This circular logging means that with a single domain controller, you might lose Active Directory data if the domain controller crashes and you have to restore from backup. Even in a small company, multiple domain controllers are critical. If you want all the users to use one domain controller most of the time, you can modify the Domain Name System (DNS) records by adjusting the priority for each domain controller. The second domain controller can then serve another function and be used for backup only when the first domain controller fails.

Active Directory Data Storage

The Active Directory database is stored in a file called Ntds.dit, which is located in the %systemroot%\NTDS folder by default. The contents of this folder are shown in Figure 15-1. This folder also contains the following files:

- **Edb.chk**   This file is a checkpoint file that indicates which transactions from the log files have been written to the Active Directory database.

- **Edb.log**   This file is the current transaction log. This log file is a fixed-length file exactly 10 megabytes (MB) in size.

- **Edbxxxxx.log**   After Active Directory has been running for a while, there might be one or more log files with the *xxxxx filename* portion being a value that is incremented in hexadecimal numbers. These log files are previous log files; whenever the current log file is filled up, the current log file is renamed to the next previous log file and a new Edb.log file is created. The old log files are automatically deleted as the changes in the log files are made to the Active Directory database. Each of these log files is also 10 MB in size.

- **Edbtmp.log**   This log is a temporary log that is used as the current log file (Edb.log) fills up. A new file named Edbtemp.log is created to store any transactions, and the Edb.log file is renamed to the next previous log file. Then the Edbtmp.log file is renamed to Edb.log. Because use of this filename is transient, it is typically not visible.

- **Edbres00001.jrs and edbres00002.jrs**   These files are reserved log files that are used only when the hard disk that contains the log files runs out of space. If the current log file fills up and the server cannot create a new log file because there is no hard disk space left, the server will flush any Active Directory transactions currently in memory to the two reserved log files and then shut down Active Directory. Each of these log files is also 10 MB in size.

- **Temp.edb**   This is a temporary file used during database maintenance and to store information about transactions that are currently in progress.

> **Note**   If you have worked with any of the recent versions of Microsoft Exchange Server, this discussion of Active Directory database components and processes will sound very familiar. The Active Directory database is the same database that is deployed with servers running Exchange Server 4 or later.

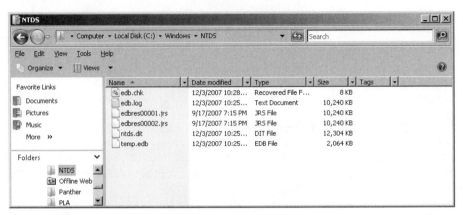

Figure 15-1   Active Directory files located in %systemroot%\NTDS.

Every modification to the Active Directory database is called a *transaction*. A transaction can consist of several steps. For example, when a user is moved from one organizational unit (OU) to another, the object must be created in the destination OU and deleted from the source OU. For the transaction to be complete, both steps must be performed successfully. If one of the steps fails, the transaction should be rolled back so that neither step is completed. When all the steps in a transaction are complete, the transaction is *committed*, or completed. By using a transaction-based model, Active Directory ensures that the database remains in a consistent state at all times.

Whenever any change is made to the Active Directory database (for example, the telephone number for a user is changed), the change is first written to a transaction log file. Because a transaction log file is essentially a text file in which the changes are written sequentially, writing to a transaction log is much quicker than writing to a database. Therefore, the use of transaction logs improves the performance of the domain controller.

After the transaction has been written to the transaction log, the domain controller loads the database page containing the user object into memory (if it is not already in memory). All changes to the Active Directory database are made in the memory of the domain controller. The domain controller will use as much memory and retain as much of the Active Directory database in memory as possible. The domain controller flushes database pages from memory only when available free memory becomes limited or when the domain controller is being shut down. The changes to the database pages are written to the database during low server-utilization periods or at server shutdown.

The transaction logs not only improve the performance of the domain controller by providing a place to rapidly write changes, they also provide some recoverability in the event of a server failure. For example, if a change is made to Active Directory, the change is written to the transaction logs and then to the database page in the server memory. If the server shuts down unexpectedly at this point, the changes in the server memory will not have been committed to the database. When the domain controller restarts, it checks the transaction logs for any transactions that have not yet been committed to the database. These changes are applied to the database as the domain controller service restarts. The checkpoint file is used during this recovery process. The *checkpoint file* is a pointer that indicates which transactions in the transaction logs have been written to the database. During the recovery process, the domain controller reads the checkpoint file to determine which transactions have been committed to the database, and it then applies all the changes that have not been committed.

> **Note**   The use of transaction logs enhances the performance of the domain controllers and improves the recovery of data in the event of an unexpected shutdown. These advantages are maximized when the transaction logs and the database are located on separate hard disks because disk performance is less likely to be a bottleneck.

Active Directory in Windows Server 2008 uses circular logging, and this configuration cannot be changed. With circular logging, only previous log files containing transactions that have not been written to the database are retained. As the information in the previous log file is committed to the database, the log file is deleted. The use of circular logging prevents you from replaying transaction logs on a restored database to make it current. Instead, replication from a second domain controller is used to bring a restored Active Directory database to the current state.

Backing Up Active Directory

The process for backing up Active Directory in Windows Server 2008 is very different from the process used in Windows Server 2003 and Windows 2000 Server. Windows Server Backup and Wbadmin.exe replace the previous Backup utility Ntbackup.exe. The new backup utility has the following changes:

- Windows Server Backup and Wbadmin.exe are not installed by default. You must install the Windows Server Backup feature to use these utilities.

- Only full volumes can be backed up. There is no option to back up only system state data, which includes Active Directory. You back up critical volumes to back up system state data.

- Backups are performed only to disk or DVD. Windows Server Backup does not perform backups to tape. If you want to perform backups to tape, you must use a third party backup solution. You can store backups on a local disk, external disk, remote share, or DVD.

- Backups are faster. Windows Server Backup performs Volume Shadow Copy Service (VSS) backups and tracks block level changes. This increases the speed of both incremental backups and full backups.

System state data is a collection of configuration data on a server. This data is tightly integrated and must be backed up and restored as a single unit. In Windows Server 2003 and Windows 2000 Server, you could back up only system state data. In Windows Server 2008, when using Windows Server Backup or Wbadmin.exe, you must back up critical volumes containing system state data. In Windows Server Backup, the option I Want To Be Able To Perform A System Recovery Using This Backup is used to automatically select all critical volumes, as shown in Figure 15-2.

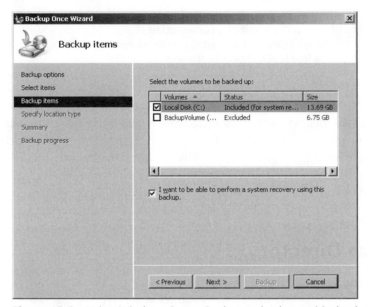

Figure 15-2   Using Windows Server Backup to back up critical volumes.

The critical volumes for a server vary depending on the roles installed on a server. The system volume hosts the boot files, such as the Boot Configuration Data (BCD) store and Bootmgr, and it is a critical volume. The boot volume with the Windows operating system is also a critical volume. Volumes hosting the following additional data are also critical:

- SYSVOL directory
- Active Directory database and log files
- Registry
- COM+ Class Registration database
- Active Directory Certificate Services database
- Cluster service information
- System files that are under Windows Resource Protection

Windows Server 2008 has an install from media (IFM) feature that can be used when installing new domain controllers. IFM uses a restored copy of Active Directory as a starting point for replication on new domain controllers rather than replicating the entire Active Directory database. This is useful for branch office servers with low bandwidth connection. The backup set for IFM is created by using Ntdsutil rather than by using Windows Server Backup or Wbadmin.exe.

> **Note**   Members of the Administrators and Backup Operators groups have the necessary rights to perform a manual backup. Only members of the Administrators group have the necessary right to perform a scheduled backup, and this right cannot be delegated.

The Need for Backups

The primary method for backing up Active Directory is replication to a second domain controller. If one domain controller in a domain fails, then other domain controllers have the same information and make that information available to clients for logon or other queries. There should always be at least two domain controllers per domain for this purpose.

Even though domain information is replicated between domain controllers, a domain controller should still be backed up regularly. You may need to restore an existing domain controller or Active Directory in the following situations:

- **Applications are configured to use a specific domain controller**   Some applications are configured to use a specific domain controller to access Active Directory. In such a case, restoring a domain controller avoids the need to reconfigure the application.

- **All domain controllers for a domain are lost**   If there is a major disaster such as a building fire, all domain controllers for a domain may be lost. In such a case, Active Directory must be restored from backup.

- **Objects are deleted**   If an Active Directory object is deleted by accident, then you can restore the deleted objects from backup. Depending on the number of objects, this may be much faster than recreating the objects.

Tombstone Lifetime

Tombstone lifetime determines how long a deleted object remains in Active Directory. As described in Chapter 14, "Monitoring and Maintaining Active Directory," when an Active Directory object is deleted, the object is not removed from Active Directory. Instead, the object is marked as deleted, most attributes are removed, the object is renamed, and the object is moved to the Deleted Objects container. This object is now referred to as a *tombstone*. These changes are replicated to all other domain controllers, and the tombstone is only removed from Active Directory after the tombstone lifetime has passed.

A backup is only valid for the length of the tombstone lifetime configured in Active Directory. You cannot restore an Active Directory backup that is older than the tombstone lifetime. This ensures that nonauthoritative restores of Active Directory function as expected. For example, if a backup that includes the user *Paul* is used to restore a domain controller after the object *Paul* has been deleted, the deleted status of *Paul* is replicated back to the restored domain controller. The deleted status of *Paul* is unchanged, because the backup is performed within the tombstone lifetime configured for Active Directory. If the domain controller were restored after the tombstone lifetime expired, then *Paul* would be restored and the deleted status of *Paul* would not exist on other domain controllers to be replicated back. The object *Paul* becomes a lingering object that exists in Active Directory even though it had been deleted. This results in an inconsistency in Active Directory, and the object must be removed.

The tombstone lifetime is configured for an entire forest. The value for the tombstone lifetime is stored in the *tombstoneLifetime* attribute of the CN=Directory Service,CN=Windows NT,CN=Services,CN=Configuration,DC=ForestRootDomain object, as shown in Figure 15-3. The default value depends on the operating system on which the forest is created, as shown in Table 15-1. These values apply only when creating a new Active Directory forest. They are not modified by upgrades or applying service packs. You can modify the default value for tombstone lifetime by using ADSIEdit.msc.

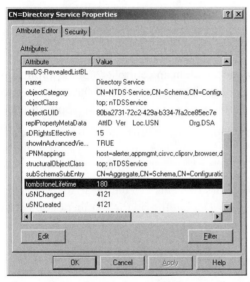

Figure 15-3   The *tombstoneLifetime* attribute for an Active Directory forest.

Table 15-1   Default Tombstone Lifetime for New Active Directory Forests

Operating System	Default Tombstone Lifetime
Windows 2000 Server	60 days
Windows Server 2003 no service pack	60 days
Windows Server 2003 SP1	180 days
Windows Server 2003 R2	60 days
Windows Server 2003 SP2	180 days
Windows Server 2008	180 days

Backup Frequency

Although the tombstone lifetime places a hard limit on the frequency of backups, you should back up the domain controllers much more frequently than the tombstone lifetime. Many issues in addition to the tombstone problem need to be considered if you are trying to restore the domain controller from a backup that is more than a couple of days old. Because the restore of Active Directory includes all the information on critical volumes, that information will be restored to a previous state. If the server has the Active Directory Certificate Services role installed, any certificates that you issued since the backup will not be included in the Active Directory Certificate Services database. If you have updated drivers or installed any new applications, they might not work because the registry has been rolled back to a previous state. Almost all companies use a backup regimen in which at least some servers are backed up every night. The domain controllers should be part of the nightly backup.

Restoring Active Directory

There are two reasons you might need to restore Active Directory. The first reason is if your database is unusable—perhaps because one of your domain controllers has experienced a hard disk failure or because the database has been corrupted to the point where it cannot be loaded. The second reason is if human error has created a problem with the directory information. For example, if someone has deleted an OU containing several hundred user and group accounts, you will want to restore the information rather than reenter all the information.

If you are restoring Active Directory because the database on one of your domain controllers is not usable, you have two options. The first option is to not restore Active Directory to the failed server at all, but rather to create another domain controller by promoting another server running Windows Server 2008 to become a domain controller. This way, you are restoring the domain controller functionality rather than restoring Active Directory on a specific domain controller. The second recovery option is to repair the server that failed and then restore the Active Directory database on that server. In this case, you will perform a nonauthoritative restore. A *nonauthoritative restore* restores the Active Directory database on the domain controller, and then all the changes made to Active Directory since the backup are replicated to the restored domain controller.

If you are restoring Active Directory because someone deleted a large number of objects in the directory, you have only one way to restore the information. You will restore the Active Directory database on one of the domain controllers using a backup that contains the deleted objects. Then you will perform an authoritative restore. During the authoritative restore, the restored data is marked so that it is replicated to all other domain controllers, overwriting the deletion of the information.

Restoring Active Directory by Creating a New Domain Controller

One of the options for restoring a domain controller after a failure is to build a new domain controller to replace a failed domain controller. If one domain controller fails, you can build a new server running Windows Server 2008 and Active Directory, or you can use an existing server and promote that server to be a domain controller. Then you can use normal Active Directory replication to populate the Active Directory database on the new domain controller.

> **Note**   When creating a new domain controller where replication is over a slow link, such as a branch office, use an IFM installation to reduce the time required for replication. An IFM installation uses an Active Directory backup created by Ntdsutil as a starting point for replication.

Creating a new domain controller is the best solution in the following situations:

- You have an available domain controller in addition to the failed server. This is an absolute requirement. If you do not have another domain controller that is available to be used as a replication partner, your only option is to restore the Active Directory database on a new or repaired domain controller.

- The time required to build the new domain controller and replicate the information from another domain controller is significantly less than the time needed to repair the failed domain controller and restore the database. This calculation depends on the size of the Active Directory database, the network connection speed between your domain controllers, and the speed with which you can rebuild and restore a domain controller. If you have a relatively small Active Directory database (less than 100 MB) and another domain controller is on the same local area network (LAN), creating another domain controller and replicating the database will be faster than repairing and restoring the failed domain controller. If you have a large database or the only available replication partner is across a slow wide area network (WAN) connection, repairing the failed domain controller and restoring the database will usually be the quicker option.

- You cannot repair the failed domain controller. Although it is possible to restore Windows Server 2008 and the Active Directory database onto a server with different hardware from the original domain controller, this process is usually difficult and can be very time-consuming. If you cannot rebuild the failed server with similar hardware, building another domain controller will usually be quicker.

Creating a new domain controller is not a good option when you must make significant changes to support the new domain controller. One example is having many applications configured to use a specific domain controller. Reconfiguring these applications to use a new domain controller may take longer than repairing or restoring the domain controller. Application reconfiguration problems can be avoided by using a hostname rather than an IP address in the application configuration. Reconfiguring a DNS record for the hostname is a fast method to begin using the IP address of a new domain controller or an alternate domain controller.

To build an additional domain controller to replace the failed server, use an existing server running Windows Server 2008 (or build a new server) and promote it to be a domain controller. During the promotion process, the directory will be replicated from one of the other domain controllers. If the failed domain controller was a global catalog (GC) server or the holder of one of the operations master roles, you will need to consider how to restore this functionality. Recovering GC servers and operations master servers is covered in detail in the section titled "Restoring Operations Masters and Global Catalog Servers" later in this chapter.

If you do choose to restore Active Directory functionality by creating a new domain controller, you still need to remove the old domain controller from the directory and from DNS. If you are planning to use the failed domain controller's name for the restored domain controller, you need to clean up the directory by using Ntdsutil before starting the recovery, as shown in Figure 15-4. If you are using a different name for the new domain controller, you can clean up the directory after installation.

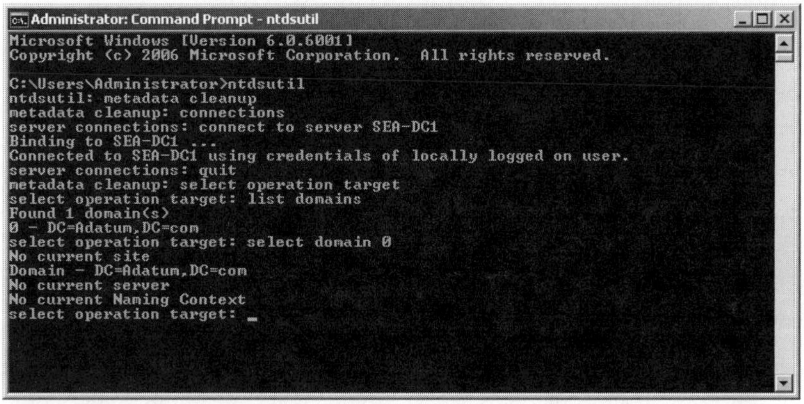

Figure 15-4   Using Ntdsutil.

To clean up the directory from a failed domain controller, follow these steps:

1. Open a command prompt.

2. Type **ntdsutil** and press Enter.

3. At the Ntdsutil prompt, type **metadata cleanup** and press Enter.

4. At the Metadata Cleanup prompt, type **connections** and press Enter. This command is used to connect to a current domain controller to make changes to Active Directory.

5. At the Server Connections prompt, type **connect to server** *servername*, where *servername* is the name of an available domain controller, and then press Enter. If you are logged in with an account that has administrative rights in Active Directory, you will be connected to that domain controller. If you do not have administrative rights, you can

use **set creds** *domain username password* to enter the credentials of a user with domain-level permissions.

6. At the Server Connections prompt, type **quit** and then press Enter. This returns you to the Metadata Cleanup prompt.

7. At the Metadata Cleanup prompt, type **select operation target** and press Enter. This command is used to select the domain, site, and domain controller so that you can remove the domain controller.

8. At the Select Operations Target prompt, type **list domains** and press Enter. All the domains in the forest are listed with a number assigned to each.

9. At the Select Operations Target prompt, type **select domain** *number*, where *number* is the domain containing the failed domain controller, and press Enter.

10. At the Select Operations Target prompt, type **list sites** and press Enter. All the sites in the forest are listed with a number assigned to each.

11. At the Select Operations Target prompt, type **select site** *number*, where *number* is the site containing the failed domain controller, and press Enter.

12. At the Select Operations Target prompt, type **list servers in site** and press Enter.

13. At the Select Operations Target prompt, type **select server** *number*, where *number* is the failed domain controller, and press Enter.

14. Type **quit** and press Enter. This returns you to the Metadata Cleanup prompt.

15. Type **remove selected server** and press Enter.

16. Click Yes to confirm removal of the server.

17. Type **quit** at each prompt to exit Ntdsutil.

> **Note**   This process with Ntdsutil is also used when you have forced the removal of Active Directory from a server by using Dcpromo /forceremoval. This command demotes a domain controller without cleaning up Active Directory metadata. When Active Directory becomes unusable for some reason, this can be an alternative to completely rebuilding a server.

In addition to cleaning up the directory object using Ntdsutil, you should clean up the DNS records for the failed domain controller. Remove all DNS records from DNS, including all domain controller records, GC server records, and primary domain controller (PDC) emulator records. (The last two will exist only if the domain controller was configured with these roles.) If you do not clean up the DNS records, clients will continue to receive the DNS information and try to connect to the domain controller. This can result in slower connections to Active Directory as clients fail over to use alternate domain controllers.

The version of Ntdsutil included in Windows Server 2008 and Windows Server 2003 SP1 automatically performs some Active Directory cleanup tasks that needed to be performed manually in previous versions:

- Removal of the NTDSA or NTDS Setting subject
- Removal of inbound AD connection objects used for replication
- Removal of the computer account
- Removal of the FRS member object used by File Replication Service
- Removal of the FRS subscriber object used by File Replication Service
- Seizure of flexible single master operations roles from the failed DC

Performing a Nonauthoritative Restore of Active Directory

A nonauthoritative restore of Active Directory is performed in two situations. When the Active Directory database on a server becomes corrupted, then performing a nonauthoritative restore of Active Directory recreates the database and allows it to function. When you perform a full recovery of a domain controller, you also use a nonauthoritative restore of Active Directory. A full recovery of a domain controller is required if the only domain controller in a domain fails. You can also perform a full recovery of a domain controller when you want the identity of a failed domain controller kept the same.

If you have made any changes to Active Directory since the backup, the backup tape will not contain those changes. However, the other domain controllers in the domain will have the most recent information. If you are rebuilding the domain controller because the server failed, the domain controller should get the changes from its replication partners after the restore is complete. For this to happen, you must perform a nonauthoritative restore.

Nonauthoritative Restore on an Existing Server

To perform a nonauthoritative restore of Active Directory, you must have a good backup of the critical volumes on the domain controller. You boot into Directory Services Restore Mode (DSRM), shown in Figure 15-5; restore the system state from the critical volumes by using Wbadmin.exe; and then reboot Windows Server 2008 normally. After the domain controller reboots, it will connect to its replication partners and begin updating its own database to reflect any domain information modified since the backup.

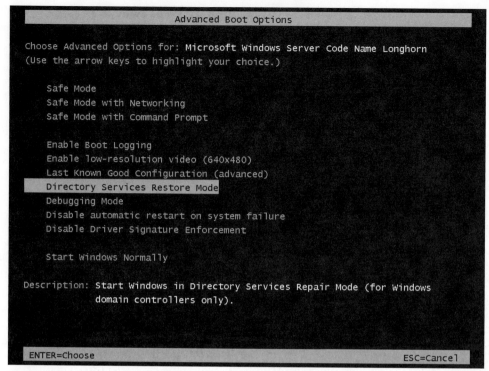

```
                       Advanced Boot Options

Choose Advanced Options for: Microsoft Windows Server Code Name Longhorn
(Use the arrow keys to highlight your choice.)

    Safe Mode
    Safe Mode with Networking
    Safe Mode with Command Prompt

    Enable Boot Logging
    Enable low-resolution video (640x480)
    Last Known Good Configuration (advanced)
    Directory Services Restore Mode
    Debugging Mode
    Disable automatic restart on system failure
    Disable Driver Signature Enforcement

    Start Windows Normally

Description: Start Windows in Directory Services Repair Mode (for Windows
            domain controllers only).


ENTER=Choose                                            ESC=Cancel
```

Figure 15-5   The Advanced Boot Options menu with DSRM.

DSRM is a version of safe mode for domain controllers on which Active Directory is stopped. This mode is required to restore Active Directory. To log on to DSRM, you must use the DSRM Administrator account that is created during the installation of Active Directory. This is a local Administrator account created during the installation of Active Directory on the domain controller. The password is set during installation and is not the same as the domain Administrator password.

> **Note**   In Windows Server 2003 and Windows Server 2008, Ntdsutil is used to reset the DSRM Administrator account password. At the Set Dsrm Password context, use the command **reset password of server** *server*, where *server* is the name of the domain controller on which you want to reset the DSRM Administrator account password. You can use *null* to represent the local server.

To perform a nonauthoritative restore of Active Directory, follow these steps:

1. Repair the failed domain controller. At this point, the server is functional, with the exception of Active Directory.

2. Restart the server and press F8 to enter the Advanced Boot Options menu.

3. Select Directory Service Restore Mode.

> **Note** As an alternative to using the Advanced Boot Options menu, you can use *bcdedit /set safeboot dsrepair* to set the default start option as Directory Services Restore Mode (DSRM). After the installation is complete, use **bcdedit /deletevalue safeboot** and reboot to start Windows normally.

4. Log on as the DSRM Administrator account. To log on as this user, enter .**Administrator** as the username.

5. Open a command prompt.

6. Type **wbadmin get versions –backuptarget:***backuplocation*, where *backuplocation* is the drive letter or UNC path storing the backup, and press Enter. This lists the backups stored in the location.

7. Take note of the version identifier of the backup you want to restore. This identifier is the time when the backup was taken.

8. Type **wbadmin start systemstaterecovery –version:***identifier* **–backuptarget:***backuplocation*, where *identifier* is the version identifier noted in step 7 and *backuplocation* is the drive letter or UNC path storing the backup, and press Enter. Figure 15-6 shows a system state restore using Wbadmin.

```
Administrator: Command Prompt - wbadmin start sysstaterecovery -version:11/16/2007-20:38 -bac...

C:\Users\Administrator.SEA-DC1>wbadmin get versions -backuptarget:E:
wbadmin 1.0 - Backup command-line tool
(C) Copyright 2004 Microsoft Corp.

Backup time: 11/16/2007 2:38 PM
Backup target: Fixed Disk labeled BackupVolume(E:)
Version identifier: 11/16/2007-20:38

C:\Users\Administrator.SEA-DC1>wbadmin start sysstaterecovery -version:11/16/200
7-20:38 -backuptarget:E:
wbadmin 1.0 - Backup command-line tool
(C) Copyright 2004 Microsoft Corp.

Do you want to start the system state recovery operation?
[Y] Yes [N] No y

Starting System State Restore [12/3/2007 11:29 AM]
Processing files to restore (This may take a few minutes)...
Processed (28) files
Processed (320) files
Processed (886) files
```

Figure 15-6   System state restore using Wbadmin.exe.

9. Type **Y** and press Enter to begin the system state restore.

10. After the restore is complete, restart the domain controller.

Full Server Recovery of a Domain Controller

Full server recovery of a domain controller is also a nonauthoritative restore of Active Directory. However, it additionally includes a full restore of the operating system and other data as well. This is appropriate when the system disk has been lost and the operating system is not functional. To perform a full server recovery of a domain controller, you must have a full server backup.

In some cases, you might need to restore the domain controller on a server that uses different hardware than was available on the original server. Although it is possible to restore Windows Server 2008 on hardware that differs from the hardware on the server that produced the backup, this process may have problems. If you try to restore Windows Server 2008 on a server with different hardware, try to choose hardware that is as compatible as possible. Also, ensure that the hard disk configuration on the new server is the same as it was on the failed server.

During a full server recovery, the operating system of the server is not functional. To provide the functionality required to perform a restore, use Windows RE. You can run Windows Recovery Environment (Windows RE) by booting from the Windows Server 2008 installation DVD. To avoid reliance on the Windows Server 2008 installation DVD, you can install Windows RE on the local hard drive to make it available in the Advanced Boot Options menu during startup.

To perform a full server recovery of a domain controller, follow these steps:

1. Boot from the Windows Server 2008 installation DVD and press a key to start from the DVD.

2. Select the appropriate language options, time and currency format, and keyboard layout, and then click Next.

3. In the Install Windows dialog box, click Repair Your Computer.

4. In the System Recovery Options dialog box, load disk drivers, if necessary, and then click Next.

5. Click Windows Complete PC Restore, as shown in Figure 15-7.

> **Note**   If a local backup cannot be found, you will receive error messages. This is normal when restoring from a network location.

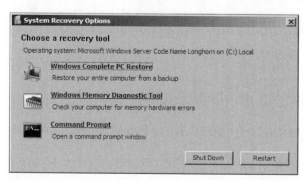

Figure 15-7   System Recovery Options in Windows RE.

6. Select the location of the backup to restore. This can be a DVD, local disk, or network location.

7. To wipe out all existing data on the server, select the Format And Repartition Disks check box.

8. To prevent disks that are not part of the restore from being deleted and recreated, click Exclude Disks and select the appropriate disks to exclude.

9. Click Next and then click Finish.

10. Select the I Confirm That I Want To Format The Disks And Restore The Backup check box and then click OK.

Performing an Authoritative Restore of Active Directory

An authoritative restore is required in situations in which deleted objects are being recovered. For example, if someone has just deleted an OU that contains several hundred users, you do not want the domain controller to simply reboot after performing the restore and then begin replication with other domain controllers. If you do, the domain controller will receive the information that the OU has been deleted from its replication partners, and by the time you open the Active Directory Users And Computers administrative tool, the OU will be deleted again.

In this scenario, you must use an authoritative restore to ensure that the restoration of the OU is replicated to the other domain controllers. When you perform an authoritative restore, you restore a backup copy of the Active Directory that was made before the data was deleted and then force that data to be replicated to all the other domain controllers. Forced replication is done by manipulating the update sequence number (USN) for the restored information. By default, when you perform an authoritative restore, the USN on the restored objects is incremented by 100,000 so that the restored object becomes the authoritative copy for the entire domain.

Restoring Computer Accounts

An authoritative restore can result in broken trust relationships between domains and computer accounts. When a computer running Microsoft Windows NT, Windows 2000, Windows XP Professional, or Windows Server 2003 is added to the domain, a password known only to the domain controllers and the member computer is created. This password is used to maintain the trust relationship between the computer and the domain. However, by default, the password is also changed every 30 days.

When you perform an authoritative restore, it restores the trust passwords that were in use when the backup was made. If the member computer has negotiated a different password for the trust, the trust relationship between the domain and the member computer will fail. NT Lan Manager (NTLM) trusts between Active Directory domains and Windows NT domains use a similar process to maintain the trust; these trusts can also fail if the older password is restored. In either case, the trust must be rebuilt. A domain trust can be rebuilt by deleting the domain trust and re-creating it. Workstation trusts with the domain can be rebuilt by using the NetDom command-line tool or by removing the workstation from the domain and then adding it back.

Performing an Authoritative Restore

The basic process for performing an authoritative restore of Active Directory is the same as a nonauthoritative restore except for one step. After the restore of Active Directory is complete in DSRM, you use Ntdsutil to specify which objects are authoritative, as shown in Figure 15-8. You can specify single objects or a subtree in the domain.

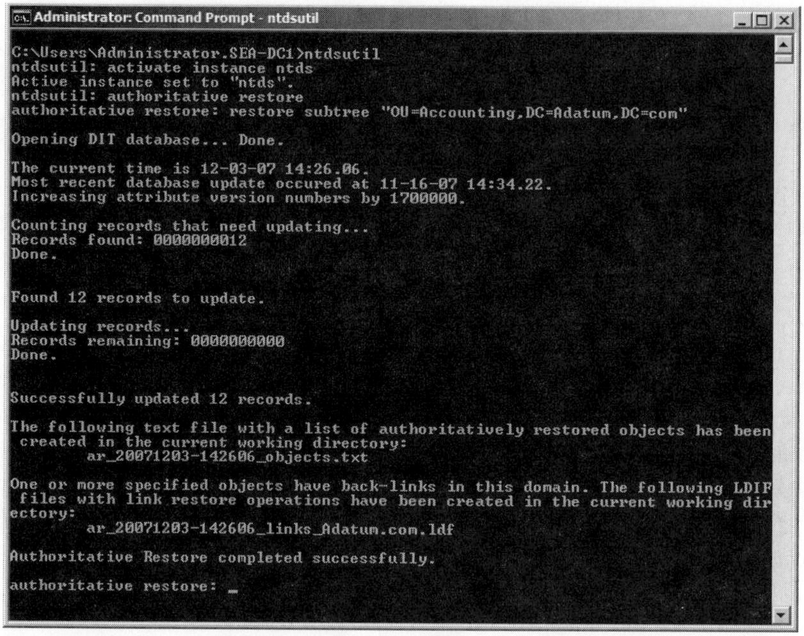

Figure 15-8   Using Ntdsutil to specify authoritative objects after a restore.

After an authoritative restore is complete, group memberships are not updated properly. The next section, "Restoring Group Memberships," describes how this is done. Ntdsutil creates an LDAP Interchange Format (LDIF) file to help perform this process. Take note of the filename during the authoritative restore.

The contents of the SYSVOL folder are not marked as authoritative when performing an authoritative restore of Active Directory. Instructions on how to perform an authoritative restore of SYSVOL contents are described in the section "Restoring SYSVOL Information."

To perform an authoritative restore, follow these steps:

1. Repair the failed domain controller. At this point, the server is functional, with the exception of Active Directory.

2. Restart the server and press F8 to enter the Advanced Boot Options menu.

3. Select Directory Service Restore Mode.

4. Log on as the DSRM Administrator account. To log on as this user, enter .**Administrator** as the username.

5. Open a command prompt.

6. Type **wbadmin get versions –backuptarget:***backuplocation*, where *backuplocation* is the drive letter or UNC path storing the backup, and then press Enter. This lists the backups stored in the location.

7. Take note of the version identifier of the backup you want to restore. This identifier is the time at which the backup was taken.

8. Type **wbadmin start systemstaterecovery –version:***identifier* **–backuptarget:***backuplocation*, where *identifier* is the version identifier noted in step 7 and *backuplocation* is the drive letter or UNC path storing the backup, and press Enter.

9. Type **Y** and press Enter to begin the system state restore.

10. After the restore is complete, type **ntdsutil** and press Enter.

11. At the Ntdsutil prompt, type **activate instance ntds** and press Enter.

12. At the Ntdsutil prompt, type **authoritative restore** and press Enter.

13. To restore a single object, at the Authoritative Restore prompt, type **restore object "***DN***"**, where *DN* is the distinguished name of the object to be authoritatively restored. The restore process specifies the location of an LDIF file for repairing backlinked objects if any are restored.

14. To restore a hierarchy of OUs, at the Authoritative Restore prompt, type **restore subtree "***DN***"**, where *DN* is the distinguished name of the OU that begins the hierarchy to be authoritatively restored. The restore process specifies the location of an LDIF file for repairing backlinked objects if any are restored.

15. Exit Ntdsutil and reboot the server.

> **Note**   The schema partition cannot be authoritatively restored.

Restoring Group Memberships

The restoration of group memberships is a complex process in Active Directory. This process has been improved beginning with Windows Server 2003, but it still requires you to be aware of where group members are located and what the forest functional level was when group members were assigned. To understand the recovery process, you also need to know how group memberships are maintained and how group memberships are replicated.

Group Membership Maintenance

Group membership is maintained in Active Directory by the use of links between the user object and the group object. These links are created based on a distinguished name tag (DNT). The DNT is a locally unique identifier for each domain object on a domain controller. Because it is local, the DNT for each object is different on each domain controller.

The membership list of a group object contains the DNTs for members of the group. Because the links are initially created on the group object, these are called *forward* links. A backlink is created on the user object to refer to the group. Backlinks are maintained by Active Directory and cannot be modified by an administrator. Backlinks are also not replicated; only forward links are replicated. Each domain controller maintains its own set of backlinks based on the forward links.

If a group membership list contains a member not in the local domain, then a phantom object is created in the local copy of Active Directory. The phantom object contains the *objectGUID*, *SID*, and *DN* attributes of the group member. This object allows a DNT to be created. The *DN* attribute of phantom objects is periodically updated by the Infrastructure Master FSMO role in the domain. The phantom object is not created on domain controllers that are global catalogs that already have copies of the original member object.

> **More Info**   For more information about links and phantom objects, see "Disaster Recovery: Active Directory Users and Groups" on the Technet Magazine Web site at *http://www.microsoft.com/technet/technetmag/issues/2007/04/ADRecovery/*.

Linked Value Replication

Windows Server 2003 introduced linked value replication (LVR) for multivalue attributes when the forest functional level is raised to Windows Server 2003 or Windows Server 2003 Interim. LVR allows individual changes in group membership to be replicated rather than the entire group membership list. This helps reduce replication traffic and stores additional metadata that simplifies the restoration of group membership.

When the forest functional level is raised to support LVR, the membership of existing groups is not automatically updated for LVR. Only changes to group membership are updated for LVR. For example, a new member of a group is stored using LVR whereas existing members are not.

When a user is restored authoritatively, the versions of Ntdsutil included with Windows Server 2003 SP1 and Windows Server 2008 use the *backlink* attribute of the restored user object to update the membership in groups created after LVR is enabled. If the restored user's membership is stored without LVR enabled, then Ntdsutil does not update the group membership automatically. Instead, Ntdsutil creates a text file listing backlinked objects that were restored and an LDIF that can be used to update the local domain appropriately for those backlinked objects. Previous to Windows Server 2003 SP1, Ntdsutil did not provide any functionality for locating backlinked objects.

> **Important**   If the authoritative restore is performed on a global catalog server, then multiple LDIF files are created. One LDIF file is created for the local domain and another for each domain in which the user was a member of a universal group.

Recovering Group Membership from Backlinks

After an authoritative restore is complete, you can restore group membership for users that were members of groups before LVR was enabled. This is done by using the LDIF files created by Ntdsutil. The process is performed only after the authoritative restore is replicated out to all replication partners. This process restores all backlinks, not just those related to group membership.

> **Note**   This process does not restore backlinks for domain local groups in other domains. Groups in the local domain and universal groups are repaired.

Follow these steps to recover group membership from backlinks:

1. After an authoritative restore is complete and the domain controller has been restarted normally, open a command prompt.

2. At the command prompt, type **repadmin /syncall** *DCName* **/a /d /A /P /q**, where *DCName* is the name of the restored domain controller, and then press Enter. This forces replication to all replication partners.

3. Change to the directory containing the LDIF file created by Ntdsutil during the authoritative restore.

4. At the command prompt, type **ldifde −i −k −f** *filename*, where *filename* is the LDIF file created by Ntdsutil, and then press Enter. Repeat this step for all LDIF files created by Ntdsutil.

> **Note**   Previous to Windows Server 2003 SP1, the Groupadd and Ldifde utilities were used to restore backlinks.

Recovering Domain Local Group Memberships in Remote Domains

To recover membership in domain local groups in remote domains, an additional process in each remote domain is required. This process uses the text file created by Ntdsutil in the domain where the user was authoritatively restored. This text file contains a list of objects with backlinks. This list of objects is used in the remote domain to generate an LDIF file specifically for that domain. It also requires a nonauthoritative restore of a domain controller in the remote domain.

Follow these steps to recover domain local group memberships in a remote domain:

1. Copy the text file created by Ntdsutil in the domain where the user accounts were authoritatively restored to a domain controller in the remote domain.

2. Perform a nonauthoritative restore on the domain controller in the remote domain and do not reboot the server.

3. While in DSRM, open a command prompt.

4. At the command prompt, type **ntdsutil** and press Enter.

5. At the Ntdsutil prompt, type **authoritative restore** and press Enter.

6. At the Authoritative Restore prompt, type **create ldif file from** *filename*, where *filename* is the name of the text file copied to the domain controller in the remote domain, and then press Enter.

7. Read the output from step 6 and take note of the LDIF filename.

8. Reboot the domain controller in the remote domain and start Windows normally.

9. Open a command prompt and change to the directory containing the LDIF file created by Ntdsutil during step 6.

10. At the command prompt, type **ldifde −i −k −f** *filename*, where *filename* is the LDIF file created by Ntdsutil, and then press Enter. Repeat this step for all LDIF files created by Ntdsutil.

Restoring Groups

When groups are authoritatively restored, the group membership is restored back to the point when the backup is taken. The authoritatively restored group membership overrides any changes that have occurred since the backup was taken. This can result in users having different rights and permissions than you expect. You should verify group membership after a restore is complete.

When users and groups are authoritatively restored at the same time, the group membership may not be correct. This happens when the restored group information replicates to a destination domain controller before the user information replicates. When the destination domain controller receives a group and notices that one or more user accounts listed in the group do not have valid user accounts, it deletes those users from the group. Later, when the user account is replicated to the destination domain controller, it is not added back to the group. If the user information replicates before the group information, the group memberships will be assigned correctly. Unfortunately, there is no way to control which objects will get replicated first.

To ensure correct group membership, perform two authoritative restores. The first authoritative restore ensures that all user and group objects exist. After replication of the first restore, a second authoritative restore of the group objects is required to ensure that the group membership is correct.

> **More Info**   For more information about restoring users and groups, see "How to Restore Deleted User Accounts and Their Group Memberships in Active Directory" in the Microsoft Knowledge Base at *http://support.microsoft.com/kb/840001/*.

Reanimating Tombstone Objects

Reanimating a tombstone object allows you to recover an Active Directory object without restoring the object from backup. This avoids the need to take a domain controller offline. However, a tombstone object has attributes stripped out of it. Consequently, a reanimated tombstone object will not have all the attributes present that an authoritatively restored object would. For example, when a user object is deleted, many attributes, such as address information, are removed. This information is not returned if a user tombstone object is reanimated.

When a user is reanimated, a number of important attributes are retained. Retention of the *objectSID* attribute allows any permissions assigned directly to the user to be retained. This is a significant advantage over recreating a deleted user account. The *objectGUID* attribute, which uniquely identifies each Active Directory object, is retained as well. This is important to preserve the relationships between objects and for applications that use this attribute.

It is possible to modify which attributes are retained in tombstone objects by modifying the schema. For each attribute that you want saved, set the third bit in the *searchFlags* attribute of the corresponding *attributeSchema* object. However, linked attributes, such as group memberships, cannot be retained even with this bit set.

> **Important**   When a user tombstone is reanimated, group membership is not restored. You must have another mechanism for restoring group membership. If group memberships are documented in your organization, you can manually recreate the group memberships.

The Reanimation Process

A tombstone object that is reanimated has some modifications made to it. The first modification is to remove the *idDeleted* attribute. The second modification is to change the *distinguishedName* attribute, which moves the object to its new location. Typically the new location of the object is based on the *lastKnownParent* attribute, which would return the object to the same OU from which it was deleted. The *objectCategory* attribute for the new object is configured as the most specific *objectClass* in the tombstone object.

To perform reanimation of a tombstone object, you must use a tool capable of modifying Active Directory objects. You can use the tool Ldp.exe to edit Active Directory objects and reanimate tombstone objects, as shown in Figure 15-9. In addition, AdRestore is specifically designed to reanimate objects and always reanimates objects to the location defined by the *lastKnownParent* attribute.

Note   AdRestore can be downloaded from the Windows Sysinternals Web site at *http://www.microsoft.com/technet/sysinternals/utilities/AdRestore.mspx.*

Figure 15-9   Using Ldp.exe to reanimate a tombstone object.

Note   Previous versions of Windows Server required you to download Ldp.exe. In Windows Server 2008, Ldp is included when the Active Directory Domain Services role is installed.

To reanimate a tombstone object with Ldp.exe, follow these steps:

1. Click Start, click Run, type **ldp**, and press Enter.

2. Click the Connection menu and click Connect.

3. Enter the name of the server and click OK.

4. Click the Connection menu and click Bind.

5. Select Logon Credentials With Sufficient Rights To Perform The Reanimation Process and click OK.

6. Click the Options menu and click Controls.

7. In the Load Predefined drop-down list, select Return Deleted Objects and click OK. This is necessary to view the Deleted Objects container.

8. Click the View menu and click Tree.

9. Select the domain in the BaseDN drop-down list and click OK.

10. Expand the domain and double-click CN=Deleted Objects. This lists all deleted objects in the domain. You can limit this by searching only for user objects if desired.

11. Right-click the object to reanimate and click Modify.

12. In the Attribute box, type **isDeleted,** click Delete, and click the Enter button.

13. In the Attribute box, type **distinguishedName**.

14. In the Values box, type the new distinguished name of the user object. For example, CN=Paul West,OU=Accounting,DC=Adatum,DC=com.

15. Click Replace and click Enter.

16. Select the Extended check box. This is required when modifying deleted objects.

17. Click Run to modify the object.

18. Click Close and close Ldp.

To reanimate a tombstone object with AdRestore, follow these steps:

1. Open a command prompt.

2. Type **adrestore** and press Enter. This lists all objects available to be restored.

3. Type **adrestore** *text*, where *text* is contained in the object name, and press Enter. This command is used to search for specific objects.

4. Type **adrestore −r** *text*, where *text* is contained in the object name, and press Enter.

5. For each object found by AdRestore, you are prompted to decide whether or not you want to reanimate the object.

> **More Info**   For more information about reanimating tombstone objects, see "Reanimating Active Directory Tombstone Objects" on the Technet Magazine Web site at *http://www.microsoft.com/technet/technetmag/issues/2007/09/Tombstones/default.aspx.*

Using the Active Directory Database Mounting Tool

Windows Server 2008 includes a new Active Directory database mounting tool (Dsamain.exe). This tool is used to expose a snapshot of Active Directory without rebooting a domain controller into DSRM. The Active Directory database mounting tool acts as a Lightweight Directory Access Protocol (LDAP) server to allow access to the snapshot. LDAP viewing tools such as Ldp.exe and ADSI Edit are used to view the contents of the snapshot.

When Active Directory information is being restored, you may need to review the contents of several backups to determine which is most appropriate. For example, you may need to review several backups to determine when a specific object was deleted. With the previous versions of Windows Server, you needed to perform a restore of system state data in DSRM to view the contents of Active Directory in a backup. In Windows Server 2008, you can restore the Active Directory database to an alternate location and expose the contents of the database by using the Active Directory database mounting tool.

You can also create snapshots of Active Directory by using Ntdsutil and then expose them by using Dsamain.exe. A snapshot created this way takes up significantly less disk space than a critical volumes backup. These snapshots are useful for auditing modified and deleted objects. Snapshots created by Ntdsutil cannot be used to restore Active Directory objects. To audit information over time, you can schedule a task that creates the Active Directory snapshots.

Managing Active Directory Snapshots

Ntdsutil can be used to create and manage snapshots of Active Directory. Snapshots are managed by using the snapshot context. You can create snapshots on domain controllers and Active Directory Lightweight Directory Services servers.

Follow these steps to create a snapshot of Active Directory by using Ntdsutil:

1. Open a command prompt.

2. At the command prompt, type **ntdsutil** and press Enter.

3. At the Ntdsutil prompt, type **snapshot** and press Enter.

4. At the Snapshot prompt, type **activate instance ntds** and press Enter.

5. At the Snapshot prompt, type **create** and press Enter. This creates a new snapshot. An identifier is listed.

Follow these steps to mount a snapshot of Active Directory by using Ntdsutil:

1. Open a command prompt.

2. At the command prompt, type **ntdsutil** and press Enter.

3. At the Ntdsutil prompt, type **snapshot** and press Enter.

4. At the Snapshot prompt, type **activate instance ntds** and press Enter.

5. At the Snapshot prompt, type **list all** and press Enter. This lists all available snapshots.

6. At the Snapshot prompt, type **mount *number***, where *number* is the snapshot you want to expose with the Active Directory database mounting tool, and then press Enter.

7. Take note of the update displayed for the mounted snapshot. This is required when exposing the snapshot with the Active Directory database mounting tool.

> **Note**   The **unmount *number*** command is used to unmount a mounted database when you are done viewing the data. The **delete *number*** command is used to delete a snapshot when it is no longer required.

Exposing and Accessing Active Directory Snapshots

The Active Directory snapshots exposed by the Active Directory database mounting tool can be those created and mounted by Ntdsutil or those restored to an alternate location by Windows Server Backup. In both cases, you specify the path to Ntds.dit and a port number for the LDAP server. The port number must be unused by other services running on the server. Port 51389 is commonly available.

By default, only Enterprise Admins and Domain Admins can access data exposed by the Active Directory database mounting tool. You can override this by using the */allowNonAdmin-Access* parameter.

The syntax for Dsamain.exe is as follows:

```
Dsamain /dbpath PathToDatabaseFile /ldapport PortNumber
```

When you access the database contents exposed by the Active Directory database mounting tool, you must connect to the port number that the Active Directory database mounting tool is running on. This will be a nondefault port that must be manually entered in Ldp.exe or ADSI Edit when you create a connection. You can also use Active Directory Users And Computers to view the exposed database by changing to a specific domain controller and specifying the appropriate port number, as shown in Figure 15-10.

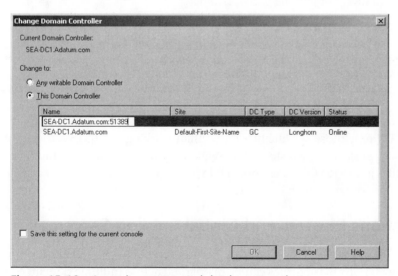

Figure 15-10   Accessing a mounted database snapshot.

While the Active Directory database mounting tool is running, the command prompt remains open. To shut down the Active Directory database mounting tool, press Ctrl+C.

Restoring SYSVOL Information

So far, the focus of this chapter has been restoring the Active Directory database—that is, the database of accounts and settings for the domain or forest. However, the SYSVOL folder on each domain controller also contains critical domain information, such as Group Policy templates and scripts used by computers or users on the network. Therefore, restoration of the SYSVOL information can be as critical as restoration of the Active Directory database.

When you perform a restore of system state from critical volumes, the SYSVOL folder is included. However, the SYSVOL folder is not replicated by Active Directory and is set as authoritative through a separate process when required. You may mark SYSVOL as authoritative when you want to recover from unauthorized group policy changes or if logon scripts have been deleted.

SYSVOL is replicated by File Replication Service (FRS) in all versions of Windows prior to Windows Server 2008 and is used in mixed environments that include Windows Server 2008 domain controllers. Windows Server 2008 uses Distributed File System (DFS) to replicate SYSVOL if the domain is at the Windows Server 2008 functional level. When FRS is used for SYSVOL replication, the BurFlags registry key is automatically configured to mark the restored replicated folders as authoritative. When DFS is used for SYSVOL replication, the *–authsysvol* option is used with Wbadmin.exe to mark the restored replicated folders as authoritative. The *–authsysvol* option is used during the nonauthoritative restore of Active Directory. In both cases, other replicated files that are restored at the same time will also be marked as authoritative, not just the SYSVOL folder.

> **More Info**   For more information about the BurFlags registry key and FRS, see "Using the BurFlags Registry Key to Reinitialize File Replication Service Replica Sets" on the Microsoft Help and Support Web site at *http://support.microsoft.com/default.aspx/kb/290762*.

If only a few files from SYSVOL are required to be restored, such as a logon script, then consider restoring only those specific files rather than marking all of SYSVOL authoritative. You can do this by performing a restore of SYSVOL to an alternate location and then copying the necessary files in to SYSVOL. Files copied into SYSVOL are treated as normal changes and will be replicated to other domain controllers.

Restoring Operations Masters and Global Catalog Servers

The operations master server roles require extra consideration when planning for disaster recovery. The operations master roles can be distributed across multiple domain controllers, but each role can be held by only one domain controller in a domain or forest at a point in time. So, restoring these roles is different from restoration for domain controllers that do not hold these roles. The actual procedures for restoring the domain controllers are essentially the same as restoring any other domain controller; the difference is the planning that must go into disaster recovery. For example, because only one domain controller can hold a particular role, you must determine how long the network will be able to operate without that operations master. In some cases, the absence of the operations master might not cause any problems for several days; in other cases, the failure might have an almost immediate effect. If you can restore the domain controller before the operations master role is needed, you can repair the domain controller and perform a nonauthoritative restore of the server. The operations master will be restored when the server is restored.

In some cases, you might decide that rebuilding the failed domain controller will take longer than your network can operate without that operations master. Or you might decide that you do not want to restore that domain controller at all, but would rather create a new domain controller and transfer the operations master role to the new domain controller. Transferring the operations master role is easy if both domain controllers are online because the domain controllers can ensure that they have completed replication before the role is transferred. However, if the operations master has failed and you need to move the role to another domain controller, you will need to seize the role.

Placement of Operations Masters

Because of the important roles that the operations master servers play on the network, you should plan the placement and management of these roles carefully. The operations masters should always be included in a regular backup regimen. Also, the operations masters should be located in the same site as at least one other domain controller to ensure that at least one other domain controller contains the same information as the operations master.

For example, if a user has just changed his or her password using a down-level client, the change was made on the PDC emulator. The PDC emulator will replicate that change to a replication partner in the same site within 15 seconds. If there is no replication partner in the same site, the password replication will not occur until the next scheduled intersite replication. If the domain controller fails before this scheduled time, the password change will not be replicated to other sites. If a domain controller is in the same site as the operations master server, the chance of incomplete replication is much less. The domain controller that is in the same site as the operations master is also the best choice for seizing the operations master role because it will have the most current information from the operations master. If you have more than one additional domain controller in the same site as the failed operations master, you can use the *repadmin /showvector namingcontext* command to determine which domain controller has the most recent updates from the failed domain controller.

To seize operations master roles by using Ntdsutil, follow these steps:

1. Open a command prompt.

2. At the command prompt, type **ntdsutil** and press Enter.

3. At the Ntdsutil prompt, type **roles** and press Enter.

4. At the Fsmo Maintenance prompt, type **connections** and press Enter.

5. At the Server Connections prompt, type **connect to server** *ServerName*, where *Server-Name* is the name of the server that you want to place the operations master role on, and press Enter.

6. At the Server Connection prompt, type **quit** and press Enter.

7. At the Fsmo Maintenance prompt, type **seize** *role*, where *role* is the operations master role you want to seize, and press Enter. The valid values for role are *schema master, domain naming master, infrastructure master, RID master*, and *PDC*.

8. Accept the warning. The server will first try to perform a normal transfer of the specified operations master role. When that fails because the domain controller cannot be contacted, the role will be seized.

9. Use the **quit** command to exit Ntdsutil.

> **Note**   Active Directory Users And Computers can also be used to seize the PDC Emulator and Infrastructure Master operations roles.

PDC Emulator

The failure of the PDC emulator has the potential to affect users almost immediately. As a consequence, you should seize the PDC emulator role quickly if it is expected to be unavailable for a period of time. When the PDC emulator is unavailable, Windows NT 4.0 backup domain controllers are unable to synchronize directory changes, and pre-Windows 2000 clients are unable change passwords. The PDC emulator is also the preferred location for making Group Policy changes and is used for password change replication.

Seizing the PDC emulator has no negative consequences. When the original PDC emulator is restored and connected to the network again, it will detect the presence of the new PDC emulator and give up the PDC emulator role. If desired, the PDC emulator role can be moved back to the original server after it is restored, but this is not required.

Schema Master

The schema master plays an essential role in a Windows Server 2008 domain, but it is also a role that is used very infrequently. The schema master is the only domain controller in which the schema can be changed. If this server fails, you will not be able to make changes to the schema until the server is restored or until the role has been seized to another domain controller.

The failure of a schema master does not affect users. In most cases, you should wait and restore the schema master rather than seizing the schema master role. If you do seize the schema master role to another domain controller, the original schema master should never be restored on the network.

Domain Naming Master

The domain naming master is another role that is infrequently used. This operations master is required only when adding or removing domains. The failure of this role does not affect users. Administrators are only affected if a new domain is being added to the forest or an old domain is being removed from the forest.

In most cases, you should wait for the original domain naming master to be restored. However, if you must add or remove a domain and you do not have time to restore the domain naming master, you can seize the role. If you do seize the domain naming master role to another domain controller, the original domain naming master should never be restored on the network.

Infrastructure Master

The infrastructure master's role is perhaps the least significant from a disaster recovery perspective. The infrastructure master monitors display-name changes for user and group accounts across multiple domains. This is an issue only when administrators are viewing group memberships. Even network administrators are unlikely to notice the failure unless a large number of accounts have been moved or renamed.

In most cases, you should wait and restore the infrastructure master role rather than seizing the infrastructure master role. If you decide to seize an infrastructure role to another domain controller in a multiple-domain environment, you should ensure that the destination domain controller is not a GC server. An infrastructure master placed on a global catalog server does not function properly. If you do seize the role, you can subsequently restore the original infrastructure master.

Relative Identity (RID) Master

The RID master is a domain-level operations master that assigns RID pools to other domain controllers as new security principals are created. If the RID master is not available for an extended period, the domain controllers might run out of RIDs to assign to new security principals. When a domain controller is out of RIDs, it cannot create new security principals, such as users and security groups.

The failure of a RID master does not affect existing users. This role only needs to be seized if you are planning to create a large number of security principals before the original RID master is restored or if you are not planning to restore the original RID master. If you do seize the RID master role to another domain controller, the original RID master should never be restored on the network.

Global Catalog Servers

Global catalog servers have no additional backup and restore considerations beyond that of a domain controller. If you restore a failed domain controller that is configured as a global catalog, then it will continue to be a global catalog server with no additional configuration required.

Fast access to global catalog servers is critical for some applications and logon processes. If a site does not have a global catalog server, performance will be degraded and errors may occur. Ideally, a site has multiple global catalog servers, in which case clients will automatically use the remaining global catalog servers when one fails. You can also manually designate another domain controller as a global catalog server after the failure.

Summary

This chapter covered the essential topic of disaster recovery in Windows Server 2008 Active Directory. Disaster recovery is one of the network administration tasks that you hope you will never need to use. However, as any experienced administrator knows, you will almost certainly need to use disaster recovery procedures at some time. This chapter began by discussing the basic data elements in Active Directory and then discussed the practices for backing up Active Directory. The rest of this chapter explained the procedures for restoring Active Directory in both authoritative and nonauthoritative modes. Reanimating tombstone objects and restoring SYSVOL were also covered. Finally, the management of the operations master roles and the special planning issues involved in restoring these roles on the network were addressed.

Best Practices

- To minimize the size of critical volume backups, do not store application or user data on critical volumes.

- Perform regular backups of critical volumes on domain controllers. This allows you to recover Active Directory or SYSVOL information. Schedule backups to ensure they are performed.

- Dedicate a volume on an internal or external hard drive for backups.

- To simplify recovery, install Windows RE on a separate partition. When Windows RE is installed on the local server, then you do not need the CD to perform a full restore.

- Test your recovery strategy in a lab environment to ensure that it works properly before a disaster occurs.

- Set an appropriate tombstone lifetime for your environment. The tombstone lifetime controls how long an Active Directory backup is valid.

- Implement multiple domain controllers in each domain to avoid the need to perform an authoritative restore of Active Directory.

- Use the Active Directory Database Mounting Tool to view the contents of Active Directory backups without performing a restore.

Additional Resources

The following resources contain additional information related to this topic.

Related Information

- For information about recovering an entire Active Directory forest, see "Planning for Active Directory Forest Recovery" in the Microsoft Download Center at *http://www.microsoft.com/downloads/details.aspx?FamilyID=AFE436FA-8E8A-443A-9027-C522DEE35D85&displaylang=en.*

- For more information about links and phantom objects, see "Disaster Recovery: Active Directory Users and Groups" on the Technet Magazine Web site at *http://www.microsoft.com/technet/technetmag/issues/2007/04/ADRecovery/.*

- For more information about restoring users and groups, see "How to Restore Deleted User Accounts and Their Group Memberships in Active Directory" in the Microsoft Knowledge Base at *http://support.microsoft.com/kb/840001/.*

- For more information about reanimating tombstone objects, see "Reanimating Active Directory Tombstone Objects" on the Technet Magazine Web site at *http://www.microsoft.com/technet/technetmag/issues/2007/09/Tombstones/default.aspx.*

- For more information about the BurFlags registry key and FRS, see "Using the BurFlags Registry Key to Reinitialize File Replication Service Replica Sets" on the Microsoft Help and Support Web site at *http://support.microsoft.com/default.aspx/kb/290762.*

Related Tools

Windows Server 2008 provides several tools that can be used for Active Directory disaster recovery. Table 15-2 lists some of these tools and their uses.

Table 15-2   Active Directory Disaster Recovery Tools

Tool Name	Description and Use
Active Directory database mounting tool (Dsamain.exe)	Use to mount Active Directory backups and snapshots as an LDAP server. This tool can be used to view the contents of backups without performing a restore.
AdRestore	Use to reanimate tombstone objects. It can be downloaded from the Windows Sysinternals Web site at *http://www.microsoft.com/technet/sysinternals/utilities/AdRestore.mspx.*

Table 15-2   Active Directory Disaster Recovery Tools *(continued)*

Tool Name	Description and Use
ADSIEdit.msc	Is a Microsoft Management Console (MMC) snap-in used to view Active Directory. It can also be used to view the contents of Active Directory snapshots that are mounted by using the Active Directory database mounting tool.
Ldifde.exe	Use to import and export LDIF files from Active Directory.
Ldp.exe	Is a tool that uses LDAP to access Active Directory. This tool can view and modify object properties that standard administrative tools such as Active Directory Users And Computers cannot. In particular, it can be used to reanimate tombstone objects. As well, Ldp.exe can be used to view the contents of Active Directory snapshots that are mounted with the Active Directory database mounting tool.
Ntdsutil.exe	Use to manage Active Directory from a command line. It can be used to mark an Active Directory restore as authoritative, remove Active Directory objects left after a domain controller fails, and seize operations master roles.
Repadmin.exe	Use to monitor and manage Active Directory replication.
Wbadmin.exe	Use to back up and restore Windows Server 2008. This tool is required for system state restores and is installed when you install the Windows Server Backup feature.
Windows Recovery Environment (Windows RE)	Is a recovery environment for Windows Server 2008 that allows you to perform a full restore of Windows Server 2008 from backup. Windows RE can be accessed by booting from the Windows Server 2008 installation DVD or from a local disk if it has been preinstalled.
Windows Server Backup	Is a graphical tool that is used to back up and restore Windows Server 2008. This tool is not functional until you install the Windows Server Backup feature.

Part V
Identity and Access Management with Active Directory

Chapter 16

Active Directory Lightweight Directory Services

Active Directory Domain Services is a flexible and powerful directory service that can address many directory services requirements for an organization. However, AD DS also has many dependencies that make its deployment and management a complex task. Because AD DS provides the core authentication and authorization services for most organizations, it can also be very difficult to make changes such as schema changes to the directory. At the same time, many organizations are deploying applications that use an external directory service. These applications may require the directory service to provide authentication services or to store application configuration information.

Although AD DS could be configured to support these applications, this may not be the best solution because of the issues related to incompatible schema change, replication traffic, or the risks of making changes to the infrastructure directory. As an alternative, Windows Server 2008 provides the Active Directory Lightweight Directory Services (AD LDS) server role, which you can use to deploy a Lightweight Directory Access Protocol (LDAP)–compliant directory service to provide support for these directory-enabled applications. AD LDS provides much of the same directory service functionality as AD DS but does not require the deployment of domains or domain controllers. AD LDS provides a much more flexible deployment model; for example, you can run multiple instances of AD LDS concurrently on a single computer, with an independently managed schema for each AD LDS instance. You can also configure AD LDS replication so that the same AD LDS data is distributed across multiple computers.

AD LDS Overview

AD LDS is designed specifically to provide directory services for directory-enabled applications. A directory-enabled application uses a directory, rather than (or in addition to) a database, flat file, or other data storage structure, to hold its data. The application may be storing configuration or application data in the directory, or it may be using the directory for authentication. AD LDS provides this functionality.

AD LDS Features

In order to provide the features required by directory-enabled applications, AD LDS includes the following features:

■ **The same architecture and the same code base as AD DS**   AD LDS provides a hierarchi-cal data store, a directory service component, and interfaces that clients can use to communicate with the directory service. This means that developers and administrators who are used to working with AD DS will be able to transfer those skills to AD LDS.

■ **Support for multiple AD LDS instances on one computer**   An AD LDS instance refers to a single running copy of the AD LDS directory service. Multiple instances of AD LDS can run simultaneously on the same computer. Each instance of the AD LDS directory service has a separate directory data store, a unique service name, a unique service description and a unique port for clients to be able to access the instance. Each instance also has a single schema, so by deploying multiple instances, you can support multiple directories with different schemas on one server.

■ **Support for multiple application directory partitions**   Application directory partitions hold the data that your applications use. You can create an application directory partition during AD LDS setup or anytime after installation. You can store multiple application directory partitions in a single instance or distribute copies of application directory partitions across multiple instances.

■ **Support for extensible schemas**   AD LDS includes several options for configuring the schema in each AD LDS instance. In addition, you can modify the schema for each instance to support application requirements.

■ **Support for directory replication**   AD LDS supports replication of directory information between AD LDS instances installed on multiple computers. In this way, you can provide high availability or provide access to the directory information in geographically dispersed locations.

AD LDS Deployment Scenarios

AD LDS is designed to complement rather than replace AD DS. AD DS provides a network authentication and management directory, whereas AD LDS is designed to be used purely as a directory service for applications. AD LDS is designed to be deployed in the following scenarios:

- **Enterprise directory store**   AD LDS can store application data in a local directory service either on the same computer as the application or on a different computer. One example of the type of application that could use AD LDS is an enterprise application that stores personalization data that is associated with corporate users who access a Web site. Storing this personalization data in AD DS would require AD DS schema changes. By using AD LDS to store application-specific data, and using user principals in AD DS for authentication and controlling access to objects in AD LDS, you can prevent a proliferation of user IDs and passwords for end users every time a new directory-enabled application is introduced to the network.

- **Extranet authentication store**   Many organizations deploy Web portal applications that require extranet access to corporate business applications but provide access for users who are outside the organization. These servers and portal applications require an authentication store to save authorization information for the users. AD LDS can provide this authentication store because it can host user objects that are not Windows security principals but that can be authenticated with LDAP simple binds.

You can also deploy AD LDS as an extranet authentication store along with Active Directory Federation Services (AD FS). This configuration enables Web single-sign-on (SSO) technologies to authenticate users to multiple Web applications with a single user account.

You can also use AD LDS to provide a directory for distributed applications that requires a configuration store with multimaster update and replication.

> **More Info**   For more information on the integration of AD LDS and AD FS, see Chapter 19, "Active Directory Federation Services."

- **As part of a directory consolidation solution**   Enterprise organizations frequently have several directories deployed. Users accounts may be located in multiple Active Directory forests, domains, and OUs, or in several identity systems and other directories, such as human resource databases, SAP databases, and telephone directories. To address this proliferation of directories, many organizations have integrated the identities by deploying a metadirectory, such as Microsoft Identity Integration Server (MIIS) or Microsoft Identity Lifecycle Manager 2007, to simplify the user experience and administrative processes. AD LDS can integrate with a metadirectory in that identities created in AD LDS can be synchronized with the metadirectory, and AD LDS can also accept identity synchronization from the metadirectory.

- **As a development environment for AD DS and AD LDS**   Because AD LDS uses the same programming model and provides virtually the same administration experience as AD DS, developers can use AD LDS when staging and testing various Active Directory–integrated applications. For example, if an application under development requires a different schema from the current AD DS schema, the application developer can use AD

LDS to build the application and test a schema update process. The application can then be ported to AD DS after the application and schema update process have been thoroughly tested.

AD LDS Architecture and Components

Because AD LDS uses much of the same code as AD DS, many of the AD LDS components are similar to the AD DS components.

AD LDS Servers

A Windows Server 2008 server with the AD LDS server role installed is called an AD LDS server. The AD LDS server role can be installed on any of the following operating systems:

- Windows Server 2008, Standard Edition, Enterprise Edition, and Datacenter Edition
- Windows Server 2008 Server Core Installation Option, Standard Edition, Enterprise Edition, and Datacenter Edition

You cannot install AD LDS on Windows Server 2008, Web Edition, or on Windows Server 2008 for Itanium-Based System.

Each AD LDS server hosts the AD LDS data store. Table 16-1 provides a description of the data store components:

Table 16-1   Data Store Components

Component	Description
Interfaces	Client computers, administrators, and other servers running AD LDS cannot communicate directly with the data store. The data store supports the following interfaces for directory clients and other directory servers to communicate with the data store: ■ Lightweight Directory Access Protocol (LDAP)—LDAP v3 is the most common interface used by directory clients to locate information in the directory store. The LDAP interface is part of Wldap32.dll. AD LDS supports LDAP v2 ("Request for Comments [RFC] 1777—Lightweight Directory Access Protocol," available at *http://www.ietf.org/rfc/rfc1777.txt*) and LDAP v3 ("RFC 2251—Lightweight Directory Access Protocol v3," available at *http://www.ietf.org/rfc/rfc2251.txt*). AD LDS supports both LDAP and secure LDAP connections. Each instance on an AD LDS server requires a unique port number. If the AD LDS server role is installed on an AD DS domain controller, the AD LDS port numbers must be different than the AD DS port number. ■ Replication (REPL) interface—The REPL interface is used by AD LDS during management access and for replication between domain controllers. This interface is accessible through Remote Procedure Calls (RPCs).

Table 16-1 **Data Store Components** *(continued)*

Component	Description
Directory Service Agent (DSA) (Adamdsa.dll)	The DSA, which runs as Adamdsa.dll on each AD LDS instance, provides the interfaces through which directory clients and other AD LDS instances gain access to the directory database. In addition, the DSA enforces directory semantics, maintains the schema, guarantees object identity, and enforces data types on attributes.
	When clients or other AD LDS Servers need to access the directory store, they use one of the supported interfaces to connect (bind) to the DSA and then search for, read, and write to AD LDS objects and their attributes.
Database layer	The database layer resides in Adamdsa.dll and provides an interface between the DSA and the directory database. The DSA, or any other application, cannot directly connect to the database; they go through the database layer. The database layer also provides an object view of the directory database, making the data accessible to the DSA as a set of hierarchical containers.
	The database layer is also responsible for the creation, retrieval, and deletion of individual records (objects), attributes within records, and values within attributes.
ESE (Esent.dll)	The Extensible Storage Engine (ESE) is a Windows component that is used by AD LDS as an interface to the database. The ESE is responsible for indexing the data in the database file and for transferring the data in and out of the database. Its purpose is to enable applications to store and retrieve data. The ESE also implements the transactional process for committing changes to the database.
Database files	The data store stores directory information in a single database file named Adamntds.dit. In addition, the data store also uses log files, to which it temporarily writes transactions before committing them to the database. By default, AD LDS data and log files are installed in %ProgramFiles%\Microsoft ADAM\instancename\data, where *instancename* is the AD LDS instance name that you specify when you create the instance.

AD LDS Instances

Each time that you install AD LDS, you create a unique AD LDS instance. Each AD LDS instance includes a configuration partition and a schema partition and can also contain one or more application partitions. Each AD LDS instance consists of the following:

- **Program files** After you install AD LDS, the program files and tools of an AD LDS instance reside in the %windir%\ADAM directory. If you install multiple instances of AD LDS on a single computer, the program files and tools in the *windir*\ADAM directory are shared by all AD LDS instances running on that computer. This means that if you apply an update to AD LDS, all instances of AD LDS are affected.

- **Data files** The data files for an AD LDS instance are installed by default in the %ProgramFiles%\Microsoft ADAM*instancename*\Data folder, where *instancename* is the name that you provide for the AD LDS instance during installation. If you install multiple instances of AD LDS on a single computer, each instance that you install has a separate data directory.

- **Registry keys**   Registry keys for AD LDS are stored in the following location: HKEY_LOCAL_MACHINE\SYSTEM\CurrentControlSet\Services\ADAM_*instancename*

- **Service name**   During setup, you assign a name to the AD LDS instance, and that name is used in the creation of the file directory structure and registry keys for AD LDS. In addition, the name that you assign is used to create the service name and service display name. For example, if you create a new instance with a name of App1, the service display name will be App1, and the service name will be ADAM_App1.

- **Service account**   Each AD LDS instance runs as a user service in the security context of the service account that is specified for that instance. The service account for an AD LDS instance is specified at installation, and it should be modified only with the Dsdbutit command-line tool.

> **Caution**   Change the AD LDS service account only with the Dsdbutil command-line tool. Changing the AD LDS service account with the Services snap-in will cause errors. For details on the options available for configuring service accounts, see the section titled "Implementing AD LDS" later in this chapter.

- **Event log**   Each AD LDS instance that is installed on a computer writes events to a unique event log. These events appear in Event Viewer, in the Applications and Services Logs folder, under ADAM (*instancename*).

- **Name:port**   For a directory-enabled application to communicate with an AD LDS instance, the application must specify the NetBIOS name, DNS name, or IP address of the computer on which AD LDS is running. In addition, the application must specify the LDAP or Secure Sockets Layer (SSL) communication port that is being used by the AD LDS instance. If you are running multiple instances of AD LDS on a computer, you must specify unique port numbers for each instance.

Directory Partitions

Each AD LDS instance uses a single directory store that is organized into logical directory partitions, or naming contexts. Each AD LDS directory store must contain a single configuration directory partition and a single schema directory partition. The directory store can contain zero or more application directory partitions.

Configuration Directory Partition

The configuration directory partition holds information about AD LDS replication scheduling and replica sets, information that defines the other partitions in the replication set, information about the users and groups in the replica set, and other information. Table 16-2 describes the default containers in the configuration directory partition.

Table 16-2   Default Containers in the Configuration Directory Partition

Container	Purpose
CN=DirectoryUpdates, CN=Configuration,CN={*GUID*}	Not currently used.
CN=Extended-Rights, CN=Configuration,CN={*GUID*}	Stores objects of the class *controlAccessRight* that applications can use to extend standard access control.
CN=ForeignSecurityPrincipals, CN=Configuration,CN={*GUID*}	Stores proxy objects for security principals that are from AD DS domains. By default, the SID for the Network Service account (if you use this account as the instance service account) and the SID for the administrator that created the instance are added to this container.
CN=LostAndFoundConfig, CN=Configuration,CN={*GUID*}	Stores configuration directory partition objects that are being created in containers that are being deleted simultaneously on other AD LDS instances in the same configuration set.
CN=NTDS Quotas, CN=Configuration,CN={*GUID*}	Stores objects of the class *msDS-QuotaControl* that contain object ownership quota assignments for the configuration directory partition. Quotas limit the number of objects that a user (including *inetOrgPerson*), group, computer, or service can own in a configuration directory partition or application directory partition.
CN=Partitions, CN=Configuration,CN={*GUID*}	Stores the cross-references to every directory partition in the configuration set, including the configuration partition, the schema partition, and all application partitions. During LDAP searches, these cross-references to directory partitions make referrals to other domains possible.
CN=Roles, CN=Configuration,CN={*GUID*}	Stores the default groups for a given partition.
CN=Services,CN=Configuration, CN={*GUID*}	Stores data for various networking services and applications.
CN=Sites,CN=Configuration, CN={*GUID*}	Identifies all the sites in the network, the AD LDS instances in those sites, and the replication topology. The contents of this container take the form of replication transports, subnets, and the first site and site link that are created, which are called Default-First-Site-Name and DEFAULT-IPSITELINK, respectively.

Note   If you add the Display Specifier schema to the instance, another container object named *CN=DisplaySpecifiers* is created in the Configuration container. This container contains the information required to display AD LDS information in administration tools like Active Directory Sites And Services.

Schema Directory Partition

The schema directory partition contains the definitions for the types of data that the directory database can hold. The definitions in the schema partition maintain data consistency for the AD LDS directory service. You can also extend the schema so that AD LDS can hold data that is specific to a particular application.

Like the AD DS schema, the AD LDS schema uses object classes and attributes to define the kinds of objects and data that can be created and stored in an AD LDS directory. However, one of the important differences between AD DS and AD LDS is that each AD LDS instance can have a unique schema. The base AD LDS schema contains only the classes and attributes that are needed to start an AD LDS instance. The schema can be extended with new classes and attributes, either by administrators or by the applications themselves. In addition, unneeded schema classes and attributes can be deactivated. As with all objects in the directory, access control lists (ACLs) protect schema objects so that only authorized users can alter the schema.

Like the AD DS schema, the AD LDS schema can be extended manually or by importing .ldf files into the schema. When you create an AD LDS instance by running the Active Directory Application Mode Setup Wizard, you can modify the default schema by importing LDIF files when you create the instance. Table 16-3 describes each of the optional AD LDS .ldf files.

Table 16-3   AD LDS .LDF Files

LDIF Filename	Description
MS-adamschemaw2k3.ldf	Used to import the entire Windows Server 2003 schema.
MS-adamschemaw2k8.ldf	Used to import the entire Windows Server 2008 schema.
MS-AdamSyncMetadata.ldf	Used to prepare the AD LDS schema to synchronize with AD DS by using ADAMSync.
MS-ADLDS-DisplaySpecifiers.ldf	Used to add the display specifiers to the AD LDS schema. Required if you want to use snap-ins such as Active Directory Sites and Services to manage AD LDS.
MS-User.ldf	Used to create user objects in the AD LDS directory.
MS-InetOrgPerson.ldf	Used to create user objects in the AD LDS directory of the *inetOrgPerson* class.
MS-UserProxy.ldf	Used to create proxy objects in AD LDS for use in bind redirection.
MS-UserProxyFull.ldf	Used to create the full proxy objects in AD LDS for use in bind redirection. If you select this file, you must also select either MS-User.ldf or MS-InetOrgPerson.ldf.
MS-AZMan.ldf	Used to prepare AD LDS for use with Windows Authorization Manager.

Note These .ldf files are located in the %windir%\ADAM directory on the AD LDS server.

You can add these .ldf files to the AD LDS instance when you create the instance by using the Active Directory Lightweight Directory Services Setup Wizard, or you can import the files by using the Ldifde utility after creating the instance. To import the files using the Ldifde utility, use the following command:

```
Ldifde –i –u –f ldffilename –s servername:port –b username domain password
–j . –c "cn=Configuration,dc=x" #configurationNamingContext
```

This command performs an .ldf import (*-i*), using the Unicode format (*-u*), and will create a log file (*-j*) in the current directory. The server name and port number identify the instance that you are modifying. If you run the command from a context other than the %windir%\ADAM directory, you must provide the full path to the .ldf file. The user credentials are not required if you run the command while logged in with an account that has permission to modify the schema. By default, the administrator who installed the AD LDS instance is the only account with this level of permissions.

The last part of the command replaces all occurrences of cn=Configuration,dc=x with the actual configuration naming context for the AD LDS instance. With AD LDS, you can use the constants *#schemaNamingContext* and *#configurationNamingContext* in place of the distinguished names of the schema directory partition and configuration directory partitions when replacing strings in .ldf files.

Note The command-line syntax for importing the .ldf files is included at the beginning of each of the .ldf files.

Application Directory Partitions

Application directory partitions hold the data that your applications use. You can create an application partition during AD LDS setup or anytime after installation. After the application directory partition is created, AD LDS holds the application partition reference objects in CN=Configuration,CN=Partitions. The actual application partitions are identified by the fully qualified name you assigned when you created the partition.

Each AD LDS directory partition has its own unique distinguished name. Unlike AD DS, which supports only DNS-style (DC=) names for top-level directory partitions, AD LDS supports both DNS-style and X.500-style names for top-level directory partitions. Table 16-4 lists the distinguished name types supported by AD LDS partitions.

Table 16-4   AD LDS Directory Partition Names

Distinguished Name	Description
C=	Country/region
CN=	Common name
DC=	Domain component
L=	Location
O=	Organization
OU=	Organizational unit (*Note:* Organizational unit containers can only be created in OU, C, O, or DC containers. You cannot create an OU in an L container.)

Note   If you are using AD LDS to create and test an application that will be deployed in AD DS, use only DC= naming components in directory partition names. Using only DC= naming components means that the naming for the directory will be consistent when you migrate the application from AD LDS to AD DS.

You can create one or more application directory partitions in a single AD LDS instance. If you do create more than one application directory partition in an instance, ensure that the applications that are using the instance require a compatible schema. Because each instance has only one schema, all application partitions use that one schema.

Although you can create and modify the data in the application partition by using tools such as ADSI Edit or Ldp.exe, you will normally create the application partition and manage data in an application directory partition through your application. During the application install, it should provide an .ldf file to create the application partition and configure the required settings on the partition objects. The application can then read and write data from the partition.

The *rootDSE* Object in AD LDS

At the root of the AD LDS directory tree is the *rootDSE* object, which is not part of any directory partition. The *rootDSE* object represents the top of the logical namespace for an AD LDS instance. The *rootDSE* attributes contain information about the AD LDS instance, including the following:

- Supported LDAP versions

- Naming contexts (directory partitions) on the server

- Alternate URLs for other servers if this server is not available

- Supported extensions, LDAP controls, and Simple Authentication and Security Layer (SASL) mechanisms

- Configuration naming context

- Highest committed USN and other replication information

To view the rootDSE object, you can connect to the *rootDSE* by using ADSI Edit. The RootDSE Properties dialog box is shown in Figure 16-1.

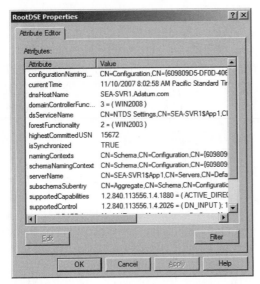

Figure 16-1 The *rootDSE* contains configuration settings for the AD LDS instance.

> **On the Disc**   To display all of the naming contexts on a server running AD LDS, use the DisplayADLDSInstances.ps1 script on the CD.

AD LDS Replication

As in AD DS, you can deploy multiple AD LDS servers and configure replication between instances running on different servers. Through replication, AD LDS copies directory data updates that are made to a directory partition on one AD LDS instance to other AD LDS instances that hold copies of the same directory partition. In this way, you can provide fault tolerance and load balancing for directory services and enable applications in different locations to use the same directory information.

AD LDS replication uses the same underlying processes and concepts as AD DS replication:

- **Multimaster replication**   With multimaster replication, you can make changes to directory data on any AD LDS instance. AD LDS replicates these changes to other members of the configuration set automatically.

- **Replication conflict resolution**   If two different users make changes to the same data on replicas of the same directory partition on two different AD LDS instances, each AD LDS instance attempts to replicate the changes, which creates a conflict. To resolve this conflict, replication partners that receive these conflicting changes use the version and a time stamp for the change. AD LDS instances accept the change with the higher version and discard the other change. If the versions are identical, AD LDS instances accept the change with the more recent time stamp.

- **Site-based replication**   Like AD DS, AD LDS uses sites to define the replication topology that is used to replicate directory updates among AD LDS instances in a configuration set. By default, when you install an AD LDS instance, a default site named Default-First-Site-Name is created, along with a site connector named DEFAULTIPSITELINK. All AD LDS replicas are placed in the default site. AD LDS preserves bandwidth between sites by minimizing the frequency of replication and by enabling you to schedule the availability of site links for replication. By default, intersite replication across each site link occurs every 180 minutes (3 hours). By creating additional sites, you can control replication traffic between company locations by configuring a replication schedule and configuring replication frequency.

- **Replication topology building**   Just like AD DS, AD LDS servers use the Knowledge Consistency Checker (KCC) and the Inter-Site Topology Generator (ISTG) to build the replication topology. The KCC automatically builds the most efficient replication topology for intrasite replication using a bidirectional ring design. This bidirectional ring topology attempts to create at least two connections to each AD LDS instance (for fault tolerance) and no more than three hops between any two AD LDS instances (to reduce replication latency). The ISTG, which runs on one domain controller in a site, builds the replication topology between sites.

> **Note**   An AD LDS configuration set maintains its own replication topology, separate from any AD DS replication topology that might also exist. Directory partitions cannot be replicated between AD LDS instances and AD DS domain controllers.

- **Optimization of intrasite replication**   Intrasite replication is optimized for speed, rather than bandwidth, because bandwidth within a site is assumed to be high speed. Intrasite replication occurs automatically on the basis of change notification, and it begins when a directory update occurs. By default, the source AD LDS instance waits 15 seconds and then sends an update notification to its closest replication partner. If the source AD LDS instance has more than one replication partner, subsequent notifications go out by default at three-second intervals to each partner. If no directory updates occur in a given time period, intrasite replication still occurs, based on a scheduled interval. By default, this scheduled interval is once per hour.

> **More Info**   For detailed information on how AD DS replication occurs, see Chapter 4, "Active Directory Domain Services Replication." With the exception of configuration sets and replication security, the replication concepts and processes are the same in AD DS and AD LDS.

Configuration Sets

One of the ways in which AD LDS replication is different than AD DS replication is in the way you define the scope of replication for a specific partition. In AD DS, the domain partition is automatically replicated to all domain controllers in the same domain, and the configuration and schema partitions are automatically replicated to all domain controllers in the same forest. In AD LDS, just like with custom application directory partitions in AD DS, you have more flexibility in how you configure the scope of replication.

In AD LDS, the replication scope is based on participation in a configuration set. A configuration set is a group of AD LDS instances that replicate a common schema partition and configuration partition. You can also configure the AD LDS instances in a configuration set to replicate one or more application directory partitions. If the AD LDS instances contain more than one application partition, you do not need to include all of the application partitions in the configuration set. However, you cannot configure replication between application directory partitions in different configuration sets.

Because you can install more than one AD LDS instance on a server, one server may participate in multiple configuration sets with replication connections to several other servers with shared configuration sets. Figure 16-2 shows an example of how configuration sets work.

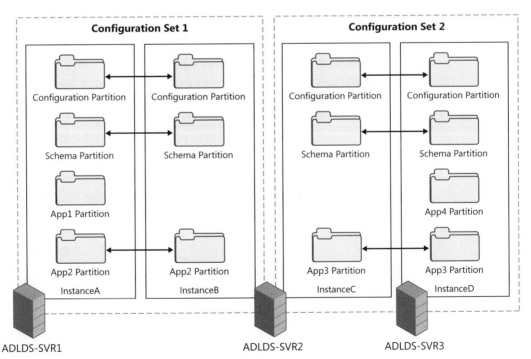

Figure 16-2   Configuration sets define the scope of AD LDS replication.

When you install an AD LDS instance by using the Active Directory Application Mode Setup Wizard, you can install a unique instance or you can install a replica of an existing instance. When you install a replica of an existing instance, you are joining that instance to a configuration set defined on another server. You can join an AD LDS instance to a configuration set only during the installation of the instance. After an AD LDS instance is created, it cannot be added to or removed from a configuration set.

> **Note** Configuration sets are purely conceptual, in that you do not need to assign a name to a configuration set, and you cannot create a configuration set and add instances later. To manage configuration sets, you must manage the instances that make up the configuration set.

AD LDS Replication Security

Another way in which AD LDS replication is different than AD DS replication is in how the replication connections and traffic are secured. Because all AD DS domain controllers are members of the same forest, they can use Kerberos security to authenticate and secure replication traffic. You can deploy the AD LDS server role on computers that are members of the same domain or forest, on computers that are in a different forest, or on computers that are not members of any domain.

This means that the AD LDS servers may not be able to use the same authentication and security mechanisms in all scenarios. To ensure replication security, AD LDS authenticates replication partners before replication, and replication authentication always occurs over a secure channel. After replication partners authenticate, all replication traffic between the two partners is encrypted. AD LDS replication partners authenticate each other by using the service account that is specified for each respective AD LDS instance. The method that is used for replication authentication within a configuration set depends on the value of the *msDS-ReplAuthenticationMode* attribute on the configuration directory partition.

Table 16-5 describes the available options for configuring security for AD LDS replication and the corresponding authentication mode (msDS-ReplAuthenticationMode) attribute value for each security level. The default replication security level for a new, unique AD LDS instance is 1, unless a local user account is specified as the AD LDS service account. If a local user account is specified as the AD LDS service account, the replication security level is 0.

Table 16-5   AD LDS Replication Security Levels

msDS-ReplAuthenticationMode Value	Authentication Method	Description
0	Negotiated pass-through	All ADAM instances in the configuration set use an identical account name and password as the ADAM service account. The configuration set can include computers that are joined to one or more workgroups or that are joined to multiple domains or forests without trust relationships.
1	Negotiated	Kerberos authentication (using SPNs) is attempted first. If Kerberos fails, NTLM authentication is attempted. If NTLM fails, the ADAM instances will not replicate.
2	Mutual authentication with Kerberos	Kerberos authentication, using service principal names (SPNs), is required. If Kerberos authentication fails, the ADAM instances will not replicate. The configuration set must be fully contained in an Active Directory domain, forest, or forest trust.

AD LDS Security

One of the requirements for an application directory is to provide security. Applications may write confidential information such as customer information to the directory, or organizations may want to limit what data users can view or edit within the directory. Because AD LDS is based on the same code as AD DS, many of the same concepts, such as authentication, authorization, users, groups, ACLs, and security tokens apply to AD LDS just like they apply to AD DS.

Security Principals in AD LDS

AD LDS security principals are any objects that have a unique SID and that can be assigned permissions to directory objects. In AD LDS, security principals can be any of the following:

- AD LDS security principals that are created in an AD LDS directory partition. An AD LDS security principal is a user or other bindable object that is created in AD LDS. By default, the AD LDS schema does not contain any user object classes and so it cannot contain any AD LDS security principals. If you add the ms-user.ldf or the ms-inetorgperson.ldf file to the schema, you can create user or inetOrgPerson objects. When you add these objects, they are automatically assigned a SID.

> **Note** By default, no AD LDS user accounts are created in an AD LDS instance or application partition. AD LDS user accounts can only be created in application directory partitions, not in the configuration or scheme partitions. In addition, AD LDS users can be assigned permissions only on objects in their own directory partition and cannot be a member of a group in any directory partition other than the one where the user account exists.

- Windows users that are defined on a local computer. User accounts from the local computer can be assigned permissions to AD LDS objects and can be added to AD LDS groups.

- Windows users that are defined in an AD DS domain. User accounts from the AD DS domain of which the AD LDS server is a member, or any trusted domain, can also be assigned permissions to AD LDS objects and can be added to AD LDS groups.

> **Note** By default, the Windows account for the administrator who installed the AD LDS instance is added to the Administrators group in the Configuration partition. If you configure AD LDS to use a Windows account as the service account, this account is added to the Instances group in the Configuration container.

Windows user accounts can be added to groups in more than one directory partition, including the configuration directory partition. In addition, Windows users can be assigned permissions on objects in multiple partitions.

> **Note** To add an AD LDS user or Windows user account to an AD LDS group, add the user account to the *multivalue member* attribute on the respective group object. You can use ADSI Edit to do this. For more information, see the "Step-by-Step Guide for Getting Started with Active Directory Lightweight Directory Services" article, located at *http://technet2.microsoft.com/windowsserver2008/en/library/141900a7-445c-4bd3-9ce3-5ff53d70d10a1033.mspx?mfr=true.*

Like AD LDS user accounts, the scope of an AD LDS group is restricted to the partition in which the group is created. The only exception to this rule is the Administrators group in the configuration directory partition, whose members have full control of all objects in all partitions.

Default Groups in AD LDS

Like AD DS, AD LDS uses user accounts and groups to provide access to information in the directory store. By default, when you install an AD LDS instance and create an application partition, a set of default groups is created in each directory partition. In addition, you can create custom groups or use AD DS or local user or group accounts to assign permissions to AD LDS data.

Table 16-6 lists the default groups created in an AD LDS instance.

Table 16-6   Default AD LDS Groups

Partition	Group	Purpose	Default Members
Configuration	Administrators	This group has full administrative permissions to the instance and all directory partitions in the instance.	The administrator that is assigned during the creation of the instance. This account must be a Windows security principal (either AD DS or local account).
Configuration	Readers	This group has Read access to the configuration partition (including the schema).	None
Configuration	Users	This group is a computed group. Use this group to assign permissions to all user accounts.	All AD LDS users that are defined in any application directory partition.
Configuration	Instances	Used for replication.	The AD LDS server account and the AD LDS service account. You should not add users to the Instances group.
Application	Administrators	This group administers the application partition in which the group resides.	Members of the Administrator's group from the configuration partition.
Application	Readers	This group has Read access to the application partition in which the group resides.	None
Application	Users	This is a computed group.	All AD LDS users from the respective application directory partition.

You can use ADSI Edit to view the AD LDS groups in the CN=Roles, CN=Configuration container. You can create additional groups in any application partition. You cannot create additional groups in the configuration partition.

Assigning Permissions in AD LDS

Like AD DS, AD LDS uses security principals and ACLs to control access to objects in AD LDS. When you install AD LDS and configure instances and partitions, a default set of permissions are assigned to the partition. Table 16-7 lists the default permissions. These permissions are inherited throughout the entire partition.

Table 16-7 Default Permissions for AD LDS Partitions

Partition	Default Permissions
Configuration	Administrators: Full Control
	Readers: Read
	Instances: five replication-related access control entries (ACE)
Schema	Administrators (from the configuration partition): Full Control
	Readers: five replication-related access control entries (ACE)
Application	Administrators: Full Control
	Readers: Read
	Instances: five replication-related access control entries (ACE)

To view the ACL configured on an AD LDS container, you can use the Dsacls.exe command, or you can use Ldp.exe. To display permissions by using the Dsacls.exe command, use the following command:

```
Dsacls \\servername:portnumber\partitionname /a
```

For example, to display the ACL for the App2 partition on an instance using port 4389 on a server named SEA-SVR1, use the following command:

```
Dsacls \\sea-svr1:4389\CN=App2,dc=Adatum,dc=com /a
```

To use Ldp.exe, connect to the AD LDS instance and bind with an account that has permissions to view the ACL. Right-click the container that you want to view, point to Advanced, and then click Security Descriptor. Figure 16-3 shows the default permissions on an application partition.

More Info   For details on how to configure permissions in AD LDS, see the section titled "Configuring Access Control" later in this chapter.

In AD LDS, as in AD DS, when a user is authenticated, AD LDS (or the LSA, depending on the type of security principal) creates a security access token for that user. An access token contains the user's name, the groups to which that user belongs, a SID for the user, and all of the SIDs for the groups to which the user belongs. The information in the access token is used to determine a user's level of access to objects whenever the user attempts to access them. The SIDs in the access token are compared with the list of SIDs that make up the discretionary access control list (DACL) for the object to ensure that the user has sufficient permission to access the object.

More Info   For details on how the access token is created, see Chapter 8, "Active Directory Domain Services Security."

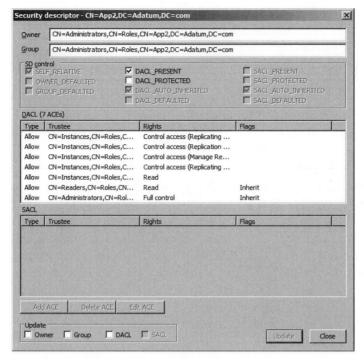

Figure 16-3   Ldp.exe can be used to view permissions in AD LDS.

Authentication in AD LDS

Like AD DS, AD LDS implements authentication to ensure the identity of users. When a user attempts to authenticate against, or bind to, AD LDS, the user might be authenticated by AD LDS, the LSA, or Active Directory, depending on the type of user attempting the bind. Table 16-8 lists the types of authentication that AD LDS supports, the types of users that are appropriate to each authentication method, and the authenticating authority that handles the authentication.

Table 16-8   Authentication Methods in AD LDS

Type of Authentication	Type of User	Description
Anonymous	Anonymous	User does not supply a password, so the user is not authenticated. By default, the only object in AD LDS to which an anonymous user has access is the *rootDSE* object.
Simple LDAP bind	AD LDS security principal	AD LDS. AD LDS accounts have access to data only in the same application partition where the user account exists.

Table 16-8   Authentication Methods in AD LDS *(continued)*

Type of Authentication	Type of User	Description
SASL bind (using Kerberos, NTLM, or negotiated)	Local Windows security principal or AD DS security principal	LSA on the local computer or AD DS. Windows accounts can be configured to have access to data in all partitions in the AD LDS instances.
Bind redirection (Simple LDAP bind to AD LDS, then SASL bind to AD DS)	AD LDS proxy object	LSA and AD DS. AD LDS proxy object accounts have access to data only in the same application partition where the proxy object exists.

Simple LDAP Bind for AD LDS Security Principals   Simple LDAP binding occurs when a user binds to AD LDS as an AD LDS security principal. This authentication method uses a simple LDAP bind; no SASL options are available with basic authentication. This simple LDAP bind uses the distinguished name of the security principal or the user principal name (UPN) of the security principal. In a simple LDAP bind, the user password is sent in plaintext format. In order to secure the authentication traffic, you must implement SSL between the client and the AD LDS server. To enable SSL, you must have certificates installed on the computer running AD LDS. In addition, the clients that connect to AD LDS should trust the certification authority (CA) that issues the certificate to the AD LDS server.

Security Alert   You can disable the requirement for SSL in basic authentication by using the ds-behavior option of the Dsmgmt.exe command-line tool. However, this is not recommended for production environment, as this means that all passwords will be sent in plaintext.

When basic authentication is used, AD LDS supports and enforces the password policy settings and account lockout settings that are provided by Windows Server 2008. For example, if the computer has a password policy configured in the local security policy, or through a domain security policy, password settings such as minimum and maximum age, complexity, and history requirements are enforced when users change their passwords.

Note   You can disable the enforcement of password policy settings in AD LDS by setting *ADAMDisablePasswordPolicies*, a value in the attribute *msDS-Other-Settings* on CN=Directory Service,CN=Windows NT,CN=Services,CN=Configuration,CN=*GUID*, to 1.

SASL Bind for Windows Security Principals   Integrated authentication occurs when a Windows security principal attempts to bind to an AD LDS instance. AD LDS does not authenticate Windows users itself. Instead, AD LDS relies on the Windows security process to authenticate the user. Integrated authentication uses SASL binds and supports, including Kerberos, NTLM, and Negotiated (default). Integrated authentication supports the use of domain\user, UPN, or distinguished name as authentication credentials.

When AD LDS receives a SASL bind request, AD LDS forwards the request to Active Directory or the LSA. If the bind request is authenticated successfully, the user account is granted a security token. AD LDS uses that token in its internal context, adds the SIDs for the AD LDS groups of which the Windows user is a member, and then performs transitive group expansion across all the application partitions. That is, AD LDS determines group memberships for the Windows user that result from the user being a member of a group that itself is a member of a different group. Access to AD LDS objects is that granted or denied based on the security token.

Bind Redirection for AD LDS Proxy Objects   AD LDS bind redirection occurs when a bind to AD LDS is attempted using a special object called a proxy object. A proxy object is an object in AD LDS that represents a security principal in Active Directory. Each proxy object in AD LDS contains the SID of a user in Active Directory. When a user attempts to bind to a proxy object, AD LDS takes the SID that is stored in the proxy object, together with the password that is supplied at bind time, and presents the SID and the password to Active Directory for authentication.

Because the initial bind request is a simple LDAP bind request, the password is presented in plaintext to AD LDS. To secure this authentication, AD LDS requires the use of SSL. Because the password that is presented to AD LDS during AD LDS bind redirection is an AD DS password that is presented in plaintext, you should not disable the requirement for SSL when using bind redirection.

AD LDS bind redirection is used when an application can perform a simple LDAP bind to AD LDS but the application still needs to associate the user with a security principal in Active Directory.

Proxy objects (and proxy object classes) do not exist by default in AD LDS. However, you can import a proxy object class into the AD LDS schema during AD LDS installation. A proxy object can be created from any object class that contains the *msDS-bindProxy* auxiliary class. The *msds-BindProxy* class possesses a single "must contain" attribute, *ObjectSid,* that holds the SID of the associated local or AD DS security principal. You can set the value of *ObjectSid* only at the time that the object is created. After a proxy object is created, the value of its *ObjectSid* attribute cannot be modified. You can set the *ObjectSid* of a proxy object to the SID of any local Windows user or to any user who is a member of a domain or forest that is trusted by the computer on which AD LDS is running.

> **More Info**   For detailed information on how to configure user accounts and authentication settings, see "Step 7: Practice Managing Authentication" in the "Step-by-Step Guide for Getting Started with Active Directory Lightweight Directory Services," located at *http://technet2.microsoft.com/windowsserver2008/en/library/141900a7-445c-4bd3-9ce3-5ff53d70d10a1033.mspx?mfr=true.*

Implementing AD LDS

AD LDS is implemented in Windows Server 2008 as a server role. To install the server role, use Server Manager to add the role. To install the server role on a Windows Server 2008 computer running Server Core, run the start /w ocsetup DirectoryServices-ADAM-ServerCore command. During the role installation, you do not need to make any installation decisions other than choosing to install the role. In order to install AD LDS, your user account must be a member of the local Administrators group.

Configuring Instances and Application Partitions

After installing the AD LDS server role, you use the Active Directory Lightweight Directory Services Setup Wizard to create AD LDS service instances. Multiple instances of AD LDS can run simultaneously on the same computer. Each instance of the AD LDS directory service has a separate directory data store, a unique service name, and a unique service description that is assigned during installation. When you run the wizard, you also have the option of creating an application directory partition.

To create a new AD LDS instance by using the Active Directory Lightweight Directory Services Setup Wizard, complete the following steps:

1. Start the Active Directory Lightweight Directory Services Setup Wizard. You can start the wizard from the Administrative Tools menu or from Server Manager.

2. On the Welcome page, click Next.

3. On the Setup Options page, you have a choice of creating a new instance or creating a replica of an existing instance, as shown in Figure 16-4. Click A Unique Instance and then click Next.

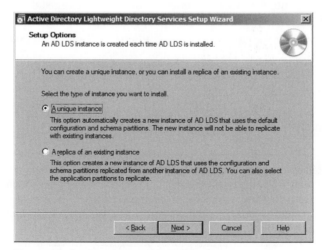

Figure 16-4   Creating an AD LDS instance.

4. On the Instance Name page, provide a name for the AD LDS instance that you are installing. The name that you choose must meet the following requirements:

   ❑ It must be different from other ADAM instances running on the same computer.

   ❑ It must be no longer than 44 characters.

   ❑ It must use characters only from the ranges of *a* through *z*, *A* through *Z*, or *0* through *9*.

   ❑ The name *ntds* cannot be used.

5. On the Ports page, specify the communications ports that the AD LDS instance uses to communicate. AD LDS can communicate using both LDAP and Secure Sockets Layer (SSL).

> **Note** If you install AD LDS on a computer where either of the default ports is in use, the Active Directory Lightweight Directory Services Setup Wizard automatically locates the first available port, starting at 50000. If you install AD LDS on an AD DS domain controller, you cannot use ports 389 and 636, or ports 3268 and 3269 on global catalog servers, as these ports are used for AD DS domain controller and global catalog lookups.

6. On the Application Directory Partition page, you can create an application directory partition during the AD LDS installation, as shown in Figure 16-5. If you do not install an application directory partition now, you must create an application directory partition manually after installation. When you create the application partition, you must provide a fully qualified partition name.

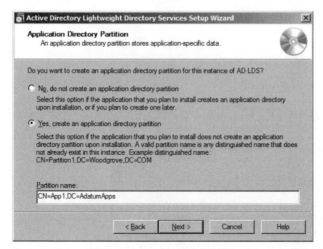

Figure 16-5 You can create an application directory partition when creating an AD LDS instance.

7. On the File Locations page, you can view and change the installation directories for AD LDS data and recovery (log) files. By default, AD LDS data and recovery files are installed in %ProgramFiles%\Microsoft ADAM*instancename*\data, where *instancename* represents the AD LDS instance name that you specified on the Instance Name page.

8. On the Service Account Selection page, select an account to be used as the service account for AD LDS. The account that you select determines the security context in which the AD LDS instance runs. The Active Directory Lightweight Directory Services Setup Wizard defaults to the Network Service account.

> **Note**   If you are installing AD LDS on a computer that is a member of a Windows Server 2000 or later domain, you can use the Network Service account even if you plan to implement replication. If you are deploying AD LDS on a computer that is a member of a workgroup, or you want to enable replication between AD LDS computers in different untrusted domains, you will need to use the identical user account on all computers as the AD LDS service account.

9. On the AD LDS Administrators page, select a user or group to become the default administrator for the AD LDS instance. The user or group that you select will have full administrative control of the AD LDS instance. By default, the Active Directory Lightweight Directory Services Setup Wizard specifies the currently logged-on user. You can change this selection to any local or domain account or group on your network.

10. On the Importing LDIF Files page, you can import schema .ldf files into the AD LDS instance, as shown in Figure 16-6.

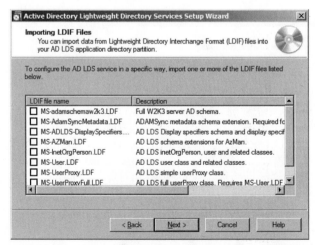

Figure 16-6   By adding .ldf files, you modify the AD LDS schema.

11. On the Ready To Install page, review your installation selections. After you click Next, the Active Directory Lightweight Directory Services Setup Wizard copies files and sets up AD LDS on your computer.

Note   If an error occurs in the Active Directory Lightweight Directory Services Setup Wizard before the Summary page, you can review the error message that appears. In addition, you can view the adamsetup.log file and the adamsetup_loader.log files in the %windir%\debug folder for information on why the installation failed.

Note   To remove an AD LDS instance, access the Programs And Features console in the Control Panel. All AD LDS instances are listed as installed programs, and you can uninstall the instance just like any other program.

AD LDS Management Tools

In most cases, after you install an AD LDS instance, you will install the application that will use the instance (in fact, the application may install AD LDS and configure the instance for you). However, you can also manage AD LDS instances by using the administration tools provided with AD LDS.

Using the ADSI Edit Tool

ADSI Edit is a Microsoft Management Console (MMC) snap-in for general administration of AD LDS. It is installed as part of the AD LDS and AD DS server roles. To use ADSI Edit to administer an AD LDS instance, you must first connect to the instance. When you open ADSI Edit for the first time, it is not connected to any directory. To connect to a directory, on the Action menu, click Connect To. On the Connection Settings screen, shown in Figure 16-7, you must provide the following information:

- **A name for this connection**   If you choose one of the well-known naming contexts, this name is filled in for you.

- **A connection point**   This can be a well-known naming context like the configuration or schema partitions, the *rootDSE* object, or the Default naming context (which only applies to AD DS domains or application directory partitions). If you want to connect to an application directory partition, you must enter the distinguished name of the application directory partition.

- **The server to which you are connecting**   If you are using a port other than the standard LDAP ports, you must also provide the port number for the connection.

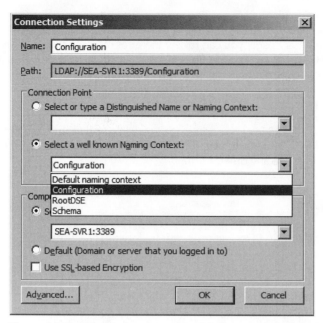

Figure 16-7 Connecting to an AD LDS instance by using ADSI Edit.

Using the Ldp.exe Tool

Ldp.exe is a tool that can be used to administer any LDAP directory service. To use Ldp.exe to administer an AD LDS instance, you must connect and bind to the instance and then display the hierarchy (tree) of a distinguished name of the instance:

1. To connect to an instance using LDP, open a command prompt and type **Ldp.exe** and then press Enter.

2. On the Connection menu, click Connect. Provide the server name and the port used for the AD LDS instance and choose whether or not to use SSL.

3. After connecting to the instance, you need to provide your credentials by binding to the instance. On the Connection menu, click Bind.

   ❑ To bind using the credentials that you logged on with, click Bind As Currently Logged-on User.

   ❑ To bind using a domain user account, click Bind With Credentials; then type the user name, password, and domain name (or the computer name if you are using a local workstation account) of the account that you are using.

   ❑ To bind using just a user name and password, click Simple Bind and type the user name and password of the account that you are using.

   ❑ To bind using an advanced method (NTLM, Distributed Password Authentication (DPA), Negotiate, or Digest), click Advanced DIGEST. Then click Advanced, and in the Bind Options dialog box, select the desired method and set other options as needed.

4. After you have been authenticated, on the View menu, click Tree. Type or select the distinguished name for the directory partition that you want to connect to.

5. To view information about the objects in the directory partition, click the object in the left pane. Detailed information about the object is displayed in the right pane, as shown in Figure 16-8.

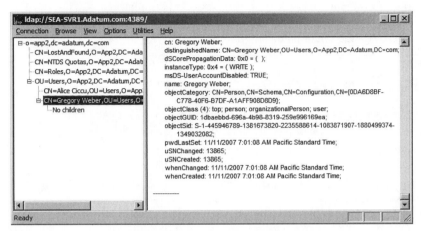

Figure 16-8   You can view details of all objects in AD LDS with Ldp.exe.

6. To edit the object, right-click the object and select one of options for modifying the object or adding child objects.

> **More Info**   For details on how to use ADSI Edit and Ldp.exe to manage AD LDS objects such as OUs, user, and group accounts, see the article titled "Working with Authentication and Access Control" in the AD LDS online help, or see the article "Step-by-Step Guide for Getting Started with Active Directory Lightweight Directory Services," located at *http://technet2.microsoft.com/windowsserver2008/en/library/141900a7-445c-4bd3-9ce3-5ff53d70d10a1033.mspx?mfr=true*.

Using the Dsdbutil Tool

Dsdbutil is a directory service management tool that provides much of the same functionality as Ntdsutil does for AD DS. With Dsdbutil, you can:

■ Backup and perform authoritative restores of AD LDS data.

■ Move the AD LDS data files.

■ Change the AD LDS service account and port numbers.

■ List all of the AD LDS instances running on a server.

To use Dsdbutil, start the utility from a command prompt. Then connect to a specific instance by typing **Activate Instance** *instancename*. To see all of the commands available in Dsdbutil, type **Help**. Like Ntdsutil, Dsdbutil also provides context sensitive help, so typing Help at any command prompt will display all of the options available in that context.

> **Note** If you add the MS-ADLDS-DisplaySpecifiers.ldf file, you can use the Active Directory Sites And Services snap-in to manage AD LDS sites. To connect to an AD LDS instance, you must provide the server name and port number.

Configuring Access Control

In AD LDS, each directory object has an access control list (ACLs) that determines which users have access to that object. By default, ACLs are assigned only at the top of each directory partition. All objects in a given directory partition inherit these ACLs. If your application required specific permissions to be assigned at different levels in the directory structure, you can use tools such as Dsacls and Ldp.exe to view and assign permissions.

Dsacls is a command-line tool that can be used to view and modify permissions in a directory like AD LDS. Dsacls uses the following syntax. The syntax is described in Table 16-9.

```
dsacls object [/a] [/d {user | group}:permissions [...]]
[/g {user | group}:permissions [...]] [/i:{p | s | t}] [/n] [/p:{y | n}]
[/r {user | group} [...]] [/s [/t]]
```

Table 16-9 Dsacls Syntax

Parameter	Description
object	This is the path to the directory services object on which to display or change the ACLs. You need to use the full LDAP name, for example: CN=AppData,OU=Software,CN=App1,DC=AdatumApps. To specify a server, add \\Servername:portnumber\ before the object. For example: \\SEA-SVR1:3389\ CN=AppData,OU=Software,CN=App1,DC=AdatumApps
/a	Displays the auditing information as well as the permissions and ownership information.
/d {user | group}:permissions:	Denies the specified permissions to a user or group.
/g {user | group}:permissions:	Grants the specified permissions to a user or group.
/i:{p | s | t} :	Specifies one of the following inheritance flags: ■ *p:* Use this option to propagate inheritable permissions one level only. ■ *s:* Use this option to propagate inheritable permissions to subobjects only. ■ *t:* Use this option to propagate inheritable permissions to this object and subobjects.
/n:	Replaces the current access on the object instead of editing it.

Table 16-9   Dsacls Syntax *(continued)*

Parameter	Description
/p:{y | n}:	This parameter determines whether or not the object can inherit permissions from its parent objects. If you omit this parameter, the inheritance properties of the object are not changed.
/r {user | group}:	Remove all permissions for the specified user or group.
/s:	Restore the security on the object to the default security for that object class.
/t:	Use this parameter to restore the security on the tree of objects to the default for each object class. This switch is valid only when you also use the */s* parameter.

Dsacls uses permissions bits in the command to configure permissions on the object. For example, dsacls provides the generic permissions: GR – Generic Read, GE – Generic Execute, GW – Generic Write, and GA – Generic All.

> **More Info**   For detailed information about how to use Dsacls to manage permissions in a directory, including details on the permission bit settings, see the Knowledge Base article "How to Use Dsacls.exe in Windows Server 2003 and Windows 2000," located at *http://support.microsoft.com/kb/281146*. You can also type **dsacls /?** at the command line.

Table 16-10 describes some sample Dsacls commands.

Table 16-10   Sample Dsacls Commands

Command	Explanation
dsacls \\SEA-SVR1:4389\O=App2, DC=Adatum,DC=com	Displays the permissions assigned to the references application partition.
dsacls \\SEA-SVR1:4389\O=App2, DC=Adatum,DC=com /G "CN=Gregory Weber, OU=Users,O=App2, DC=Adatum,DC=com ":SD	Grants the user *Gregory Weber* the special Delete permission on the object O=App2.
dsacls "\\SEA-SVR1:4389\O=App2, DC=Adatum,DC=com" /D "CN=Alice Ciccu, OU=Users,O=App2, DC=Adatum, DC=com ":SDDCDT	Denies the Delete, Delete Child, and Delete Tree permissions on the O=App2 object for the user *Alice Ciccu*.

You can also use Ldp.exe to configure permissions on AD LDS objects. To configure permissions using LDP, complete the following steps:

1.   Open Ldp.exe and then connect and bind to an AD LDS instance.

2.   On the View menu, click Tree View and then select the directory partition that you are connecting to.

3.   Right-click the directory partition object for which you want to modify the permissions, click Advanced, and then click Security Descriptor. The Security Descriptor dialog box displays all access control entries (ACEs) and their assigned access rights over the selected directory partition object.

4.   Click anywhere in the discretionary access control list (DACL) and then click Add
     ACE. See Figure 16-9. Type the distinguished name of the user account and select the
     appropriate permissions. You can also choose to allow or deny permissions and
     configure permission inheritance.

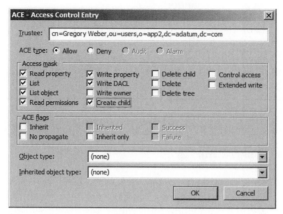

Figure 16-9   Configuring permissions by using Ldp.exe.

Configuring Replication

Like AD DS, AD LDS uses replication to provide redundancy, geographic distribution,
and load balancing for AD LDS instances. As described earlier, AD LDS uses many of the
same concepts and processes to implement replication as AD DS.

Creating AD LDS Replicas

To configure AD LDS replication, you start by creating additional replicas of the AD LDS
instance. The replica can only be configured when you create the instance. All AD LDS
instances in a configuration set replicate a common configuration directory partition and a
common schema directory partition, plus any number of application directory partitions.

To create an AD LDS instance and join it to an existing configuration set, use the Active
Directory Lightweight Directory Services Wizard to create a replica AD LDS instance. You
need to know the DNS name of the server running an AD LDS instance that belongs to the
configuration set, as well as the LDAP port that was specified when the instance was created.
You can also supply the distinguished names of specific application directory partitions that
you want to copy from the configuration set to the AD LDS instance that you are creating.

To create a replica AD LDS instance by using the Active Directory Lightweight Directory
Services Setup Wizard, complete the following steps:

1.   Start the Active Directory Lightweight Directory Services Setup Wizard. On the
     Welcome page, click Next.

2.   On the Setup Options page, click A Replica Of An Existing Instance (see Figure 16-4).

3. On the Instance Name page, configure an instance name. AD LDS instance names have to be unique on a given computer. Also, the instance name can (but does not need to) match the instance name of other replicas.

4. On the Ports page, configure the port numbers for the instance. These port numbers define the ports clients will use to connect to the server, so it is recommended but not required that you use the same ports as the existing instance.

5. On the Joining a Configuration Set page, provide the host name or DNS name of the computer where the first AD LDS instance is installed. Then, type the LDAP port number in use by the first AD LDS instance. This port number must match the port number configured on the existing instance.

6. On the Administrative Credentials for the Configuration Set page, click the account that is used as the AD LDS administrator for your first AD LDS instance.

7. On the Copy Application Directory Partition page, select the application directory partitions that you want to replicate to the new AD LDS instance. See Figure 16-10.

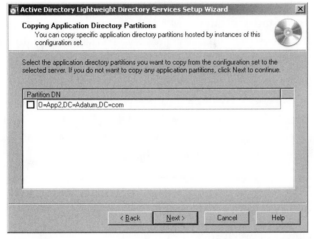

Figure 16-10   When creating an AD LDS replica, you can add application directory partitions to the replica.

8. Accept the default values on the remaining Active Directory Lightweight Directory Services Set Wizard pages by clicking Next on each page and then click Finish on the Completing The Active Directory Application Mode Setup Wizard page.

Note   You can also install an AD LDS instance by using the Install From Media feature. To do this, back up a copy of the AD LDS data store on the source AD LDS server and restore the files to an alternate location that is accessible from the server where you are configuring a replica. Then start the Active Directory Lightweight Directory Services Setup Wizard by typing **%windir%\adam\adaminstall /adv** at a command prompt. When you start the wizard in advanced mode, you are given the choice of copying the application information from a restored copy of the data store.

Configuring AD LDS Sites

Just like AD DS, as soon as you configure a replica of an existing AD LDS instance, the KCC on both servers begin to create the replication topology and replication will occur. Also, just like AD DS, you can use sites to manage replication traffic between AD LDS instances. If you are deploying AD LDS instances in geographically dispersed locations, you can configure separate sites for each location and then configure site links to manage replication traffic between the sites.

Important   Two important differences between using sites in AD LDS compared to sites in AD DS are that AD LDS clients are not site-aware, and AD LDS does not provide any means for automating client connections to AD LDS instances in the client's location. AD LDS does not use SRV records to help clients locate AD LDS instances. Although you can configure subnets for AD LDS instances and associate sites with subnets, clients do not make use of this information. This means that, if you do deploy AD LDS instances in separate locations, you must configure the AD LDS clients to connect to the local AD LDS instance.

To manage AD LDS sites, you must install the MS-ADLDS-DisplaySpecifiers.ldf file in the instance. You can then use the Active Directory Sites and Services snap-in to connect to your AD LDS instance so that you can define site objects and move the directory objects between sites.

To connect to an AD LDS instance by using Active Directory Sites and Services, open the MMC, right-click Active Directory Sites and Services, and then click Change Domain Controller. Specify the name and the port number of the server that holds the AD LDS instances in the configuration set for which you want to create site objects.

After you have connected to the AD LDS instance, you can:

- Create site objects.
- Move AD LDS instances between sites.
- Configure replication frequency within a site.
- Configure the replication schedule and frequency for intrasite replication by configuring site links.

Note   The steps for configuring these objects in AD LDS are identical to the steps for completing these tasks in AD DS. To review these steps, go to the online help in Active Directory Sites And Services or see Chapter 4.

Backing Up and Restoring AD LDS

After deployment, AD LDS will contain important application data or configuration information. In order to ensure that you can recover from a data loss or server failure, you need to include AD LDS in your regular backup routine and be prepared to restore AD LDS data to the same server, or on another server.

Backing Up AD LDS

You should back up AD LDS data and log files regularly to ensure the continued availability of data to applications and users in the event of a system failure.

> **Note**   One option for providing high availability for AD LDS instances is to deploy multiple replicas of the same instance. If one replica fails, clients can still connect to the second replica. In addition, you can deploy AD LDS on a network load balanced cluster so that you do not need to reconfigure AD LDS clients in the event of a server failure.

By default, each instance of AD LDS running on an AD LDS server stores its database file, Adamntds.dit, and the associated log files in %program files%\Microsoft ADAM*instance_name*\data, where *instance_name* is the AD LDS instance name. To ensure that the AD LDS data is backed up regularly, include these files as part of the regular backup plan of your organization.

> **Important**   AD LDS is less server dependent than AD DS. You can back up AD LDS data on one server and restore it to a different server if the original server fails. As well, you do not need to back up or restore system state data on a server to recover the AD LDS data store.

You can use Windows Server Backup or any other backup program that enables you to back up open files to back up the AD LDS data. You should leave the AD LDS instance running during the backup.

You can also use the Dsdbutil.exe command-line tool to back up the AD LDS instance. With the Dsdbutil.exe tool, you can back up and create installation media for individual AD LDS instances, rather than just backing up the AD LDS files or backing up entire volumes that contain the AD LDS instance.

> **Note**   If you have Ntdsutil installed on the AD LDS server, you can set the focus for Ntdsutil to an AD LDS instance by activating the instance. You can then use Ntdsutil to manage the AD LDS instance.

To back up an AD LDS instance by using Dsdbutil.exe, complete the following steps:

1. Open a command prompt, type **dsdbutil** and then press Enter.

2. At the dsdbutil: prompt, type **activate instance** *instancename* and then press Enter, where *instancename* is the name of the AD LDS instance that you want to back up or create the installation media for.

3. At the dsdbutil: prompt, type **ifm** and then press Enter.

4. At the ifm: prompt, type **create full** *filepathname* and then press Enter, where *filepathname* is the location where the backup will be stored. Dsbdutil will create a snapshot of the AD LDS data store and back it up to the backup location. The Dsbdutil backup consists of just the Adamntds.dit file.

Restoring AD LDS

If the AD LDS server fails or the data store files are lost or corrupted, you can use the same backup tools to recover the data store. Depending on the situation, you may need to use slightly different processes to recover the AD LDS instance data.

Restore an Existing AD LDS Instance   If the AD LDS server fails, or the database is lost on the server, you can simply perform a regular restore of the AD LDS data to restore the AD LDS instance to its state at the time when its backup was created. If the AD LDS server fails, you first need to repair and restart the server. You must stop the AD LDS instance before you run the restore operation. In addition, because the AD LDS restore will overwrite any files in the instance directory, you should copy any files out of the directory before completing the restore.

> **Caution**   You can restore an AD LDS instance by using Windows Server Backup without stopping the instance. However, if you do, Windows Server Backup leaves the restored files in a pending state, and it does not write the files to disk until the computer reboots. In this situation, any directory changes that are made to the running AD LDS instance after Windows Server Backup is run are lost.

To restore an existing AD LDS instance, complete the following steps:

1. Stop the AD LDS instance that you want to restore. You can stop the instance in the Services snap-in or by using a command such as sc stop *instancename*, where *instancename* is the name of the AD LDS instance.

2. Use your backup tool to restore the AD LDS files. Ensure that you restore the files to the same location as the original files and that you overwrite the original files.

3.   Start the AD LDS instance. When you restart the instance, it will start using the restored files.

> **Note**   You cannot use Windows Server Backup to restore an existing AD LDS instance with a backup that was created with the Dsdbutil.exe tool. To restore a backup that was created using the Dsbdutil tool, you can just stop the AD LDS instance and copy the file created by the Dsbdutil backup back to the original directory.

Restore an AD LDS Instance to a New Server   If the AD LDS server has failed and you cannot repair it, you can restore the AD LDS data to a new server. To do this, you must first create a new AD LDS instance on the server by using exactly the same settings as the original AD LDS instance. When creating the new instance, ensure that you use the same instance name and the same location for storing the data. Do not create any application partitions for the data while creating the instance.

After creating the instance, stop the instance and then use the backup tool to restore the backed up data store. If your backup was created using Dsbdutil, copy the file created by Dsbdutil to the appropriate directory and restart the instance.

Authoritatively Restore an AD LDS Instance

Like AD DS, you can also perform authoritative restores of AD LDS data that has been accidentally deleted or modified. If the AD LDS data is not replicated to another server, you can just perform a normal restore. However, if the AD LDS data is replicated to another server, you must authoritatively restore those objects so that the correct version of the objects is replicated.

To authoritatively restore directory data, first perform a normal restore. Then, before restarting the AD LDS instance, run the Dsdbutil tool to mark directory objects for authoritative restore. When an object is marked for authoritative restore, its update sequence number is changed so that the number is higher than any other update sequence number in the configuration set. This ensures that any data you restore is properly replicated throughout the configuration set.

To perform an authoritative restore, complete these steps:

1.   Stop the AD LDS instance and restore the data. Depending on how you performed the backup, you can restore the data by using your backup tool or by using Dsbdutil.

2.   Before restarting the instance, start the Dsbdutil tool and activate the AD LDS instance that you want to restore by typing **Dsbdutil activate** *instancename*.

3.   Type **authoritative restore**.

4. At the authoritative restore: prompt, type one of the following commands:

❑ **restore object** *dn*   This command performs authoritative restore of a directory object whose distinguished name is represented by dn. For example, to restore a specific user account, you could type **restore object "CN=Gregory Weber,OU=Users,O=App2,DC=Adatum,DC=com"**.

❑ **restore subtree** *dn*   This command performs an authoritative restore of the directory subtree whose distinguished name is represented by *dn*. For example, to restore an OU, you could type **restore subtree "OU=Users,O=App2,DC=Adatum, DC=com"**.

5. Exit Dsdbutil and restart the AD LDS instance.

Configuring AD DS and AD LDS Synchronization

One of the most common ways to integrate AD DS and AD LDS is to use AD DS user accounts when configuring authorization in AD LDS. To implement this level of integration, you do not need to perform any additional steps beyond installing AD LDS on a computer that is either part of the same AD DS domain as the user accounts or in a trusted domain. When installed on a domain member, the AD DS users accounts can be directly assigned to ACLs in AD LDS or added to AD LDS groups that are assigned to ACLs.

Another option for integrating AD DS and AD LDS is to configure synchronization from AD DS to AD LDS. This option can significantly decrease the administrative effort required to administer the AD DS instance. For example, if you are deploying AD LDS in a perimeter network, you may not want to install AD LDS on a server that is a member of an internal domain. However, you may still want to use internal user accounts to assign permissions to the AD LDS data, or the application using AD LDS may require the internal accounts. By configuring synchronization from AD DS to AD LDS, you can automate the process of creating the user accounts in the AD LDS instance.

Adamsync and Exchange Server 2007

One of the interesting scenarios in which Adamsync can be implemented is when you deploy Exchange Server 2007 servers running the Edge Transport server role. The Edge Transport server role is designed to be deployed on servers that are located in a perimeter network and on servers that are not members of your AD DS domain. The Edge Transport servers use AD LDS to store configuration information for implementing spam filtering as well as other configuration information.

In order to implement spam filtering based on specific user names or the safe sender lists configured by individual users, you need to replicate data from AD DS to the AD LDS instance used by the Edge Transport server role. You can do this by configuring Adamsync. Exchange Server 2007 provides Windows PowerShell scripts for implementing the Adamsync synchronization. If your organization is planning to implement Adamsync synchronization for another application, and that application does not provide similar scripts, review the Exchange scripts to see how you may be able to automate the Adamsync configuration.

To prepare an AD LDS instance for synchronization, you need to first ensure that the appropriate schema extensions have been installed on the AD LDS instance. In order to enable synchronization, you need to add the MS-adamschemaw2k3.ldf file (for synchronizing with Windows Server 2003 Active Directory) or the MS-adamschemaw2k8.ldf file (for synchronizing with Windows Server 2008 AD DS). You also need to add the MS-AsamSync-Metadata.ldf file to the AD LDS schema.

Direct from the Field: Using ADSchemaAnaylzer to Create .ldf Files

One of the issues that you can run into when you are implementing Adamsync is that you may have modified the AD DS schema. The MS-adamschemaw2k3.ldf and the MS-adamschemaw2k8.ldf files contain only the default schema objects that are included in Windows Server 2003 or Windows Server 2008. If you have made changes to the AD DS schema, or if you have implemented directory aware applications such as Exchange Server 2007, you cannot just import these files into AD LDS.

In order to create an .ldf file that includes all of the schema changes in your AD DS forest, you can use the ADSchemaAnaylzer tool. This tool is installed with the AD LDS administration tools, and is located in the %windir%/ADAM folder. Use the tool to load the target schema from a domain controller in your domain and then load the base schema from the AD LDS instance. When the AD LDS schema is imported, ADSchemaAnalyzer compares the two and finds any differences. Then, use the Mark All Non-present Elements As Included option on the Schema menu to add the differences to an .ldf file. You can then create and save the file and use the Ldifde command to import the file into the AD LDS instance.

For more details on the ADSchemaAnalyzer tool, see the ADSchemaAnalyzer article at *http://technet2.microsoft.com/windowsserver/en/library/7fac5191-27d3-43dd-99c6-bb8ad044e7b91033.mspx?mfr=true*.

To implement Adamsync synchronization, complete these steps:

1. To add the .ldf files to the schema, open a command prompt, switch to the %windir%\ADAM directory, and then use the following command:

```
ldifde -i -u -f ldf_filename -s server:port -b user_name domain password
-j . -c "cn=Configuration,dc=X" #configurationNamingContext
```

In this command, replace *ldf_filename* with MS-adamschemaw2k3.ldf (to import the Windows Server 2003 schema) or with MS-adamschemaw2k8.ldf (to import the Windows Server 2008 schema).

2. To add the <MS-AdamSyncMetadata.ldf file, use the following command:

```
ldifde -i -s server:port -c CN=Configuration,DC=X
#ConfigurationNamingContext -f MS-AdamSyncMetadata.ldf
```

3. Open the MS-AdamSyncConf.xml file located in the %windir%\ADAM directory with Notepad. Make the following changes to the contents of the configuration file:

   ❑ Replace the value of *<source-ad-name>* with the name of the source AD DS domain controller.

   ❑ Replace the value of *<source-ad-partition>* with the distinguished name of the source domain.

   ❑ Replace the value of *<source-ad-account>* with the name of an account in the Domain Admins group of the source domain.

   ❑ Replace the value of *<account-domain>* with the fully qualified Domain Name System (DNS) name of the source domain.

   ❑ Replace the value of *<target-dn>* with the name of the partition of the target AD LDS instance. This value must use a partition name and cannot use a container inside the partition.

   ❑ Replace the value of *<base-dn>* with the base distinguished name of the container in the source AD DS domain from which you want to import users. For example, if you want to import only users from a specific OU, change this value to something like "*OU=NYC,DC=Adatum,DC=com*".

4. Save the file with an .xml extension, using a different filename.

On the Disc   For an example of a modified Adamsync configuration file, see the file ADatumSync.xml on the CD. This file imports all objects from the NYC OU in the ADatum.com domain to the O=App2,DC=Adatum,DC=com directory partition.

Note   You can modify other settings in the file to define which attributes are replicated to AD LDS. For a complete description on the file syntax, see "Adamsync Configuration File XML Reference," located at *http://technet2.microsoft.com/windowsserver/en/library/d4b6dbdc-eb53-4229-9118-b7d80c9125671033.mspx?mfr=true*.

5. The next step is to prepare the AD LDS instances for replication by installing the Adamsync instance. To do this, at the command prompt, type the following command, where *xml_file* is the name of the file that you created in the previous step:

    `adamsync /install server:port .\xml_file`

    If this file is not in the %windir%\ADAM directory, you must provide the full path to the file.

6. After running the Adamsync /install command, type the following command where *xml_file* is the name of the file that you used in the previous step:

    `adamsync /delete .\xml_file`

    This command deletes the configuration file from the ADAM instance. This is required if the user needs to update the .xml file or restart the sync process.

7. After you prepare the AD LDS instance for synchronization, you can initiate synchronization from the specified AD DS forest to the AD LDS instance. To do this, type the following command, where *configuration_dn* is the root of the application directory partition to which you are synchronizing the data:

    `adamsync /sync server:port configuration_dn /log Adamsynclog.txt`

> **Note**   You can perform additional synchronization tasks such as aging searches (where AD LDS is searched for objects deleted in AD DS) or synchronizing just specific objects with Adamsync. For a complete list of the options available with Adamsync, type **Adamsync /?** in a command prompt focused on %windir%\ADAM or review the AD LDS management console online help.

Summary

AD LDS is designed to complement the functionality provided by AD DS by providing a directory service that is very much like AD DS in many ways, but is designed to provide an application-specific directory. AD LDS provides more deployment flexibility than AD DS, as you can run multiple instances on a single computer, which enables multiple schemas and application partitions on one server.

Best Practices

- To help maintain AD LDS replication security, use the highest level of replication security that your environment can support. If you must use the domain account as an AD LDS service account, ensure that it is configured with a highly complex password.

- In AD DS environments, run AD LDS on member servers rather than on domain controllers whenever possible. If you run AD LDS on a domain controller in an Active Directory environment, do not use the Network Service account as the AD LDS service account. Instead, use a domain user account that does not have administrative privileges.

Additional Resources

The following resources contain additional information and tools related to this chapter.

- Chapter 4, "Active Directory Domain Services Replication," goes into detail on how AD DS replication works. Most of the same concepts and configuration tasks also apply to configuring AD LDS replication.

- The Active Directory Lightweight Directory Services subsite on the Windows Server 2008 Technical Library site provides technical information and step by step guides for implementing AD LDS in a test environment. The site is located at *http://technet2.microsoft.com/windowsserver2008/en/servermanager/activedirectorylightweightdirectoryservices.mspx.*

- The "Active Directory Application Mode Technical Reference" at *http://technet2.microsoft.com/windowsserver/en/library/74d58697-970a-45db-9139-ebcd3db051181033.mspx?mfr=true* provides details on ADAM as implemented in Windows Server 2003. Most of the concepts have not changed significantly in Windows Server 2008.

- The "Step-by-Step Guide for Getting Started with Active Directory Lightweight Directory Services" article, located at *http://technet2.microsoft.com/windowsserver2008/en/library/141900a7-445c-4bd3-9ce3-5ff53d70d10a1033.mspx?mfr=true*, provides detailed steps for configuring user and group accounts in AD LDS.

- The Knowledge Base article "How to Use Dsacls.exe in Windows Server 2003 and Windows 2000," located at *http://support.microsoft.com/kb/281146,* provides details on how to manage permissions by using Dsacls.exe.

- For a complete description on the Adamsync file syntax, see "Adamsync Configuration File XML Reference," located at *http://technet2.microsoft.com/windowsserver/en/library/d4b6dbdc-eb53-4229-9118-b7d80c9125671033.mspx?mfr=true.*

Related Tools

Windows Server 2008 provides several tools that can be used when managing AD LDS. Table 16-11 lists some of these tools and their uses.

Table 16-11   AD LDS Management Tools

Tool Name	Description and Use
Active Directory Lightweight Directory Services Installation Wizard	Use to configure AD LDS instances and replicas
Active Directory Sites And Services	Use to configure AD LDS sites and replication
Dsdbutil.exe	Use to manage the AD LDS data store files and to manage AD LDS server settings
ADSI Edit	Use to view and modify the contents of AD LDS partitions
Ldp.exe	Use to view and modify the contents of AD LDS partitions

Resources on the CD

- DisplayADLDSInstances.ps1 is a Windows PowerShell script that lists all naming contexts or partitions on your AD LDS server.

- AdatumSync.xml is a preconfigured .xml file that illustrates the format of the AdamSync configuration file.

Related Help Topics

- "Checklist: Manage Group Memberships" in Active Directory Lightweight Directory Services help

- "Working with Authentication and Access Control" in Active Directory Lightweight Directory Services help

- "Checklist: Synchronize Data from AD DS to AD LDS" in Active Directory Lightweight Directory Services help

Chapter 17

Active Directory Certificate Services

Active Directory Certificate Services (AD CS) is the Microsoft implementation of public key infrastructure (PKI). PKI deals with the components and processes for issuing and managing digital certificates that are used for encryption and authentication. It is not mandatory to implement AD CS as part of a Windows Server 2008 Active Directory structure. However, many organizations find it useful to deploy this service internally rather than relying on an external provider.

This chapter begins by providing an overview of AD CS and how it can be used. It then discusses how to implement AD CS and manage the certificates that are issued by AD CS. Finally, the overall design of an AD CS implementation is reviewed.

Active Directory Certificate Services Overview

AD CS is the component of Windows Server 2008 that can be used to issue and manage digital certificates. The digital certificates issued by AD CS can be used for encrypting file system (EFS), e-mail encryption, secure sockets layer (SSL), and authentication. A server with AD CS installed is referred to as a certification authority (CA).

Digital certificates are used for *asymmetrical encryption*, which requires two keys. The first key is the private key, which is securely stored by the user or computer that a digital certificate has been issued to. The second key is the public key that is distributed to other users and computers. The data encrypted by one key can only be decrypted by the other key. This relationship ensures protection of the encrypted data. Each key is sufficiently large to prevent computation of the private key via possession of the public key.

Public Key Infrastructure Components

PKI, in general, has a number of components such as certification authorities, management tools, and certificate revocation lists. In addition to those general PKI components, AD CS also includes certificate templates that can be used to automate the issuance of certificates to users and computers.

Certificate and CA Management Tools

Windows Server 2008 includes a number of graphical and command-line tools for managing certificates and CAs. Most client certificate management is performed by using the Certificates MMC snap-in shown in Figure 17-1. This snap-in can manage the certificates for users, the local computer, or services. Some of the management tasks include generating a certificate request, installing new certificates, renewing certificates, installing trusted root certificates, and exporting certificates for backup. To help automate the generation of certificate requests, you can use the Certreq.exe command-line utility. This utility can be used in scripts.

Note   The Certificates snap-in is also available on Windows Vista and Windows XP computers. The Certreq.exe utility is included with Windows Vista and as part of the Windows Server 2003 Service Pack 1 Administration Tools Pack.

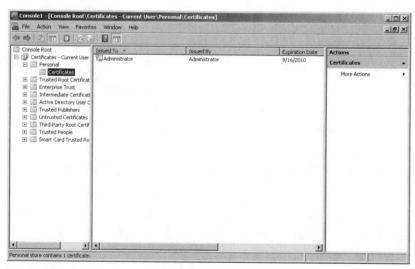

Figure 17-1   The Certificates MMC snap-in.

Direct from the Source: Enabling CryptoAPI 2.0 Diagnostic Logging

Windows Vista and Windows Server 2008 have been shipped with a new built-in feature called CryptoAPI 2.0 Diagnostics that is designed to troubleshoot Public Key Infrastructure issues. In previous versions of Windows, only certain events regarding PKI would get logged in the event logs. The new diagnostic logging allows PKI administrators and application developers to capture detailed events with the application programming interfaces (APIs) that are used by PKI during operations such as certificate revocation checking, certificate chaining, and opening a certificate store (plus many more).

There are a couple of ways to enable diagnostic logging. From the event viewer, administrators can navigate to the following location:

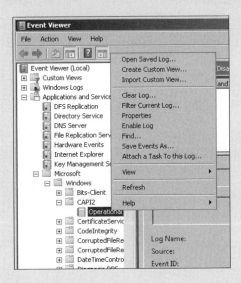

From there, right-click Operational and select the option Enable Log.

Another method you can use to enable or disable logging is the Wevutil.exe command-line tool. To enable logging, type the following command:

Wevtutil.exe sl Microsoft-Windows-CAPI2/Operational /e:true

To disable logging, type this command:

Wevtutil.exe sl Microsoft-Windows-CAPI2/Operational /e:false

When diagnostic logging is enabled, detailed events will be seen in the operational log. An administrator can then filter the log for the relevant events or save it as a custom view to monitor future events.

> For more information about Wevtutil.exe, see *http://technet2.microsoft.com/windowsserver2008/en/library/d4c791e0-7e59-45c5-aa55-0223b77a48221033.mspx?mfr=true.*
>
> *Bob Drake*
>
> *Microsoft Directory Services Team*

The Certification Authority snap-in, shown in Figure 17-2, is used to manage the CAs running AD CS. By using this snap-in, you can view issued and revoked certificates, pending and failed certificate requests, or certificate templates. You can also view and approve pending certificate requests and revoke certificates that have been compromised. Finally, you can view and modify the properties of the CA.

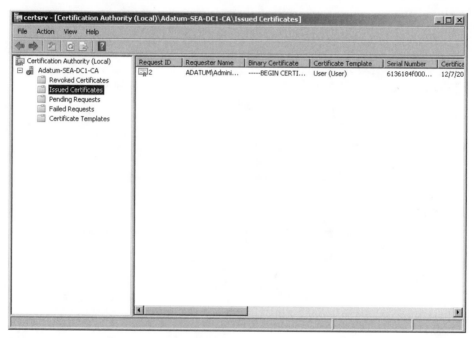

Figure 17-2   The Certification Authority MMC snap-in.

The Enterprise PKI snap-in, shown in Figure 17-3, is used to view the status of CAs in an organization. It allows you to quickly view the status of multiple CAs and drill down to view potential problems. This snap-in was available as part of the Windows Server 2003 Resource Kit Tools as PKIView.

The Certutil.exe command-line utility allows you to perform many of the same tasks as the certificates snap-in and the Certification Authority snap-in. However, this tool can be used in scripts to automate certificate management on servers and workstations. Certutil.exe can also perform CA management tasks.

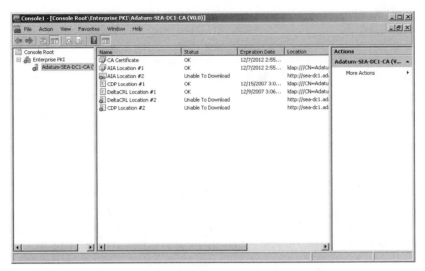

Figure 17-3 The Enterprise PKI MMC snap-in.

Digital Certificates

Whereas PKI requires the use of both a public key and a private key, only the public key is included in the certificate. This allows the certificate to be publicly distributed and available for verification. The private key is held in the public key-enabled application or on the local computer. Windows stores private keys in user profiles.

The digital certificate contains information about the subject that requested the certificate. This allows certificates to be used to verify the identity of the person or computer holding the private key. For example, a digital certificate for a Web server includes the hostname name or IP address of the Web server. Information about the CA that issued the certificate is also included to allow for verification of validity with that CA.

Certificates also include information about the validity of certificates. This includes how the certificate can be used and the time period for which it is valid. For example, a certificate may be limited to being used for Encrypting File System (EFS). Certificates are valid only for a certain period of time, typically two years or less. After a certificate is expired, it cannot be used.

More Info The specific format of certificates issued by a Windows Server 2008 CA is X.509 version 3. For detailed information about X.509 version 3 and PKI, see "RFC 3280: Internet X.509 Public Key Infrastructure Certificate and Certificate Revocation List (CRL) Profile" at *http://www.ietf.org/rfc/rfc3280.txt*.

Certification Authorities

CAs are the PKI component that issues digital certificates to users and computers. When organizations implement digital certificates, they must consider whether to implement an internal CA by using AD CS or an external CA. The primary advantage of an internal CA is cost. There is no additional cost for each certificate issued. In contrast, when an external CA is used, there is a charge for each certificate issued. If hundreds or thousands of certificates are being issued, this is a significant concern. However, for simple applications such as an SSL certificate for a single server, the administrative cost of maintaining a CA will likely be higher that the cost of the certificate.

When you are implementing services using digital certificates for external clients, an internal CA is not automatically trusted by external clients. When an internal CA is untrusted by external clients, the application may display warning messages or not work at all. An example of a warning message is shown in Figure 17-4. Internal CAs are automatically trusted by internal clients because the trusted root certificate of the internal CA is distributed to domain members. Many external CAs are automatically trusted by internal clients and external clients. External CAs that are part of the Microsoft Root Certificate Program are automatically trusted by Windows operating systems.

> **Note** The trusted root certificate for an Internal CA is automatically distributed to clients via Group Policy if it is an Enterprise Root CA. Otherwise, you can manually configure Group Policy to distribute the trusted root certificate.

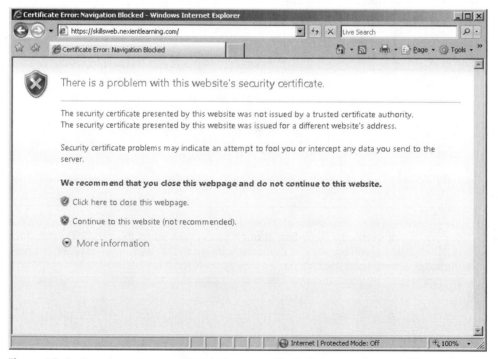

Figure 17-4 Error message caused by using a certificate from an untrusted CA.

Certificate Revocation List

A certificate revocation list (CRL) is a list of certificates that have been revoked by an administrator before their expiration date. This can be done any time a certificate is no longer trusted or use of the certificate is no longer needed. In the case of a partner using a certificate for authentication, a certificate may be revoked if the business relationship is severed. A certificate may also be revoked if the private key of the certificate has been compromised.

Certificate Templates

Certificate templates are used to control the process of creating certificates. Certificate templates define a wide variety of certificate characteristics, such as certificate purpose, validity period, renewal period, cryptographic service provider, subject name format, and included extensions. Certificate templates can also be used to automate the enrollment process for certificates by defining which users have access to the template. You can also define rules for renewal.

Certificate and CRL Distribution Points

Distribution points are locations where certificates and CRLs can be accessed by users and computers. For certificates, Active Directory can be a distribution point where certificates are published. When the Certificates snap-in is used to request a certificate from an enterprise CA, the response is automatically retrieved and installed by the Certificates snap-in. When a certificate request is made by using Web enrollment, the response is retrieved from the certificate services Web site.

CRLs are periodically downloaded by computers to ensure that they have an updated list of revoked certificates that should not be trusted even though the certificates have not expired. Previous versions of Windows Server distributed the CRL by making it available on the Certificate Services Web site and in Active Directory. AD CS on Windows Server 2008 supports both of these methods, as well as Online Certificate Status Protocol (OSCP).

Public Key-Enabled Applications

To use certificates for encryption or digital signatures, your applications must support the use of PKI. For example, to send e-mail with a digital signature, the e-mail client must support the use of certificates. In addition, a Web server must support the use of certificates to encrypt connections by using Secure Sockets Layer (SSL). If an application is not public key-enabled, you cannot use certificates for encryption and digital signatures.

Certification Authorities

A CA is responsible for managing the issuance of certificates. As part of this process, the identity of certificate requestor is verified. Requestor identity can be verified manually or automatically. Manual verification prevents automatic issuance of certificates and forces an administrator to intervene. For example, manual verification may require an administrator to verify employee status before issuing a certificate. Windows Server 2008 CAs (also, Windows 2000 Server and Windows Server 2003 CAs) can automatically verify status in combination with certificate templates. When a user logs in and has the necessary permissions to access a template, the verification process is automated for the user and administrator.

CAs are also responsible for managing and maintaining certificate revocation. Revoking a certificate is initiated manually by an administrator. After the certificate is revoked, the CA publishes that revocation into the CRL and makes certificate status available through OCSP.

CA Hierarchy

The issue of trust is central to planning the implementation of PKI. Specifically, the CAs issuing certificates must be trusted by the clients using those certificates. Windows clients include a list of trusted root certification authorities. Any certificates issued by a trusted root certification authority are trusted by Windows clients. Windows clients also trust any certificate issued by a CA authorized by the trusted root certificate authorities.

The first Windows Server 2008 CA implemented in your organization is a root CA. If the root CA is an enterprise CA, then the root CA's self-signed certificate is automatically distributed to the Windows clients in the Active Directory forest as a trusted root certificate. Therefore, Windows clients in the Active Directory forest will automatically trust certificates issued by an internal CA. If a stand-alone root CA is used, then you must configure the distribution of the trusted root certificate for the root CA.

In smaller organizations, only a single CA may be required. In larger organizations, there may be large number of CAs with specific roles. When a second Windows Server 2008 CA is installed, the CA certificate for the second CA is signed by the trusted root CA. Therefore, all Windows clients in the Active Directory forest will trust certificates issued by the second CA. The second CA could authorize a third CA, whose certificates would also be trusted by the Windows clients in the Active Directory forest. Using this process, you can build a CA hierarchy that meets the needs of your organization. All CAs installed in a hierarchy after the root CA are called *subordinate CAs*.

Enterprise and Stand-Alone CAs

Windows Server 2008 CAs can be installed as stand-alone or enterprise CAs. The primary difference between the two is Active Directory integration. An enterprise CA automatically integrates with Active Directory. This provides the opportunity to automate certificate enrollment and automatically add the root and subordinate CAs to the proper Certification Authority stores on domain computers. Stand-alone CAs can be integrated with Active Directory in limited ways, such as publishing configuration data into Active Directory, but integration must be manually configured. Detailed characteristics are shown in Table 17-1.

Table 17-1   CA Characteristics

Stand-Alone CA	Enterprise CA
Configuration can be stored in Active Directory.	Configuration is always stored in Active Directory.
CA certificate and CRL can be manually published in Active Directory.	CA certificate, CRL, and Delta CRL are automatically published in Active Directory.
Issues certificates by Web enrollment only, by default.	Issues certificates by Web enrollment or Certificates MMC.
User identification is manually typed in by the user.	User identification is retrieved from Active Directory.
Certificates are manually approved.	Certificates can be approved manually or automatically.
Certificates cannot be published to Active Directory.	Certificates can be automatically published to Active Directory.
Stand-alone servers can be used.	Domain servers must be used.
Certificate templates are not used.	Certificate templates are used.
Members of the local Administrators group can install.	Only members of the Enterprise Administrators or the Domain Admins group of the forest root domain can install.

Offline CAs

If a CA is compromised, all certificates issued by the CA are also considered to be compromised and must be revoked. Consequently, the security of a CA is very important. An offline CA offers increased security because it is not connected to the network. An offline CA is also not a domain member and therefore cannot be an enterprise CA.

Certificate requests to an offline CA must be presented on physical media such as a floppy disk or USB drive. This makes an offline CA impractical for issuing certificates to a large number of users. It also prevents automatic enrollment or integration with Active Directory. Most offline CAs are root CAs, with subordinate CAs responsible for certificate enrollment. The subordinate CAs would be enterprise CAs that can use Active Directory and certificate templates to simplify certificate enrollment.

> **Note**   Offline certificate requests can be created by using Certreq.exe. Windows Vista and Windows Server 2008 include support for creating offline certificate requests in the Certificates MMC snap-in.

Certificate Services Deployment Scenarios

AD CS is implemented only if you want to deploy one or more internal CAs. If you are planning to use certificates issued by an external third-party CA, then there is no need for AD CS. An external CA is used in most cases when clients outside the organization need to trust the certificates. An external CA is likely to be used in these scenarios:

■ Securing e-mail with encryption or digital signatures

■ Securing Web sites with SSL certificates

An internal CA is well-suited to scenarios with a client that is already within the organization and can easily be configured to trust the internal CA. AD CS could be used as an internal CA in the following scenarios:

❑ **Securing files with EFS**   AD CS can be used to issue certificates to all EFS users and to create a recovery key. Key archival and recovery is also important when using AD CS to implement EFS.

❑ **Securing internal Web applications**   AD CS can be used to issue SSL certificates to internal Web servers. The internal clients will trust the internal CA.

❑ **Enhance security on wireless networks**   AD CS can be configured as part of the system and performs 802.1X authentication for wireless devices. When 802.1X authentication is used, wireless clients are authenticated before they are allowed access to the network. This is supported by the Network Device Enrollment Service (NDES), which allows devices to obtain certificates from AD CS.

❑ **Enhance user logon security with smart cards**   AD CS can be used to issue certificates that are stored on smart cards and used to log on. Security is enhanced because two-factor authentication is now in place. Users must provide the smart card and a personal identification number (PIN). Support for smart cards is enhanced in Windows Server 2008 with the introduction of a restricted enrollment agent. This allows an authorized individual to configure smart cards for specific individuals or groups. For example, a local IT support person could configure smart cards for all of the users in a remote location. In previous versions of Windows, an enrollment agent could not be restricted.

 Note   The restricted enrollment agent is available in Windows Server 2008 Enterprise.

Implementing AD CS

AD CS is a complex product with various options for implementations. The implementation options for root and subordinate CAs vary, and you need to be aware of the process for each. Web enrollment is commonly used in many environments and must be configured. You must also manage certificate revocation by using either certificate revocation lists or OCSP. Finally, you must be aware of how to perform key archival and recovery.

Installing AD CS Root Certification Authorities

The installation options for a CA should be documented before you begin installation. This ensures that the correct options are selected during installation and also aids in disaster recovery. In Server Manager, you add the Active Directory Certificate Services role. You must define the following options:

- **Role Services**   The only role service that is required to configure a root CA is the Certification Authority role service. This configures the server to issue certificates. Certification Authority Web Enrollment is also required to accept certificate requests and issue certificates on a stand-alone root CA. The Online Certificate Status Protocol and Microsoft Simple Certificate Enrollment Protocol are more likely to be installed on subordinate CAs than the root CA.

- **Setup Type**   The setup type is defined as Enterprise or Stand-alone. If you are planning to make the root CA an offline root CA, then you should select stand-alone. It is possible to change between an enterprise and stand-alone CA, but such a switch requires reinstallation and restoring from backup.

- **CA Type**   The CA type is defined as Root CA or Subordinate CA. Root CA is selected when installing the first CA in the hierarchy.

- **Private Key**   You can create a new private key or use an existing private key. Create a new private key for a new root CA installation. Use an existing private key when restoring a failed CA.

- **Cryptography**   You must select the cryptographic service provider, hash algorithm, and key length. Ensure that the settings you select are compatible with any other systems that this CA needs to interact with. For example, some third-party CAs have a maximum key length of 2048 bits.

> **Note**   The built-in cryptographic service providers are sufficient for most purposes, but developers also have the option to develop their own. This is often done by smart card vendors. For more information on writing cryptographic service providers, see "Writing a CSP" at *http://msdn2.microsoft.com/en-us/library/aa388213(VS.85).aspx.*

- **CA Name**   You should have a standard naming convention for all CAs. The CA name can be a maximum of 64 characters. By default, the CA name includes the computer name, but this is not required. The fully qualified domain name of the CA should not be used as the CA name. This is to prevent malicious users from easily identifying the root CA for an organization.

- **Validity Period** The most important consideration for the validity period is that a CA cannot issue certificates that are valid for longer than its own certificate is valid for. The default validity period is 5 years, and therefore, certificates issued to subordinate CAs and clients are valid for a maximum of 5 years from the date of installing the root CA. It is common to extend the validity period for a root CA to 10 or even 20 years to provide flexibility. You can renew the certificate for the root CA at any time by using the Certificate Services Web pages or the Certification Authority MMC snap-in.

- **Database and Log Location** In most cases, a root CA issues a low number of certificates. Consequently, performance is not much of an issue and the default location for the database and log files on the %systemroot% drive is acceptable. The database stores certificates issued by the CA, private keys archived by the CA, certificates revoked by the CA, and all certificate requests ever received by the CA.

> **Note** The name of a server cannot be changed after AD CS is installed. To change the name of a server, AD CS must be removed, the name must be changed, and then AD CS must be reinstalled.

CAPolicy.inf

To ensure standardized installation for CAs, you can use a CAPolicy.inf file. This file contains settings used during installation and certificate renewal. This file is read during installation or renewal of a CA when it is placed in the %Windir% folder. You can define these settings:

- **Certification practice statement (CPS)** This is a text-based statement that describes the process used to issue certificates. This statement is visible in the CA certificate, but including this statement is not a technical requirement. To implement a CPS, you must use a CAPolicy.inf file. To avoid limits on length, it is common practice to include a URL that points to a full CPS rather than including CPS text.

- **CRL publication intervals** This allows you to define how often the CRL for this CA is updated during installation. Otherwise, you can modify this parameter in the Certification Authority MMC snap-in.

- **CA renewal settings** During renewal of a certificate using the Certification Authority MMC snap-in, the existing configuration is reused. Defining CA renewal settings in CAPolicy.inf allows you to change the key length and validity period, and determine whether a new key pair is issued.

- **Paths for the CRL distribution point and Authority Information Access (AIA)** Because a root CA is typically not available to clients, you may not want to include the locations of the CRL distribution point and AIA in the CA certificate. You can disable these extensions in the CAPolicy.inf file. AIA indicates where the CA certificate for the CA can be obtained.

> **More Info**   For more information about the CAPolicy.inf file, see "CAPolicy.inf Syntax" on the Technet Web site at *http://technet2.microsoft.com/windowsserver/en/library/25127c1f-4880-4764-85e8-226ce41588881033.mspx?mfr=true.*

Hardware Security Modules

To increase the security of private keys on a CA, you can use a Hardware Security Module (HSM). An HSM is capable of storing private keys in hardware, which is more secure than storing them on disk. An HSM can also provide functionality that is normally provided by software, such as key generation, key archival and recovery, and random number generation. Because these functions are offloaded from the server CPU, server performance is increased.

Installing AD CS Subordinate Certification Authorities

The installation of a subordinate CA is approximately the same process as installing a root CA, with one exception: a subordinate CA must obtain a CA certificate from the root CA. In most cases, a subordinate CA will be an enterprise CA to allow integration with Active Directory and the use of certificate templates. As with the installation of a root CA, the installation options for a subordinate CA should be planned well in advance of beginning the installation.

When the subordinate CA requests a certificate from the root CA, the process varies depending on whether the root CA is offline, online, enterprise, or stand-alone. If the root CA is an online enterprise CA, then the certificate can be obtained automatically during the installation of the subordinate CA. If the root CA is a stand-alone CA, then the request for a CA certificate must be saved to file and submitted to the root CA. The response from the root CA must also be imported into the AD CS installation wizard. If a stand-alone root CA is online, the certificate request and response can be obtained over the network. If the stand-alone root CA is offline, the certificate request and response must be saved to removable storage for transport between the root CA and the subordinate CA.

Configuring Web Enrollment

Certification Authority Web Enrollment is implemented in AD CS as a role service. You can install the role service during initial installation or after installation. When you install Certification Authority Web Enrollment, a number of additional role services and features are required. You are prompted to install these additional features and role services if they are not already installed. These features and role services are required:

- **Web Server (IIS)**   The Web server and management tools are installed. This includes support for ASP pages and .NET extensibility required to run the dynamic Web pages that are part of Certification Authority Web Enrollment.

- **Windows Process Activation Service**   This includes the .NET environment.

After installation, no configuration of the Certification Authority Web Enrollment is required. However, if the virtual directory for accessing the Web enrollment pages is accidentally removed or modified, it can be managed by using Certutil.exe. The command *certutil -vroot* recreates the virtual directories if required. The command *certutil -vroot delete* removes the virtual directories if required. It may be useful to remove and recreate these virtual directories if the default configuration has been modified.

Configuring Certificate Revocation

It is important that public key-enabled applications only accept valid certificates. This ensures that the certificate can be trusted and consequently that the holder of the certificate can be trusted. The following checks are performed on a certificate to ensure validity:

- **Valid date**   A certificate is checked to ensure that the current date is between the valid from and valid to dates.

- **Certificate content and format**   The certificate must be a valid X.509 certificate with all required fields completed.

- **Signature check**   The digital signature of the root CA is used to verify that the certificate has not been modified.

- **Root check**   The certificate must be issued by a trusted root CA.

- **Policy validation and critical extensions**   The application may require that a specific policy be in place. Or an application may reject a certificate with an extension marked as critical that the application does not understand.

In addition to these validation checks, a revocation check can be performed. You revoke a certificate when you want to invalidate it before reaching the end of its validity period. The following are some reasons you may want to revoke a certificate:

- Compromise of the private key of a certificate

- Compromise of the private key of the issuing CA

- Change in business relationship with an external party

- Change in employment status of an employee

- Fraud used to obtain a certificate

Windows Server 2008 supports both CRLs and an Online Responder for verifying the revocation status of a certificate. CRLs are the traditional method used to provide revocation data. The Online Responder is new in Windows Server 2008.

CRL Configuration

A CRL is a list of revoked certificates that a public key-enabled application can use to verify that a certificate is valid. There are two types of CRLs: a base CRL and a delta CRL. The *base CRL* is a list of all certificates revoked as of a specific time. The *delta CRL* lists all certificates revoked since the last base CRL. The base CRL and delta CRL are combined to provide the entire list of revoked certificates. By default, a base CRL is published once per week and a delta CRL is published once per day. You can modify this schedule to suit unique organizational needs by using the Certification Authority MMC snap-in to view the properties of the Revoked Certificates folder, as shown in Figure 17-5.

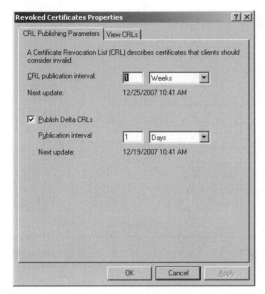

Figure 17-5   CRL publishing parameters.

The purpose of using a delta CRL is to reduce the network traffic associated with downloading CRLs to client computers. When a CA has been operating for some time, the base CRL may become quite large. Downloaded delta CRLs will be much smaller by comparison, much as a differential backup is smaller than a full backup.

> **Note**   Windows 2000 clients are not capable of using delta CRLs and use only the base CRL. If you have Windows 2000 clients on your network, you should ensure that the base CRL is updated often enough to support those clients.

By default, CRLs for stand-alone CAs are available only through the Certification Authority Web Enrollment pages at *http://server/certsrv/*. However, you can define an LDAP Path for the CRL and manually publish the CRL to Active Directory using CertUtil. You can also make it available through HTTP at an alternate location if it is an offline CA. The CRLs published by enterprise CAs are available through the Certificate Authority Web Enrollment pages and Active Directory, as shown in Figure 17-6.

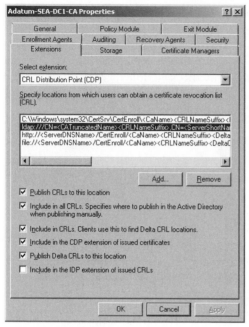

Figure 17-6   CRL configuration.

Direct from the Source: How to Determine If the CRL Is Cached Locally on a System

Sometimes we are asked how to verify that the latest CRL has been downloaded on the local systems. It is important to understand that there are always at least two different CRL caches. The SYSTEM has a CRL cache and the currently logged-on user has a CRL cache. When you attempt to determine if the CRL has been cached, it is important to understand this.

If the application is running in the user's context, it can look at the User CRL cache and the SYSTEM (*Local Computer*) CRL cache. However, if the application is running under the systems context, then it can look only at the SYSTEM CRL cache.

There are two different ways to determine this information:

- Use CertUtil -URLCache CRL
- Use the Certificates snap-in

To verify the CRL download by using the Certificates Snap-in, perform the following steps:

1. Add the proper store to the MMC snap-in and then add the proper store at the top node, such as the *Certificates (Local Computer)* node.

2. Right-click the *Certificates (Local Computer)* node, select View, and then click Options.

3. Click to select the Physical Certificate Stores check box.

If you are looking for the CRL for the root CA, then look in the following location: Certificates (*Local Computer*)\Trusted Root Certification Authorities\Registry\Certificate Revocation List. Note that this location is visible only because you chose to show Physical Certificate Stores. Also, this is the location where you would import the CRL via the GUI.

If you are looking for the CRL for an intermediate CA (Subordinate or Issuing CA), then look in the following location: Certificates (*Local Computer*)\Intermediate Certification Authorities\Registry\Certificate Revocation List. Note that this location is visible only because you chose to show Physical Certificate Stores. Also, this is the location where you would import the CRL via the GUI.

Note that you need to look in different stores depending on what the CRL is for.

Rob Greene

Support Escalation Engineer

Commercial Technical Support–Platforms

Direct from the Source: How to Import a CRL to a Local Machine

If you are in a situation in which certain systems do not have direct access to the CRL locations, you can manually add or script the CRLs into a local system.

To add the CRL to the certificate store for the local computer account, you will need to run one of the following commands:

- **Root CA CRL**   If this is a CRL for a root CA, type the following:

  CertUtil -AddStore ROOT <Root CA CRL Filename>

- **Intermediate, Subordinate, and Issuing CA CRL**   If this is a CRL for an Intermediate CA type the following:

  CertUtil -AddStore CA <Intermediate CA CRL Filename>

These two commands will add the CRL to the local computer's CRL cache and not the user's CRL cache.

Another method of publishing a CRL would be to publish the CRL to Active Directory. Then when Group Policy Refresh occurs, the new CRLs would be added to the appropriate store. To do this, type the following command:

CertUtil -f -DSPublish <CRL Filename> <DSConfigPath>

Rob Greene

Support Escalation Engineer

Commercial Technical Support–Platforms

Online Responder Configuration

An *Online Responder* is a server that supports using OCSP for checking the revocation status of certificates. OCSP is an alternative to CRLs. OCSP does not require periodic downloading of a CRL. Clients send a query to obtain the validity of a specific certificate instead. This can significantly reduce the network traffic associated with traditional downloading of complete CRLs. This also allows up-to-the-moment status information to be used by clients. However, if many repetitive queries are performed, then OSCP may increase overall network usage when compared with CRLs that are cached locally.

Note   Windows Server 2008 and Windows Vista are the only Windows operating systems to include an OSCP client that can verify certificate status by checking an online responder.

This is the process for checking certificate validity with an Online Responder:

1. Local memory and disk caches are searched for a previous cached OCSP response that is still valid.

2. If no cached OCSP response is found, then the client sends an HTTP GET request. If the GET method is not supported by the Online Responder, then the client will retry with an HTTP POST request.

3. The Online Responder searches the local cache and CRL to check the status of the certificate being verified and sends a digitally signed response.

4. When the response is received, the client then verifies the signature on the response to ensure that it is valid.

Installing an Online Responder   To configure a Windows Server 2008 CA as an Online Responder, you install the Online Certificate Status Protocol role service for the AD CS role. If not already installed, you will be prompted to install the Web Server (IIS) and Windows Process Activation Service that are also required by the Certification Authority Web Enrollment role service. There are no configuration options when installing the Online Certificate Status Protocol role service.

The installation process for the Online Certificate Status Protocol role service creates the OSCP virtual directory in IIS. You can use the *certutil -vocsproot* command to recreate this virtual directory if necessary. You can also use the *certutil -vocsproot -delete* command to delete this virtual directory.

Configuring CAs   After installation, you need to configure the Authority Information Access (AIA) extension of the CAs issuing certificates to include the URL for the Online Responder. OSCP clients use this URL for verifying the status of certificates. This is done by using the Certification Authority MMC snap-in to access the Extensions tab in the Properties of a CA. The URL you need to add is *http://servername/ocsp*. For this new entry, you should also select the Include In The AIA Extension Of Issued Certificates and Include In The Online Certificate Status Protocol (OCSP) Extension check boxes. Only certificates issued after this configuration is performed can be verified by using OCSP.

Configuring an OCSP Response Signing Certificate   When responses from an Online Responder are signed, they can be signed with the CA certificate of the Online Responder or by using a delegated signing key. Using the CA certificate requires no additional configuration. Using a delegated signing key requires you to enroll for an OCSP Response Signing certificate. A delegated signing key has the following characteristics:

- **A shorter validity period than a CA certificate**   A validity period of two weeks is recommended. This is done to reduce the risks associated with a compromised key.

- **Includes the id-pkix-ocsp-nocheck extension**   This prevents clients from verifying the revocation status of the Online Responder's certificate to increase overall performance by reducing network traffic. When this extension is included, it is important to keep the validity period of the certificate short.

- **Does not include CRL distribution point and AIA extensions**   These are not required, because revocation status is not verified.

- **Includes the id-kp-PCSPSigning enhanced key usage**   This indicates to OCSP clients that the response is signed by using a delegated signing key rather than a CA key.

In Windows Server 2008, enterprise CAs include an OCSP Response Signing certificate template. This template can be assigned to the CA with no further configuration required other than the necessary security permissions to allow enrollment or autoenrollment. A stand-alone CA is unable to use the OCSP Response Signing certificate template, and you must use Certreq.exe in combination with a customized INF file to create an OCSP Response Signing certificate.

> **More Info** For the detailed steps on how to obtain an OCSP Response Signing certificate from a stand-alone CA, see the section titled "Enrolling for an OCSP Response Signing Certificate Against a Stand-Alone CA" in *Installing, Configuring, and Troubleshooting the Microsoft Online Responder* at *http://technet2.microsoft.com/windowsserver2008/en/library/ 045d2a97-1bff-43bd-8dea-f2df7e270e1f1033.mspx*.

Configuring Revocation Information You must configure revocation information for an Online Responder. This configures an Online Responder to respond to OCSP requests for certificates issued by a specific CA. Multiple revocation configurations can be configured for the Online Responder to support multiple CAs. You use the Online Responder Management MMC snap-in to create a revocation configuration. When creating the revocation configuration, you identify the CA by selecting the CA certificate from Active Directory, the local certificate store, or a file.

Next, you select the signing certificate for OCSP responses, as shown in Figure 17-7. Automatically Select A Signing Certificate allows the wizard to select an appropriate certificate from the local certificate store or autoenroll to obtain an OCSP signing certificate. Manually Select A Signing Certificate prevents the wizard from assigning a certificate. You must manually assign a certificate after the wizard is complete. When Use The CA Certificate For The Revocation Configuration is selected, requests are signed with the CA certificate rather than an OCSP signing certificate. This option can only be selected if the Online Responder is running on the CA.

> **Note** Autoenrollment for computers must be enabled to allow the Online Responder to autoenroll for the OCSP signing certificate. This is not enabled by default. See the section "Configuring Certificate Autoenrollment" for more information.

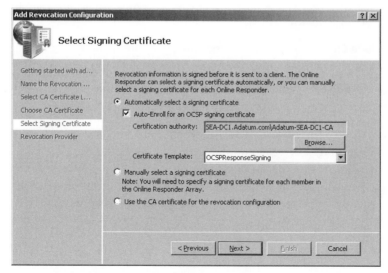

Figure 17-7 Selecting the signing certificate.

Online Responder Arrays   When Online Responders are used to provide revocation status for certificates, it is critical that they are available all of the time. This is critical because Online Responders are providing current status information. If they cannot be reached, then revocation status cannot be determined and public key-aware applications may fail. CRLs are cached locally, so availability is less of a concern.

To provide fault tolerance for Online Responders, they can be configured in an array that synchronizes configuration information between the members. This simplifies the configuration of the Online Responders. To be fault-tolerant, CAs must be configured with the URL for all Online Responders in the array. Requests are not automatically distributed among members in the array.

Managing Key Archival and Recovery

Key archival and recovery is the process used to archive and recover private keys. Windows stores user private keys in the user profile. If this profile is lost for any reason, the private key is lost along with it. If the key has been archived, then it can be recovered to a profile on the same or a different computer without loss of functionality. For example, if the profile on a workstation is deleted, the key can be recovered to a new profile and then all encrypted data can be accessed.

When certificates are issued, you can select an option to prevent private key export. This prevents anyone from exporting private key and using it in a new location. This is typically done for sensitive certificates such as CA certificates where the risk of the key being accessed and used from an alternate location would result in a high cost. However, you must also balance out the risk of a key being lost with no method to recover it and the associated cost. For example, without an archived key, you may not be able to recover encrypted data.

Manual Key Archival

If the certificate is configured to support private key export, individual users can export their certificates and private keys to a file by using the Certificates MMC snap-in. During export, a password is entered to encrypt the file to prevent unauthorized users from importing the file. The encrypted file can then be placed on removable storage until needed. When needed, the key can be imported by using the Certificates MMC snap-in. Here are some recommendations for manual key archival:

- When you export a key manually, you should use the strongest available encryption to secure it.

- Physically secure the removal storage with the encrypted file to add a further layer of security beyond a password.

- If you import a key temporarily for a specific purpose, be sure to remove it when you are done.

Manual key archival is suitable when only a few keys need to be archived. In general, large organizations require an automated solution for key archival that can be centrally managed.

Automatic Key Archival

A CA running on Windows Server 2008 is capable of performing key archival for the certificates that it issues. This is also referred to as *key escrow*. Key archival is a feature of Windows Server 2008 Enterprise and Datacenter editions.

Designate Key Recovery Agents   A key recovery agent (KRA) is a user that is capable of recovering keys from the CA after they have been archived. The first step in configuring key archival is the designation of KRAs. There should be a limited number of KRAs in any organization, and each KRA should be approved by your organization.

KRAs are designated by issuing a Key Recovery Agent certificate. A Key Recovery Agent certificate template is included with Windows Server 2008 for this purpose. Configure the Key Recovery Agent certificate template with the necessary permissions for the specific people you want to enroll for the certificate. Then publish the Key Recovery Agent certificate template.

After the certificate template is ready, the designated users can enroll for a Key Recovery Agent certificate by using the Certificates MMC snap-in, CA Enrollment Web pages, or autoenrollment. Autoenrollment is not recommended because some manual intervention is preferred in this highly sensitive process. You cannot download the Key Recovery Agent certificate by using the Certificates MMC snap-in unless autoenrollment is enabled.

Note   When a Key Recovery Agent certificate request is approved, the certificate is added to the local certificate store on the CA and the Active Directory object for the user that requested the certificate.

Enable Key Archival on the CA   To enable key archival on the CA, you add a recovery agent to the CA, as shown in Figure 17-8. After enabling key archival, certificates services must be restarted for the change to take effect. How KRAs are implemented depends on the number of recovery agents you have elected to use and the number of KRA certificate you have configured.

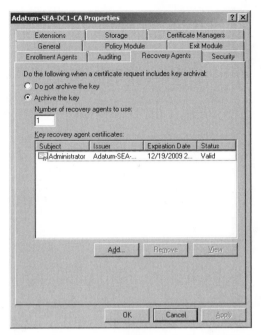

Figure 17-8   Recovery agents for key archival.

If the number of recovery agents selected matches the number of KRA certificates, then all recovery agents are able to recover all keys. If the number of recovery agents is less than the number of KRA certificates, then a round-robin selection method is used to determine which recovery agents can recover which keys. In this case, to recover a key from the database, you must first determine the recovery agents that are capable of recovering the key.

Configure Certificate Templates   The KRA for a private key is configured when a certificate is issued. This is an option that is configured in the certificate template for certificate, as shown in Figure 17-9. The option Archive Subject's Encryption Private Key indicates that the private key for certificates created from this template will be archived. The option Use Advanced Symmetric Algorithm To Send The Key To The CA is new in Windows Server 2008 and forces the client and server to use the AES encryption algorithm to secure the private key.

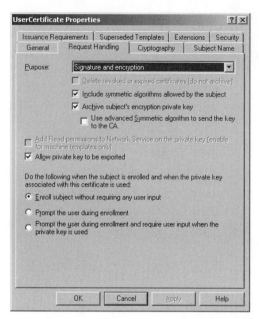

Figure 17-9   Configuring key archival in a certificate template.

> **Note**   The option Allow Private Key To Be Exported must be selected to allow manual key archival to be performed.

Recover an Archived Key   Recovering an archived key is a manual process that may require the cooperation of multiple people depending on the security configuration of AD CS in your organization. If role separation is enforced, then a Certification Manager must work with the KRA to obtain the key. If role separation is not enforced, then any user with the permission to manage the CA can work with the KRA to obtain the key.

The first step in recovery is finding candidate certificates for recovery and extracting the recovery Binary Large Object (BLOB). You can find the certificate you want to recover by using the Certification Authority MMC snap-in or the Certutil.exe utility. To find candidate certificates for recovery, the Certificate Manager requires the Common Name, User Principal Name, down-level name (domain\logon), certificate serial number, or certificate thumbprint. Use the command *certutil -getkey <searchtext> <filename>* to obtain a list of certificates issued to a user. The *searchtext* can be the user Common Name, User Principal Name, or down-level name. If the user has only a single certificate, then this will extract the BLOB for key recovery to the specified file name.

If there are multiple certificates for a user, then use the certificate serial number or certificate thumbprint as the search text for the *certutil* command to extract the recovery BLOB. Both the certificate serial number and certificate thumbprint uniquely identify the certificate.

The recovery BLOB is the certificate in PKCS #7 format. The contents are encrypted and include the public key. Next, the KRA can extract the private key from the recovery BLOB. The output of the *certutil -getkey* command identifies the KRAs for a certificate if required.

To recover the private key from the recovery BLOB, the KRA uses the command *certutil -recoverkey <filename> <output.pfx>*. The *filename* is the recovery BLOB previously created. The *output.pfx* is a generic file name that can be used for the output of the private key recovery. The output file is in PKCS #12 format and should have the .pfx extension. You will be prompted for a password to secure the output file during creation. Also be aware that the KRA certificate must be in the local certificate store where the recovery is being performed, or the recovery will fail.

> **Note**   If the KRA certificate was created using a new CryptoAPI Next Generation (CNG) algorithm, then that algorithm must be specified during recovery with the option *-csp "CryptographicStorageProvider."*

Import the Recovered Key   After the private key has been recovered to file, the user can import it into the user profile. The user can do this by using the Certificates MMC snap-in or Certutil. The command when using Certutil is *certutil -importPFX <output.pfx>*. After import, the private key is recovered to the user's certificate store and the user can use the certificate again.

Managing Certificates in AD CS

AD CS includes several features to help you manage certificates. Certificate templates are used to define certificate settings that can be used by many clients during certificate creation. Certificate autoenrollment can automate the entire certificate enrollment process so that no end user or administrator intervention is required. Group Policy settings can be used to manage how certificates are accepted by clients. And finally, credential roaming can be used to support certificates when users roam between workstations.

Configuring Certificate Templates

Certificate templates are used in the creation of certificates on enterprise CAs. The settings in a certificate template are incorporated into the certificates issued by the CA. In addition, security settings on a certificate template define which users or computers are allowed to enroll for that particular certificate type.

Windows Server 2008 supports three versions of certificate templates. Version 1 templates are the only templates available in Windows Server 2008 Standard edition. You can modify the security configuration of version 1 templates to control manual certificate enrollment, but you cannot modify other template settings and certificate autoenrollment is not possible. If you are using Windows Server 2008 Enterprise or Datacenter edition, then version 2 and version 3 templates are available.

Version 2 certificate templates allow you to modify certificate templates to suit your organization and allow for certificate autoenrollment. Version 3 templates are new in Windows Server 2008 and include the ability to specify additional cryptographic settings that are only supported by a Windows Server 2008 CA. If you want to modify the settings of a version 1 certificate template, you can create a version 2 or version 3 certificate template by copying a version 1 certificate template. Alternatively, you can create an entirely new certificate template.

> **Note**   Windows Server 2008 includes many certificate templates for various purposes. You can read the description of each and view the details of each by using the Certificate Templates MMC snap-in.

Direct from the Source: Version 3 Templates

From the introduction of PKI with Windows Server 2000, certificate templates have provided an easy solution for automatically enrolling certificates for both users and computers. The original templates that shipped with Windows Server 2000 were called version 1 (v1) templates. These templates could not be modified or customized to suit the unique needs of an environment. When Windows Server 2003 came out, the templates were upgraded to version 2 (v2) templates. If a certificate authority was installed on an Enterprise edition of Windows, these templates could be customized to the desired settings and needs. Windows Server 2008 introduces version 3 (v3) templates, which are even more flexible than previous versions.

The version 3 templates now support the use of CNG (Cryptography API: Next Generation) Suite-B cryptographic algorithms. This new technology enhances the security features of cryptography and increases the overall functionality by enabling the use of the new algorithms through a Key Service Provider or KSP. Currently only Windows Vista and Windows Server 2008 support the new asymmetric algorithms, which include:

- Elliptic-Curve Digital Signature Algorithm (ECDSA) P256, P384, P521
- Elliptic-Curve Diffie-Hellman (ECDH) P256, P384, P521
- RSA
- AES

The hash algorithms included are MD2, MD4, MD5, SHA1, SHA256, SHA384, and SHA512. With the implementation of version 3 templates and the CNG technologies, the KSP is capable of extensive auditing that was not previously available. The KSP now audits key imports and exports, secret key validation failures, failures in encryption, and key-pair generation failures, to name a few. Additional auditing is possible by running the following command:

```
Auditpol /set /subcategory:"other system events" /success:enable /failure:enable
```

> For more information about version 3 templates, CNG features, and Suite B cryptography, read the information at the following Web sites:
>
> ■ *http://msdn2.microsoft.com/en-us/library/ms683902(VS.85).aspx*
>
> ■ *http://msdn2.microsoft.com/en-us/library/bb204775(VS.85).aspx*
>
> ■ *http://www.nsa.gov/ia/industry/crypto_suite_b.cfm?MenuID=10.2.7*
>
> *Bob Drake*
>
> *Microsoft Directory Services Team*

Configure Certificate Template Security

The permissions configured for certificate templates, shown in Figure 17-10, determine which users are able to modify, view, and create certificates based on certificate templates. These permissions are available to be assigned:

■ **Full Control**   The user or group can modify all template attributes, including permissions.

■ **Read**   The user or group can find the certificate when attempting to enroll.

■ **Write**   The user or group can modify all template attributes, except permissions.

■ **Enroll**   The user or group can enroll for a certificate based on the template. Read permission must also be assigned.

■ **Autoenroll**   The user or group can automatically receive a certificate based on this template through autoenrollment. Read and Enroll permissions must also be assigned.

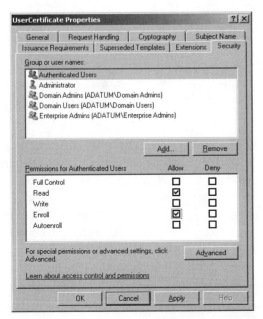

Figure 17-10   Certificate template permissions.

When assigning permissions in a multidomain environment, use global and universal groups rather domain local groups. When permissions are assigned to domain local groups, CAs in other domains will not be able to utilize those permissions.

Deploy Certificate Templates

Certificate templates are stored in Active Directory and replicated to all domain controllers in the Active Directory forest. The time required to replicate certificate templates will vary depending on your environment. Allow sufficient time for new certificate templates to replicate before configuring CAs to use the new template.

Certificate templates are published on a CA to make them available for enrollment. This is done in the Certificate Templates node of the Certificate Authority MMC snap-in. In general, you should publish a certificate template to at least two CAs in the forest to ensure at least one is available at all times. In organizations with multiple physical locations, you should consider publishing a certificate template on a CA at each physical location.

Update Certificate Templates

There is no method for modifying existing certificates. When you want to change the settings on a certificate for users, you must first update the certificate template used to create the certificates and then reissue certificates to the users. When you update a certificate template, you can modify an existing certificate template or create a new certificate template that supercedes the existing certificate template. Updating certificate templates does not affect certificates that are already issued.

In general, you modify an existing certificate template when only minor changes are required. You can do this only if the certificate template is version 2 or version 3. Updating security permissions does not require you to reissue certificates because it does not affect the contents of the certificates. When changes affect the contents of the certificates, they must be reissued.

Superceding a certificate template allows you to create an entirely new certificate template to replace one or more existing certificate templates. A new certificate template is configured with the templates it is superceding, as shown in Figure 17-11. Certificates must be reissued for the new settings to take effect.

Reissuing certificates is done when certificates are renewed. The renewal period for a certificate is typically much shorter than the certificate lifetime to allow these types of changes to be made automatically. You can also force certificate holders to reenroll before the renewal period is up by using the Certificate Templates snap-in. Right-click the existing certificate and select *Reenroll All Certificate Holders*. Existing user certificates will be updated the next time the client verifies the contents of the certificate against the template. Forcing reenrollment can only be done for version 2 and version 3 certificate templates.

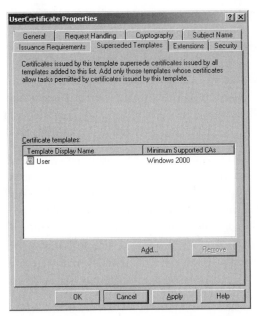

Figure 17-11   Superseded Templates tab.

Certificate Validity for Stand-alone CAs

For enterprise CAs, the validity period for a certificate is defined in the certificate template. The default validity period for certificates issued by a stand-alone CA is one year. To increase the validity period of a stand-alone CA, you can edit the registry by using the following steps:

1.   Open RegEdit.

2.   Locate the following registry key:

HKEY_LOCAL_MACHINE\System\CurrentControlSet\Services\CertSvc\ Configuration\<CAName>\

3.   Edit the *ValidityPeriod* key and enter one of these: days, weeks, months, or years.

4.   Edit the *ValidityPeriodUnits* key and enter a numeric value matching the number of days, weeks, months, or years that the certificates should be valid for.

5.   Restart Active Directory Certificate Services.

Note   You can also use Certutil.exe to modify the validity period, as described in "Certutil Tasks for Configuring a Certificate Authority (CA)" at *http://technet2.microsoft.com/ windowsserver/en/library/0133c888-9277-4f3e-beed-0e73bcdf5b381033.mspx?mfr=true*.

Configuring Certificate Autoenrollment

When a large number of certificates are being issued in your organization, the management process can be overwhelming and expensive. A Windows-based PKI solution solves this problem with autoenrollment. Autoenrollment allows a Windows CA to issue certificates without any administrator or user intervention. This simplifies the process of issuing certificates for EFS, smart cards, or e-mail, and also reduces costs. Autoenrollment applies on to version 2 and 3 certificate templates.

Version 1 certificate templates can be used to generate certificates automatically for computers through Automatic Certificate Request Service (ACRS). When ACRS is used, a version 1 certificate template is configured in a Group Policy object (GPO). There are no certificate templates settings that apply. The GPO settings apply only to computer accounts, not user accounts. You must link the GPO with the domain, site, or OU with the computers you want to receive the certificate. The Group Policy setting to configure is Computer Configuration\ Policies\Windows Settings\Security Settings\Public Key Policies\Automatic Certificate Request Settings.

By contrast, Autoenrollment is configured as a combination GPO settings and settings within the certificate template. A GPO setting is used to enable autoenrollment, and then security on the certificate templates determines which certificates are obtained. The GPO settings for version 2 or 3 certificate templates can be used to autoenroll certificates for both user and computer accounts. You must link the GPO to the domain, site, or OU with the computers you want to receive the certificate. The Group Policy setting to configure is *<Computer or User>* Configuration\Policies\Windows Settings\Security Settings\Public Key Policies\Certificate Services Client – Auto-Enrollment, as shown in Figure 17-12.

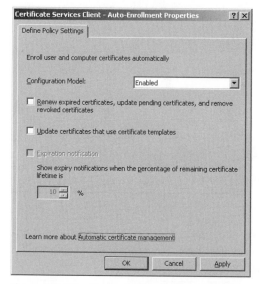

Figure 17-12   Group Policy settings for autoenrollment

The Configuration Model options for the GPO can be enabled, disabled, or not configured. Enabled turns on autoenrollment for the affected clients. The Renew Expired Certificates, Update Pending Certificates, And Remove Revoked Certificates option allows autoenrollment for renewals and pending certificates, and also automatically removes revoked certificates. The Update Certificates That Use Certificate Templates option allows autoenrollment to update certificates when an existing certificate template is superceded. You can also configure the Expiration Notification that indicates to users when their certificates are going to expire.

Within version 2 or 3 certificate templates, you can configure settings that impact autoenrollment. On the Request Handling tab, previously shown in Figure 17-9, you can determine the level of user input that is required during autoenrollment. The Enroll Subject Without Requiring Any User Input option is required when issuing certificates to computers and service accounts. It is preferred in most cases when issuing certificates to users, because it will allow the certificate to be created automatically in the background without any user intervention. The Prompt The User During Enrollment option forces users to interact with the enrollment process. The Prompt The User During Enrollment And Require User Input When The Private Key Is Used option has the user enter a password during enrollment, and the password is required each time that the user utilizes the private key associated with the certificate. This additional security ensures that the private key can be utilized only by the user and only at the expected times.

The Issuance Requirements tab of the certificate template, shown in Figure 17-13, defines whether enrollment requests are approved automatically or whether intervention is required. The option CA Certificate Manager Approval requires enrollment requests for this template to be approved by a CA manager before the certificate is issued. The option This Number Of Authorized Signatures requires requestors to sign the enrollment request with a digital signature containing the same issuance and application policies that are defined for this certificate template. If more than one signature is required, then autoenrollment is disabled for the certificate template. The option to require a Valid Existing Certificate rather than the Same Criteria For Enrollment allows users to renew their certificate without intervention by a CA manager or requiring authorized signatures.

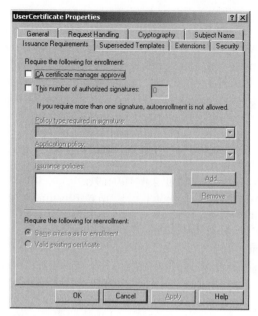

Figure 17-13   Issuance Requirements tab of a certificate template.

Managing Certificate Acceptance with Group Policy

You can use Group Policy to automatically distribute trusted root certification authorities to client computers. This is the best way to ensure that clients trust certificates from a CA that is not automatically included with the Windows client. The GPO setting to distribute trusted root certification authorities is Computer Configuration\Policies\Windows Settings\Security Settings\Public Key Policies\Trusted Root Certification Authorities. Windows Server 2008 introduces a number of other GPO settings that can be useful for managing certificate acceptance. For example, Windows Server 2008 adds a new setting to distribute trusted publishers that are used to verify software that is being installed and executed. The setting for trusted publishers is Computer Configuration\Policies\Windows Settings\Security Settings\Public Key Policies\Trusted Publishers.

Internally, you can control the revocation of certificates that are no longer trusted. A list of revoked certificates can be distributed through a CRL or OCSP. Windows Server 2008 includes a GPO setting for Untrusted Certificates. These are certificates from external CAs that you cannot revoke, but want to indicate are untrusted. The GPO setting is Computer Configuration\Policies\Windows Settings\Security Settings\Public Key Policies\Untrusted Certificates.

Many options for managing validation have also been added in the Computer Configuration\Policies\Windows Settings\Security Settings\Public Key Policies\Certification Path Validation Settings setting. The Stores tab can be used to restrict the ability of users to add trusted root CAs to their computers. The Trusted Publishers tab can be used to control whether users, administrators, or only enterprise administrators can modify the list of trusted publishers for software. The Network Retrieval tab can be used to configure timeout values that are used when performing OCSP requests. The Revocation tab can be used to configure how long OSCP and CRLs remain valid.

Configuring Credential Roaming

In some environments like telemarketing firms, users frequently roam from computer to computer. Because certificates are stored in the profiles on each computer, this makes certificates difficult to use in such an environment. One solution is *roaming user profiles*, where user profiles are uploaded to a network location on each logout and downloaded during login. However, roaming profiles contain a lot of data in addition to the certificate store and may create long logon times.

Credential roaming is a system that allows user certificates and their private keys to move from one computer to another without using roaming profiles. The first time the user logs on, the user certificates in the local certificate store are published to their user account in Active Directory. If there are published certificates in Active Directory that are newer than the local certificates, the local certificate store is updated with the certificates from Active Directory. From this point on, any new certificates issued to the user are published to Active Directory from the local store. When the user logs on to another computer, the certificates from Active Directory are synchronized to the local certificate store for use. Credential roaming is triggered each time a certificate is changed in the local certificate store, when the computer is locked or unlocked, and when Group Policy is refreshed.

> **Note**   Credential roaming and roaming user profiles should not be used at the same time.

> **Note**   To use credential roaming, a client must be Windows XP SP2, Windows Server 2003 SP1, Windows Vista, or Windows Server 2008.

The GPO setting to control credential roaming is User Configuration\Policies\Windows Settings\Security Settings\Public Key Policies\Certificate Services Client – Credential Roaming, as shown in Figure 17-14. The Maximum Tombstone Credentials Lifetime In Days option determines how long a certificate remains in Active Directory after it has been deleted from the local certificate store. The Maximum Number Of Credentials Per User option limits the number of certificates that can be roamed. The Maximum Size (In Bytes) Of A Roaming Credential option limits the maximum size of a certificate and private key that are roamed. The Roam Stored User Names And Passwords option is new in Windows Server 2008 and allows locally stored user names and passwords for resources such as Web sites to be roamed. However, user names and passwords can only be roamed between Windows Vista computers.

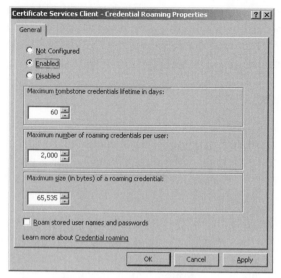

Figure 17-14 Certificate Services Client – Credential Roaming GPO setting.

Designing an AD CS Implementation

The design of AD CS should be carefully planned before implementation. If changes are made to the design after implementation, the alterations could require many certificates to be reissued. Part of the design process is determining the CA hierarchy that will be used. You must also determine the certificate templates that will be used to support enrollment. Finally, you must plan how certificate distribution and revocation will be performed.

Designing a CA Hierarchy

The *CA hierarchy* is the organization of CAs within your organization. The design of your CA hierarchy determines how certificates will be issued and managed by your organizations. Before designing your CA hierarchy, you must determine exactly how PKI will be used in your organization.

Prepare to Design a CA Hierarchy

Before you can design a CA hierarchy, you must determine the project scope, applications in use, technical requirements, and business requirements. When determining the scope, the design can be for the overall hierarchy or just a portion of the hierarchy. Which scope is selected will be based on how PKI is managed in your organization and whether or not PKI is already implemented in your organization. For example, an organization with an existing PKI may need to design only additional infrastructure. An organization without an existing PKI needs to design the entire infrastructure from the ground up.

The applications you use PKI for will help determine how PKI is implemented. For example, it is likely that user certificates will be distributed by autoenrollment to streamline the process. However, certificates issued to Web servers are likely to be done manually. You may implement the Network Device Enrollment Service to support the implementation of 802.1X for authentication of network devices.

The technical requirements include those related to security and administration. The CA design must adhere to any security policies that are in place for your organization. This may include hardware storage modules for enhanced security. You must also determine who will manage the CA infrastructure. Centralizing administration may not be practical for large organizations. Large organizations will likely delegate at least some CA management tasks to local administrators.

The business requirements include availability and legal requirements. Business needs will dictate the level of fault tolerance that is required for CAs. For example, if your PKI supports applications running 24 hours per day and 7 days per week, then fault tolerance will be important. This may require multiple CAs in some locations. However, if certificates are only issued occasionally in your organization, then a single CA may be sufficient. Legal requirements will vary depending on whether or not you support external users and which applications are in use. Each organization should independently determine its legal obligations.

Hierarchy Types

When your deployment is entirely internal, then you will use a root CA hierarchy, as shown in Figure 17-15. All CAs are trusted back to a common root CA. By creating a hierarchy, you can allocate specific roles to the various CAs. For example, the issuing CAs at the lowest level of the hierarchy can be specialized for specific types of certificates or by geographic location. The higher-level CAs can be offline as required for security.

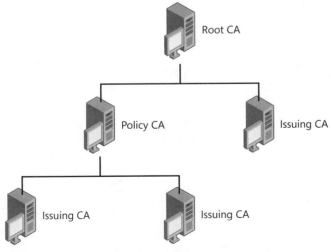

Figure 17-15   Root CA hierarchy.

Within a root hierarchy, large organizations often implement three tiers. The first tier is the root CA. The second tier is policy CAs. A *policy CA* defines rules to which its subordinate CAs must adhere. This can be used to define policies that affect all subordinate CAs for a physical region or organizational division. Finally, the third level is issuing CAs that issue certificates to users, computers, and devices.

In many cases, two organizations will already have existing PKI infrastructures that need to be integrated. In this case you will use a cross-certification hierarchy, as shown in Figure 17-16. A CA in the first organization issues a subordinate CA certificate to a CA in the second organization. A CA in the second organization also issues a subordinate CA certificate to the CA in the first organization. In this way, certificates issued by either organization are trusted by both organizations. The main drawback to this configuration is the complete trust of the other organization that is required.

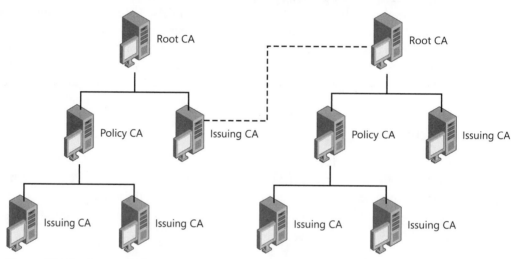

Figure 17-16   Cross-certification CA hierarchy.

CA Hierarchy Roles

A typical CA hierarchy has three levels. This number of levels is optimal for allowing flexibility in application. Moving beyond three levels offers little additional flexibility and results in unnecessary complexity.

The first level is the root CA. The root CA issues its own certificate and authorizes the policy CAs. If the root CA is compromised, then all certificates issued by the entire hierarchy are compromised.

The second level is policy CAs. A policy CA enforces the policies and procedures for issuing certificates. The role of a policy CA is to authorize issuing CAs. Multiple policy CAs are required only when different polices are used for issuing certificates to different user groups. For example, two departments may have varying rules.

The third level is issuing CAs. Issuing CAs are responsible for issuing certificates to clients. An issuing CA must always be online and is typically an enterprise CA to simplify administration. Issuing CAs can be organized by certificate use, location, department, or user type. If a CA is dedicated to issuing certificates for EFS, that would be organization based on certificate use. If a CA is dedicated to issuing certificates for external users, that would be organization based on user type.

The actual number of levels in your CA hierarchy will depend on the needs of your organization. In a very low-security environment with a minimal number of certificates issued, only a single root CA may be used to issue certificates. As security requirements increase and as the number of certificates issued grows, then a second, third, or even fourth layer can be added. When there are multiple levels, the use of an offline root and policy CAs is recommended.

Role Separation for Management

Role separation divides the management roles for Windows-based PKI. It is important to track which roles have been assigned to which users, because they must work together to manage the PKI. If a user has been assigned more than one role, usage of any of the roles will fail. The following roles have been created for management:

- **CA administrator**   This role configures certificate services, including designating certificate managers and renewing certificates.
- **Certificate manager**   This role issues and revokes certificates.
- **Auditor**   This role can review the security event log for events related to certificate services.
- **Backup operator**   This role can backup the CA database, CA configuration, and CA key pair.

Role separation is not enabled by default. To enable role separation, use the command *certutil -setreg ca\RoleSeparationEnabled 1*. Certificate Services must be restarted for this change to take effect.

Designing Certificate Templates

Designing certificate templates is a matter of selecting the options in the certificate templates that best meet your organizational needs. Even though the options you select will be specific to your organization, there are some broad recommendations for certain settings.

Validity and Renewal Periods

A certificate can be used until the end of its validity period unless it is revoked. It is important to match the validity period with the use of the certificate. For example, the validity period of a CA certificate is typically long, because a CA can only issue certificates with a validity period ending at or before the validity periods of its own CA certificate. Certificates used for authentication typically have a shorter validity period of one year or less to avoid revocation when possible.

The renewal period for a certificate determines how long before the end of the certificates validity period the client will attempt to renew the certificate. Renewing before the end of the validity period ensures that a minor interruption in CA service will not prevent certificates from being renewed. If the renewal period is more than 20 percent of the total certificate validity period, the certificate will not be renewed until 80 percent of the validity period has passed.

Certificate Purpose

When defining the certificate purpose in a certificate template, the key is to accurately determine exactly what you want the certificate to be used for. In part, this will depend on how you want to control user activity.

One method is to identify all purposes that may be required by your users and then issue a generic user certificate that supports all of those purposes. However, in such a case, all users will be able to use the certificate for all purposes, and you lose the ability to restrict which applications groups of users can use.

The alternative is to create specialized certificate templates for specific purposes and then grant permission to those certificate templates only for groups of users that you want to authorize to use specific applications. This is more secure and provides more control. However, this also requires additional administrative overhead to maintain the various templates.

The purpose of a certificate is defined on the Extensions tab of a certificate template. There are two extensions that can be used to define the certificate purpose: Application Policies and Extended Key Usage (EKU). Application Policies are Microsoft-specific, whereas EKU is used by third-party CAs. If both are part of a certificate template, they should be configured with exactly the same settings.

Subject Name Requirements

The subject of a certificate is the user or computer that is requesting the certificate. You can determine how the subject name for a certificate is derived, as shown in Figure 17-17. In most cases, the subject name will be built from Active Directory. This is required to support autoenrollment. The subject name format can be based on either the fully distinguished name or the common name of the requestor. Using the fully distinguished name guarantees that the subject name is unique.

If a computer or user account does not have some of the information that is required, then issuance of the certificate will fail. For example, if the e-mail address is part of a subject name, then a missing e-mail address in the user object will prevent the certificate from being issued. This error will appear in the Certification Authority MMC snap-in in the Failed Requests Node.

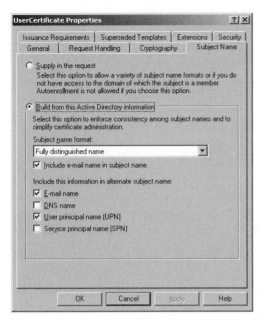

Figure 17-17   Subject Name settings in a certificate template.

If you select the Supply In The Request option, then users will be prompted for the subject name during enrollment. This option requires that users understand the certificate enrollment process and select an appropriate name. In most cases, this option should not be used and it cannot be used with autoenrollment.

Issuance Policies

Issuance policies are identifiers included in a certificate that describe to what level the certificate is trusted by your organization. The application of issuance policies is not technically enforced; it relies on your organization implementing the appropriate level of security when the certificate is issued. Windows Server 2008 includes the following issuance policies and allows for the creation of custom issuance policies: All issuance policies, European Qualified Candidate, High Assurance, Medium Assurance, Low Assurance, and Secure Signature Creation Device Qualified Candidate.

Issuance Security

You can raise issuance security by requiring certificate manager approval or by signing requests. Requiring certificate manager approval forces a certificate manager to manually validate all requests by approving them. This provides the certificate manager with the opportunity to perform additional identity checks. Signing requests validate the identity of the certificate requestor.

Designing Certificate Distribution and Revocation

Certificate distribution and revocation procedures will be based on the specific needs of your organization. Certificate distribution must allow users to enroll for necessary certificates with a minimum of effort. Certificate revocation must provide current information without overwhelming network resources.

Certificate Distribution

Certificate distribution determines how clients will obtain certificates. This includes the type of enrollment and interface for enrollment. Whenever possible, you should use auto-enrollment for issuing large numbers of certificates. This significantly reduces administrative burdens and user frustration. However, this is only possible when using an enterprise CA for clients that are part of Active Directory.

The Certificates MMC snap-in is useful for obtaining certificates from an enterprise CA. It reads the available certificate templates from Active Directory and presents only options that are available for the user that certificates are being obtained for. This is also only available for clients that are part of Active Directory.

The CA Web Enrollment pages are required when a requestor is not part of Active Directory or when a stand-alone CA is issuing the certificates. The CA Web Enrollment pages are also required for some special cases such as enrollment and retrieval of KRA certificates.

Certificate Revocation

Windows Server 2008 includes both CRLs and OCSP for checking revocation status of certificates. CRL distribution is automatic for Active Directory clients. Clients that are not a part of Active Directory can download the CRL from the CA Web Enrollment pages. However, it is unlikely that client will complete such a manual process. OCSP can be used for clients that are part of Active Directory and those that are not.

In general, OCSP has better network performance when certificate checks are infrequent. CRLs result in less network traffic when there are many certificate checks because the CRLs are cached locally.

Summary

AD CS is the Microsoft implementation of a certification authority. It includes management tools such as Enterprise PKI and the Certification Authority snap-in. A CA can be an enterprise CA or stand-alone. An enterprise CA integrates with Active Directory and can use certificate templates for autoenrollment. The first CA installed is a root CA. Additional CAs in the same hierarchy are subordinate CAs.

You can configure Web Enrollment to allow users to obtain certificates through a Web page. A CRL is used by clients to verify the validity of a certificate. You can also configure an online responder to provide certificate status information. Key archival can be implemented to automatically archive private keys for certificates issued by a Windows Server 2008 CA.

Certificate templates are used to determine which certificate types a user or computer can obtain. They are also used as part of certificate autoenrollment. The certificate templates available to users are controlled by permissions assigned to the certificate templates. Credential roaming allows certificates to move with users from computer to computer and avoid the need for roaming user profiles.

Best Practices

- Verify that an external CA is automatically trusted by clients before purchasing a certificate issued by that CA.

- Use an internal CA for internal applications where it is easy to configure clients to trust the internal CA.

- Use an offline root CA to increase security.

- Use an enterprise CA for issuing certificates to allow for autoenrollment.

- Use autoenrollment to issue large numbers of certificates to users or computers.

- Use key archival and recovery to allow for the recovery of lost private keys.

- Use an Online Responder to allow immediate verification of certificate status.

- Use CRL distribution to support Windows 2000, Windows XP, and Windows Server 2003 clients.

- Use credential roaming when users move regularly from one computer to another.

- Use multiple layers of CA in the hierarchy to increase security.

Additional Resources

The following resources contain additional information and tools related to this chapter.

Related Information

- The Active Directory Certificate Services Web page is at *http://technet2.microsoft.com/ windowsserver2008/en/servermanager/activedirectorycertificateservices.mspx.*

- For more information about using Wevtutil.exe, see *http://technet2.microsoft.com/ windowsserver2008/en/library/d4c791e0-7e59-45c5-aa55-0223b77a48221033.mspx?mfr=true.*

- For detailed information about X.509 version 3 and PKI, see "RFC 3280: Internet X.509 Public Key Infrastructure Certificate and Certificate Revocation List (CRL) Profile" at *http://www.ietf.org/rfc/rfc3280.txt.*

- For more information on writing cryptographic service providers, see "Writing a CSP" at *http://msdn2.microsoft.com/en-us/library/aa388213(VS.85).aspx.*

- For the detailed steps on how to obtain an OCSP Response Signing certificate from a stand-alone CA, see the section titled "Enrolling for an OCSP Response Signing Certificate Against a Stand-Alone CA" in *Installing, Configuring, and Troubleshooting the Microsoft Online Responder* at *http://technet2.microsoft.com/windowsserver2008/en/library/045d2a97-1bff-43bd-8dea-f2df7e270e1f1033.mspx.*

Related Tools

Windows Server 2008 provides several tools that can be used when managing AD CS. Table 17-2 lists some of these tools and their uses.

Table 17-2   AD CS Management Tools

Tool Name	Description and Use
Certificate Templates snap-in	Use to manage certificate templates
Certificates snap-in	Use to manage certificates issued to users, computers, and services
Certification Authority snap-in	Use to manage Windows CAs
Certreq.exe	Use to create and manage certificate requests from a command line.
Certutil.exe	Use to manage certificates and CAs at a command line
Enterprise PKI snap-in	Use to view the status of all CAs in an organization
Group Policy Management console	Use to modify GPOs and configure computers for autoenrollment or credential roaming
Online Responder snap-in	Use to manage Online Responders for an entire organization
Wevtutil.exe	Use to access event log information from the command line

Chapter 18

Active Directory Rights Management Services

In this chapter:

Most information technology professionals agree that protecting digital information is often a difficult and challenging task. Organizations spend increasing amounts to implement multiple layers of security, such as perimeter firewalls to protect access to the network and encryption and authentication technologies to help secure network communication. Documents are typically protected by using carefully designed security groups and access control lists (ACLs) that specify who can access information and the level of access allowed.

Even with all of these security methods implemented, organizations tend to forget that recipients are still free to do whatever they want with the information they receive. After access is granted, there are often no additional restrictions to control what recipients can do with the data or where it can be sent. Relying on individuals' discretion to determine the manner in which they use and share confidential information can introduce an unacceptable degree of risk into an organization's security model. For example, it is easy for a user to forward a sensitive e-mail message to unintended recipients or misuse a confidential document in an unauthorized manner (such as unauthorized copying, modifying, or printing).

In addition to the mishandling of documents, organizations also have to consider the latest laws related to privacy and information disclosure. Many countries have introduced government legislation that ensures the privacy and protection of personal data, such as identifiable health information or the disclosure of financial information. It is critical that this private information is secure and that even authorized users are limited to being able to perform tasks that ensure that confidentiality requirements are met.

This chapter introduces Active Directory Rights Management Services (AD RMS) as a solution to help protect your organization's digital content. This chapter describes how AD RMS works and how to implement and manage the solution to protect information for users located within internal, external, and inter-organizational locations.

AD RMS Overview

Your organization's overall security strategy must incorporate methods for maintaining security, protection, and validity of company data and information. This includes not only controlling access to the data, but also how the data is used and distributed to both internal and external users. Your strategy may also include methods to ensure that the data is tamper-resistant and that the most current information is valid based on the expiration of outdated or time-sensitive information.

AD RMS enhances your organization's existing security strategy by applying persistent usage policies to digital information. A *usage policy* specifies trusted entities, such as individuals, groups of users, computers, or applications. These entities are only permitted to use the information as specified by the rights and conditions configured within the policy. Rights can include permissions to perform tasks such as read, copy/paste, print, save, forward, and edit. Rights may also be accompanied by conditions, such as when the usage policy expires for a specific entity. Usage policies remain with the protected data at all times to protect information stored within your organization's intranet, as well as information sent externally via e-mail or transported on a mobile device.

> **Note**   Do not confuse Rights Management with Digital Rights Management (DRM). DRM refers to a separate technology used to protect multimedia content, such as music, videos, and e-books, and is not related to AD RMS.

AD RMS Features

An AD RMS solution is typically deployed throughout the organization with the goal of protecting sensitive information from being distributed to unauthorized users. The addition of AD RMS–enabled client applications such as the 2007 Office system or AD RMS–compatible server roles such as Exchange Server 2007 and Microsoft Office SharePoint Server 2007 provides an overall solution for the following uses:

- **Enforcing document rights**   Every organization has documents that can be considered sensitive information. Using AD RMS, you can control who is able to view these sensitive files and prevent readers from accessing selected application functions, such as printing, saving, copying, and pasting. If a group of employees is collaborating on a document and frequently updating it, you can configure and apply a policy that includes an expiration date of document rights for each published draft. This helps to ensure that all involved parties are using only the latest information—the older versions will not open after they expire.

- **Protecting e-mail communication**   Microsoft Office Outlook 2007 can use AD RMS to prevent an e-mail message from being accidentally or intentionally mishandled. When a user applies an AD RMS rights policy template to an e-mail message, numerous tasks can be disabled, such as forwarding the message, copying and pasting content, printing, and exporting the message.

Direct from the Source: Integrating AD RMS and Office SharePoint Server 2007

AD RMS integrates with Microsoft Office SharePoint Server 2007 to give you tight control over business data by imposing access restrictions at the document library level. When a user navigates to a rights-protected document library and attempts to download a document, Office SharePoint Server 2007 binds the permissions configured for the document library to the document. As a result, there's a direct mapping between Office SharePoint Server 2007 and document permissions, translating Office SharePoint Server 2007 roles related to the document into AD RMS permissions on the document itself.

Brian M. Lich

Technical Writer

Windows Server Security

Note   AD RMS works well to protect digital data from misuse. However, it does not protect against attacks such as third-party screen capture programs or use of a digital camera to take a picture of sensitive online information. It is important to treat AD RMS as an additional layer to the overall protection and security of your digital information. Other security measures should still be implemented, such as the configuration of appropriate access control lists (ACLs) and secure desktop management.

Depending on your security requirements, you may have already implemented a number of technologies to secure digital content. Technologies such as Access Control Lists (ACLs), Secure Multipurpose Internet Mail Extensions (S/MIME), or the Encrypted File System (EFS) can all be used to help secure e-mail and company documents. However, AD RMS still provides additional benefits and features in protecting the confidentiality and use of the data stored within the documents. Table 18-1 provides a feature comparison with other common technologies that are typically implemented within a corporate environment.

Table 18-1   AD RMS Feature Comparison

Feature	RMS	ACLs	S/MIME Signing	S/MIME Encryption	EFS
Verifies the identity of the publisher	No	No	Yes	No	No
Differentiates permissions by user	Yes	Yes	No	No	No
Prevents unauthorized viewing	Yes	Yes	No	Yes	Yes
Encrypts protected content	Yes	No	No	Yes	Yes
Offers content expiration	Yes	No	No	No	No

Table 18-1 AD RMS Feature Comparison *(continued)*

Feature	RMS	ACLs	S/MIME Signing	S/MIME Encryption	EFS
Controls content reading, forwarding, saving, modifying, or printing by user	Yes	Can be set to modify, write, or read only	No	No	No
Extends protection beyond initial publication location	Yes	No	Yes	Yes	Yes, for folders stored on NTFS-formatted volumes and marked for encryption

AD RMS Components

The implementation of an AD RMS solution consists of several components, some of which are optional. The size of your organization, scalability requirements, and data sharing requirements all affect the complexity of your specific configuration. Figure 18-1 provides an illustration of the primary components that contribute to an AD RMS solution.

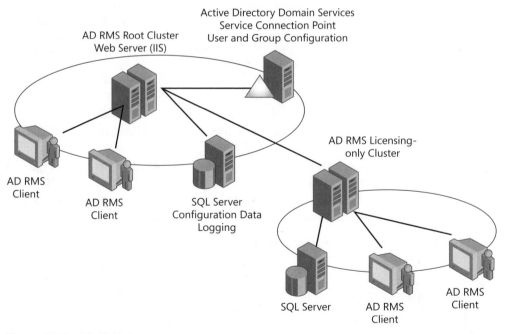

Figure 18-1 AD RMS components.

AD RMS Root Cluster

The AD RMS root cluster is the primary component of an RMS deployment and is used to manage all certification and licensing requests for clients. There can be only one root cluster in each Active Directory forest that contains at least a single Windows Server 2008 server that runs the AD RMS server role. You can add multiple servers to the cluster to be used for redundancy and load balancing. During initial installation, the AD RMS root cluster performs an automatic enrollment that creates and signs a server licensor certificate (SLC). The SLC is used to grant the AD RMS server the ability to issue certificates and licenses to AD RMS clients. In previous versions of RMS, the SLC had to be signed by the Microsoft Enrollment Service over the Internet. This required Internet connectivity from either the RMS server or from another computer to be used for offline enrollment of the server. Windows Server 2008 AD RMS has removed the requirement to contact the Microsoft Enrollment Service. Windows Server 2008 includes a server self-enrollment certificate that is used to sign the SLC locally. This removes the previous requirement for an Internet connection to complete the RMS cluster enrollment process.

> **Note**   Do not confuse the AD RMS root cluster with the failover clustering feature of Windows Server 2008.

Web Services

Each server that is installed with the AD RMS server role also requires a number of Web-related server roles and features. The Web Server (IIS) server role is required to provide most of the AD RMS application services, such as licensing and certification. These IIS-based services are called *application pipelines*. The Windows Process Activation Service and Message Queuing features are also required for AD RMS functionality. The Window Process Activation Service is used to provide access to IIS features from any application that hosts Windows Communication Foundation services. Message Queuing provides guaranteed message delivery between the AD RMS server and the SQL Server database. All transactions are first written to the message queue and then transferred to the database. If connectivity to the database is lost, the transaction information will be queued until connectivity resumes. During the installation of the AD RMS server role, you specify the Web site on which the AD RMS virtual directory will be set up. You also provide the address used to enable clients to communicate with the cluster over the internal network. You can specify an unencrypted URL, or you can use an SSL certificate to provide SSL-encrypted connections to the cluster.

Licensing-only Clusters

A licensing-only cluster is optional and is not part of the root cluster; however, it relies on the root cluster for certification and other services (it cannot provide account certification services on its own). The licensing-only cluster is used to provide both publishing licenses and use licenses to users. A licensing-only cluster can contain a single server, or you can add multiple servers to provide redundancy and load balancing. Licensing-only clusters are typically deployed to address specific licensing requirements, such as supporting unique rights-management requirements of a department or supporting rights management for external business partners as part of an extranet scenario.

> **Note**   For standard scenarios, it is preferable to use only a root cluster and join multiple servers to this configuration. This is because root and licensing-only servers cannot be used in the same load-balancing pool and the combination may become difficult to manage.

Active Directory Domain Services (AD DS)

The AD RMS server role is configured on a Windows Server 2008 server. The server must be a member of an Active Directory domain with domain controllers running Windows Server 2000 SP3, Windows Server 2003, or Windows Server 2008. AD DS is also used for hosting the Service Connection Point (SCP). The SCP is a registered object in the Configuration partition within Active Directory. It is used to provide intranet-based domain clients the ability to automatically discover the URL of the AD RMS cluster. You can register the AD RMS service connection point during the installation of the AD RMS server role, or you can register it postinstallation using the AD RMS Admin console. In order to perform the registration, you must be a member of the Enterprise Admins security group in Active directory. You should plan to register the SCP when you are ready for the users to start using AD RMS.

> **Note**   Any user or group that is to use or publish content that is protected with AD RMS must have an e-mail address configured in Active Directory Domain Services.

Database Services

AD RMS requires a database to store configuration information, such as configuration settings, templates, user keys, and server keys. Logging information is also stored within the database. SQL Server is also used to keep a cache of expanded group memberships obtained from Active Directory to determine if a specific user is a member of a group. For production environments, it is recommended that you use a database server such as SQL Server 2005 or later. For test environments, you can use an internal database that is provided with Windows Server 2008; however, the internal database only supports a single-server root cluster.

AD RMS Client

Any client computer that is to take part in the AD RMS environment requires the AD RMS Client software. The Windows Vista and Windows Server 2008 operating systems both include the AD RMS client component built into the operating system. If your client computers consist of Windows XP, Windows 2000, or Windows Server 2003, you can download a compatible version of the AD RMS client from the Microsoft Download Center.

The AD RMS client includes a component called the *lockbox*. The lockbox stores all necessary keys and credentials used to perform encryption, decryption, signing, and validation necessary to publish and use rights-protected information. The lockbox is activated when a user attempts to publish or use any rights-protected data.

In addition to the AD RMS client, end-users require applications that support rights-management features. These are examples of applications that support rights management:

- Microsoft Office Professional Edition 2003 for creating rights-protected information. All editions will allow you to consume rights-protected content.

- Microsoft Office 2007 Enterprise, Ultimate, and Professional Plus editions for creating rights-protected information. All editions will allow you to consume rights-protected content.

- Windows Mobile 6

- Microsoft Office SharePoint Server 2007

- Microsoft Exchange Server 2007 with Service Pack 1

More Info   The Active Directory Rights Management Services Software Development Kit (SDK) provides documentation and sample code that enables developers to customize the AD RMS environment and to create AD RMS-enabled applications. You can find the AD RMS SDK at *http://msdn2.microsoft.com/en-us/library/bb968798(VS.85).aspx*.

How AD RMS Works

Server and client components of an AD RMS solution use various types of eXtensible rights Markup Language (XrML)–based certificates and licenses to ensure trusted connections and protected content. XrML is an industry standard that is used to provide rights that are linked to the use and protection of digital information. Rights are expressed in an XrML license attached to the information that is to be protected. The XrML license defines how the information owner wants that information to be used, protected, and distributed.

More Info   For more information about the XrML standards, see the XrML Web site at *http://www.xrml.org/*.

Several types of XrML-based certificates are used during the server and client enrollment processes. Table 18-2 provides a summary of those certificates.

Table 18-2 AD RMS Certificates Used for Server and Client Enrollment

Certificate	Description	Security Content
Server Licensor certificate (SLC)	Created when the AD RMS server role is installed and configured on the first server of an AD RMS root cluster. Windows Server 2008 AD RMS performs a self-enrollment that has the server self-enrollment certificate (included with Windows Server 2008) sign the SLC. This ensures that any licenses issued to machines and users are verified and trusted by a valid root cluster. If you add any additional servers to the root cluster, each will share the SLC. If you deploy licensing-only clusters, these will generate their own unique SLC.	Contains the public key of the server.
Machine certificate	This is created on the client computer the first time a user consumes a rights-protected document or the first time the user attempts to protect a document using an AD RMS–enabled application. During this process, the AD RMS client enrolls with the root cluster to create this certificate, create a public and private key pair, and activate the client lockbox.	Contains the public key of the activated computer. The private key is stored in the computer lockbox.
Rights account certificate (RAC)	The RAC is used to identify the users who are trusted entities within an AD RMS system. When a user attempts to perform an AD RMS–based task, the AD RMS root cluster issues an RAC that associates the user to the computer or device being used. In order to obtain an RAC, the user must have an e-mail address listed in the E-mail field of the user object in Active Directory. By default, a standard RAC is valid for 365 days. Temporary RACs are valid for 15 minutes.	Contains the public key of the user and the private key of the user encrypted with the public key of the activated computer.
Client Licensor certificate (CLC)	If client computers will be used to publish rights-protected information when they are not connected to the corporate network (offline publishing), a local enrollment process is required. Client computers enroll with the root cluster and receive rights management client licensor certificates (CLC), which enable users to publish rights-protected information from those computers without being connected to the corporate network. This allows the user to sign publishing licenses and use licenses via the lockbox.	Contains the client licensor public key and the client licensor private key, which is encrypted by the public key of the user requesting the CLC. Also contains the public key of the Root or licensing-only cluster that issued the certificate (which is signed by the private key of the cluster that issued the certificate.)

Note You can view the machine certificate, RAC, and CLC in the following location on the user's workstation:

Windows XP/2003: %UserProfile%\Local Settings\Application Data\Microsoft\DRM

Windows Vista/2008: %UserProfile%\AppData\Local\Microsoft\DRM

After machine and client activation has take place, users can then apply rights-management policies to information or consume data that is already rights-protected. Both of these tasks require specific types of certificates as described in Table 18-3.

Table 18-3 AD RMS Licenses Used for Publishing or Consuming Data

License	Description	Security Content
Publishing license (PL)	Issued by either a server in an AD RMS cluster or by a CLC through the lockbox. The PL sets the policy (names principals, rights, and conditions) for acquiring a use license (UL) for rights-protected information.	Contains the symmetric keys used for decrypting the content, which is encrypted with the public key of the server that issued the license.
		The PL also contains the URL of the AD RMS Licensing service.
Use license (UL)	Issued only by a server in an AD RMS cluster, it grants an authorized user with valid RAC rights to consume rights-protected information based on policy established in the PL.	Contains the symmetric key for decrypting the content, which is encrypted with the public key of the user.

For the most part, machine and user enrollment and the publishing and use of rights-protected information happen in the background with very little user interaction. However, it is still important to understand the flow of the various processes. Figure 18-2 provides an illustration of how AD RMS works when users publish or consume rights-protected information.

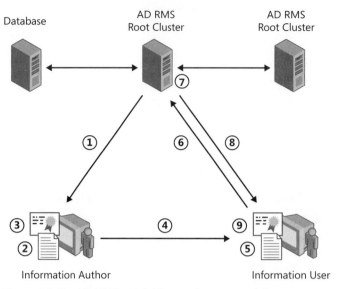

Database

AD RMS
Root Cluster

AD RMS
Root Cluster

Information Author

Information User

Figure 18-2 AD RMS publishing and usage workflow.

1. The author receives an RAC and a CLC from the AD RMS root cluster (or licensing-only cluster) the first time he or she tries to rights-protect information. This is a one-time step that establishes the user's AD RMS credential (which is the RAC) and enables offline publishing of rights-protected information (using the CLC) in the future.

2. Using an AD RMS-enabled application, an author creates a file and specifies a set of usage rights and conditions for that file. A publishing license that contains the usage policies is then generated.

3. The application encrypts the file with a symmetric key, which is then encrypted by the public key of the author's AD RMS cluster. The key is inserted into the publishing license, and the publishing license is bound to the file. Only the author's AD RMS cluster can issue use licenses to decrypt this file. If the author has used offline publishing, another copy of the symmetric key is encrypted by the public key of the author's client licensor certificate and included in the publishing license. The result of this additional encryption step is the creation of an owner license that allows the author to consume the content without licensing it from an AD RMS server.

4. The author distributes the file.

5. A recipient receives a rights-protected file through a regular distribution channel and opens it using an AD RMS–enabled application or browser. If the recipient does not have an RAC on the current computer, this is the point at which one will be issued.

6. The application sends a request for a use license to the AD RMS cluster that issued the publishing license for the protected information. The request includes the recipient's account certificate (which contains the recipient's public key) and the publishing license (which contains the symmetric key that encrypted the file).

7.   The AD RMS root cluster (or licensing-only cluster) confirms that the recipient is autho-rized, checks that the recipient is a named user, and creates a use license. During this process, the server decrypts the symmetric key by using the private key of the server, re-encrypts the symmetric key by using the public key of the recipient, and then adds the encrypted symmetric key to the use license. This step ensures that only the intended recipient can decrypt the symmetric key and thus decrypt the protected file. The server also adds any relevant conditions to the use license, such as the expiration date or an application or operating system exclusion.

8.   When the confirmation is complete, the AD RMS Root or licensing-only cluster server returns the use license to the recipient's client computer.

9.   After receiving the use license, the application examines both the license and the recipient's account certificate to determine if any certificate in either chain of trust requires a revocation list. If so, the application checks for a local copy of the revocation list that has not expired. If necessary, it retrieves a current copy of the revocation list. The application then applies any revocation conditions that are relevant in the current context. If no revocation condition blocks access to the file, the application renders the data, and the user may exercise the rights he or she has been granted.

AD RMS Deployment Scenarios

To meet specific organizational requirements, AD RMS can be deployed in a number of different scenarios. Each of these scenarios offers unique considerations to ensure a secure and effective rights-management solution. These are some possible deployment scenarios:

- Providing AD RMS for the corporate intranet

- Providing AD RMS to users over the Internet

- Integrating AD RMS with Active Directory Federation Services

Deploying AD RMS within the Corporate Intranet

A typical AD RMS installation takes place in a single Active Directory Forest. However, there may be other specific situations that require additional consideration. For example, you may need to provide rights-management services to users throughout a large enterprise with multiple branch offices. For scalability and performance reasons, you might choose to implement licensing-only clusters within these branch offices. You may also have to deploy an AD RMS solution for an organization that has multiple Active Directory forests. Since each forest can only contain a single root cluster, you will have to determine appropriate trust policies and AD RMS configuration between both forests. This will effectively allow users from both forests to publish and consume rights-management content. The configuration of trust policies for inter-forest or inter-organizational deployment scenarios is discussed in the section titled "Implementing AD RMS" later in this chapter.

Deploying AD RMS to Users over the Internet

Most organizations have to support a mobile computing workforce, which consists of users that connect to organizational resources from remote locations over the Internet. To ensure that mobile users can perform rights-management tasks, you have to determine how to provide external access to the AD RMS infrastructure. One method is to place a licensing-only server within your organization's perimeter network. This will allow external users to obtain use and publishing licenses for protecting or viewing information. Another common solution is to use a reverse proxy server such as Microsoft Internet Security and Acceleration (ISA) Server 2006 to publish the extranet AD RMS cluster URL. The ISA server will then handle all requests from the Internet to the AD RMS cluster and passes on the requests when necessary. This is a more secure and effective method, so it is typically recommended over placing licensing servers within the perimeter network location.

Deploying AD RMS with Active Directory Federation Services

Windows Server 2008 includes the Active Directory Federation Services (AD FS) server role, which is used to provide trusted inter-organizational access and collaboration scenarios between two organizations. AD RMS can take advantage of the federated trust relationship as a basis for users from both organizations to obtain RAC, use, and publishing licenses. In order to install AD RMS support for AD FS, you will need to have already deployed an AD FS solution within your environment. This scenario is recommended if one organization has AD RMS and the other does not. If both have AD RMS, trust policies are typically recommended. More information about configuring AD FS support is discussed in the section titled "Federated Identity Support" later in this chapter.

Implementing AD RMS

Regardless of which scenario you intend to use for rights-management services, you will always begin with the installation of the initial AD RMS root cluster. After the root cluster is in place, you can then determine how to address specific requirements such as providing external access to the AD RMS environment. This section describes how to deploy and configure AD RMS components to ensure an effective and secure rights-management solution.

Preinstallation Considerations Before Installing AD RMS

During the installation process for the AD RMS server role, you will be asked to provide a number of configuration values that you should determine beforehand. There are also several requirements that must be met in order for a successful implementation. These points should be considered before installing AD RMS:

- The AD RMS server role should be installed on a member server in the same Active Directory domain as the user accounts that will be participating in the rights-management solution. It is possible to install AD RMS on a domain controller; however, you must add the AD RMS service account to the Domain Admins group, which may pose a security risk.

■   You will need to create a domain user account that will be specified during installation as the AD RMS service account. This account does not require any additional permission other than a standard user account.

■   The user account that will be used to install the AD RMS server role must be a different account than the one specified as the AD RMS service account and must be able to query the Active Directory domain. Also, if the AD RMS service connection point is to be registered during the installation, the user account that will be used to install AD RMS must be a member of the Active Directory Enterprise Admins group or equivalent.

■   If an external database is being used for the AD RMS cluster, the user installing AD RMS must have the right to create new databases. Also, if Microsoft SQL Server 2005 is used, the user account must be a member of the System Administrators database role.

■   During installation, you will be asked to provide a URL for the AD RMS cluster. Be sure to use a URL that is different than the computer name and one that will represent the entire AD RMS cluster. You should also create a DNS alias (CNAME) record for the AD RMS cluster URL, as well as a separate CNAME record for the computer hosting the configuration database. CNAMEs provide flexibility in the event that a hardware failure takes place or a computer's name is changed.

■   If you intend to secure communication to and from the AD RMS cluster using SSL, be sure to obtain the required SSL certificate from a trusted root certification authority. You do have an option to use a self-signed certificate; however, there are a number of limitations and this option is not recommended for a production environment.

Installing AD RMS Clusters

The AD RMS server role is an option that is available with the Windows Server 2008 operating system. You can use the Initial Configuration Tasks or Server Manager to install the role and configure the AD RMS root cluster. You will need to be a member of the local Administrators group, or equivalent, in order to complete the installation.

The following is a high-level outline that describes the installation of an AD RMS cluster:

1.   Open the Server Manager (or use the Initial Configuration Tasks page), click the Roles node, and click Add Roles. The Add Roles Wizard starts.

2.   On the Select Server Roles page, select Active Directory Rights Management Services. You are prompted to add additional required role services and features. These include the Web Server (IIS) role service as well as the Windows Process Activation Service and Message Queuing features. Figure 18-3 shows an illustration of the Add Roles Wizard with the appropriate roles selected.

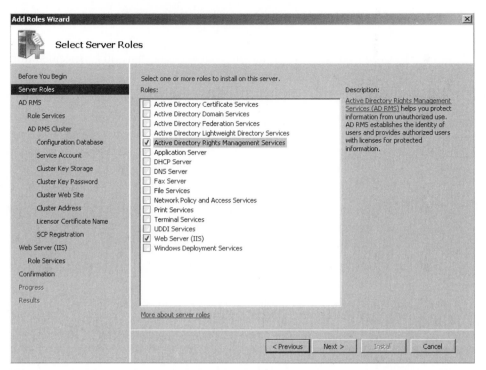

Figure 18-3   Selecting the Active Directory Rights Management Services and Web Server (IIS) roles.

3.   On the Select Role Services page, you are provided the option to select the role services to install for Active Directory Rights Management Services. There are two options:

   ❑   **Active Directory Rights Management Server**   This is the required role service that installs the AD RMS components required to publish and consume rights-protected information.

   ❑   **Identity Federation Support**   This is an optional role service that is used for providing rights-protected content integration with Active Directory Federation Services. If you select this role service, you will also be prompted to add specific Active Directory Federation Services role services to the server.

4.   On the Create Or Join An AD RMS Cluster page, you have two options:

   ❑   **Create A New AD RMS Cluster**   If you are implementing a new AD RMS deployment, you would select this option to create an AD RMS root cluster for certification and licensing purposes. If an existing AD RMS root cluster is detected within the Active Directory forest, you would then select this option to create a new licensing-only cluster.

   ❑   **Join An Existing AD RMS Cluster**   If an existing root or licensing-only cluster is already deployed, you can use this option to add another server to the cluster. You will need to provide the name of an existing AD RMS configuration database as well as the name of the database server.

5. On the Select Configuration Database page, you configure the database that will be used to store configuration and policy information. This page provides you with two options:

    ❑   **Use Windows Internal Database On This Server**   If you are implementing AD RMS on a single server for a small environment or for a test lab, you can select this option. Note that this option does not allow for more servers to join the AD RMS cluster, and so if you require future scalability, choose the other option.

    ❑   **Use A Different Database Server**   This option allows you to specify the server name and database instance for the configuration database. It is recommended that you use a database server such as Microsoft SQL Server 2005 or above.

6. On the Specify Service Account page, you specify the account that the AD RMS cluster will use to communicate with other services on the computer and throughout the network. This account requires only standard domain user permission. This account will automatically be added to the AD RMS service group and will be provided with the default permissions for that group.

7. On the Configure AD RMS Cluster Key Storage page, you specify where you want to store the AD RMS cluster key. The AD RMS cluster key is used to sign certificates and licenses issued by the cluster. It is also used in disaster recovery scenarios and by other AD RMS servers as they join the cluster. You are provided with two options for storing the cluster key:

    ❑   **Use AD RMS Centrally Managed Key Storage**   When the AD RMS cluster key is generated, the next step of the wizard asks you to provide a cluster key password to protect the key (which you must remember for disaster recovery purposes). The AD RMS cluster key is stored in the configuration database and will be automatically shared by AD RMS servers joining the cluster.

    ❑   **Use CSP Key Storage**   For advanced security, you can choose to store the AD RMS cluster key to a cryptographic service provider (CSP). This provides the best security option, but it does require you to manually provide the key when new servers join the cluster. If you choose this option, the next step of the wizard asks you to select the CSP and choose whether to create a new key with the CSP or use an existing key with the selected CSP (the latter option is typically used in a recovery scenario).

8. On the Select AD RMS Cluster Web Site page, you can select a Web site for the AD RMS virtual directory. Typically you would use the Default Web Site on a server that is only running the AD RMS server role.

9. The Specify Cluster Address page allows you to specify how AD RMS clients will communicate with the cluster. You can choose to use an SSL-encrypted connection or

you can specify an unencrypted connection. You will also provide the internal address and port that will be used for the cluster. It is recommended that you use an SSL-encrypted connection. In order to do so, the next step in the wizard provides the ability to either choose an existing certificate that has already been issued by a certification authority or create a self-signed certificate. A self-signed certificate is only recommended for small-scale deployments because you will need to manually install the certificate on all clients that communicate with the server. Figure 18-4 shows the configuration of an SSL-encrypted connection.

Note   The internal address needs to be a fully qualified domain name that resolves to the AD RMS cluster. You should not specify a server name, but rather an alias that represents the entire cluster. This will then allow you to easily add Network load balancing or additional servers to the cluster at a later time. Also note that you cannot change this address or port number after AD RMS is installed, so it is important to decide on this FQDN before deployment.

Note   If you are planning to integrate AD RMS with AD FS, you must choose the SSL-encrypted connection. Otherwise, you have to reinstall AD RMS.

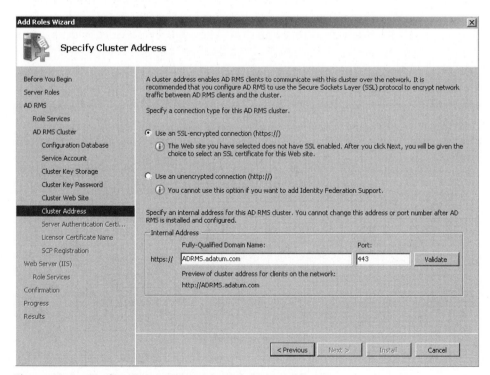

Figure 18-4   Configuring an SSL-encrypted cluster address.

10.   On the Name the Server Licensor Certificate page, enter a name that will be used for identifying the SLC.

11.   On the Register AD RMS Service Connection Point page, you are provided with two options:

❑   **Register The AD RMS Service Connection Point Now**   If you are a member of the Enterprise Admins group in Active Directory, you can have the AD RMS installation automatically configure the AD RMS service connection point. Recall that this Active Directory object is required for AD RMS–enabled clients to resolve intranet URLs for the AD RMS cluster.

❑   **Register The AD RMS Service Connection Point Later**   If you are not a member of the Enterprise Admins group, or if you do not yet want the AD RMS cluster to be automatically discoverable by clients, you can select this option.

12.   If you have selected to install Identity Federation Support, you will be asked to enter the federation server name that will communicate with the AD RMS server. If you did not choose to install Identify Federation Support, this option will not be available.

13.   The final step is to configure the Web Server (IIS) role service. Generally you would keep the recommended settings specified in the Select Role Services page; however, you do have the option to add or remove specific role service settings as required.

After the installation is complete, you will need to log off and then log on again in order to update your security token and be able to administer the AD RMS server. After logging back on, you can then administer the server by using the Active Directory Rights Management Services console, as shown in Figure 18-5.

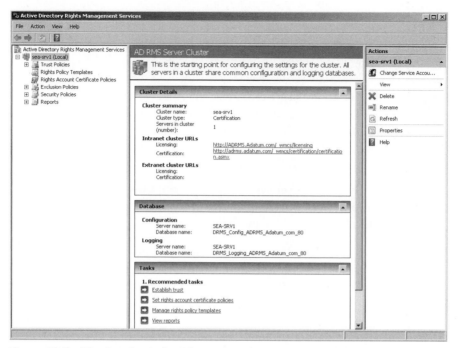

Figure 18-5   Viewing the Active Directory Rights Management Services console.

Configuring the AD RMS Service Connection Point

As mentioned previously, the service connection point (SCP) is required for clients to be able to automatically discover the AD RMS cluster URL. There is only one SCP per Active Directory forest. When an AD RMS client attempts to use rights-management features on a computer, the AD RMS client application queries the SCP to find the URL of the AD RMS cluster. After finding the AD RMS cluster, the client downloads an RAC and can then participate in publishing and consuming rights–protected information.

The SCP is typically registered during the installation of the AD RMS root cluster, but if you (or the individual that installed the AD RMS server) are not a member of the Enterprise Admins group, this task may have to take place as a separate step.

After installation, the SCP can be registered or changed from the cluster Properties box in the Active Directory Rights Management Services console. In order to perform this task, membership is required in the AD RMS Enterprise Administrators and the Enterprise Admins groups in Active Directory. Figure 18-6 provides an illustration of the dialog box used to modify the SCP registration.

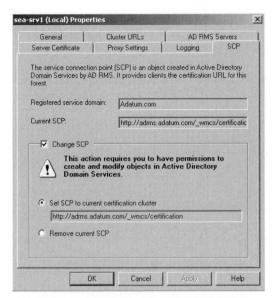

Figure 18-6   Modifying the SCP registration.

Working with AD RMS Clients

After the AD RMS cluster is deployed and the SCP configured, your next step is to ensure that all clients that are to participate in the rights-management solution have the appropriate AD RMS client software installed. If your clients consist of mainly Windows Vista or Windows Server 2008 operating systems, then this step is easy, since the AD RMS client is already installed and provided with the client operating system.

If your client operating systems consist of Windows XP, Windows 2000, or Windows Server 2003, you will need to download a compatible version of the AD RMS client from the Microsoft Download Center and then determine an appropriate deployment method to have it installed on the computers that will take part in the AD RMS environment. Many organizations will choose to use Systems Management Server (SMS), System Center Configuration Manager (SCCM), or Group Policy to deploy the RMS client. In order to deploy the client using these methods, you must extract the Windows Installer files from the executable package using the following command syntax (note that the example uses the SP2 version of the RMS client):

```
WindowsRightsManagementServicesSP2-KB917275-Client-ENU.exe /x
```

When you provide the /x switch, you will be prompted for a location to extract the files. These two files are required to be deployed to the clients:

- **MSDrmClient.msi**   This is the installation file for the RMS client. This file should be deployed first, which will remove any previous versions and then install the new version of the client.

■ **RMSClientBackCompat.msi**   This file associates the new RMS client to RMS-enabled applications such as Microsoft Office. This should be installed after the MSDrm-Client.msi file is deployed.

You might also decide to deploy the executable file using a script or batch file. You can deploy the RMS client using an unattended installation method by using the following command:

```
WindowsRightsManagementServicesSP2-KB917275-Client-ENU.exe
-override 1 /I MsDrmClient.msi REBOOT=ReallySuppress /q -override 2 /I
RmClientBackCompat.msi REBOOT=ReallySuppress /q
```

Note   In addition to installing the client, do not forget that each user object is required to have the *E-mail* attribute configured on the General tab of the user Properties dialog box in Active Directory.

Configuring Client Service Discovery

When a network client attempts to use a rights-management feature of a compatible application, the AD RMS client queries the service connection point in Active Directory to retrieve the URL pipeline of the Certification virtual directory located on the AD RMS root cluster. The URL pipeline is in the following format: http(s)://*<server or cluster name>*/_wmcs/Certification.

Note   You will be prompted for credentials each time you attempt to connect to the AD RMS cluster. To address this, you can add the AD RMS cluster URL to the Local intranet security zone for all users who will be participating in the AD RMS infrastructure. You can configure this as a Group Policy setting to affect multiple clients as required.

During the creation or consumption of rights-protected content, the AD RMS client retrieves and looks for the URL to the Licensing virtual directory on the AD RMS cluster. The URL pipeline for licensing requests is in the following format: http(s)://*<server or cluster name>*/_wmcs/Licensing.

There may be times when you will need to override the default service discovery process and force a client to contact a specific AD RMS cluster that is different from the one published in the SCP. For example, if you deploy licensing-only AD RMS clusters for scalability purposes, you will need to override the default configuration on the clients with the licensing-only clusters deployed so that the AD RMS root cluster is no longer contacted to acquire use or publishing licenses.

You can override the default service discovery process by adding the following registry entry on the client workstations that are participating in the AD RMS environment:

HKEY_LOCAL_MACHINE\Software\Microsoft\MSDRM\ServiceLocation

The keys listed in Table 18-4 are used for overriding the activation or licensing services to use a specified AD RMS cluster.

Table 18-4   Keys Used for Overriding Activation or Licensing Services

Key Name	Data Type	Syntax	Description
Activation	REG_SZ	http(s)://<*cluster name*>/_wmcs/certification (where <*cluster name*> is the URL of the root cluster that should be used for certification)	Used to override the default AD RMS certification service that is configured in the SCP
Enterprise-Publishing	REG_SZ	http(s)://<*cluster name*>/_wmcs/licensing (where <*cluster name*> is the URL of the licensing-only cluster)	Used to override the default AD RMS licensing service

Most applications that contain rights-management features also provide a way to identify specific licensing servers to be used for publishing or consuming rights-protected information. This prevents you from having to change the global settings for service discovery, but still provides unique settings for a specific application. For example, to specify a licensing server for Microsoft Office 2007, you can add or modify the following registry entry:

Hive: *HKEY_LOCAL_MACHINE\Software\Microsoft\Office\12.0\Common\DRM*

Value: *CorpLicenseServer*

Type: *REG_SZ*

Entry: *http(s)://<server or cluster name>/_WMCS/licensing*

Creating Rights-Protected Content with Microsoft Office

Both Microsoft Office 2003 Professional Edition and Microsoft Office 2007 (Enterprise, Ultimate, and Professional Plus editions) work together with the AD RMS client to enable the creation and use of rights-protected content. You can apply rights to a document using the following methods:

- For Microsoft Office Professional Edition 2003, click the File menu and then point to Permission. You can then select an appropriate template to apply that specifies the rights required for the document.

- For Microsoft Office 2007, click the Office button and then point to Prepare. You can then point to the Restrict Permission option to select an appropriate rights policy template to apply to the document.

Depending on the rights policy template being used, the user applying the permissions may have the Permission dialog box open. This box provides the ability to specify who has Read or

Change permission to the document. As shown in Figure 18-7, Don has Read permissions, and Terry has Change permissions to the document.

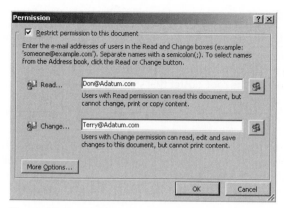

Figure 18-7   Restricting permissions on a document.

Clicking the More Options button provides additional permissions, as shown in Figure 18-8 and described in Table 18-5.

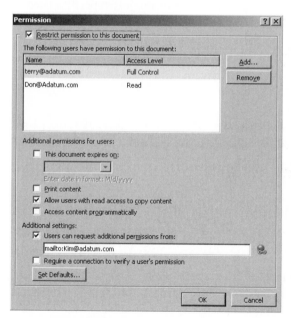

Figure 18-8   Additional permissions and settings for users.

Table 18-5   Permission and Setting Options

Permission or Setting	Description
Restrict Permission To This Document	Provides the option for enabling or disabling the permissions applied to the document.
The Following Users Have Permission To This Document	You can click the Add button or the Remove button to modify the list of users that have permissions and settings as configured in this dialog box.
This Document Expires On	Provides the ability to set an expiration date for the document. After the expiration date, the users will no longer have any rights to open the document.
Print Content	Adds the permission to be able to print the document.
Allow Users With Read Access To Copy Content	Adds the permission to copy content and paste it to another location or document.
Access Content Programmatically	Adds permission for services or scripts to access the content.
Users Can Request Additional Permissions From	You can use this option to provide the e-mail address of the individual that users can request additional permissions for content access and modification.
Require A Connection To Verify A User's Permission	You can use this check box to ensure that users can only open this document if a user can be verified by the AD RMS cluster. This verification is done every time the file is opened, and so do not enable this setting for offline users.
Set Defaults	You can click the Set Defaults button to save common permission settings for future use.

When a user attempts to consume rights-protected content, a permission notification box is displayed. As shown in Figure 18-9, you can see that the notification provides the URL to the licensing pipeline for credential verification and obtaining a use license.

Figure 18-9   Viewing the permission notification.

The user will then be restricted to the permissions as outlined in the use policy, which can be viewed by clicking the View Permission button, as shown in Figure 18-10. Notice that Don@ADatum.com has View and Copy permissions assigned to the document.

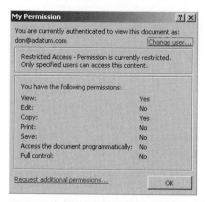

Figure 18-10   Viewing permissions assigned to a rights-protected document.

Note   For users that do not have Microsoft Office to view rights-protected documents, you can install the Rights Management Add-on for Internet Explorer. This add-on provides the ability to view, but not alter, rights-protected information. You can download the Rights Management Add-on for Internet Explorer at *http://www.microsoft.com/downloads/ details.aspx?FamilyID=B48F920B-5AF0-46B4-994F-2F62582CC86F&displaylang=en.*

Administering AD RMS

The complexity and design of your AD RMS environment will dictate the specific administration tasks to complete after the initial deployment of your AD RMS root cluster. If your organization consists of multiple Active Directory forests, you may need to integrate multiple AD RMS deployments. You might also have external users or organizational partnerships that you need to consider in order to enable sharing and collaboration of rights-protected information. Another major set of administration tasks is to ensure security of the AD RMS environment including the application of exclusion policies, security policies, and the configuration and deployment of rights policy templates.

This section describes each of these administration tasks and provides information to help maintain and administer an effective and secure AD RMS deployment throughout your network environment.

Managing Trust Policies

A standard implementation of AD RMS provides rights-management protection for documents created and consumed within an organization. However, there are many scenarios that require the configuration of trust policies. A trust policy allows for the processing of licensing requests for content that was rights-protected by a different AD RMS cluster in another Active Directory forest or another organization. There are three main types of trust policies that can be configured to address specific scenarios:

■   Trusted user domains

■   Trusted publishing domains

■   Federated Identity Support

Trusted User Domains

A trusted user domain configuration allows recipients from an AD RMS cluster in another organization or Active Directory forest to obtain use licenses from your AD RMS cluster. For example, a large enterprise organization may consist of multiple Active Directory forests that contain multiple AD RMS installations. Each AD RMS installation may be configured to trust the other AD RMS installations by establishing one another as trusted user domains. A trusted user domain can also be established between two organizations in order to provide sharing and collaboration for published rights-protected content. A trusted user domain is typically one of the following entities:

■   Another Active Directory forest in your organization

■   A partner's AD RMS installation

■   Windows Live ID service

By default, an AD RMS cluster will not service requests from any user whose RAC has been issued by another AD RMS installation. For example, consider this scenario: Kim@NWtraders.com sends rights-protected content to Don@ADatum.com. Don attempts to open the content, which results in his RAC (issued by his organization's AD RMS installation) and the publishing license to be sent to the cluster URL listed in the publishing license. The licensing cluster at NWTraders.com will receive Don's request for a use license; however, that request will fail unless the licensing cluster can verify his RAC. By configuring another AD RMS cluster as a trusted user domain, you can verify that the user requesting a use license is originating from a trusted user domain.

To configure a trusted user domain, you must open the Active Directory Rights Management Services console and import a trusted user domain .bin file. The .bin file contains the Server Licensor Certificate of the AD RMS cluster to be trusted. The .bin file is created by selecting the Internal domain certificate from the Trusted User Domains node and then clicking Export trusted user domain from the Actions pane. The file can then be saved and provided to the administrator who is configuring the integration between the two AD RMS clusters.

When a .bin file is obtained from a trusted domain, you can import the file by selecting the trusted user domains node and then clicking Import Trusted User Domain in the Actions pane. As shown in Figure 18-11, the .bin file obtained from A. Datum Corporation is being imported. A display name is provided in order to specifically identify the trusted user domain.

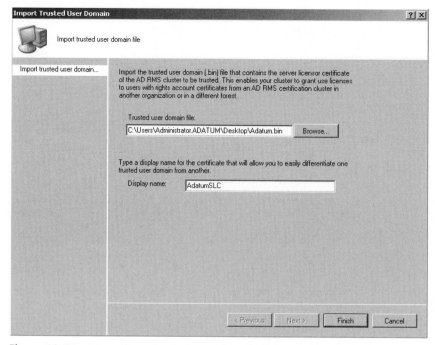

Figure 18-11 Importing a trusted user domain file.

By importing the server licensor certificate of another AD RMS cluster, you are now able to verify that a user who may be requesting a use license is originating from a trusted user domain. Figure 18-12 describes the interaction between trusted user domains.

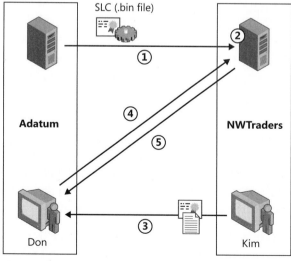

Figure 18-12 Trusted user domain interaction.

1. ADatum exports and sends the server licensor certificate (.bin file) to NWTraders.

2. NWTraders imports the .bin file and specifies ADatum as a trusted user domain.

3. Kim (an employee at NWTraders) sends Don a rights-protected document.

4. Don receives the content and, in his attempt to open it, sends his RAC and publishing license to the licensing server at NWTraders.

5. The AD RMS cluster at NWTraders is aware that the ADatum domain is a trusted user domain and can use the imported SLC to verify Don's RAC and issue him a use license.

> **Note**   The licensing pipeline is initially configured with only Windows Authentication enabled. In order for a user from another domain to be able to request a use license, the user must be able to authenticate to the server running IIS. This can be established by configuring an Active Directory trust relationship with the other Forest, enabling anonymous authentication on the licensing pipeline in IIS, or by creating shadow accounts used for authentication.

Trusted Publishing Domains

By default, an AD RMS cluster is only capable of issuing use licenses for rights-protected information that contains a publishing license issued by the same AD RMS cluster. However, there may be scenarios that require you to configure your AD RMS cluster to have the ability to issue use licenses against publishing licenses that were issued by a different AD RMS cluster. For example, A. Datum Corporation acquires Northwind Traders, and it has been decided that there is no need to maintain two AD RMS installations. Northwind Traders can export its SLC and private key, which will be imported into the ADatum AD RMS cluster. This will designate Northwind Traders as a trusted publishing domain within the ADatum AD RMS cluster. As a result, the ADatum AD RMS cluster will be able to decrypt publishing licenses and issue use licenses for all rights-protected content that had been originally managed by the RMS installation at Northwind Traders.

To configure a trusted publishing domain, you must open the Active Directory Rights Management Services console and import a trusted publishing domain file. The domain file is an XML-based file that contains the Server Licensor Certificate, cluster key, and any rights policy templates of the AD RMS cluster to be trusted. The XML file is created by selecting the SLC listed under the trusted publishing domains node and then clicking Export Trusted Publishing Domain in the Actions pane. You also must provide a password, which is used to provide additional security and encrypt the trusted publishing domain file. If you are importing the file into an RMS cluster that contains a previous version of RMS, you can select the check box next to Saved As V1 Compatible Trusted Publishing Domain File. The file can then be saved and provided to the administrator who will import the trusted publishing domain file into the target AD RMS cluster. Figure 18-13 shows the dialog box used for exporting the trusted publishing domain file.

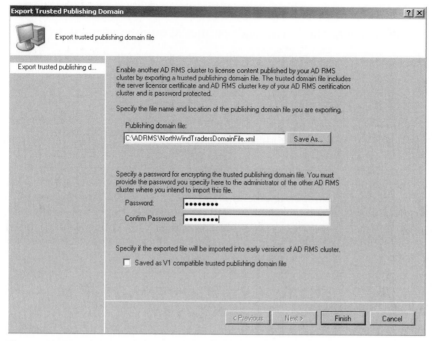

Figure 18-13   Exporting the trusted publishing domain file.

When a trusted publishing domain file is obtained, you can import the file by selecting the Trusted Publishing Domains node and then clicking Import Trusted Publishing Domain in the Actions pane.

Figure 18-14 describes the interaction between trusted publishing domains.

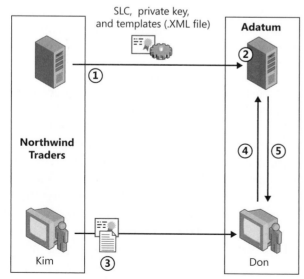

Figure 18-14   Trusted publishing domain interaction.

1. Northwind Traders exports its SLC, private key, and rights policy templates to ADatum in XML format.

2. ADatum imports the XML file and specifies Northwind Traders as a trusted publishing domain.

3. Kim (an employee at Northwind Traders) sends Don a rights-protected document that originally had a publishing license assigned by the RMS cluster at Northwind Traders.

4. Don receives the content and, in his attempt to open it, sends his RAC and publishing license to his local AD RMS licensing cluster at ADatum.

5. The AD RMS cluster at ADatum can decrypt the publishing license issued by the Northwind Traders RMS cluster and confirms that Don is named in the publishing license. It then issues a use license to Don.

> **Note**   In order for the publishing license to route to the AD RMS cluster at the ADatum location, DNS records will need to be modified so that the URL in the publishing license is resolved to the IP of the ADatum-based licensing cluster instead of the licensing cluster located at Northwind Traders.

Federated Identity Support

Windows Server 2008 AD RMS supports the ability to leverage the federated trust created between two forests or two organizations through the use of Active Directory Federation Services (AD FS). This allows for the use of a single AD RMS infrastructure for all members of the federated trust. A user wanting to publish or consume rights-protected information can use the account credentials established by the federated trust relationship for obtaining an RAC from an AD RMS cluster.

> **More Info**   For more information about Active Directory Federation Services, refer to Chapter 19, "Active Directory Federation Services."

Identity Federation Support is an optional component that has to be installed when the AD RMS server is installed. If you choose to install the Identity Federation Support Role Service, you will also be prompted to include the Active Directory Federation Services Claims-aware Agent as a supporting role service. During the installation, you will also be required to specify the federation server that the AD RMS cluster will communicate with.

> **Note**   Communication between the AD FS server and the AD RMS cluster requires an SSL-encrypted connection. It is recommended that you use a certificate issued by a certification authority trusted by all clients taking part in the AD RMS solution. You can create a self-signed certificate for small-scale or test scenarios; however, you must manually install the certificate on all clients communicating with the servers.

After installing the Identity Federation Support role service, a new node will appear in the Active Directory Rights Management Services console. You can select the Federated Identity Support node and enable Active Directory Federation Service, as shown in Figure 18-15.

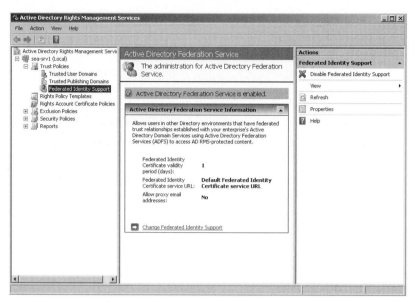

Figure 18-15   Viewing the Federated Identity Support node.

By default, any RAC issued to a federated identity has a unique validity period of one day. This can be modified by accessing the Federated Identity Support Properties box. You can also configure a specific location of an AD RMS certification server that should be used to issue RACs to external users. Figure 18-16 shows an illustration of the Federated Identity Support Properties box.

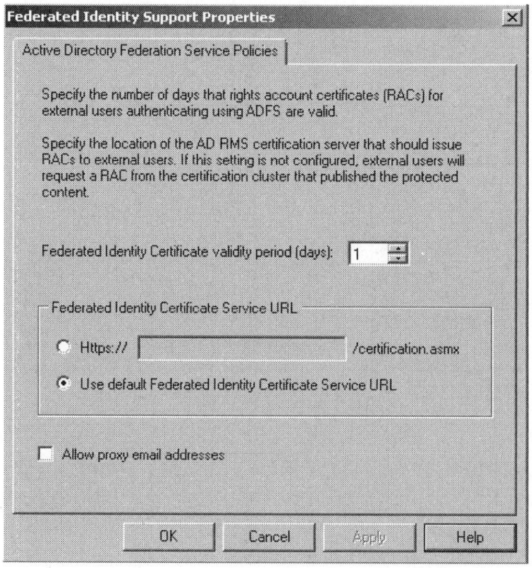

Figure 18-16   Configuring Active Directory Federation Service Policies.

> **Important**   Be sure to consider the impact of enabling proxy e-mail addresses through a federated trust. If this is allowed, it is possible for a malicious user to spoof the identity of a user and access rights-protected content. This feature is disabled, by default.

Managing Rights Policy Templates

When using an AD RMS–enabled application to publish protected content, a user applies a specific rights policy template selected from a list of available templates. AD RMS administrators create and manage the rights policy templates that are available to an AD RMS–enabled application. To create and manage Rights Policy Templates, you select the Rights Policy Templates node in the Active Directory Rights Management Services console. There are two types of rights policy templates that can be configured:

- **Distributed Rights Policy Templates**   When you configure a distributed rights policy template, the template is made available to users to apply rules and conditions to protected content. If you need to retire a distributed template, you can select the template and then archive the template to remove it from general use.

- **Archived Rights Policy Templates**   An archived rights policy template is a template that is not available to users. Typically, an archived template is used to design templates or create starter templates that can then be copied, modified, and distributed to AD RMS clients. A rights policy template can also be archived when it should not be used to publish new content, but is still required because of older content still available with this template applied.

By default, all rights policy templates are stored in the configuration database used by AD RMS. However, templates can also be copied to a shared folder and then deployed to workstations to provide local access to the rights policy templates and allow for offline creation of rights-protected content.

Creating a New Distributed Rights Policy Template

Use the following steps to create a new distributed rights policy template:

1. In the Active Directory Rights Management Services console, select Rights Policy Templates and then click Create Distributed Rights Policy Template.

2. On the Add Template Identification Information page, select the language that is supported on your client computers. When you click Add, you can specify the Language and then provide a Name and Description for the template. Figure 18-17 illustrates the template identification information for a new template named Adatum Internal Use Only.

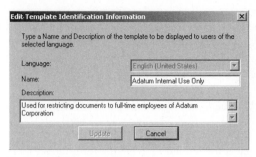

Figure 18-17   Specifying the template identification information.

3. On the Add User Rights page, you can specify rights for users or groups within the organization. You have the choice of specifying the e-mail address for a user or group, or you can choose to apply this template to everyone who can acquire an RAC (including AD FS and Windows live ID users) by selecting Anyone. You also have the option to grant the author of the document full control right with no expiration and to provide a URL that can be used to grant user requests for additional rights. A rights request URL is typically in the form of a mailto: URL for users to request additional rights via an e-mail message.

4. On the Specify Expiration Policy page, you can specify conditions for Content expiration and Use License expiration.

5. On the Specify Extended Policy page, you can configure the following options:

    ❑ **Enable Users To View Protected Content Using A Browser Add-On**   This allows users to view protected information with the Information Rights Management Add-on for Internet Explorer. If you do not select this option, the content can only be viewed using the application that created it.

    ❑ **Require A New Use License Every Time Content Is Consumed (Disable Client-Side Caching)**   Select this option if you want users to have to connect to the AD RMS cluster and acquire a new use license each time they open content based upon this template. If this option is not selected, a client can use a cached version of the use license to consume content.

    ❑ **If You Would Like To Specify Additional Information For Your AD RMS-Enabled Application, You Can Specify Them Here As Name-Value Pairs**   This option provides the ability to add application-specific settings to the policy template.

6. On the Specify Revocation Policy, you can specify whether or not protected content may be revoked based upon a revocation list. You can enable the feature and provide a location where the revocation list and file containing the public key is located.

7. After a rights policy template has been created, you can access a rights summary report by selecting the new template and then clicking View Rights Summary. Figure 18-18 shows an illustration of the User Rights Summary report.

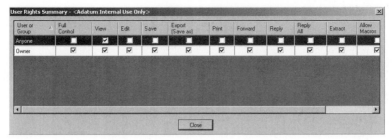

Figure 18-18   Viewing the User Rights Summary report.

> **Note**   Creating a new archived rights policy template follows the same process and steps as the creation of a distributed rights policy template.

Distributing Rights Policy Templates

In order for users to create rights-protected information using a rights policy template, they need to have access to the template. Rights policy templates can be made available from a shared network location for use by internal network users. For mobile users who are not connected to the network at all times, you can copy the templates to a location on the local computer. The AD RMS client built into Windows Server 2008 and Windows Vista SP1 has the ability to automatically detect and update local copies of rights policy templates.

> **How It Works: Distributing AD RMS Rights Policy Templates Automatically with Windows Server 2008 and Windows Vista SP1**
>
> To ease administration of AD RMS rights policy templates, Windows Server 2008 and Windows Vista with Service Pack 1 (SP1) introduces a new template distribution pipeline on all servers in the AD RMS cluster. This new pipeline allows an AD RMS client to request the rights policy templates from the cluster and store them locally on the AD RMS client.
>
> AD RMS rights policy templates are requested from the AD RMS client by using a scheduled task. Two scheduled tasks are available: automated or manual. The manual scheduled task can be run at any time. The automated scheduled task is configured to run one hour after a user logs into the computer and every morning at 03:00. This scheduled task is disabled by default. You can enable it by using the Task Scheduler Control Panel or by using a Group Policy object.
>
> For AD RMS clients that are not running Windows Vista with SP1 or Windows Server 2008, you must still distribute the rights policy templates manually from a central location. For more information about distributing AD RMS rights policy templates, see the "Creating and Deploying Active Directory Rights Management Services Rights Policy

Templates Step-by-Step Guide" at *http://technet2.microsoft.com/windowsserver2008/en/ library/909a3fa6-a7c5-4c86-9468-2b77b72c54841033.mspx.*

Brian M. Lich

Technical Writer

Windows Server Security

Use the following steps to specify a location for rights policy templates and to export the templates to that location:

1. Create a folder on the server as a deployment point to store the exported rights policy templates. You should have Full Control For Everyone on the Share as well as the following permissions on the folder itself:

    ❑ AD RMS Service Group – Modify

    ❑ System – Modify

    ❑ Users – Read

2. In the Active Directory Rights Management Services console, select Rights Policy Templates and then click Change Distributed Rights Policy Templates File Location. Select the check box next to Enable Export and then provide the UNC path to the shared folder that will contain the exported templates. Figure 18-19 provides an illustration of the Rights Policy Templates dialog box. When you click OK, an XML version of the template is exported from the configuration database into the shared folder location.

Figure 18-19 Specifying the location for exported templates.

After you export the rights policy templates to the shared folder location, you will need to configure registry settings on each client computer to point to the local template store. You also have to copy the rights policy templates from the shared folder location on the server to the local template store on each client. For Windows Server 2008 and Windows Vista SP1, you will not have to copy the files manually, as a scheduled task will copy them to the local template store automatically.

The client registry configuration may depend on the type of application being used to protect information. These methods are commonly used to configure the registry settings:

- **Deploy registry settings through Group Policy**   You can use Group Policy preferences or specific application-based Group Policy ADM or ADMX templates to configure registry settings to reflect the location of the template store.

- **Manually configure the registry settings**   You can manually modify the registry to specify the path to the local template store on a client computer. To do this, you must create the following key:

  HKEY_CURRENT_USER\SOFTWARE\Microsoft\Office\12.0\Common\DRM\ AdminiTemplatePath

  Type: REG_EXPAND_SZ

  Recommended Value: %allusersprofile%\Application Data\Microsoft\DRM\ <templatefoldername>

> **Note**   The listed key is for Office 2007. If you are configuring Office 2003, substitute 12.0 with 11.0. Also, for Windows Vista, the recommended value is %userprofile%\ AppData\Local\Microsoft\DRM.

When the AdminTemplatePath registry setting has been configured on each client machine, users will then be able to apply any templates that are available in the local template store to documents that are to be rights-protected. Figure 18-20 shows an example of the Adatum Internal Use Only template being applied to an Office Word 2007 document.

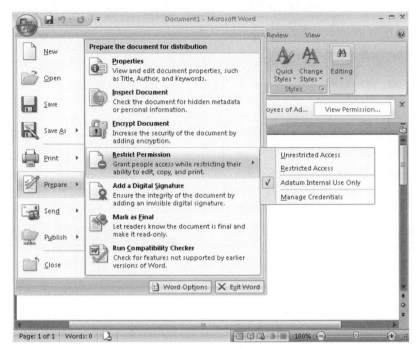

Figure 18-20   Applying a custom rights policy template.

Configuring Exclusion Policies

An exclusion policy enables the ability to exclude specific entities from acquiring certificates and license requests from the AD RMS cluster. Unlike revocation, exclusion does not invalidate the entity. Any existing licenses associated with excluded entities are still valid, but new licensing requests are denied. Four types of exclusion policies can be configured:

- **Users**   You can specify a User Exclusion list that defines which user accounts are not trusted by the AD RMS cluster. When you enable user exclusion, you can specify the user name (in the form of an e-mail address) or the public key of the user's RAC to be excluded on the server.

- **Applications**   You can exclude specific applications from being trusted by the AD RMS server. For example, you may only want to provide rights-management support for a specific version of Microsoft Office. To prevent other versions of Microsoft Office from participating in the AD RMS environment, you can specify the Application filename, minimum version, and maximum version.

- **Lockbox**   You can configure an exclusion policy to ensure that only a specific minimum version of the AD RMS lockbox is being used. Any user with a lockbox version less than the specified version will not be able to obtain RACs or use licenses from the AD RMS cluster.

- **Windows versions** For security reasons, most organizations should be moving away from supporting Windows 98 Second Edition and Windows Millennium Edition. To ensure that these two operating systems are not used in the AD RMS environment, you can configure an exclusion policy to prevent users of these operating systems from obtaining use licenses from the AD RMS cluster.

Configuring Security Policies

The Security Policies node of the Active Directory Rights Management Services console contains a number of security-related features, such as the configuration of super users, changing the cluster key password, and a feature to grant all users full access to protected content. You need to carefully consider the impact on your security model before modifying any of these options, as the results may affect the security of the entire AD RMS cluster.

Managing Super Users

The Super Users group is a specified group that is granted full owner rights in all use licenses issued by the AD RMS cluster. This essentially provides members of the Super Users group full control over all rights-protected content managed by the cluster. This group is typically used as a data recovery mechanism to gain access to expired content or to content protected by a user that has left the organization.

The Super Users group is not enabled by default and should only be enabled when data recovery is required.

To set up a Super Users group, you can perform the following tasks:

1. In Active Directory Users And Computers, create a security group that will be used for the super group. You will also need to provide an e-mail address for the group.

2. In the Active Directory Rights Management Services console, expand the Security Policies node, and then click Super Users.

3. In the Actions pane, click Enable Super Users.

4. In the details pane, click Change Super Users Group.

5. In the Super Users dialog box, type the e-mail address for the Active Directory security group that will be used as the super group.

Figure 18-21 illustrates the configuration of a Super Users group. Notice that *ADRMSSupergroup@Adatum.com* has been configured. Any members of this group will have full owner rights to content managed by this AD RMS cluster.

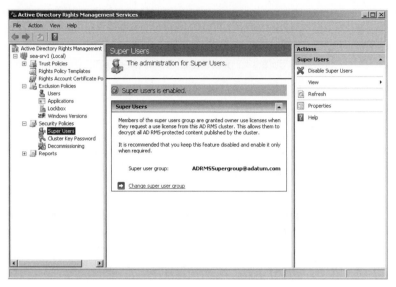

Figure 18-21 Configuring a Super Users group.

You can monitor the enabling and use of the Super Users group by accessing the Application log in the Event Viewer and looking for the events as listed in Table 18-6.

Table 18-6 Events Related to the Super Users Group

Event ID	Source	Description
163	Active Directory Rights Management Services	The Active Directory Rights Management Services (AD RMS) Super Users group has been enabled.
49	Active Directory Rights Management Services	A use license was granted to a user belonging to the Super Users group. The user has the following e-mail address: %1.
		E-mail address: %1.
		A use license is used to consume rights-protected content.

Changing the Cluster Key Password

When you first deploy a new AD RMS cluster, you determine a method for protecting the AD RMS cluster key (AD RMS cluster key protection or the use of a hardware- or software-based CSP). If you were to choose AD RMS cluster key protection, you have to provide a strong password that is used to encrypt the cluster key in the configuration database.

There may be situations where you have to change the cluster key password. This can be performed from the Cluster Key Password node of the Active Directory Rights Management console. If you do reset the password, you must be sure to reset the cluster key password on every AD RMS server in the cluster to ensure proper functionality.

> **Note**   You cannot change the password from a remote console; it has to be changed from the console launched locally on the AD RMS server.

Decommissioning AD RMS

In the event that you need to remove the entire AD RMS cluster from your organization, you need to first decommission the cluster. Decommissioning automatically grants all users full access to all content that was previously protected with the cluster. Users can then save the content without rights-protection.

> **Caution**   When a cluster is decommissioned, it cannot be restored to its previous configuration, and it cannot be reversed. Use with caution!

To decommission AD RMS, perform the following steps:

1. On the AD RMS server, browse to %systemdrive%\inetpub\wwwroot_wmcs\ decommission. Grant the Everyone group Read and Execute permissions on the Decommissioning.asmx file.

2. From within the Active Directory Rights Management Services console, browse to the Security Policies node and then select Decommissioning.

3. In the Actions pane, click Enable Decommissioning.

4. In the details pane, click the Decommission button. Repeat for all servers in the cluster.

5. Export the server licensor certificate and then uninstall the AD RMS server role from the server. Note that this should only be done after you are confident that all rights-protected content has been decrypted.

Viewing Reports

Windows Server 2008 AD RMS provides reports that can be used for gathering statistics or for troubleshooting client certification or licensing issues. These are some of the reports that can be viewed:

- **Statistics Report**   Provides information about the total user accounts certified, domain user accounts certified, and federated identities certified.

- **System Health**   Provides information on the number of total, successful, and failed requests for service location, client licensor certificates, or certification within a given timeframe. Figure 18-22 illustrates an example of a System Health Report.

- **Troubleshooting**   Provides similar information as provided by the System Health report; however, it allows you to get information regarding a specific user and timeframe.

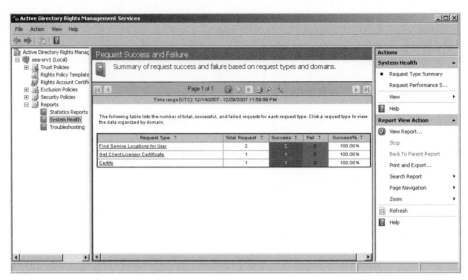

Figure 18-22 Viewing the System Health report.

 Note To view the System Health and Troubleshooting reports, you have to download and install the Microsoft Report Viewer Redistributable 2005. A link is provided within the details pane of the Active Directory Rights Management Services console.

Summary

This chapter introduced Active Directory Rights Management Services (AD RMS) as a way to protect digital content within an organization. Through the use of certification and use certificates, users can apply rights-management permissions on information to prevent unauthorized reading, copying, printing, or forwarding. AD RMS can be used to protect content for users located within the Intranet and users located over the Internet, or it can integrate with Active Directory Federation Services. This chapter also described how to implement and administer an AD RMS environment. Administration tasks include configuring Trust Policies, deploying Rights Policy Templates, applying exclusion policies, and modifying security policies. You can also view statistical and troubleshooting reports to determine the number of users and the health of the AD RMS environment.

Additional Resources

The following resources contain additional information and tools related to this chapter.

Related Information

- Chapter 19, "Active Directory Federation Services," for more information about how to use Active Directory Federation Services

- "Microsoft Windows Rights Management Services Client with Service Pack 2-x86" at *http://go.microsoft.com/fwlink/?LinkId=76880*

- "Microsoft Windows Rights Management Services Client with Service Pack 2-x64" at *http://go.microsoft.com/fwlink/?LinkId=76882*

- "Microsoft Windows Rights Management Services Client with Service Pack 2-IA64" at *http://go.microsoft.com/fwlink/?LinkId=76884*

- "XrML," at *http://www.xrml.org/*

- "Active Directory Rights Management Services SDK" at *http://msdn2.microsoft.com/en-us/library/bb968798(VS.85).aspx*

- "Rights Management Add-on for Internet Explorer" at *http://www.microsoft.com/downloads/details.aspx?FamilyID=B48F920B-5AF0-46B4-994F-2F62582CC86F&display-lang=en*

- "Windows Rights Management Services" at *http://go.microsoft.com/fwlink/?LinkId=14149*

- Active Directory Rights Management Services Technical Library at *http://go.microsoft.com/fwlink/?LinkId=51479*

- Active Directory Rights Management Services Events and Errors Troubleshooting at *http://technet2.microsoft.com/windowsserver2008/en/library/8a2b240e-e426-4c37-8ca4-55a5aaad6fb91033.mspx*

- Active Directory Rights Management Services Installed Help on the Web at *http://technet2.microsoft.com/windowsserver2008/en/library/c70ba42a-272d-4e99-940f-bf7f30277ae41033.mspx*

- Windows Rights Management Services Technical Library at *http://go.microsoft.com/fwlink/?LinkId=68637*

- Active Directory Rights Management Services Scripting API at *http://msdn2.microsoft.com/en-us/library/bb968797(VS.85).aspx*

Active Directory Federation Services

Active Directory Domain Services (AD DS) provides a full-featured directory service for securing and managing an organization's internal network resources. AD DS can also be extended to users outside the organization so that it can be used to authenticate user requests for Web access, authenticate remote connections to Exchange Servers, and authenticate remote access connections. However, because AD DS provides a central store for all users' accounts, AD DS services are extended only to those users with accounts.

Many organizations have established partnerships or working relationships with other organizations that require users from one organization to access information or applications in another organization. AD DS can be extended to provide this level of access by implementing forest trusts. However, forest trusts require that domain controllers in both organizations are able to communicate with each other. If the organizations are connected only by a public Internet connection, establishing forest trusts will raise security concerns.

Microsoft has developed Active Directory Federation Services (AD FS) to address some of these inter-organization access scenarios. AD FS, which was first released with Windows Server 2003 R2, is designed to enable secure access to Web-based applications within an organization and between organizations without the dependency on external or forest trusts between those organizations. With AD FS, IT departments can maintain complete administrative autonomy while still enabling collaboration between organizations. For example, each organization in an AD FS Federated Web SSO business-to-business scenario can manage its own user and group accounts in a way that is transparent to the other organization. Each organization can also manage access to the Web-based applications that it deploys. In this way, AD FS makes it possible for the user accounts from one organization to access the application in the other organization, while still allowing full administrative control to each organization's IT departments.

AD FS also simplifies the user experience by providing users with a Web-based, single sign-on (SSO) experience when they access extranet Web sites or sites on the Internet that are accessible through federation partnerships. This means that users need only authenticate once to their organization's directory service in order to gain access to multiple Web-based applications that may be hosted within that organization's perimeter network or in another organization.

AD FS Overview

In order to provide SSO access to Web-based applications located in different organizations or on different networks in the same organization, IT departments are deploying identity federation solutions. Windows Server 2008 AD FS is an identity federation solution. *Identity federation solutions* provide a standards-based technology for collaborating with other organizations.

Identity Federation

Identity federation is a means by which organizations can enable user access to resources between different organizations or between different server platforms. One of the goals of an identity federation solution is to allow organizations to manage their own directories while still securely exchanging authentication and authorization information between organizations. Another important goal for identity federation solutions is to enable SSO to multiple Web-based applications.

To establish an identity federation partnership, both partners agree to create a federation trust relationship between the two organizations. As a part of the trust, the partners also define what resources will be accessible to the other organization, and how access to the resources will be enabled. For example, an organization may choose to implement an identity federation solution that enables a sales representative to access information from a supplier's database through a Web application hosted on the supplier's network. The administrator for the sales organization is responsible for ensuring that the appropriate sales representatives are members of the group needing access to the supplier's database. The administrator at the supplier's organization ensures that the partner's employees have access only to the data they require.

In an identity federation solution, user identities and their associated credentials are stored, owned, and managed by the organization where the user is located. As part of the identity federation trust, each organization also defines how user identities will be securely shared to provide access to resources. Each partner must define the services that it makes available to trusted partners and customers and also must define which other organizations and users it trusts, what types of credentials and requests it accepts, and how privacy policies ensure that private information is not accessible across the trust.

Identity federation can be implemented in the following scenarios:

- **Business-to-Business (B2B)**   Organizations work with partners, suppliers, and contractors that they trust. These partnerships can include standard vendor relationships as well as outsourcing relationships for internal functions such as benefits, human resources, or travel bookings. Federation trust relationships allow organizations to work together more efficiently, without the overhead of managing identities in different organizations. In this type of relationship, federation becomes the equivalent of electronic data interchange (EDI), except that it uses standard Internet protocols, making trust development simpler to manage and less expensive to maintain. In addition, identity federation provides single sign-on, which allows users to sign in using their corporate credentials without exposing the credentials to the business partner.

  In AD FS, the B2B scenario mentioned here is comparable to the Federated Web SSO design described later in this chapter.

- **Business-to-Employee (B2E)**   An organization may want to provide resources over the Internet to their employees while those employees are out of the office or provide access to business applications in a perimeter network to users inside the organization. For example, organizations might create information portals to provide consolidated information to users by integrating different back-end systems. AD FS can be used to provide secure access to the application while enabling single sign-on access for the users.

  In AD FS, the B2E scenario mentioned here is comparable to the Federated Web SSO with Forest Trust design described later in this chapter.

- **Business-to-Consumer (B2C)**   An organization may want to provide resources over the Internet to individual users who are not employees and who may not have user accounts in any partner organization forest. In this scenario, the organization can create user accounts for the customers in AD DS or AD LDS and then allow those users to authenticate once and access multiple applications.

  In AD FS, the B2C scenario mentioned here is comparable to the Web SSO design described later in this chapter.

Web Services

Identity federation is based on the Web services industry standards. *Web services standards* are a set of specifications used for building connected applications and services whose functionality and interfaces are exposed to potential users located in different organizations and using different platforms. Web services are based on the following standards:

- Most Web services use Extensible Markup Language (XML) to transmit data through HTTP. XML allows developers to create their own customized tags, which enable the definition, transmission, validation, and interpretation of data between applications and between organizations.

- Web services expose useful functionality to Web users through a standard Web protocol. In most cases, the protocol used is SOAP (Simple Object Access Protocol). SOAP is the communications protocol for XML Web services. SOAP is a specification that defines the XML format for messages—essentially, it describes what a valid XML document looks like.

- Web services provide a way to describe their interfaces in enough detail to allow a user to build a client application to talk to them. This description is usually provided in an XML document called a *Web Services Description Language (WSDL) document.* In other words, a WSDL file is an XML document that describes a set of SOAP messages and how the messages are exchanged.

- Web services are registered so that potential users can find them easily. This is done with Universal Description Discovery And Integration (UDDI). A *UDDI directory entry* is an XML file that describes a business and the services it offers. There are three parts to an entry in the UDDI directory. The "white pages" describe the company offering the service: name, address, contacts, etc. The "yellow pages" include industrial categories based on standard taxonomies such as the North American Industry Classification System and the Standard Industrial Classification. The "green pages" describe the interface to the service in enough detail for someone to write an application to use the Web service.

The Web services model is based on the idea that enterprise systems are often written in different programming languages, with different programming models, which run on and are accessed from many different types of devices. Web services are a means of building distributed systems that can connect and interact with one another easily and efficiently across the Internet, regardless of what language they are written in or which platform they run on. As long as the applications use SOAP and XML to communicate, provide a WSDL document that describes how to interface with the application, and provide UDDI directory information for how to locate the application, the applications can interoperate across all platforms.

The Web services specifications include protocols that provide security, reliable messaging, and transactions in a Web services environment. The specifications build on top of the core underlying XML and SOAP standards. AD FS implements two of the WS-Security standards:

- **WS-Federation**   The WS-Federation specification defines how individuals and enterprises can authenticate each other quickly on many heterogeneous IT infrastructures. This specification defines mechanisms to allow different security realms to federate by allowing and brokering trust of identities, attributes, and authentication between participating Web services. AD FS implements the WS-Federation specification by enabling the creation of trust policies between organizations. The trust policies define how an organization will grant access to resources to users in the other organization. AD FS also enables organizations to create claims, which define the user account properties that are sent between organizations to provide authentication and authorization information.

■ **WS-Federation Passive Requestor Profile**   The WS-Federation Passive Requestor Profile is an implementation of WS-Federation, and it proposes a standard protocol for how passive requestors (such as Web browsers) can submit authentication information between trusted partners and how the applications can gain access to resources in partner organizations. Within this protocol, Web service requestors are expected to understand the new security mechanisms and be capable of interacting with Web service providers. AD FS implements the passive requestor profile. In an AD FS deployment, Web browsers must be able to connect to various components in the AD FS infrastructure using HTTPS connections. The Web browser must then be able to authenticate the user in the home organization and then forward the required authentication credentials to Web service applications in the partner organization.

> **More Info**   For more information on the Web services specifications, see the article "Web Services Specifications" located at *http://msdn2.microsoft.com/en-us/webservices/ aa740689.aspx*. One of the benefits of using open standards such as Web services is that AD FS can interoperate with other applications that use the same standards. For examples of how you can implement AD FS with other identity federation solutions, see the Active Directory Federation Services Web site at *http://technet2.microsoft.com/windowsserver/en/technologies/ featured/adfs/default.mspx*.

AD FS Components

In order to implement AD FS, you need to deploy several components on computers running Windows Server 2008 or Windows Server 2003 R2. Depending on the deployment scenario, some or all of these components will be required. Figure 19-1 shows some of the AD FS components.

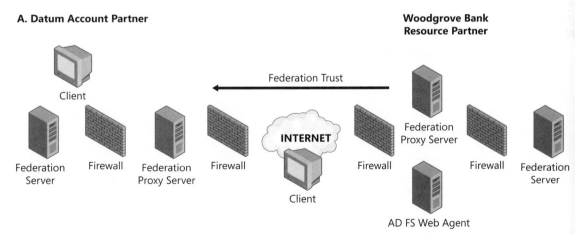

Figure 19-1   AD FS includes several components that can be distributed across multiple servers in different organizations.

Federation Trusts

A *federation trust* is the AD FS implementation of a business-level agreement or partnership between two organizations or between two security realms in the same organization. In AD FS, you create a federation trust between two organizations so that users in one organization can access resources in another organization, or so that users can access resources across any other organization or technical boundaries. The federation trust enables authentication requests that are made to the Web server in the resource partner organization to flow successfully through the federation trust from users who are located in the account partner organization.

> **Note** A federation trust is established between two federation servers running the Federation Service. These trusts are not related to the trusts that can be established between Windows NT or Active Directory Domain Services (AD DS) domains.

Account Partner

An *account partner* is the organization partner in the federation trust that hosts and manages the user accounts used in the relationship. Accounts are stored in AD DS, Active Directory Application Mode (ADAM), or AD LDS. The federation server in the account partner issues security tokens that make assertions about users; for example, the token may indicate that the user is a manager. These tokens can then be presented across a federation trust to access resources in the resource partner organization.

Resource Partner

A resource partner is the second organization partner in the federation trust relationship. The resource partner physically houses the Web servers that host one or more Web-based applications. The resource partner trusts the account partner to authenticate users and provide security tokens. The resource partner servers then make authorization decisions based on the security tokens that are produced by the account partner.

> **Note** Figure 19-1 shows a Federation Web SSO design in which the account partner and resource partner roles are clearly defined. In the Federation Web SSO or Web SSO designs, one organization may be both the account partner and the resource partner.

Federation Service

The Federation Service is one of the role services available when you install the AD FS server role on a Windows Server 2008 computer. The Federation Service is the AD FS component that functions as a security token service. All implementations of AD FS require at least one Federation Service to be installed. In a Federation Web SSO design, a federation server is required for both the account partner and resource partner organizations.

When configured as an account partner, the Federation Service allows users to access resources at partner organizations. The Federation Service provides the following functionality:

1. Collect and verify user credentials against AD DS or AD LDS. A user's authentication requests are sent to the federation server, which verifies that the user account can be authenticated against the directory service.

2. Populate a set of organization claims based on LDAP attributes stored for the account in a directory service. An AD FS claim is a statement made about a user that is understood by both partners in an AD FS federation scenario. For example, if the federation trust uses the user's group membership to provide access to applications, the federation server will add the group membership attribute to the security token.

3. Map organization claims to an agreed set of outgoing federation claims for the resource partner. As part of the federation trust configuration, organizations will agree on how to map attributes in the account organization to information that can be used to make resource access decisions in the resource organization. For example, members of a managers group in the account partner may be provided with more access to the application than members of other groups. The federation server adds this mapping information to the security token.

4. Package the claims into a digitally signed security token. The security token is provided to the Web client that is requesting access to the application in the resource organization.

When configured as a resource partner, the Federation Service enables access to the Web application. The Federation Service on the resource partner performs these tasks:

1. Verifies security tokens. When the user provides a security token from the federation server on the account partner, the resource Federation Service verifies the claims information presented by the user to ensure that it came from a trusted account partner.

2. Maps incoming claims into the equivalent resource organization claims. For example, the incoming claim may indicate that the user is a member of the managers group. The resource Federation Service maps that information to a claim that is understood by the Web application to provide access required by sales managers.

3. Packages the organization claims into a new digitally signed security token that is returned to the Web client. The Web client then presents this token to the Web application.

Federation Claims

Federation claims are created by the Federation Service and are assertions about a user based on information retrieved from an LDAP directory store. The claims data is stored in attributes held for a particular user and may include information about which groups a user is a member of or any other attribute-based information, such as a user's title. These claims are used by the resource Federation Service to make decisions about the level of access granted to the user.

Federation Service Proxy

A *Federation Service Proxy* is another role service that you can install separately on a Windows Server 2008 computer. The server that hosts the Federation Service Proxy service is also referred to as a federation server proxy. The federation server proxy is usually deployed in a perimeter network to protect a federation server at either the account partner or the resource partner, or both. By implementing a federation server proxy, you can avoid exposing the federation servers directly to the Internet.

A federation server proxy communicates with a protected Federation Service on the client's behalf. When the federation server proxy is protecting an account partner, it collects user credential information from browser clients and passes the request to the Federation Service. When the federation server proxy is protecting a resource partner, it relays requests by and for Web-based applications to the Federation Service.

AD FS Web Agents

AD FS–enabled Web servers consume security tokens and either allow or deny a user access to a Web application. To accomplish this, the AD FS–enabled Web server requires a relationship with a resource Federation Service so that it can direct the user to the Federation Service as needed. The AD FS Web Agent provides that connection between the application and the Federation Service.

The AD FS Web Agent is implemented as an ISAPI extension in Internet Information Services (IIS) 7.0. AD FS Web Agents support two different types of applications:

- **Claims-aware applications**   If applications have been especially written or modified to understand claims, they are known as *claims-aware applications*. When used with claims-aware applications, the AD FS Web Agent can make claims available directly to an application which is coded to know how to use them (typically, what access to provide to a user who presents a particular claim).

- **Windows token-based applications**   Older applications, sometimes known as *legacy applications*, are not coded to understand claims. Instead, these applications can make authorization decisions based on security principal SIDs and access control lists. In such cases, the application can be configured to create a Windows NT security token for the user making the request that matches a user from the resource partner directory service. To restrict access to the application, you must then configure the access control lists on the resource being accessed to use the Windows NT security token.

Servers that have either of the AD FS Web Agents installed are also referred to as AD FS–enabled Web servers.

AD FS Deployment Designs

AD FS can be deployed in many different situations and can be used to provide access to many different applications running in different locations and on different server platforms. However, all of the AD FS designs break down into the following scenarios:

- Business-to-Business
- Business-to-Employee
- Business-to-Consumer

These business scenarios do not appear as configuration options in AD FS when you install or configure the AD FS components. In fact, AD FS provides more than one option for implementing the business scenarios. There are three possible designs in AD FS:

- **Web Single Sign-on (SSO) Design**   In a Web SSO scenario, one organization deploys one or more Web-based applications that need to be accessed by users both inside and outside the organization. By implementing AD FS, these applications can be accessed by users after a single authentication. The Web SSO deployment option is suitable for both B2E and B2C scenarios.

- **Federated Web SSO Design**   In a Federated Web SSO solution, two organizations, or two security realms in a single organization, provide access to applications in one organization to users in another organization. The Federated Web SSO deployment option is suitable for B2B scenarios.

- **Federated Web SSO with Forest Trust Design**   In a Federated Web SSO solution, an organization is using multiple forests to manage user accounts but still wants to use AD FS to provide the SSO feature. This deployment option is primarily used for B2E scenarios.

When you add account and resource partners to a Federation Service, you are asked whether you would like to implement the Federated Web SSO or the Federated Web SSO with Forest Trust deployment option. The Web SSO deployment option is implied in an AD FS deployment.

Web SSO Design

In a Web SSO design, users must authenticate only once to access multiple AD FS–secured applications. In this design, users may be external employees or customers, or they may be internal employees. In a Web SSO design, no federation trust exists because there are no partners. Typically, you deploy this design when you want to provide an employee or customer access to one or more AD FS–secured applications over the Internet. With the Web SSO design, an organization that typically hosts an AD FS–secured application in a perimeter network can maintain a separate store of customer accounts in the perimeter network, which makes it easier to isolate customer accounts and employee accounts. You can manage the local accounts for customers in the perimeter network by using either AD DS or AD LDS as the account store.

To implement the Web SSO design, you must install at least one federation server and a Web server running the AD FS Web Agent. Since you do not have a second federation server to act as the account partner, you do not add an account partner in the AD FS. Instead, you add a local account store to this single federation server so that it not only protects an application, but it also requests user authentication and provides the security tokens to provide access to the application.

The account store you choose may be the internal or external directory. A common scenario in a B2E deployment is to use an internal directory service such as AD DS. If you are deploying the Web SSO design, you are more likely to use AD LDS as the account store and locate the AD LDS server in the perimeter network. You can even deploy both options on one federation server. If you have employee accounts in the AD DS and external accounts in AD LDS, you could add two account stores to your AD FS configuration. These would be searched in the specified order to find where the user account is located.

Figure 19-2 shows how the traffic flows in a Web SSO design. In this example, the organization has deployed AD LDS as the account store. This solution uses a single federation server and AD LDS server, hosted in the corporate network, with a federation server proxy and Web server in the perimeter network.

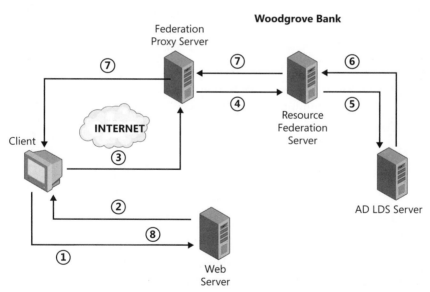

Figure 19-2   The Web SSO design option can provide access to a Web application for customers.

The following steps describe how resource access works in this deployment:

1. A Woodgrove Bank customer uses a Web browser to make a request over HTTPS to access an application running on the Web server in the perimeter network at Woodgrove Bank.

2. The AD FS Web Agent intercepts the request and checks to see if the client has an AD FS authentication cookie that allows access to the application. Because the client does not have this cookie, the client request is refused, and the client is redirected to the federation proxy server.

3. The client sends an HTTPS request to the federation proxy server. The client is redirected to the federation proxy server authentication page, and the client is prompted for logon credentials.

4. The federation proxy server accepts the credentials, and the request is passed through to the resource Federation Service.

5. The resource federation server goes directly to a local account store, AD LDS, to request authentication for the user.

6. AD LDS authenticates the user if it can. The resource federation server retrieves attributes from AD LDS by LDAP and builds the security token and the AD FS authentication token for the AD FS–enabled Web server application.

7. The authentication information and other information is placed in a claim and passed back to the client, via the proxy, with a redirect message telling the client to present the security token to the original URL.

8. The AD FS Web Agent receives the request, validates the signed tokens, and, if successful, issues another AD FS authentication cookie and forwards the request to the Web service process, which provides access to the application based on the claims.

Federated Web SSO Design

The Federated Web Single Sign-On (SSO) design in Active Directory Federation Services (AD FS) is used to provide secure communication between organizations. Typically, this design is used when two organizations agree to create a federation trust relationship to allow users in one organization (the account partner organization) to access Web-based applications, which are secured by AD FS, in the other organization (the resource partner organization).

In a typical Federation Web SSO design, one organization has deployed an application that needs to be accessible to the users in the other organization. In a federation trust, this organization is the resource partner. The resource partner needs to ensure the security of the application. Securing the application means that the organization can ensure that only authorized users can access the application. In addition, the resource organization may also want to configure different levels of access, so that some users get access to more application components or can perform more actions than others. In Figure 19-3, Woodgrove Bank is the resource partner.

The other organization in the Federation Web SSO design hosts the user accounts that need access to the application in the resource partner organization. This organization is called the *account partner*. The account partner wants to maintain full control of the user and group accounts in its organization and wants to limit what types of information about the users is made available to other organizations. In Figure 19-3, A. Datum is the account partner.

In a Federation Web SSO design implementation, both organizations must configure at least one federation server, and the resource organization must also configure a Web server running the application and the AD FS Web Agent. Both organizations may also implement a federation server proxy.

> **Note**   Figure 19-3 shows the AD FS components involved in a Federation Web SSO design. Federation Service proxies are not included in the figure in order to simplify the diagram. If the organizations did deploy a federation server proxy, all communication between the client and the federation server would be proxied through the federation server proxy.

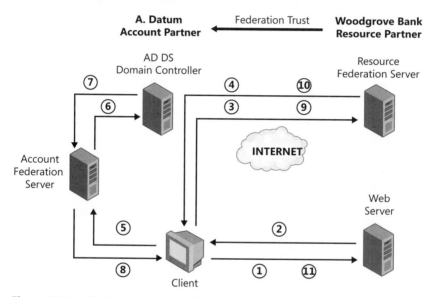

Figure 19-3   The Federated Web SSO design can provide access to a Web application between organizations.

The following steps describe the Federated Web SSO traffic flow:

1. A user at A. Datum uses a Web browser to make a request over HTTPS to access an application running on the Web server at Woodgrove Bank.

2. The AD FS Web Agent installed on the Web server intercepts the request and checks to see if the client has presented a cookie legitimizing the request. If the user has not yet authenticated, the client will not have this cookie. In this case, the AD FS Web Agent uses a HTTP 302 redirect message to redirect the client to the resource federation server hosted at Woodgrove Bank. The AD FS Web Agent is not aware of the federation trust, so it must redirect the client request to the federation server.

3. The client sends an HTTPS request to the resource federation server. The resource Federation Service must now determine where the account is held for this use—this is known as the *home realm discovery*. Based on the federation trust configuration, which includes information such as the UPN or e-mail address, the resource federation server will determine that the home realm is A. Datum.

4. The client is redirected again, this time to the account federation server at A. Datum.

5. The client sends an HTTPS request to the account Federation Service.

6. The user is authenticated by using Windows integrated authentication or by providing credentials when prompted by the federation server.

7. AD DS authenticates the user and sends the success message back to the federation server, along with other information about the user stored in the directory (attributes, group memberships, and so on), which will be used to generate the user's claims.

8. The claims data is placed in a digitally signed security token and given to the client as an authentication cookie, with a further redirect back to the resource Federation Service.

9. The client sends the security token to the resource Federation Service, which validates that the security token comes from a trusted partner. If it did, the federation server will issue a home realm cookie so that future requests will not have to go through the home realm discovery process again, until the cookie expires.

10. If successful, the federation server creates and signs a new token of its own to issue to the client, as a resource partner cookie, with a final redirect back to the original URL requested.

11. The Web Agent receives the request, validates the signed tokens, and, if successful, issues a further cookie and forwards the request to the Web service process.

Federated Web SSO with Forest Trust Design

The Federated Web SSO with Forest Trust design combines two Active Directory forests in a single organization. Typically, you use this design when you want to provide employees on the corporate network and remote employees with federated access to AD FS–secured applications in the perimeter network, while using each employee's standard corporate domain credentials.

In a Federated Web SSO with Forest Trust design, the organization deploys two AD DS forests, one in the internal network and one in the perimeter network. A one-way forest trust is configured between the perimeter forest and the corporate forest so that employee user accounts that are on the internal forest may be used to access the application installed on a server in the perimeter network forest. This scenario is most frequently used when you use Windows NT token-based applications. A Windows NT token-based application requires that a security principal exists so that the AD FS token can be mapped to it. By deploying two forests, you can configure the security principal account in the internal forest.

> **Note**   If a trust is not in place between the internal forest and the perimeter forest and the application in the perimeter network is a Windows NT token-based application, you can create shadow accounts or groups in the perimeter network forest. Users will then use these accounts to gain access to the application.

The Federated Web SSO with Forest Trust design can provide access to AD FS protected resources for both internal and external employees. Figure 19-4 illustrates the traffic flow in the scenario in which users are located outside the organization.

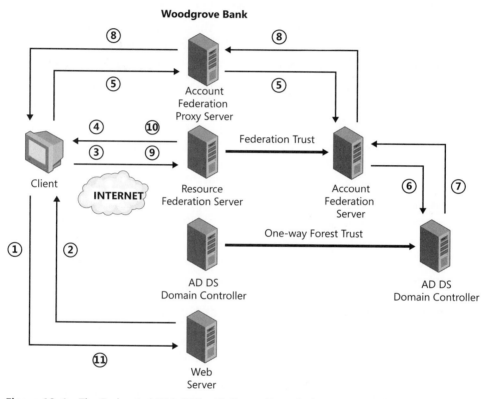

Figure 19-4   The Federated Web SSO with Forest Trust design can provide access to a Web application in a perimeter forest.

The following steps describe the processes:

1. A Woodgrove Bank employee, who is outside the office, uses a Web browser to make a request over HTTPS to access an application running on the Web server in the perimeter network.

2. The AD FS Web agent intercepts the request. Because the client does not have the required cookie, the AD FS Web Agent redirects the client to the resource federation server.

3. The client sends an HTTPS request to the resource federation server.

4. The resource federation server redirects the client to the account federation proxy server.

5. The account federation proxy server requests the user credentials and then passes the request through to the account federation server.

6. The account federation server forwards the authentication request to the AD DS domain controller.

7. Active Directory authenticates the user, if it can, and sends the success message back to the account federation server along with other information about the user stored in the directory (attributes, group memberships, and so on), which will be used to generate the user's claims.

8. If the authentication is successful, the authentication information and other information is wrapped up in a claim and passed back to the client, via the proxy, with a redirect message telling the client to present the security token to the resource Federation Service.

9. The Web browser presents the security token to the resource federation server. The resource federation server builds the security token and AD FS authentication token for the Web application.

10. The resource federation server provides the tokens to the Web browser and redirects the client to connect to the AD FS Web application.

11. The Web Agent receives the request and the AD FS authentication cookie. Because the application is a Windows NT token-based rather than a claims-aware application, the application must build an impersonation Windows NT token from the security token. The application then uses this Windows NT token to impersonate the user account and provide the appropriate level of access.

If the user is located inside the organization, the same process is followed, with the exception that the account federation proxy server is not used to authenticate the user. Because the user is already on the internal network, the Web browser can communicate directly with the account federation server.

Implementing AD FS

After choosing an AD FS design, you will implement AD FS by installing and configuring the AD FS components on computers running Windows Server 2008. This section describes how to deploy and configure federation servers, federation server proxies, and AD FS–enabled Web servers. It also describes the different types of AD FS applications (claims-aware and Windows NT token-based) and describes how to implement each type of application.

Note This section describes how to deploy AD FS in the Federated Web SSO design. This deployment option is the most complicated scenario that includes the maximum number of AD FS components. The actual components that you require and the way you configure them depend on the AD FS design.

AD FS Deployment Requirements

In order to deploy AD FS, you must first make sure that your corporate network infrastructure is configured to support AD FS requirements.

Network Requirements

In order to deploy AD FS, you must ensure that the following network requirements are met:

- **TCP/IP connectivity** For AD FS to function, TCP/IP network connectivity must exist between the client, the AD DS or AD LDS servers, and the computers that host the Federation Service, the Federation Service Proxy, and the AD FS Web Agents. Because all client requests use HTTPS, you must ensure HTTPS connectivity between the client and all servers running AD FS roles required by the client.

- **DNS requirements** In order for AD FS to function, you must ensure that the client computers can resolve the names of all of the servers running AD FS components. You need to ensure that name resolution works in the following ways:

  - ❏ Client computers from the Internet or from account organizations must be able to resolve the DNS names for the Web servers running the AD FS Web Agent. The clients will connect to these servers to start the process of AD FS authentication and authorization and to access the application after the user has been authenticated. Client computers must also be able to resolve the DNS names for federation proxy servers or federation servers.

  - ❏ If you are enabling AD FS access for internal users and any AD FS servers are deployed in the perimeter network, the client computers on the internal network must be able to resolve the IP addresses for AD FS servers.

  - ❏ Federation proxy servers must be able to resolve the names of the federation servers in order to forward client requests. You can enable this name resolution by using host files on the federation proxy servers or by implementing DNS in the perimeter network with the appropriate zones.

Client Web Browser requirements

Almost any current Web browser with JScript enabled can work as an AD FS client. Microsoft has tested Internet Explorer 5 or newer browsers, including Internet Explorer 7, Mozilla Firefox, and Safari on Apple Macintosh. Jscript should be enabled for the Web browsers.

AD FS creates authentication cookies that must be stored on client computers to provide SSO functionality. Therefore, the client browser must be configured to accept cookies. Authentication cookies are always Secure Hypertext Transfer Protocol (HTTPS) session cookies that are written for the originating server. If the client browser is not configured to allow these cookies, AD FS cannot function correctly.

AD FS uses three types of cookies that assist in authentication and authorization tasks during a session:

- **Authentication cookie** The *authentication cookie* facilitates single sign-on (SSO) to resources located at the resource partner. Authentication cookies can be issued by both the Federation Service and the AD FS Web Agent. When issued by the account Federation Service, the security token in a cookie holds the organization claims for the client. The organization claims may be mapped to outgoing claims for a particular resource.

   After the resource Federation Service validates the client once, the authentication cookie is written to the client. Further authentication takes place through use of the cookie rather than through repeated collection of the client credentials.

   The AD FS Web Agent can authenticate and use cookies that are issued by the account federation server. The Web server receives a cookie when the client connects to the Web server. Then, the AD FS Web Agent can authenticate this cookie and use the claims that it contains. The authentication cookie is always a session cookie and is signed but not encrypted, which is one reason that use of Transport Layer Security and Secure Sockets Layer (TLS/SSL) in AD FS is mandatory.

- **Account partner cookie** The *account partner cookie* facilitates SSO. After the resource partner has confirmed that the authentication cookie provided by the account partner is valid, the account partner cookie is written to the client. Further interactions use the information in this cookie rather than prompting the client for account partner membership information again. The account partner cookie is set as a result of the account partner discovery process. The account partner cookie is a long-lived, persistent cookie. It is neither signed nor encrypted.

- **Sign-out cookie** The *sign-out cookie* facilitates sign-off. Whenever the Federation Service issues a token, the token's resource partner or target server is added to the sign-out cookie. When it receives a sign-off request, the federation server or federation server proxy sends requests to each of the token target servers asking them to clean up any authentication artifacts, such as cached cookies, that the resource partner or Web server may have written to the client. In the case of a resource partner, it sends a cleanup request to any application Web servers that the client has used. The sign-out cookie is always a session cookie. It is neither signed nor encrypted.

Account Store Requirements

AD FS requires at least one account store to be used for authenticating users and extracting security claims for those users. AD FS supports two types of account stores: AD DS and AD LDS.

AD DS You can use AD DS as the account store if your organization is the account partner and you want to allow locally stored identities to access federated applications (both claims-aware applications and Windows NT token-based applications) in a resource partner. If your organization is the resource partner, you will need to use AD DS to grant access permissions for Windows NT token-based applications to federated users. In this scenario, each federated user must be mapped to a resource account or resource group in a local AD DS domain. You can add only one AD DS account store to AD FS.

For AD FS to operate successfully, Active Directory domain controllers in either the account partner organization or the resource partner organization must be running Windows 2000 Server SP4 with critical updates, Windows Server 2003 SP1, Windows Server 2003 R2, or Windows Server 2008.

AD LDS You can also use AD LDS or ADAM as the account store if you want to allow locally stored identities to access federated applications (both claims-aware applications and Windows NT token-based applications) located in a resource partner. If your organization is the resource partner, you cannot use AD LDS to map federated users to local resource accounts or resource groups.

You can add multiple AD LDS account stores to AD FS. When a federation server needs to authenticate a user, it will use the first account store configured to request authentication for the user. If the store does not contain the account for the user, the federation server will query the other stores in the order in which you have configured them.

The computers that host the ADAM account store must be running Windows 2000 Server with Service Pack 4 (SP4) or higher, Windows Server 2003 with Service Pack 1 (SP1), or Windows Server 2003 R2. To install AD LDS, the computer must be running Windows Server 2008.

Web Server Requirements

IIS is a mandatory requirement for all AD FS server components. When you choose to install any of the AD FS server role services and the Web Server (IIS) server role is not installed, you are prompted to add the required IIS components.

> **Note** AD FS also requires that .NET Framework 2.0 and ASP.NET be installed on the computer. .NET Framework 2.0 is installed by default on Windows Server 2008 computers, and ASP.NET is installed when the Web Server (IIS) server role is installed.

Public Key Infrastructure (PKI) Requirements

In order to secure the communications between all of the AD FS components, AD FS requires that all Web sites that accept user authentication traffic or security tokens be configured with server authentication certificates. These certificates are used for account partner and resource partner authentication and for authentication between federation servers and federation server proxies. This means that you must obtain the required digital certificates from a certification authority (CA). You can use a trusted third party CA or an internal Active Directory Certificate Services (AD CS) CA to issue these certificates.

Certificates Used by Federation Servers   Federation servers perform both server-based and client-based functions that require the use of specific types of certificates:

- **Token-signing certificate**   Each federation server uses a *token-signing certificate* to digitally sign all security tokens that it produces. Because each security token is digitally signed by the account partner, the resource partner can verify that the security token was in fact issued by the account partner and that it was not modified. This helps prevent attackers from forging or modifying security tokens to gain unauthorized access to resources. Digital signatures on security tokens are also used within the account partner when more than one federation server is used. In this situation, the digital signatures verify the origin and integrity of security tokens that are issued by other federation servers within the account partner. The digital signatures are verified with verification certificates. Each token-signing certificate contains a private key that is associated with the certificate.

> **Note**   If you install more than one federation server in a server farm, you can assign the same token-signing certificate to each federation server, or you can assign a unique certificate to each server. To simplify and decrease the cost of your deployment, you should install the same token-signing certificate on all federation servers. For more details on planning a federation server farm deployment, see the "AD FS Design Guide" located at *http://go.microsoft.com/fwlink/?LinkId=91898*.

- **Verification certificate**   A *verification certificate* is used to verify that a security token was issued by a valid federation server and that it was not modified. A verification certificate is actually the token-signing certificate of another federation server. To verify that a security token was issued by a given federation server and not modified, the federation server must have a verification certificate for the federation server that issued the security token. For example, if the federation server at A. Datum issues a security token and sends the security token to a federation server at Woodgrove Bank, the Woodgrove Bank federation server must have a verification certificate (which is the A. Datum federation server's token-signing certificate). Unlike a token-signing certificate, a verification certificate does not contain the private key that is associated with the certificate.

The root CA certificate for the verification certificates must be trusted by the resource partners and Web Agents that trust the federation server. In addition, the certificate revocation lists (CRLs) of the certificate must be accessible to resource partners and Web Agents that trust the federation server.

> **Note**   The resource federation server must have access to the token-signing certificate for the account federation server. You will import the certificate when you create an account partner on the resource federation server.

■   **SSL server authentication certificate**   The federation server uses an SSL server authentication certificate to secure Web services traffic for communication with Web clients or the federation server proxy.

The root CA for all SSL server authentication certificates must be trusted by any federation server proxies and Web Agents that trust this federation server, and the CRLs must be accessible for all the certificates in the chain, from the server authentication certificate to the root CA certificate. In addition, the subject name that is used in the server authentication certificate must match the Domain Name System (DNS) name of the Federation Service endpoint Uniform Resource Locator (URL) in the trust policy.

Direct from the Source: Troubleshooting Certificate Revocation Issues

Certificate issues are among the top five AD FS troubleshooting hot spots for the product support team at Microsoft. One particular AD FS–related certificate issue centers on a known routine process that checks for the validity of a certificate by comparing it to a certificate authority-issued list of revoked certificates. This process, in the world of public key infrastructure (PKI), is known as certificate revocation list (CRL) checking.

The revocation verification setting configured for an account partner on a federation server is used by the federation server to determine how revocation verification will be performed for tokens sent by that account partner. The revocation verification setting of the federation server itself, configured on the *Trust Policy* node of the AD FS snap-in, is used by the federation server and by any AD FS Web Agent bound to the federation server to determine how the revocation verification process will be performed for the federation server's own token-signing certificate. The verification process will make use of CRLs imported on the local machine or that are available through the CRL distribution point.

When troubleshooting certificate issues, it is important to be able to quickly disable revocation checking to help you locate the source of the problem. For example, this can be helpful in deployment scenarios where there are no CRLs available for the token-signing certificates.

To help troubleshoot CRL checking issues, the AD FS product team has provided a method within the AD FS snap-in in Windows Server 2008 that allows you to adjust or disable how revocation checking behaves within the scope of a Federation Service. For example, you can set revocation checking to check for the validity of all the certificates in a certificate chain or only the end certificate in the certificate chain.

Nick Pierson

Senior Technical Writer, Microsoft

Certificates Used by Federation Server Proxies   Federation server proxies use SSL to secure communication to both the federation servers and to Web clients. These certificates include:

- **SSL client authentication certificates**   Each federation server proxy uses an SSL client authentication certificate to authenticate to the Federation Service. A copy of the federation server proxy client authentication certificate is stored on both the federation server proxy and in the trust policy of the federation server. However, only the federation server proxy stores the private key that is associated with the federation server proxy client authentication certificate.

- **SSL server authentication certificates**   The federation server proxy uses SSL server authentication certificates to secure Web services traffic for communication with Web clients.

Certificates Used by the AD FS Web Agent   Each Web server that hosts the AD FS Web Agent uses SSL server authentication certificates to securely communicate with Web clients. These certificates are requested and installed through the Internet Information Services snap-in or can be installed through Group Policy or autoenrollment if you have deployed AD CS.

Note   You can also choose to use client certificates for client computers that connect to federation servers, federation proxy servers, or the Web servers. Client authentication provides an extra level of security, but it also requires that you distribute certificates to all client computers that will be connecting to your AD FS environment. If you are deploying AD FS only for employees who only use client computers that are members of the internal AD DS forest, you can automate the certificate distribution by enabling autoenrollment in AD CS. For details on how to do this, see Chapter 17, "Active Directory Certificate Services."

Direct from the Field: Choosing a Certification Authority

You can address the certificate requirements for AD FS by purchasing certificates from a public certification authority (CA), by using an internal CA that is part of an AD CS implementation, or by using self-signed certificates. Table 19-1 lists advantages and disadvantages with each option.

Table 19-1   Advantages and Disadvantages for CA Options

CA Type	Explanation
Public CA	Advantages: ■ Client computers will already trust the root CA, so certificates can be chained to the root without further configuration. ■ The public CA provides full certificate and certificate revocation management services. Disadvantages: ■ The certificates issued by public CAs are more expensive than self-signed certificates or certificates issued by internal CAs. ■ If security policies used by the public CA are not sufficient, there is an increased security risk.

Table 19-1   Advantages and Disadvantages for CA Options *(continued)*

CA Type	Explanation
Internal CA	Advantages: ■ Revocation is managed internally, so certificates can be centrally revoked if a private key is compromised. ■ By managing your own CA, you have more flexibility in how you manage certificate distribution. ■ By managing your own CA, you have complete control over the security of the implementation. Disadvantages: ■ Implementing an internal CA can be complicated, and the complexity can introduce security problems if incorrectly managed. ■ Although the certificates issued by internal CAs are free, the cost of implementing and managing a CA implementation can be much more costly than buying certificates from a public CA. ■ Client computers will not automatically trust the root CA, so you must add certificates for the trusted root to client machines where necessary.
Self-signed certificates	Advantages: ■ Self-signed certificates can be deployed without any PKI infrastructure. ■ Certificates are free. Disadvantages: ■ Centralized revocation lists are not available. If the private key of the certificate is compromised, each relying party must be notified manually to change to a new certificate and stop relying on the existing one. ■ Client computers will not automatically trust the self-signed certificate, so you must add certificates for the trusted root to client machines where necessary. ■ Self-signed certificates are not part of a certificate trust page, so each self-signed cert must be explicitly trusted by a relying party.

Because the SSL certificates assigned to the Web servers and federation servers are going to be accessed by a large number of clients, it is recommended that you use a public CA for any SSL certificates. The token-signing certificates need to be trusted only by the servers running AD FS role services, so you could consider using either an internal CA or a self-signed certificate. If your organization is an account partner and expects to have many resource partners, an internal CA will usually be better because of the need for centralized revocation and trust management. If an organization will have few resource partners, self-signed certificates are often a better choice due to costs and complexity concerns.

Implementing AD FS in a Federation Web SSO Design

After verifying that your environment meets all of the prerequisites, you are ready to start installing the AD FS components. This section provides a description of the process for doing so.

Implementing Federation Web SSO Design Overview

In order to implement the Federation Web SSO design, you need to complete the following procedures:

Preparing the Environment

1. Install the Web Server (IIS) server role on all servers participating in the AD FS deployment. Although you can install this server role as part of the AD FS server role installment, you should perform this step first if you want to configure the required server certificates before installing AD FS.

> **Note** The steps for installing the Web Server role will not be included in the following sections. For details, see the Server Manager and Internet Information Services Online Help.

2. Obtain the required authentication certificates for each server participating in the AD FS scenario and configure the applicable Web sites on each server to require SSL. This task includes the Web servers and all AD FS–related servers. If you choose to use a self-signed certificate, you can install the certificate at the same time that you are installing AD FS.

    In order for AD FS to function, the following certificate requirements must be configured:

    ❑ The token-signing certificate used by the account partner must be imported on the resource federation server. To do this, export the token-signing certificate on the account federation server to a file and have it available to import on the resource federation server when you create a new account partner.

    ❑ The server authentication certificate for the resource federation server must be trusted by the AD FS Web server. If you are using a public CA for the resource federation sever, the certificate will be trusted. If you are using an internal CA, you will need to export the certificate on the resource federation server and import it to the Trusted Root Certificate Authorities folder on the AD FS Web server.

    ❑ If you are using a federation proxy server, the proxy server must be configured with a client certificate that is trusted by the corresponding federation server.

> **Note** The steps for importing and exporting the server certificates will not be included in the following sections. For details, see the Internet Information Services Online Help or the AD FS Deployment Guide at *http://go.microsoft.com/fwlink/ ?LinkId=91899.*

3. Install the Federation Service role service. Install the AD FS Federation Service role service on the designated account partner and resource partner servers. During this process, you can create a self-signed token-signing certificate used to secure tokens used for authentication.

4. Install the Federation Service Proxy role service. Install the AD FS Federation Service Proxy role service on the designated account partner and resource partner servers.

5. Install the AD FS Web Agent. The AD FS Web Agent is installed and configured on the Web server running the claims-aware or Windows NT token-based application.

Configuring the Account Federation Partner   Configuring the Federation Service for the account environment includes a number of tasks:

1. Configure the trust policy. Configuring the trust policy includes entering the appropriate Federation Service URI and the Federation Service endpoint URL for the account federation environment.

2. Configure the organization claims. On the account side, organization claims are a standard set of claims that are populated from an either AD DS or AD LDS. The organization claims map AD DS or AD LDS attributes to AD FS objects that are understood by the federation servers.

3. Add and configure account stores. The user accounts used by the account partner must be stored in either AD DS or AD LDS. By adding the account store to AD FS, you enable the account federation server to access the user accounts.

4. Add and configure a resource partner. Adding a resource partner represents the configuration of the relationship between the account and resource partner organizations.

> **Note**   On both the account partner and resource partner, you can export the federation trust policy settings to an .xml file and then use the file to configure many of the settings on the partner federation server.

5. Create outgoing claim mapping (transformations) for the resource partner. After establishing a federated trust between two organizations, you may need to map, or transform, the account partner's organization claims into claims that can be consumed by the resource partner application.

Configuring the Resource Federation Partner   Configuring the Federation Service for the resource environment includes a number of tasks:

1. Configure the trust policy. Configuring the trust policy includes entering the appropriate Federation Service URI and the Federation Service endpoint URL for the resource federation environment.

2. Configure the organization claims. In order for the resource to make appropriate access decisions, organization claims must be added to the resource Federation Service.

3. Add and configure an AD FS application. The AD FS resource partner provides the shared resource. The application must be added to the Federation Service so that the federation server can redirect client requests to the appropriate Web server.

4. Add and configure an account partner. Adding an account partner represents the configuration of the relationship between the account and resource partner organizations. This relationship is established by configuring the account partner settings and by importing the verification certificate from the account partner.

5. Create an incoming claim mapping for the application. This task transforms the incoming organization claims from the account partner to map to the organization claims for the resource partner.

Configuring the Web Server and Web-based Applications   As part of the AD FS deployment, you will also need to configure the Web server and Web-based applications. This task includes setting up either a claims-aware application or a Windows NT token-based application. Depending on the type of application configured, specific application and Web server configuration settings may be required.

> **On the Disc**   An AD FS deployment can have many components and many different configurations. As you plan your AD FS deployment, use the AD FS Documentation.xls spreadsheet located on the companion CD to document each component.

Deploying Federation Servers

To install the Federation Service, ensure that all of the prerequisite components are installed and configured on the server, and then complete the following steps:

1. From Server Manager, right-click Roles and then click Add Roles to start the Add Roles Wizard.

2. On the Before You Begin page, click Next.

3. On the Select Server Roles page, click Active Directory Federation Services. Click Next two times.

4. On the Select Role Services page (see Figure 19-5), select the Federation Service check box. If you are prompted to install additional Web Server (IIS) or Windows Process Activation Service role services, click Add Required Role Services to install them and then click Next.

5. On the Choose A Server Authentication Certificate For SSL Encryption page, choose the certificate that you want to use for SSL encryption and then click Next. If you already have a certificate configured for the Default Web Site, this page is not displayed. If you do not have a certificate configured, then you can choose to use a self-signed certificate.

6. On the Choose A Token-Signing Certificate page (see Figure 19-6), choose the certificate that you want to use to sign the tokens issued by this server and then click Next.

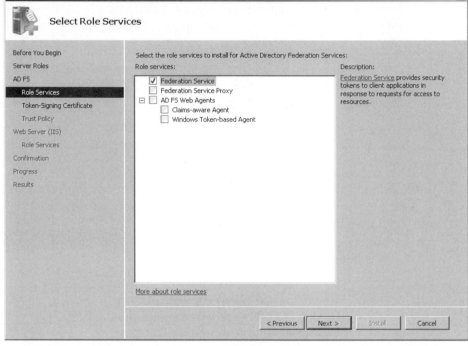

Figure 19-5 Installing the AD FS server role includes choosing the specific role services to install.

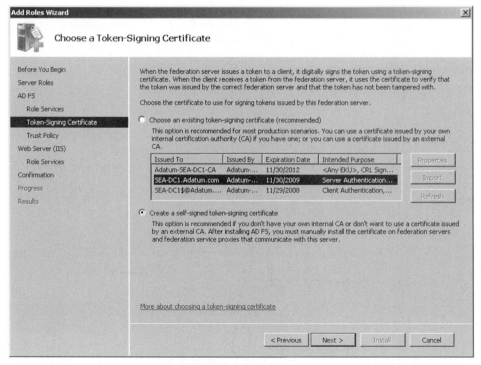

Figure 19-6 Token-signing certificates can be installed certificates or self-signed certificates.

> **Note**   Remember that the token-signing certificate configured on the account partner must be imported on the resource federation server and federation proxy server. You should export the token-signing certificate to a file or wait to export the certificate with the trust policy export.

7. On the Select Trust Policy page, choose whether to create a new trust policy or import an existing policy and then complete the installation of the Web Server (IIS) server role.

Direct from the Source: Limiting Federation Service Deployment Using Group Policy

In Windows Server 2003 R2, AD FS did not provide control mechanisms that prevented users from installing or configuring their own Federation Service. In Windows Server 2008, AD FS administrators can now turn on Group Policy settings that prevent nonauthorized federation servers in their domain. This new setting helps to satisfy the needs of an IT department when they want to enforce compliance or legal process requirements.

After the Group Policy setting has been enabled, the value *DisallowFederationService* is inserted into the registry key on each federation server in that domain. Before an AD DS–domain–joined computer running the Windows Server 2008 operating system can install the Federation Service server role, the server will first check to make sure that the **Don't allow non-authorized federation servers in this domain** Group Policy setting is enabled. If it is enabled, the installation of the Federation Service will fail. If it is not enabled, which is the default setting, installation of a Federation Service will be allowed and the installed Federation Service will function normally.

The registry key value is only checked when the trust policy file is loaded, so there may be a delay between the update that brings down the policy and when the Federation Service observes the policy. By default, the policy is read when a file change notification is received and also once every hour.

Note that this feature only applies to Windows Server 2008 federation servers and does not affect new or existing installations of a Federation Service in Windows Server 2003 R2.

Lu Zhao

Program Manager, Microsoft

Deploying Federation Service Proxy Servers

By using a federation server proxy, you can avoid exposing your federation servers directly on the Internet. In most cases, you will deploy the federation proxy server in a perimeter network with the federation servers on the internal network.

There are two configuration options that you need to consider if you are implementing federation proxy servers:

- **Modifying the federation proxy URL** When you install an account or a resource federation server, you configure a Uniform Resource Identifier (URI) in the trust policy, which identifies the Uniform Resource Locator (URL) the users will be redirected to when they try to connect to the federation server. These URIs are used as follows:

  - ❏ The AD FS Web Agents on the IIS servers are configured with the URI of the resource federation server.

  - ❏ The resource federation server is configured with the URI for the account federation server.

  - ❏ The account federation server is configured with the URI for the resource federation server.

  When you add a federation server proxy, the endpoint on the federation server URIs must be changed accordingly, so that client computers are redirected to the federation server proxy rather than trying to connect directly to the federation server.

- **Configure the federation proxy server client certificate** The federation proxy server must have a certificate for client authentication chained to a root CA that is trusted by the federation server it is protecting. The federation proxy server will have both a public and a private key for this certificate, and the certificate must be exported (without the private key) and imported into the trust policy of the federation server it is protecting.

To install the Federation Service Proxy role service, ensure that all of the prerequisite components are installed and configured on the server and then complete the following steps:

1. From Server Manager, right-click Roles and then click Add Roles to start the Add Roles Wizard.

2. On the Before You Begin page, click Next.

3. On the Select Server Roles page, click Active Directory Federation Services. Click Next two times.

4. On the Select Role Services page (see Figure 19-5), select the Federation Service Proxy check box. If you are prompted to install additional Web Server (IIS) or Windows Process Activation Service role services, click Add Required Role Services to install them and then click Next.

5. On the Specify Federation Server page, type the fully qualified name of the federation server used by this proxy and then click Validate to ensure that the proxy server can communicate with the federation server. Click Next.

6. On the Choose A Client Authentication Certificate page, choose the certificate that you want to use for client authentication and then click Next. If you do not have a certificate configured, then you can choose to use a self-signed certificate.

> **Note**   The client certificate used by the federation proxy server must be added to federation server configuration, so you should export the client certificate to a file.

7. Complete the installation of the Web Server (IIS) server role.

After you complete the installation, the Federation Service Proxy component is configured with default settings that include the URL for the federation server and default settings for client logon, logoff, and account partner discover pages. If you want to modify these settings or configure enhanced logging for troubleshooting, use the Active Directory Federation Service snap-in on the federation proxy server.

Deploying the AD FS Web Agent

To deploy the AD FS Web Agent role service, ensure that all of the prerequisite components are installed and configured on the server and then complete the following steps:

1. From Server Manager, right-click Roles and then click Add Roles to start the Add Roles Wizard.

2. On the Before You Begin page, click Next.

3. On the Select Server Roles page, click Active Directory Federation Services. Click Next two times.

4. On the Select Role Services page (see Figure 19-5), choose either the Claims-Aware Agent check box or the Windows Token-Based Agent check box or both. The selection you make depends on the type of application you are installing on the server. Click Next.

5. Continue with the installation of the Web Server (IIS) server role. If you are using a self-signed server authentication certificate, on the Select Role Services page, in addition to the preselected check boxes, select the Client Certificate Mapping Authentication check box and then click Next. The Client Certificate Mapping Authentication component is required for IIS to create a self-signed server authentication certificate.

Configuring the Account Partner Federation Service

After installing the AD FS role services, you can move on to configuring the AD FS components in the account and resource partners.

Configuring the Trust Policy

A trust policy defines parameters that will be applied to all federation servers within the same AD FS security realm. To configure the trust policy, complete these steps:

1. Start the Active Directory Federation Services snap-in. Expand Federation Service, right-click Trust Policy, and then click Properties.

2. On the Trust Policy (see Figure 19-7), specify the following:

   ❑ Federation Services URI. This value uniquely identifies the AD FS installation. This value will be provided to the resource partner.

   > **Important**   The Federation Services URI is case-sensitive. You must enter this value on the resource federation server using the same case. To ensure that the value is entered correctly, you should export the trust policy file after creating it and provide it to your resource partners.

   ❑ Federation Service Endpoint URL. This is the URL to which the client is redirected by the Web Agent on the Web server. If you are using a federation server proxy, this URL must point to the federation server proxy server. If you are not using a federation server proxy, this value will point to the federation server.

   ❑ Token-Signing Verification Certificate in use. You can add or remove token-signing verification certificates (without the private key) that are used by account partners to validate the digital signature on the security tokens. By adding the certificate to the trust policy, it will be included when you export the policy in preparation for handing the policy file to a resource partner.

   ❑ Federation proxy server client authentication certificates available. You can add the client authentication certificates (without the private key) for federation server proxy computers.

   ❑ Claims transformation module DLL being used. Use this option if you have created a .dll file to manage the claim transformations between the resource and account partners.

   ❑ Event log levels. You can configure whether or not errors, warning, and audit events will be logged.

   ❑ Validity periods for tokens and policy refresh.

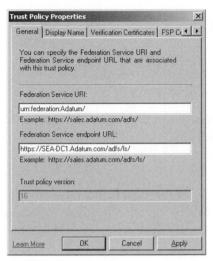

Figure 19-7   The trust policy settings define the URI and URL required for AD FS clients.

Managing Trust Policy Files

By right-clicking Federation Service and clicking Properties, you can view the location where the server will store the trust policy file. By default, the file is stored in the c:\Windows\SystemData\ADFS folder. If there is more than one computer hosting the Federation Service at a single federation partner organization operating in a server farm, they will share the same trust policy file. When you install additional federation servers in the organization, use this policy file to configure the servers. For details on how to configure Federation Service farms, see the "AD FS Design Guide" located at *http://go.microsoft.com/fwlink/?LinkId=91898*.

After creating the policy, you can also export the policy to an XML file so that you can provide the information to resource partners. To do this, right click Trust Policy and click Export Basic Partner Policy; then provide a filename and location. The exported policy includes the display name, URL, and URI, as well as the verification certificate. By providing this file to your resource partners, you do not need to provide them with the certificate as a separate file, and you can ensure that all of the information is entered correctly.

Configuring Organization Claims

An AD FS claim is a statement made about a user that is understood by both partners in an AD FS federation scenario. In a federation scenario, the AD FS organization claim is first created on the account partner. When the user authenticates to the federation server, the federation server extracts the information from AD DS or AD LDS that will be used to create the claim. For example, if the claim is a group claim (which means that the Web Agent at the resource partner will make authorization decisions based on which group the user belongs to), the federation server will extract the group information from the directory service and provide it to the client as part of the security token.

On the account partner, you create organization claims to define the types of criteria that will be included in the claim. Three types of claims are supported by the Federation Service:

- **Identity claims**   Identity claims are configured by default when you install the Federation Service. *Identity claims* are used to ensure that a specific user has been authenticated from a trusted federation partner's directory store. There are three types of identity claims:

  - ❑ *UPN claims* indicate a Kerberos-style user principal name (UPN), for example: user@adatum.com. Only one claim may be the UPN type. When you configure the account partner, you can specify a list of user principal name (UPN) domains and suffixes that may be accepted from the account partner. If a UPN identity is received whose domain part is not in the list, the request is rejected.

  - ❑ *E-mail claims* indicate RFC 2822–style e-mail names of the form user@adatum.com. Only one claim may be the e-mail type. When you configure the account partner, you can specify a list of e-mail domains and suffixes that may be accepted from the account partner. As with the UPN claim, if an e-mail identity is received whose domain part is not in the list, the request is rejected.

  - ❑ *Common name claims* indicate an arbitrary string that is used for personalization. Examples include *John Smith* or *A. Datum Employee*. Only one claim may have the common name type. It is important to note that there is no mechanism for guaranteeing the uniqueness of the common name claim. Therefore, use caution when using this claim type for authorization decisions. When you configure the account partner, you can specify whether or not common name claims can be received from the account partner.

> **Note**   The three identity claims may not be mapped; they are simply passed through if they are enabled. If more than one of the three identity claim types is present in a token, the identity claims are prioritized by UPN, e-mail, then common name.

- **Group claims**   A *group claim* is a type of claim that maps a group membership in AD DS or AD LDS to a specific authorization role. For example, you might map the Finance-Managers group to a group claim on the account partner. On the resource partner, the Web application will then make authorization decisions based on the group claim. When you configure the resource partner, you can specify a set of incoming group claims that may be accepted from the account partner. You can also associate Authorization Manager roles with group claims that may be used to provide authorization to the Web application.

- **Custom claims**   *A custom claim* contains custom information about a user; for example, an employee ID number. This information is retrieved via LDAP from the user account attributes and mapped to a custom name in the claim. When you configure the resource partner, you can specify a set of incoming names of custom claims that are accepted from the account partner. If an incoming custom claim is encountered that has no mapping, it is discarded.

> **Security Alert**   You can use any attribute stored in the account store when creating a common name claim. For example, if your organization stores employee numbers, bank account numbers, or social insurance numbers in the directory, you could create claims using this information. However, some of this information may be private, and legal constraints may apply to distributing this information to other organizations.

To create new organization claims, right-click Organization Claims, point to New, and click Organization Claim (see Figure 19-8). Creating the organization claim essentially creates a placeholder for the claim, which is only useful after you add one or more account stores to the Federation Service and configure claim mappings.

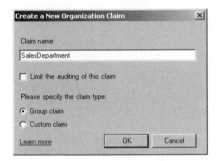

Figure 19-8   Configuring a group organization claim enables you to map groups from the account store to AD FS objects.

Adding an Account Store

A federation server that is to be used for authentication in any of the federation scenarios must have at least one account store. To add an account store, right-click Account Store under My Organization in the AD FS console, point to New, and click Account Store. By default, the Add Account Store Wizard will add an account store for the AD DS domain to which the federation server belongs. You can add only one AD DS account store.

You can add additional AD LDS account stores. When you add AD LDS account stores, you must specify this information:

- The display name for the AD LDS account store.

- The account store URI, in the ldap://*servername* format.

■ The server name, IP address, and port number (see Figure 19-9). Because you can run multiple instances of AD LDS on one server, and you can configure different port numbers for each instance, you must provide the appropriate port number for each instance.

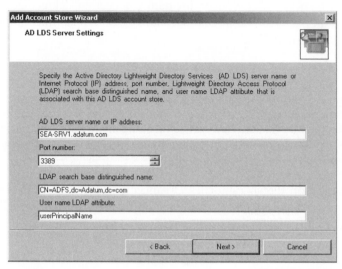

Figure 19-9   You need to provide information about the AD LDS instance when creating the account store.

■ The LDAP user object attribute containing the user name. For example, if you are using a UPN identity claim, you would use *userPrincipalName*.

■ Search base. This setting is optional. If a subtree is specified, searches are performed on the specified subtree. Otherwise, the entire directory tree is searched.

■ Identity claims. When you configure the store, you can also configure which types of identity claims will be supported by the AD LDS store and which user attributes contain the expected information.

■ Client timeout. This setting is optional. This refers to the maximum time that the Federation Service waits for a response from the AD LDS server before timing out the connection. The default is 5 *seconds*.

Adding Group and Custom Claims Extractions

After configuring the account stores, which contain user accounts and groups, you can configure claims extractions to use the information stored in the LDAP directory to populate a user's claims. When you create a claims extraction, you are mapping an attribute linked to the user account in the account store to an AD FS claim that can be consumed by the AD FS process.

Note   You do not have the option of creating claims extractions for the identity claims. These attributes are assigned to specific user accounts.

There are two types of claims extractions:

- **Group Claims Extractions**   For group claims extractions, you associate membership of a group in the directory store with an organization claim. For example, you could map the FinanceManagers group from AD DS to the FinanceManagers organization claim (see Figure 19-10). This means that all members of the FinanceManagers group will have the FinanceManagers claim attached to their security token when they connect to the Web application in the resource partner.

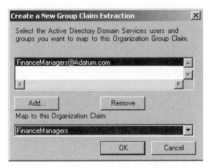

Figure 19-10   Configuring a group claim extraction maps groups from the account store to AD FS claims.

- **Custom Claims**   For custom claims, you map an attribute in the directory with a custom organization claim, whose name is simply a string value that fits well with the organization that configured it. For example, an organization claim called *Department* might be associated with the *department* attribute in AD DS.

Adding a Resource Partner

Up to this point, the whole process for configuring AD FS on an account partner has not considered the resource partner at all. In fact, the process for configuring the resource partner is the same as configuring the account partner up to this point. However, in order to create the link between the account partner and the resource partner, you must create a resource partner on the account federation server.

There are two methods you can use to add a resource partner:

- Configure the resource manually in the AD FS console.

- Import the resource partner information from an XML configuration file that the resource partner has previously exported and made available. (The XML file simply includes the information that would have to be entered manually otherwise.)

To manually configure a resource partner, you must provide the information configured in the trust policy of the resource partner. To configure the resource partner, expand Partner Organizations in the AD FS console, right-click Resource Partners, select New, and click Resource

Partner. In the Add Resource Partner Wizard, you need to provide the following information, as shown in Figure 19-11:

- Display name.

- Federation Service URI.

- Federation Service endpoint URL.

- Federation Scenario. You can choose either the Federated Web SSO or the Federated Web SSO with Forest Trust option.

- Identity claim. You can choose whether you will send UPN claims, e-mail claims, or common name claims to the resource partner. You must choose at least one, but you can choose all three.

- UPN suffix mapping. If you choose to use UPN suffixes, you can choose to replace all suffixes with alternate suffixes. For example, the Federation Service at Woodgrove Bank may require that all suffixes use the WoodgroveBank.com format. A. Datum can configure the resource partner settings to replace all ADatum.com UPNs with WoodgroveBank.com.

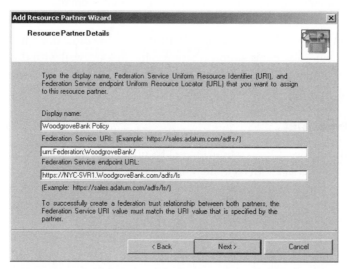

Figure 19-11   Configuring a resource partner creates one side of the trust between the account and resource partners.

Important   The information that you provide must exactly match the information configured on the resource partner, including the case for the Federation Service URI.

Direct from the Source: Using Import/Export Functionality to Create Federation Trusts More Efficiently

There's no doubt about it—setting up a federation trust between two organizations can be a daunting task, due to the many sequential steps involved in manually setting up both partners for successful AD FS communications. In this scenario, both administrators are equally responsible for entering values and addresses (that is, URIs, URLs, and claims) within the AD FS snap-ins that are unique to their respective company's federation environment.

After this initial setup phase has been completed, each administrator must then provide these values to the administrator in the other organization so that a federation trust can be properly established. Even when these values are sent to the intended partner administrator, there is the distinct possibility that an administrator could accidentally type a value incorrectly and inadvertently cause himself or herself many hours of headaches trying to locate the source of the problem with the new trust.

In Windows Server 2008, improvements have been made that will allow each partner administrator to export their generic trust policy as well as their partner trust policy into a small XML-format file that can be forwarded easily in e-mail to a partner administrator in another organization. The generic trust policy contains the Federation Server Display Name, URI, Federation Server Proxy URL, and any Verification Certificates information, and the partner trust policy file also includes information about each of the claims. With this in mind, the second half of the federation trust can then be quickly established by importing the partner's trust policy and mapping the claims.

This "export and e-mail" process adds the following benefits for the partner administrator who receives the XML file:

- Expedites the process of establishing a federation trust, since the administrator can choose to "import" the contents of the XML file in the Add Partner Wizard and then simply click through the wizard pages to verify that the imported settings are suitable

- Eliminates the additional step of importing the account verification certificate because the import process will do this automatically

- Provides Easy Claim mapping

- Eliminates the possibility of manual typing errors

You can test-drive this new functionality by walking through the Windows Server 2008 version of the *AD FS Step-by-Step Guide*.

Nick Pierson

Senior Technical Writer, Microsoft

Adding Outgoing Claim Mappings

After creating the resource partner, you can also configure outgoing claim mappings. Outgoing claim mappings are used to convert the internal organization claims used by the account partner into group or custom claims that are specific to the resource partner. Each organization may be using different names for the claims. For example, A. Datum may have an organization claim for FinanceManagers, but Woodgrove Bank may use a corresponding claim called AdatumFinanceManagers. By creating the outgoing claim mapping, you can convert the account partner organization claim into a claim that fits your resource partner's requirements.

> **Note** By configuring outgoing claim mappings, you can reuse the same organization claim with multiple resource partners. For example, the FinanceManagers organization claim may map to the AdatumFinanceManagers claim for Woodgrove Bank, but it could map to a completely different claim for another resource organization.

On the account partner, you must add outgoing claims for each resource partner and map them to the organization claims already added. To create an outgoing Group Claim Mapping, right-click the resource partner name, select New, and click Outgoing Group Claim Mapping (see Figure 19-12). You can also create outgoing custom claim mappings.

Figure 19-12 Configuring an outgoing claim mapping maps claims from the account partner to claims for the resource partner.

Configuring Resource Partner AD FS Components

The resource Federation Service partner protects access to at least one application resource. The resource federation server receives claims from the account federation server, extracts them and verifies that they match the set of incoming claims allowed, maps them to its own organization claims, and adds them to a new token, which it signs with its token-signing certificate to be sent to the Web Agent installed on the IIS server on which the application is hosted.

Many of the initial steps in configuring the resource partner are similar to configuring the account partner:

1. Configure the trust policy. Configuring the trust policy on a resource partner is identical to configuring the trust policy on an account partner.

2. Configure organization claims. On the resource partner, the organization claims are used to define access to applications. The organization claims are the actual claims used by claims-aware applications to make authorization decisions. You have the same options for configuring organization claims as you do on the account partner. You can create any number of organization claims and then enable some or all of these on each individual application the resource federation server is protecting.

3. Configure account stores (optional) and claims extractions. In a pure B2B federation scenario, you do not need to configure an account store on the resource federation server. However, if you want to provide access to the same resources to your own employees or customers via the same federation mechanism already in place, you will need to configure an account store and assume the role of an account provider. After configuring the account stores, you may also need to configure group and custom claim extractions to match the directory information with the claims used by the application.

Configuring Applications

In order for a resource federation server to protect access to an application, you must define the application to the federation server. When you configure an application on the federation server, you have two options:

- **Claims-aware applications**   When you set up a claims-aware application, all of the information about a given identity is contained in the token that is presented by the application. When an application is presented with a valid token, the claims-aware application can make authorization decisions based on the claims in the token. This means that a user account in the resource AD DS is not required to access a claims-aware application.

- **Windows NT token-based application**   When you set up a Windows NT token-based application, you can map claims in incoming AD FS tokens to either user accounts or groups in the local AD DS user store in the resource partner. The user accounts or groups are also known as resource accounts or resource groups. The application then uses the resource accounts or groups to perform authorization.

> **More Info**   For more information about how to configure Windows NT token-based accounts, see the section titled "Configuring AD FS for Windows NT Token-based Applications" later in this chapter.

To add an application, right-click the Applications node under My Organization, point to New, and click Application. This will start the Add Application Wizard, where you will need to provide the following information:

- **The application type**   Choose either claims-aware application or Windows NT token-based application.

- **Application display name and URL**   The URL must be the same as the actual URL used to access the application.

- **Supported identity claims**   You can choose whether the application supports UPN claims, e-mail claims, or common name claims. You must choose at least one, but you can choose all three.

After creating the application, you can access the application properties to configure the mechanism used to protect the security tokens sent to the application. By default, Public Key Infrastructure (PKI) is selected, which means that the Federation Service uses its token-signing certificate to protect security tokens for this application. You can also choose to use a Domain service account. When you select this option, the Federation Service uses a Kerberos request to protect security tokens for this application. If you select this option, you must specify a service principal name (SPN) for the target service account. For the AD FS Web Agent for claims-aware applications, the SPN must be registered for the application pool identity for the protected application.

You can also choose what types of authentication are supported by the application. By default, all the options Windows integrated authentication, user name and password authentication, and certificate or TLS/SSL client authentication are enabled.

Adding Account Partners

A resource partner would typically have one or more account partners configured. Just like configuring a resource partner on the account partner, you can configure the account partner manually or by importing a policy that has been exported from the account partner.

Account partners digitally sign the security tokens they generate and the tokens are specifically designed for the resource Federation Service to receive and trust. For this reason, you must provide the token-signing certificate when you configure the account partner on the resource partner. When you configure the account partner, you will need to provide the following information:

- Display name.
- Federation Service URI.
- Federation Service endpoint URL.
- The account partner token-signing certificate. If you import the XML file from the account partner, these first values are configured. You are also given a choice whether you want to use the token-signing certificate included in the XML file or a different certificate.

- The scenario you are implementing—a Federated Web SSO or Federated Web SSO with Forest Trust design.

- The types of identity claims that the account partner will provide.

- The UPN and e-mail suffixes that will be accepted from the account partner.

Adding Incoming Claim Mappings

Incoming group claim mappings convert group or custom claims that are sent by an account partner into a claim that the resource partner uses to make authorization decisions. For example, the incoming claim from A. Datum may include the AdatumFinanceManager claim. However, the application may be configured to use a claim named CustomerManagers to provide the right level of access to the application. By configuring the incoming claim, you can map the claim provided by the account partner to a claim that can be consumed by the application.

To consume the outgoing custom claims on the account partner, you also can configure incoming custom claim mappings. For example, an account partner might send a security token for a user that contains a custom claim of EmployeeID. Because the resource partner cannot make authorization decisions based on the user's EmployeeID, you might configure an incoming custom claim mapping that converts the custom claim from EmployeeID to a custom claim called CustomerID.

> **Note**   Incoming group claim mappings must be created for all incoming group claims, even if the claims are transformed to their original value. For example, if the incoming claim is AdatumFinanceManager, and the resource partner can use a user's membership in the AdatumFinanceManager group to make authorization decisions, you must still create a group claim mapping. In this case, the group claim mapping is used to transform AdatumFinance-Manager to AdatumFinanceManager, effectively leaving the claim unchanged.

How It Works: Understanding Claims

With all of this discussion about claims, it can be confusing to understand how all of the claims fit together. To illustrate how the claims work together, examine Figure 19-13.

This figure shows the end-to-end use of the organization claims. In this example, the A. Datum AD FS administrators have created a FinManagers organization claim and then used a group claim extraction to link the FinanceManagers group from AD DS to the FinManagers organization claim. However, Woodgrove Bank needs to be able to distinguish among the finance managers from different organizations, so it requires that any claims for the A. Datum finance managers must be identified as AdatumManagers. Therefore, the A. Datum administrators must create an outgoing group claim mapping that maps the FinManagers organization claim to the AdatumManagers claim.

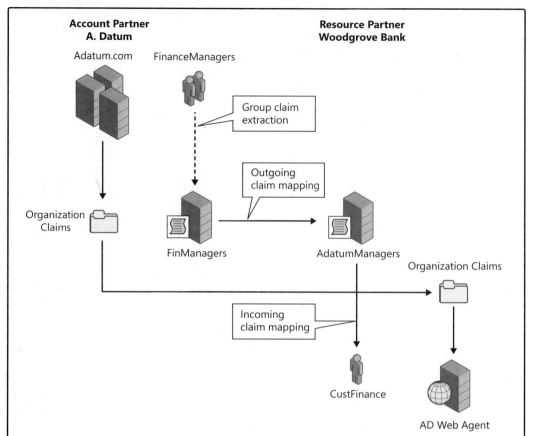

Figure 19-13   Claims are passed from account partner to resource partner through several mappings.

When a claim mapping is created and named in one partner, it is critical that the other partner name their claim mapping exactly the same. For example, in this scenario, A. Datum is mapping an outgoing group claim mapping to AdatumManagers. Woodgrove Bank must configure an incoming group claim mapping that uses AdatumManagers. The shared claim name creates the link between the two federation servers.

At Woodgrove Bank, the Web application has been configured to use a claim named CustFinance when making authorization decisions. Therefore, the Woodgrove Bank AD FS administrators need to configure an incoming group claim that accepts the AdatumManagers claim and transforms it into a claim named CustFinance for the Web application.

So in the end, the members of the FinanceManagers AD DS group at A. Datum get all of the access assigned to the CustFinance claim on the Woodgrove Bank Web server.

Outgoing and incoming group claim mappings enable a layer of abstraction between the two federation partners. For example, the account partner may be hesitant to share the internal AD DS group names with the federation partner. In addition, the federation partner may not want to share the internal claim details used by its applications with the account partner. If you configure an outgoing claim mapping on the account partner, the internal AD DS group structure is hidden. If you configure an incoming claim mapping on the resource partner, the application claims are also not visible. The resource partner and account partner just have to agree on the name and authorization requirements of the claim that is being sent between the two organizations.

Configuring AD FS for Windows NT Token-based Applications

Most of the description for implementing AD FS so far has focused on configuring AD FS to use a claims-based application. However, many organizations already have Windows NT token-based applications, and it will take some time for all of those applications to be rewritten to claims-based applications. This section provides details on how to configure AD FS to use Windows NT token-based applications.

Windows NT token-based or legacy applications cannot directly consume AD FS claims. Rather, all of the resources on the Web server are secured by using access control lists (ACLs) that include the SIDs for security principals from the resource AD DS forest or from a trusted forest. This means that the Web Agent protecting a token-based application must accept the claim from the resource federation server and then use the information in the claim to find a corresponding AD DS user account or group. The Web Agent then creates an access token using that AD DS account and grants permissions based on the user or group account SID.

To enable access to the token-based applications, you need to configure the organization claims on the resource federation server that maps the organization claim to a resource user or group. For example, the CustomerManagers organization claim at Woodgrove Bank may be mapped to the CustManagers@WoodgroveBank.com group (see Figure 19-14).

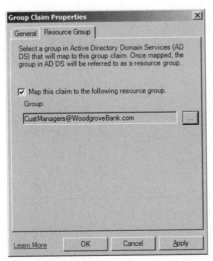

Figure 19-14   Mapping a resource group to an organization claim enables token-based applications to use the claim.

There are two options for implementing the resource user or group accounts to enable access to token-based applications:

- Use user and group accounts from the forest where the AD FS resource federation server is installed or from a trusted domain. This option is feasible in a B2E deployment because the employees are likely to have accounts in the forest where AD FS resides already, and they may be using the same credentials to authenticate to other Web-based resources. This option is also possible if you are using the Federation Web SSO with Forest Trust design, because the perimeter network forest will trust the user accounts from the internal forest.

- Use resource user and groups accounts. Resource accounts and groups are created in the resource forest purely to enable authorization to the token-based applications. When using resource user and group accounts, the account is not used for authentication—the user must still authenticate to the account federation server, and the normal process of creating the claims still applies.

One of the issues with using resource accounts is that you may need to create many different resource accounts if your organization has several token-based applications and the account partners use many different user accounts to access the application. To simplify this process, AD FS provides the following resource account methods:

- **Resource accounts**   In this method, a single security principal, usually a user account, created in Active Directory is used to map to a single federated user. This option provides detailed user level access control but also requires the creation of a unique resource account for each user that will be accessing the application.

- **Resource groups**   In this method, a single security group created in AD DS is mapped to incoming group claims. This method requires much less effort to implement, as it eliminates the need to create and manage separate resource accounts for each federated user. One resource group can support an unlimited number of federated users that are mapped to it. The primary disadvantage of using this method is that the resource organization cannot control access based on individual users, and it has to trust that the account organization is only adding appropriate users to the group claim.

- **Group-to-UPN mapping**   In this method, a group of federated users is mapped to the UPN of a user account that is created in the resource forest. This option eliminates the need to create and manage separate resource accounts for each federated user. The primary disadvantage of using this option is the lack of granularity in auditing. Because multiple users will be using the same group for accessing the application, you cannot audit individual user access.

> **Note**   One of the options for decreasing the administrative effort required to manage resource accounts is to use an identity provisioning tool such as Microsoft Identity Lifecycle Manager (ILM) 2007 to automate the process of creating the required accounts. Another option is to use a claims transform module to automatically create accounts and remove them when the session is finished.

In order to implement resource groups, you may also need to add UPN suffixes to the resource forest. For example, if users in the WoodgroveBank.com forest are using a UPN of User@WoodgroveBank.com, and the UPN is not being mapped to a UPN already accepted by the resource forest, you will need to add the WoodgroveBank.com UPN to the resource forest.

Implementing a Web SSO Design

The Web SSO design is less complex than the Federated Web SSO design because the Web SSO design includes only the following components:

■ Only one federation server is required. In this design, the federation server operates both as the account partner and resource partner.

■ A federation proxy server is optional in this deployment.

■ A Web server with the AD FS Web Agent installed and an installed claims-aware or Windows NT token-based application is required.

To complete the Web SSO design, complete the following high-level steps:

1. Prepare the environment. This includes installing the Web Server (IIS) server role on each computer and configuring the Web server certificates, as well as the Federation Service and Federation Service Proxy role services.

2. Configure the federation server by completing this process:

   a. Configure the trust policy. The steps are identical to configuring the trust policy in the Federated Web SSO design.

   b. Configure the organization claims. In the Web SSO design, the federation server is operating as both the account server and resource server. This means that the organization claims will be populated from either AD DS or AD LDS.

   c. Add and configure account stores. The user accounts must be stored in either AD DS or AD LDS, so one or more account stores need to be added to the federation server. When users access the application, they will be authenticated against the account store to start the process of creating the security token.

   d. Create claim mappings for the application. The organization claims must be mapped into claims that can be consumed by the application. As with the Federated Web SSO design, if you are using Windows NT token-based applications, you will need to implement resource groups by using AD DS accounts in the forest where the federation server is deployed or by using resource accounts.

   e. Add and configure an application. As the resource partner, the application provides access to the shared resource. The application must be added to the Federation Service so that the federation server can redirect client requests to the appropriate Web server.

Implementing a Federated Web SSO with Forest Trust Design

Implementing the Federated Web SSO with Forest Trust design is another option when deploying AD FS. Just like the Web SSO deployment, the Federated Web SSO with Forest Trust design is still primarily used for B2E or B2C deployments, but it has the extra complexity of requiring two AD DS forests. The primary reason for choosing a Federated Web SSO with Forest Trust design is to enable the use of Windows NT token-based applications that use the user's internal forest credentials to make authorization decisions. By using a forest trust, you do not need to create resource user or group accounts in the perimeter AD DS forest.

A Federated Web SSO with Forest Trust design requires the following components:

- Two federation servers. In this design, one federation server will operate as the account partner and a second federation server will operate as the resource partner. Even though both federation servers are deployed in the same organization, they are deployed in separate forests. Federation proxy servers are optional in this deployment.

- Two AD DS forests. A one-way (or two-way) forest trust configured so that the internal forest is trusted by the external forest.

- A Web server with the AD FS Web Agent installed and a claims-aware or Windows NT token-based application installed.

To deploy the Federated Web SSO with Forest Trust design, complete the following high-level steps:

1. Prepare the environment. This includes installing the Web Server (IIS) server role on each computer and configuring the Web server certificates, as well as the Federation Service role server and federation role server proxies.

2. Configure a forest trust between the perimeter network forest and the internal forest. This trust will be used so that Windows NT token-based applications can make authorization decisions based on internal AD DS accounts.

3. Configure the account federation partner. In this scenario, the account federation partner is the federation server that is located on the internal network and runs on a server that is a member of the internal AD DS forest. To configure the Federation Service, complete the following steps:

    a. Configure the trust policy.

    b. Configure the organization claims. The organization claims will be populated from the internal AD DS forest.

    c. Add and configure account stores. The user accounts will be stored in the internal AD DS forest so the default AD DS account store must be added to the federation server.

    d. Configure the organization group or custom claim extractions. Map the AD DS groups to the appropriate organization group or custom claims.

    e.   Add and configure a resource partner. In this case, the resource partner is the federation server in the perimeter network forest.

    f.   Create outgoing claim mapping for the resource partner. Configure the organization claims into claims that can be consumed by the resource partner application.

4.   Configuring the resource federation partner. In this scenario, the resource federation partner is the federation server that is located on the perimeter network and runs on a server that is a member of the perimeter AD DS forest. To configure the Federation Service, complete the following steps:

    a.   Configure the trust policy.

    b.   Configure the organization claims.

    c.   Add and configure an AD FS application. Although you can use a claims-aware application in this scenario, most applications will likely be Windows NT token-based applications.

    d.   Add and configure an account partner.

    e.   Create an incoming claim mapping for the application.

    f.   Deploy the application on the Web servers.

    g.   Assign access control rights to federated user accounts.

Summary

AD FS provides a way to extend the authentication and authorization services provided by AD DS to users outside the organization. With AD FS, you can deploy Web-based applications and enable SSO access to those applications without requiring that all users have user accounts in your internal AD DS forest. This enables collaboration scenarios with other organizations, customers, or remote employees who are accessing the applications from outside the office.

Best Practices

- Deploy federation servers that use your internal AD DS forest as an account store on your internal network. This is important, because federation servers have full authorization to grant security tokens. Therefore, they should have the same protection as a domain controller. Then, deploy federation server proxy servers in the perimeter network to protect the federation server.

- To provide an addition level of security, leave all resource user accounts disabled. If that is not an option, then add all resource user accounts to a security group and deny the security group permission to log on locally on the AD FS Web server.

Additional Resources

- Chapter 18, "Active Directory Rights Management Services," describes how to integrate AD FS with AD RMS. By using this feature, you can use the AD FS federated identities within an AD RMS deployment to protect content as it is distributed between organizations.

- The Active Directory Federation Services site on the Windows Server 2008 Technical Library site provides design and deployment information and step-by-step guides for implementing AD FS in a test environment. The site is located at *http://technet2.microsoft.com/windowsserver2008/en/servermanager/activedirectory-federationservices.mspx.*

- The Active Directory Federation Services Web site on the Windows Server 2003 TechCenter provides detailed information on how to configure AD FS with other identity federation products such as IBM Tivoli Federated Identity Manager and CA SiteMinder Federation Security Services. The site is located at *http://technet2.microsoft.com/windowsserver/en/technologies/featured/adfs/default.mspx.*

- The "AD FS Design and Deployment Guide," which can be downloaded from *http://www.microsoft.com/downloads/details.aspx?FamilyID=b92ea722-0c30-4ea6-bd45-7e5934b870cf&DisplayLang=en*, provides detailed information on how to design and deploy an AD FS implementation, including how to deploy multiple servers in a federation server farm configuration.

- Configure Web SSO authentication by using AD FS (Office SharePoint Server) guide, available at *http://technet2.microsoft.com/Office/en-us/library/61799f9a-da01-4c11-b930-52e5114324451033.mspx?mfr=true.* This document describes how to configure Microsoft Office SharePoint Server 2007 to use AD FS.

- For detailed troubleshooting information, see the Active Directory Federation Services section of the Windows Server 2008 Troubleshooting Web site, located at *http://technet2.microsoft.com/windowsserver2008/en/library/acc299c9-3bff-4c2d-b4af-78d772012b101033.mspx?mfr=true.*

Resources on the CD

- The AD FS Documentation.xls spreadsheet can be used to document the AD FS deployment in your organization.

Related Help Topics

- "Troubleshooting AD FS" in Active Directory Federated Directory Services help

- "Understanding AD FS Terminology" in Active Directory Federated Directory Services Help

About the Authors

Stan Reimer is president of S. R. Technical Services Inc., where he works as an enterprise consultant, trainer, and writer. As a consultant, Stan has designed and implemented Exchange Server and Active Directory for some of the largest companies in Canada. As a trainer, Stan specializes in creating and teaching customized Exchange Server, Active Directory, and security courses. As a writer, Stan is the lead author for the *Active Directory for Microsoft Windows Server 2003 Technical Reference* (Microsoft Press, 2003) and other Exchange Server and ISA Server books, as well as the author of many Microsoft Learning courses. Stan lives and works in Winnipeg, but his heart (and frequently his mind) live in a cottage on Big Whiteshell Lake. You can reach Stan at Stanr@srtech.ca.

Conan Kezema received his Bachelor of Education degree in 1994 and realized the importance of computer technology and the need for experienced high-level technical educators. He subsequently obtained the Microsoft Certified Systems Engineer and Microsoft Certified Trainer designations. For the past 12 years, Conan has been involved in the computer technology field as an educator, systems consultant, network systems architect, and technical writer. For the past four years, Conan has been associated with S. R. Technical Services Inc. as a subject matter expert, instructional designer, and technical writer on numerous Microsoft-related projects. To contact Conan for training, consulting, or technical writing opportunities, you can e-mail him at ckezema@sasktel.net.

Mike Mulcare works for the Microsoft Corporation as the senior product manager for online learning products. During his eight years with Microsoft, Mike has developed numerous courses on directory services and Windows server networking, as both an instructional designer and subject matter expert. He is the coauthor, with Stan Reimer, of *Active Directory for Microsoft Windows Server 2003 Technical Reference* (Microsoft Press, 2003). Mike is originally from New York state and now resides in Seattle, Washington, with his wife and three sons. He has been in the software consulting and training industry since 1990.

Byron Wright is an owner of Conexion Networks, where he performs network consulting, computer systems implementation, and technical training. Byron is also a sessional instructor for the Asper School of Business at the University of Manitoba, teaching management information systems and networking. Byron has authored a number of books on Windows servers, Windows Vista, and Exchange Server. He currently resides in Winnipeg, Manitoba, with his wife and two daughters, but was born and raised in Saskatoon, Saskatchewan. You can reach Byron at byron@conexion.ca.

Index

A

Access control entries (ACEs)
  description of, 274–275
  in Active Directory object access, 328–329
  in AD LDS, 647
  Ldp.exe to view, 334–336
Access control lists (ACLs)
  dynamic DNS and, 79
  for GPO settings, 406–407
  groups and, 366
  in AD LDS, 646–648
  integrated zones and, 75
  of organizational units, 59
  overview of, 273–275
  schema objects and, 626
  security filtering and, 433
  selective authentication and, 169
  Web server resources secured by, 785
Access denied errors, 133
Access tokens
  authentication from, 327
  for security, 276, 282
  in AD LDS, 636
  migration and, 251
Account administrative model, 155
Account domains, 178
Account lockout, 110
  attributes of, 7
  Default Domain Policy control of, 7
  domain number and, 175
  fine-grained password policies and, 528
  in AD LDS, 638
  policy for, 516
  security policy boundaries and, 47
Account management, 326
Account Operators group, 317
Account partner in AD FS, 773–781
  account store in, 776–777
  adding, 783
  claims extractions in, 778
  cookies for, 761
  definition of, 750
  federation service configured as, 750
  in federation Web SSO scenario, 755–756, 768
  organization claims in, 775–776

  outgoing claims mappings in, 780–781
  resource partner in, 778–780
  trust policy in, 773–774
Account policies, 514–518
Account properties for user object, 360–361
Account store
  adding, 776–777
  Federation Services requirements for,
    761–762
  forest as, 790
Accounts organizational units, 197
Activation
  file extension, 487, 496–497
  overriding RMS cluster, 723
  Windows Process Activation Service
    for, 673
Active Directory Application Mode (ADAM),
    15, 750, 762
Active Directory Application Mode Setup
    Wizard, 626, 632
Active Directory Certificate Services (AD CS),
    130, 294, 762
Active Directory Client Extension, 301
Active Directory Diagnostic tool, 256–257
Active Directory Domain Services (AD DS),
    3–11. See also Administration, delegating;
    also Domain Name System (DNS); also
    Installing AD DS; also Migrating to AD DS
  account partner and, 761–762
  accounts stored in, 750
  AD LDS synchronization with, 654–657
  auditing of, 6
  database mounting tool in, 9
  fine-grained password policies in, 7–8
  read-only domain controllers (RODC) in, 3–5
  restartable, 9
  Rights Management Services (RMS)
    and, 708
  user interface improvements of, 10–11
Active Directory Domain Services (AD DS),
    components of, 19–62
  data store, 20–22
  domain controllers, 22
  domains, 46–50
  forests, 50–51

System Requirements

To use this book's companion CD-ROM, you need a computer equipped with the following minimum configuration:

- Microsoft Windows Server 2008, Windows Vista, Windows Server 2003, or Windows XP

- 1 GHz 32-bit (x86) or 64-bit (x64) processor (depending on the minimum requirements of the operating system)

- 1 GB of system memory (depending on the minimum requirements of the operating system)

- A hard disk partition with at least 1 GB of available space

- Appropriate video output device

- Keyboard

- Mouse or other pointing device

- Optical drive capable of reading CD-ROMs

- Microsoft Office 2003 or Microsoft Office 2007

In addition, the companion CD-ROM includes scripts that are written in VBScript (with a .vbs file extension) and Windows PowerShell (with a .ps1 file extension). The Windows PowerShell scripts require that you have Windows PowerShell installed and that you have configured Windows PowerShell to run unsigned scripts. In order to run these scripts, your system must meet the following additional requirements:

- On Windows Server 2008, install the Windows PowerShell feature.

- Windows XP SP2, Windows Server 2003 SP1, or Windows Vista: To install Windows PowerShell on these operating systems, download and install Windows PowerShell from the "How to Download Windows PowerShell 1.0" Web page located at *http://www.microsoft.com/windowsserver2003/technologies/management/powershell/download.mspx.*

- To enable Windows PowerShell to run unsigned scripts, start Windows PowerShell and then type **Set-ExecutionPolicy RemoteSigned**. When you run a Windows PowerShell script, you need to provide the full path to the script.

- To use the VBScript scripts, double-click them, or execute them directly from a command prompt.

What do you think of this book?

We want to hear from you!

Do you have a few minutes to participate in a brief online survey?

Microsoft is interested in hearing your feedback so we can continually improve our books and learning resources for you.

To participate in our survey, please visit:

www.microsoft.com/learning/booksurvey/

...and enter this kit's ISBN-10 number (appears above barcode on bottom of box*).
As a thank-you to survey participants in the United States and Canada, each month we'll randomly select five respondents to win one of five $100 gift certificates from a leading online merchant. At the conclusion of the survey, you can enter the drawing by providing your e-mail address, which will be used for prize notification only.

Thanks in advance for your input. Your opinion counts!

* Where to find the ISBN-10 on bottom of box

ISBN-13: 000-0-0000-0000-0
ISBN-10: 0-0000-0000-0

00000

0 000000 000000

Example only. Each kit has unique ISBN.

Microsoft Press